Windows® 7

Administrator's Pocket Consultant

William R. Stanek

PHI Learning Private Limited

New Delhi-110001

2009

This Indian Reprint—Rs. 395.00
(Original U.S. Edition—Rs. 1788.00)

WINDOWS® 7 ADMINISTRATOR'S POCKET CONSULTANT
by William R. Stanek

This Eastern Economy Edition is the authorized unabridged reprint published by PHI Learning Private Limited, © 2010 by arrangement with original publisher, Microsoft Press, a division of Microsoft Corporation, Redmond, Washington, U.S.A.

This edition is authorised for sale in Bangladesh, Bhutan, India, Maldives, Nepal, Pakistan, and Sri Lanka only.

ISBN-978-81-203-3960-6

The export rights of this book are vested solely with the publisher.

Published by Asoke K. Ghosh, PHI Learning Private Limited, M-97, Connaught Circus, New Delhi-110001 and Printed by Rajkamal Electric Press, Plot No. 2, Phase IV, HSIDC, Kundli-131028, Sonepat, Haryana.

Contents

What do you think of this book? We want to hear from you!

Microsoft is interested in hearing your feedback so we can continually improve our books and learning resources for you. To participate in a brief online survey, please visit:

microsoft.com/learning/booksurvey

Introduction

Writing *Windows 7 Administrator's Pocket Consultant* was a lot of fun—and a lot of work. As I set out to write this book, my initial goals were to determine how Windows 7 was different from Windows Vista and Windows XP and what new administration options were available. As with any new operating system—but especially with Windows 7—I had to do a great deal of research and a lot of digging into the operating system internals to determine exactly how things work.

When you start working with Windows 7, you'll see at once that the operating system is different from earlier releases of Windows. What won't be apparent, however, is just how different Windows 7 is from its predecessors—and that's because many of the most significant changes to the operating system are below the surface. These changes affect the underlying architecture, as well as the user interfaces, and they were some of the hardest for me to research and write about.

Because Administrator's Pocket Consultants are meant to be portable and readable—the kind of book you use to solve problems and get the job done wherever you might be—I had to carefully review my research to make sure I focused on the core aspects of Windows 7 administration. The result is the book you hold in your hands, which I hope you'll agree is one of the best practical, portable guides to Windows 7. Toward that end, the book covers everything you need to perform the core administrative tasks for computers running Windows 7.

Because my focus is on giving you maximum value in a pocket-size guide, you don't have to wade through hundreds of pages of extraneous information to find what you're looking for. Instead, you'll find exactly what you need to address a specific issue or perform a particular task. In short, the book is designed to be the one resource you turn to whenever you have questions regarding Windows 7 administration. It zeroes in on daily administration procedures, frequently used tasks, documented examples, and options that are representative while not necessarily inclusive.

One of the goals for this book is to keep its content concise so that it remains compact and easy to navigate while at the same time packing it with as much information as possible to make it a valuable resource. Instead of a hefty 1,000-page tome or a lightweight, 100-page quick reference, you get a valuable resource guide that can help you quickly and easily perform common tasks, solve problems, and implement everyday solutions for systems and users.

Who Is This Book For?

Windows 7 Administrator's Pocket Consultant covers all editions of Windows 7. The book is designed for:

- Current Windows system administrators.
- Accomplished users who have some administrator responsibilities.
- Administrators upgrading to Windows 7 from earlier releases of Windows.
- Administrators transferring from other platforms.

To pack in as much information as possible, I had to assume that you have basic networking skills and a basic understanding of Windows operating systems. As a result, I don't devote entire chapters to understanding Windows basics, Windows architecture, or Windows networks. I do, however, cover desktop customization, mobile networking, TCP/IP configuration, user profiles, and system optimization. The book also goes into depth on troubleshooting, and I've tried to ensure that each chapter, where appropriate, has troubleshooting guidelines and discussions to accompany the main text. From the start, troubleshooting advice is integrated into the book—instead of being captured in a single, catchall troubleshooting chapter inserted as an afterthought. I hope that after you read these chapters and dig into the details, you'll be able to improve the overall experience of your users and reduce downtime.

How Is This Book Organized?

Windows 7 Administrator's Pocket Consultant is designed to be used in daily administration, and as such, the book is organized by job-related tasks rather than by Windows 7 features. The books in the Administrator's Pocket Consultant series are down-and-dirty, in-the-trenches books.

Speed and ease of reference are essential elements of this hands-on guide. The book has an expanded table of contents and an extensive index for finding answers to problems quickly. Many other quick reference features have been added as well. These features include step-by-step instructions, lists, tables with fast facts, and extensive cross-references.

Conventions Used in This Book

I've used a variety of elements to help keep the text clear and easy to follow. You'll find code listings in monospace type, except when I tell you to actually type a command. In that case, the command appears in **bold** type. When I introduce and define a new term, I put it in *italics*.

Other conventions include the following:

Note To provide additional details about a particular point that needs emphasis

Tip To offer helpful hints or additional information

Caution To warn you when there are potential problems you should look out for

Real World To provide real-world advice when discussing advanced topics

I truly hope you find that *Windows 7 Administrator's Pocket Consultant* provides everything you need to perform the essential administrative tasks on Windows 7 systems as quickly and efficiently as possible. You are welcome to send your thoughts to me at williamstanek@aol.com. Thank you.

Find Additional Content Online

As new or updated material becomes available that complements this book, it will be posted online on the Microsoft Press Online Windows Server and Client Web site. The type of material you might find includes updates to book content, articles, links to companion content, errata, sample chapters, and more. This Web site is available at *http://microsoftpresssrv.libredigital.com/serverclient/* and is updated periodically.

You'll also find discussion about the book at *www.williamstanek.com*. Follow me on Twitter at WilliamStanek.

Support

Every effort has been made to ensure the accuracy of this book. Microsoft Press provides corrections for books through the World Wide Web at the following address:

http://www.microsoft.com/mspress/support

If you have comments, questions, or ideas about this book, please send them to Microsoft Press using either of the following methods:

Postal mail:
Microsoft Press
Attn: Editor, *Windows 7 Administrator's Pocket Consultant*
One Microsoft Way
Redmond, WA 98052-6399

E-mail:
mspinput@microsoft.com

Please note that product support isn't offered through these addresses. For support information, visit Microsoft's Web site at *http://support.microsoft.com/*.

CHAPTER 1

Introduction to Windows 7 Administration

Like Windows Vista, the Windows 7 operating system is different from Windows XP and earlier versions of Windows. Not only is Windows 7 more versatile than Windows XP, but it builds on the revolutionary architecture introduced with Windows Vista. The most significant architectural changes include:

- User account controls and elevation of privilege
- Modularization and disk imaging
- Preinstallation and preboot environments

This chapter covers getting started with Windows 7 and explores the extent to which control and privilege changes affect working with and managing computers running Windows 7. Chapter 2, "Deploying Windows 7," shows you how the other architectural changes simplify the task of deploying Windows 7. Throughout this and the other chapters in this book, you'll also find detailed discussions of manageability changes that enhance all aspects of computer management. Although this book focuses on Windows 7 administration, the tips and techniques discussed throughout the text can help anyone who supports, develops for, or works with Windows 7.

Keep in mind that this book is meant to be used in conjunction with *Windows Server 2008 Administrator's Pocket Consultant*, Second Edition (Microsoft Press, 2010). In addition to coverage of broad administration tasks, server-focused books in the Administrator's Pocket Consultant series examine directory services administration, data administration, and network administration. This book, on the other hand, zeroes in on user and system administration tasks. You'll find detailed coverage of the following topics:

- Customizing the operating system and Windows environment
- Configuring hardware and network devices
- Managing user access and global settings
- Configuring laptops and mobile networking
- Using remote management and remote assistance capabilities
- Troubleshooting system problems

Also, it is important to note that just about every configuration option in the Windows operating system can be controlled through Group Policy. Rather than add caveats to every discussion that feature A or B can be configured only if allowed in Group Policy, I'm going to assume you are smart enough to understand the global impact of Group Policy on system configuration and management. I'm also going to assume you are familiar with the command line and Windows PowerShell. This will allow me to focus on essential tasks for administration.

Getting Started with Windows 7

Windows 7 is the latest release of the Windows operating system for client computers. The main editions of Windows 7 include:

- **Windows 7 Starter** A budget edition of Windows 7 for casual users as well as emerging markets. It is compatible with the latest applications and devices and is more reliable and secure than earlier releases of Windows are. However, it is extremely limited compared to other editions.
- **Windows 7 Home Basic** A budget edition of Windows 7 for home users. It includes a basic set of entertainment features but does not include features for joining a domain.
- **Windows 7 Home Premium** An enhanced edition of Windows 7 that includes a premium set of entertainment features but does not include features for joining a domain.
- **Windows 7 Professional** A basic edition of Windows 7 for business users. It includes a basic set of management features as well as features for joining a domain.
- **Windows 7 Enterprise** An enhanced edition of Windows 7 for business users. It includes an extended set of management features as well as features for joining a domain.
- **Windows 7 Ultimate** An enhanced edition of Windows 7 that includes the best of the available features in the home and business editions as well as features for joining a domain.

Windows 7 natively supports image-based installation and deployment. Thanks to the new hardware-independent architecture in Windows 7, which is discussed later in this chapter, all editions of Windows 7 except Windows 7 Starter support both 32-bit and 64-bit hardware. This means that every product edition except Starter can be used with computers that have either 32-bit or 64-bit architecture. Computers with 32-bit x86 architecture can have up to 4 gigabytes (GB) of RAM. Computers with 64-bit architecture can have up to 8 GB of RAM on Home Basic; 16 GB of RAM on Home Premium; and more than 128 GB on the Professional, Enterprise, and Ultimate editions. The Professional, Enterprise, and Ultimate editions also provide multiprocessor support.

Table 1-1 provides an overview of the differences between the various Windows 7 editions. A detailed list is provided at *www.williamstanek.com/windows7/*.

TABLE 1-1 Windows 7 Feature Differences

FEATURE	HOME BASIC	HOME PREMIUM	PROFESSIONAL	ENTERPRISE	ULTIMATE
Aero user interface		X	X	X	X
BitLocker Drive Encryption				X	X
Complete PC Backup			X	X	X
Desktop deployment tools			X	X	X
Dual processor support (not counting processor cores)			X	X	X
Encrypting File System			X	X	X
File and printer sharing connections	10	20	20	20	20
Network Access Protection client			X	X	X

FEATURE	HOME BASIC	HOME PREMIUM	PROFESSIONAL	ENTERPRISE	ULTIMATE
Network And Sharing Center	X	X	X	X	X
Parental controls	X	X			X
Policy-based Quality of Service for networking			X	X	X
Premier Support, covered under			X	X	
Scheduled backups	Limited	X	X	X	X
Software Assurance, available under			X	X	X
Subsystem for UNIX-based applications				X	X
Tablet PC		X	X	X	X
User interface multiple language installs				X	X
Volume licensing keys			X	X	
Virtual machine licenses (4)				X	X
Windows Fax And Scan			X	X	X
Windows Media Center	X	X	X	X	X
Wireless network provisioning			X	X	X

Windows XP and earlier releases of the Windows operating system could not be upgraded from one edition to another, but Microsoft provides an easy upgrade path from the basic editions to the enhanced editions of Windows 7, using either Windows Anytime Upgrade or the Deployment Image Servicing and Management tool. Table 1-2 provides an overview of the upgrade paths. As the table shows, you have several options for upgrading the most basic editions to the enhanced editions within each version. To determine which version of Windows 7 you are using, click Start, right-click Computer, and then click Properties. The edition of Windows 7 you are using is displayed under Windows Edition.

TABLE 1-2 Upgrade Paths for Windows 7 Editions

VERSION OF WINDOWS	UPGRADES TO	UPGRADES TO
HOME VERSION	**WINDOWS 7 HOME PREMIUM**	**WINDOWS 7 ULTIMATE**
Windows 7 Home Basic	Yes	Yes
Windows 7 Home Premium		Yes
PROFESSIONAL VERSION	**WINDOWS 7 ENTERPRISE**	**WINDOWS 7 ULTIMATE**
Windows 7 Professional	Yes	Yes
Windows 7 Enterprise		Yes

With Windows Anytime Upgrade, you can buy an upgrade disc at a retail store, use the built-in feature to enter a valid product key for an upgrade, or buy the upgrade online. To use the built-in Windows Anytime Upgrade feature, click Start and then click Control Panel. In Control Panel, click System And Security, and then click Windows Anytime Upgrade. To complete the upgrade, follow the instructions provided. You'll need the Windows 7 distribution media. The distribution media contains the components for all Windows 7 versions, and it is the product key you provide that unlocks and installs the features for a specific version.

> ***NOTE*** **Separate distribution media is provided for 32-bit and 64-bit editions of Windows 7. To install the 32-bit edition of Windows 7 on an x86-based computer, you need to use the 32-bit distribution media. To install the 64-bit edition of Windows 7 on an x64-based computer, you need to use the 64-bit distribution media. Generally, if you are running a 32-bit operating system and want to install a 64-bit operating system (on hardware that supports both), you need to restart the computer and boot from the installation media. The same is generally true if you want to install a 32-bit operating system on a computer running a 64-bit operating system. Note also that Microsoft has developed a separate edition for computers with IA64 processors. This edition is called Windows 7 for Itanium-Based Systems.**

The Deployment Image Servicing and Management tool (DISM) ships with business editions of Windows 7. Using DISM, you can manage online and offline images of the Windows operating system, including images for deployment and those for virtual machines. Windows Image (.wim) files are used to deploy Windows 7. Virtual hard disk (.vhd) files are used with virtual machines. The same commands work on WIM and VHD files.

As you'll learn more about in Chapter 2, you can use DISM to:

- Add and remove packages. Packages can include language packs, patches, utilities, and so on.
- Enable and disable Windows features.
- Add and remove third-party device drivers.

You can run DISM at an elevated administrator command prompt by following these steps:

1. Click Start, point to All Programs, and then click Accessories.
2. Right-click the Command Prompt shortcut on the menu, and then click Run As Administrator.

   If you see the User Account Control prompt, proceed as you normally would to allow the application to run with administrator privileges.
3. In the Command Prompt window, enter **dism /?** to view available options for DISM.
4. To view commands available for working with online images, enter **dism /online /?**.

Although DISM is designed to work primarily with offline images and images you've mounted, you can use some DISM commands to get important information about the live operating system running on a computer. Table 1-3 provides an overview of DISM Online subcommands you can use with live operating systems. For example, if you want to display a list of Windows editions to which a computer can be upgraded, you can enter the following command:

```
dism /online /get-targeteditions
```

TABLE 1-3 DISM Online Commands for Live Operating Systems

SUBCOMMAND	DESCRIPTION
/Disable-Feature /featurename:*FeatureName*	Disables a specified feature. Feature names are case sensitive.
/Enable-Feature /featurename:*FeatureName*	Enables a specified feature. Feature names are case sensitive.
/Get-CurrentEdition	Displays the currently installed edition of Windows.
/Get-DriverInfo /driver:*DriverName.inf*	Displays information about a specified third-party driver that is installed in the driver store. Driver names are not case sensitive.

SUBCOMMAND	DESCRIPTION
/Get-Drivers	Displays information about all third-party drivers that are installed in the driver store.
/Get-FeatureInfo /featurename:*FeatureName*	Displays information about a specified feature. Feature names are case sensitive.
/Get-Features	Displays information about Windows features that are installed.
/Get-Intl	Displays information about the default system user interface language, system locale, default time zone, keyboard language, and installed languages.
/Get-PackageInfo /packagename:*PackageName*	Displays information about a specified package. Package names are case sensitive.
/Get-Packages	Displays information about Windows packages that are installed.
/Get-TargetEditions	Lists the Windows editions that the operating system can be upgraded to.

Windows 7 ships with Windows PowerShell 2.0. When you've configured PowerShell for remoting, you can execute commands on remote computers in a variety of ways. One technique is to establish a remote session with the computers you want to work with. The following example and partial output shows how you can check the Windows edition on remote computers:

```
$s = new-pssession -computername engpc15, hrpc32, cserpc28
invoke-command -session $s {dism.exe /online /get-currentedition}
```

```
Deployment Image Servicing and Management tool
Version: 6.1.7350.0

Image Version: 6.1.7350.0

Current Edition : Ultimate
The operation completed successfully.
```

NOTE With the New-PSSession command, you use the –ComputerName parameter to specify the remote computers to work with by DNS name, NetBIOS name, or IP address. When working with multiple remote computers, separate each computer name or IP address with a comma. For more information on working with Windows PowerShell 2.0 and using remoting, see Chapter 4, "Using Sessions, Jobs, and Remoting," in ***Windows PowerShell 2.0 Administrator's Pocket Consultant*** (Microsoft Press, 2009).

Understanding 64-Bit Computing

Since it was introduced for Windows operating systems, 64-bit computing has changed substantially. Not only do computers running 64-bit versions of Windows perform better and run faster than their 32-bit counterparts, they are also more scalable because they can process more data per clock cycle, address more memory, and perform numeric calculations faster. Windows 7 supports two different 64-bit architectures:

- **x64** This architecture is based on 64-bit extensions to the x86 instruction set, which is implemented in AMD Opteron (AMD64) processors, Intel Xeon processors with 64-bit extension technology, and other processors. This architecture offers native 32-bit processing and 64-bit extension processing, allowing simultaneous 32-bit and 64-bit computing.
- **IA64** This architecture is based on the Explicitly Parallel Instruction Computing (EPIC) processor architecture, which is implemented in Intel Itanium (IA64) processors and other processors. This architecture offers native 64-bit processing, allowing 64-bit applications to achieve optimal performance.

Sixty-four-bit computing is designed for performing operations that are memory intensive and that require extensive numeric calculations. With 64-bit processing, applications can load large data sets entirely into physical memory (that is, RAM), which reduces the need to page to disk and increases performance substantially. The EPIC instruction set enables Itanium-based processors to perform up to 20 operations simultaneously.

Currently, the prevalent firmware interfaces are:

- Basic input/output system (BIOS)
- Extensible Firmware Interface (EFI)
- Unified Extensible Firmware Interface (UEFI)

Itanium-based computers differ in many fundamental ways from computers based on the x86 and x64 specifications. While Itanium-based computers use EFI and the GUID partition table (GPT) disk type, computers based on x86 use BIOS and the master boot record (MBR) disk type. Computers based on x64 use UEFI wrapped around BIOS or EFI, as discussed in "Navigating and Understanding Firmware Options" in Chapter 10. This means that there are differences in the way you manage computers with these architectures, particularly when it comes to setup and disk configuration. However, with the increasing acceptance and use of UEFI and the ability of Windows 7 to use both MBR and GPT disks regardless of firmware type, the underlying chip architecture won't necessarily determine what firmware type and disk type a computer uses. This decision is in the hands of the hardware manufacturer.

NOTE Techniques for using MBR and GPT disks are covered in detail in Chapter 12, "Managing Disk Drives and File Systems." Generally, BIOS-based computers use MBR for booting or for data disks and GPT only for data disks. EFI-based computers can have both GPT and MBR disks, but you must have at least one GPT disk that contains the EFI system partition (ESP) and a primary partition or simple volume that contains the operating system for booting.

In most cases, 64-bit hardware is compatible with 32-bit applications; however, 32-bit applications perform better on 32-bit hardware. Windows 64-bit editions support both 64-bit and 32-bit applications using the Windows on Windows 64 (WOW64) x86 emulation layer. The WOW64 subsystem isolates 32-bit applications from 64-bit applications. This prevents file system and registry problems. The operating system provides interoperability across the 32-bit/64-bit boundary for the Component Object Model (COM) and for basic operations such as cutting, copying, and pasting using the Clipboard. However, 32-bit processes cannot load 64-bit dynamic-link libraries (DLLs), and 64-bit processes cannot load 32-bit DLLs.

In the shift to 64-bit computing, you may want to track which computers in the enterprise support 64-bit operating systems, which computers are already running 64-bit operating systems, or both. With Windows PowerShell you can:

- Determine whether a computer has a 64-bit operating system installed by using the OSArchitecture property of the Win32_OperatingSystem object. An example and sample output follow:

```
get-wmiobject -class win32_operatingsystem | format-list
osarchitecture
```

```
osarchitecture : 32-bit
```

- Determine whether a computer supports a 64-bit operating system by using the Name and Description properties of the Win32_Processor object.

```
get-wmiobject -class win32_processor | format-list name,
description
```

```
name        : Intel(R) Core(TM)2 Quad CPU          @ 2.66GHz
description : x64 Family 6 Model 15 Stepping 7
```

Here, the first sample output tells you the computer is running a 32-bit version of Windows. The second sample output tells you the computer has an x64 processor. As a result, you know the computer can be upgraded to a 64-bit version of Windows 7.

Rather than check each computer individually, you can create a script to do the work for you. For sample scripts and complete walkthroughs, see Chapter 9, "Inventorying and Evaluating Windows Systems," in *Windows PowerShell 2.0 Administrator's Pocket Consultant*.

Installing Windows 7

Windows 7 Professional, Enterprise, and Ultimate editions are the only editions intended for use in Active Directory domains. When you install Windows 7 on a computer with an existing operating system, you can perform a clean installation or an upgrade. The major differences between a clean installation and an upgrade are the following:

- **Clean installation** With a clean installation, the Windows Setup program completely replaces the original operating system on the computer, and all user and application settings are lost. You should use a clean installation when the operating system cannot be upgraded, the system must boot to multiple operating systems, a standardized configuration is required, or when no operating system is currently installed.
- **Upgrade installation** During an upgrade, user settings are retained, existing applications and their settings are kept, and basic system configuration is not required. An upgrade installation should be used when you have computers running the Windows operating system that support upgrading to Windows 7 and you want to minimize disruption by maintaining the existing settings, user information, and application configurations.

The way an upgrade works depends on the operating system being upgraded. When you are upgrading from Windows Vista, Windows Setup performs an in-place upgrade. Upgrade copies are available for Windows XP, but you can't perform an in-place upgrade. When you are upgrading from Windows XP, you need to use Windows Easy Transfer to transfer your files and settings and then run Windows Setup. Windows Setup will then perform a clean installation of the operating system. Afterward, you need to reinstall your applications.

Preparing for Windows 7 Installation

To install Windows 7, you can boot from the Windows distribution media, run Setup from your current Windows operating system, perform a command-line installation, or use one of the automated installation options.

There are two basic approaches to setting up Windows 7—interactively or as an automated process. An interactive installation is what many people regard as the regular Windows installation—the kind where you walk through the setup process and enter a lot of information. It can be performed from distribution media (by booting from the distribution media or running Windows Setup from a command line). The default Windows setup process when booting from the retail Windows 7 DVD is interactive, prompting you for configuration information throughout the process.

There are several types of automated setup, which actually have administrator-configurable amounts of user interaction. The most basic form of unattended setup you can perform is an unattended installation using only answer files. An answer file contains all or part of the configuration information usually prompted for during a standard installation process. You can create unattended answer files using Windows System Image Manager, which is provided in the Windows Deployment Toolkit (available at *www.download.microsoft.com*). To take unattended setup a step further, you can use Windows Deployment Services, as discussed in Chapter 2.

The standard setup program for Windows 7 is Setup.exe. You can run Setup.exe from the Windows operating system to upgrade the current version or to install Windows 7 to a different partition. On BIOS-based (x86) systems, you can boot from the distribution media to initiate the setup process. On IA64 Itanium-based systems, you start Setup through the EFI shell by running the \IA64\Setupldr.efi Setup boot loader on the DVD (or the equivalent). Other than the partitioning method, Setup for an IA64 system works the same as for the 32-bit x86 and 64-bit x64 versions.

When you are working with Windows 7 on x86-based systems, you should be aware of the special types of drive sections used by the operating system.

- **Active** The active partition or volume is the drive section for system cache and startup. Some removable media devices may be listed as having an active partition.
- **Boot** The boot partition or volume contains the operating system and its support files. The system and boot partition or volume can be the same.
- **System** The system partition or volume contains the hardware-specific files needed to load the operating system. As part of software configuration, the system partition or volume can't be part of a striped or spanned volume.

Partitions and volumes are essentially the same thing. Two different terms are used at times, however, because you create partitions on basic disks and you create volumes on dynamic disks. On an x86-based computer, you can mark a partition as active by using the Disk Management snap-in.

Although the active, boot, and system volumes or partitions can be the same, each is required nonetheless. When you install Windows 7, the Setup program assesses all the hard disk drive resources available. Typically, Windows 7 puts boot and system files on the same drive and partition and marks this partition as the active partition. The advantage of this configuration is that you don't need multiple drives for the operating system and can use an additional drive as a mirror of the operating system partitions.

There are a number of differences when installing to the IA64 Itanium-based hardware platform. The IA64 Extended Firmware Interface starts up by loading a firmware-based boot menu. IA64 disks have a partition structure, called a globally unique identifier (GUID) partition table, or GPT. This partition structure differs substantially from the 32-bit platform MBR–based partitions.

GPT–based disks have two required partitions and one or more optional (OEM or data) partitions (up to 128 total):

- EFI system partition (ESP)
- Microsoft reserved partition (MSR)
- At least one data partition

The IA64 boot menu presents a set of options, one of which is the EFI shell. The EFI shell provides an operating environment supporting the FAT and FAT32 file systems, as well as configuration and file management commands. To view a list of partitions on an IA64-based computer, use the Map command. In the output of the Map command, *blk* designates partition blocks and *fs#* designates readable file systems. You can change to a partition by entering the partition block number followed by a colon. Type **dir** to view files in the partition. EFI has a boot maintenance manager that allows you to configure the boot menu.

As discussed in Chapter 2, when you install Windows 7, the Setup program will automatically create a Windows Recovery Environment (Windows RE) partition and install additional components that can be used for recovery and troubleshooting in that partition. As a result, the Windows recovery tools are always available on computers running Windows 7. These tools include:

- **Startup Repair** Repairs problems that prevent Windows from starting. If the boot manager or a corrupted system file is preventing startup, the tool is started automatically and will initiate repair of the computer.
- **System Restore** Restores Windows to a state at an earlier point in time. If a configuration change or application installation is preventing startup and restore points are available, you can use this feature to restore Windows to a state prior to the change.
- **System Image Recovery** Performs a full recovery of the computer by using a system image created previously. If Startup Repair, System Restore, and other troubleshooting techniques fail to restore the computer and you have a system image for recovery, you can use this feature to restore the computer from the backup image.
- **Windows Memory Diagnostics** Performs diagnostics on the computer's memory. If memory hardware errors are causing startup or other problems with the computer, you can use this tool to identify the problem.

As an administrator, you can use these tools to recover computers. If a remote user can't start Windows, you can talk the user through the process of starting Windows RE and initiating recovery. You do this by having the user access the Advanced Boot Options menu as discussed in "Repairing and Recovering a Computer" in Chapter 17.

Performing a Windows 7 Installation

Before you install Windows 7 on a computer, you should determine whether the underlying hardware meets the requirements for physical memory, processing power, and graphics capabilities. Microsoft provides both minimum requirements and recommended requirements. Requirements for memory and graphics are measured in megabytes (MB) and gigabytes (GB); requirements for processors are measured in gigahertz (GHz).

Windows 7 requires:

- A 1 GHz or faster 32-bit (x86) or 64-bit (x64) processor
- At least 1 GB RAM (32-bit) or 2 GB RAM (64-bit)
- A DirectX 9 graphics processor with a WDDM 1.0 or higher driver

NOTE **Microsoft recomends that a computer have available disk space of at least 16 GB (32-bit) or 20 GB (64-bit). Various features in Windows 7, such as protection points, which include previous versions of files and folders that have been modified, can quickly increase the size requirements. For optimal performance of the hard disk, you need at least 15 percent free space at all times and adequate space for the paging file, which might be up to twice the size of the system's RAM. Also, if you are doing an in-place upgrade, the Windows.old folder will contain folders and files from the previous installation.**

Any computer that meets or exceeds the hardware requirements can run Windows 7. You can perform an interactive installation of Windows 7 by completing these steps:

1. Start the Windows 7 Setup program by using one of the following techniques:
   - For a new installation, turn on the computer and insert the Windows 7 distribution media into the computer's DVD-ROM drive. When prompted, press a key to start the Setup program from the DVD.
   - For an upgrade, start the computer and log on using an account with administrator privileges. Insert the Windows 7 distribution media into the computer's DVD-ROM drive. The Windows 7 Setup program should start automatically. If Setup doesn't start automatically, use Windows Explorer to access the distribution media and then double-click Setup.exe.
2. Click Install Now to start the installation. Setup will copy temporary files and then start. If you are starting the installation from an existing operating system and are connected to a network or the Internet, choose whether to get updates during the installation. Either click Go Online To Get The Latest Updates For Installation or click Do Not Get The Latest Updates For Installation.

   TIP **You don't have to get updates during the installation. If you decide not to get updates, you can update the computer later using the Windows Update feature.**

3. Read the license terms. If you agree, click I Accept The License Terms, and then click Next.
4. Specify the installation type as Upgrade or Custom (Advanced). Select Upgrade if you want to upgrade the previously installed operating system to Windows 7. Otherwise, select Custom (Advanced) to install a clean copy of Windows 7.

NOTE When you install a clean copy of Windows 7 on a computer running an earlier version of Windows, Setup moves folders and files for the previous installation to a folder named Windows.old, and the previous installation will no longer run.

5. When prompted for an installation location, choose the disk drive on which you want to install the operating system, and then click Next.

   TIP During installation, on the Where Do You Want To Install Windows page, you can access a command prompt by pressing Shift+F10. This puts you in the MinWinPC environment used by Setup to install the operating system, and you have access to many of the same command-line tools that are available in a standard installation of Windows 7.

6. If the disk you've selected contains a previous Windows installation, you'll see a prompt telling you that existing user and application settings will be moved to a folder named Windows.old and that you must copy these settings to the new installation to use them. Click OK.

   Setup will then start the installation. During this process, Setup copies the full disk image of Windows 7 to the disk you've selected and then expands it. Afterward, Setup installs features based on the computer's configuration and any hardware that Setup detects. This process requires several automatic restarts. When Setup finishes the installation, the operating system will be loaded and the system will be set up for first use.

7. When prompted, choose your country or region, your time and currency format, and your keyboard layout. Click Next.
8. You must next create a local machine account that will be created as a computer administrator account. Type a user name.
9. Type a computer name, and then click Next.
10. Type and then confirm a password. Enter a password hint. Click Next.

    TIP Passwords for user accounts should be fairly complex. You make passwords difficult to guess and crack by using a combination of all available character types, including lowercase letters, uppercase letters, numbers, and symbols.

11. With retail versions of Windows 7, you typically have to provide a product key. If prompted for a product key, enter the product key. By default the computer will automatically activate Windows the next time you connect to the Internet. Click Next.
12. Select a Windows Update option for the computer. Usually, you'll want to use the recommended settings to allow Windows 7 to automatically install all available updates and security tools as they become available. If you choose Ask Me Later, Windows Update will be disabled.
13. Review the date and time settings, and then make changes as necessary. Click Next.

14. If a network card is detected during setup, networking components are installed automatically. Depending on your location type, click Home, Work, or Public Network. Windows 7 will then configure networking for this location. Afterward, Windows 7 will prepare your desktop.

You may have trouble installing Windows 7 for a variety of reasons. Possible solutions to common problems follow in problem/solution format.

- **You can't boot from the Windows 7 installation media** Although most computers can boot from DVD, sometimes this capability is disabled in firmware. Set the boot order in firmware so that the DVD drive appears ahead of hard disk drives and other bootable media. For more information, see Chapter 10, "Managing Firmware, Boot Configuration, and Startup."
- **You can't select a hard disk during setup** Although the Windows 7 installation media contains drivers for most disk controllers, you may have a disk controller for which a default driver isn't available. Insert media containing the required drivers and then click Load Drivers on the Where Do You Want To Install Windows page. If the driver is on an internal hard drive, press Shift+F10 to access a command prompt and then use Xcopy to copy the driver files to a USB flash device or other removable media. You can then click Load Drivers to load the drivers from the media.
- **You forgot to modify the hard disk configuration prior to starting the installation** On the Where Do You Want To Install Windows page, click Drive Options (Advanced). You can then use the options provided to create, delete, and format partitions as necessary. If you need to shrink or extend a partition (even during an upgrade), press Shift+F10 to access a command prompt and then use Disk Part to work with the partition. You can extend and shrink partitions without having to delete them. You also can use Disk Part to change the disk type and partition style. For more information on Disk Part, see Chapters 10, 11, and 12 in *Windows Command-Line Administrator's Pocket Consultant*, Second Edition (Microsoft Press, 2008).

Running Windows 7

When the operating system starts after installation, you can log on and access the desktop. By default, Windows 7 stores user profile data under %SystemDrive%\Users\%UserName%. Within the user profile folder, each user who logs on to the system has a personal folder, and that personal folder contains additional folders. These folders are the default locations for storing specific types of data and files and include:

- **AppData** User-specific application data (in a hidden folder)
- **Contacts** Contacts and contact groups
- **Desktop** The user's desktop
- **Downloads** Programs and data downloaded from the Internet

- **Favorites** The user's Internet favorites
- **Links** The user's Internet links
- **My Documents** The user's document files
- **My Music** The user's music files
- **My Pictures** The user's pictures
- **My Videos** The user's video files
- **Saved Games** The user's saved game data
- **Searches** The user's saved searches

NOTE **%SystemDrive% and %UserName% refer to the *SystemDrive* and *UserName* environment variables, respectively. The Windows operating system has many environment variables, which are used to refer to user-specific and system-specific values. Often, I'll refer to environment variables by using this syntax: %VariableName%. If you've upgraded to Windows 7 from an earlier version of Windows, the user's personal folder will also contain symbolic links (which look like shortcuts) to the folders and settings used by that earlier version. A symbolic link is a pointer to a file or folder that often is created for backward compatibility with applications that look for a folder or file in a location that has been moved. You can create symbolic links by using the Mklink command-line utility. At a command prompt, enter mklink /? to learn the available options.**

In addition to personal folders, Windows 7 uses personal libraries. A library is simply a collection of files and folders that are grouped together and presented through a common view. Standard libraries include:

- **Documents** Collects a user's My Documents data and Public Documents data.
- **Music** Collects a user's My Music data and Public Music data.
- **Pictures** Collects a user's My Pictures data and Public Pictures data.
- **Videos** Collects a user's My Videos data and Public Videos data.

You can create new libraries to act as views to various collections of data by right-clicking the Libraries node in Windows Explorer, pointing to New, and then clicking Library.

CAUTION **When you work with libraries, it is important to remember that they are only representations of collected data. Windows 7 creates merged views of files and folders that you add to libraries. The libraries themselves do not contain any actual data, and any action you take on a file or folder within a library is performed on the source file or folder.**

Windows 7 provides themes that allow you to easily customize the appearance of menus, windows, and the desktop. You can select a theme by clicking Start and then clicking Control Panel. In Control Panel, click the Change The Theme link under Appearance And Personalization, and then choose the theme you want to use. Windows Aero adds improved visual design and enhanced dynamic effects to the interface. If you want to use fewer advanced features, choose the Windows Classic or Windows 7 Basic theme.

It is important to point out, however, that the interface enhancements that can be used on a computer depend on which Windows 7 edition is installed and the computer's hardware.

Using Action Center and Activating Windows

Windows 7 has a redesigned desktop with many additional customization options. By default, when you log on, the operating system displays an Action Center summary icon in the notification area. This icon has a flag with a red circle with an X in it. Action Center is a program that monitors the status of important security and maintenance areas. If the status of a monitored item changes, Action Center updates the notification icon as appropriate for the severity of the alert. If you move the mouse pointer over this icon, you see a summary of all alerts. If you click this icon, Windows displays a dialog box with a summary listing of each alert or action item that needs your attention. Click an alert or action item link to open your default Web browser and display a possible solution. Click the Open Action Center link to display the Action Center.

If you've disabled Action Center notifications on the taskbar, you can start Action Center by following these steps:

1. Click Start, and then click Control Panel.
2. In Control Panel, click the System And Security category heading link.
3. Click Action Center.

Action Center, shown in Figure 1-1, provides an overview of the computer's status and lists any issues that need to be resolved. If a problem has a solution, you can view the solution by clicking the View Problem Response button. For example, if a computer is experiencing a problem with the Intel Active Management Technology and this problem can be resolved by installing a newer driver, clicking View Problem Response displays a page providing more information about the problem and a link to download and install the latest driver, as shown in Figure 1-2. When you've resolved a problem, you can elect to archive the message for future reference by selecting the Archive This Message check box before you click OK to close the More Information page.

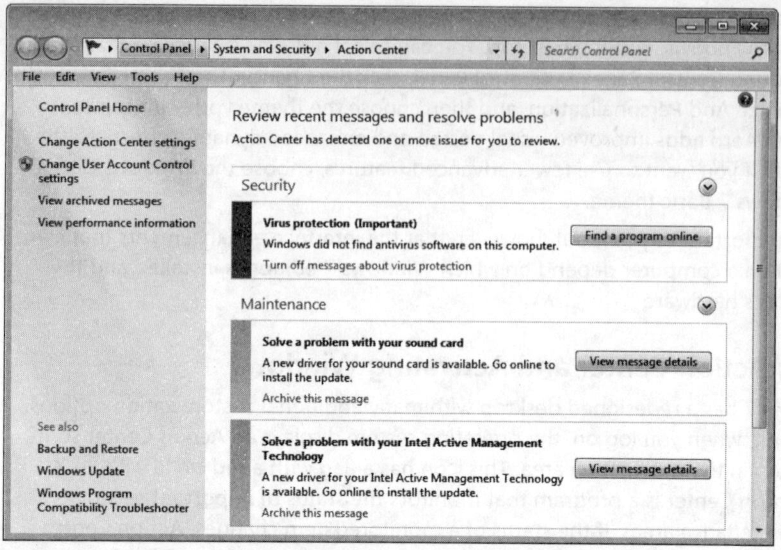

FIGURE 1-1 The Action Center window

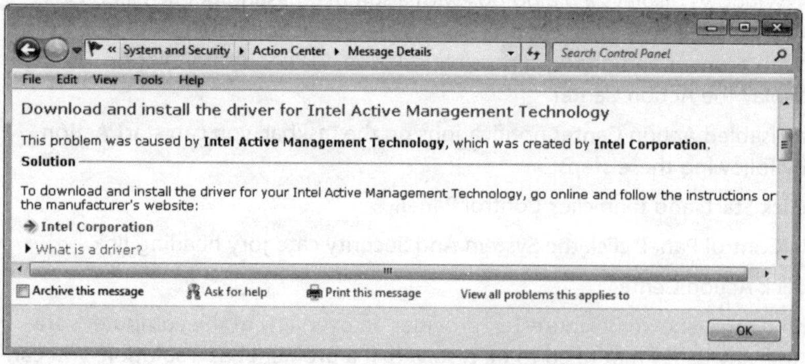

FIGURE 1-2 Getting more information about a problem

In Action Center's left pane, you have options for performing the following tasks:

- **Change Action Center Settings** When you click this option, you can turn alert messages on or off. Alert messages are divided into two categories: security and maintenance. Security alerts you can turn on or off include those related to Windows Update, Internet security settings, the network firewall, spyware and related programs, User Account Control, and virus programs. Maintenance alerts you can turn on or off include those related to Windows Backup, checking for updates, and Windows troubleshooting. Quick links are provided to allow you to configure settings for the Customer Experience Improvement Program, problem reporting, and Windows Update.

- **Change User Account Control Settings** When you click this option, you can modify the way User Account Control works. Select Always Notify to always notify the current user when programs try to install software or make changes to the computer and when the user changes Windows settings. Select Default to notify the current user only when programs try to make changes to the computer and not when the user changes Windows settings. Selecting the Notify Me Only When ... (Do Not Dim My Desktop) option works the same as the default setting but prevents User Account Control from switching to the secure desktop. Select Never Notify to turn off all User Account Control notification prompts. For more information, see Chapter 5, "Managing User Access and Security."
- **View Archived Messages** Displays messages you archived from Action Center about computer problems.
- **View Performance Information** Click this option to view the computer's performance rating and determine whether there are any issues causing performance problems. The computer's base score is determined according to the worst performing component. For example, if the computer's primary hard disk has a slow data-transfer rate, the computer will have a low score in this area, and the base score will reflect this as well. To improve performance, you would need to upgrade the computer's primary hard disk. If you think the performance rating isn't accurate, click Re-Run The Assessment to have Windows recheck the computer's performance.

Windows 7 Professional and Enterprise editions support volume licensing. Although volume-licensed versions of Windows 7 might not require activation or product keys, retail versions of Windows 7 require both activation and product keys. You can determine whether Windows 7 has been activated by clicking Start and then clicking Control Panel. In Control Panel, click System And Security, and then click System. On the System page, read the Windows Activation entry. This entry specifies whether you have activated the operating system. If Windows 7 has not been activated and you are connected to the Internet, select Activate Windows Now under Windows Activation to start the Windows Activation wizard. In the wizard, click Activate Windows Online Now.

Unlike with Windows XP and earlier versions of Windows, the product key provided during installation of Windows 7 can be changed as necessary to stay in compliance with your licensing plan. To change the product key, follow these steps:

1. Click Start, and then click Control Panel. In Control Panel, click System And Security, and then click System.
2. In the System window, under Windows Activation, click Change Product Key.
3. In the Windows Activation window, type the product key and then click Next.
4. If the product key is accepted, you'll need to reactivate Windows by clicking Activate Windows Online Now. If the product key you provide is not accepted or is for a different edition of Windows 7, you need to provide a valid product key before you can activate Windows.

Running Windows 7 in Groups and Domains

Computers running Windows 7 can be members of a homegroup, a workgroup, or a domain. A homegroup is a loose association of computers on a home network. Computers in a homegroup share data that can be accessed using a password common to the users in the homegroup. You set the homegroup password when you set up the homegroup and can modify the password as necessary at any time.

A workgroup is a loose association of computers in which each computer is managed separately. A domain is a collection of computers that you can manage collectively by means of domain controllers, which are servers running Windows that manage access to the network, to the directory database, and to shared resources.

Homegroups are available only when a computer running Windows 7 is connected to a home network. Workgroups and domains are available only when a computer running Windows 7 is connected to a work network. You'll learn how to manage networking and network connections in Chapter 15, "Configuring and Troubleshooting TCP/IP Networking." To change the network location type for the network to which a computer currently is connected, follow these steps:

1. Click the Network icon in the notification area, and then click the Open Network And Sharing Center link. If the Network icon is not displayed, click Start and then click Control Panel. In Control Panel, click Network And Internet, and then click Network And Sharing Center.
2. Under View Your Active Networks, click Work Network, Home Network, or Public Network.
3. In the Set Network Location dialog box, select Work Network, Home Network, or Public Network, as appropriate, and then click Close.

Some aspects of Windows 7 vary depending on whether a computer is a member of a homegroup, workgroup, or domain.

The sections that follow discuss these differences as they pertain to User Account Control, logon, fast user switching, and password management.

Understanding User Account Control in Windows 7

In a homegroup or workgroup, a computer running Windows 7 has only local machine accounts. In a domain, a computer running Windows 7 has both local machine accounts and domain accounts. Windows 7 has two primary types of local user accounts:

- **Standard** Standard user accounts can use most software and can change system settings that do not affect other users or the security of the computer.
- **Administrator** Administrator user accounts have complete access to the computer and can make any changes that are needed.

Windows 7 includes User Account Control as a way to enhance computer security by ensuring true separation of standard user and administrator user accounts.

Because of the User Account Control feature in Windows 7, all applications run using either standard user or administrator user privileges. Whether you log on as a standard user or as an administrator user, you see a security prompt by default whenever you run an application that requires administrator privileges. The way the security prompt works depends on Group Policy settings (as discussed in "Optimizing User Account Control and Admin Approval Mode" in Chapter 5) and whether you are logged on with a standard user account or an administrator user account.

When you are logged on using a standard user account, you are asked to provide a password for an administrator account, as shown in Figure 1-3. In a homegroup or workgroup, each local computer administrator account is listed by name. To proceed, you must click an account, type the account's password, and then click Submit.

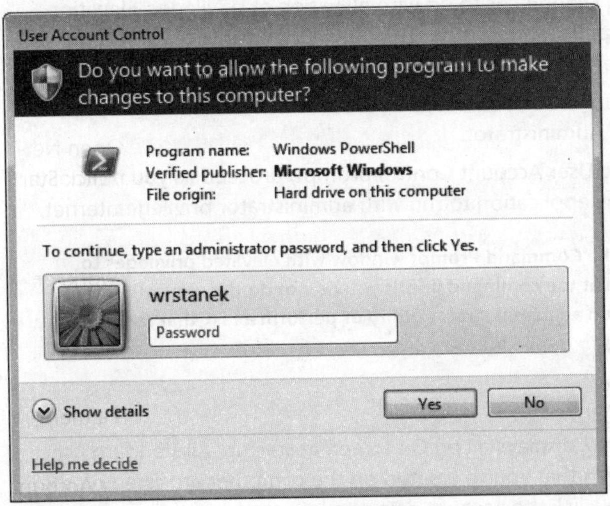

FIGURE 1-3 Prompting for administrator privileges

In a domain, the User Account Control dialog box does not list any administrator accounts, so you must know the user name and password of an administrator account in the default (log on) domain or a trusted domain to continue. When Windows prompts you, type the account name, type the account's password, and then click OK. If the account is in the default domain, you don't have to specify the domain name. If the account is in another domain, you must specify the domain and the account name by using the format *domain\username*, such as cpandl\williams.

When you are logged on using an administrator user account, you are asked to confirm that you want to continue, as shown in Figure 1-4. You can click Yes to allow the task to be performed or click No to stop the task from being performed. Clicking Show Details shows the full path to the program being executed.

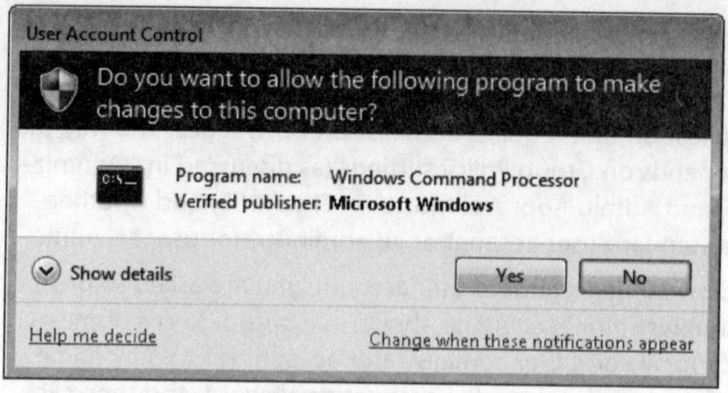

FIGURE 1-4 Prompting for confirmation to continue

An important related change has to do with elevation of privileges. Elevation allows a standard user application to run with administrator privileges. You can run applications with elevated privileges by following these steps:

1. Right-click the application's shortcut on the menu or on the desktop, and then click Run As Administrator.
2. When you see the User Account Control prompt, proceed as you normally would to allow the application to run with administrator privileges.

NOTE **You must run the Command Prompt window with elevated privileges to perform administration at the command line. If you do not do this, you will see an error when you try to run an administrator utility or perform a task that requires administrator privileges.**

Logging on to Windows 7

In a workgroup, Windows 7 displays a Log On screen at startup. All standard user and administrator accounts that you've created on the computer are listed on the Log On screen. To log on, click the account name you want to use. If the account is password protected, you must click the account name, type the account password, and then click the arrow button.

In a domain, Windows 7 displays a blank startup screen after initializing the operating system. You must press Ctrl+Alt+Del to display the Log On screen. By default, the last account to log on to the computer is listed in *computer\username* or *domain\username* format. To log on to this account, you type the account password and then click the arrow button. To log on to a different account, click the Switch User button, press Ctrl+Alt+Del, and then click Other User. The logon information you must provide depends on what type of account you are using.

- If the account is in the default domain, type the user name and password and then click the arrow button.
- If the account is in another domain, you must specify the domain and the account name by using the format *domain\username*, such as cpandl\williams.

- If you want to log on to the local machine, type ***.\username***, where *username* is the name of the local account, such as .\williams.

Using Fast User Switching with Windows 7

Windows 7 supports fast user switching in domain, homegroup, and workgroup configurations. When a user is logged on to a computer running Windows 7, you can use fast user switching to allow another user to log on without requiring the current user to log off.

To switch users, press Ctrl+Alt+Del, and then click the Switch User button. In a workgroup, the Log On screen is displayed as at startup. In a domain, a screen appears with the message "Press Ctrl+Alt+Del To Log On," and you must press Ctrl+Alt+Del again to display the Log On screen.

Managing User Account Passwords with Windows 7

Unlike Windows XP and earlier versions of Windows, Windows 7 provides fast and easy ways to manage user account passwords. You can easily perform the following tasks:

- Change the current user's password
- Change the password for another domain or local computer account
- Create a password reset disk
- Reset a user's password

These tasks are discussed in the sections that follow.

CHANGING THE CURRENT USER'S PASSWORD

You can change the current user's password by completing the following steps:

1. Press Ctrl+Alt+Del, and then click the Change A Password option.

   NOTE **In a domain, the current user's domain account name is listed in *domain\username* format. In a homegroup or workgroup, the current user's local account name is listed.**

2. Type the current password for the account in the Old Password text box.
3. Type and confirm the new password for the account in the New Password and the Confirm Password text boxes.
4. Click the arrow button to confirm the change.

CHANGING OTHER ACCOUNT PASSWORDS

You can change the password for a domain or a local account other than the current user's account by completing these steps:

1. Press Ctrl+Alt+Del, and then click the Change A Password option.
2. Click in the User Name text box, and then type the name of the account.

NOTE For a domain account, specify the domain and the account name using the format *domain\username*, such as cpandl\williams. For a local computer account, type **.\username**, where *username* is the name of the local account, such as .\williams.

3. Type the current password for the account in the Old Password text box.
4. Type and confirm the new password for the account in the New Password and the Confirm Password text boxes.
5. Click the arrow button to confirm the change.

CREATING AND USING A PASSWORD RESET DISK

Passwords for domain users and local users are managed in different ways. In domains, passwords for domain user accounts are managed by administrators. Administrators can reset forgotten passwords using the Active Directory Users And Computers console.

In homegroups and workgroups, passwords for local machine accounts can be stored in a secure, encrypted file on a password reset disk, which can be either a floppy disk or a USB flash device. You can create a password reset disk for the current user by completing these steps:

1. Press Ctrl+Alt+Del, and then click the Change A Password option.
2. Click Create A Password Reset Disk to start the Forgotten Password wizard.
3. In the Forgotten Password wizard, read the introductory message and then click Next.

   You can use a floppy disk or a USB flash device as your password key disk. To use a floppy disk, insert a blank, formatted disk into drive A, and then select Floppy Disk Drive (A:) in the drive list. To use a USB flash device, select the device you want to use in the drive list. Click Next.
4. Type the current password for the logged on user in the text box provided, and then click Next.
5. After the wizard creates the password reset disk, click Next, remove the disk, and then click Finish.

Be sure to store the password reset disk in a secure location because anyone with access to the disk can use it to gain access to the user's data. If a user is unable to log on because he or she has forgotten the password, you can use the password reset disk to create a new password and log on to the account using this password.

REAL WORLD You can use BitLocker To Go to protect and encrypt USB flash devices and other removable media drives. When a user is logged on, protected media can be unlocked using a password or a smart card with a smart card PIN. However, when a user isn't logged on, the protected drive cannot be accessed. Because of this, you shouldn't protect password reset disks with BitLocker To Go. For more information, see Chapter 11, "Using TPM and BitLocker Drive Encryption."

RESETTING A USER'S PASSWORD

You can reset a password by following these steps:

1. On the Log On screen, click the arrow button without entering a password, and then click OK. The Reset Password option should be displayed. If the user has already entered the wrong password, the Reset Password option might already be displayed.
2. Insert the disk or USB flash device containing the password recovery file, and then click Reset Password to start the Reset Password wizard.
3. In the Reset Password wizard, read the introductory message and then click Next.
4. Select the device you want to use in the drive list, and then click Next.
5. On the Reset The User Account Password page, type and confirm a new password for the user.
6. Type a password hint, and then click Next. Click Finish.

Power Plans, Sleep Modes, and Shutdown

Power options have changed in Windows 7. By default, computers running Windows 7 use the Balanced power plan, and this power plan turns off the display and puts the computer in sleep mode automatically after a specified period of time passes with no user activity.

When entering the sleep state, the operating system automatically saves all work, turns off the display, and puts the computer in sleep mode. Sleep mode is a low-power consumption mode in which the state of the computer is maintained in the computer's memory, and the computer's fans and hard disks are turned off.

Windows 7 saves the computer state before entering sleep mode, and you don't need to exit programs before you do this. Because the computer uses very little energy in the sleep state, you don't have to worry about wasting energy.

TIP **Sleep mode works in a slightly different way with mobile computers. Often you can turn off and turn on mobile computers by closing or opening the lid. When you close the lid, the laptop enters the sleep state. When you open the lid, the laptop wakes up from the sleep state. If while the laptop is in the sleep state, the laptop's battery runs low on power, the state of the computer is saved to the hard disk and then the computer shuts down completely. This final state is similar to the hibernate state used in Windows XP.**

To view or modify the default power options, click Start and then click Control Panel. In Control Panel, click System And Security, and then, under Power Options, click Change When The Computer Sleeps. As shown in Figure 1-5, you can use the options provided to specify when the display is turned off and when the computer goes to sleep for the power plan that is active. Click Save Changes to save your changes.

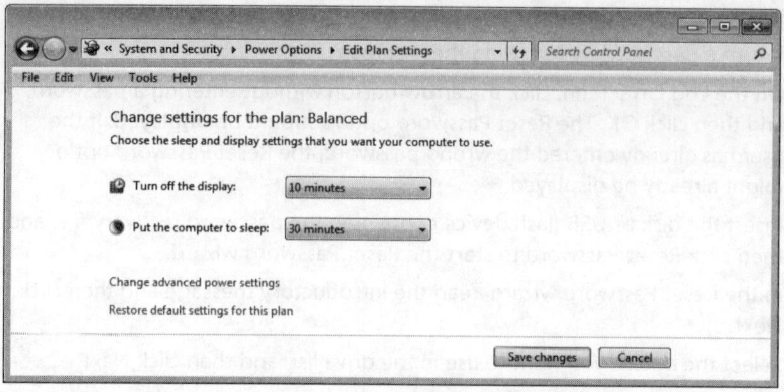

FIGURE 1-5 Configure power options to meet the needs of your users.

You can cause most computers to enter the sleep state by clicking the Start button, clicking the options button to the right of Shutdown, and then clicking Sleep. To wake the computer from the sleep state, you can move the mouse or press any key on the keyboard. Note that some computers have separate power and sleep buttons on their case. The way these buttons work can be set through the power plan options.

There are instances in which a computer can't use the sleep state. The system hardware, state, and configuration can affect the way the power and sleep buttons work. Some computer hardware doesn't support the sleep state. In this case, the computer can't use the sleep state. This is also the case when the computer has updates installed that require a restart or you've installed programs that require a restart. Additionally, if an administrator has reconfigured the power options on the computer and set the power button, the sleep button, or both to alternative actions, the computer will use those actions instead of the default shutdown and sleep actions.

> ***CAUTION*** **When working with computers in the sleep state, keep in mind that the computer is still drawing power. You should never install hardware inside the computer or connect devices to the computer when it is in the sleep state. To avoid possible confusion regarding the sleep state and the power-down state, be sure to unplug a computer running Windows 7 before installing or connecting devices. The only exceptions are external devices that use USB, IEEE 1394 (FireWire), or eSATA ports. You can connect USB, FireWire, and eSATA devices without shutting down the computer.**

To change the default setting for the power button, click Start and then click Control Panel. In Control Panel, click System And Security, and then, under Power Options, click Choose What The Power Buttons Do. As shown in Figure 1-6, you can then use the options provided to specify what happens when you press the power button and what happens when you press the sleep button. Optionally, you can click

Change Settings That Are Currently Unavailable, and then select Require A Password to require a password on wakeup. Click Save Changes to save your changes.

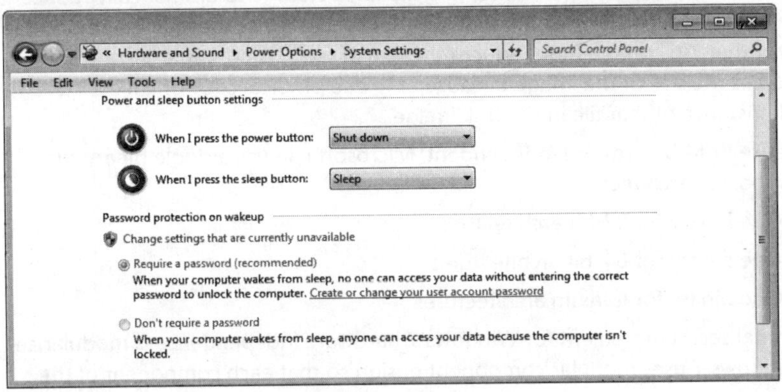

FIGURE 1-6 Configure power button options.

Windows 7 Architecture

If you want to truly know how Windows 7 works and what makes it tick, you need to dig under the hood. Windows 7 doesn't boot from an initialization file. Instead, the operating system uses the Windows boot manager to initialize and start the operating system.

The boot environment dramatically changes the way the operating system starts. The boot environment was created by Microsoft to resolve several prickly problems related to boot integrity, operating system integrity, and firmware abstraction. The boot environment is loaded prior to the operating system, making it a preoperating system environment. As such, the boot environment can be used to validate the integrity of the startup process and the operating system itself before actually starting the operating system.

The boot environment is an extensible abstraction layer that allows the operating system to work with multiple types of firmware interfaces without requiring the operating system to be specifically written to work with these firmware interfaces. Rather than updating the operating system each time a new firmware interface is developed, firmware interface developers can use the standard programming interfaces of the boot environment to allow the operating system to communicate as necessary through the firmware interfaces.

Firmware interface abstraction is the first secret ingredient that makes it possible for Windows 7 to work with BIOS-based and EFI-based computers in exactly the same way, and this is one of the primary reasons Windows 7 achieves hardware independence. You'll learn more about the boot environment in Chapter 2 and in Chapter 10.

The next secret ingredient for Windows 7 hardware independence is Windows Imaging Format (WIM). Microsoft distributes Windows 7 on media using WIM disk images. WIM uses compression and single-instance storage to dramatically reduce the size of image files. Using compression reduces the size of the image in much the same way that Zip compression reduces the size of files. Using single-instance storage reduces the size of the image because only one physical copy of a file is stored for each instance of that file in the disk image.

Because WIM is hardware independent, Microsoft can use a single binary for each supported architecture:

- One binary for 32-bit architectures
- One binary for 64-bit architectures
- One binary for Itanium architectures

The final secret ingredient for Windows 7 hardware independence is modularization. Windows 7 uses modular component design so that each component of the operating system is defined as a separate independent unit or module. Because modules can contain other modules, various major features of the operating system can be grouped together and described independently of other major features. Because modules are independent from each other, modules can be swapped in or out to customize the operating system environment.

Windows 7 includes extensive support architecture. At the heart of this architecture is built-in diagnostics and troubleshooting. Microsoft designed built-in diagnostics and troubleshooting to be self-correcting and self-diagnosing, and failing that, to provide guidance while you are diagnosing problems.

Windows 7 includes network awareness and network discovery features. Network awareness tracks changes in network configuration and connectivity. Network discovery controls a computer's ability to detect other computers and devices on a network.

Network awareness allows Windows 7 to detect the current network configuration and connectivity status, which is important because many networking and security settings depend on the type of network to which a computer running Windows 7 is connected. Windows 7 has separate network configurations for domain networks, private networks, and public networks and is able to detect:

- When you change a network connection
- Whether the computer has a connection to the Internet
- Whether the computer can connect to the corporate network over the Internet

Unlike all earlier versions of Windows, Windows Firewall in Windows 7 supports connectivity to multiple networks simultaneously and multiple active firewall profiles. Because of this, the active firewall profile for a connection depends on the type of connection.

If you disconnect a computer from one network switch or hub and plug it into a new network switch or hub, you might inadvertently cause the computer to think it is on a different network, and depending on Group Policy configuration, this could cause the computer to enter a lockdown state in which additional network security settings are applied. As shown in Figure 1-7, you can view the network connection status in the Network And Sharing Center. In Control Panel, under Network And Internet, click Network And Sharing Center to access this management console.

TIP **Through the DirectAccess feature, computers running Windows 7 can now directly access corporate networks wherever they are as long as they have access to the Internet, and best of all users don't need to initiate VPN connections. The feature relies on DirectAccess servers being configured on the corporate network and DirectAccess being enabled in Group Policy. For more information, see Chapter 16, "Managing Mobile Networking and Remote Access."**

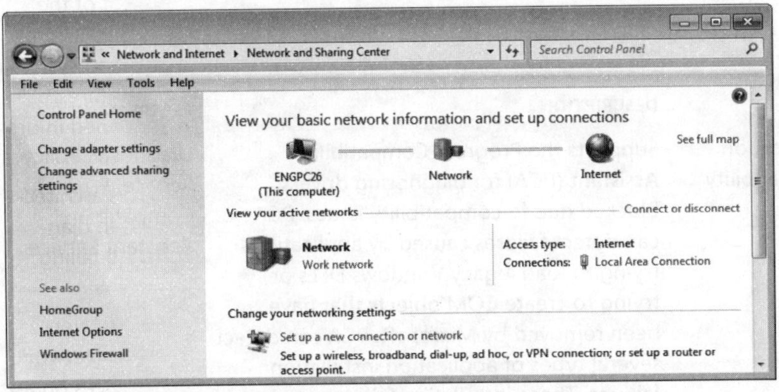

FIGURE 1-7 Determine the network state.

Windows 7 tracks the identification status of all networks to which the computer has been connected. When Windows 7 is in the process of identifying a network, the Network And Sharing Center shows the Identifying Networks state. This is a temporary state for a network that is being identified. After Windows 7 identifies a network, the network becomes an Identified Network and is listed by its network or domain name in the Network And Sharing Center.

If Windows 7 is unable to identify the network, the network is listed with the Unidentified Network status in the Network And Sharing Center. In Group Policy, you can set default location types and user permissions for each network state, as well as for all networks, by using the policies for Computer Configuration under Windows Settings\Security Settings\Network List Manager Policies.

When you are working with the Network And Sharing Center, you can attempt to diagnose a warning status by using Windows Network Diagnostics—another key component of the diagnostics and troubleshooting framework. To start diagnostics, click the warning icon in the network map or click Troubleshoot Problems, and then click Internet Connections. Windows Network Diagnostics then attempts to identify the network problem and provide a possible solution.

The Windows diagnostics and troubleshooting infrastructure offers improved diagnostics guidance, additional error reporting details, expanded event logging, and extensive recovery policies. Although Windows XP and earlier versions of Windows include some help and diagnostics features, those features are, for the most part, not self-correcting or self-diagnosing. Windows 7, on the other hand, can detect many types of hardware, memory, and performance issues and resolve them automatically or help users through the process of resolving them.

As shown in Table 1-4, Windows diagnostics and troubleshooting features are divided into 15 broad diagnostics areas. In Group Policy, you can configure how these features work by using the Administrative Templates policies for Computer Configuration under System\Troubleshooting And Diagnostics.

TABLE 1-4 Key Diagnostics Areas in Windows 7

DIAGNOSTIC AREA	DESCRIPTION	REQUIREMENTS
Application compatibility	Supports the Program Compatibility Assistant (PCA) for diagnosing drivers blocked due to compatibility issues. PCA can detect failures caused by applications trying to load legacy Windows DLLs or trying to create COM objects that have been removed by Microsoft. PCA can detect several types of application installation failures. These installation failures can be related to applications that do not have privileges to run as an administrator but must be installed with elevated privileges as well as applications that fail to launch child processes that require elevation. In this case, PCA provides you with the option to restart the installer or the update process as an administrator.	Diagnostic Policy Service, Program Compatibility Assistant Service
Boot performance	Supports automatic detection and trouble-shooting of issues that affect boot perfor-mance. Root causes of boot performance issues are logged to the event logs. Can also assist you in resolving related issues.	Diagnostic Policy Service

DIAGNOSTIC AREA	DESCRIPTION	REQUIREMENTS
Corrupted file recovery	Supports automatic detection, troubleshooting, and recovery of corrupted files. If Windows detects that an important operating system file is corrupted, Windows attempts notification and recovery, which requires a restart in most cases for full resolution.	Diagnostic Policy Service
External support	Supports the Microsoft Support Diagnostic Tool (MSDT) for collecting and sending diagnostic data to a support professional to resolve a problem. Msdt.exe is stored in the %SystemRoot%\System32 folder and through policy settings can be configured for local and remote troubleshooting or remote troubleshooting only.	Diagnostic Policy Service
Fault-tolerant heap	Supports automatic detection and correction of common memory management issues related to the heap used by the operating system.	Diagnostic Policy Service
Memory leak	Supports automatic detection and troubleshooting of memory leak issues. A memory leak occurs if an application or system component doesn't completely free areas of physical memory after it is done with them.	Diagnostic Policy Service
MSI corrupted file recovery	Supports automatic detection, troubleshooting, and recovery of corrupted MSI applications. If Windows detects that application files are corrupted, Windows attempts notification and recovery.	Diagnostic Policy Service
Performance PerfTrack	Supports automated tracking and reporting of responsiveness events to Microsoft's Software Quality Management (SQM) team.	

DIAGNOSTIC AREA	DESCRIPTION	REQUIREMENTS
Resource exhaustion	Supports automatic detection and troubleshooting to resolve issues related to running out of virtual memory. Can also alert you if the computer is running low on virtual memory and identify the processes consuming the largest amount of memory, allowing you to close any or all of these high-resource-consuming applications directly from the Close Programs To Prevent Information Loss dialog box. An alert is also logged in the event log.	Diagnostic Policy Service
Scheduled maintenance	Supports diagnostics that run periodically via the Task Scheduler to detect and resolve system problems.	Task Scheduler Service
Scripted diagnostics	Supports Action Center and controls whether users can access troubleshooting content and troubleshooting tools.	
Shutdown performance	Supports automatic detection and troubleshooting of issues that affect shutdown performance. Root causes of shutdown performance issues are logged to the event logs. Can also assist you in resolving related issues.	Diagnostic Policy Service
Standby/resume performance	Supports automatic detection and troubleshooting of issues that affect standby/resume performance on desktop computers. Root causes of standby/resume performance issues are logged to the event logs. Can also assist you in resolving related issues.	Diagnostic Policy Service
System responsiveness	Supports automatic detection and troubleshooting of issues that affect the overall responsiveness of the operating system. Root causes of responsiveness issues are logged to the event logs. Can also assist you in resolving related issues.	Diagnostic Policy Service

Other diagnostics features of Windows 7 include:

- Restart Manager
- Action Center and troubleshooters
- Startup Repair tool
- Performance Diagnostics console
- Windows Memory Diagnostics

In Windows XP and earlier versions of Windows, an application crash or hang is marked as Not Responding, and it is up to the user to exit and then restart the application. Windows 7 attempts to automatically resolve the issues related to unresponsive applications by using Restart Manager. Restart Manager can shut down and restart unresponsive applications automatically. In many cases, this means that you may not have to intervene to try to resolve issues with frozen applications.

A failed installation and nonresponsive conditions of applications and drivers are also tracked through Action Center. Should such an event occur, the Action Center notification icon will show a red circle with an X through it. If you click the notification icon, Windows 7 displays a summary report of current issues. As discussed previously, you can click the link provided to open a possible solution or to get more information. If these processes fail, access the Action Center main window and then scroll down to display the Troubleshooting and Recovery links.

Clicking Troubleshooting opens the Troubleshooting window. As shown in Figure 1-8, several troubleshooters are provided. These troubleshooters can help users quickly resolve common problems without requiring administrator support. The troubleshooters include:

- Programs for compatibility issues with applications designed for earlier versions of Windows.
- Hardware And Sound for issues with hardware devices, audio recording, and audio playback.
- Network And Internet for issues with connecting to networks and accessing shared folders on other computers.
- Appearance And Personalization for issues with the display appearance and personalization settings. To quickly resolve display issues with Aero, click Display Aero Desktop Effects.
- System And Security for issues with Windows Update, power usage, and performance. Click Run Maintenance Tasks to clean up unused files and shortcuts and perform other routine maintenance tasks.

To resolve startup problems, Windows 7 uses the Startup Repair tool (StR), which is installed automatically and started when a system fails to boot. After it is started, StR attempts to determine the cause of the startup failure by analyzing startup logs and error reports. Then StR attempts to fix the problem automatically. If StR is unable to resolve the problem, it restores the system to the last known working state and then provides diagnostic information and support options for further troubleshooting.

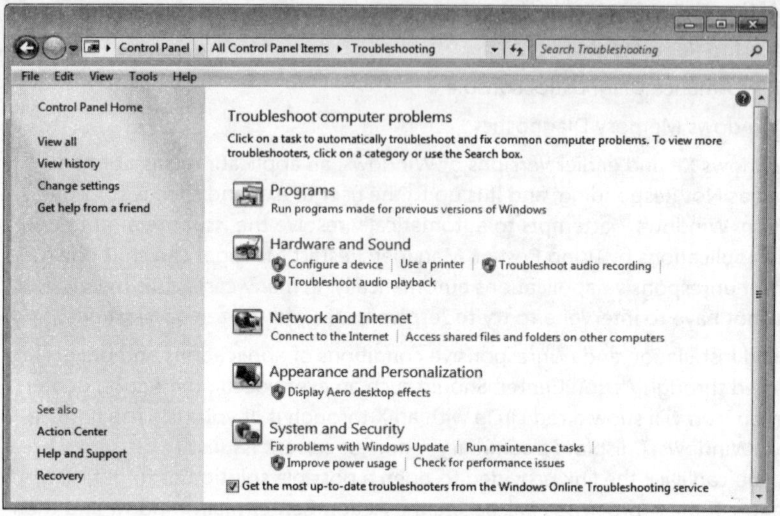

FIGURE 1-8 Access the troubleshooters to fix common problems.

Startup Repair performs many tests during diagnostics and troubleshooting. These tests can take anywhere from 5 to 30 minutes or more depending on the configured hardware, and they include these specific tests:

- **Check for updates** Determines whether newly applied updates are affecting startup.
- **System disk test** Determines whether there is a problem with the system disk that is preventing startup. If so, StR can attempt to repair any missing or corrupt files.
- **Disk failure diagnosis** Determines whether any of the configured disks have failed.
- **Disk metadata test** Determines whether any of the available disks have a problem with their metadata that is preventing startup. The metadata associated with a disk depends on how a disk is partitioned and the file system format of disk partitions.
- **Target OS test** Determines whether the operating system you are attempting to start has a specific issue that is preventing startup.
- **Volume content check** Examines the content of disk volumes to ensure that volumes are accessible.
- **Boot manager diagnosis** Determines whether there is a problem with the boot manager or boot manager entries that are preventing startup.

- **System boot log diagnosis** Examines system boot log entries from previous startups to see if there are specific errors that might be related to the startup issue.
- **Event log diagnosis** Examines event log entries to see if there are specific errors that might be related to the startup issue.
- **Internal state check** Checks the current internal state of the preboot environment.
- **Boot status test** Checks the current boot status in the preboot environment.
- **Setup state check** Determines whether the computer is in a setup state.
- **Registry hives test** Checks the computer's registry hives.
- **Windows boot log diagnosis** Examines the Windows boot log entries to see if there are specific errors that might be related to the startup issue.
- **Bug check analysis** Performs a basic bug check analysis of the operating system.
- **Access control test** Determines whether access controls in the preboot environment are preventing startup of the operating system.
- **File system test (chkdsk)** Performs a basic file system test using Chkdsk.
- **Software install log diagnosis** Examines software installation log entries to see if there are specific errors that might be related to the startup issue.
- **Fallback diagnosis** Determines whether any flags have been set that indicate the computer should fall back to a previous state to correct the startup issue. If so, StR will attempt to restore the previous state.

Error detection for devices and failure detection for disk drives also is automated. If a device is having problems, hardware diagnostics can detect error conditions and either repair the problem automatically or guide the user through a recovery process. With disk drives, hardware diagnostics can use fault reports provided by disk drives to detect potential failure and alert you before this happens. Hardware diagnostics can also help guide you through the backup process after alerting you that a disk might be failing.

Windows 7 can automatically detect performance issues, which include slow application startup, slow boot, slow standby/resume, and slow shutdown. If a computer is experiencing degraded performance, Windows diagnostics can detect the problem and provide possible solutions. For advanced performance issues, you can track related performance and reliability data in the Performance Monitor console, which can be opened from the Administrative Tools menu.

Windows 7 can also detect issues related to memory leaks and failing memory. If you suspect that a computer has a memory problem that is not being automatically detected, you can run Windows Memory Diagnostics manually by completing the following steps:

1. Click Start, type **mdsched.exe** in the Search box, and then press Enter.
2. Choose whether to restart the computer and run the tool immediately or schedule the tool to run at the next restart.
3. Windows Memory Diagnostics runs automatically after the computer restarts and performs a standard memory test. If you want to perform fewer or more tests, press F1, use the Up and Down Arrow keys to set the Test Mix as Basic, Standard, or Extended, and then press F10 to apply the desired settings and resume testing.
4. When testing is completed, the computer restarts. You'll see the test results when you log on.

If a computer crashes because of failing memory and Memory Diagnostics detects this, you are prompted to schedule a memory test the next time the computer is started.

CHAPTER 2

Deploying Windows 7

With Windows 7, you can deploy custom builds to computers through manual and automated processes. To deploy Windows using manual processes, you need to create the required boot and installation images and optionally create recovery images. To automate the deployment process, you need to install Windows Deployment Services. Whether you use a completely manual process, a completely automated process, or some combination of the two, you'll perform similar administrative tasks. These tasks require you to understand and use:

- Windows Preinstallation Environment (Windows PE)
- Windows Recovery Environment (Windows RE)
- Windows Imaging tools
- Windows Deployment Services

I discuss these technologies in this chapter and show you how to use them to deploy Windows 7.

Working with Windows PE

Windows Preinstallation Environment replaces MS-DOS as the preinstallation environment for Windows operating systems. Windows Vista and Windows 7 installation is based entirely on Windows PE and disk imaging. You also can use Windows PE to start computers and prepare for installation.

Understanding Windows PE

Windows 7 and Windows Server 2008 Release 2 use Windows PE 3.0. Windows PE 3.0 is a bootable startup environment that provides operating system features for the following:

- **Installation** When you install Windows 7, the graphical tools that collect system information during the setup phase are running within Windows PE.
- **Deployment** When a new computer performs a network boot, the built-in Preboot Execution Environment (PXE) client can connect to a Windows Deployment Services server, download a Windows PE image across the network, and then run deployment scripts within this environment.
- **Recovery** Windows PE enables you to access and run the Startup Repair tool if Windows 7 fails to start because of a corrupted system file.
- **Troubleshooting** You can manually start Windows PE to perform troubleshooting or diagnostics testing if Windows 7 is experiencing problems that can't otherwise be diagnosed.

Windows PE is modular and extensible, and it provides full access to partitions formatted using the file allocation table (FAT) or NTFS file system. Because Windows PE is built from a subset of Windows components, you can run many Windows applications, work with hardware devices, and communicate across Internet Protocol (IP) networks. Several command-line tools are available in Windows PE, including:

- **BCDBoot** A tool that initializes the boot configuration data (BCD) store and allows you to copy boot environment files to the system partition
- **Bootsect** A tool for creating and working with boot sectors on hard disks and flash drives
- **DiskPart** A tool for creating and working with disks, partitions, and volumes
- **DISM** An advanced tool for servicing and maintaining images
- **Drvload** A support tool for adding device drivers and dynamically loading a driver after Windows PE has started
- **ImageX** A tool for capturing and applying Windows images
- **Net** A set of support commands that enables you to manage local users, start and stop services, and connect to shared folders
- **Netcfg** A tool that configures network access
- **Oscdimg** A tool for creating CD and DVD ISO image files
- **Wpeinit** A tool that initializes Windows PE every time it boots

For deployment, you can execute these tools from configuration scripts to perform key configuration tasks. As examples, you can:

- Use Netcfg to configure network access.

- Use Drvload to install a driver and use the hardware without restarting the computer.
- Run DiskPart to partition and format the computer's hard disk.
- Use Net Share to connect to a shared folder containing the Windows 7 Setup files.
- Run the Windows 7 Setup program to install the operating system.

You can get the Windows PE build environment in the Windows OEM Preinstallation Kit (Windows OPK), the Windows Automated Installation Kit (Windows AIK), or the Windows PE Kit. To use Windows PE to create boot and installation environments for Windows 7, you must use the version of these kits for Windows 7. Because these kits are often updated, look for the one for the service pack you are currently using.

Included in these kits are separate 32-bit and 64-bit editions of Windows PE. You use the 32-bit edition to prepare 32-bit versions of Windows 7. You use the 64-bit edition to prepare 64-bit versions of Windows 7.

As with Windows 7 itself, Windows PE can be contained within a disk image. When you store a Windows 7 image in a disk image, the only way to start Windows 7 is to copy the full image to the computer's hard disk. When you store Windows PE in a disk image, however, you can start Windows PE from the image without having to copy it to the computer's hard disk. This enables you to store Windows PE disk images on bootable media, such as a DVD or USB flash drive, and then start Windows PE directly from that media. The Windows 7 distribution media uses this technique to load Windows PE into RAM during setup of the operating system.

You can load Windows PE into RAM as well, which might be necessary for troubleshooting. When you do this, the Windows PE boot loader creates a virtual RAM disk in memory and then copies a compressed version of Windows PE to the RAM disk. Afterward, the boot loader mounts the RAM disk as if it were a disk drive and starts Windows PE. Running Windows PE from RAM enables you to write temporary files to the virtual RAM disk, which isn't possible when running from read-only media such as a CD. It also enables you to remove the Windows PE media after Windows PE has started and then insert different media into the computer's CD-ROM or DVD-ROM drive or USB flash drive.

When working with Windows PE, keep the following in mind:

- Windows PE requires a computer with a VESA-compatible display and a minimum of 256 megabytes (MB) of RAM. During startup, if Windows PE can't detect the video settings, it uses a screen resolution of 640 × 480 pixels. Otherwise, it uses the highest resolution possible.
- Windows PE supports Plug and Play (PnP) devices. Hardware devices can be detected and installed while Windows PE is running. This means that you can install any PnP device that has a driver in the driver store, including removable media and hard disk devices.

- Windows PE supports both IPv4 and IPv6. Although you can access shared folders on other computers from Windows PE, other computers cannot access files or folders on a computer running Windows PE.
- Windows PE always starts with the default drive letter assignments. This means that drive letter assignments aren't persistent between sessions.
- Windows PE discards online changes to the registry. This means changes to the registry aren't persistent between sessions. To make permanent changes to the registry, you must mount the Windows PE image and make changes using the Registry editor.
- Windows PE doesn't support the Microsoft .NET Framework or Windows on Windows 64 (WOW64) subsystem. This means you cannot use .NET applications on any version of Windows PE, 16-bit applications on 32-bit versions of Windows PE, or 32-bit applications on 64-bit versions of Windows PE.
- Windows PE automatically restarts after running for 72 hours. This behavior is a safeguard to prevent Windows PE from being used as a general-purpose operating system.

You can boot Windows PE from the Boot.wim file on the Windows distribution media. When Windows PE initializes, the Wpeinit command is called to initialize PnP devices and start the network connection.

Configuring Windows PE

Windows PE supports several configuration files that control startup and operation. These files can be configured to start custom shell environments or perform specified tasks. The available configuration files include:

- **BCD store** The boot configuration data (BCD) store file contains boot settings for Windows PE.
- **Startnet.cmd** The StartNet script configures network startup. You can add commands to this script to customize startup.
- **Unattend.xml** The unattended installation file can be used to automate the installation process for Windows PE.
- **Winpeshl.ini** The Windows PE shell initialization file contains the default interface for Windows PE. By modifying this file you can define a custom shell environment.

At startup, computers running Windows 7 enter the preboot environment prior to the loading of the operating system. The preboot environment uses Windows Boot Manager to control the boot experience and determine which boot applications are run. The standard boot application for Windows 7 is Windows boot loader. Windows boot loader is responsible for accessing entries in the BCD store. Entries in the BCD store contain boot configuration parameters and control how the operating system is started.

The BCD store is used to abstract the underlying firmware, thereby making it easier for Windows 7 to work with new firmware models such as the Extensible Firmware Interface (EFI). The BCD store also provides the foundation for a variety of new features in Windows 7, including the Startup Repair tool and Multi-User Install shortcuts, which can be launched in the preboot environment.

The BCD store is contained in a file called the BCD registry file. The BCD registry file is located in the \Boot\Bcd directory of the active partition on BIOS-based computers and in the EFI system partition on EFI-based computers. The BCD store contains multiple entries on most computers. These entries include:

- One Windows Boot Manager entry. Because there is only one boot manager, there is only one boot manager entry in the BCD store.
- One Windows boot loader application entry for each Windows 7 operating system installed on the computer.
- One legacy operating system entry.

The legacy operating system entry is not for a boot application. Instead, this entry uses Ntldr and Boot.ini to start up a version of the Windows operating system released prior to Windows Vista. You will use the legacy operating system entry to start up Windows Server 2003, Windows XP, and earlier releases if they are installed on a computer. For more information on firmware and the BCD store, see Chapter 10, "Managing Firmware, Boot Configuration, and Startup."

Windows PE operates in the Windows PE setup configuration pass of the Windows installation process. During this setup pass, Windows PE looks for an Unattend.xml file. If one exists, Windows PE looks for and reads sections of this file that are used to automate Windows PE setup. You can use the Windows System Image Manager utility, included in the Windows AIK, to create and manage Unattend.xml files. You also can create Unattend.xml files yourself using a text editor.

Windows PE looks for the Unattend.xml file in the root directory on the boot device. After you create the file, copy the file to the root directory on the Windows PE boot device. You also can specify the location of this file in the StartNet script or by using the Wpeutil command.

You can initialize Windows PE by using the Winpeshl.ini file. This file is located in the %SystemRoot%\System32 folder in the Windows PE image. In this file, you can specify the path and executable name of a custom shell application that you want to run when Windows PE starts. The Windows Recovery Environment included in Windows 7 is simply a custom Windows PE image that runs a custom shell application.

Preparing a Build Environment

Installing the Windows OPK, Windows AIK, or Windows PE Kit will install the Windows PE build and imaging tools you need to create Windows PE images. You can download the Windows AIK from the Microsoft Download site (*http://download.microsoft.com/*). Next, burn the kit to a DVD or mount it using virtual DVD software.

If the Setup program doesn't start automatically, browse the DVD, and then click StartCD.exe to start the setup process.

After you install a kit, you'll find the following folders (where *Version* can be Windows OPK, Windows AIK, or Windows PE Kit):

- **%SystemRoot%\Program Files*Version*\Tools** Contains the *Version* program files.
- **%SystemRoot%\Program Files*Version*\Tools\amd64** Contains ImageX source files for 64-bit x64 computers.
- **%SystemRoot%\Program Files*Version*\Tools\x86** Contains ImageX source files for 32-bit x86 computers.
- **%SystemRoot%\Program Files*Version*\Tools\ia64** Contains ImageX source files for Itanium-based computers.
- **%SystemRoot%\Program Files*Version*\Tools\Image Manager** Contains Windows System Image Manager and related files.
- **%SystemRoot%\Program Files*Version*\Tools\PETools** Contains the Windows PE source files and optional components.
- **%SystemRoot%\Program Files*Version*\Tools\Servicing** Contains the servicing files.
- **%SystemRoot%\Program Files*Version*\Tools\USMT** Contains the User State Migration Toolkit and related files for x86 and x64 computers.

Before you can create a build, you need to set up the build environment. In the Tools folder is a command-line script called Copype.cmd. You can use this script to create your Windows PE build environment. The build environment contains the build scripts and source files that you can customize and then use to create new Windows PE images.

Whenever you work with the tools in the kit, you should use the Deployment Tools command prompt. This prompt has the environment settings for working with the kit you installed and can be started by completing the following steps:

1. Click Start, point to All Programs, and then click either Microsoft Windows OPK, Microsoft Windows AIK, or Microsoft Windows PE Kit as appropriate.
2. Right-click Deployment Tools Command Prompt, and then click Run As Administrator.

To set up a build environment for 32-bit x86 computers, enter the following command:

```
copype x86 c:\winpe_x86
```

To set up a build environment for 64-bit x64 computers, enter the following command:

```
copype amd64 c:\winpe_x64
```

To set up a build environment for Itanium-based computers, enter the following command:

```
copype ia64 c:\winpe_ia64
```

These commands set up the build environment under C:\Winpe_x86, C:\Winpe_x64, and C:\Winpe_ia64, respectively. The C:\Winpe_x86 folder contains files for 32-bit Windows PE. The C:\Winpe_x64 folder contains files for 64-bit Windows PE. The C:\Winpe_ia64 folder contains files for Itanium-based Windows PE. You can specify alternative directories if you want, but using these standard names might be helpful for other administrators in your organization.

In the build directories, you'll find ISO and Mount subdirectories. The ISO directory contains all the necessary files to build an .iso file by using the Oscdimg tool. This directory also includes the following subdirectories: Boot, EFI, and Sources. The Mount directory is an empty directory that you can use to mount Windows PE images by using the ImageX tool.

ImageX has a number of subcommands that you can use when working with Windows image files. These subcommands include the following:

- **imagex /append** Appends a volume image to an existing Windows image file. *ImagePath* sets the path of the volume image to be captured. *WIMFile* sets the path of the existing WIM file. *ImageName* sets the unique name for the image. *Description* sets the descriptive text. The /Boot option marks the volume image as bootable (only for Windows PE images). The /Check option enables WIM integrity checking, and /Config *Config*.ini specifies a configuration file to use for excluding files and setting compression options. The /Norpfix option disables reparse point path fixup. The /Scroll option scrolls output for redirection. The /Temp option specifies the path where temporary files are stored, and /Verify enables verification of file resources.

```
imagex {Options} /append ImagePath WIMFile "ImageName"
["Description"]

{Options}
[/boot] [/check] [/config config.ini] [/norpfix] [/scroll] [/temp]
[/verify]
```

```
imagex /append c: d:\images\windows.wim "Drive C"
```

- **imagex /apply** Applies a volume image to a specified path. *WIMFile* sets the path of the WIM file containing the volume image. *ImageIndex* identifies the image within the WIM file by its index position. *ImageName* sets the name that identifies the image within the WIM file. *ImagePath* sets the path where the image will be applied. The /Ref *Splitwim*.swm option enables a reference to split WIM files.

```
imagex {Options} /apply WIMFile {ImageIndex | ImageName} ImagePath

{Options}
[/check] [/norpfix] [/ref splitwim.swm] [/scroll] [/temp] [/verify]
```

```
imagex /apply d:\images\windows.wim 1 c:\
```

- **imagex /capture** Captures a volume image from a drive to a new Windows image file. *ImagePath* sets the path to the volume image to be captured. *WIMFile* sets the path of the new WIM file. *ImageName* sets the unique name for the image being captured. *Description* sets the text that provides additional reference information. The /Compress Maximum option sets the compression level to maximum, and /Compress Fast enables fast compression.

```
imagex {Options} /capture ImagePath WIMFile "ImageName"
["Description"]

{Options}
[/boot] [/check] [/compress {maximum | fast | none}]
[/config] [/norpfix] [/scroll] [/temp] [/verify]
```

```
imagex /capture c: d:\images\windows.wim "Drive C"
```

- **imagex /cleanup** Deletes all the resources associated with a mounted image that has been abandoned. This command will not unmount currently mounted images, nor will it delete images that can be recovered via the imagex /remount command.

```
imagex /cleanup
```

```
imagex /cleanup
```

- **imagex /commit** Commits the changes made to a mounted image without unmounting the image. *MountPath* sets the path of the mounted image to commit. *ImageName* sets the image name. The /Append option captures the changes you've made and creates a new image with those changes. If the /Append option is set, a unique image name must be provided.

```
imagex [/append] /commit MountPath ["ImageName"]
```

```
imagex /commit c:\mount
imagex /commit /append c:\mount "New Image"
```

- **imagex /delete** Deletes the specified volume image from a Windows image file with multiple volume images. *WIMFile* sets the path of the WIM file containing the specified image. *ImageIndex* sets the number that identifies the image within the WIM file. *ImageName* sets the name that references the image within the WIM file.

```
imagex [/check] [/temp] /delete WIMFile {ImageIndex | ImageName}
```

```
imagex /delete d:\images\windows.wim 1
```

- **imagex /dir** Displays a list of the files and folders within a specified volume image. *WIMFile* sets the path of the WIM file containing the specified image. *ImageIndex* sets the number that identifies the image within the WIM file. *ImageName* sets the name that identifies the image within the WIM file.

```
imagex /dir WIMFile {ImageIndex | ImageName}
```

```
imagex /dir d:\images\windows.wim 1
```

- **Imagex /export** Exports a copy of the specified image to another Windows image file. *SourceFile* sets the path of the WIM file that contains the image to be copied. *SourceNumber* sets the number that identifies the image within the source WIM. *SourceName* sets the name that identifies the image within the source WIM. *DestFile* sets the path of the WIM file that will receive the image copy. *DestName* sets the unique name for the image in the destination WIM. If *SourceName* is set to "*", then all images are exported to *DestFile*.

```
imagex {Options} /export SourceFile {SourceNumber | SourceName}
DestFile DestName

{Options}
[/boot] [/check] [/compress {maximum | fast | none}]
[/ref splitwim.swm] [/temp]
```

```
imagex /export d:\images\windows.wim 1 d:\images\win_copy.wim
"Exported Image"
```

- **imagex /info** Returns the stored descriptions for the specified Windows image file or volume image. *ImgFile* sets the path of the WIM file to be queried for information. *ImgNumber* sets the number that identifies an image within the WIM file. *ImgName* sets the name that identifies an image within the WIM file. *NewName* sets the new unique name for the specified image. *NewDesc* sets the new description for the specified image. The /XML option returns the output as XML.

```
imagex {Options} /info ImgFile {ImgNumber | ImgName} [NewName]
[NewDesc]

{Options}
[/boot] [/check] [/temp] [/xml]
```

```
imagex /info d:\images\windows.wim
```

- **imagex /mount** Mounts a Windows image with read-only permission to a specified path. *WIMFile* sets the path of the WIM file containing the specified image. *ImageIndex* identifies the image within the WIM file by its index position. *ImageName* identifies the image within the WIM file by its name. *ImagePath* sets the path where the specified image will be mounted. When used without parameters, this subcommand lists all mounted images.

```
imagex [/check] /mount [WIMFile {ImageIndex | ImageName} ImagePath]
```

```
imagex /mount d:\images\windows.wim 2 c:\mount
```

- **imagex /mountrw** Mounts a Windows image with read/write permission to a specified path. *WIMFile* sets the path of the WIM file containing the specified image. *ImageIndex* identifies the image within the WIM file by its index position. *ImageName* identifies the image within the WIM file by its name. *ImagePath* sets the path where the specified image will be mounted. When used without parameters, this subcommand lists all mounted images.

```
imagex [/check] /mountrw [WIMFile {ImageIndex | ImageName}
ImagePath]
```

```
imagex /mountrw d:\images\data.wim 2 c:\mount
```

- **imagex /remount** Recovers an orphaned mount path. *ImagePath* sets the path to be remounted. When used without parameters, this subcommand lists all mounted images.

```
imagex /remount [ImagePath]
```

```
imagex /remount c:\mount
```

- **imagex /split** Splits an existing Windows image file into multiple read-only split WIM (SWM) files. *WIMFile* sets the path of the WIM file to split. *DestFile* sets the path of the split file or files. *Size* sets the maximum size in megabytes for each created file.

```
imagex [/check] /split WIMFile DestFile Size
```

```
imagex /split d:\images\windows.wim d:\images\splitdata.swm 600
```

- **imagex /unmount** Unmounts a Windows image from the specified path. *ImagePath* sets the path to be unmounted. The /Commit option saves the changes before unmounting the image. If uncommitted changes exist, this subcommand must use either the /Commit or the /Discard option. When used without parameters, this subcommand lists all mounted images.

```
imagex /unmount [[/commit | /discard] ImagePath]
```

```
imagex /unmount /commit c:\mount
```

If you want to manipulate Windows images on a computer that does not have an appropriate kit installed, you must copy Dism.exe, Imagex.exe, Oscdimg.exe, Wimmount.sys, Wimmount.inf, and Wimserv.exe to that computer. Next, you must install the mounting driver by right-clicking the Wimmount.inf file, and then clicking Install. You must then place Dism.exe, Imagex.exe, Oscdimg.exe, and Wimserv.exe in your local path. To do this, copy them to the %SystemRoot%\System32 directory.

Creating a Build: The Essentials

When you set up the build environments for Windows PE, you create base images for Windows PE. The traditional way to customize Windows PE builds is to use the PeImg utility. However, the Deployment Image Servicing and Management tool (DISM) replaces PeImg and provides a more robust solution for working with builds. To create custom builds using DISM, you need to do the following:

1. Mount the image.
2. Customize the image.
3. Unmount the image.
4. Capture the image to a Windows Imaging (.wim) file.
5. Create a bootable ISO (.iso) image.

In the sections that follow, I discuss these processes. Whenever you work with the tools in the kit, you should use the Deployment Tools command prompt. This prompt has the environment settings for working with the kit you installed and can be started by completing the following steps:

1. Click Start, point to All Programs, and then click either Microsoft Windows OPK, Microsoft Windows AIK, or Microsoft Windows PE Kit as appropriate.
2. Right-click Deployment Tools Command Prompt, and then click Run As Administrator.

Mounting a Windows PE Image

After you set up the build environment, you need to mount one of the base images. This allows you to customize your Windows PE images.

- To prepare 32-bit Windows PE for customization, mount the base image in the build folder by entering **imagex /apply c:\winpe_x86\iso\sources\boot.wim *n* c:\winpe_x86\mount**, where *n* is the index position of the image number within the Boot.wim file to be applied, and the directory path provided is the location in which to copy the image contents.

- To prepare 64-bit Windows PE for customization, mount the base image in the build folder by entering **imagex /apply c:\winpe_x64\iso\sources\boot.wim *n* c:\winpe_x64\mount**, where *n* is the index position of the image number within the Boot.wim file to be applied, and the directory path provided is the location in which to copy the image contents.
- To prepare Itanium-based Windows PE for customization, mount the base image in the build folder by entering **imagex /apply c:\winpe_ia64\iso\sources\boot.wim *n* c:\winpe_ia64\mount**, where *n* is the index position of the image number within the Boot.wim file to be applied, and the directory path provided is the location in which to copy the image contents.

NOTE **There are several other ways to mount images for customization. For example, you can use ImageX /MountRW to mount images. The syntax is the same as with ImageX /Apply. DISM has /Mount-wim and /Unmount-wim options as well. For more information, see the section "Customizing Windows Images" later in this chapter.**

When you mount an image file, you'll see output similar to the following:

```
ImageX Tool for Windows
Copyright (C) Microsoft Corp. All rights reserved.

Mounting: [c:\winpe_x86\iso\sources\boot.wim, 1] ->
[c:\winpe_x86\mount\]...

[ 100% ] Mounting progress

Successfully mounted image.

Total elapsed time: 10 sec
```

If ImageX is unable to mount the image, you should check to be sure that you started the Deployment Tools command prompt and are working as an administrator. If you are, check the image file properties and ensure that the security settings are configured correctly.

Once an image is mounted, you can browse its contents. Simply use Windows Explorer to access the folder to which you've mounted the image. When working with Windows PE, keep in mind that Windows PE images include a limited subset of Windows components—specifically, only those components required to start the computer and prepare for installation. Windows Recovery Environment differs from a standard Windows PE configuration only because it includes additional components that can be used for recovery and for troubleshooting startup.

Customizing a Windows PE Image

You can customize a mounted boot or installation image using the DISM utility. You work with mounted images by using the subcommands of Dism /image. DISM options designed for servicing Windows PE images are listed in Table 2-1. Some other options can be used with Windows PE as well, and you'll find a complete list of other available options later in the chapter in Tables 2-4 and 2-5.

TABLE 2-1 Common DISM Options for Windows PE Images

OPTION	DESCRIPTION	EXAMPLE
/Get-PESettings	Displays a list of Windows PE settings in the mounted Windows PE image. The list includes current profiling state, scratch space settings, and target path settings.	Dism /image:C:\winpe_x86\mount /Get-PESettings
/Get-Profiling	Displays the status of the profiling feature.	Dism /image:C:\winpe_x86\mount /Get-Profiling
/Get-ScratchSpace	Displays the configured amount of Windows PE system volume scratch space. This setting represents the amount of writable space available on the Windows PE system volume when booted in RAM disk mode.	Dism /image:C:\winpe_x86\mount /Get-ScratchSpace
/Get-TargetPath	Displays the target path of the Windows PE image. The target path represents a path to the root of the Windows PE image at boot time.	Dism /image:C:\winpe_x86\mount /Get-TargetPath
/Set-ScratchSpace:*Size*	Sets the available scratch space in megabytes. Valid values are 32, 64, 128, 256, and 512.	Dism /image:C:\winpe_x86\mount /Set-ScratchSpace:256
/Set-TargetPath:*Path*	When you are booting to a hard disk, this option sets the location of the Windows PE image on the disk. The path must start with a letter (any letter from C to Z) and must be followed by :\.	Dism /image:C:\winpe_x86\mount /Set-TargetPath:X:\

OPTION	DESCRIPTION	EXAMPLE
/Enable-Profiling	Enables profiling so that you can create your own profiles. By default, profiling is disabled.	Dism /image:C:\winpe_x86\mount /Enable-Profiling
/Disable-Profiling	Turns off profiling.	Dism /image:C:\winpe_x86\mount /Disable-Profiling
/Apply-Profiles:*Path*	Applies a profile and removes files that are not used in the custom profile. Critical boot files are not deleted. A Windows PE image that has been customized using any profile is not serviceable.	Dism /image:C:\winpe_x86\mount /Apply-Profiles: C:\profiles\prof.txt

If you mount an image using the following command:

```
imagex /apply c:\winpe_x86\iso\sources\boot.wim 1 c:\winpe_x86\mount\
```

you'll work with the image via the mount point:

```
c:\winpe_x86\mount\
```

All Windows PE images have the following settings:

- **Profiling status** Specifies whether profiling is enabled or disabled.
- **Scratch space** Specifies the amount of memory to allocate to the Windows PE work space, such as 32 MB.
- **Target path** Specifies the target path used when you boot the Windows PE image, such as X:\.

To review the settings of the mounted image, enter the following command:

```
dism /image:ImagePath /Get-PESettings
```

where *ImagePath* is the path to the image you've mounted, such as:

```
dism /image:c:\winpe_x86\mount\ /get-pesettings
```

By default, Windows PE allocates 32 MB of writable memory for its work space. You can increase the work space up to 512 MB by typing the following at a command prompt:

```
dism /image:ImagePath /Set-ScratchSpace:Size
```

where *ImagePath* is the path to the image you've mounted, and *Size* is the work space size in megabytes. Valid values for *Size* are 32, 64, 128, 256, and 512. The following example sets the work space to 128 MB:

```
dism /image:c:\winpe_x86\mount\  /Set-ScratchSpace:128
```

You might want to increase the amount of memory allocated to the work space if you plan to use profiling or run nonstandard applications in the Windows PE environment. If Windows PE runs out of memory, applications might become unresponsive.

There are many other things you can do with Windows PE images. You can get information about all installed drivers by entering the following command:

```
dism /image:c:\winpe_x86\mount\ /get-drivers /all
```

> ***NOTE*** **When a DISM option expects you to provide a working value, follow the option name with a colon and then specify the required value. Don't insert a space between the colon and the value.**

To add a third-party driver to Windows PE images, you use /Add-Driver. The basic syntax is:

```
dism /image:MountPoint /add-driver /Driver:InfPath
```

where *MountPoint* is the path where the image is mounted, and *InfPath* is the path for the .inf file for the driver, for example:

```
dism /image:c:\winpe_x86\mount\ /add-driver
/driver:c:\drivers\remmedia\rem.inf
```

If a common folder has subdirectories containing drivers to add, you can specify the base folder to search recursively by using the following syntax:

```
dism /image:MountPoint /add-driver /driver:BaseFolder /recurse
```

where *MountPoint* is the path where the image is mounted, and *BaseFolder* is the folder to search for drivers, such as:

```
dism /image:c:\winpe_x86\mount\ /add-driver /driver:c:\drivers /recurse
```

> ***TIP*** **With x64 and Itanium-based computers, you must use signed drivers by default. To force DISM to accept unsigned drivers, add the /ForceUnsigned option.**

To add applications to a Windows PE image, simply use Copy or Xcopy to copy the necessary application files to the appropriate subdirectory. For example, you can copy Imagex.exe to the root directory of the image by using the following command:

```
xcopy "C:\Program Files\Windows AIK\Tools\x86\Imagex.exe"
c:\winpe_x86\mount\
```

You can get information about packages installed in a Windows PE image by using the /Get-Packages option. The basic syntax is:

```
dism /image:MountPoint /get-packages
```

such as:

```
dism /image:c:\winpe_x86\mount\ /get-packages
```

To add packages, you use the /Add-Package option. The available packages you can install include those listed in Table 2-2. The basic syntax for adding packages is:

```
dism /image:MountPoint /add-package /PackagePath:PathtoCab
```

Here is an example:

```
dism /image:C:\winpe_x86\mount /Add-Package /PackagePath:"C:\Program Files\
Windows AIK\Tools\PETools\x86\WinPE_OCs\winpe-wmi.cab"
```

TABLE 2-2 Common Windows PE Packages

PACKAGE NAME	DESCRIPTION
WinPE-FONTSupport-*Language*.cab	Installs fonts for the specified language: ja-jp, ko-kr, zh-cn, zh-hk, or zh-tw
WinPE-HTA.cab	Installs HTML application support
WinPE-LegacySetup.cab	Installs the legacy setup package
WinPE-MDAC.cab	Installs Microsoft Data Access Component support
WinPE-Scripting.cab	Installs Windows Script Host support
WinPE-Setup-Client.cab	Installs the client setup package (as long as you have already installed the main setup package)
WinPE-Setup.cab	Installs the main setup package
WinPE-Setup-Server.cab	Installs the server setup package (as long as you have already installed the main setup package)
WinPE-SRT.cab	Installs the Windows Recovery Environment component (Windows OPK only)
WinPE-WDS-Tools.cab	Installs the Windows Deployment Services tools package
WinPE-WMI.cab	Installs Windows Management Instrumentation (WMI) support

The base Windows PE image does not contain all the packages listed in the table. You must use the DISM tool to install the additional packages you want to use. The packages are located in the \Windows OPK\Tools\PETools*ProcType* or \Windows AIK\Tools\PETools*ProcType* directory, where *ProcType* is amd64, ia64, or x86. When you install font support for additional languages, be sure the required language resources are installed on the client computer. The language resources are located in a language-specific subfolder of the \Windows OPK\Tools\PETools*ProcType* or \Windows AIK\Tools\PETools*ProcType* directory.

Once you install language support, you can specify the user interface language you want by using the /SetUILang option. For example, if you want to use U.S. English, enter:

```
dism /image:c:\winpe_x86\mount /Set-UILang:en-US
```

You can verify the language settings by using the /Get-Intl option, such as:

```
dism /image:c:\winpe_x86\mount /Get-Intl
```

After you have made all the necessary changes, you can unmount the image and commit your changes. The basic syntax is:

```
imagex /unmount MountPath /commit
```

Here is an example: :

```
imagex /unmount c:\winpe_x86\mount /commit
```

NOTE **If you unmount an image without committing the changes, your changes will be discarded.**

Now you have a customized Windows PE image. You can replace the default Windows PE image in the ISO directory with your customized image by entering the following command:

```
copy c:\winpe_x86\boot.wim c:\winpe_x86\ISO\sources\boot.wim
```

Capturing a Build

After your Windows PE image is ready, you can use the following ImageX command to capture the image into a Windows Imaging (.wim) file:

```
imagex /boot /capture c:\winpe_x86\mount c:\winpe_x86\iso\sources\boot.wim
"Primary WinPE Build"
```

Here, the /Boot option marks the image as bootable, and the /Capture option captures the contents of C:\Winpe_x86\Mount and creates an image file in the C:\Winpe_x86\ISO\Sources directory. "Primary WinPE Build" is the descriptive name of the bootable image file (Boot.wim).

NOTE **WIM images can be bootable or installable. Generally, bootable images, used with Windows PE, are stored in Boot.wim files, and installable images, used to deploy Windows, are stored in Install.wim files. Install.wim files can include multiple editions of Windows. The standard Windows 7 distribution media contains a Boot.wim file and an Install.wim file. The Boot.wim file loads Windows PE to start the computer and prepare for installation. The Install.wim file contains the Windows image needed to install Windows 7.**

The ISO\Sources directory is a standard build directory used for staging Windows PE images. The ISO directory also has Boot and EFI subdirectories, which are required for creating bootable media. After you've staged the boot image, you can create bootable media that uses the image or you can import the image into Windows Deployment Services.

Optimizing a Build

Profiling tracks the required components for a build and then allows you to optimize a build image. To use profiling, you must install the WinPE-WMI package and enable the feature by using the /Enable-Profiling option in the Windows PE image. Enabling profiling turns on logging of the files and features that are used when you boot to the Windows PE image.

After you boot to the Windows PE image, test all the features you are going to use in the actual environment. Testing the features shows the related files as being used in the profile log. You can save the profile using Wpeutil SaveProfile before ending the Windows PE session. The basic syntax is:

```
wpeutil saveprofile SaveLocation "Description"
```

where *SaveLocation* is the file path where the profile should be stored, and *Description* is a description of the profile, for example:

```
wpeutil saveprofile x:\st-profile.txt "Optimization Profile"
```

Next, you need to mount the image and apply the profile. The basic syntax for applying a profile to a mounted image is:

```
dism /image:ImagePath /apply-profiles:ProfilePath
```

where *ImagePath* is the path to the image you've mounted, and *ProfilePath* is the path to the profile you want to use to optimize the image, such as:

```
dism /image:c:\winpe_x86\mount\ /apply-profiles:c:\st-profile.txt
```

Once you've optimized the image, unmount the image and commit the changes. Note that applying a profile turns off the profiling features and marks the image so that it can no longer be serviced.

Creating a Bootable ISO Image and Bootable Media

Use the Oscdimg utility to create an ISO image that can be burned to a DVD. With single boot entry images, you can use the following options:

- –b*BootFile*, where *BootFile* specifies the file that will be written in the boot sectors of the disk.
- –p*PlatformID*, where *PlatformID* is either 0 for BIOS-based platforms or EF for EFI-based platforms. The default is 0 for BIOS-based platforms.
- –e specifies not to use floppy-disk emulation, generally needed if you also specify the –p option.

The following command creates an ISO image for the build staged previously:

```
oscdimg -n -bc:\winpe_x86\etfsboot.com
c:\winpe_x86\iso c:\winpe_x86\winpe.iso
```

Here, C:\Winpe_x86\Etfsboot.com is the path to the boot file that will be written to the boot sector, C:\Winpe_x86\ISO is the path to the folders for the ISO image, and C:\Winpe_x86\Winpe.iso is where the ISO image will be created. After you create the ISO image, you can burn the ISO image to a DVD by using a CD/DVD burning application such as Roxio Media Creator or Nero Media Burner.

To generate multiboot entry images, such as those required for EFI-based systems, you use the –bootdata option. The basic syntax is:

```
-bootdata:NumberOfEntries#Defaultbootentry#Bootentry2#...#BootentryN
```

Here, *NumberOfEntries* specifies the number of boot entries, where each multiboot entry is separated by a number sign (#) and options within a boot entry are separated using a comma (,). Boot entry options in the order they are used are:

- p*PlatformID,* where *PlatformID* is either 0 for BIOS-based platforms or EF for EFI-based platforms.
- e specifies not to use floppy-disk emulation.
- b*BootFile,* where *BootFile* is the path to the file that will be written in the boot sectors of the disk.

Knowing this, you can build a Windows PE x64 ISO image that supports both EFI and BIOS firmware by entering the following command:

```
oscdimg "-bootdata:2#p0,e,betfsboot.com#pEF,e,befisys.bin -u2 -udfver102
-o c:\winpe_x64\ISO c:\winpe_x64\winpe_2X.iso"
```

Here, –bootdata sets the boot information for EFI and BIOS, and –UDFVer sets the required UDF version. You set C:\Winpe_x64\ISO as the path to the folders for the ISO image, and C:\Winpe_x64\Winpe_2X.iso is where the ISO image will be created. After you create the ISO image, you can burn the ISO image to a DVD using a CD/DVD burning application.

NOTE **The default UDF version is 1.50. The setting –udfver102 writes UDF revision 1.02, which is supported on Windows 98 and later; –udfver150 writes UDF revision 1.50, which is supported on Windows 2000 and later; and –udfver200 writes UDF revision 2.00, which is supported on Windows XP and later.**

Creating a Bootable USB Flash Drive

You can create bootable Windows PE images on USB flash drives as long as the flash drive has the capacity to store the entire Windows image. You might need to modify computer firmware to allow booting from USB disk devices. For more information on configuring firmware, see Chapter 10.

To create a bootable USB flash drive, insert the device into a USB port, and then use the DiskPart utility to prepare the device. The commands you need to run are as follows:

1. At an elevated administrator command prompt, enter **diskpart**, and then enter **list disk**. Note the disk number and size of the USB flash drive.
2. Enter **select disk *n***, where *n* is the device you are preparing.
3. Enter **clean** to wipe the device and remove all contents.
4. Enter **create partition primary size=*size***, where *size* is the size in MB of the USB flash drive listed previously.
5. Enter **select partition 1** to select the partition you just created, and then enter **active** to mark the new partition as active.
6. Enter **format fs=fat32** to format the partition with the FAT32 file system.
7. Enter **assign** to assign the next available drive letter to the USB flash drive, and then enter **exit** to quit DiskPart. Note the drive letter assigned in the output. Don't exit the command prompt.
8. Write a new boot sector to the USB flash drive by entering **bootsect /nt60 *e*: /force**, where *e*: is the drive letter of the USB flash drive.

   NOTE **Bootsect is in the PeTools\x86 and PeTools\amd64 folders within the build. Use the version of Bootsect that supports the type of Windows PE image you are creating.**

9. Copy the contents of your ISO folder to the USB flash drive by entering **xcopy /echry c:\winpe_x86\iso*.* *e*:**.

When the copy is complete, remove your USB flash drive. The USB flash drive is now bootable Windows media.

NOTE **Some USB flash drives do not support this preparation process, and you might not be able to make the device bootable in this way. The devices that do not support this process are typically set so they are recognized as removable media devices and not USB disk devices. Because of this, you might need to refer to the device manufacturer's Web site for formatting documentation and tools.**

Booting to an Image from a Hard Disk

By booting Windows PE from a hard disk and loading it into RAM, you can perform a refresh installation of Windows 7. Once you've booted Windows PE, you can repartition system disks and install the new Windows image. You can also use Windows PE as a Windows Recovery Environment to recover unbootable systems.

To boot Windows PE from a hard disk, follow these steps:

1. Boot the computer from prepared Windows PE media.

2. At the command prompt, enter **diskpart**, and then enter **list disk**. Note the disk number of the primary disk. Typically the primary disk is disk 0.
3. Enter **select disk *n***, where *n* is the primary disk.
4. Enter **clean** to wipe the disk and remove all contents.
5. Enter **create partition primary size=*size***, where *size* (in MB) creates a partition large enough to hold the Windows PE source files.
6. Enter **select partition 1** to select the partition you just created, and then enter **active** to mark the new partition as active.
7. Enter **format fs=fat32** to format the partition with the FAT32 file system.
8. Enter **exit** to quit DiskPart. Don't exit the command prompt.
9. Write a new boot sector to the disk by entering **bootsect /nt60 *c*:**, where *c*: is the drive letter of the primary drive you formatted.

   NOTE **Bootsect is in the PeTools\x86 and PeTools\amd64 folders within the build. Use the version of Bootsect that supports the type of Windows PE image you are creating.**

10. Copy the contents of your ISO folder to the drive by entering **xcopy /echry x:*.* *c*:**.

Adding Windows PE Images to Windows Deployment Services

When you've set up Windows Deployment Services on your network, you can add a Windows PE image to Windows Deployment Services so that you can easily deploy the image. To do this, follow these steps:

1. On a management computer or a server running Windows Deployment Services, start the Windows Deployment Services console by clicking Start, pointing to All Programs, Administrative Tools, and then clicking Windows Deployment Services.
2. In the Windows Deployment Services console, expand the Servers node and select the server you want to work with. Right-click the server's Boot Images folder, and then click Add Boot Image.
3. On the Image File page, enter the path to the Windows PE image, and then click Open.
4. On the Image Metadata page, type a name and description for the image, and then click Next.
5. On the Summary page, click Next to add the image to Windows Deployment Services. When the import operation is complete, click Finish.

Working with Windows RE

Windows Recovery Environment (RE) is a Windows PE image with recovery extensions installed. After you create a customized Windows RE image, you can deploy the image by creating bootable media that uses the image or by importing the image into Windows Deployment Services.

To enable rapid recovery, Windows RE is installed with Windows 7 automatically. If you've added a custom Windows RE to the installation image, your custom environment is available to users. Normally, you configure Windows RE on a hard disk partition other than the one containing the Windows installation. This ensures that Windows RE is separate from the operating system.

Creating a Customized Windows RE Image

In Windows 7, users can initiate image-based recovery without having to first start Windows RE manually. The Recovery control panel allows users to back up their personal data and then restarts the system into Windows RE, where the image recovery application is launched automatically.

You can create a custom Windows RE image by completing the following steps:

1. Click Start, point to All Programs, and then click either Microsoft Windows OPK, Microsoft Windows AIK, or Microsoft Windows PE Kit as appropriate.
2. Right-click Deployment Tools Command Prompt, and then click Run As Administrator.
3. Make directories for mounting the image. At the command prompt, do the following:
    a. Enter **c:**, and then enter **mkdir c:\win7**.
    b. Enter **cd win7**, and then enter **mkdir mount**. You will use this directory to mount the Windows 7 image.
    c. Enter **mkdir mountre**. You will use this directory to mount the Windows Recovery Environment.
4. Insert the Windows 7 distribution media into the DVD-ROM drive, and then copy the Windows install image from the distribution media to your hard disk by entering **copy *e*:\sources\install.wim c:\win7**, where *e*: is the drive designator for the DVD-ROM drive.
5. Mount the Windows 7 image on the distribution media by entering **imagex /mountrw *e*:\sources\install.wim c:\win7\mount**.
6. Copy the original Windows RE image from the mounted image by entering **copy c:\sources\mount\windows\system32\recovery\winre.wim c:\win7**.

7. Unmount the Windows 7 image by entering **imagex /unmount c:\win7\mount**.
8. Mount the Windows RE image by entering **imagex /mountrw c:\win7\winre.wim c:\win7\mountre**.
9. Customize the Windows RE image as necessary by using the techniques discussed in the section "Customizing a Windows PE Image" earlier in the chapter. Be sure to add the following package to the image: WinPE-SRT-Package. This package is required.
10. Unmount the customized Windows RE image, and then save your changes by entering **imagex /unmount /commit c:\win7\mountre**.
11. Mount the Windows 7 image you copied previously to the C:\Win7 directory by entering **imagex /mountrw c:\win7\install.wim c:\win7\mount**.
12. Overwrite the original Windows RE image in the Windows 7 image with your customized Windows RE image by entering **copy c:\win7\winre.wim c:\win7\mount\Windows\System32\recovery**.
13. Save the changes to the Windows 7 image by entering **imagex /unmount c:\win7\mount /commit**.

Now you have a bootable Windows RE image in the C:\Win7\Winre.wim file and Windows 7 distribution media containing a bootable Windows RE image. You can create Windows RE recovery media using the C:\Win7\Winre.wim file as discussed in the next section.

Creating Windows RE Recovery Media

After you create a custom Windows RE image, you can create bootable Windows RE images on CD-ROM, DVD-ROM, or USB flash drives. Then, if a computer fails to start, you can start the computer by using this recovery media and attempt to fix the computer. The procedures to create recovery media are the same as those for creating Windows PE images. The key difference is that you create your ISO image from a Windows RE image rather than a Window PE image.

To set up a build environment for Windows RE on 32-bit computers, complete the following steps:

1. Click Start, point to All Programs, and then click either Microsoft Windows OPK, Microsoft Windows AIK, or Microsoft Windows PE Kit as appropriate.
2. Right-click Deployment Tools Command Prompt, and then click Run As Administrator.
3. At the command prompt, enter **copype x86 c:\winrec_x86**.

You now have a build environment for Windows RE on 32-bit computers. You can create build environments for x64 and Itanium-based computers as well if you need to.

After you set up the build environment, create a customized Windows RE environment as discussed in the previous section, "Creating a Customized Windows RE Image." Next, copy the Windows RE image to the build environment by entering the following command:

```
copy c:\win7\winre.wim c:\winrec_x86\ISO\sources\boot.wim
```

You must name the Windows RE image file Boot.wim. This ensures that you can boot computers using the image.

Use the Oscdimg utility to create an ISO image that can be burned to a DVD. The following command creates an ISO image for the Windows RE image created previously:

```
oscdimg -n -bc:\winrec_x86\etfsboot.com c:\winrec_x86\iso
c:\winrec_x86\winrec.iso
```

Here, C:\Winrec_x86\Etfsboot.com is the path to the Etfsboot.com script required to create the ISO image, C:\Winrec_x86\ISO is the path to the folders for the ISO image, and C:\Winrec_x86\Winrec.iso is the path and file name of the ISO image that will be created. After you create the ISO image, you can burn the ISO image to a DVD by using a CD/DVD burning application such as Roxio Media Creator or Nero Media Burner.

To build a Windows RE x64 ISO image that supports both EFI and BIOS firmware, enter the following command:

```
oscdimg "-bootdata:2#p0,e,betfsboot.com#pEF,e,befisys.bin -u2 -udfver102
-o c:\winrec_x64\ISO c:\winrec_x86\winrec_2X.iso"
```

Here, –bootdata sets the boot information for EFI and BIOS, and –UDFVer sets the required UDF version. You set C:\Winrec_x64\ISO as the path to the folders for the ISO image, and C:\Winrec_x64\Winrec_2X.iso is the path and file name of the ISO image that will be created. After you create the ISO image, you can burn the ISO image to a DVD using a CD/DVD burning application.

You can create bootable Windows RE images on USB flash drives as well. The procedure is the same as described in "Creating a Bootable USB Flash Drive" earlier in the chapter. Instead of copying a Windows PE image, copy your Windows RE image.

Adding Windows RE Images to Windows Deployment Services

When you've set up Windows Deployment Services on your network, you can add a Windows RE image to Windows Deployment Services so that you can easily deploy the image. To do this, follow these steps:

1. On a management computer or a server running Windows Deployment Services, start the Windows Deployment Services console by clicking Start,

pointing to All Programs, Administrative Tools, and then clicking Windows Deployment Services.

2. In the Windows Deployment Services console, expand the Servers node and select the server you want to work with. Right-click the server's Boot Images folder, and then click Add Boot Image.
3. On the Image File page, enter the path to the Windows RE image, and then click Open.
4. On the Image Metadata page, type a name and description for the image, and then click Next.
5. On the Summary page, click Next to add the image to Windows Deployment Services. When the import operation is complete, click Finish.

Deploying Windows with a Customized Windows RE

Windows RE is included with Windows 7. When you deploy a Windows computer, you can set up a recovery image. To do this, you must partition the hard disk with a recovery partition, copy the recovery image to this partition, and then create an association between the recovery image and the Windows 7 installation.

A Windows RE image can be installed on GUID partition table (GPT) disks that have the PARTITION_MSFT_RECOVERY_GUID attribute and on master boot record (MBR) disks with the type 0x7 or 0x27. With 0x27 disks, the recovery partition must be at the beginning of the disk. The partition used by Windows RE must be a primary partition formatted as NTFS on the same disk as the partition containing the Windows installation.

The recovery partition can be the same as the system partition, but it is better to separate the partitions. You should size the recovery partition so that it is appropriate for the size of the recovery image. Check the size of your modified Windows 7 installation image to help you size the partition. With a full recovery image, you normally need a recovery partition of between 9 and 10 gigabytes (GB).

To set up a computer with MBR hard disks for a recovery partition, follow these steps:

1. Start the computer using bootable Windows PE media. The Windows PE into which you boot must include the WinPE-SRT package. Normally, this package is available only in the Windows OPK.
2. At the Windows PE command prompt, enter **diskpart**, and then enter **list disk**. Note the disks that are available and their sizes. Disk 0 will need enough space for the recovery partition and the partition on which you will install Windows.
3. Enter **select disk 0**, and then enter **clean** to wipe the disk and remove all contents.
4. Create the system partition by entering **create partition primary size=*size***, where *size* is the size in megabytes of the system partition, such as size=250.

5. Format the system partition by entering **format=fat32 label="System" quick**. Make the system partition the active partition by entering **active**, and then assign drive letter S by entering **assign letter=s**.
6. Create the recovery partition by entering **create partition primary size=*size* id=27**, where *size* is the size in megabytes of the recovery partition, such as size=1000, and the value id=27 creates a hidden recovery partition.
7. Enter **format=ntfs label="Recovery" quick** to format the recovery partition with the NTFS file system.
8. Enter **assign letter=r** to assign the drive letter R for the recovery partition.
9. Create the Windows installation partition by entering **create partition primary size=*size***, where *size* is the size in megabytes of the Windows installation partition, such as size=2000.
10. Format the Windows partition by entering **format=ntfs label="Windows" quick**, and then enter **assign letter=c** to assign the drive letter C for the Windows partition.
11. Enter **exit** to quit DiskPart. Don't exit the command prompt.

To set up a computer with GPT hard disks for a recovery partition, follow these steps:

1. Start the computer using bootable Windows PE media. The Windows PE into which you boot must include the WinPE-SRT package. Normally, this package is available only in the Windows OPK. For Unified Extensible Firmware Interface (UEFI)-based computers, you must start Windows PE by using the EFI boot-mode option in the EFI shell.
2. At the prompt, enter **diskpart**, and then enter **list disk**. Note the disks that are available and their sizes. Disk 0 will need enough space for the recovery partition and the partition on which you will install Windows.
3. Enter **select disk 0**, and then enter **clean** to wipe the disk and remove all contents. For UEFI-based computers, you will need to set the GPT disk information by entering **convert gpt**.
4. Create the EFI system partition by entering **create partition efi size=*size***, where *size* is the size in megabytes of the EFI system partition, such as size=200.
5. Format the EFI system partition by entering **format=fat32 label="System" quick**, and then assign drive letter S by entering **assign letter=s**.
6. Create the MSR partition by entering **create partition msr size=*size***, where *size* is the size in megabytes of the MSR partition, such as size=128.
7. Create the recovery partition by entering **create partition primary size=*size***, where *size* is the size in megabytes of the recovery partition, such as size=1000.

8. Identify the partition as a recovery partition by entering **set id="de94bba4-06d1-4d40-a16a-bfd50179d6ac"**.
9. Format the recovery partition by entering **format=ntfs label="Recovery" quick**, and then assign drive letter R by entering **assign letter=r**.
10. Create the Windows installation partition by entering **create partition primary**. Because you don't specify a size, the partition will fill the remainder of the disk.
11. Enter **format=ntfs label="Windows" quick** to format the partition with the NTFS file system.
12. Enter **assign letter=c** to assign the drive letter C for the Windows partition.
13. Enter **exit** to quit DiskPart. Don't exit the command prompt.

Now that you've configured the computer's hard disks, you can deploy Windows. One way to do this is to complete the following steps:

1. Insert the media or connect to the network location containing the Windows 7 image you are deploying.
2. Use ImageX to apply the Windows 7 image. For example, if the installation image is on the E drive, you would enter **imagex /apply e:\images\install.wim 1 c:**.
3. You can use BCDBoot to copy system files to the system partition and update the BCD store. To do this, enter **cd c:\windows\system32**, and then enter **bcdboot c:\windows /l en-us /s s:**. The /l option sets the locale. The /s option specifies the drive designator for the system partition.
4. Copy the Windows RE image to partition 1. For example, if the installation image is on the E drive, you would enter **copy e:\images\winre.wim r:**.
5. Create an association between the Windows RE image and the Windows 7 installation using Reagentc.exe. For example, enter **reagentc.exe /setreimage /path r:**.

TIP **Optionally, you can map a keyboard key or a custom hardware button to launch Windows RE directly when the key or button is pressed during startup of the system. To map the key or button, add the /Bootkey option when using Reagentc.exe to associate the Windows RE image to the Windows 7 installation. For example, enter reagentc.exe /setreimage /path r: /bootkey *ScanCode*, where *ScanCode* is the four-digit hexadecimal scan code of the keyboard key or custom hardware button.**

NOTE **Normally, the Windows RE installation will be complete when the user finalizes the installation. However, if you need to start the computer in audit mode before completing the installation and you are not generalizing the installation again by using the Sysprep tool, you can complete the Windows RE installation during audit mode. At the command prompt, enter reagentc.exe /enable /auditmode.**

Another way to deploy Windows is to use separate images for each partition. Let's say you capture separate images using the following steps:

1. Start the computer using bootable Windows PE media. For UEFI-based computers, you must start Windows PE by using the EFI boot-mode option in the EFI shell.
2. At the Windows PE command prompt, enter **diskpart**, then enter **select disk 0**, and then enter **list volume**. Note the partition information provided. If any partition you want to capture doesn't have a drive letter, you need to select the volume and then assign a drive letter. For example, if the recovery partition is volume 0 and it doesn't have a drive letter, enter **select volume 0**, and then enter **assign letter=r**.
3. Enter **cd c:\windows\system32** to change to the directory containing the ImageX tool.
4. Capture images for each customized partition. If you have separate Windows, system, and recovery partitions, you could use the following commands:

```
imagex /capture c:\ c:\win-partition.wim "Windows partition"

imagex /capture s:\ c:\sys-partition.wim "System partition"

imagex /capture r:\ c:\rec-partition.wim "Recovery partition"
```

5. Connect to your distribution share by using the Net Use command, such as **net use Z: \\ImageShare\Images**. Copy the WIM files to the network share by using the following commands:

```
copy c:\win-partition.wim Z:\

copy c:\sys-partition.wim Z:\

copy c:\rec-partition.wim Z:\
```

Now you can apply the separate images using the following steps:

1. Start the computer using bootable Windows PE media. For UEFI-based computers, you must start Windows PE by using the EFI boot-mode option in the EFI shell.
2. Insert media or connect to the network location containing images you are deploying. You can connect to a network location with Net Use—for example, **net use Z: \\ImageShare\Images**.
3. At the Windows PE command prompt, enter **diskpart**, enter **select disk 0**, and then enter **list volume**. Note the partition information provided. If any partition you want to apply an image to doesn't have a drive letter, you need to select the volume and then assign a drive letter. For example, if the recovery partition is volume 0 and it doesn't have a drive letter, enter **select volume 0**, and then enter **assign letter=r**.

4. Enter **cd c:\windows\system32** to change to the directory containing the ImageX tool.
5. Use ImageX to apply the Windows partition image. For example, if the installation image is on the Z drive, you would enter **imagex /apply z:\win-partition.wim 1 c:**.
6. Use ImageX to apply the system partition image. For example, if the system partition image is on the Z drive, you would enter **imagex /apply z:\sys-partition.wim 1 s:**.
7. Use ImageX to apply the recovery partition image. For example, if the recovery partition image is on the Z drive, you would enter **imagex /apply z:\rec-partition.wim 1 r:**.

Creating Windows Images for Deployment

Windows 7 builds on the enhanced architecture in Windows Vista. This architecture is both language independent and hardware independent. Windows 7 achieves language independence through its modular component design, and it achieves hardware independence through its imaging format. In a modular component design, each component is designed as a smaller, independent unit that performs a particular task or function. Thanks to modularization, every component of the operating system, from device drivers to language packs and service packs, can be created as a module that can be selectively swapped in or out to customize the operating system environment.

Understanding Windows Imaging

When you update Windows 7 by adding or removing features, applying hotfixes, or installing service packs, you are simply modifying the set of modules available. And because these modules are independent, you can make these changes without impacting the system as a whole. Because language packs are separate modules as well, you can easily implement different language configurations without needing separate installations for each language.

Microsoft distributes Windows 7 on media with Windows Imaging Format (WIM) disk images. WIM uses compression and single-instance storage to dramatically reduce the size of image files. Compression reduces the size of the image in much the same way that Zip compression reduces the size of files. Using single-instance storage reduces the size of the image because only one physical copy of a file is stored for each instance of that file in the disk image. Because WIM is hardware independent, Microsoft can ship one binary for 32-bit architectures and one binary for 64-bit architectures. A separate binary is available for Itanium-based computers.

Windows 7 can be installed through either automated or interactive setup. You can automate the installation of Windows 7 in several ways. You can:

- **Create an unattended installation answer file** Windows 7 uses a standards-based single-format answer file. This file, called Unattend.xml, is written in XML, making it easier to process using standard tools. By creating a custom answer file and then running Setup using this answer file, you can perform unattended installations of Windows 7. The Setup program can then install the operating system from a distribution share or from media.

- **Use Sysprep image-based installation** Requires running the System Preparation command-line tool (Sysprep.exe) on a computer that you want to use as the master deployment computer and then creating a disk image of this computer's configuration. Sysprep is stored in the %SystemRoot%\System32\Sysprep folder. The Windows Automated Installation Kit (Windows AIK) includes Windows System Image Manager and ImageX to help you use Sysprep for deployments. You use Windows System Image Manager to create answer files for unattended installations. You use ImageX to create and manage disk images.

By using WIM as its disk-imaging format and taking advantage of the modular design of Windows 7, ImageX significantly reduces the number of disk images that must be maintained. You no longer need to maintain multiple hardware-dependent disk images or multiple language-dependent disk images. Instead, you typically need only a single disk image for each chip architecture used in your organization. You can then use different installation scripts to customize the operating system installation as necessary.

WIM has other advantages over earlier disk image formats as well. WIM enables you to modify and maintain disk images offline, which means you can add or remove optional components and drivers or perform updates without having to create a new disk image. To do this, you mount the disk image as a folder and then use Windows Explorer or other tools to update, manage, or remove files as necessary.

Windows System Image Manager, ImageX, and Sysprep provide several different ways to automate deployment. Here are the basic steps:

1. Set up and configure Windows 7 on a computer not being used for normal operations, and then install and configure any necessary components and applications.
2. Run Sysprep to prepare the computer for capture. Sysprep removes unique identifiers from the computer and designates it as a master deployment computer. At the end of this process, the computer no longer has identifying information that allows it to be logged on to and used within a domain or workgroup.
3. Use the ImageX /Capture option to capture the disk image and store this image on media or in a distribution share. The image can be maintained offline by using the ImageX /Mountrw option to mount the image in read/write mode so that you can make any necessary changes. Use the ImageX /Unmount command to unmount the image when you are finished making changes.

You also can mount images using DISM /Mount-WIM and unmount images using DISM /Unmount-WIM. DISM provides functionality for manipulating images. You can set product keys, perform upgrades, add or remove drivers, set language and locale information, add or remove packages and features, and clean up images.

4. Use Windows System Image Manager to create your unattended installation answer files. You can then create deployment scripts that configure the computer, run Setup using the answer file, and apply the disk image you've previously created.
5. Run your deployment script to configure the computer and install the operating system.

Creating a Windows Install Image

The primary tool you use to prepare Windows install images is Sysprep. Before you use Sysprep on any computer, keep in mind that Sysprep removes unique identifiers from the computer you are preparing and designates it as a master deployment computer. At the end of this process, the computer no longer has identifying information that allows it to be logged on to and used within a domain or workgroup. After you create your install image, you can reinstall Windows and then start using the source computer again.

On all editions of Windows 7, Sysprep is stored in the %SystemRoot%\System32\Sysprep folder. Table 2-3 provides an overview of key options for Sysprep.

NOTE **All editions of Windows 7 must be activated within a specified period of time, even if you are using volume activation with Key Management Service (KMS) servers. When you use the /Generalize option for the first time, Sysprep sets the initial Windows activation grace period, providing 30 days to activate the system once it is deployed. When a system exceeds its grace period, you can run Sysprep /Generalize again to reset the activation grace period, providing an additional 30 days to activate the system. You can do this up to three times. However, generalizing a system removes all unique identifiers, clears system restore points, and removes the event logs.**

TIP **When you are using Key Management Service (KMS), you can return a computer to its initial activation state by using the Slmgr.vbs script with the –Rearm option. This option resets the activation period and reinitializes some activation parameters, including the computer's unique machine ID. The number of times you can reset the activation period in this way depends on how many times you've reset the activation period previously using Sysprep /Generalize. The maximum number of times you can reset the activation period is three.**

TABLE 2-3 Key Options for Sysprep

OPTION	DESCRIPTION
/Audit	Sets the computer to start in audit mode. In audit mode, you can add drivers and applications to the operating system. You also can use audit mode to test the installation before deploying it.
/Generalize	Prepares the Windows installation to be imaged by removing all unique system identifiers. The computer's security identifier (SID) is reset, system restore points are cleared, and event logs are removed. The next time the computer starts, a new SID is created.
/Oobe	Sets the computer to start in welcome mode, which is the mode in which users will receive the deployed computer.
/Reboot	Restarts the computer.
/Shutdown	Turns off and shuts down the computer after Sysprep finishes preparing the computer.
/Quiet	Runs Sysprep without displaying on-screen confirmation messages. Use this mode if you automate Sysprep.
/Quit	Closes Sysprep after running the specified command.
/Unattend: *AnswerFile*.xml	Applies settings in an answer file during an unattended installation, where *AnswerFile*.xml is the name of the answer file.

To prepare a computer, log on to the system you want to configure as a custom image and use as the basis for other computer images. Configure the computer by modifying the settings, installing applications, and making any necessary changes. Once you've configured a computer's components, you can use Sysprep to prepare it for use as an image.

Sysprep has a command-line mode and a graphical user interface mode. Every time you use Sysprep, Sysprep looks for:

- A clean-up action, which is to enter either the System Out-of-Box Experience (OOBE) mode or the System Audit mode on the next restart, and optionally to generalize the system.
- A shutdown option, which is either to quit, to reboot, or to shutdown after running the specified command.

Before you can start and use Sysprep, you must open an elevated administrator command prompt and then enter **cd %systemroot%\system32\sysprep**.

Using Sysprep, you can generalize a computer and set it to start in OO
on the next reboot by using the settings shown in Figure 2-1 or by enterin

```
sysprep /oobe /generalize /quit
```

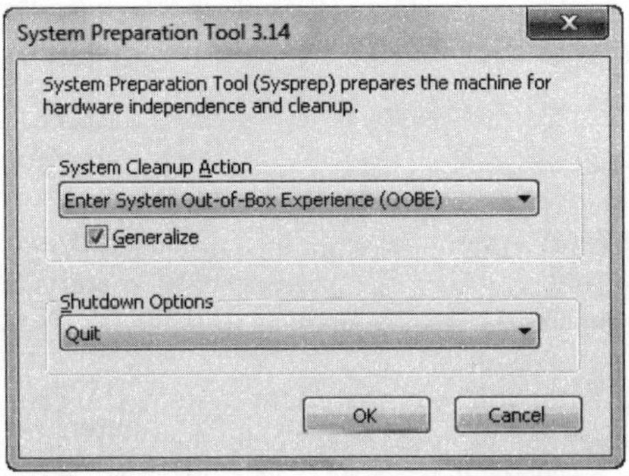

FIGURE 2-1 Generalize the computer and set OOBE mode.

If you want to install additional applications and modify the configuration after generalizing the computer, you can set the computer to restart in System Audit mode as shown in Figure 2-2 or by entering the following:

```
sysprep /audit /generalize /reboot
```

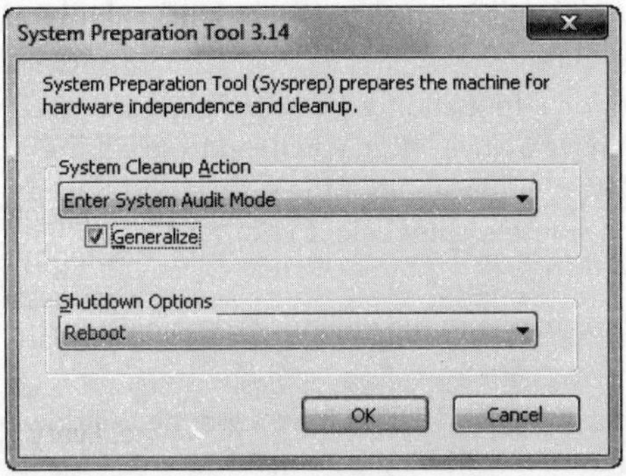

FIGURE 2-2 Generalize the computer and set audit mode.

You can then make any necessary changes. These changes will be tracked so that they can be applied when the system is deployed. When you have finished modifying the computer, you can finalize the operating system by setting the computer to shut down and start in OOBE mode on the next reboot as shown in Figure 2-3 or by entering the following:

```
sysprep /oobe /shutdown
```

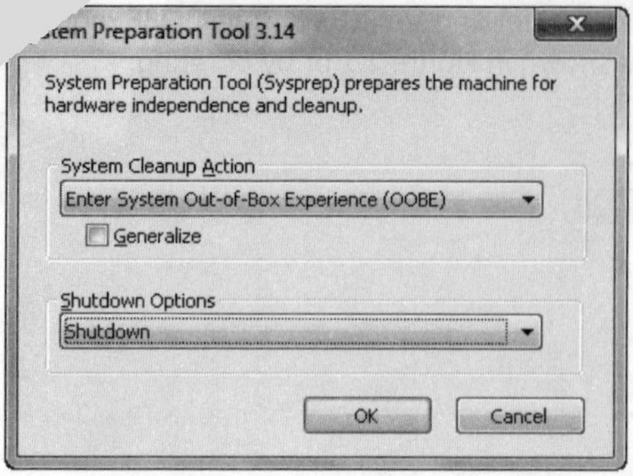

FIGURE 2-3 After auditing set OOBE mode and shutdown.

The system is then ready for imaging. After you've prepared the system, you can import the image into Windows Deployment Services for later deployment, or you can capture the image and deploy it manually. You'll learn more about Windows Deployment Services later in the chapter. To capture the image manually, follow these steps:

1. Start the computer using bootable Windows PE media. For UEFI-based computers, you must start Windows PE by using the EFI boot-mode option in the EFI shell.
2. At an elevated administrator command prompt, enter **diskpart**, and then enter **list disk**. Note the number of the disk you want to use. Enter **select disk *n***, where *n* is the disk you want to use.
3. Enter **list volume**. Note the partition information provided. If any partition you want to capture doesn't have a drive letter, you need to select the volume and then assign a drive letter. For example, if the system partition is volume 1 and it doesn't have a drive letter, enter **select volume 1**, and then enter **assign letter=s**.
4. Enter **cd c:\windows\system32** to change to the directory containing the ImageX tool.
5. Capture images for each customized partition. If you have separate Windows and system partitions, you could use the following commands:

```
imagex /capture c:\ c:\win-partition.wim "Windows partition"

imagex /capture s:\ c:\sys-partition.wim "System partition"
```

6. Connect to your distribution share by using the Net Use command, such as **net use Z: \\ImageShare\Images**. Copy the WIM files to the network share by using the following commands:

```
copy c:\win-partition.wim Z:\
```

```
copy c:\sys-partition.wim Z:\
```

You can apply the separate images by using the following steps:

1. Start the computer using bootable Windows PE media. For UEFI-based computers, you must start Windows PE by using the EFI boot-mode option in the EFI shell.
2. Insert media or connect to the network location containing images you are deploying. You can connect to a network location with Net Use, such as **net use Z: \\ImageShare\Images**.
3. At the Windows PE command prompt, enter **diskpart**, enter **select disk 0**, and then enter **list volume**. Note the partition information provided. If any partition you want to apply an image to doesn't have a drive letter, you need to select the volume and then assign a driver letter. For example, if the recovery partition is volume 0 and it doesn't have a drive letter, enter **select volume 0**, and then enter **assign letter=r**.
4. Enter **cd c:\windows\system32** to change to the directory containing the ImageX tool.
5. Use ImageX to apply the Windows partition image. For example, if the installation image is on the Z drive, you would enter **imagex /apply z:\win-partition.wim 1 c:**.
6. Use ImageX to apply the system partition image. For example, if the system partition image is on the Z drive, you would enter **imagex /apply z:\sys-partition.wim 1 s:**.
7. Restart the computer and log on.

Configuring and Using Windows Deployment Services

You can use Windows Deployment Services to deploy Windows 7 over a network by using the Preboot Execution Environment (PXE). Once you've set up Windows Deployment Services, you can install Windows 7 on any client computer that supports PXE and has network boot enabled in firmware simply by turning it on while it is connected to the network. For client computers that don't support PXE, you can create boot discs using the Oscdimg utility as discussed earlier in the chapter.

Setting Up Windows Deployment Services

Windows Deployment Services running on Windows Server 2008 or later operates in native mode, in which only Windows PE boot environments and Windows image files are supported. Your Windows Deployment Services server must be either a member of an Active Directory domain or a domain controller in an Active Directory domain. Your network also must have Dynamic Host Configuration Protocol (DHCP) servers and Domain Name System (DNS) servers.

To install Windows Deployment Services on a server running Windows Server 2008 or later, follow these steps:

1. Start Server Manager by clicking the related option on the Quick Launch toolbar. In Server Manager, select the Roles node, and then click Add Roles to start the Add Roles wizard.
2. In the Add Roles wizard, click Next. On the Select Server Roles page, select Windows Deployment Services, and then click Next. Read the overview of Windows Deployment Services, and then click Next again.
3. On the Select Role Services page, the Deployment Server and Transport Server roles are selected for you automatically. You need both roles. Click Next, and then click Install.

After you install Windows Deployment Services, you must register the deployment server and configure it by completing the following steps:

1. Start the Windows Deployment Services console by clicking Start, pointing to All Programs, Administrative Tools, and then clicking Windows Deployment Services.
2. In the console tree, expand the Servers node. If you are logged on to the deployment server, the server should be listed automatically. If the server isn't listed, right-click Servers in the console tree, and then click Add Server. In the Add Servers dialog box, choose the server to add to the console, and then click OK.
3. In the console tree, right-click the Server, and then click Configure Server. When the Configuration wizard starts, review the Before You Begin tasks and ensure that the network is prepared as specified. You need a DHCP server with an active scope and an active DNS server. You also need to be sure that the server has a partition formatted with NTFS.
4. On the Remote Installation Folder Location page, enter the path for the image store, and then click Next. The folder must be a partition on an NTFS drive, and in most cases it shouldn't be the same partition as the one containing the system files. If you chose a folder on the system partition, click Yes when prompted to confirm that you really want to do this.
5. On the PXE Server Initial Settings page, choose one of the following options to specify which clients the server will respond to:
   - **Do Not Respond To Any Client Computers** Choose this option if you don't want the server to respond to any client computers.
   - **Respond Only To Known Client Computers** Choose this option if you want the server to respond only to known clients that have been prestaged. Prestaging a computer requires that an administrator create a managed computer account in Active Directory before booting the client so that it can be installed over the network.

- **Respond To All Client Computers** Choose this option if you want the server to respond to unknown clients as well as known clients. An unknown client is a client that hasn't been prestaged. By default, if you allow responding to unknown clients, the security settings on the Windows Image file determine who can install clients. You can limit this to administrators by also selecting Require Administrator Approval For Unknown Clients.

6. When you click Next, the wizard configures the server. Before you click Finish, consider whether you want to set up images now or later. You must have at least one install image and one boot image on your server before you can boot a client using the PXE and install an operating system.
   - If you want to set up images now, insert the Windows 7 distribution media into the DVD-ROM drive, and then click Finish. Continue with the rest of the steps in this procedure.
   - If you want to set up images later, clear Add Image Files, and then click Finish. Skip the rest of the steps in this procedure.
7. The Add Image Wizard starts. On the Image File page, enter the path to the root of the installation DVD that contains the images you want to add, such as E:\ to access the E drive. Alternatively, click Browse to select the root path. Click Next.
8. An image group is a collection of images that share common file resources and security. On the Image Group page, specify a name for your first image group, and then click Next twice. The wizard will then add the boot and install images from the distribution media.

TIP **You can modify the way the server responds to clients at any time. In the Windows Deployment Services console, right-click the server, and then click Properties. In the Properties dialog box, select the response technique you want, and then click OK.**

Importing Images

Once you've configured Windows Deployment Services, you can import any available boot and install images. These images can then be used to deploy client computers.

You can import bootable images directly from Windows source files or from your custom boot images. To add boot images, complete the following steps:

1. On your server running Windows Deployment Services, start the Windows Deployment Services console by clicking Start, pointing to All Programs, Administrative Tools, and then clicking Windows Deployment Services.
2. Insert the Windows 7 distribution DVD or bootable image into the DVD-ROM drive, or make an installation source available to the server over the network.

3. In the Windows Deployment Services console, expand the Servers node and select the server you want to work with. Right-click the server's Boot Images folder, and click Add Boot Image.
4. On the Image File page, enter the path to the root of the installation DVD or click Browse to select the boot image, and then click Open. For example, if the Windows distribution media is on the E drive, you can select the default boot image by selecting E:\Source\Boot.wim. Click Next.
5. On the Image Metadata page, type a name and description for the image, and then click Next.
6. On the Summary page, click Next to add the image to Windows Deployment Services. When the import operation is complete, click Finish.

You can import install images directly from Windows source files. To add install images, complete the following steps:

1. On your server running Windows Deployment Services, start the Windows Deployment Services console by clicking Start, pointing to All Programs, Administrative Tools, and then clicking Windows Deployment Services.
2. Insert the Windows 7 distribution media into the DVD-ROM drive, or make an install source available to the server over the network.
3. In the Windows Deployment Services console, expand the Servers node and select the server you want to work with. Right-click the server's Install Images folder, and then click Add Image Group.
4. Enter a name for the image group, and then click OK. This creates a store location for storing similar groups of images.
5. Right-click the server's Install Images folder, and then click Add Install Image. Choose the Image Group you created previously, and then click Next.
6. On the Image File page, click Browse to select the install image, and then click Open. For example, if the Windows distribution media is on the E drive, you can select the default install image by selecting E:\Source\Install.wim. Click Next.
7. On the List Of Available Images page, choose the image to import, and then click Next.
8. On the Summary page, click Next to add the image to Windows Deployment Services. When the import operation is complete, click Finish.

Installing Windows from an Image

To install Windows from Windows Deployment Services, follow these steps:

1. Configure the computer's firmware to boot from the network, and then restart the computer.
2. When the computer starts and the boot loader prompts you, press F12 to download and start the Windows Deployment Services client.

3. On the Windows Deployment Services page, choose a locale and keyboard layout, and then click Next.
4. When prompted to connect to the Windows Deployment Services server, enter the account name and password to use for the connection, and then click OK.
5. On the Select The Operating System You Want To Install page, choose an operating system image to install, and then click Next.
6. On the Where Do You Want To Install Windows page, choose a partition on which to install Windows, and then click Next. If you want to repartition the disk, click Drive Options (Advanced) before clicking Next. You can then configure the disk partitions.
7. Windows Setup will then install Windows. You are prompted for required settings that are not specified in an unattended setup answer file.

Capturing Images

You can use Windows Deployment Services to deploy custom images you've created as well as the default images from the Windows distribution media. When you create your own boot and install images, you can import them as discussed in the section "Importing Images" earlier in the chapter. You also can capture images.

First, you need a capture boot image. You can create a capture boot image by completing the following steps:

1. In the Windows Deployment Services console, expand the Servers node and select the server you want to work with. Next, click the server's Boot Images folder to select it and display available boot images.
2. Right-click the boot image to use as the capture boot image, and then click Create Capture Boot Image.
3. On the Capture Image Metadata page, enter a name and description for the capture boot image, and then specify the location and file name of the image to create, such as C:\Images\Win_capture.wim.
4. Click Finish.

To capture an image, you must:

1. Use Windows Deployment Services to install an existing image on a computer, as described in "Installing Windows from an Image."
2. Customize the image.
3. At the command prompt, enter **cd %systemroot%\system32\sysprep**, and then enter **sysprep /oobe /generalize /reboot**.
4. When the computer starts and the boot loader prompts you, press F12 to download and start the Windows Deployment Services client.
5. In Windows Boot Manager, select the capture boot image.

6. When the Windows Deployment Services Image Capture Wizard starts, click Next.
7. On the Image Capture Source page, select the volume or volumes to capture in the Volume To Capture list, and then provide a name and description for the image. Click Next to continue.
8. On the Image Capture Destination page, click Browse, and then choose the location where you want to store the captured image. In the File Name text box, type a name for the image using the .wim file name extension. Click Save.
9. Click Upload Image To WDS Server. Type the name of the server, and then click Connect. If you are prompted for credentials, provide a user name and password for an account that can access the server.
10. In the Image Group list, choose the image group in which to store the image, and then click Finish.

Managing Access and Prestaging Computers

You can manage images using DISM and the techniques discussed previously. To prevent unauthorized users from installing images, you can:

- Prestage computers and allow only known computers to be deployed
- Modify the security settings of image files so that only appropriate personnel can access them
- Enable administrator approval for client installation

Prestaging Computers

Prestaging computers involves creating computer accounts in Active Directory prior to their use. By prestaging a computer, you control exactly which clients and servers can communicate with each other. Before you prestage computers, you should be sure that Windows Deployment Services is configured to accept requests only from known computers. To do this, follow these steps:

1. In the Windows Deployment Services console, expand the Servers node. Right-click the server you want to work with, and then select Properties.
2. On the PXE Response Settings tab, click Respond Only To Known Client Computers, and then click OK.

To prestage a computer, you need to know the computer's globally unique identifier (GUID). A computer's GUID comes from the active network adapter on the computer and must be entered in the format {*dddddddd-dddd-dddd-dddd-dddddddddddd*}, where *d* is a hexadecimal digit, such as {AEFED345-BC13-22CD-ABCD-11BB11342112}.

You can obtain the required identifier in several ways. In some cases, manufacturers print a label with the GUID and attach the label to the computer. However, don't forget that the GUID is valid only for the network adapter that shipped with the computer. If you replace the adapter, the new adapter will have a new GUID.

To obtain the GUID for the installed network adapter, you can check the computer's firmware. If a remote computer is started, you can enter the following command at a Windows PowerShell prompt:

```
get-wmiobject win32_networkadapter | format-list guid
```

Write down or copy the GUID associated with the network adapter connected to the local area network.

To prestage computers, follow these steps:

1. In Active Directory Users And Computers, right-click the OU or container where the computer will be staged, click New, and then click Computer.
2. Type a name for the computer, and then click Next. Alternatively, click Change to choose the user or group with permission to join this computer to the domain, and then click Next.
3. On the Managed page, select This Is A Managed Computer, type the computer's GUID, and then click Next. The GUID can be found in the system firmware or it might be posted on the computer case.
4. On the Host Server page, choose the Windows Deployment Services server that will service this client. Click Next, and then click Finish.

Modifying Image File Security

To modify the security settings on an image file, open Windows Explorer. Right-click the image file, and then click Properties. In the Properties dialog box, use the options on the Security tab to configure the security settings you want to use. Alternatively, you can configure security settings on the Image Group folder in which the image file is stored. These settings will then be inherited by the images in the Image Group folder.

Requiring Administrator Approval

Instead of prestaging computers or using image file security, you can require administrator approval before allowing computers to be installed from images. To require administrator approval rather than modify security settings on image files, you can do the following:

1. In the Windows Deployment Services console, expand the Servers node. Right-click the server you want to work with, and then click Properties.
2. On the PXE Response Settings tab, select Respond To All (Known And Unknown) Client Computers.
3. Select For Unknown Clients, Notify Administrator And Respond After Approval, and then click OK.

Now computers that are booted from the network will enter a pending state. Before the installation can proceed, an administrator can approve or reject the request.

To approve a request, complete the following steps:

1. In the Windows Deployment Services console, select the server you want to work with. Next, click the server's Pending Devices folder to select it and display a list of computers waiting for approval.
2. Right-click the computer, and then click Approve.

To reject a request, complete the following steps:

1. In the Windows Deployment Services console, select the server you want to work with. Next, click the server's Pending Devices folder to select it and display a list of computers waiting for approval.
2. Right-click the computer, and then click Reject.

Customizing Windows Images

You can customize a mounted boot or install image using the DISM utility. Available options for DISM are summarized in Table 2-4. All components in an image are managed via the component store.

TABLE 2-4 Key Options for the DISM Utility

COMMAND TYPE/COMMAND	DESCRIPTION
GENERAL COMMANDS	
/Cleanup-Wim	Deletes resources associated with mounted Windows images that are corrupt.
/Commit-Wim	Saves changes to a mounted Windows image.
/Get-MountedWimInfo	Displays information about mounted Windows images.
/Get-WimInfo	Displays information about images in a Windows image file.
/Image	Specifies the path to the root directory of an offline Windows image.
/Mount-Wim	Mounts an image from a Windows image file.
/Online	Targets the running operating system.
/Remount-Wim	Recovers an orphaned Windows mount directory.
/Unmount-Wim	Unmounts a mounted Windows image.

COMMAND TYPE/COMMAND	DESCRIPTION
ADDITIONAL OPTIONS	
/English	Displays command-line output in English.
/Format	Specifies the report output format.
/LogLevel	Specifies the output level shown in the log (1–4).
/LogPath	Specifies the log file path.
/NoRestart	Suppresses automatic reboots and reboot prompts.
/Quiet	Suppresses all output except for error messages.
/ScratchDir	Specifies the path to a scratch directory.
/SysDriveDir	Specifies the path to the system loader file named BootMgr.
/WinDir	Specifies the path to the Windows directory.

Once you mount an image, you are able to work with the mounted image using the Dism /Image subcommands listed in Table 2-5. These subcommands allow you to upgrade the image to a higher edition, add and remove device drivers, specify time zones and language UI options, display patches and installed MSI applications, add and remove packages, and more.

TABLE 2-5 Important Subcommands for Mounted and Offline Images

SUBCOMMANDS	DESCRIPTION
/Add-Driver	Adds driver packages to an offline image.
/Add-Package	Adds packages to the image.
/Apply-Unattend	Applies an *AnswerFile*.xml file to an image.
/Check-AppPatch	Displays information if the MSP patches are applicable to the mounted image.
/Cleanup-Image	Performs cleanup and recovery operations on the image.
/Disable-Feature	Disables a specific feature in the image.
/Enable-Feature	Enables a specific feature in the image.
/Gen-LangIni	Generates a new Lang.ini file.
/Get-AppInfo	Displays information about a specific installed MSI application.

SUBCOMMANDS	DESCRIPTION
/Get-AppPatches	Displays information about all applied MSP patches for all installed applications.
/Get-AppPatchInfo	Displays information about installed MSP patches.
/Get-Apps	Displays information about all installed MSI applications.
/Get-CurrentEdition	Displays the editions of the specified image.
/Get-DriverInfo	Displays information about a specific driver in an offline image or a running operating system.
/Get-Drivers	Displays information about all drivers in an offline image or a running operating system.
/Get-FeatureInfo	Displays information about a specific feature.
/Get-Features	Displays information about all features in a package.
/Get-Intl	Displays information about the international settings and languages.
/Get-PackageInfo	Displays information about a specific package.
/Get-Packages	Displays information about all packages in the image.
/Get-TargetEditions	Displays a list of Windows editions that an image can be upgraded to.
/Remove-Driver	Removes driver packages from an offline image.
/Remove-Package	Removes packages from the image.
/Set-AllIntl	Sets all international settings in the mounted offline image.
/Set-Edition	Upgrades the Windows image to a higher edition.
/Set-InputLocale	Sets the input locales and keyboard layouts to use in the mounted offline image.
/Set-LayeredDriver	Sets the keyboard layered driver.
/Set-ProductKey	Populates the product key into the offline image.
/Set-SetupUILang	Defines the default language that will be used by Setup.
/Set-SKUIntlDefaults	Sets all international settings to the default values for the specified SKU language in the mounted offline image.
/Set-SysLocale	Sets the language for non-Unicode programs (also called system locale) and font settings in the mounted offline image.

SUBCOMMANDS	DESCRIPTION
/Set-TimeZone	Sets the default time zone in the mounted offline image.
/Set-UILang	Sets the default system UI language that is used in the mounted offline image.
/Set-UILangFallback	Sets the fallback default language for the system UI in the mounted offline image.
/Set-UserLocale	Sets the user locale in the mounted offline image.

The Deployment Image Servicing and Management tool provides commands for working with WIM images. The syntax for mounting images is:

```
dism /mount-wim /wimfile:Path /index:Index /mountdir:MountPath
```

where *Path* is the full path to the WIM image, *Index* is the index position of the image number of the image within the .wim file to apply, and *MountPath* is the directory location where you'd like to mount the image, such as:

```
dism /mount-wim /wimfile:c:\winpe_x86\iso\sources\boot.wim /index:1
/mountdir:c:\win7
```

You can then modify the image as necessary. To commit your changes at any time, you can use Dism /Commit-Wim as shown in the following example:

```
dism /commit-wim /mountdir:c:\win7
```

Here, you commit changes to the WIM images mounted in the C:\Win7 directory.

To unmount a WIM file, you can use Dism /Unmount-Wim as shown in the following example:

```
dism /unmount-wim /mountdir:c:\win7
```

Here, you unmount the WIM image that was mounted and committed in the C:\Win7 directory. If there are uncommitted changes you must commit or discard changes when you unmount a WIM image. Add /Commit to commit changes or /Discard to discard changes. This affects only the changes you haven't previously committed.

CHAPTER 3

Configuring User and Computer Policies

Group Policy is a set of rules that you can apply to help manage users and computers. In Windows 7, Group Policy includes both managed settings, referred to as *policy settings*, and unmanaged settings, referred to as *policy preferences*. Policy settings enable you to control the configuration of the operating system and its components. Policy preferences enable you to configure, deploy, and manage operating system and application settings. The key difference between policy settings and policy preferences is enforcement. Group Policy strictly enforces policy settings. Group Policy does not strictly enforce policy preferences.

In this chapter, I show you how to use policy settings. In the next chapter, I show you how to use policy preferences.

Group Policy Essentials

You use policy settings to control the configuration of the operating system and also to disable options and controls in the user interface for settings that Group Policy is managing. Most policy settings are stored in policy-related branches of the registry. The operating system and compliant applications check these branches to determine whether—and how—various aspects of the operating system are controlled.

Two types of Group Policy are available: local Group Policy and Active Directory–based Group Policy. Local Group Policy is used to manage settings for a local machine only. Active Directory–based Group Policy is used to manage the settings of computers throughout sites, domains, and organizational units (OUs). Group Policy simplifies administration by giving administrators centralized control over privileges, permissions, and capabilities of users and computers. Careful management of policies is essential to proper operations. Policy settings are divided into two broad categories: those that apply to computers and those that apply to users. Computer policies are normally applied during system startup, and user policies are normally applied during logon.

During startup and logon, policies are applied in an exact sequence, which is often important to keep in mind when troubleshooting system behavior. When multiple policies are in place, they are applied in the following order:

1. Local policies
2. Site policies
3. Domain policies
4. OU policies
5. Child OU policies

By default, if policy settings conflict, settings applied later take precedence and overwrite previous policy settings. For example, OU policies take precedence over domain policies. As you might expect, there are exceptions to the precedence rule that enable administrators to block, oversee, and disable policies.

The Group Policy client service isolates Group Policy notification and processing from the Windows logon process, which reduces the resources used for background processing of policy, increases overall performance, and enables delivery and application of new Group Policy files as part of the update process without requiring a restart.

Unlike Windows XP, Windows 7 doesn't use the trace logging functionality in Userenv.dll. Instead, Windows 7 writes Group Policy event messages to the system log. In addition, the Group Policy operational log replaces previous Userenv logging. When you are troubleshooting Group Policy issues, you use the detailed event messages in the operational log rather than the Userenv log. In Event Viewer, you can access the operational log under Applications And Services Logs\Microsoft\Windows\GroupPolicy\Operational.

Windows 7 uses Network Location Awareness instead of ICMP protocol (ping). With Network Location Awareness, a computer is aware of the type of network to which it is connected and can also be responsive to changes in the system status or network configuration. By using Network Location Awareness, the Group Policy client can determine the computer state, the network state, and the available network bandwidth for slow-link detection. As a result, the Group Policy client has a better understanding of the operational environment and can better determine which policies should be applied when.

Accessing and Using Local Group Policies

Local Group Policy applies to any user or administrator who logs on to a computer that is a member of a workgroup, as well as to any user or administrator who logs on locally to a computer that is a member of a domain.

A computer running Windows 7 can have one or more local policy objects associated with it. Local Group Policy is managed through the local Group Policy object (GPO). The local GPO is stored on individual computers in the %SystemRoot%\System32\GroupPolicy folder. Additional user-specific and group-specific local GPOs are stored in the %SystemRoot%\System32\GroupPolicyUsers folder.

When using computers in a stand-alone configuration rather than a domain configuration, you might find multiple local GPOs useful. You can implement one local GPO for administrators and another local GPO for nonadministrators and then no longer have to explicitly disable or remove settings that interfere with your ability to manage a computer before performing administrator tasks. In a domain configuration, however, you might not want to use multiple local GPOs. In domains, most computers and users already have multiple GPOs applied to them, and adding multiple local GPOs to this already varied mix can make it confusing to manage Group Policy.

Windows 7 has three layers of local GPOs:

- **Local Group Policy** Local Group Policy is the only local GPO that allows both computer configuration and user configuration settings to be applied to all users of the computer.
- **Administrators and Non-Administrators local Group Policy** Administrators and Non-Administrators local Group Policy contains only user configuration settings. This policy is applied based on whether the user account being used is a member of the local Administrators group.
- **User-specific local Group Policy** User-specific local Group Policy contains only user configuration settings. This policy is applied to individual users and groups.

These layers of local GPOs are processed in the following order: local Group Policy, Administrators and Non-Administrators local Group Policy, user-specific local Group Policy.

Because the available User Configuration settings are the same among all local GPOs, a setting in one GPO might conflict with a setting in another GPO. Windows 7 resolves conflicts in settings by overwriting any previous setting with the last read and most-current setting. The final setting is the one Windows 7 uses. When Windows 7 resolves conflicts, only the enabled or disabled state of settings matters. A setting of Not Configured does not affect the state of the setting from a previous policy application. To simplify domain administration, you can disable processing of local GPOs on computers running Windows 7 by enabling the Turn Off Local Group Policy Objects Processing policy setting in a domain GPO. In Group Policy, this setting is located under the Administrative Templates policies for Computer Configuration under \System\Group Policy.

> **NOTE** If enabled, local GPOs are always processed. However, they have the least precedence, which means their settings can be superseded by site, domain, and OU settings.

The only local policy object that exists on a computer by default is the local GPO. You can create and manage other local policy objects by using the Group Policy Object Editor. Because local Group Policy is a subset of Group Policy, there are many things you can't do locally that you can do in a domain setting. First, you can't manage any policy preferences. Second, you can manage only a subset of policy settings. Beyond these fundamental differences, local Group Policy and Active Directory–based Group Policy are managed in much the same way.

To work with local GPOs, you must use an administrator account. The quickest way to access the top-level local GPO on a local computer is to type the following command at a command prompt:

```
gpedit.msc /gpcomputer: "%ComputerName%"
```

This command starts the Group Policy Management Editor in a Microsoft Management Console (MMC) with its target set to the local computer.

You can also manage the top-level local GPO on a computer by following these steps:

1. Click Start, type **mmc** in the Search box, and then press Enter.
2. In Microsoft Management Console, click File, and then click Add/Remove Snap-In.
3. In the Add Or Remove Snap-Ins dialog box, click Group Policy Object Editor, and then click Add.
4. In the Select Group Policy Object dialog box, click Finish (because the local computer is the default object). Click OK.

As shown in Figure 3-1, you can now manage local Group Policy settings by using the options provided. Because local Group Policy does not have policy preferences, you will not find separate Policies and Preferences nodes under Computer Configuration and User Configuration.

You can create and manage other local policy objects as necessary. To create or access other local GPOs, follow these steps:

1. Click Start, type **mmc** in the Search box, and then press Enter. In Microsoft Management Console, click File, and then click Add/Remove Snap-In.
2. In the Add Or Remove Snap-Ins dialog box, click Group Policy Object Editor, and then click Add.
3. In the Select Group Policy Object dialog box, click Browse. In the Browse For A Group Policy Object dialog box, click the Users tab.

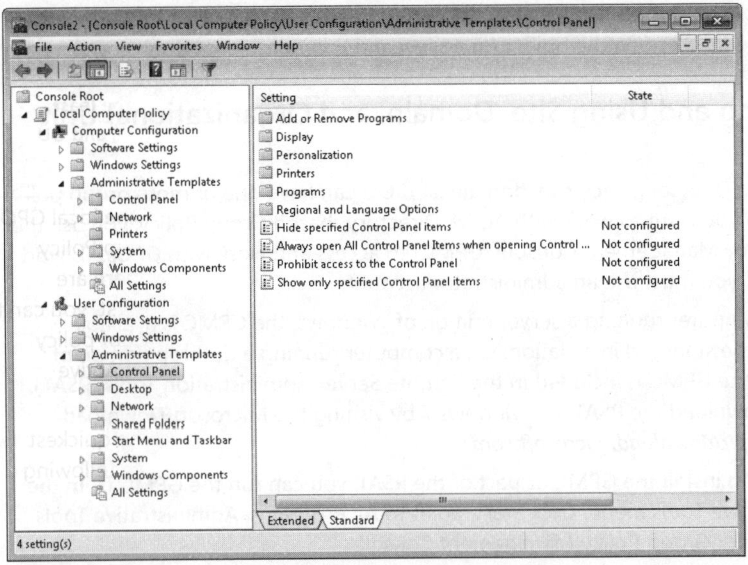

FIGURE 3-1 Accessing the top-level local GPO.

4. On the Users tab, shown in Figure 3-2, the entries in the Group Policy Object Exists column specify whether a particular local policy object has been created. Do one of the following:

   - Select Administrators to create or access the Administrators local GPO. You select Administrators instead of the Administrator user to ensure that the policy is applied to all local administrators.
   - Select Non-Administrators to create or access the Non-Administrators local GPO.
   - Select the local user whose user-specific local GPO you want to create or access.

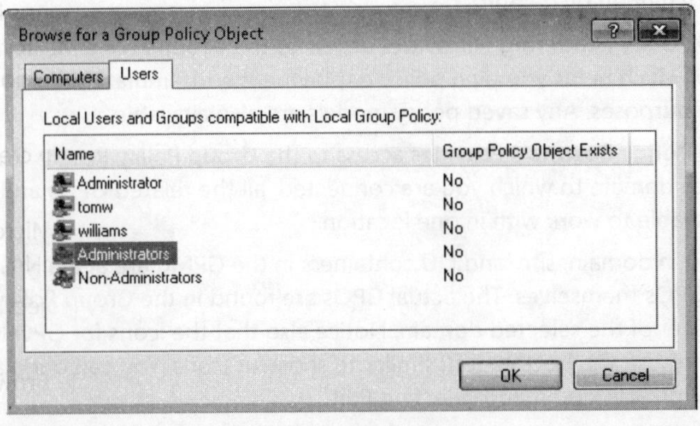

FIGURE 3-2 Accessing additional local GPOs

5. Click OK. If the selected object doesn't already exist, it will be created. Otherwise, you'll open the object for review and editing.

Accessing and Using Site, Domain, and Organizational Unit Policies

With Active Directory, each site, domain, and OU can have one or more group policies. When you want to work with Active Directory–based Group Policy, you use the Group Policy Management Console (GPMC) to access and work with GPOs. To work with GPOs, you must use an administrator account.

On a computer running a server edition of Windows, the GPMC is available as part of the standard installation. On a computer running a desktop edition of Windows, the GPMC is included in the Remote Server Administration Tools (RSAT). You can download the RSAT for Windows 7 by visiting the Microsoft Download Center (*http://download.microsoft.com/*).

Once you install the GPMC as part of the RSAT, you can run the GPMC from the Administrative Tools menu. Click Start, point to All Programs, Administrative Tools, and then click Group Policy Management Console.

As shown in Figure 3-3, the left pane of the GPMC has two top-level nodes by default: Group Policy Management (the console root) and Forest (a node representing the forest to which you are currently connected, which is named after the forest root domain for that forest). When you expand the Forest node, you see the following nodes:

- **Domains** Provides access to the policy settings for domains in the forest being administered. You are connected to your logon domain by default; you can add connections to other domains. If you expand a domain, you can access the Default Domain Policy GPO, the Domain Controllers OU (and the related Default Domain Controllers Policy GPO), and GPOs defined in the domain.
- **Sites** Provides access to the policy settings for sites in the related forest. Sites are hidden by default.
- **Group Policy Modeling** Provides access to the Group Policy Modeling Wizard, which helps you plan policy deployment and simulate settings for testing purposes. Any saved policy models are also available.
- **Group Policy Results** Provides access to the Group Policy Results Wizard. For each domain to which you are connected, all the related GPOs and OUs are available to work with in one location.

GPOs found in domain, site, and OU containers in the GPMC are actually GPO links and not GPOs themselves. The actual GPOs are found in the Group Policy Objects container of the selected domain. Notice also that the icons for GPO links have a small arrow at the bottom left, similar to shortcut icons. You can open a GPO for editing by right-clicking it and selecting Edit.

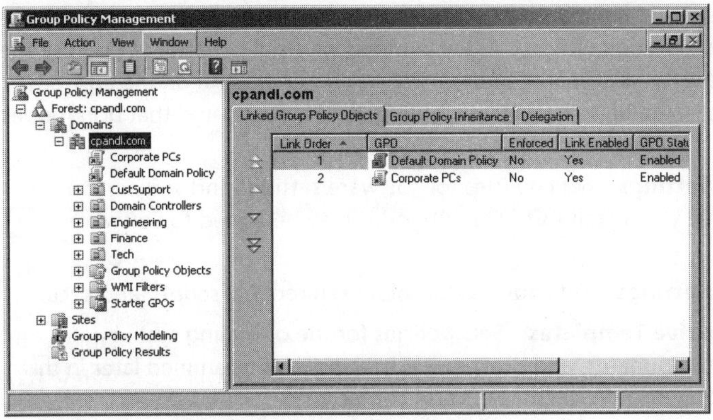

FIGURE 3-3 Access GPOs for domains, sites, and OUs.

Once you've selected a policy for editing or created a new policy, use the Group Policy Management Editor to work with the GPOs. As Figure 3-4 shows, the Group Policy Management Editor has two main nodes:

- **Computer Configuration** Enables you to set policies that should be applied to computers, regardless of who logs on.
- **User Configuration** Enables you to set policies that should be applied to users, regardless of which computer they log on to.

NOTE **Keep in mind that user configuration options set through local policy objects apply only to computers on which the options are configured. If you want the options to apply to all computers that the user might use, you must use domain, site, or OU policies.**

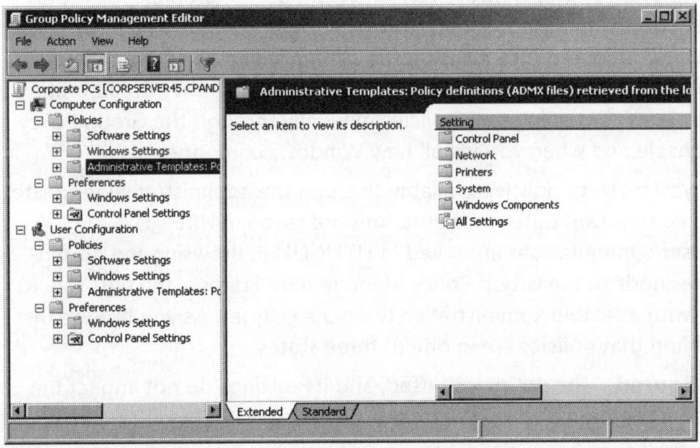

FIGURE 3-4 Group Policy options depend on the type of policy you're creating and the add-ons installed.

You will find separate Policies and Preferences nodes under Computer Configuration and User Configuration. When you are working with policy settings, you use the Policies node. The options available under a Policies node depend on the add-ons installed and which type of policy you're creating. You'll usually find that both nodes have subnodes for the following:

- **Software Settings** Sets policies for software settings and software installation. When you install software, subnodes may be added to Software Settings.
- **Windows Settings** Sets policies for folder redirection, scripts, and security.
- **Administrative Templates** Sets policies for the operating system, Windows components, and programs. These policies, examined later in this chapter, apply specifically to users and computers.

Configuring Policies

To manage users and computers, you need to configure the administrative template policies. These policies provide easy access to registry-based policy settings that control the operating system, Windows components, and programs. Although earlier versions of Windows that support Group Policy use administrative template (ADM) files with a proprietary markup language to store registry-based policy settings, Windows 7 uses a standards-based XML file format called ADMX. Unlike ADM files, which are stored in the GPO to which they relate, ADMX files are stored in a central repository. In domains, central storage of ADMX files makes it easier to work with and manage the files.

Viewing Policies and Templates

As shown in Figure 3-5, you can view the currently configured templates in the Group Policy Management Editor's Administrative Templates node, which contains policies that can be configured for local systems, OUs, domains, and sites. Different sets of templates are found under Computer Configuration and User Configuration. You can add templates containing new policies manually through the Group Policy Management Console and when you install new Windows components.

Any changes you make to policies available through the administrative templates are saved in the registry. Computer configurations are saved in HKEY_LOCAL_MACHINE, and user configurations are saved in HKEY_USER. Browsing the Administrative Templates node in the Group Policy Management Editor is the best way to become familiar with available administrative template policies. As you browse the templates, you'll find that policies are in one of three states:

- **Not Configured** The policy isn't used, and its settings do not impact the existing configuration on the computer.
- **Enabled** The policy is active, and its settings are saved in the registry.

- **Disabled** The enabled behavior of the policy is not on. The policy may have a specific disabled behavior that is contrary to its enabled setting. This setting is saved in the registry.

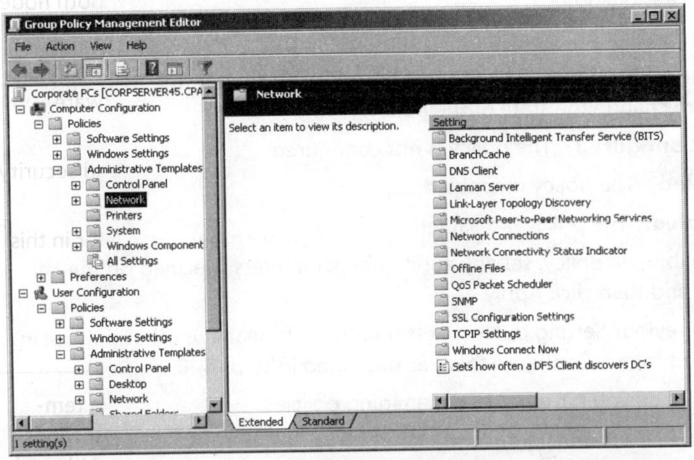

FIGURE 3-5 Set user and computer policies through administrative templates.

Enabling, Disabling, and Configuring Policies

In the Group Policy Management Editor, you'll find administrative templates in two nodes: Computer Configuration and User Configuration. In most cases, the policies in these areas don't overlap or conflict with each other. If there is a conflict, however, computer policies have precedence, which means that the computer policy is enforced. Later in this chapter, you'll find details on commonly used policies and how to employ them.

Before you can work with policies, you must access the Group Policy Management Editor for the site, domain, or OU you want to work with. To access a GPO for a domain or OU, follow these steps:

1. In the GPMC, expand the entry for the forest you want to work with, and then expand the related Domains node.
2. Expand the node for the domain you want to work with, and then expand the related Group Policy Objects node.
3. Right-click the GPO that you want to work with, and then select Edit. This opens the GPO for editing in the Group Policy Management Editor.

Once you've opened a GPO in the Group Policy Management Editor, you can enable, disable, and configure policies by completing the following steps:

1. Under the Computer Configuration or User Configuration node (whichever applies for the type of policy you want to set), access the Administrative Templates folder.

2. In the left pane, click the subfolder containing the policies you want to work with. The related policies are displayed in the right pane.
3. Double-click a policy (or right-click a policy and select Properties) to display its Properties dialog box.
4. Click the Explain tab to see a description of the policy, if one is provided.
5. To set the policy's state, click the Setting tab, and then use the following options to change the state of the policy:
   - **Not Configured** The policy is not configured.
   - **Enabled** The policy is enabled.
   - **Disabled** The policy is disabled.
6. If you enable the policy, set any additional parameters specified on the Setting tab, and then click Apply.
7. Use the Previous Setting or Next Setting button to manage other policies in the current folder. Configure them as described in steps 4–6.
8. Click OK when you have finished managing policies.

Adding or Removing Templates

You can add or remove template folders in the Group Policy Management Editor. To do this, complete the following steps:

1. Access the Group Policy Management Editor for the site, domain, or OU you want to work with.
2. In the Computer Configuration or User Configuration node, right-click the Administrative Templates folder, and then click Add/Remove Templates. This displays the Add/Remove Templates dialog box.
3. To add a template, click Add. Then, in the Policy Templates dialog box, select the template you want to add, and then click Open.
4. To remove a template, select the template, and then click Remove.
5. When you have finished adding and removing templates, click Close.

Working with File and Data Management Policies

Every system administrator needs to be familiar with file and data management policies, which affect the amount of data a user can store on systems, how offline files are used, and whether the System Restore feature is enabled.

Configuring Disk Quota Policies

Policies that control disk quotas are applied at the system level. You access these policies using the Administrative Templates policies for Computer Configuration under System\Disk Quotas. The available policies are summarized in Table 3-1.

TABLE 3-1 Disk Quota Policies

POLICY NAME	DESCRIPTION
Apply Policy To Removable Media	Determines whether to extend quota policies to NTFS volumes on removable media. If you do not enable this policy, quota limits apply only to fixed media drives.
Default Quota Limit And Warning Level	Sets a default quota limit and warning level for all users. This setting overrides other settings and affects only new users of a volume.
Enable Disk Quotas	Turns disk quotas on or off for all NTFS volumes on the computer and prevents users from changing the setting.
Enforce Disk Quota Limit	Specifies whether quota limits are enforced. If quotas are enforced, users are denied disk space if they exceed the quota. This setting overrides settings on the Quota tab for the NTFS volume.
Log Event When Quota Limit Exceeded	Determines whether an event is logged when users reach their limit and prevents users from changing their logging options.
Log Event When Quota Warning Level Exceeded	Determines whether an event is logged when users reach the warning level.

Whenever you work with quota limits, you'll want to use a standard set of policies on all systems. Typically, you won't need to enable all the policies. Instead, you can selectively enable policies and then use the standard NTFS features to control quotas on various volumes. If you want to enable quota limits, use the following technique:

1. Access Group Policy for the system, site, domain, or OU you want to work with. Next, access the Disk Quotas node using the Administrative Templates policies for Computer Configuration under System\Disk Quotas.
2. Double-click Enable Disk Quotas. Select Enabled, and then click OK.
3. Double-click Enforce Disk Quota Limit. If you want to enforce disk quotas on all NTFS volumes residing on this computer, select Enabled. Otherwise, select Disabled, and then set specific limits on a per-volume basis, as discussed in Chapter 14, "Maintaining Data Access and Availability." Click OK.
4. Double-click Default Quota Limit And Warning Level. The Default Quota Limit And Warning Level dialog box, shown in Figure 3-6, appears. Select Enabled.

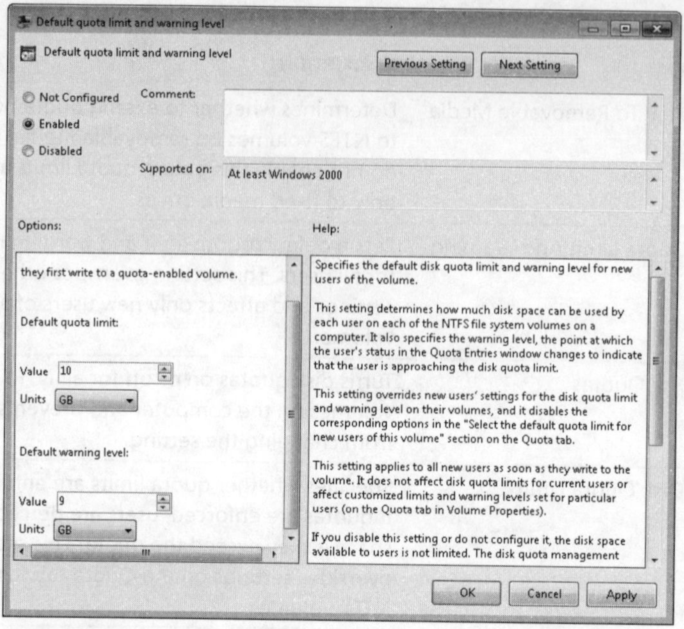

FIGURE 3-6 Use the Default Quota Limit And Warning Level dialog box to establish disk quota values.

5. Scroll the Options slide down. Under Default Quota Limit, set a default limit that is applied to new users when they first write to the quota-enabled volume. The limit does not apply to current users and does not affect current limits. On a corporate network share, such as a share used by all members of a team, a good limit is between 1 gigabyte (GB) and 3 GB. Of course, this depends on the size of the data files the users routinely work with. Graphic designers and data engineers, for example, might need much more disk space.
6. Scroll the Options slider down to set a warning limit as well. A good warning limit is about 90 percent of the default quota limit, meaning that if you set the default quota limit to 1 GB, you should set the warning limit to 900 MB. Click OK.
7. Double-click Log Event When Quota Limit Exceeded. Select Enabled so that limit events are recorded in the application log. Click OK.
8. Double-click Log Event When Quota Warning Exceeded. Select Enabled so that warning events are recorded in the application log. Click OK.
9. Double-click Apply Policy To Removable Media. Select Disabled so that the quota limits apply only to fixed media volumes on the computer. Click OK.

Configuring System Restore Policies

System Restore is designed to save the state of system volumes and enable users to restore a system in the event of a problem. It is a helpful feature for the average user, but it can use a tremendous amount of disk space. As you'll learn in Chapter 6, "Configuring Windows 7 Computers," you can turn System Restore off for individual drives or for all drives on a computer.

In the Group Policy console, you'll find the System Restore policies under the Administrative Templates policies for Computer Configuration under System\System Restore. Through System Restore policies, you can override and disable management of this feature. The following policies are available:

- **Turn Off System Restore** If you enable this policy, System Restore is turned off and can't be managed using the System utility or the System Restore Wizard. If you disable this policy, System Restore is enforced and cannot be turned off.
- **Turn Off Configuration** If you enable this policy, you prevent configuration of the System Restore feature. Users can't access the Settings dialog box but can still turn off System Restore. If you disable this policy, users can access the Settings dialog box but can't manipulate it, and they can still turn off System Restore.

To configure System Restore policies, follow these steps:

1. Access Group Policy for the system, site, domain, or OU you want to work with. Next, access the System Restore node using the Administrative Templates policies for Computer Configuration under System\System Restore.
2. To enable or disable System Restore, double-click Turn Off System Restore. Select either Enabled or Disabled, and then click OK.
3. To enable or disable configuration of System Restore, double-click Turn Off Configuration. Select either Enabled or Disabled, and then click OK.

Configuring Offline File Policies

Offline file policies are set at both the computer and the user level, and there are identically named policies at each level. If you work with identically named policies at both levels, keep in mind that computer policies override user policies and that these policies may be applied at different times.

The primary policies you'll want to use are summarized in Table 3-2. As the table shows, most offline policies affect access, synchronization, caching, and encryption. You'll find Offline File policies under Administrative Templates for Computer Configuration in Network\Offline Files and under Administrative Templates policies for User Configuration in Network\Offline Files.

TABLE 3-2 Offline File Policies

POLICY TYPE	POLICY NAME	DESCRIPTION
Computer	Allow Or Disallow Use Of The Offline Files Feature	Forces enabling or disabling of the offline files feature and prevents overriding by users. Enables administrative control of offline file settings for a system.
Computer	At Logoff, Delete Local Copy Of User's Offline Files*	At logoff, cleans up the offline file cache on the local computer.
Computer	Configure Slow-Link Mode	Controls how slow links are used. Enabled: slow-link values for each shared folder used with offline files are configured. Disabled: offline files will not use slow-link mode.
Computer	Configure Background Sync	Controls background synchronization on slow links. Enabled: Background synchronization occurs periodically to synchronize files in shared folders between the client and server. Disabled: default behavior for background synchronization is used.
Computer	Default Cache Size*	Limits the size of automatically cached offline files and prevents users from changing related options. Enabled: you can set a cache size. Disabled: the limit is 10 percent of drive space.
Computer	Enable Transparent Caching	Controls caching of network files over slow links. Enabled: optimizes caching on the client to reduce the number of transmissions over slow links. Disabled: transparent caching is not used.
Computer	Encrypt The Offline Files Cache	Determines whether offline files are encrypted to improve security.
Computer	Exclude Files From Being Cached	Allows you to specify file extensions of file types that should not be cached.

POLICY TYPE	POLICY NAME	DESCRIPTION
Computer	Files Not Cached*	Lists types of files, by file extension, that cannot be used offline.
Computer	Limit Disk Space Used By Offline Files	Limits the amount of disk space that can be used to store offline files.
Computer	Subfolders Always Available Offline*	Makes subfolders available offline when the parent folder is available offline.
Computer	Turn On Economical Application Of Administratively Assigned Offline Files	Determines how administratively assigned files and folders are synced at logon. Enabled: only new files and folders are synced at logon. Disabled: all files and folders are synced at logon.
Computer/User	Action On Server Disconnect*	Specifies how the system responds when the file-hosting server becomes unavailable. The Work Offline action ensures that offline files are available.
Computer/User	Administratively Assigned Offline Files	Uses a Universal Naming Convention (UNC) path to specify files and folders that are always available offline.
Computer/User	Event Logging Level*	Ensures that offline file events are logged in the application log.
Computer/User	Prevent Use Of Offline Files Folder*	Prevents users from accessing the Offline Files folder. Users can't view or open copies of cached files, but they can work offline.
Computer/User	Prohibit "Make Available Offline" For These Files And Folders*	Prohibits users from making specific files and folders available offline. Enter UNC paths to resources.
Computer/User	Prohibit User Configuration Of Offline Files*	Prevents users from enabling, disabling, and configuring offline files. This locks down the default settings for offline files.
Computer/User	Remove "Make Available Offline"	Prevents users from making files available offline.

POLICY TYPE	POLICY NAME	DESCRIPTION
Computer/User	Synchronize All Offline Files Before Logging Off*	Forces full synchronization before users log off and prevents them from changing synchronization timing.
Computer/User	Synchronize All Offline Files When Logging On*	Forces full synchronization when users log on and prevents them from changing synchronization timing.
Computer/User	Synchronize Offline Files Before Suspend*	Forces synchronization before a computer goes into standby or hibernate mode. You can specify quick or full synchronization.

** Does not apply to Windows 7, Windows Server 2008 Release 2, or later*

Setting Offline File Configuration Policies

Offline file configuration can be easily controlled through Group Policy. You can allow users to specify which files and folders should be available offline, prevent them from configuring offline file features on their own, and allow them to work offline but not access other cached resources. Follow these steps to set offline file configuration policies:

1. Access Group Policy for the system, site, domain, or OU you want to work with. Most offline file policies can be configured for either computer or user policy (with user policy having precedence by default) by using the Offline Files node. You can access the policies for offline files using either the Administrative Templates policies for Computer Configuration under Network\Offline Files or the Administrative Templates policies for User Configuration under Network\Offline Files, unless specifically noted otherwise.
2. To control the availability of offline files, double-click Allow Or Disallow Use Of The Offline Files Feature. Select either Enabled or Disabled, and then click OK. Users can now select specific files and folders that they want to have available when working offline. To prevent user selection of files and assign specific offline files to be used, you need to prohibit this feature and administratively assign offline files.
3. To prevent users from changing offline file configuration settings, double-click Prohibit User Configuration Of Offline Files, and then select Enabled. Once this policy is set, users can't configure offline file options.
4. To prevent users from accessing the Offline Files folder but still allow them to work offline, double-click Prevent Use Of Offline Files Folder, and then select Enabled. Once you select this option, users cannot use the Offline Files folder to view or open copies of cached files. They can, however, save current work and continue to use active files when offline.

Administratively Controlling Offline Files and Folders

You can administratively control which files and folders are available for offline use. Typically, you'll want to do this on file servers or other systems sharing resources on the network. You can use several techniques to administratively control which resources are available offline.

You can prevent users from making files available offline and instead assign specific offline resources by following these steps:

1. Access Group Policy for the system you want to work with. Next, access the Offline Files node using the Administrative Templates policies for Computer Configuration under Network\Offline Files or the Administrative Templates policies for User Configuration under Network\Offline Files.
2. To prevent users from making files available offline, double-click Remove "Make Available Offline." Select Enabled, and then click OK. Once this policy is enforced, users are unable to specify files for use offline.
3. To assign resources that are automatically available offline, double-click Administratively Assigned Offline Files. Select Enabled, and then click Show. In the Show Contents dialog box, specify resources according to their UNC path, such as \\corpserver\data. Figure 3-7 shows a list of resources that have been added to the Show Contents dialog box.

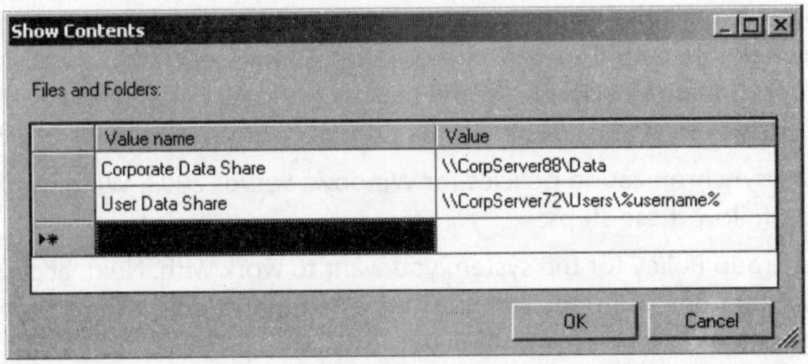

FIGURE 3-7 Use the Show Contents dialog box to specify resources according to their UNC path.

CAUTION **You should carefully consider which resources are automatically made available offline. The more resources you assign through this technique, the more network traffic is generated to maintain offline file caches.**

For computers running Windows XP, you can make specific files automatically available and prevent others from being used offline by following these steps:

1. Access Group Policy for the system that you want to work with. Next, access the Offline Files node using the Administrative Templates policies for Computer Configuration under Network\Offline Files or the Administrative Templates policies for User Configuration under Network\Offline Files.

2. To assign resources that are available offline automatically, double-click Administratively Assigned Offline Files. Select Enabled, and then click Show. In the Show Contents dialog box, specify resources according to their UNC path, such as \\corpserver\data.
3. To specify resources that users should not be able to make available offline, double-click Prohibit "Make Available Offline" For These Files And Folders. Select Enabled, and then click Show. In the Show Contents dialog box, specify resources according to their UNC path, such as \\corpserver\data. This setting doesn't prevent automatic caching of resources assigned through step 2.
4. Click OK until all open dialog boxes are closed.

Setting Offline File Synchronization Policies

Offline file synchronization can be controlled using the Sync Center, which is accessed by clicking Start, pointing to All Programs or Programs, Accessories, and then clicking Sync Center. However, you can set specific synchronization timing and techniques through policies. Normally, resources are fully synchronized (meaning that all files are checked to be sure they are complete and current) or quickly synchronized (meaning files are checked to be sure they are complete, but file contents are not examined for currency).

In Windows 7, offline files are synchronized automatically, with background synchronization used whenever a computer is connected to a slow network. A slow network is any network with a latency of more than 80 milliseconds. You can prevent a computer running Windows 7 from entering the slow-link mode and using background synchronization by disabling the Configure Slow-Link Mode policy.

To configure synchronization policies for Windows Server 2003, Windows XP, and Windows 2000, follow these steps:

1. Access Group Policy for the system you want to work with. Next, access the Offline Files node using the Administrative Templates policies for Computer Configuration under Network\Offline Files.
2. The policies that control synchronization are Synchronize All Offline Files When Logging On, Synchronize All Offline Files Before Logging Off, and Synchronize Offline Files Before Suspend. Double-click the policy related to the synchronization technique that you want to use. Select Enabled. For the Synchronize Offline Files Before Suspend policy, be sure that the appropriate option under Action is selected, either Full or Quick. Click OK.

TIP **A full synchronization ensures that the latest version of the user's offline files is stored prior to the suspend operation. Quick synchronization ensures that all the offline files are available but not necessarily in the most current version.**

Setting Offline File Cache Policies

Careful configuration of the offline file cache is essential to managing the system and network overhead generated by offline file usage. In Sync Center, you can specify a maximum file cache size, whether the cache is encrypted for security, and which file types should never be cached, as discussed in the sections "Configuring Disk Usage Limits for Offline Files" and "Managing Encryption for Offline Files" in Chapter 14. To configure related policies for the offline file cache for older computers, follow these steps:

1. Access Group Policy for the system you want to work with. Next, access the Offline Files node using the Administrative Templates policies for Computer Configuration under Network\Offline Files.
2. To set the cache size, double-click Default Cache Size. Select Enabled, and then use the Default Cache Size dialog box, shown in Figure 3-8, to set the default cache size. The value entered is the percentage of disk space times 10,000, meaning that if you enter 1,500, the cache can use up to 15 percent of the space on the system drive.

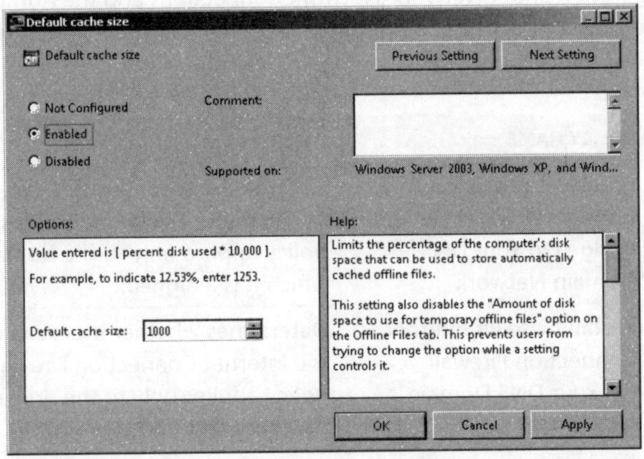

FIGURE 3-8 Set a default cache size for offline files in the Default Cache Size dialog box.

NOTE **If you don't configure the Default Cache Size policy or if you disable it, the cache size limit is 10 percent of the space on the system drive.**

3. To specify file types that are not cached, double-click Files Not Cached, and then select Enabled. Next, in the Extensions field, type a semicolon-separated list of file extensions to exclude. Each extension must be preceded by an asterisk and a period. You could enter *.wbk; *.tmp; *.lnk; *.ndx to block caching of many temporary file types.
4. To encrypt the cache, double-click Encrypt The Offline Files Cache, and then select Enabled. Once this policy is enabled, all existing and new files in the

cache are encrypted. The user can see his or her own files, but other users will not be able to use them.

Working with Access and Connectivity Policies

Access and connectivity policies control network connections, dial-up connections, and Remote Assistance configurations. These policies affect a system's connectivity to the network as well as remote access to the system.

Configuring Network Policies

Many network policies are available. Network policies that control Internet Connection Sharing, Internet Connection Firewall, Windows Firewall, and Network Bridge are configured at the computer level. Network policies that control local area network (LAN) connections, TCP/IP configuration, and remote access are configured at the user level. The primary policies that you'll want to use are summarized in Table 3-3. You'll find network policies under the Administrative Templates policies for Computer Configuration under Network\Network Connections and the Administrative Templates policies for User Configuration under Network\Network Connections.

TABLE 3-3 Network Policies

POLICY TYPE	POLICY NAME	DESCRIPTION
Computer	Prohibit Installation And Configuration Of Network Bridge On Your DNS Domain Network	Determines whether users can install and configure network bridges. This policy applies only to the domain in which it is assigned.
Computer	Prohibit Use Of Internet Connection Firewall On Your DNS Domain Network*	Determines whether users can enable the Internet Connection Firewall. This policy applies only to the domain in which it is assigned.
Computer	Prohibit Use Of Internet Connection Sharing On Your DNS Domain Network*	Determines whether administrators can enable and configure connection sharing. This policy applies only to the domain in which it is assigned.
Computer	Require Domain Users To Elevate When Setting A Network's Location	Determines whether the elevation prompt is displayed prior to setting a network's location.

POLICY TYPE	POLICY NAME	DESCRIPTION
Computer	Route All Traffic Through The Internal Network	Used with DirectAccess. Determines whether remote computers access the Internet via the internal corporate network or via their own Internet connection.
User	Ability To Change Properties Of An All User Remote Access Connection	Determines whether users can view and modify the properties of remote access connections available to all users of the computer.
User	Ability To Delete All User Remote Access Connections*	Determines whether users can delete remote access connections available to all users of the computer.
User	Ability To Enable/Disable A LAN Connection*	Determines whether users can enable or disable LAN connections.
User	Prohibit Access To Properties Of A LAN Connection*	Determines whether users can change the properties of LAN connections.
User	Prohibit Access To Properties Of Components Of A Remote Access Connection*	Determines whether users can access and change properties of components used by remote access connections.
User	Prohibit Deletion Of Remote Access Connections	Determines whether users can delete remote access connections.
User	Prohibit TCP/IP Advanced Configuration*	Determines whether users can access advanced TCP/IP settings.

** Does not apply to Windows 7, Windows Server 2008 Release 2, or later*

As shown in Table 3-3, network policies for computers are designed to restrict actions on an organization's network. When you enforce these restrictions, users are prohibited from using features such as Internet Connection Sharing in the applicable domain. This is designed to protect the security of corporate networks, but it doesn't prevent users with laptops, for example, from taking their computers home and using these features on their own networks. To enable or disable these restrictions, follow these steps:

1. Access Group Policy for the resource you want to work with. Next, access the Network Connections node using the Administrative Templates policies for Computer Configuration under Network\Network Connections.

2. Double-click the policy that you want to configure. Select Enabled or Disabled, and then click OK.

User policies for network connections usually prevent access to certain configuration features, such as the advanced TCP/IP property settings. To configure these policies, follow these steps:

1. Access Group Policy for the resource you want to work with. Next, access the Administrative Templates policies for User Configuration under Network\Network Connections.
2. Double-click the policy that you want to configure. Select Enabled or Disabled, and then click OK.

Configuring Remote Assistance Policies

Remote Assistance policies can be used to prevent or permit use of remote assistance on computers. Typically, when you set Remote Assistance policies, you'll want to prevent unsolicited offers for remote assistance while allowing requested offers. You can also force a specific expiration for invitations through policy rather than by setting this time limit through the System Properties dialog box of each computer. To improve security, you can use strong invitation encryption. This enhancement, however, limits who can answer Remote Assistance invitations to only those running Windows Vista or later releases of Windows.

To configure policy in this manner, follow these steps:

1. Access Group Policy for the computer you want to work with. Next, access the Administrative Templates policies for Computer Configuration under System\Remote Assistance.
2. Double-click Solicited Remote Assistance. Select Enabled. When enabled, this policy allows authorized users to solicit remote assistance.
3. You can now specify the level of access for assistants. The Permit Remote Control Of This Computer selection list has two options:
   - **Allow Helpers To Remotely Control The Computer** Permits viewing and remote control of the computer.
   - **Allow Helpers To Only View This Computer** Permits only viewing; assistants cannot take control to make changes.
4. Next, as shown in Figure 3-9, use the Maximum Ticket Time (Value) and Maximum Ticket Time (Units) fields to set the maximum time limit for remote assistance invitations. The default maximum time limit is 1 hour. Click OK.

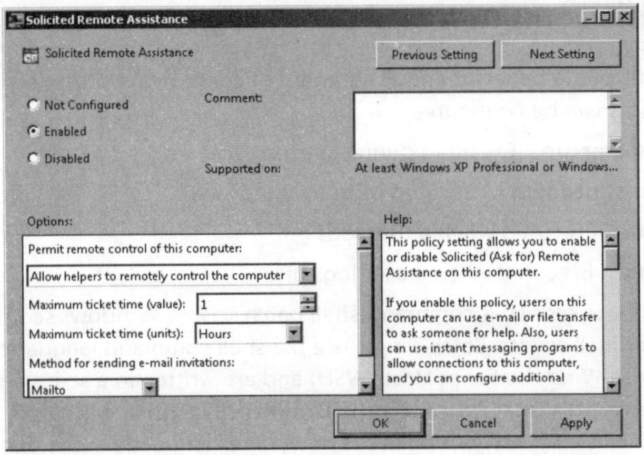

FIGURE 3-9 Set a time expiration limit for Remote Assistance invitations.

REAL WORLD **The method for sending e-mail invitations can be set to Mailto or Simple MAPI. Mailto is a browser-based mail submission technique in which the invitation's recipient connects through an Internet link. Simple MAPI uses Messaging Application Programming Interface (MAPI) for sending the e-mail invitation as an attachment to an e-mail message. As long as computers can establish a connection with each other over port 80 and you're using a standard e-mail program such as Microsoft Outlook or Windows Mail, you'll probably want to use Mailto.**

5. Double-click Offer Remote Assistance. In the Offer Remote Assistance dialog box, select Disabled. Disabling this policy prevents unsolicited assistance offers. Click OK.
6. If you want to use strong invitation encryption and limit connections so they can come only from computers running Windows Vista, Windows 7, or later releases of Windows, double-click Allow Only Vista Or Later Connections. In the Allow Only Vista Or Later Connections dialog box, select Enabled. Click OK.

To prevent remote assistance and remote control, follow these steps:

1. Access Group Policy for the computer you want to work with. Next, access the Administrative Templates policies for Computer Configuration under System\Remote Assistance.
2. Double-click Solicited Remote Assistance. Select Disabled, and then click Previous Setting or Next Setting, as appropriate.
3. In the Offer Remote Assistance dialog box, select Disabled, and then click OK.

Working with Computer and User Script Policies

Script policies control the behavior and assignment of computer and user scripts. Four types of scripts can be configured:

- **Computer startup** Executed during startup
- **Computer shutdown** Executed prior to shutdown
- **User logon** Executed when a user logs on
- **User logoff** Executed when a user logs off

You can write these scripts as command-shell batch scripts, Windows scripts, or Windows PowerShell scripts. Batch scripts use the shell command language. Windows scripts use Windows Script Host (WSH) and are written in a scripting language such as Microsoft Visual Basic Scripting Edition (VBScript) or Microsoft JScript. Windows PowerShell scripts are written in the PowerShell language. Note that policy preferences can in many cases eliminate the need to use computer and user scripts.

Controlling Script Behavior Through Policy

Policies that control script behavior are found under the Administrative Templates policies for Computer Configuration under System\Scripts and the Administrative Templates policies for User Configuration under System\Scripts. Through policy, you can control the behavior of startup, shutdown, logon, and logoff scripts. The key policies that you'll use are described in Table 3-4. As you'll see, there are numerous options for configuring script behavior.

TABLE 3-4 Computer and User Script Policies

POLICY TYPE	POLICY NAME	DESCRIPTION
Computer	Maximum Wait Time For Group Policy Scripts	Sets the maximum time to wait for scripts to finish running. The default value is 600 seconds (10 minutes).
Computer	Run Shutdown Scripts Visible	Displays shutdown scripts and their instructions as they execute.
Computer	Run Startup Scripts Asynchronously	Allows the system to run startup scripts simultaneously rather than one at a time.
Computer	Run Startup Scripts Visible	Displays startup scripts and their instructions as they execute.
Computer	Run Windows PowerShell Scripts First At Computer Startup, Shutdown	Determines whether Windows PowerShell scripts are run before other types of scripts at startup and shutdown.

Computer/ User	Run Windows PowerShell Scripts First At User Logon, Logoff	Determines whether Windows PowerShell scripts are run before other types of scripts at logon and logoff.
Computer/ User	Run Logon Scripts Synchronously	Ensures the system waits for logon scripts to finish before displaying the Windows interface.
User	Run Legacy Logon Scripts Hidden	Hides logon scripts configured through the System Policy Editor in Windows NT 4.
User	Run Logoff Scripts Visible	Displays logoff scripts and their instructions as they execute.
User	Run Logon Scripts Visible	Displays logon scripts and their instructions as they execute.

Although you can control script behavior in many ways, you'll usually want scripts to behave as follows:

- Windows PowerShell scripts should run first.
- Logon and startup scripts should run simultaneously (in most cases).
- All scripts should be hidden rather than visible.
- The system should wait no more than 1 minute for a script to complete (in most cases).

To enforce this behavior, follow these steps:

1. Access Group Policy for the computer you want to work with. Next, access the Administrative Templates policies for Computer Configuration under System\Scripts.
2. Double-click Run Windows PowerShell Scripts First At Computer Startup, Shutdown. Select Enabled, and then click OK.
3. Double-click Run Windows PowerShell Scripts First At User Logon, Logoff. Select Enabled, and then click OK.
4. Double-click Run Logon Scripts Synchronously. Select Disabled, and then click OK.
5. Double-click Run Startup Scripts Asynchronously. Select Enabled, and then click OK.
6. Double-click Run Startup Scripts Visible. Select Disabled, and then click OK.
7. Double-click Run Shutdown Scripts Visible. Select Disabled, and then click OK.

8. Double-click Maximum Wait Time For Group Policy Scripts. Select Enabled, and then enter a value of 60 for the wait time in the Seconds field. Click OK.
9. Access the Administrative Templates policies for User Configuration under System\Scripts.
10. Double-click Run Legacy Logon Scripts Hidden. Select Enabled, and then click OK.
11. Double-click Run Logon Scripts Visible. Select Disabled, and then click OK.
12. Double-click Run Logoff Scripts Visible. Select Disabled, and then click OK.
13. Double-click Run Windows PowerShell Scripts First At User Logon, Logoff. Select Enabled, and then click OK.

Assigning Computer Startup and Shutdown Scripts

Computer startup and shutdown scripts can be assigned as part of Group Policy. In this way, a computer and all its users—or all computers that are members of the site, domain, or OU—execute scripts automatically when they're started or shut down.

To assign computer scripts, follow these steps:

1. For easy management, copy the scripts you want to use to the Scripts\Startup or Scripts\Shutdown folder for the related policy. Scripts are stored in the %SystemRoot%\Sysvol\Sysvol*%UserDnsDomain%*\Policies*GUID*\Machine folder on domain controllers and %WinDir%\System32\GroupPolicy\Machine on Windows 7 workstations.
2. Access the Group Policy console for the resource you want to work with. Then access policies for Computer Configuration under Windows Settings\Scripts.
3. To work with startup scripts, right-click Startup and then select Properties. To work with shutdown scripts, right-click Shutdown and then select Properties.
4. Click Show Files. If you copied the computer scripts to the correct location, you should see the scripts you want to assign.
5. Click Add to assign a script. This opens the Add A Script dialog box. In the Script Name field, type the name of a script you copied to the Scripts\Startup or the Scripts\Shutdown folder for the related policy. In the Script Parameters field, enter any command-line arguments to pass to the command-line script or parameters to pass to the scripting host for a WSH script. Repeat this step to add other scripts.
6. During startup or shutdown, scripts are executed in the order in which they're listed in the Properties dialog box. Click Up or Down to reposition scripts as necessary.
7. If you want to edit the script name or parameters later, select the script in the scripts list, and then click Edit.
8. To delete a script, select the script in the scripts list and then click Remove.

Assigning User Logon and Logoff Scripts

User scripts can be assigned as part of Group Policy. In this way, all users who access a computer or are members of the site, domain, or OU execute scripts automatically when they log on or log off.

To assign user scripts, complete the following steps:

1. Copy the scripts you want to use to the Scripts\Logon or the Scripts\Logoff folder for the related policy. User scripts are stored in the %SystemRoot%\Sysvol\Sysvol*%UserDnsDomain%*\Policies*GUID*\User folder on domain controllers and under %WinDir%\System32\GroupPolicy\User on Windows 7 workstations.
2. Access the Group Policy console for the resource you want to work with. Then access policies for User Configuration under Windows Settings\Scripts.
3. To work with logon scripts, right-click Logon and then click Properties. To work with logoff scripts, right-click Logoff and click Properties.
4. Click Show Files. If you copied the user scripts to the correct location, you should see the scripts you want to assign.
5. Click Add to assign a script. This opens the Add A Script dialog box. In the Script Name field, type the name of a script you copied to the Scripts\Logon or the Scripts\Logoff folder for the related policy. In the Script Parameter field, enter any command-line arguments to pass to the command-line script or parameters to pass to the scripting host for a WSH script. Repeat this step to add other scripts.
6. During logon or logoff, scripts are executed in the order in which they're listed in the Properties dialog box. Click Up or Down to reposition scripts as necessary.
7. If you want to edit the script name or parameters later, select the script in the scripts list, and then click Edit.
8. To delete a script, select the script in the scripts list, and then click Remove.

Working with Logon and Startup Policies

Windows 7 provides a set of policies to control the logon process, some of which allow you to configure the way programs run at logon. This makes them similar to logon scripts in that you can execute specific tasks at logon. Other policies change the view in the welcome and logon screens. The main logon and startup policies that you'll use are available using Administrative Templates policies for Computer Configuration and User Configuration under System\Logon and are summarized in Table 3-5.

TABLE 3-5 Logon and Startup Policies

POLICY TYPE	POLICY NAME	DESCRIPTION
Computer	Always Use Custom Logon Background	Allows use of a custom logon background.
Computer	Always Use Classic Logon	This overrides the default simple logon screen and uses the logon screen displayed in previous versions of Windows.
Computer	Always Wait For The Network At Computer Startup And Logon	Requires the computer to wait for the network to be fully initialized. At startup, this Group Policy is fully applied rather than applied through a background refresh. At logon, this means the user account cannot be authenticated against cached credentials and must be authenticated against a domain controller.
Computer/User	Do Not Process The Legacy Run List	Disables running legacy run-list applications other than those set through the System Policy Editor in Windows NT 4.
Computer/User	Do Not Process The Run-Once List	Forces the system to ignore customized run-once lists.
Computer/User	Run These Programs At User Logon	Sets programs that all users should run at logon. Use the full file path (unless the program is in %SystemRoot%).

Using Classic Logon vs. Simple Logon

The simple logon window is implemented in Windows 7. It is the default mechanism for authentication, and although that view can be useful, some users might prefer to see only the classic logon window. To use classic logon rather than simple logon, follow these steps:

1. Access Group Policy for the computer you want to work with. Next, access the Administrative Templates policies for Computer Configuration under System\Logon.
2. Double-click Always Use Classic Logon. Select Enabled, and then click OK.

NOTE **For more details, see the "Controlling Logon: Welcome Screens and Classic Logons" section of Chapter 5.**

Setting Policy-Based Startup Programs

Although users can configure their startup applications separately, it usually makes more sense to handle this through Group Policy, especially in an enterprise in which the same applications should be started by groups of users. To specify programs that should start at logon, follow these steps:

1. Access Group Policy for the computer you want to work with. Next, access the Administrative Templates policies for Computer Configuration under System\Logon.
2. Double-click Run These Programs At User Logon. Select Enabled.
3. Click Show. In the Show Contents dialog box, specify applications using their full file or UNC path, such as C:\Program Files (x86)\Internet Explorer\Iexplore.exe or \\DCServ01\Apps\Stats.exe.
4. Close all open dialog boxes.

Disabling Run Lists Through Policy

Using Group Policy, you can disable legacy run lists as well as run-once lists. Legacy run lists are stored in the registry in HKEY_LOCAL_MACHINE\SOFTWARE\Microsoft\Windows\CurrentVersion\Run and HKEY_CURRENT_USER\Software\Microsoft\Windows\CurrentVersion\Run.

Run-once lists can be created by administrators to specify programs that should run the next time the system starts but not on subsequent restarts. Run-once lists are stored in the registry under HKEY_LOCAL_MACHINE\SOFTWARE\Microsoft\Windows\CurrentVersion\RunOnce and HKEY_CURRENT_USER\Software\Microsoft\Windows\CurrentVersion\RunOnce.

To disable run lists, follow these steps:

1. Access Group Policy for the computer you want to work with. Next, access the Administrative Templates policies for Computer Configuration under System\Logon or the Administrative Templates policies for User Configuration under System\Logon.
2. Double-click Do Not Process The Run Once List. Select Enabled, and then click OK.
3. Double-click Do Not Process The Legacy Run List. Select Enabled, and then click OK.

CHAPTER 4

Automating Windows 7 Configuration

Group Policy preferences enable you to automatically configure, deploy, and manage operating system and application settings, including settings for data sources, mapped drives, environment variables, network shares, folder options, and shortcuts. When you are deploying and setting up computers, you'll find that working with Group Policy preferences is easier than configuring the same settings manually on each computer, in Windows images, or through scripts used for startup, logon, shutdown, and logoff.

In this chapter, I introduce essential tasks for understanding and managing Group Policy preferences. In upcoming chapters, I show you how to put individual policy preferences to work to automate the configuration of your Windows computers whether you work in a small, medium, or large enterprise.

Understanding Group Policy Preferences

You configure preferences in Active Directory–based Group Policy. Local Group Policy does not have preferences. Group Policy does not strictly enforce policy preferences, nor does Group Policy store preferences in the policy-related branches of the registry. Instead, Group Policy writes preferences to the same locations in the registry that an application or operating system feature uses to store the related setting. This approach allows you to use preferences with applications and operating system features that aren't Group Policy–aware.

Preferences do not disable application or operating system features in the user interface to prevent their use. Users can change settings that you've configured with policy preferences. However, preferences overwrite existing settings, and there is no way to recover the original settings.

As it does with policy settings, Group Policy refreshes preferences at a regular interval, which is every 90 to 120 minutes by default. This means that periodically the preferences you've configured will be reapplied to a user's computer. Rather than allowing a refresh, you can prevent Group Policy from refreshing individual preferences by choosing to apply preferences only once.

The way you use policy preferences depends on whether you want to enforce the item you are configuring. To configure an item without enforcing it, use policy preferences, and then disable automatic refreshes. To configure an item and enforce the specified configuration, use policy settings or configure preferences, and then enable automatic refreshes.

Because preferences apply to both computer configuration and user configuration settings, you will find a separate Preferences node under Computer Configuration and User Configuration. In both configuration areas, you'll find two top-level subnodes:

- **Windows Settings** Used to manage general operating system and application preferences
- **Control Panel Settings** Used to manage Control Panel preferences

Table 4-1 provides an overview of the available preferences and where they are located within the configuration areas and the top-level subnodes.

TABLE 4-1 Configurable Preferences in Group Policy

PREFERENCE TYPE	LOCATION	POLICY CONFIGURATION AREA
Applications	Windows Settings	User
User Data Source, Data Sources	Control Panel Settings	User
System Data Source, Data Sources	Control Panel Settings	Computer and User
Devices	Control Panel Settings	Computer and User
Dial-Up Connection, Network Options	Control Panel Settings	Computer and User
Drive Maps	Windows Settings	User
User Variable, Environment	Windows Settings	Computer and User
System Variable, Environment	Windows Settings	Computer and User
Files	Windows Settings	Computer and User
Folders	Windows Settings	Computer and User

PREFERENCE TYPE	LOCATION	POLICY CONFIGURATION AREA
Ini Files	Windows Settings	Computer and User
File Type, Folder Options	Control Panel Settings	Computer
Open With, Folder Options	Control Panel Settings	User
Advanced Folder Options, Folder Options	Control Panel Settings	User
Local Users And Groups	Control Panel Settings	Computer and User
Network Shares	Windows Settings	Computer
Power Options	Control Panel Settings	Computer and User
TCP/IP Printer, Printers	Control Panel Settings	Computer and User
Local Printer, Printers	Control Panel Settings	Computer and User
Shared Printer, Printers	Control Panel Settings	User
Regional Options	Control Panel Settings	User
Registry	Windows Settings	Computer and User
Immediate Task, Scheduled Tasks	Control Panel Settings	Computer and User
Scheduled Task, Scheduled Tasks	Control Panel Settings	Computer and User
Services	Control Panel Settings	Computer
Shortcuts	Windows Settings	Computer and User
Start Menu	Control Panel Settings	User
VPN Connection, Network Options	Control Panel Settings	Computer and User

Configuring Group Policy Preferences

Policy preferences are configured and managed differently from policy settings. You define preferences by specifying a management action, an editing state, or both.

Working with Management Actions

Most preferences support the following management actions:

- **Create** Creates a preference item on a user's computer. The preference item is created only if it does not already exist.

- **Replace** Deletes an existing preference item and then re-creates it, or creates a preference item if it doesn't already exist. With most preferences, you have additional options that control exactly how the Replace operation works. Figure 4-1 shows an example.
- **Update** Modifies designated settings in a preference item. This action differs from the Replace action in that it updates only settings defined within the preference item. All other settings remain the same. If a preference item does not exist, the Update action creates it.
- **Delete** Deletes a preference item from a user's computer. With most preferences, you have additional options that control exactly how the Delete operation works. Often, the additional options will be the same as those available with the Replace operation.

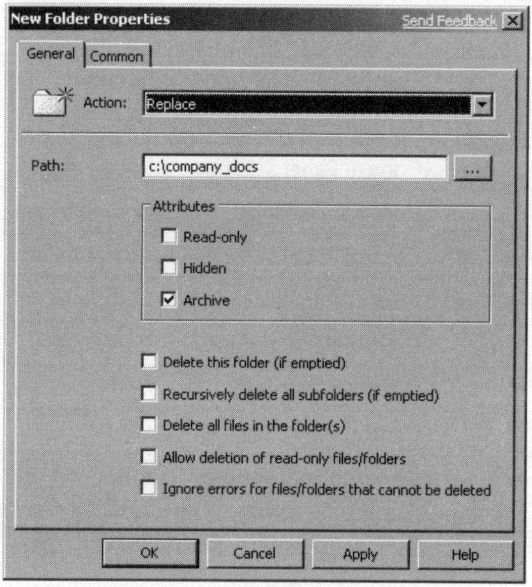

FIGURE 4-1 Set the management action.

The management action controls how the preference item is applied, or the removal of the item when it is no longer needed. Preferences that support management actions include those that configure the following:

- Applications
- Data sources
- Drive maps
- Environment

- Files
- Folders
- Registry
- Shortcuts
- Network shares

Working with Editing States

A small set of preferences supports editing states, which present graphical user interfaces from Control Panel utilities. With this type of preference, the item is applied according to the editing state of each setting in the related interface. The editing state applied cannot be reversed, and there is no option to remove the editing state when it is no longer applied.

Preferences that support editing states include those that configure the following:

- Folder options
- Internet settings
- Power options
- Regional options
- Start menu settings

Because each version of an application and the Windows operating system can have a slightly different user interface, the related options are tied to a specific version. For example, you must configure folder option preference items separately for Internet Explorer 7 and Internet Explorer 8.

By default, when you are working with this type of preference, every setting in the interface is processed by the client computer and applied, even if you don't specifically set the related value. This effectively overwrites all existing settings applied through this interface. As shown in Figure 4-2, the editing state of each related option is depicted graphically:

- A sold green line indicates that the setting will be delivered and processed on the client
- A dashed red line indicates that the setting will not be delivered or processed on the client

When limited space on the interface prevents underlining, a green circle is displayed as the functional equivalent of the solid green line (meaning that the setting will be delivered and processed on the client) and a red circle is used as the functional equivalent of a dashed red line (meaning that the setting will not be delivered or processed on the client). Figure 4-3 shows these conventions.

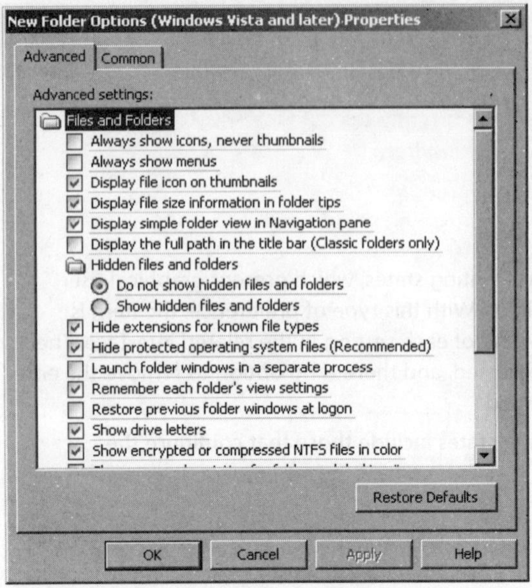

FIGURE 4-2 Note the editing state indicators.

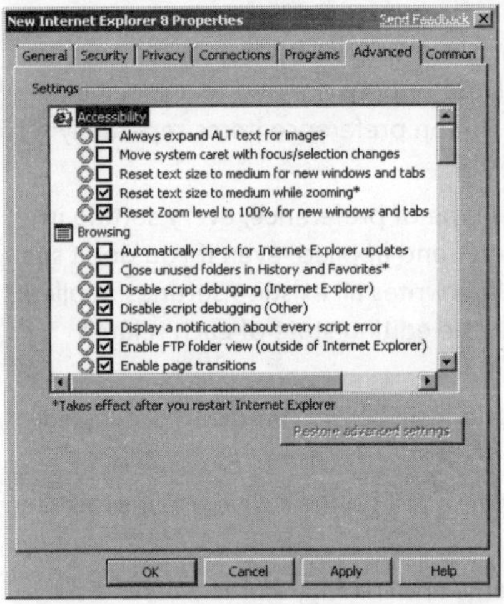

FIGURE 4-3 Alternative editing state indicators

You can use the following function keys to manage the editing state of options:

- **F5** Enables processing of all settings on the selected tab. This is useful if you disabled processing of some settings and later decide that you want all settings on a tab to be processed.

- **F6** Enables processing of the currently selected setting on the selected tab. This is useful if you disabled a setting and later decide you want the setting to be processed.
- **F7** Disables processing of the currently selected setting on the selected tab. This is useful to prevent one setting from being processed on the client.
- **F8** Disables processing of all settings on the selected tab. This is useful to prevent all settings on a tab from being processed on the client. It is also useful if you want only a few settings to be enabled.

NOTE **Keep in mind that the value associated with an option is separate from the editing state. Setting or clearing an option will not change the editing state.**

Working with Alternative Actions and States

A few preferences support neither management actions nor editing states. Preferences of this type include those that configure devices, immediate tasks, and services.

With devices, as shown in Figure 4-4, you use the Action list to enable or disable a particular type of device. With immediate tasks, the related preference creates a task. The task runs and is then deleted automatically. With services, you use the related preference to configure an existing service.

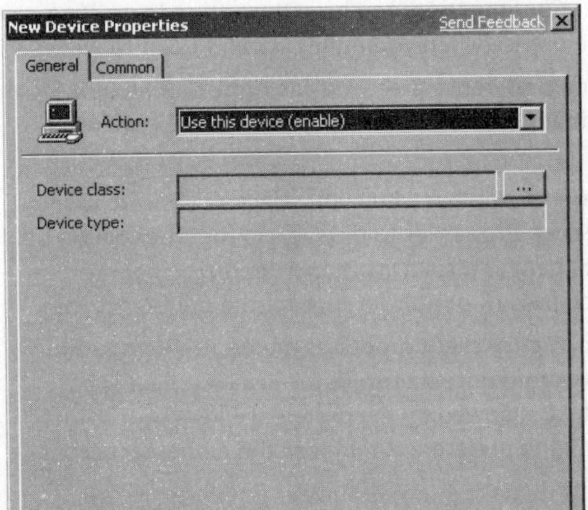

FIGURE 4-4 Set the action to enable or disable the device.

Managing Preference Items

To view and work with preferences, you must open a Group Policy object (GPO) for editing in the Group Policy Management Editor, as discussed in Chapter 3 "Configuring User and Computer Policies." Then you can manage preferences for either computers or users using the following techniques:

- If you want to configure preferences that should be applied to computers, regardless of who logs on, double-click the Computer Configuration node, double-click the Preferences node, and then select the preference area you want to work with.
- If you want to configure preferences that should be applied to users, regardless of which computer they log on to, double-click the User Configuration node, double-click the Preferences node, and then select the preference area you want to work with.

Creating and Managing a Preference Item

You manage preference items separately by selecting the preference area and then working with the related preference items in the details pane. While you are viewing a particular preference area, you can create a related item by right-clicking an open space in the details pane, pointing to New, and then selecting the type of item to create. Only items for the selected area are available. For example, if you are working with Printers under Computer Configuration, you have the option to create a TCP/IP Printer or Local Printer preference when you right-click and point to New.

Once you've created items for a preference area, you can right-click an individual item to display a shortcut menu that allows you to manage the item. Figure 4-5 shows an example.

Similar options are displayed on the toolbar when you select an item. In addition to right-clicking an item and selecting Properties to display its Properties dialog box, you can double-click a preference item to display its Properties dialog box. You can then use the Properties dialog box to view or edit settings for the preference item.

On client computers, the Group Policy client processes preference items according to their precedence order. The preference item with the lowest precedence (the one listed last) is processed first, followed by the preference item with the next lowest precedence, and so on until the preference item with the highest precedence (the one listed first) is processed.

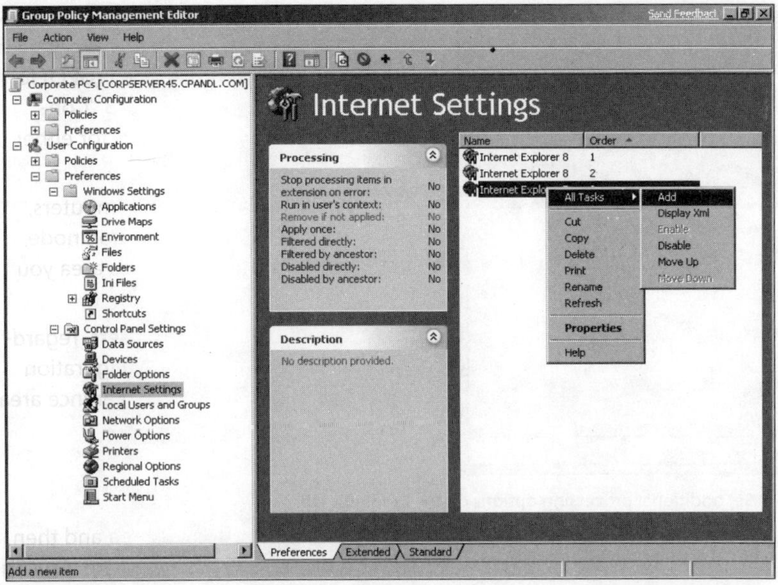

FIGURE 4-5 Manage preference items using the Group Policy Management Editor and the shortcut menu.

Processing occurs in precedence order to ensure that preference items with higher precedence have priority over preference items with lower precedence. If there is any conflict between the settings applied in preference items, the settings written last win. To change the precedence order, select a preference area in the console tree, and then click the preference item that you want to work with in the details pane. You'll then see additional options on the toolbar. These options include:

- Move The Selected Item Up
- Move The Selected Item Down

To lower the precedence of the selected item, click Move The Selected Item Down. To raise the precedence of the selected item, click Move The Selected Item Up.

Setting Common Tab Options

All preference items have a Common tab on which you'll find options that are common to preference items. Although the exact list of common options can differ from item to item, most preference items have the options shown in Figure 4-6.

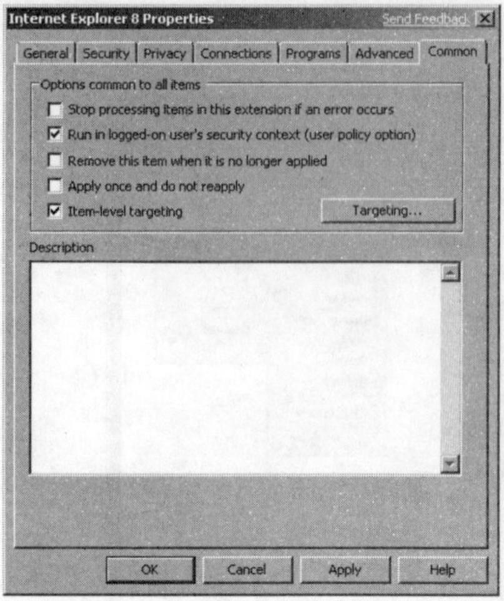

FIGURE 4-6 Set additional processing options on the Common tab.

These common options are used as follows:

- **Stop Processing Items In This Extension If An Error Occurs** By default, if processing of one preference item fails, processing of other preference items will continue. To change this behavior, you can select Stop Processing Items In This Extension If An Error Occurs. With this option selected, a preference item that fails prevents the remaining preference items within the extension from being processed for a particular GPO. This setting doesn't affect processing in other GPOs.
- **Run In Logged-On User's Security Context** By default, the Group Policy client running on a computer processes user preferences within the security context of either the Winlogon account (for pre–Windows Vista computers) or the System account (for Window Vista or later computers). In this context, a preference extension is limited to the environment variables and system resources available to the computer. Alternatively, the client can process user preferences in the security context of the logged-on user. This allows the preference extension to access resources as the user rather than as a system service, which might be required when using drive maps or other preferences for which the computer might not have permissions to access resources or might need to work with user environment variables.
- **Remove This Item When It Is No Longer Applied** By default, when the policy settings in a GPO no longer apply to a user or computer, the policy settings are removed because they are no longer set in the Group Policy area of the registry. Default preference items are not removed automatically, however, when a GPO no longer applies to a user or computer. To change this behavior, you may be able to set this option for a preference item. When this option is selected, the preference extension determines whether a

preference item that was in scope is now out of scope. If the preference item is out of scope, the preference extension removes the settings associated with the preference item.

REAL WORLD Generally, preferences that support management actions can be removed when they no longer apply, but preferences that support editing states cannot be removed when they no longer apply. If you select Remove This Item When It Is No Longer Applied, the management action is set as Replace. As a result, during Group Policy processing, the preference extension performs a Delete operation followed by a Create operation. Then, if the preference item goes out of scope (meaning it no longer applies) for the user or computer, the results of the preference item are deleted (but not created). Item-level targeting can cause a preference item to go out of scope as well.

- **Apply Once And Do Not Reapply** Group Policy writes preferences to the same locations in the registry that an application or operating system feature uses to store the related setting. As a result, users can change settings that were configured using policy preferences. However, by default, the results of preference items are rewritten each time Group Policy is refreshed to ensure that preference items are applied as administrators designated. You can change this behavior by setting this option. When this option is selected, the preference extension applies the results of the preference item one time and does not reapply the results.
- **Item-Level Targeting** Item-level targeting allows you to filter the application of a preference item so that the preference item applies only to selected users or computers. When the Group Policy client evaluates a targeted preference, each targeting item results in a true or false value. If the result is true, the preference item applies and is processed. If the result is false, the preference item does not apply and is not processed. When this option is selected, click the Targeting button to display the Targeting Editor, and then configure targeting as appropriate.

REAL WORLD Targeting items are evaluated as a logical expression. The logical expression can include environment variables as long as the environment variables are available in the current user context. After you create your logical expression, you'll need to ensure that the expression makes sense. In addition, if you hard code a value when you meant to use an environment variable, the targeting will not work as expected.

CHAPTER 5

Managing User Access and Security

Computers running Windows 7 can be configured to be members of a homegroup, a workgroup, or a domain. When a workstation is configured as a member of a homegroup or a workgroup, user access and security are configured on the workstation itself. When a workstation is configured as a member of a domain, user access and security are configured at two levels: the local system level and the domain level. User access can be configured at the local system level for a specific machine and at the domain level for multiple systems or resources throughout the current Active Directory forest. In this chapter, you'll learn how to manage local system access and local accounts. For further discussion of configuring domain access and permissions, see *Windows Server 2008 Administrator's Pocket Consultant,* Second Edition (Microsoft Press, 2010). Keep in mind that every task examined in this chapter and throughout this book can be performed through a local logon or a remote desktop connection.

Understanding User and Group Accounts

Windows 7 provides user accounts and group accounts (of which users can be members). User accounts are designed for individuals. Group accounts, usually referred to as *groups,* are designed to simplify the administration of multiple users. You can log on with a user account, but you can't log on with a group account.

Two general types of user accounts are defined in Windows 7:

- **Local user accounts** User accounts defined on a local computer are called *local user accounts*. These accounts have access to the local computer only. You add or remove local user accounts with Control Panel's User Accounts options or with the Local Users And Groups utility. Local Users And Groups is accessible through Computer Management, a Microsoft Management Console (MMC) snap-in.
- **Domain user accounts** User accounts defined in Active Directory are called *domain user accounts*. Through single sign-on, these accounts can access resources throughout a forest. When a computer is a member of an Active Directory domain, you can use it to create domain user accounts by using Active Directory Users And Computers. This MMC tool is available on the Administrative Tools menu when you install the Remote Server Administrator Tools on your Windows 7 computer.

Both local user accounts and domain user accounts can be configured as standard user accounts or administrator accounts. A standard user account on a local computer has limited privileges, and an administrator account on a local computer has extended privileges.

Local User Account Essentials

All user accounts are identified with a logon name. In Windows 7, this logon name has two parts:

- **User name** The display text for the account
- **User computer or domain** The computer or domain in which the user account exists

For the user Williams, whose account is created for the computer ENGPC85, the full logon name for Windows 7 is ENGPC85\Williams. With a local computer account, Williams can log on to his local workstation and access local resources but is not able to access domain resources.

When working with domains, the full logon name can be expressed in two different ways:

- The user account name and the full domain name separated by the At sign (@). For example, the full logon name for the user name Williams in the domain technology.microsoft.com would be *Williams@technology.microsoft.com*.
- The user account name and the domain separated by the backslash symbol (\). For example, the full logon name for Williams in the technology domain would be technology\Williams.

Although Windows 7 displays user names when describing account privileges and permissions, the key identifiers for accounts are security identifiers (SIDs). SIDs are unique identifiers generated when security principals are created. Each SID combines a computer or domain security ID prefix with a unique relative ID for the user. Windows 7 uses these identifiers to track accounts and user names independently. SIDs serve many purposes, but the two most important are to enable you to easily change user names and to delete accounts without worrying that someone might gain access to resources simply by re-creating an account.

When you change a user name, you tell Windows 7 to map a particular SID to a new name. When you delete an account, you tell Windows 7 that a particular SID is no longer valid. Even if you create an account with the same user name later, the new account won't have the same privileges and permissions as the previous one because the new account will have a new SID.

User accounts can also have passwords and certificates associated with them. Passwords are authentication strings for an account. Certificates combine a public and private key to identify a user. You log on with a password interactively, whereas you log on with a certificate by using its private key, which is stored on a smart card and read with a smart card reader.

When you install Windows 7, the operating system installs default user accounts. You'll find several built-in accounts, which have purposes similar to those of accounts created in Windows domains. The key accounts are the following:

- **Administrator** Administrator is a predefined account that provides complete access to files, directories, services, and other facilities. You can't delete or disable this account. In Active Directory, the Administrator account has domainwide access and privileges. On a local workstation, the Administrator account has access only to the local system.
- **Guest** Guest is designed for users who need one-time or occasional access. Although guests have only limited system privileges, you should be very careful about using this account because it opens the system to potential security problems. The risk is so great that the account is initially disabled when you install Windows 7.

By default, these accounts are members of various groups. Before you modify any of the built-in accounts, you should note the property settings and group memberships for the account. Group membership grants or limits the account's access to specific system resources. For example, Administrator is a member of the Administrators group and Guest is a member of the Guests group. Being a member of a group makes it possible for the account to use the privileges and rights of the group.

In addition to the built-in accounts, Windows 7 has several pseudo-accounts that are used to perform specific types of system actions. The pseudo-accounts are available only on the local system. You can't change the settings for these accounts with the user administration tools, and users can't log on to a computer with these accounts. The pseudo-accounts available include the following:

- **LocalSystem** LocalSystem is used for running system processes and handling system-level tasks. This account grants the logon right Log On As

A Service. Most services run under the LocalSystem account. In some cases, these services have privileges to interact with the desktop. Services that need fewer privileges or logon rights run under the LocalService or NetworkService account. Services that run as LocalSystem include Background Intelligent Transfer Service, Computer Browser, Group Policy Client, Netlogon, Network Connections, Print Spooler, and User Profile Service.

- **LocalService** LocalService is used for running services that need fewer privileges and logon rights on a local system. By default, services that run under this account are granted the right Log On As A Service and the privileges Adjust Memory Quotas For A Process, Change The System Time, Change The Time Zone, Generate Security Audits, and Replace A Process Level Token. Services that run as LocalService include Application Layer Gateway Service, Remote Registry, Smart Card, SSDP Discovery Service, TCP/IP NetBIOS Helper, and WebClient.
- **NetworkService** NetworkService is used for running services that need fewer privileges and logon rights on a local system but must also access network resources. Like services that run under LocalService, services that run by default under the NetworkService account are granted the right Log On As A Service and the privileges Adjust Memory Quotas For A Process, Generate Security Audits, and Replace A Process Level Token. Services that run under NetworkService include BranchCache, Distributed Transaction Coordinator, DNS Client, Remote Desktop Services, and Remote Procedure Call (RPC). NetworkService can also authenticate to remote systems as the computer account.

Group Account Essentials

Windows 7 also provides groups, which you use to grant permissions to similar types of users and to simplify account administration. If a user is a member of a group that has access to a resource, that user has access to the same resource. You can give a user access to various work-related resources just by making the user a member of the correct group. Although you can log on to a computer with a user account, you can't log on to a computer with a group account. Because different Active Directory domains or local computers might have groups with the same name, groups are often referred to by *Domain\GroupName* or *Computer\GroupName* (for example, Technology\GMarketing for the GMarketing group in a domain or on a computer named Technology).

Windows 7 uses the following three types of groups:

- **Local groups** Defined on a local computer and used on the local computer only. You create local groups with Local Users And Groups.
- **Security groups** Can have security descriptors associated with them. You use a Windows server to define security groups in domains, using Active Directory Users And Computers.

- **Distribution groups** Used as e-mail distribution lists. They can't have security descriptors associated with them. You define distribution groups in domains using Active Directory Users And Computers.

As with user accounts, group accounts are tracked using unique SIDs. This means that you can't delete a group account and re-create it and then expect that all the permissions and privileges remain the same. The new group will have a new SID, and all the permissions and privileges of the old group will be lost.

When you assign user access levels, you have the opportunity to make the user a member of the following built-in or predefined groups:

- **Administrators** Members of this group are local administrators and have complete access to the workstation. They can create accounts, modify group membership, install printers, manage shared resources, and more. Because this account has complete access, you should be very careful about which users you add to this group.
- **Backup Operators** Members of this group can back up and restore files and directories on the workstation. They can log on to the local computer, back up or restore files, and shut down the computer. Because of how this account is set up, its members can back up files regardless of whether the members have read/write access to the files. However, they can't change access permissions on the files or perform other administrative tasks.

  Backup Operators have privileges to perform very specific administrative tasks, such as backing up file systems. By default, no other group or user accounts are members of the operator groups. This is to ensure that you grant explicit access to the operator groups.
- **Cryptographic Operators** Members can manage the configuration of encryption, IP Security (IPSec), digital IDs, and certificates.
- **Event Log Readers** Members can view the event logs on the local computer.
- **Guests** Guests are users with very limited privileges. Members can access the system and its resources remotely, but they can't perform most other tasks.
- **Network Configuration Operators** Members can manage network settings on the workstation. They can also configure TCP/IP settings and perform other general network configuration tasks.
- **Performance Log Users** Members can view and manage performance counters. They can also manage performance logging.
- **Performance Monitor Users** Members can view performance counters and performance logs.
- **Power Users** In earlier versions of Windows, this group is used to grant additional privileges, such as the capability to modify computer settings and install programs. In Windows 7, this group is maintained only for compatibility with legacy applications.

- **Remote Desktop Users** Members can log on to the workstation remotely using Remote Desktop Services. Once members are logged on, additional groups of which they are members determine their permissions on the workstation. A user who is a member of the Administrators group is granted this privilege automatically. (However, remote logons must be enabled before an administrator can remotely log on to a workstation.)
- **Replicator** Members can manage the replication of files for the local machine. File replication is primarily used with Active Directory domains and Windows servers.
- **Users** Users are people who do most of their work on a single Windows 7 workstation. Members of the Users group have more restrictions than privileges. They can log on to a Windows 7 workstation locally, keep a local profile, lock the workstation, and shut down the workstation.

In most cases, you configure user access by using the Users or Administrators group. You can configure user and administrator access levels by setting the account type to Standard User or Administrator, respectively. While these basic tasks can be performed using Control Panel's User Accounts page, you make a user a member of a group by using Local Users And Groups under Computer Management.

Domain vs. Local Logon

When computers are members of a domain, you typically use domain accounts to log on to computers and the domain. All administrators in a domain have access to resources on the local workstations that are members of the domain. Users, on the other hand, can access resources only on the local workstations they are permitted to log on to. In a domain, any user with a valid domain account can by default log on to any computer that is a member of the domain. Once logged on to a computer, the user has access to any resource that his or her account or the groups to which the user's account belongs are granted access. This includes resources on the local machine as well as resources in the domain.

You can restrict logons to specific domain workstations on a per-user basis by using Active Directory Users And Computers. In Active Directory Users And Computers, right-click the user account and then click Properties. On the Account tab of the user's Properties dialog box, click Log On To, and then use the options in the Logon Workstations dialog box to designate the workstations to which the user is permitted to log on.

When you work with Windows 7, however, you aren't always logging on to a domain. Computers configured in workgroups have only local accounts. You might also need to log on locally to a domain computer to administer it. Only users with a local user account can log on locally. When you log on locally, you have access to any resource on the computer that your account or the groups to which your account belongs are granted access.

Managing User Account Control and Elevation Prompts

User Account Control (UAC) represents a significant change in the way in which user accounts are used and configured. It affects which privileges standard users and administrator users have, how applications are installed and run, and much more. In this section, I'll extend the discussion in Chapter 1, "Introduction to Windows 7 Administration," and provide a comprehensive look at how UAC affects user and administrator accounts. This is essential information to know when managing Windows 7 systems.

> ***NOTE*** **Learning how UAC works will help you be a better administrator. To support UAC, many aspects of the Windows operating system had to be reworked. Some of the most extensive changes have to do with how applications are installed and run. In Chapter 9, "Installing and Maintaining Programs," you'll find a complete discussion of how the architectural changes affect programs running on Windows 7.**

Redefining Standard User and Administrator User Accounts

In Windows XP and earlier versions of Windows, malicious software programs can exploit the fact that most user accounts are configured as members of the local computer's Administrators group. Not only does this allow malicious software to install itself, but it also allows malicious software to use these elevated privileges to wreak havoc on the computer, because programs installed by administrators can write to otherwise secure areas of the registry and the file system.

To combat the growing threat of malicious software, organizations have locked down computers, required users to log on using standard user accounts, and required administrators to use the Run As command to perform administrative tasks. Unfortunately, these procedural changes can have serious negative consequences on productivity. A person logged on as a standard user under Windows XP can't perform some of the most basic tasks, such as changing the system clock and calendar, changing the computer's time zone, or changing the computer's power management settings. Many software programs designed for Windows XP simply will not function properly without local administrator rights—these programs use local administrator rights to write to system locations during installation and during normal operations. Additionally, Windows XP doesn't let you know beforehand when a task you are performing requires administrator privileges.

UAC seeks to improve usability while at the same time enhancing security by redefining how standard user and administrator user accounts are used. UAC represents a fundamental shift in computing by providing a framework that limits the scope of administrator-level access privileges and requires all applications to run in a specific user mode. In this way, UAC prevents users from making inadvertent changes to system settings and locks down the computer to prevent unauthorized applications from being installed or performing malicious actions.

Because of UAC, Windows 7 defines two levels of user accounts: standard and administrator. Windows 7 also defines two modes (run levels) for applications: standard user mode and administrator mode. Although standard user accounts can use most software and can change system settings that do not affect other users or the security of the computer, administrator user accounts have complete access to the computer and can make any changes that are needed. When an administrator user starts an application, her access token and its associated administrator privileges are applied to the application, giving her all the rights and privileges of a local computer administrator for that application. When a standard user starts an application, her access token and its associated privileges are applied to the application at run time, limiting her to the rights and privileges of a standard user for that application. Further, all applications are configured to run in a specific mode during installation. Any tasks run by standard-mode applications that require administrator privileges not only are identified during setup but require user approval to run.

In Windows 7, the set of privileges assigned to standard user accounts has changed. Tasks that standard user accounts can perform include:

- Installing fonts, viewing the system clock and calendar, and changing the time zone.
- Changing the display settings and the power management settings.
- Adding printers and other devices (when the required drivers are installed on the computer or are provided by an IT administrator).
- Downloading and installing updates (when the updates use UAC-compatible installers).
- Creating and configuring virtual private network (VPN) connections. VPN connections are used to establish secure connections to private networks over the public Internet.
- Installing Wired Equivalent Privacy (WEP) to connect to secure wireless networks. The WEP security protocol provides wireless networks with improved security.

Windows 7 also defines two run levels for applications: standard and administrator. Windows 7 determines whether a user needs elevated privileges to run a program by supplying most applications and processes with a security token. If an application has a standard token, or an application cannot be identified as an administrator application, elevated privileges are not required to run the application, and Windows 7 starts it as a standard application by default. If an application has an administrator token, elevated privileges are required to run the application, and Windows 7 prompts the user for permission or confirmation prior to running the application.

The process of getting approval prior to running an application in administrator mode and prior to performing tasks that change system configuration is known as *elevation*. Elevation enhances security and reduces the impact of malicious software by notifying users before they perform any action that could impact system settings and by preventing applications from using administrator privileges without first notifying users. Elevation also protects administrator applications from attacks by standard applications. For more information on elevation and how UAC works with applications, see Chapter 9.

By default, Windows 7 switches to the secure desktop prior to displaying the elevation prompt. The secure desktop restricts the programs and processes that have access to the desktop environment, and in this way reduces the possibility that a malicious program or user could gain access to the process being elevated. If you don't want Windows 7 to switch to the secure desktop prior to prompting for elevation, you can choose settings that use the standard desktop rather than the secure desktop. However, this makes the computer more susceptible to malware and attack.

Optimizing User Account Control and Admin Approval Mode

Every computer has a built-in local Administrator account. This built-in account is not protected by UAC, and using this account for administration can put your computer at risk. To safeguard computers in environments in which you use a local Administrator account for administration, you should create a new local Administrator account and use this account for administration.

UAC can be configured or disabled for any individual user account. If you disable UAC for a user account, you lose the additional security protections UAC offers and put the computer at risk. To completely disable UAC or to reenable UAC after disabling it, the computer must be restarted for the change to take effect.

Admin Approval Mode is the key component of UAC that determines whether and how administrators are prompted when running administrator applications. The default way that Admin Approval Mode works is as follows:

- All administrators, including the built-in local Administrator account, run in and are subject to Admin Approval Mode.
- Because they are running in and subject to Admin Approval Mode, all administrators, including the built-in local Administrator account, see the elevation prompt when they run administrator applications.

If you are logged on as an administrator, you can modify the way UAC works for all users by completing the following steps:

1. In Control Panel, click System And Security. Under the Action Center heading, click Change User Account Control Settings.
2. On the User Account Control Settings page, shown in Figure 5-1, use the slider to choose when to be notified about changes to the computer, and then click OK. Table 5-1 summarizes the available options.

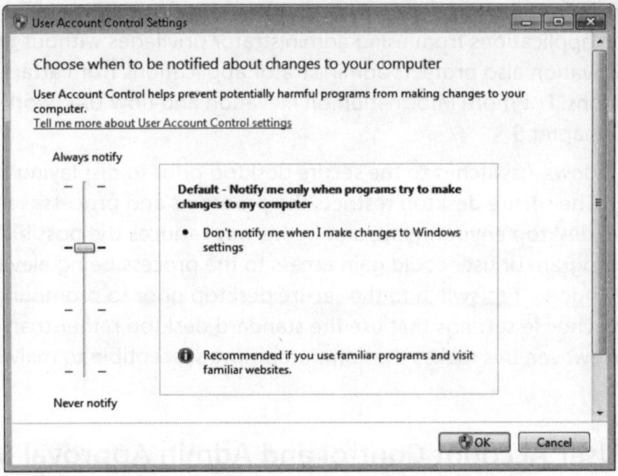

FIGURE 5-1 The User Account Control Settings page

TABLE 5-1 User Account Control Settings

OPTION	DESCRIPTION	WHEN TO USE	USES THE SECURE DESKTOP?
Always Notify	Always notifies the current user when programs try to install software or make changes to the computer and when the user changes Windows settings.	Choose this option when a computer requires the highest security possible and users frequently install software and visit unfamiliar Web sites.	Yes
Default	Notifies the current user only when programs try to make changes to the computer and not when the user changes Windows settings.	Choose this option when a computer requires high security and you want to reduce the number of notification prompts that users see.	Yes
Notify Me Only When ... (Do Not Dim My Desktop)	Same as Default but also prevents UAC from switching to the secure desktop.	Choose this option when users work in a trusted environment with familiar applications and do not visit unfamiliar Web sites.	No

OPTION	DESCRIPTION	WHEN TO USE	USES THE SECURE DESKTOP?
Never Notify	Turns off all UAC notification prompts.	Choose this option when security is not a priority and users work in a trusted environment with programs that are not certified for Windows 7 because they do not support UAC.	No

In Group Policy, you can manage Admin Approval Mode and elevation prompting by using settings under Computer Configuration\Windows Settings\Security Settings\Local Policies\Security Options. These security settings are:

- **User Account Control: Admin Approval Mode For The Built-In Administrator Account** Determines whether users and processes running as the built-in local Administrator account are subject to Admin Approval Mode. By default, this feature is enabled, which means the built-in local Administrator account is subject to Admin Approval Mode and also subject to the elevation prompt behavior stipulated for administrators in Admin Approval Mode. If you disable this setting, users and processes running as the built-in local administrator are not subject to Admin Approval Mode and therefore not subject to the elevation prompt behavior stipulated for administrators in Admin Approval Mode.
- **User Account Control: Allow UIAccess Applications To Prompt For Elevation Without Using The Secure Desktop** Determines whether User Interface Accessibility (UIAccess) programs can automatically disable the secure desktop for elevation prompts used by a standard user. If you enable this setting, UIAccess programs, including Windows Remote Assistance, can disable the secure desktop for elevation prompts.
- **User Account Control: Behavior Of The Elevation Prompt For Administrators In Admin Approval Mode** Determines whether administrators subject to Admin Approval Mode see an elevation prompt when running administrator applications, and also determines how the elevation prompt works. By default, administrators are prompted for consent when running administrator applications on the secure desktop. You can configure this option so that administrators are prompted for consent without the secure desktop, prompted for credentials with or without the secure desktop (as is the case with standard users), or prompted for consent only for non-Windows binaries. You can also configure this option so that administrators are not prompted at all, in which case an administrator will be elevated automatically. No setting will prevent an administrator from right-clicking an application shortcut and selecting Run As Administrator.

- **User Account Control: Behavior Of The Elevation Prompt For Standard Users** Determines whether users logged on with a standard user account see an elevation prompt when running administrator applications. By default, users logged on with a standard user account are prompted for the credentials of an administrator on the secure desktop when running administrator applications or performing administrator tasks. You can also configure this option so that users are prompted for credentials on the standard desktop rather than the secure desktop, or you can deny elevation requests automatically, in which case users will not be able to elevate their privileges by supplying administrator credentials. The latter option doesn't prevent users from right-clicking an application shortcut and selecting Run As Administrator.
- **User Account Control: Run All Administrators In Admin Approval Mode** Determines whether users logged on with an administrator account are subject to Admin Approval Mode. By default, this feature is enabled, which means administrators are subject to Admin Approval Mode and also subject to the elevation prompt behavior stipulated for administrators in Admin Approval Mode. If you disable this setting, users logged on with an administrator account are not subject to Admin Approval and therefore are not subject to the elevation prompt behavior stipulated for administrators in Admin Approval Mode.
- **User Account Control: Only Elevate UIAccess Applications That Are Installed in Secure Locations** Determines whether UIAccess programs must reside in a secure location on the file system to elevate. If enabled, UIAccess programs must reside in a secure location under %SystemRoot%\Program Files, %SystemRoot%\Program Files(x86), or %SystemRoot%\Windows\System32.
- **User Account Control: Only Elevate Executables That Are Signed And Validated** Determines whether applications must be signed and validated to elevate. If enabled, only executables that pass signature checks and have certificates in the Trusted Publisher store will elevate. Use this option only when the highest security is required and you've verified that all applications in use are signed and valid.

In a domain environment, you can use Active Directory–based Group Policy to apply the security configuration you want to a particular set of computers. You can also configure these settings on a per-computer basis using local security policy. To do this, follow these steps:

1. Click Start, point to All Programs, Administrative Tools, and then click Local Security Policy.
2. In the Local Security Policy console tree, under Security Settings, expand Local Policies, and then select Security Options, as shown in Figure 5-2.

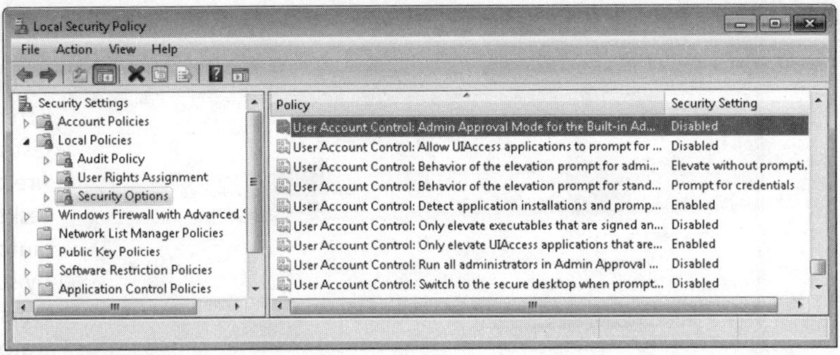

FIGURE 5-2 The Local Security Policy console

3. Double-click the setting you want to work with, make any necessary changes, and then click OK. Repeat this step to modify other security settings as necessary.

Managing Local Logon

All local computer accounts should have passwords. If an account is created without a password, anyone can log on to the account, and there is no protection for the account. However, a local account without a password cannot be used to remotely access a computer.

The sections that follow discuss how to create and work with local user accounts. Every workstation computer has local computer accounts, whether the computer is a member of a homegroup, a workgroup, or a domain.

Creating Local User Accounts in a Homegroup or Workgroup

For a computer that is a member of a homegroup or a workgroup, you can create a local user account by following these steps:

1. In Control Panel, under the User Accounts heading, click Add Or Remove User Accounts. This displays the Manage Accounts page.

   As Figure 5-3 shows, the Manage Accounts page lists all configurable user accounts on the local computer by account type and with configuration details. If an account has a password, it is labeled Password Protected. If an account is disabled, it is listed as being off.
2. Click Create A New Account. This displays the Create New Account page.
3. Type the name of the local account. This name is displayed on the Welcome screen and Start menu.
4. Set the type of account as either Standard User or Administrator. To give the user full permissions on the local computer, select Administrator.
5. Click Create Account.

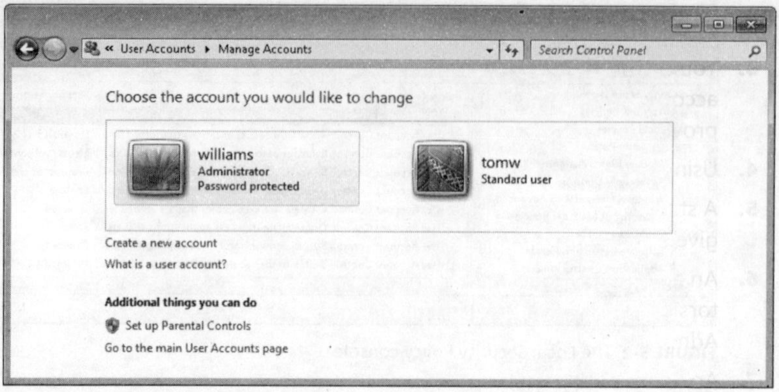

FIGURE 5-3 In a homegroup or workgroup, use the Manage Accounts page in Control Panel to add or remove local user accounts.

Granting Access to an Existing Domain Account to Allow Local Logon

If a user needs to be able to log on locally to a computer and has an existing domain account, you can grant the user permission to log on locally by completing the following steps:

1. In Control Panel, under the User Accounts heading, click the Change Account Type link. This displays the User Accounts dialog box. As Figure 5-4 shows, the User Accounts dialog box lists all configurable user accounts on the local computer by domain and with group membership details.

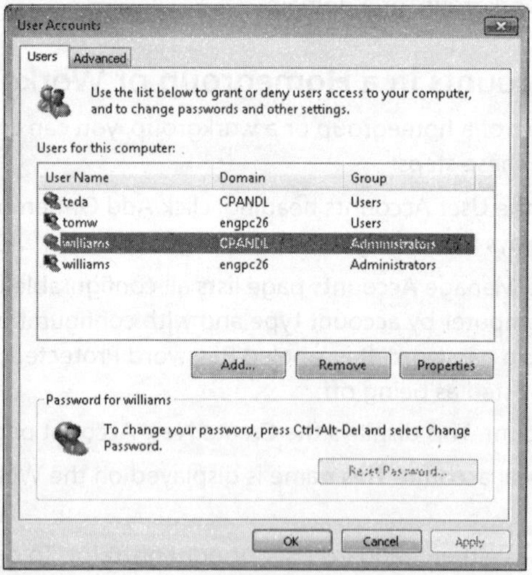

FIGURE 5-4 Use the User Accounts dialog box to manage local user accounts on a computer that is a member of a domain.

2. Click Add. This starts the Add New User wizard.
3. You are creating a local computer account for a user with an existing domain account. Type the user's domain account name and domain in the fields provided.
4. Using the options provided, select the type of user account.
5. A standard user account is created as a member of the local Users group. To give the user the permissions of a normal user, select Standard User.
6. An administrator account is created as a member of the local Administrators group. To give the user full permissions on the local computer, select Administrator.
7. An Other account is created as a member of a group you specify. To give the user the permissions of a specific group, select Other, and then select the group.
8. Click Finish. If you need to set other permissions or add the user to other local groups, follow the steps specified in the section "Managing Local User Accounts and Groups."

Changing Local User Account Types

The User Accounts utility provides an easy way to change account types for local users. You can also quickly set one of the default account types. For more advanced control, however, you need to use Local Users And Groups to assign group membership to individual accounts. (See the section "Adding and Removing Local Group Members.")

In a homegroup or workgroup, you can change the account type for a local computer user by completing the following steps:

1. In Control Panel, under the User Accounts heading, click Add Or Remove User Accounts. This displays the Manage Accounts page.
2. Click the account you want to change, and then click Change The Account Type.
3. On the Change Account Type page, set the level of access for the user as either Standard User or Administrator, and then click Change The Account Type.

In a domain, you can change the account type for a local computer user by completing the following steps:

1. In Control Panel, click User Accounts. On the User Accounts page, click Change Account Type. This displays the User Accounts dialog box.
2. On the Users tab, click the user account you want to work with, and then click Properties.
3. In the Properties dialog box, click the Group Membership tab.

4. Set the type of account as Standard User or Administrator, or select Other and then select the group you want to use.
5. Click OK twice.

Creating Passwords for Local User Accounts

In a homegroup or workgroup configuration, local user accounts are created without passwords by default. This means that a user can log on simply by clicking his account name on the Welcome screen or by clicking OK on the classic Log On To Windows screen. To improve security, all local accounts should have passwords.

For the easiest management of local accounts, log on to each account that should have a password, and then use the User Accounts utility to assign a password to the account. If you are logged on as the user when you create a password, you don't have to worry about losing encrypted data. If you create a password without logging on as the user, the user will lose access to his or her encrypted files, encrypted e-mail, personal certificates, and stored passwords. This occurs because the user's master key, which is needed to access his or her personal encryption certificate and unlock this data, is encrypted with a hash that is based on an empty password. So when you create a password, the hash doesn't match, and there's no way to unlock the encrypted data. The only way to resolve this is to restore the original settings by removing the password from the account. The user should then be able to access his or her encrypted files. Again, this issue is related only to local user accounts for computers and not to domain user accounts.

TIP **Only the User Accounts utility allows you to assign a password hint, which can be helpful in recovering a forgotten or lost password. Another technique for recovering a password is a password reset disk, which can be a floppy disk or a USB flash drive. It is important to note that these are the only techniques you should use to recover passwords for local user accounts unless you want to risk data loss. Why? Although you can create, reset, or remove a password from a user account, doing so deletes any personal certificates and stored passwords associated with this account. As a result, the user will no longer be able to access his or her encrypted files or private e-mail messages that have been encrypted with his or her personal key. In addition, he or she will lose stored passwords for Web sites and network resources. It is also important to note that this is an issue only for local user accounts. Administrators can change or reset passwords for domain user accounts without affecting access to encrypted data.**

You can create a password for a local user account by completing the following steps:

1. Log on as the user whose password you want to create. In Control Panel, under the User Accounts heading, click Add Or Remove User Accounts. This displays the Manage Accounts page.

2. Click the account you want to work with. To prevent possible data loss, this should be the same account as the account with which you logged on. Any account that has a current password is listed as Password Protected. Any account without this label doesn't have a password.

3. Click Create A Password. Type a password, and then confirm it, as illustrated in Figure 5-5. Afterward, type a unique password hint. The password hint is a word or phrase that can be used to obtain the password if it is lost or forgotten. This hint is visible to anyone who uses the computer.

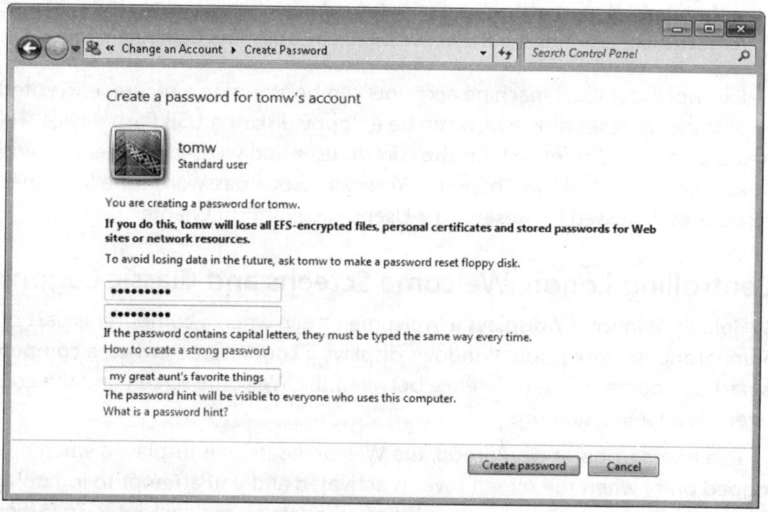

FIGURE 5-5 Create a password with a password hint.

4. Click Create Password.

Recovering Local User Account Passwords

As discussed previously, in order to preserve access to any encrypted data and stored passwords that a user might have, it is preferable to try and recover a user password rather than change or remove the password.

Windows 7 provides two ways to recover user passwords:

- **Password hint** A hint can be accessed on the Welcome screen. Ordinarily, the Welcome screen is displayed when the computer is started and no one is logged on. If someone is logged on to the workstation, ask him or her to log off. Click the user's name to display the Password prompt, and then click the blue enter button to display the password hint. Hopefully, the password hint will help the user remember the password. If it doesn't, you need to use a password reset disk.

- **Password reset disk** Password reset disks can be created for any local user account with a password. They enable anyone to change the password of the related local account without needing to know the old password. Because anyone with access to these disks can change account passwords, you should store password reset disks in a secure location. If users are allowed to create their own password reset disks, be sure they know how important the disks are.

NOTE **Passwords for domain users and those for local users are managed differently. Administrators manage passwords for domain user accounts and can reset forgotten passwords using the Active Directory Users And Computers console.**

Passwords for local machine accounts can be stored in a secure, encrypted file on a password reset disk, which can be a floppy disk or a USB flash device. You can create a password reset disk for the current user as discussed in "Creating and Using a Password Reset Disk" in Chapter 1. You can reset a password for a local machine account as discussed in "Resetting a User's Password" in Chapter 1.

Controlling Logon: Welcome Screens and Classic Logons

By default, Windows 7 displays a Welcome screen when a computer is part of a homegroup or workgroup. Windows displays a Logon screen when a computer is part of a domain. The difference between the Welcome screen and the Logon screen is an important one.

In a homegroup or workgroup, the Welcome screen is displayed when no one is logged on or when the screen saver is activated and you attempt to log on again. On the Welcome screen, you see a list of accounts on the computer. To log on with one of these accounts, click the account and type a password if required. Contrary to what many people think, the Welcome screen doesn't display all the accounts that have been created on the computer. Some accounts, such as Administrator, are hidden from view automatically.

The Welcome screen is convenient because it displays a list of available accounts and enables you to log on by clicking an account name. To enhance security in a homegroup or workgroup by not giving a list of accounts, you can use the Logon screen instead of the Welcome screen. In a domain, the Logon screen is displayed automatically when no one is logged on or when the screen saver is activated and you attempt to log on again. The Logon screen requires users to type a logon name rather than selecting an account from a list of available accounts.

The Logon screen has several features that you can control. By default, the name of the last user to log on is displayed in the User Name field of the Log On To Windows dialog box. Hiding the user name of the last user to log on can improve security by requiring users to know a valid account name for the computer. To do this, start the Local Security Policy tool from the Administrative Tools menu or type **secpol.msc** at an elevated command prompt. Then, under Local Policies\Security

Options, double-click Interactive Logon: Do Not Display Last User Name. Click Enabled, and then click OK.

You can configure whether the Welcome screen is used through the Always Use Classic Logon setting in Group Policy. You have the following options:

- Enable the policy to use the Logon screen rather than the Welcome screen.
- Disable the policy to use the Welcome screen.
- Use Not Configured to use the default configuration (the Welcome screen).

In a domain environment, you can use Active Directory–based Group Policy to apply the security configuration you want to a particular set of computers. You can also configure this setting on a per-computer basis by using local security policy. To configure a homegroup or workgroup computer to use the Logon screen rather than the Welcome screen, use the Group Policy Object Editor, which is an MMC snap-in. You can add this snap-in to an empty console and configure a computer to use the Logon screen by following these steps:

1. Click Start, type **gpedit.msc**, and then press Enter. This opens the Local Group Policy Editor with the top-level Local Group Policy object open for editing.
2. In the editor, expand Local Computer Policy, Computer Configuration, Administrative Templates, System, Logon. (See Figure 5-6.)

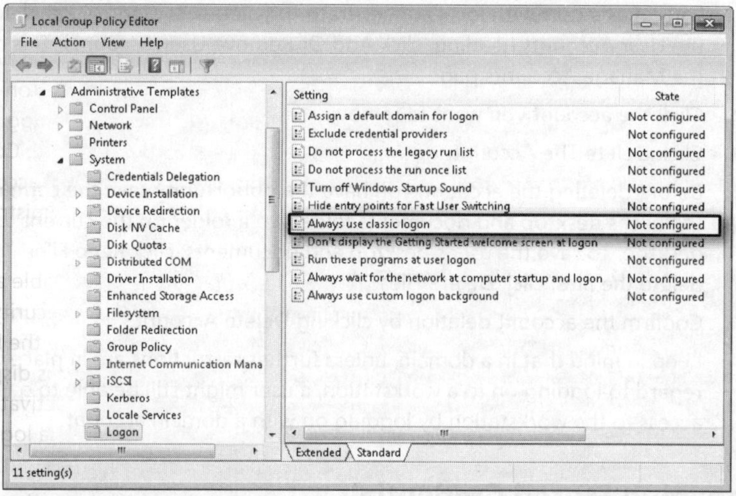

FIGURE 5-6 Enable the Always Use Classic Logon setting to use the Logon screen rather than the Welcome screen.

3. Double-click Always Use Classic Logon.
4. Select Enabled, and then click OK.

In a domain, by default you cannot bypass the requirement to press Ctrl+Alt+Del to access the Log On To Windows dialog box. You can eliminate this requirement, but it is a poor security practice. To do so, in the Local Security Policy tool, expand Local Policies\Security Options, and then double-click Interactive Logon: Do Not Require Ctrl+Alt+Del. Click Enabled, and then click OK.

Removing Accounts and Denying Local Access to Workstations

Domain administrators are automatically granted access to local resources on workstations. Other users aren't granted access to local resources on workstations other than to the computers to which they are permitted to log on. As workstations are moved around an organization, you might find that previous owners of a workstation still have access to its resources or that users who were granted temporary access to a workstation were never removed from the access list.

In a domain, you can control the workstations to which users can log on by using the account properties in Active Directory Users And Computers. Double-click the account to display the Properties dialog box. On the Account tab, click the Log On To button.

In a homegroup or workgroup, you can remove a user's local account and effectively deny logon by completing these steps:

1. Log on as a user with local administrator privileges. In Control Panel, under the User Accounts heading, click Add Or Remove User Accounts. This displays the Manage Accounts page.
2. Click the account you want to remove.
3. Click Delete The Account.
4. Before deleting the account, you have the opportunity save the contents of the user's desktop and documents folders to a folder on the current user's desktop. To save the user's desktop and documents, click Keep Files. To delete the files, click Delete Files.
5. Confirm the account deletion by clicking Delete Account.

   Keep in mind that in a domain, unless further restrictions are in place with regard to logging on to a workstation, a user might still be able to gain access to the workstation by logging on with a domain account.

Managing Stored Credentials

In Windows 7, you can use Credential Manager to store credentials that can be used to try to automatically log on users to servers, Web sites, and programs. Credentials are stored in an electronic vault (called the Windows vault) that provides easy logon to essential resources, wherever they might be located. If you find that a user frequently has problems logging on to protected resources, such as the company intranet or an external Internet site, you can create a stored credential for each resource that the user works with.

Credential Manager supports three types of stored credentials:

- **Windows credential** A credential that uses standard Windows authentication (NTLM or Kerberos) and includes a resource location, logon account name, and password.
- **Certificate-based credential** A credential that includes a resource location and uses a certificate saved in the Personal store in Certificate Manager for authentication.
- **Generic credential** A credential that uses basic or custom authentication techniques and includes a resource location, logon account name, and password.

The following sections examine techniques for working with stored credentials.

Adding Windows or Generic Credentials

Each user account has a unique Windows vault. Entries in the Windows vault are stored in the user's profile settings and contain information needed to log on to protected resources. If you are logged on to a domain account when you create a Windows vault entry, and the account has a roaming profile (instead of a local or mandatory profile), the information stored in the Windows vault entry is available when you log on to any computer in the domain. Otherwise, the information in the Windows vault entry is available only on the computer on which you create the entry.

> ***REAL WORLD*** **When your organization has computers that are in workgroups or homegroups rather than part of your domain, you'll find that stored credentials can save everyone a lot of time. For example, if Ted uses a computer that is a member of a workgroup for his daily activities but needs to access several different servers in several different locations or domains, you can make this process easier by creating a Windows credential for each resource. Now, no matter how Ted accesses the servers, he can be authenticated automatically and without having to provide alternate credentials. For example, if Ted maps a network drive to FileServer84 and you've set up a credential for this server, Ted doesn't have to select the Connect Using Different Credential option and then provide alternate credentials.**

To add an entry to the current logged-on user's Windows vault, follow these steps:

1. Log on as the user whose Windows vault entries you want to manage. In Control Panel, click User Accounts, and then click Credential Manager.

   On the Credential Manager page, shown in Figure 5-7, you'll see a list of current entries by credential type (if there are any credentials).

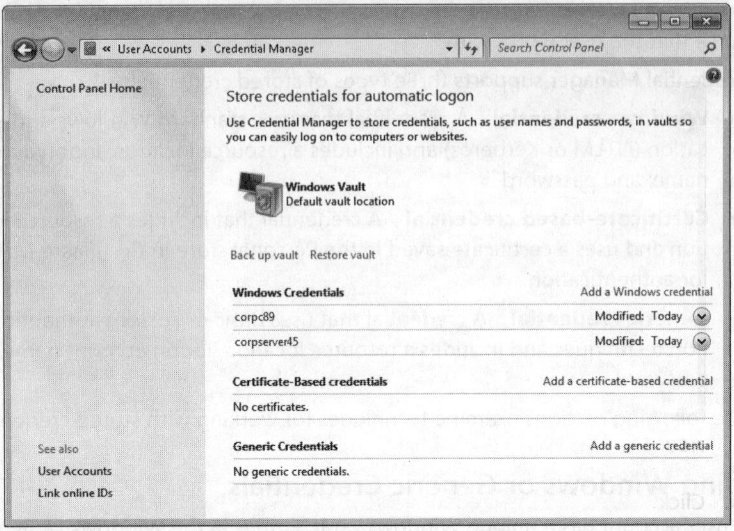

FIGURE 5-7 Review the currently available credentials and options.

2. Click Add A Windows Credential or Add A Generic Credential as appropriate for the type of credential you are creating. Then use the options provided to configure the credential (as shown in Figure 5-8). The available fields are as follows:

   - **Internet Or Network Address** The network or Internet resource for which you are configuring the Windows vault entry. This can be a server name, such as fileserver86; a fully qualified domain name for an Internet resource, such as www.microsoft.com; or an address containing a wildcard, such as *.microsoft.com. When you use a server name or fully qualified domain name, the entry is used for accessing a specific server or service. When you use a wildcard, the entry is used for any server in the specified domain. For example, the entry *.microsoft.com could be used to access *www.microsoft.com*, *ftp.microsoft.com*, *smtp.microsoft.com*, and *extranet.microsoft.com*.
   - **User Name** The user name required by the server, including any necessary domain qualifiers. To use the default domain for a resource, enter only the user name, such as Williams. For a nondefault domain, type the full domain and account name, such as technology\Williams. For an Internet service, type the full service account name, such as Williams@msn.com.
   - **Password** The password required by the server. One of the things most users forget is that whenever they change their password on the server or service, they must also change their password in their Windows vault. If a user forgets to change the password in the Windows vault, repeated

attempts to log on or connect to the server or service might result in the account being locked.

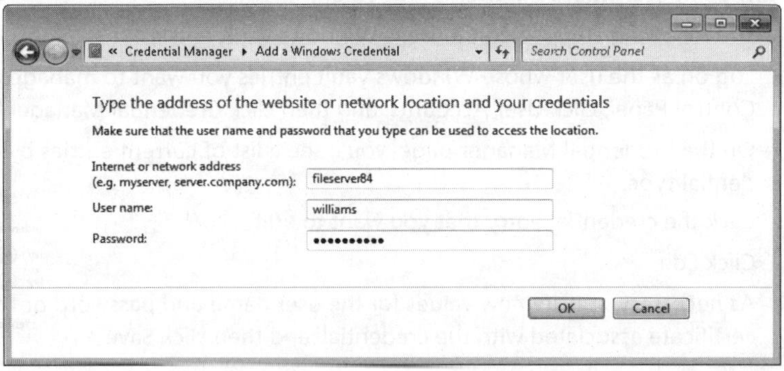

FIGURE 5-8 Create the Windows vault entry by setting the necessary logon information.

4. Click OK to save the credential.

Adding Certificate-Based Credentials

The Personal certificate store in the user's profile stores certificates that have been issued to authenticate the user. Once you've added a certificate for the user, you can create a credential that uses the certificate to access a resource.

To add an entry for a certificate-based credential to the currently logged-on user's Windows vault, follow these steps:

1. Log on as the user whose Windows vault entries you want to manage. In Control Panel, click User Accounts, and then click Credential Manager.
2. On the Credential Manager page, you'll see a list of current entries by credential type (if there are any credentials).
3. Click Add A Certificate-Based Credential. In the Internet Or Network Address field, enter the name of the network or Internet resource for which you are configuring the Windows vault entry. This can be a server name, a fully qualified domain name for an Internet resource, or an address containing a wildcard.
4. Click Select Certificate. In the Select Certificate dialog box, click the personal certificate that you want to use for the resource, and then click OK.
5. Click OK again to save the credential.

Editing Windows Vault Entries

You can edit Windows vault entries at any time, but keep in mind that local Windows vault entries are visible only on the computer on which they were created. This means that if you want to modify an entry, you must log on to the local workstation where the entry was created. The only exception is for users with roaming profiles. When a user has a roaming profile, Windows vault entries can be edited from any computer where the user is logged on.

Use the following steps to edit a user's Windows vault entries:

1. Log on as the user whose Windows vault entries you want to manage. In Control Panel, click User Accounts, and then click Credential Manager.

   On the Credential Manager page, you'll see a list of current entries by credential type.
2. Click the credential entry that you want to edit.
3. Click Edit.
4. As necessary, specify new values for the user name and password or the certificate associated with the credential, and then click Save.

Backing Up and Restoring the Windows Vault

You can back up a user's stored credentials by backing up the Windows vault. After you back up the Windows vault, you can restore the credentials or transfer them to a new computer simply by restoring the Windows vault. In most cases, you should back up the Windows vault to removable media.

To back up a user's Windows vault, follow these steps:

1. Log on as the user whose Windows vault entries you want to manage. In Control Panel, click User Accounts, and then click Credential Manager.

   On the Credential Manager page, you'll see a list of current entries by credential type.
2. Click Back Up Vault.
3. On the Stored User Names And Passwords page, click Browse. Use the Save Backup File As dialog box to select a save location and specify a name for the credential backup file. Credential backup files are saved with the .crd file extension. Click Save.
4. Click Next. Press Ctrl+Alt+Delete to switch to the secure desktop. When prompted, enter and confirm a password for the credential backup file.
5. Click Next, and then click Finish.

To restore a user's Windows vault on the same or different computer, follow these steps:

1. Log on as the user whose Windows vault entries you want to manage. In Control Panel, click User Accounts, and then click Credential Manager.
2. On the Credential Manager page, click Restore Vault.

3. On the Stored User Names And Passwords page, click Browse. Use the Open Backup File As dialog box to select the location and file in which you saved the credential backup files, and then click Open.
4. Click Next. Press Ctrl+Alt+Delete to switch to the secure desktop. When prompted, enter the password for the credential backup file.
5. Click Next, and then click Finish.

Removing Windows Vault Entries

When a user no longer needs a Windows vault entry, you should remove it. To remove a user's Windows vault entry, follow these steps:

1. Log on as the user whose Windows vault entries you want to manage. In Control Panel, click User Accounts, and then click Credential Manager.

   On the Credential Manager page, you'll see a list of current entries by credential type.
2. Click the credential entry that you want to remove.
3. Click Remove From Vault. When prompted to confirm the action, click Yes.

As stated previously, local Windows vault entries can be removed only on the computer on which they were created. When a user has a roaming profile, however, Windows vault entries can be deleted from any computer to which the user is logged on.

Managing Local User Accounts and Groups

Local user accounts and groups are managed much like domain accounts. You can create accounts, manage their properties, reset accounts when they are locked or disabled, and so on. In addition to being able to manage local user accounts with Control Panel, you can create local user accounts with Local Users And Groups or with policy preferences. You should:

- Use Local Users And Groups to manage local user accounts on one computer.
- Use policy preferences to manage local user accounts on multiple computers throughout a domain.

When working with policy preferences, you can manage users and groups through Computer Configuration entries or User Configuration entries. Use Computer Configuration if you want to configure preferences that should be applied to computers regardless of who logs on. Use User Configuration if you want to configure preferences that should be applied to users regardless of which computer they log on to.

Creating Local User Accounts

You can access Local Users And Groups and create a user account by completing the following steps:

1. Click Start, point to All Programs, Administrative Tools, and then click Computer Management. Alternatively, open Control Panel, click System And Security, scroll down, click Administrative Tools, and then double-click Computer Management.
2. Right-click the Computer Management entry in the console tree, and then click Connect To Another Computer on the shortcut menu. You can now select the Windows 7 workstation whose local accounts you want to manage. (Domain controllers do not have local users or groups.)
3. Under the System Tools node, double-click the Local Users And Groups node to expand it, and then select Users. In the details pane, you should see a list of the currently defined user accounts.
4. Right-click Users, and then click New User. This opens the New User dialog box, shown in Figure 5-9.

   The fields in the dialog box are used as follows:

   - **User Name** The logon name for the user account. This name should follow the conventions for the local user name policy.
   - **Full Name** The full name of the user, such as William R. Stanek.
   - **Description** A description of the user. Normally, you would type the user's job title, such as Webmaster. You could also type the user's job title and department.
   - **Password** The password for the account. This password should follow the conventions of your password policy.
   - **Confirm Password** A field to ensure that you assign the account password correctly. Simply retype the password to confirm it.
   - **User Must Change Password At Next Logon** If this check box is selected, the user must change the password upon logon.
   - **User Cannot Change Password** If this check box is selected, the user can't change the password.
   - **Password Never Expires** If this check box is selected, the password for this account never expires. This setting overrides the local account policy.
   - **Account Is Disabled** If this check box is selected, the account is disabled and can't be used. Use this field to temporarily prevent anyone from using an account.

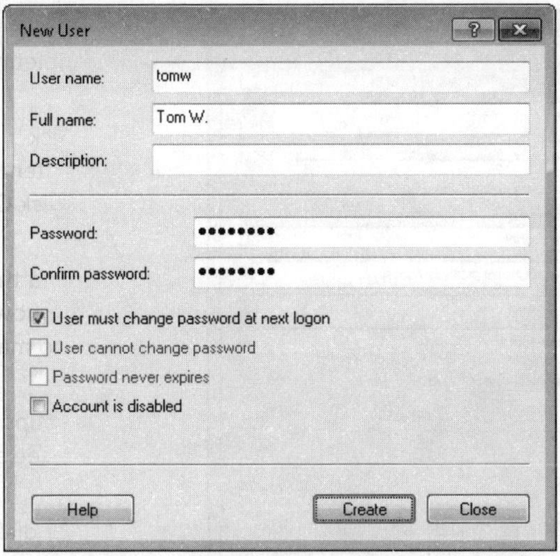

FIGURE 5-9 Configure new workstation accounts using the New User dialog box in Local Users And Groups.

5. Click Create when you have finished configuring the new account.

You can access Group Policy and use a preference item to create a user account by completing the following steps:

1. Open a Group Policy object (GPO) for editing in the Group Policy Management Editor. To configure preferences for computers, expand Computer Configuration\Preferences\Control Panel Settings, and then select Local Users And Groups. To configure preferences for users, expand User Configuration\Preferences\Control Panel Settings, and then select Local Users And Groups.
2. Right-click the Local Users And Groups node, point to New, and then select Local User. This opens the New Local User Properties dialog box, shown in Figure 5-10.
3. In the Action list, select Create. The rest of the fields in the dialog box are used as described in the previous procedure.
4. Use the options on the Common tab to control how the preference is applied. In most cases, you'll want to create the new account only once. If so, select Apply Once And Do Not Reapply.
5. Click OK. The next time Group Policy is refreshed, the preference item will be applied as appropriate for the Group Policy object in which you defined the preference item.

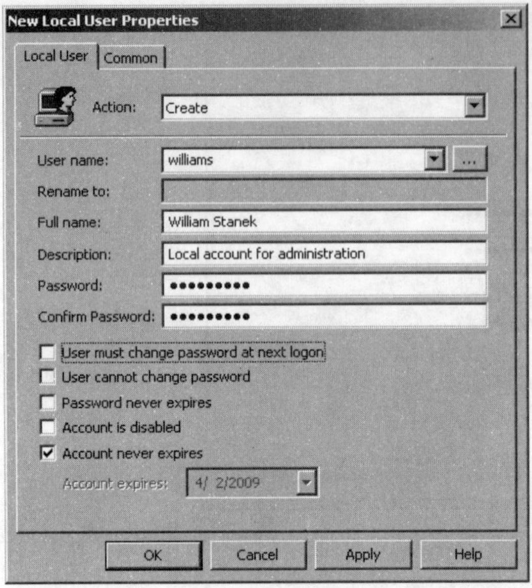

FIGURE 5-10 Configure new local user accounts in Group Policy.

Creating Local Groups for Workstations

You create local groups with Local Users And Groups or with Group Policy. You can access Local Users And Groups and create a local group by completing the following steps:

1. Click Start, point to All Programs, Administrative Tools, and then click Computer Management. Alternatively, open Control Panel, click System And Security, scroll down, click Administrative Tools, and then double-click Computer Management.
2. Right-click the Computer Management entry in the console tree, and then click Connect To Another Computer on the shortcut menu. You can now select the Windows 7 workstation whose local accounts you want to manage. (Domain controllers do not have local users or groups.)
3. Under the System Tools node, double-click the Local Users And Groups node to expand it, and then select Groups. In the details pane, you should see a list of the currently defined group accounts.
4. Right-click Groups, and then select New Group. This opens the New Group dialog box, shown in Figure 5-11.

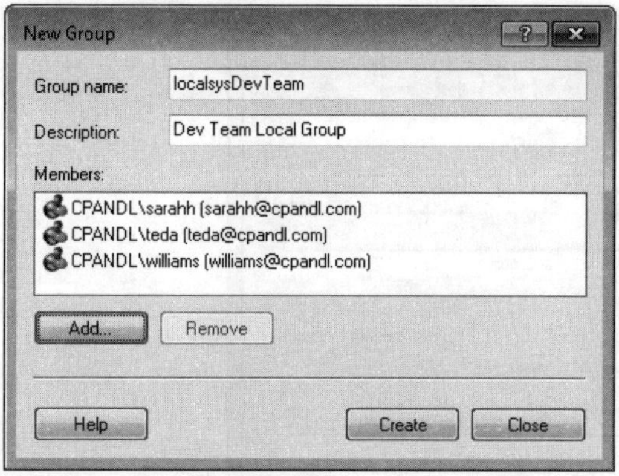

FIGURE 5-11 The New Group dialog box enables you to add a new local group to a Windows 7 workstation.

5. After you type a name and description for the group, click the Add button to open the Select Users dialog box and add names to the group.
6. In the Select Users dialog box, click Locations to select the computer or domain in which the user accounts you want to work with are located.
7. Type the name of a user you want to use in the Enter The Object Names To Select field, and then click Check Names. If matches are found, select the account you want to use, and then click OK. If no matches are found, update the name you entered and try searching again. Repeat this step as necessary, and then click OK when you have finished.
8. The New Group dialog box is updated to reflect your selections. If you made a mistake, select a name and remove it by clicking Remove.
9. Click Create when you have finished adding or removing group members.

You can access Group Policy and use a preference item to create a local group by completing the following steps:

1. Open a Group Policy object (GPO) for editing in the Group Policy Management Editor. To configure preferences for computers, expand Computer Configuration\Preferences\Control Panel Settings, and then select Local Users And Groups. To configure preferences for users, expand User Configuration\Preferences\Control Panel Settings, and then select Local Users And Groups.
2. Right-click the Local Users And Groups node, point to New, and then select Local Group. This opens the New Local Group Properties dialog box, shown in Figure 5-12.

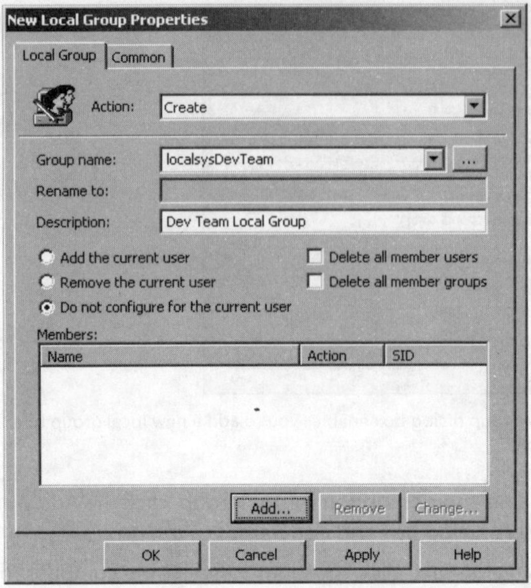

FIGURE 5-12 Configure new local group accounts in Group Policy.

3. In the Action list, select Create. Enter a name and description for the group.
4. Specify whether the current user should be added or removed as a member of the group, or select Do Not Configure For The Current User.
5. To add members to the group, click Add. In the Local Group Member dialog box, click the browse button (the one with the three dots). Use the Select User, Computer Or Group dialog box to select a user or group to add to the local group, and then click OK twice. Repeat this step as necessary.
6. Use the options on the Common tab to control how the preference is applied. In most cases, you should create the new account only once. If so, select Apply Once And Do Not Reapply.
7. Click OK. The next time Group Policy is refreshed, the preference item will be applied as appropriate for the Group Policy object in which you defined the preference item.

Adding and Removing Local Group Members

You use Local Users And Groups to add or remove local group members. Complete the following steps:

1. Expand Local Users And Groups in Computer Management, and then select the Groups folder in the left pane. Double-click the group with which you want to work.

2. Click the Add button to add user accounts to the group. This opens the Select Users dialog box. In the Select Users dialog box, type the name of a user you want to use in the Enter The Object Names To Select field, and then click Check Names. If matches are found, select the account you want to use, and then click OK. If no matches are found, update the name you entered and try searching again. Repeat this step as necessary, and then click OK.
3. Use the Remove button to remove user accounts from the group. Simply select the user account you want to remove from the group, and then click Remove.
4. Click OK when you have finished.

You can access Group Policy and use a preference item to add or remove members from a local group by completing the following steps:

1. Open a Group Policy object (GPO) for editing in the Group Policy Management Editor. To configure preferences for computers, expand Computer Configuration\Preferences\Control Panel Settings, and then select Local Users And Groups. To configure preferences for users, expand User Configuration\Preferences\Control Panel Settings, and then select Local Users And Groups.
2. Right-click the Local Users And Groups node, point to New, and then select Local Group. This opens the New Local Group Properties dialog box.
3. In the Action list, select Update to update the group's settings, or select Replace to delete the group and then re-create it exactly as you specify. If you update a group, you can enter a new name in the Rename To box.
4. Specify whether the current user should be added or removed as a member of the group, or select Do Not Configure For The Current User.
5. Specify whether all existing member users, all existing member groups, or both should be deleted.
6. To add or remove group members, click Add. In the Local Group Member dialog box, in the Action list, select Add To This Group if you are adding a member, or select Remove From This Group if you are removing a member. Next, click the browse button (the one with the three dots). Use the Select User, Computer Or Group dialog box to select a user or group to add to the local group, and then click OK twice. Repeat this step as necessary.
7. Use the options on the Common tab to control how the preference is applied, and then click OK. The next time policy is refreshed, the preference item will be applied as appropriate for the Group Policy object in which you defined the preference item.

Enabling or Disabling Local User Accounts

Local user accounts can become disabled for several reasons. If a user forgets his password and tries to guess it, he might exceed the account policy for bad logon attempts. Another administrator could have disabled the account while a user was on vacation. When an account is disabled or locked out, you can enable it by using the methods described here.

When an account is disabled, you can enable it on a local computer by completing the following steps:

1. Expand Local Users And Groups in Computer Management, and then select the Users folder in the left pane.
2. In the right pane, double-click the user's account name, and then clear the Account Is Disabled check box.
3. Click OK.

When an account is locked out, you can enable it on a local computer by completing the following steps:

1. In Local Users And Groups, select the Users folder in the left pane.
2. In the right pane, double-click the user's account name, and then clear the Account Is Locked Out check box.
3. Click OK.

You can enable or disable accounts and set other account options through policy preferences by completing the following steps:

1. Open a Group Policy object (GPO) for editing in the Group Policy Management Editor. To configure preferences for computers, expand Computer Configuration\Preferences\Control Panel Settings, and then select Local Users And Groups. To configure preferences for users, expand User Configuration\Preferences\Control Panel Settings, and then select Local Users And Groups.
2. In the right pane, double-click the user's account name to open the related Properties dialog box.
3. Select Update in the Action list. Make any necessary changes, and then click OK. The next time policy is refreshed, the preference item will be applied as appropriate for the Group Policy object in which you defined the preference item.

Creating a Secure Guest Account

In some environments, you might need to set up a Guest account that can be used by visitors. Most of the time, you'll want to configure the Guest account on a specific computer or computers and carefully control how the account can be used. To create a secure Guest account, I recommend that you perform the following tasks:

- **Enable the Guest account for use.** By default, the Guest account is disabled, so you must enable it to make it available. To do this, access Local Users And Groups in Computer Management, and then select the Users folder. Double-click Guest, and then clear the Account Is Disabled check box. Click OK.

- **Set a secure password for the Guest account.** By default, the Guest account has a blank password. To improve security on the computer, you should set a password for the account. In Local Users And Groups, right-click Guest, and then select Set Password. Click Proceed at the warning prompt. Type the new password and then confirm it. Click OK twice.
- **Ensure that the Guest account cannot be used over the network.** The Guest account shouldn't be accessible from other computers. If it is, users at another computer could log on over the network as a guest. To prevent this, start the Local Security Policy tool from the Administrative Tools menu, or type **secpol.msc** at the command prompt. Then, under Local Policies\User Rights Assignment, check that the Deny Access To This Computer From The Network policy lists Guest as a restricted account.
- **Prevent the Guest account from shutting down the computer.** When a computer is shutting down or starting up, it is possible that a guest user (or anyone with local access) could gain unauthorized access to the computer. To help deter this, you should be sure that the Guest account doesn't have the Shut Down The System user right. In the Local Security Policy tool, expand Local Policies\User Rights Assignment, and ensure that the Shut Down The System policy doesn't list the Guest account.
- **Prevent the Guest account from viewing event logs.** To help maintain the security of the system, the Guest account shouldn't be allowed to view the event logs. To be sure this is the case, start Registry Editor by typing **regedit** at a command prompt, and then access the HKLM\SYSTEM\CurrentControlSet\services\Eventlog key. Here, among others, you'll find three important subkeys: Application, Security, and System. Make sure each of these subkeys has a DWORD value named RestrictGuestAccess with a value of 1.

Renaming Local User Accounts and Groups

When you rename an account, you give it a new label. Because the SID for the account remains the same, the permissions and properties associated with the account don't change. To rename an account while you are accessing a local computer, complete the following steps:

1. In Local Users And Groups, select the Users or Groups folder, as appropriate.
2. Right-click the account name, and then click Rename. Type the new account name, and then click a different entry.

To rename an account using Group Policy, complete the following steps:

1. Open a Group Policy object (GPO) for editing in the Group Policy Management Editor. To configure preferences for computers, expand Computer Configuration\Preferences\Control Panel Settings, and then select Local Users And Groups. To configure preferences for users, expand User Configuration\Preferences\Control Panel Settings, and then select Local Users And Groups.

2. Do one of the following:
   - If a preference item already exists for the user or group, double-click the user or group name to open the related Properties dialog box. Select Update in the Action list. In the Rename To box, type the new account name, and then click OK.
   - If a preference item doesn't already exist for the user or group, you need to create one using the techniques discussed previously. Because you want to rename the user or group, select Update in the Action list, and then type the new account name in the Rename To box.

Deleting Local User Accounts and Groups

Deleting an account permanently removes it. Once you delete an account, if you create another account with the same name, you can't automatically get the same permissions because the SID for the new account won't match the SID for the account you deleted.

Because deleting built-in accounts can have far-reaching effects on the workstation, Windows 7 doesn't let you delete built-in user accounts or group accounts. In Local Users And Groups, you can remove other types of accounts by selecting them and pressing the Delete key or by right-clicking and then clicking Delete. When prompted, click Yes.

NOTE **When you delete a user account using Local Users And Groups, Windows 7 doesn't delete the user's profile, personal files, or home directory. If you want to delete these files and directories, you have to do it manually.**

To delete an account using Group Policy, complete the following steps:

1. Open a Group Policy object (GPO) for editing in the Group Policy Management Editor. To configure preferences for computers, expand Computer Configuration\Preferences\Control Panel Settings, and then select Local Users And Groups. To configure preferences for users, expand User Configuration\Preferences\Control Panel Settings, and then select Local Users And Groups.
2. Do one of the following:
   - If a preference item already exists for the user or group, double-click the user or group name to open the related Properties dialog box. Select Delete in the Action list. On the Common tab, set the appropriate options, such as Apply Once And Do Not Reapply, and then click OK.
   - If a preference item doesn't already exist for the user or group, you need to create one for the user or group using the techniques discussed previously. Be sure to select Delete in the Action list, and then select the appropriate options on the Common tab.

Managing Remote Access to Workstations

Windows 7 has several remote connectivity features. With Remote Assistance, users can send invitations to support technicians, enabling the technicians to service a computer remotely. With Remote Desktop, users can connect remotely to a computer and access its resources. In this section, you'll learn how to configure Remote Assistance and Remote Desktop. Typically, neither the Remote Assistance feature nor the Remote Desktop feature is enabled, and you must enable these features manually.

Remote Assistance and Remote Desktop can function through Network Address Translation (NAT) firewalls. Remote Assistance also has built-in diagnostic tools. To allow for easier troubleshooting and escalation of support issues, two different support staff can connect to a remote computer simultaneously. When troubleshooting requires restarting the computer, Remote Assistance sessions are reestablished automatically after the computer being diagnosed reboots.

Prior to using Remote Assistance, you may want users to use the Problem Steps Recorder to create a step-by-step record of a problem they are experiencing. The Problem Steps Recorder is very easy to use. To start and use the Problem Steps Recorder, a user needs to complete the following steps:

1. To start the Problem Steps Recorder, have the user click Start, type **psr**, and then press Enter. Once the tool is started, the user can prepare the environment and then begin recording the problem.
2. To turn on recording, the user clicks Start Record. Once recording has started, the user can perform the action that isn't working and click Add Comment to add comments as she works.
3. When the user experiences the problem and the related errors have been displayed, she can stop recording by clicking Stop Record.
4. When the user stops recording, the Save As dialog box is displayed. The user selects a save location and name for the Zip file that contains the record of the problem in an .mht file.
5. The user can send the Zip file to a support technician in an e-mail message or by copying it to a file share. To review the recorded problem steps, you double-click the Zip file to display its contents in Windows Explorer and then double-click the enclosed .mht file to open it in Internet Explorer.
6. You'll then see screen captures for all the steps the user took while the problem was being recorded. After the screen captures, you'll find additional details for each step that are generated automatically. You can use this information along with any user comments to help you troubleshoot the problem.

Configuring Remote Assistance

Remote Assistance is a useful feature for help desks, whether in-house or outsourced. A user can allow support personnel to view and take control of his or her desktop. This feature can be used to walk users through a complex process or to manage system settings while they watch the progress of the changes. The key to Remote Assistance is in the access levels you grant.

When enabled, Remote Assistance is configured by default to let support personnel view and control computers. Because users can send assistance invitations to internal and external resources, this could present a security concern for organizations. To reduce potential security problems, you might want to allow support staff to view but not control computers. A new restriction for Windows 7 is to allow connections only from computers running Windows 7 or later. This option is helpful to limit any possible compatibility issues and to ensure that any security enhancements in Windows 7 or later operating systems are available within Remote Assistance sessions.

Another key aspect of Remote Assistance you can control is the time limit for invitations. The default maximum time limit is 6 hours; the absolute maximum time limit you can assign is 30 days. Although the intent of a multiple-day invitation is to give support personnel a time window in which to respond to requests, it also means that they could use an invitation to access a computer over a period of 30 days. For instance, suppose you send an invitation with a 30-day time limit to a support person who resolves the problem the first day. That person would still have access to the computer for another 29 days, which wouldn't be desirable for security reasons. To reduce the risk to your systems, you'll usually want to reduce the default maximum time limit considerably—say, to 1 hour. If the problem is not solved in the allotted time period, you can issue another invitation.

To configure Remote Assistance, follow these steps:

1. In Control Panel, click System And Security, and then click System.
2. On the System page, click Remote Settings in the left pane. This opens the System Properties dialog box with the Remote tab displayed, as shown in Figure 5-13.
3. To disable Remote Assistance, clear the Allow Remote Assistance Connections To This Computer check box, and then click OK. Skip the remaining steps.
4. To enable Remote Assistance, select Allow Remote Assistance Connections To This Computer.

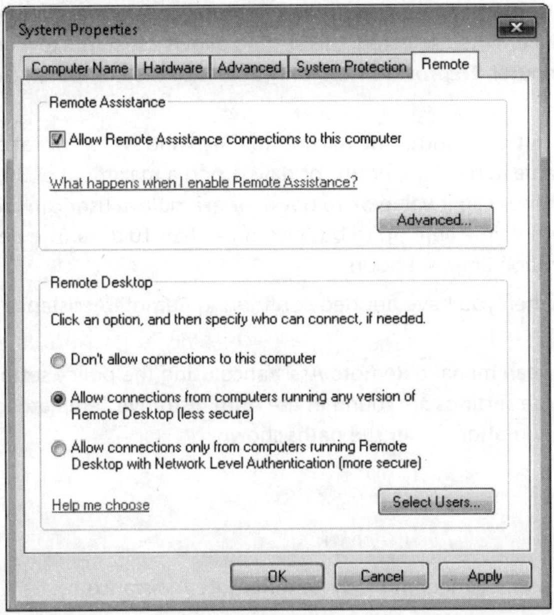

FIGURE 5-13 Use the Remote tab options to configure remote access to the computer.

5. Click Advanced. This displays the Remote Assistance Settings dialog box, shown in Figure 5-14.

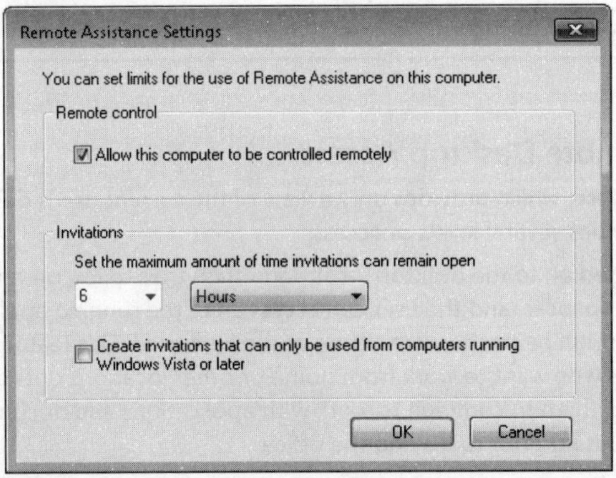

FIGURE 5-14 The Remote Assistance Settings dialog box is used to set limits for Remote Assistance.

6. The Allow This Computer To Be Controlled Remotely option sets limits for Remote Assistance. When selected, this setting allows assistants to view and control the computer. To provide view-only access to the computer, clear this check box.
7. The Invitations options control the maximum time window for invitations. You can set a value in minutes, hours, or days, up to a maximum of 30 days. If you set a maximum limit value of 10 days, for example, a user can create an invitation with a time limit up to but not more than 10 days. The default maximum expiration limit is 6 hours.
8. Click OK twice when you have finished configuring Remote Assistance options.

In Group Policy, you can manage Remote Assistance using the policy settings shown in Table 5-2. These settings are found in the Administrative Templates policies for Computer Configuration under the paths shown.

TABLE 5-2 Policy Settings for Managing Remote Assistance

SETTING	PATH
Allow Only Vista Or Later Connections	\System\Remote Assistance
Do Not Allow Windows Messenger To Be Run	\Windows Components\Windows Messenger
Offer Remote Assistance	\System\Remote Assistance
Solicited Remote Assistance	\System\Remote Assistance
Turn On Session Logging	\System\Remote Assistance

Configuring Remote Desktop Access

Unlike Remote Assistance, which provides only a view of the current user's desktop, Remote Desktop provides several levels of access:

- If a user is logged on to the desktop locally and then tries to log on remotely, the local desktop locks, and the user can access all of the running applications just as though he or she were sitting at the keyboard. This feature is useful for users who want to work from home or other locations outside the office, enabling them to continue to work with applications and documents that they were using prior to leaving the office.
- If a user is listed on the workstation's Remote Access list and is not otherwise logged on, he or she can initiate a new Windows session. The Windows session behaves as though the user were sitting at the keyboard. It can even be used when other users are also logged on to the computer. In this way, multiple users can share a single workstation and use its resources.

Remote Desktop is not enabled by default. You must specifically enable it to allow remote access to the workstation. When it is enabled, any member of the Administrators group can connect to the workstation. Other users must be placed on a remote access list to gain access to the workstation. To configure remote access, follow these steps:

1. In Control Panel, click System And Security, and then click System.
2. On the System page, click Remote Settings in the left pane. This opens the System Properties dialog box to the Remote tab.
3. To disable Remote Desktop, select Don't Allow Connections To This Computer, and then click OK. Skip the remaining steps.
4. To enable Remote Desktop, you have two options. You can:
   - Select Allow Connections From Computers Running Any Version Of Remote Desktop to allow connections from any version of Windows.
   - Select Allow Connections Only From Computers Running Remote Desktop With Network Level Authentication to allow connections only from Windows 7 or later computers (and computers with secure network authentication).
5. Click Select Users. This displays the Remote Desktop Users dialog box, shown in Figure 5-15.

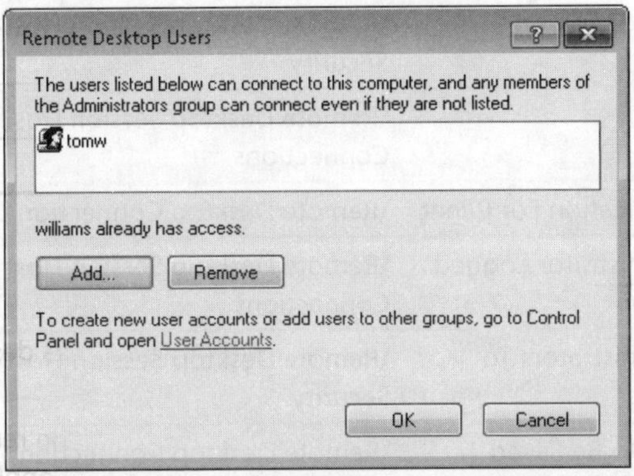

FIGURE 5-15 Specify the additional users allowed to make Remote Desktop connections.

6. To grant Remote Desktop access to a user, click Add. This opens the Select Users dialog box. In the Select Users dialog box, click Locations to select the computer or domain in which the users you want to work with are located. Type the name of a user you want to work with in the Enter The Object Names To Select field, and then click Check Names. If matches are found, select the account you want to use and then click OK. If no matches are

found, update the name you entered and try searching again. Repeat this step as necessary, and then click OK.

7. To revoke remote access permissions for a user account, select the account and then click Remove.
8. Click OK twice when you have finished.

Windows Firewall must be configured to allow inbound Remote Desktop exceptions. You can configure this on a per-computer basis in Windows Firewall for the domain profile and the standard profile. In Group Policy, you can configure this exception and manage Remote Desktop by using the policy settings shown in Table 5-3. These settings are found in the Administrative Templates policies for Computer Configuration under the path shown.

TABLE 5-3 Policy Settings for Managing Remote Desktop

SETTING	COMPUTER CONFIGURATION PATH
	PATHS UNDER WINDOWS COMPONENTS\ REMOTE DESKTOP SERVICES
Allow .Rdp Files From Unknown Publishers	\Remote Desktop Connection Client
Allow .Rdp Files From Valid Publishers And User's Default .Rdp Settings	\Remote Desktop Connection Client
Always Prompt For Password Upon Connection	\Remote Desktop Session Host\ Security
Automatic Reconnection	\Remote Desktop Session Host\ Connections
Configure Server Authentication For Client	\Remote Desktop Connection Client
Deny Logoff Of An Administrator Logged In To The Console Session	\Remote Desktop Session Host\ Connections
Do Not Allow Local Administrators To Customize Permissions	\Remote Desktop Session Host\ Security
Do Not Allow Passwords To Be Saved	\Remote Desktop Connection Client
Limit Maximum Color Depth	\Remote Desktop Session Host\ Remote Session Environment
Limit Maximum Display Resolution	\Remote Desktop Session Host\ Remote Session Environment
Limit Maximum Number Of Monitors	\Remote Desktop Session Host\ Remote Session Environment

SETTING	COMPUTER CONFIGURATION PATH
Limit The Size Of The Entire Roaming User Profile Cache	\Remote Desktop Session Host\ Profiles
Require Use Of Specific Security Layer For Remote (Rdp) Connections	\Remote Desktop Session Host\ Security
Set Client Connection Encryption Level	\Remote Desktop Session Host\ Security
Set Compression Algorithm For Rdp Data	\Remote Desktop Session Host\ Remote Session Environment
Specify Sha1 Thumbprints Of Certificates Representing Trusted .Rdp Publishers	\Remote Desktop Connection Client
	OTHER PATHS
Disable Remote Desktop Sharing	\Windows Components\NetMeeting
Windows Firewall: Allow Inbound Remote Desktop Exceptions	\Network\Network Connections\ Windows Firewall\Domain Profile
Windows Firewall: Allow Inbound Remote Desktop Exceptions	\Network\Network Connections\ Windows Firewall\Standard Profile

Making Remote Desktop Connections

As an administrator, you can make Remote Desktop connections to Windows servers and workstations. With Windows 2000 Server, Remote Desktop connections are enabled by installing Terminal Services and then configuring Terminal Services in remote access mode. With Windows XP Professional and later versions, Remote Desktop is installed automatically, but it is normally not enabled until you do so as discussed in the preceding section of this chapter. Once remote access is enabled on a computer, all administrators have remote access to that computer. Other users can be granted remote access as well.

To make a Remote Desktop connection to a server or workstation, follow these steps:

1. At a command prompt, type **mstsc**, or click Start, point to All Programs, Accessories, and then click Remote Desktop Connection. Click the Options button. This displays the Remote Desktop Connection dialog box, shown in Figure 5-16.

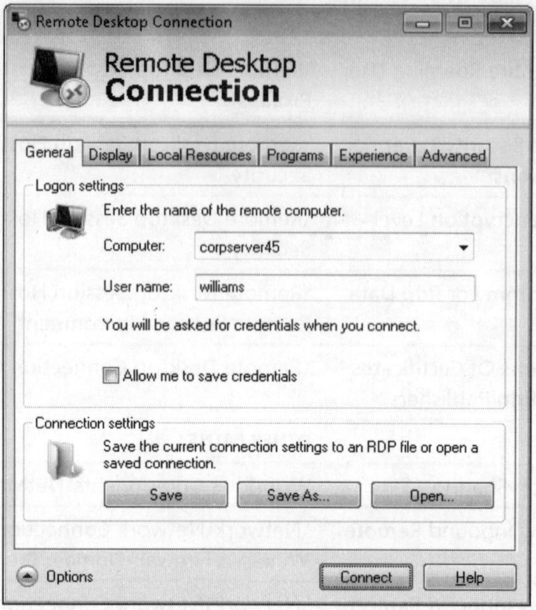

FIGURE 5-16 In the Remote Desktop Connection dialog box, type the name of the computer to which you want to connect, and then click Connect.

2. In the Computer field, type the name of the computer to which you want to connect. If you don't know the name of the computer, use the drop-down list to choose an available computer, or select Browse For More in the drop-down list to display a list of domains and computers in those domains.
3. Specify additional options as necessary. If you've configured stored credentials for the computer, your saved credentials will be used automatically. You can edit or delete the credentials as necessary.
4. Click Connect. If you haven't previously stored credentials for the computer, type your credentials when prompted, and then click OK. If the connection is successful, you'll see the Remote Desktop window on the selected computer, and you'll be able to work with resources on the computer. In the case of a failed connection, check the information you provided and then try to connect again.

NOTE **Clicking Options in the Remote Desktop Connection dialog box displays additional options for creating and saving connections. These options enable you to change the display size for the Remote Desktop, manage connections to local resources (such as printers, serial ports, and disk drives), run programs automatically on connection, and enable or disable local caching and data compression.**

CHAPTER 6

Configuring Windows 7 Computers

One of your primary responsibilities as an administrator is to manage the operating system configuration. Managing Windows 7 is very different from managing Windows XP and earlier versions of the Windows operating system, and these differences all stem from the important architectural changes introduced in Windows Vista and optimized in Windows 7. These changes include:

- A modular architecture and binaries distributed using Windows Imaging Format (WIM) disk images. Because of this, you can use the Deployment Image Servicing and Management tool (DISM) to manage packages, drivers, features, and internationalization settings in Windows Image (.wim) files or in virtual hard disk (.vhd) files. Disk Management and DiskPart have both been updated to work with .vhd files.
- A preboot environment in which Windows Boot Manager is used to control startup and load the boot application that you've selected. Because of this, Windows 7 doesn't use Ntldr and Boot.ini to load the operating system, as early versions of Windows did, and you have new boot options. For example, you can boot a computer to an operating system on a .vhd file. One way you do this is to create a basic boot image that uses Xcopy to copy the required .vhd file to a specified drive on startup.
- A user privilege and access control handler called User Account Control (UAC) is used to manage which processes can run and how applications interact with the operating system. Because of this, Windows 7 handles user privileges and access controls differently than earlier versions of Windows.

As you learned in Chapter 5, "Managing User Access and Security," you can optimize or turn off UAC prompting, but this doesn't disable other UAC features, such as application virtualization.

Beyond these changes, you need to know how to use redesigned tools and options to configure Windows 7, and that's what I discuss in this chapter.

Supporting Computers Running Windows 7

To successfully manage a computer, diagnose problems, and troubleshoot support issues, you need to know how the computer is configured. Support tools you can use to get information on a computer's configuration include:

- **Computer Management** Provides access to important system, services, and storage-management tools.
- **Performance Console** Allows you to monitor system performance and determine whether there are any issues causing performance problems.
- **Resource Monitor** Allows you to view detailed usage information for system resources, including processors, memory, disks, and networking. Use Resource Monitor when you need more information than Task Manager provides.
- **System** Allows you to view basic information about a computer and manage system properties.
- **System Information** Displays detailed system statistics about configuration and resource availability. You can also use System Information to troubleshoot system problems.
- **Task Manager** Allows you to view usage information for system resources.

In this section, I'll discuss techniques for working with these tools.

Working with the Computer Management Console

The Computer Management console is designed to handle core system administration tasks on local and remote systems. If you've added the Administrative Tools menu to the Start menu, you can start the Computer Management console by clicking Start, pointing to Administrative Tools, and then clicking Computer Management. You can also start the Computer Management console by following these steps:

1. Click Start, and then click Control Panel. Select Category in the View By list.
2. Click System And Security.
3. Click Administrative Tools, and then double-click Computer Management.

As Figure 6-1 shows, the main window has a multipane view similar to Windows Explorer. You use the console tree in the left pane for navigation and tool selection. The Actions pane, which can be displayed on the far right, is similar to the shortcut menu that is displayed when you right-click an item. To display or close the Actions pane, click the Show/Hide Action Pane button on the console toolbar. Tools are divided into three broad categories:

- **System Tools** General-purpose tools for managing systems and viewing system information
- **Storage** Provides access to drive management tools
- **Services And Applications** Used to view and manage the properties of services and applications installed on a server

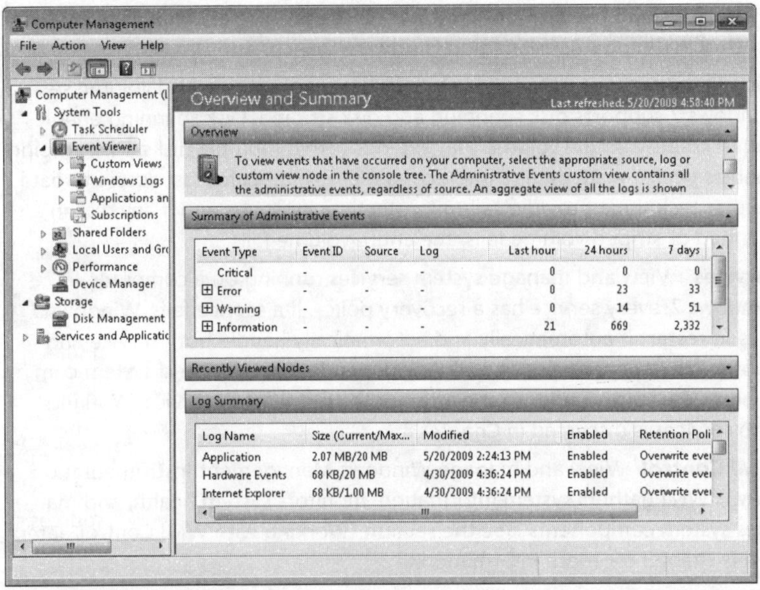

FIGURE 6-1 Use the Computer Management console to manage network computers and resources.

Within these categories are the following tools:

- **Task Scheduler** View and manage scheduled tasks. Scheduled tasks are used to automate processes such as disk cleanup or diagnostics testing. Scheduled tasks and automation are discussed in Chapter 17, "Handling Maintenance and Support Tasks."
- **Event Viewer** View the event logs on the selected computer. Event logs record important events that have taken place on the computer and can be used to determine if a computer has configuration issues or other types of problems. Events and event logs are covered in Chapter 17.
- **Shared Folders** View and manage shared folders as well as related sessions and open files. Shared folders are discussed in Chapter 13, "Managing File Security and Resource Sharing."

- **Local Users And Groups** Manage local users and local user groups on the selected computer. Each client computer has both local users and local groups, which are separate from domain users and groups. Working with local users and groups is covered in Chapter 5.
- **Performance** Provides monitoring and reporting tools that you can use to determine a computer's current performance and to track performance over time.
- **Device Manager** Use as a central location for checking the status of any device installed on a computer and for updating the associated device drivers. You can also use it to troubleshoot device problems. Managing devices is covered in Chapter 8, "Managing Hardware Devices and Drivers."
- **Disk Management** Manages hard disks, disk partitions, and volume sets. Windows 7 supports disk spanning and disk striping. Disk spanning enables you to create a single volume that extends across multiple disks. Disk striping enables you to write data stripes across multiple disks for fast access to data. Neither technique provides failure protection, however, and if any disk in a spanned or striped volume fails, the entire volume fails.
- **Services** View and manage system services running on a computer. In Windows 7, every service has a recovery policy. If a service fails, Windows 7 tries to restart it automatically and automatically handle both service and nonservice dependencies as well. Any dependent services and system components are started prior to the attempt to start a failed service. Working with services is discussed in Chapter 8.
- **WMI Control** View and manage Windows Management Instrumentation (WMI). WMI gathers system information, monitors system health, and manages system components. See the section "Working with WMI Control" later in this chapter for more information.

When working with Computer Management, you can select a remote computer to manage by completing the following steps:

1. Right-click the Computer Management entry in the console tree, and then click Connect To Another Computer. This opens the Select Computer dialog box.
2. Select Another Computer, and then type the fully qualified name of the computer you want to work with, such as cspc85.microsoft.com, where cspc85 is the computer name and microsoft.com is the domain name. Or click Browse to search for the computer you want to work with.
3. Click OK.

Getting Basic System and Performance Information

You use the System console to view and manage system properties. To access the System console, follow these steps:

1. Click Start, and then click Control Panel.
2. In Control Panel, click System And Security.
3. Click System.

As Figure 6-2 shows, the System console is divided into four basic areas that provide links for performing common tasks and a system overview. These four areas are:

- **Windows Edition** Shows the operating system edition and version.
- **System** Lists the processor, memory, performance rating, and type of operating system installed on the computer. The type of operating system is listed as 32 bit or 64 bit.
- **Computer Name, Domain, And Workgroup Settings** Provides the computer name and description as well as the domain, homegroup, or workgroup details. If you want to change any of this information, click Change Settings, and then click the Network ID button in the System Properties dialog box.
- **Windows Activation** Shows whether you have activated the operating system and the product key. If Windows 7 isn't activated yet, click the link provided to start the activation process, and then follow the prompts. If you want to change the product key, click Change Product Key, and then provide the new product key.

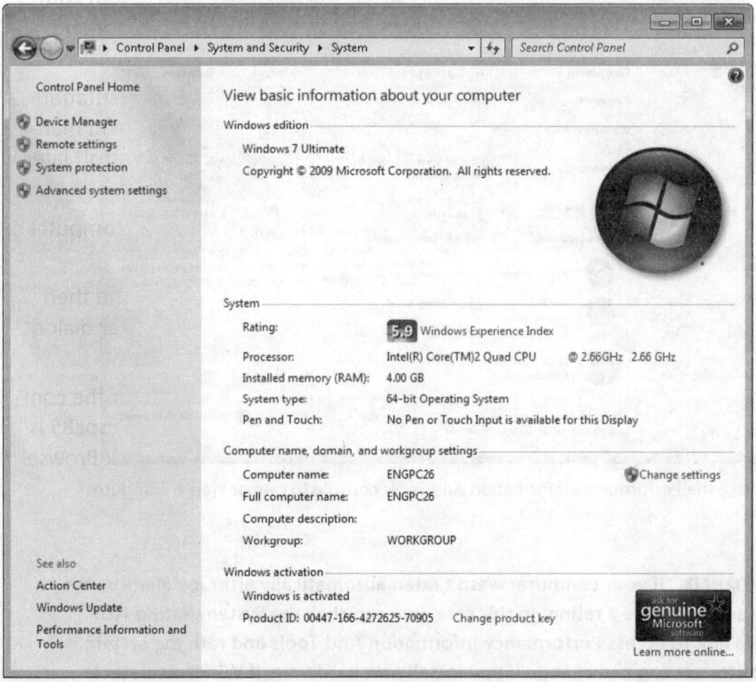

FIGURE 6-2 Use the System console to view and manage system properties.

When you're working in the System console, links in the left pane provide quick access to key support tools, including the following:

- Device Manager
- Remote Settings
- System Protection
- Advanced System Settings

Clicking Change Settings under Computer Name, Domain, And Workgroup Settings displays the System Properties dialog box. Using System Properties to manage a computer's configuration is discussed later in this chapter in the section "Managing System Properties."

A computer's Windows Experience Index rating is important in determining which operating system features the computer supports. In most cases, the Windows Setup program rates a computer's performance after completing installation. To view more information about a computer's rating, you can click the Windows Experience Index link under System to access Performance Information And Tools, shown in Figure 6-3.

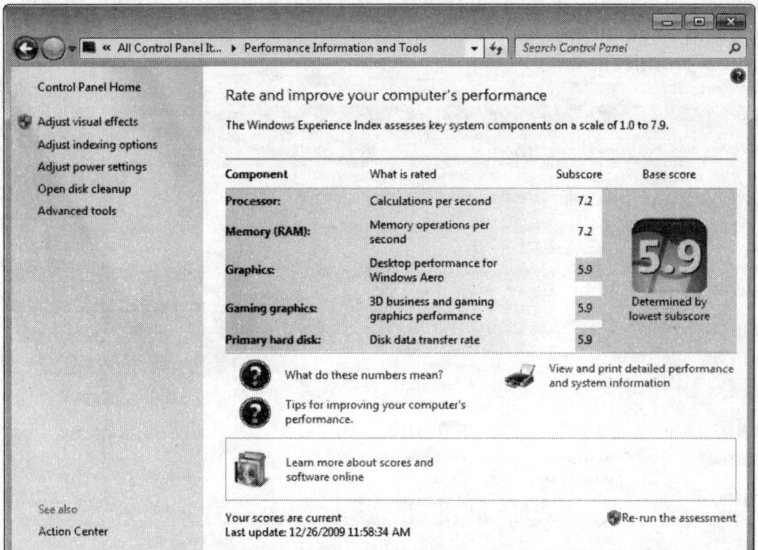

FIGURE 6-3 Use the Performance Information And Tools console to rate or view a computer's performance.

REAL WORLD **If your computer wasn't rated automatically after installation, the computer won't have a rating. In this case, you can click the System Rating Not Available link to access Performance Information And Tools and rate the system. A computer's rating can change if you install new hardware. If Windows detects**

hardware configuration changes, you'll be notified that "Your Windows Experience Index needs to be refreshed." In this case, click the link provided to access Performance Information And Tools, and then click Refresh Now to refresh the performance rating.

You also can access Performance Information And Tools by clicking Start, clicking Control Panel, selecting either Small Icons or Large Icons in the View By list, and then clicking Performance Information And Tools. This page shows the system's overall rating and lists the subscore for installed hardware in five categories:

- Processor
- Memory
- Graphics
- Gaming Graphics
- Primary Hard Disk

Windows 7 uses the computer's overall rating and subratings to determine which personalization features should be configured. If a computer has a low rating, Windows 7 will recommend turning off some features, such as Aero glass, to improve system performance. Based on performance over time, Windows 7 may also recommend turning off or modifying other features to improve performance.

TIP **Several factors can adversely affect the performance rating, including the primary disk running low on free disk space. If you install new hardware on a computer or resolve a performance issue, such as low disk space, that affects the computer rating, you can click Refresh Now or Re-Run The Assessment to update the computer's performance rating.**

In Performance Information And Tools, the left pane provides quick access to several helpful configuration areas, including:

- **Adjust Visual Effects** Opens the Performance Options dialog box, which you can use to manage visual effects, processor scheduling, virtual memory, and Data Execution Prevention.
- **Adjust Indexing Options** Opens the Indexing Options dialog box, which you can use to manage indexing locations and index settings.
- **Adjust Power Settings** Opens the Power Options dialog box, which you can use to manage power plans, what the power buttons do, when to turn off the display, and when the computer sleeps.

One of the handiest options in Performance Information And Tools is the Advanced Tools link in the left pane. Clicking this link opens the page shown in Figure 6-4, where you have quick access to the system maintenance tools. This page gives you direct access to the following:

- Task Manager, which is normally opened by pressing Ctrl+Alt+Delete.

- Resource Manager, which is normally opened by clicking the Resource Manager button in Task Manager.
- Advanced system details for System Information, which is normally accessed by running Msinfo32.
- System diagnostics reports, which are normally generated only as part of advanced diagnostics.

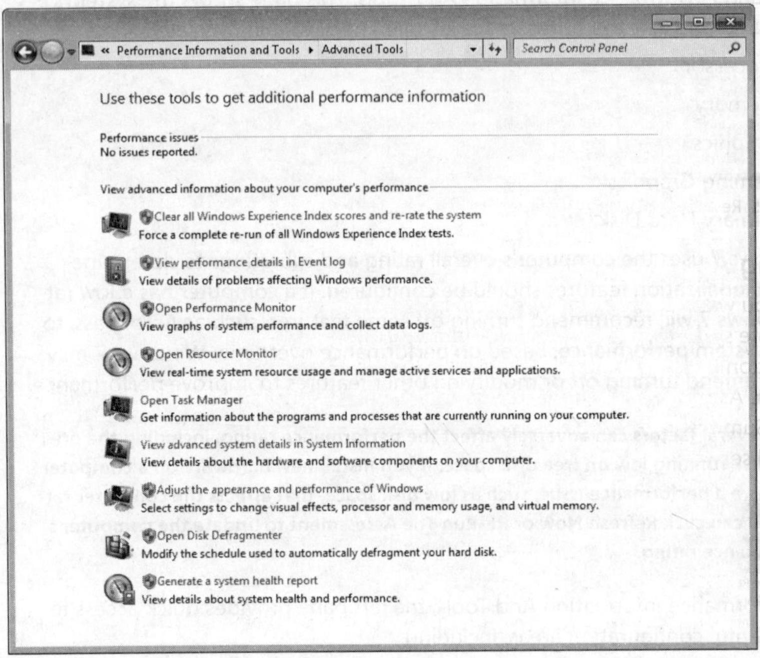

FIGURE 6-4 Access additional tools for working with the computer.

If you are logged on as an administrator, you can generate a system diagnostics report by clicking Generate A System Health Report. Generating the report can take about 1 minute (or longer). The report details the status of hardware resources, system response times, and processes on the computer, as well as system information and configuration data (see Figure 6-5). The report also includes suggestions for correcting problems, maximizing performance, and reducing overhead. You can save the report as an HTML document by clicking File, Save As, and then using the Save As dialog box to select a save location and file name for the report. You can send the report as an attachment to an e-mail message by clicking File, Send To.

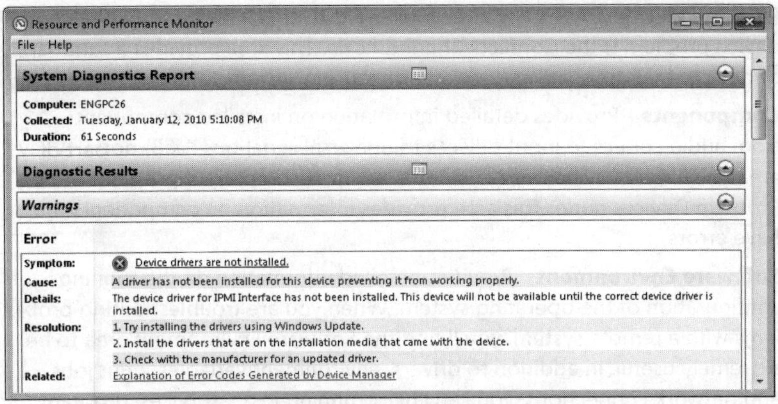

FIGURE 6-5 Review the diagnostics report to help resolve performance problems.

Getting Advanced System Information

When you want to get detailed system information or check computer information on remote systems, use System Information (Msinfo32.exe). You can access system information by clicking Start, typing **msinfo32** into the Search box, and then pressing Enter. As shown in Figure 6-6, you can view system summaries by selecting the System Summary node. All the configuration statistics provided are collected using the WMI service.

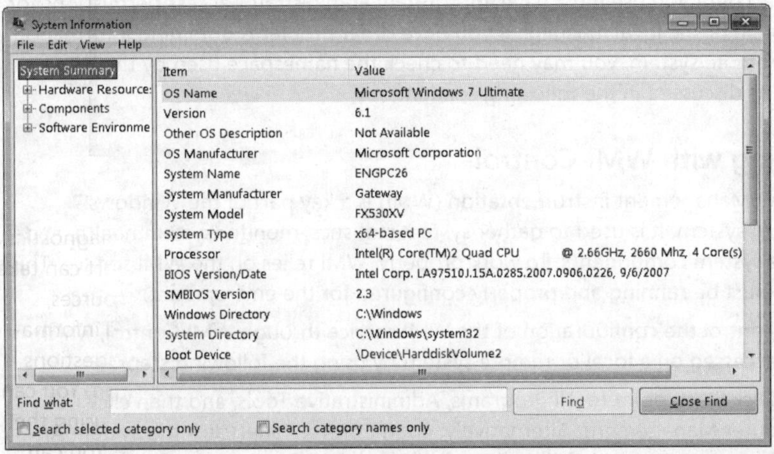

FIGURE 6-6 Advanced system information can help you troubleshoot system configuration problems.

The System Information tool provides detailed information on several major areas of the operating system:

- **Hardware Resources** Provides detailed information on input/output (I/O), interrupt requests (IRQs), memory, direct memory access (DMA), and

Plug and Play devices. A key area you'll want to check if a system is having a device problem is the Conflicts/Sharing node. This area provides a summary of devices that are sharing resources or causing system conflicts.

- **Components** Provides detailed information on installed components, from audio codecs to input devices to universal serial bus (USB) ports. A key area you'll want to check if a system is having a component problem is the Problem Devices node. This area provides information on components that have errors.
- **Software Environment** Provides detailed information on the running configuration of the operating system. When you are troubleshooting problems with a remote system, you'll find the Software Environment area to be extremely useful. In addition to drivers, environment variables, print jobs, and network connections, you can check running tasks, services, program groups, and startup programs.

If you want to browse configuration information for a remote computer, follow these steps:

1. Open System Information. Select Remote Computer on the View menu. This displays the Remote Computer dialog box.
2. In the Remote Computer dialog box, select Remote Computer On The Network.
3. Type the computer name in the field provided, and then click OK.

The account you use must have appropriate administrator access permissions for the domain or the local machine. If you have other problems obtaining information from a remote system, you may need to check the namespace used by the WMI service, as discussed in the following section.

Working with WMI Control

Windows Management Instrumentation (WMI) is a key part of the Windows 7 operating system. It is used to gather system statistics, monitor system health, and manage system components. To work properly, WMI relies on the WMI service. This service must be running and properly configured for the environment.

You control the configuration of the WMI service through WMI Control, which can be accessed on a local or remote system by using the following steps:

1. Click Start, point to All Programs, Administrative Tools, and then click Computer Management. Alternatively, open Control Panel, click the System And Security category heading link, click Administrative Tools, and then double-click Computer Management.
2. Right-click the Computer Management entry in the console tree, and then select Connect To Another Computer. You can now choose the system that has the services you want to manage.

3. Expand the Services And Applications node by clicking the plus sign (+) next to it. Next, click WMI Control to select it. (This is required for the control to be read in.) Right-click WMI Control, and then select Properties. You can now use the WMI Control Properties dialog box to configure WMI.

As shown in Figure 6-7, the WMI Control Properties dialog box has the following tabs:

- **General** Fields on this tab provide summary information for the system and WMI. WMI uses the credentials of the current user to obtain system information.
- **Backup/Restore** Statistics gathered by WMI are stored in a repository. By default, this repository is located in %SystemRoot%\System32\Wbem\Repository. These statistics are automatically backed up at regular intervals. You can back up or restore the repository manually by using the fields on this tab.
- **Security** Security settings determine who has access to different levels of WMI statistics. By default, the Administrators group has full access to WMI, and the Authenticated Users group has permissions to execute methods, enable accounts, and write gathered statistics.
- **Advanced** Advanced settings determine the default namespace for WMI. The default namespace is used in WMI scripting when a full namespace path isn't set for a WMI object. You can change the default setting by clicking Change, selecting a new default namespace, and then clicking OK.

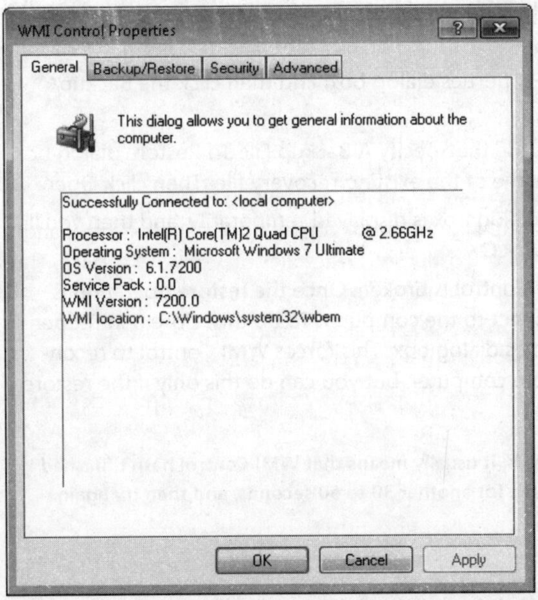

FIGURE 6-7 WMI Control is used to manage the configuration of the WMI service.

NOTE WMI maintains error logs that can be used for troubleshooting problems with the WMI service. These logs are stored by default in %SystemRoot%\System32\Wbem\Logs. WMI maintenance files, logs, and repositories can use a considerable amount of disk space on a system. On average, these files used 65 megabytes (MB) on my test systems—the bulk of this (40–50 MB) to maintain repository backup files.

Information gathered by WMI is stored in a collection of system files called a repository. By default, the repository files are stored under %SystemRoot%\System32\Wbem\Repository. The repository is the heart of WMI and the Help And Support services framework. Information is moved through the repository by using a staging file. If repository data or the staging file becomes corrupt, WMI might not function properly. This condition is usually temporary, but you can safeguard against it by backing up the repository file manually.

To back up the WMI repository manually, complete the following steps:

1. Open the WMI Control Properties dialog box, and then click the Backup/Restore tab.
2. Click Back Up Now. Next, use the Specify A Name For Your Backup File dialog box to set the file location and name of the WMI backup file. Click Save.
3. The Backup In Progress dialog box is displayed while the recovery file is being created. The recovery file is saved with a .rec extension, and its size depends on how much information is being stored. Usually this file is between 20–30 MB in size.

If you later need to restore the WMI repository from a backup file, complete these steps:

1. Open the WMI Control Properties dialog box, and then click the Backup/Restore tab.
2. Click Restore Now. Next, use the Specify A Backup File To Restore dialog box to set the location and name of the existing recovery file. Then click Open.
3. The Restore In Progress dialog box is displayed temporarily, and then you'll see a warning prompt. Click OK.
4. Your connection to WMI Control is broken. Once the restore operation is complete, you can reconnect to the computer. To do this, close and reopen the WMI Control Properties dialog box. This forces WMI Control to reconnect to the local or remote computer, but you can do this only if the restore operation is complete.

   NOTE If the connection fails, it usually means that WMI Control hasn't finished restoring the repository. Wait for another 30 to 60 seconds, and then try again.

Using System Support Tools

Windows 7 provides a wide range of support tools. Tools that are available include the following:

- **Backup (Sdclt.exe)** Runs Backup And Restore, which you can use to back up and restore user and system files. See Chapter 17 for more information.
- **Built-In Diagnostics** Scans the system, examining hardware components and software configurations for problems. This information can be used to troubleshoot and resolve performance and configuration issues. Working with diagnostics tools is discussed in this chapter and in other chapters throughout this book.
- **DirectX Diagnostic Tool (Dxdiag.exe)** Runs a diagnostic tool that you can use to troubleshoot problems with Microsoft DirectX. DirectX is used to speed up the performance of applications, provided that the system hardware supports this feature.
- **Disk Cleanup (Cleanmgr.exe)** Runs the Disk Cleanup utility, which examines disk drives for files that aren't needed. By default, Disk Cleanup examines temporary files, the Recycle Bin, and various types of offline files to see whether there are files that can be deleted.
- **Disk Defragmenter (Dfrgui.exe)** Runs the Disk Defragmenter utility, which examines disk drives for fragmentation and can then be used to defragment the drive. A drive with many fragmented files can reduce the system's performance. See Chapter 12, "Managing Disk Drives and File Systems," for more information about this utility.
- **File Signature Verification Utility (Sigverif.exe)** Used to check operating system files that have been digitally signed. Any critical files that aren't digitally signed are displayed in a results list. The complete list of system files checked is available in a log file stored in %SystemRoot%\Sigverif.txt.
- **Offer Remote Assistance** Enables you to offer remote assistance to a user. If the user accepts the offer, you can troubleshoot problems on his system as discussed in Chapter 17.
- **Remote Assistance** Enables you to create a remote assistance invitation that can be used to get remote help from a technician. Remote Assistance is discussed in detail in Chapter 17.
- **System Configuration (Msconfig.exe)** Enables you to manage system configuration information. You can configure normal, diagnostic, and selective startup as well.
- **System Restore (Rstrui.exe)** Opens the System Restore utility, which can be used to create restore points or roll back a system to a specific restore point. The System Restore utility is discussed in Chapter 17.

The tools you might want to take a closer look at now include Disk Cleanup, File Signature Verification, and System Configuration.

Working with Disk Cleanup

Disk Cleanup checks disk drives for files that aren't needed. You can start to work with Disk Cleanup by completing the following steps:

1. Click Start, point to Programs or All Programs, Accessories, System Tools, and then select Disk Cleanup.

   NOTE **The executable for Disk Cleanup is Cleanmgr.exe. To run Disk Cleanup directly, click Start, type cleanmgr in the Search box, and then press Enter.**

2. If the computer has multiple hard disk drives, the Drive Selection dialog box is displayed. Use the Drives drop-down list to choose the drive you want to clean up, and then click OK.

   Disk Cleanup then examines the selected drive, looking for temporary user files that can be deleted and user files that are candidates for deletion. The more files on the drive, the longer the search process takes.

   When Disk Cleanup finishes its initial run, you can add temporary system files that can be deleted and system files that are candidates for deletion by clicking Clean Up System Files, selecting a system drive to examine, and then clicking OK. You will then see a report similar to the one shown in Figure 6-8. File categories that you might see in the report include the following:

   - **Downloaded Program Files** Contains programs downloaded for use by your browser, such as ActiveX controls and Java applets. These files are temporary and can be deleted.
   - **Files Discarded By Windows Upgrade** Contains files from a previous upgrade that were not identified as Windows system files. After you've saved any necessary data from previous Windows installations, including user data, you can use this option to remove the related files and free up space.
   - **Hibernation File Cleaner** Contains details about the state of the computer when it enters hibernation. If the computer doesn't use hibernation, you can remove this file to free up space.
   - **Microsoft Office Temporary Files** Contains temporary files and logs used by Microsoft Office. These files can be deleted to free up space.
   - **Offline Files** Contains local copies of network files that you've designated for offline use. These files are stored to enable offline access and can be deleted.
   - **Offline Web Pages** Contains local copies of Web pages that you've designated for offline use. These files are stored to enable offline access and can be deleted.
   - **Previous Windows Installation(s)** Saved under %SystemDrive%\Windows.old, these files are from previous Windows installations. After

you've saved any necessary data from previous Windows installations, including user data, you can use this option to remove the related files and free up space.

- **Temporary Offline Files** Contains temporary data and work files for recently used network files. These files are stored to enable working offline and can be deleted.
- **Recycle Bin** Contains files that have been deleted from the computer but not yet purged. Emptying the Recycle Bin permanently removes the files.
- **Temporary Files** Contains information stored in the Temp folder. These files are primarily temporary data or work files for applications.
- **Temporary Internet Files** Contains Web pages stored to support browser caching of pages. These files are temporary and can be deleted.
- **Thumbnails** Contains thumbnails of pictures, videos, and documents created by Windows 7. When you first access a folder, Windows 7 creates thumbnails of pictures, videos, and documents. These thumbnails are saved so that they can be quickly displayed the next time you open the folder. If you delete thumbnails, they are re-created the next time you open the folder.

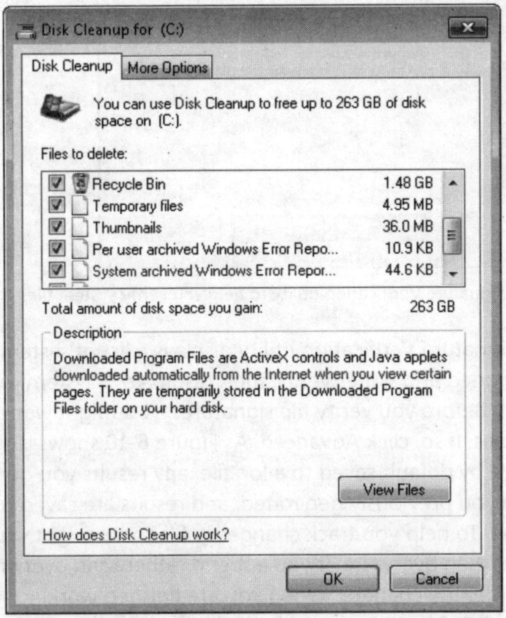

FIGURE 6-8 Use Disk Cleanup to help you find files that can be deleted.

3. Use the check boxes provided in the Files To Delete list to choose files that you want to remove. Then click OK. When prompted to confirm the action, click Yes.

Verifying System Files with File Signature Verification

Critical files used by the operating system are digitally signed. Digital signatures help prove the authenticity of these files and ensure that it is easy to track changes that might cause problems on a system. When you are having problems that cannot easily be explained, such as happens when a system becomes unstable after an application is installed, it is a good idea to verify that critical system files haven't been changed. You can do this by using the File Signature Verification utility.

The executable file for the File Signature Verification utility is Sigverif.exe. You can start and work with the File Signature Verification utility by completing the following steps:

1. Click Start, type **sigverif**, and then press Enter. This starts the File Signature Verification utility, as shown in Figure 6-9.

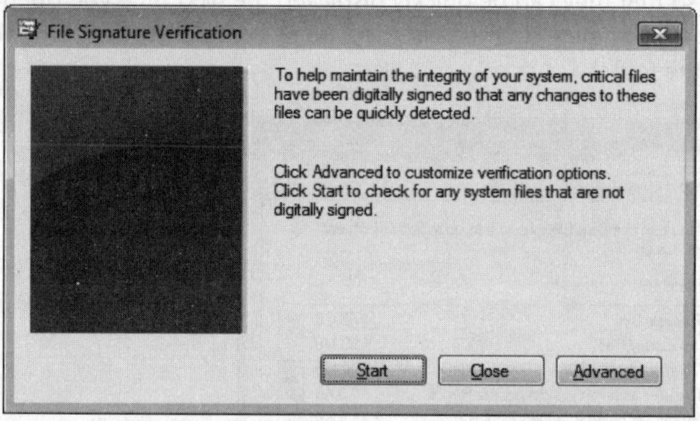

FIGURE 6-9 Use the File Signature Verification utility to help you verify system files.

2. By default, the File Signature Verification utility displays a list of system files that aren't digitally signed and writes verification results to %SystemRoot%\System32\Sigverif.txt. Before you verify file signatures, you might want to specify logging options. If so, click Advanced. As Figure 6-10 shows, the verification results are by default saved to a log file, any results you generate overwrite any results you previously generated, and results are saved to a log file named Sigverif.txt. To help you track changes in files, you might want to append results rather than overwrite. If you append rather than overwrite, you can more easily identify changes. When you are finished working with the logging options, click OK to return to the main window.

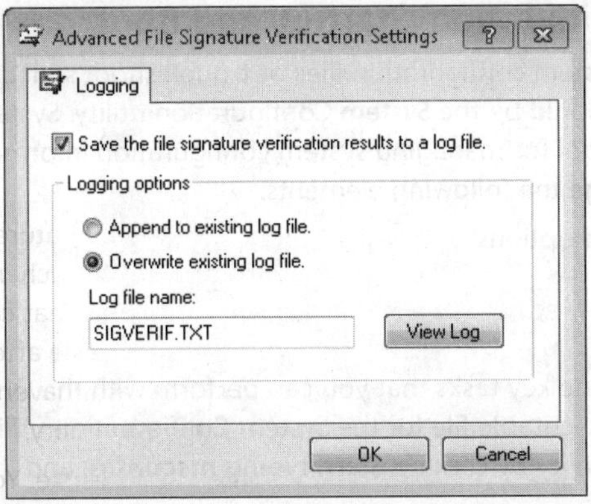

FIGURE 6-10 Modify the default logging options as necessary.

3. Click Start to run the File Signature Verification utility. In the results, shown in Figure 6-11, notice the list of files displayed in the File Signature Verification utility report. These files don't have digital signatures and could have been maliciously replaced by other programs of the same name. Click Close to return to the main window. If you suspect a problem, review event logs and other error reports to see if any of these files show up in the error reports.

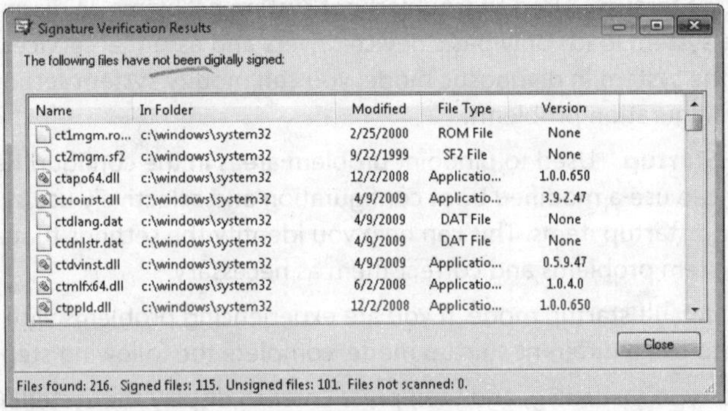

FIGURE 6-11 Review the verification results.

4. If you want to review the verification log, click Advanced, and then click View Log. You also can use Microsoft Notepad to open the verification log, which is located in %SystemRoot%\System32\Sigverif.txt by default. Check the log to see if there are files that have been altered since they were installed. Files are listed by status, such as Signed and Not Signed. Note the modification date and version of the file. If a computer has been having problems since a certain date, and critical files were changed on this date, this could be the source of the problem. For example, perhaps a program was installed that overwrote a critical file with an older version.

Managing System Configuration, Startup, and Boot

Whether you want to update system configuration files or troubleshoot startup problems, your tool of choice should be the System Configuration utility. System Configuration is an integrated tool for managing system configuration information. Using this utility, you can manage the following elements:

- Operating system startup options
- Startup applications
- Service-startup options

The following sections examine key tasks that you can perform with the System Configuration utility. The executable file for the System Configuration utility is Msconfig.exe. You can run the utility by clicking Start, typing **msconfig**, and then pressing Enter.

Understanding Startup Modes and Troubleshooting System Startup

You can use the System Configuration utility to select the startup mode for a computer. The following three startup modes are available:

- **Normal Startup** Used for normal system operations. In this mode, the operating system loads all system configuration files and device drivers and runs all startup applications and enabled services.
- **Diagnostic Startup** Used to troubleshoot system problems. In diagnostic mode, the system loads only basic device drivers and essential services. Once you start the system in diagnostic mode, you can modify system settings to resolve configuration problems.
- **Selective Startup** Used to pinpoint problem areas in the configuration. Here, you can use a modified boot configuration and selectively use system services and startup items. This can help you identify the settings that are causing system problems and correct them as necessary.

Normal is the default startup mode. If you are experiencing problems with a system and want to use a different startup mode, complete the following steps:

1. Click Start, type **msconfig**, and then press Enter to display the System Configuration utility, shown in Figure 6-12.
2. On the General tab, select either Diagnostic Startup or Selective Startup. If you choose Selective Startup, you can use the following options to specify the items that you want the system to use:
   - **Load System Services** Tells the system to load Windows services on startup. If you select this option, use the settings on the Services tab to specify which services are started.
   - **Load Startup Items** Tells the system to run applications designated for startup at boot time. If you select this option, you can enable and disable startup applications by using the options on the Startup tab.

- **Use Original Boot Configuration** Tells the system to process the original boot configuration on startup instead of one you've created by modifying the boot settings with the System Configuration utility.

NOTE **If you make changes on the Boot, Services, or Startup tab, the Selective Startup option and related suboptions are automatically selected on the General tab.**

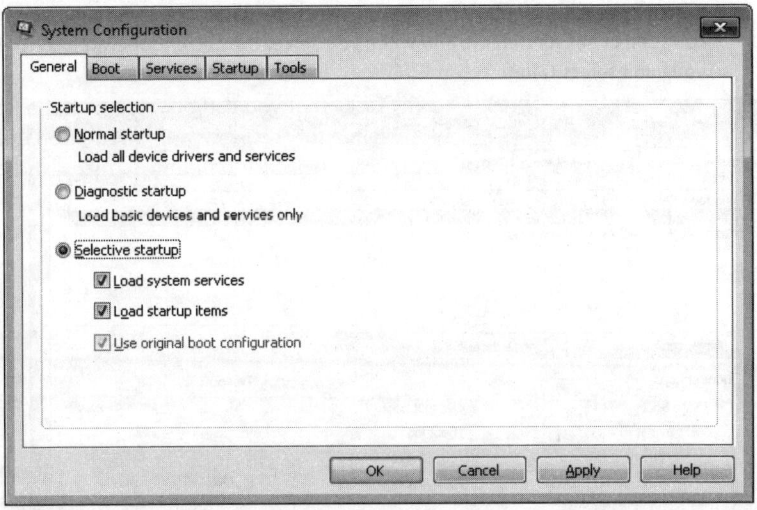

FIGURE 6-12 Use the System Configuration utility's General tab to control system startup.

3. When you are ready to continue, click OK, and then reboot the system. If you have problems rebooting the system, restart the system in Safe mode and then repeat this procedure. Safe mode appears automatically as an option after a failed boot.

Changing Boot Options

Windows 7 uses the Windows Boot Manager and a boot application to start up the operating system. Windows 7 doesn't use Boot.ini or other boot files in a standard configuration. When troubleshooting, you can use the options on the System Configuration utility's Boot tab to control the boot partition, boot method, and boot options used by the operating system.

As shown in Figure 6-13, when you start the System Configuration utility and click the Boot tab, the operating systems that are bootable on the computer are listed. To specify that an operating system other than the current one should be used, you simply click the related operating system entry. When working with operating system entries, you can select the following options:

- **Set As Default** Sets the currently selected boot partition as the default partition. The default partition is selected automatically if you don't choose an option before the timeout interval.

- **Timeout** Sets the amount of time the computer waits before using the default boot partition.
- **Delete** Deletes an operating system entry. The entry cannot be easily re-created, so only delete an entry if absolutely necessary.

NOTE **On a computer with a single operating system, the Set As Default and Delete buttons are not enabled because there is no other operating system to switch to or from. Similarly, when you select the default operating system, you can't select Set As Default, and when you select the current operating system, you can't select Delete.**

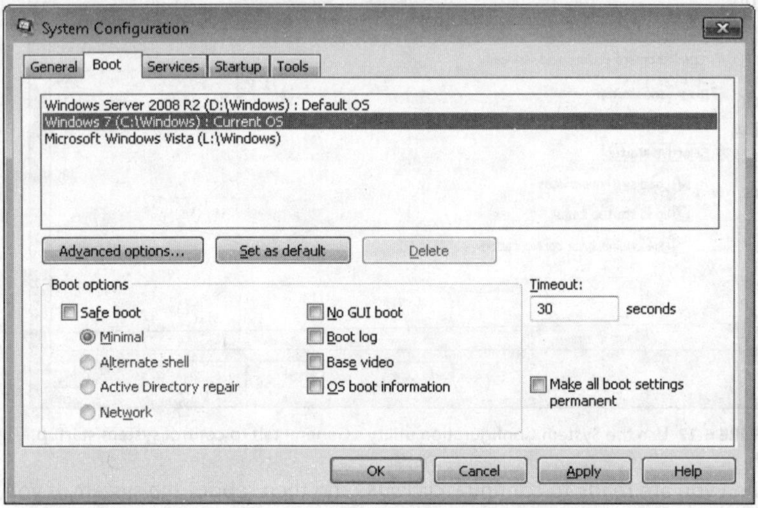

FIGURE 6-13 The Boot tab controls the boot partition, boot method, and boot options used by the operating system.

You can also set the following boot options:

- **Safe Boot** Starts the computer in Safe mode with additional flags for minimal, network, and alternate shell minimal boots, as well as the directory service repair state (Dsrepair). Once you successfully boot a system in Safe mode, you can modify system settings to resolve configuration problems.
- **No GUI Boot** Boots the computer to the Windows prompt and doesn't load the graphical components of the operating system. Booting to the prompt is useful when you are having problems with the graphical components of Windows 7.
- **Boot Log** Turns on boot logging so that key startup events are written to a log.
- **Base Video** Forces the computer to use video graphics adapter (VGA) display settings. Use this mode when you are trying to resolve display settings,

such as when the display mode is set to a size that the monitor cannot display.

- **OS Boot Information** Starts the computer using verbose output so that you can view the details of startup activities prior to the loading of Windows graphical components.

Any changes you make are stored as modified boot configuration data by the System Configuration utility. After you make changes and click OK, you can restart the computer to apply the temporary changes. To go back to a normal startup after you've made and applied changes, you must select Normal Startup on the General tab and then click OK. You must then reboot the system so that the normal settings are used.

If you click the Advanced Options button on the Boot tab, you can set boot options for processors, maximum memory, PCI locking, and debugging by using the BOOT Advanced Options dialog box, shown in Figure 6-14. Use these options for troubleshooting. For example, if you suspect a problem is related to multiple processors, you can specify 1 as the number of processors to use. If you suspect a problem is due to memory beyond the first 4 gigabytes (GB), you can specify the maximum memory to use as 4,096 MB. After you are done troubleshooting, you should remove these options to restore normal operations.

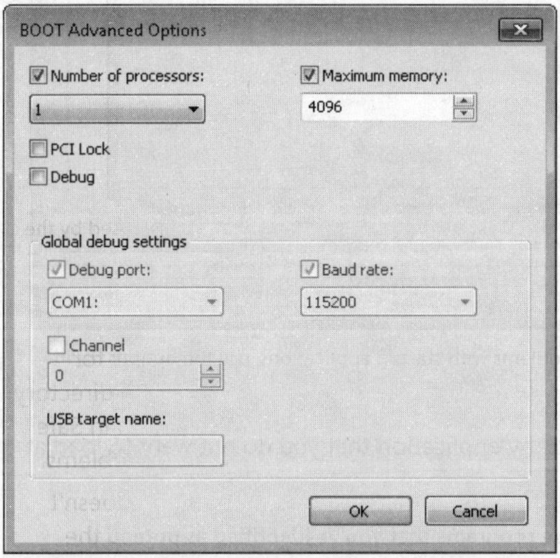

FIGURE 6-14 Set advanced boot options for troubleshooting.

On the Boot tab, to make any of the standard or advanced boot options you select permanent, select the Make All Boot Settings Permanent check box before clicking OK. In most cases, you won't want troubleshooting or debugging options to be permanent, so be sure to clear these options first.

Enabling and Disabling Startup Applications for Troubleshooting

If you suspect that an application loaded at startup is causing problems with the system, there is an easy way to diagnose this. Disable the program from starting automatically, and then reboot the system. If the problem is no longer present, you might have pinpointed the problem and could remedy it by permanently disabling the automatic startup of this program. If the problem still occurs, you might want to repeat this process with other startup applications.

To disable startup applications, follow these steps:

1. Click Start, type **msconfig**, and then press Enter to display the System Configuration utility.
2. Click the Startup tab. As shown in Figure 6-15, this tab displays a list of programs that load at startup.

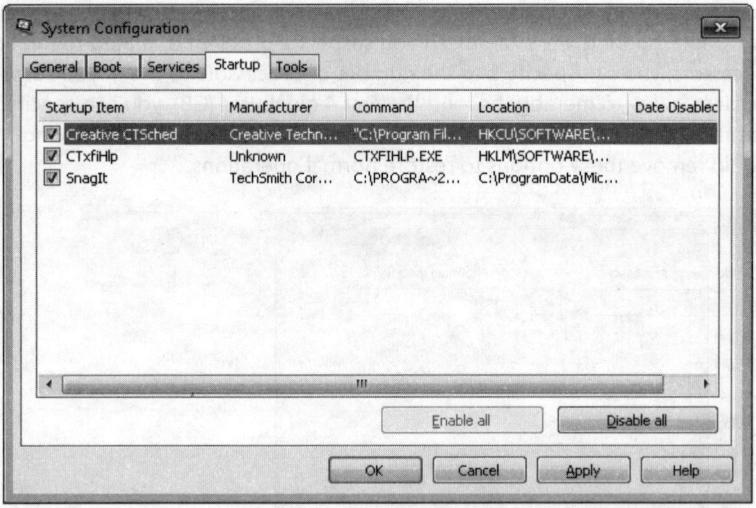

FIGURE 6-15 To troubleshoot problems with startup applications, use the options on the Startup tab.

3. Clear the check box next to any application that you do not want to load at startup.

   CAUTION **Disable only those programs that you've identified as potential problems, and do so only if you know how they are used by the operating system. If you don't know what a program does, don't disable it. Sometimes you can learn more about a startup program by following its command path and then examining its base installation folder.**

4. Click OK. You need to reboot the system to check the changes, so if you are prompted to restart the system, click Yes. Otherwise, reboot manually.

5. Repeat this procedure as necessary to pinpoint the program causing the system problems. If you can't identify an application as the cause of the problem, the trouble might be with a Windows component, service, or device driver.

Enabling and Disabling Services for Troubleshooting

Just as applications that start automatically can cause problems on a system, so can services that automatically start. To help troubleshoot service problems, you can temporarily disable services by using the System Configuration utility and then reboot to see whether the problem goes away. If it does, you might have pinpointed it. You can then permanently disable the service or check with the service vendor to see if an updated executable is available for the service.

To temporarily disable services, follow these steps:

1. Click Start, type **msconfig**, and then press Enter to display the System Configuration utility.
2. Click the Services tab. As shown in Figure 6-16, this tab displays a list of all services installed on the computer and includes the state of the service, such as Running or Stopped, and from where the service originated. To more easily find non-Microsoft services, select Hide All Microsoft Services.

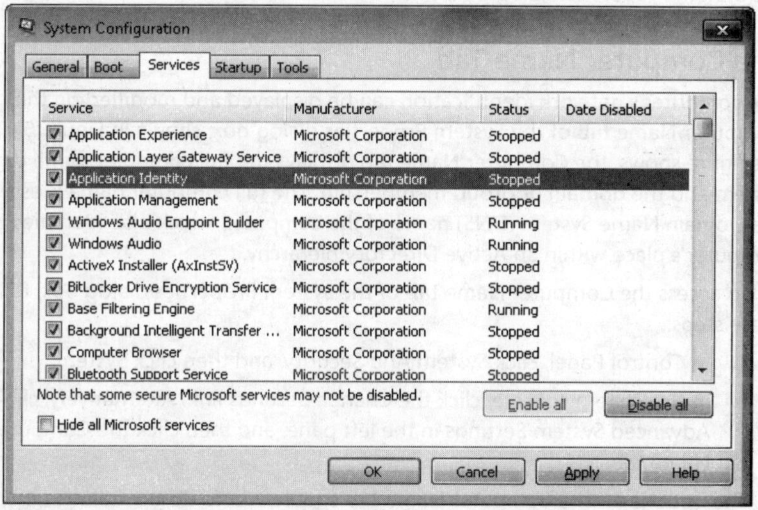

FIGURE 6-16 To troubleshoot problems with Windows services, use the options on the Services tab.

3. Clear the check box next to any service that you do not want to run at startup.

CAUTION Disable only those services that you've identified as potential problems and only if you know how they are used by the operating system. If you don't know what a service does, don't disable it. You can learn the specific purpose of a service by using the Services utility on the Administrative Tools menu. Select the service to view its description on the Extended tab, or double-click the service to read its description on the General tab of the related properties dialog box.

4. Click OK. You need to reboot the system to check the changes, so if you are prompted to restart the system, click Yes. Otherwise, reboot the system manually.
5. Repeat this procedure as necessary to pinpoint the service causing the system problems. If you can't identify a service as the cause of the problem, the trouble might be caused by a Windows component, a startup application, or a device driver.

Managing System Properties

You use the System Properties dialog box to manage system properties. The following sections examine key areas of the operating system that can be configured using the System Properties dialog box.

The Computer Name Tab

The computer's network identification can be displayed and modified on the Computer Name tab of the System Properties dialog box, shown in Figure 6-17. As the figure shows, the Computer Name tab displays the full computer name of the system and the domain or group membership. The full computer name is essentially the Domain Name System (DNS) name of the computer, which also identifies the computer's place within an Active Directory hierarchy.

To access the Computer Name tab of the System Properties dialog box, follow these steps:

1. In Control Panel, click System And Security, and then click System.
2. In the System console, click the Change Settings link. Alternatively, click Advanced System Settings in the left pane, and then click the Computer Name tab.

The options on the Computer Name tab enable you to do the following:

- **Join a computer to a domain** Click Network ID to start the Join A Domain Or Workgroup wizard, which guides you through modifying network access information for the computer.
- **Change a computer's name** Click Change to change the computer's name and the domain or group associated with the computer.

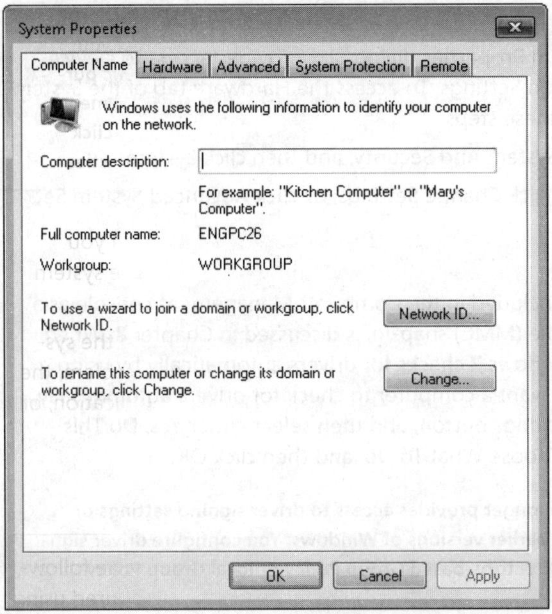

FIGURE 6-17 Use the Computer Name tab to display and configure system identification.

REAL WORLD **Before you try to join a computer to a domain, be sure that the IP address configuration, including the DNS settings, are correct for the network to which the computer is connected. For client computers to use the DNS, the computer must have an appropriate computer name and a properly configured primary DNS suffix. Rather than using names that are cute or arbitrary, you should decide on a naming scheme that is meaningful to both users and administrators. In DNS, the computer's name serves as its host name, and the primary DNS suffix determines the domain to which it is assigned for name resolution purposes. Any unqualified host names that are used on a computer are resolved using the primary DNS suffix. For example, if you are logged on to a computer with a primary DNS suffix of tech.cpandl.com and you ping CorpSvr28 from a command prompt, the computer directs the query to corpsvr28.tech.cpandl.com.**

By default, the primary DNS suffix is the domain in which the computer is a member. You can change a computer's primary DNS suffix if necessary. For example, if a computer's primary DNS suffix is seattle.tech.cpandl.com, you might want the computer to use the primary DNS suffix of cpandl.com to simplify name resolution in this large DNS hierarchy. To change a computer's primary DNS suffix, click Change on the Computer Name tab, and then click More. Enter the primary DNS suffix you want to use in the text box provided, and then close all open dialog boxes by clicking OK three times.

The Hardware Tab

The Hardware tab in the System Properties dialog box provides access to Device Manager and Device Installation Settings. To access the Hardware tab of the System Properties dialog box, follow these steps:

1. In Control Panel, click System And Security, and then click System.
2. In the System console, click Change Settings, or click Advanced System Settings in the left pane.
3. Click the Hardware tab.

The Device Manager, also included in the Computer Management console as a Microsoft Management Console (MMC) snap-in, is discussed in Chapter 8. When you connect a new device, Windows 7 checks for drivers automatically by using Windows Update. If you don't want a computer to check for drivers automatically, click the Device Installation Settings button, and then select either Yes, Do This Automatically or No, Let Me Choose What To Do, and then click OK.

> ***NOTE*** **The Hardware tab no longer provides access to driver signing settings or hardware profiles, as it did in earlier versions of Windows. You configure driver signing settings through Active Directory–based Group Policy or local Group Policy.**

The Advanced Tab

The Advanced tab in the System Properties dialog box provides access to controls for many of the key features of the Windows operating system, including application performance, virtual memory usage, user profile, environment variables, and startup and recovery.

> ***NOTE*** **User profiles contain global user settings and configuration information. They are created the first time a user logs on to a local computer or domain and are different for local and domain accounts. A user's profile maintains the desktop environment so that it is the same each time the user logs on. You'll find an extensive discussion on user profiles in Chapter 11, "Managing Existing User and Group Accounts," in *Windows Server 2008 Administrator's Pocket Consultant,* Second Edition (Microsoft Press, 2010).**

Setting Windows Performance

Many graphics enhancements have been added to the Windows 7 interface. These enhancements include many visual effects for menus, toolbars, windows, and the taskbar. You can configure Windows performance by completing the following steps:

1. In Control Panel, click System And Security, and then click System.
2. In the System console, click Change Settings, or click Advanced System Settings in the left pane.

3. To display the Performance Options dialog box, click the Advanced tab in the System Properties dialog box, and then click Settings in the Performance panel.
4. The Visual Effects tab is selected by default. You have the following options for controlling visual effects:
   - **Let Windows Choose What's Best For My Computer** Enables the operating system to choose the performance options based on the hardware configuration. For a newer computer, the effect of selecting this option will probably be identical to using the Adjust For Best Appearance option. The key distinction, however, is that this option is chosen by Windows based on the available hardware and its performance capabilities.
   - **Adjust For Best Appearance** When you optimize Windows for best appearance, you enable all visual effects for all graphical interfaces. Menus and the taskbar use transitions and shadows. Screen fonts have smooth edges. List boxes have smooth scrolling. Folders use Web views, and more.
   - **Adjust For Best Performance** When you optimize Windows for best performance, you turn off the resource-intensive visual effects, such as slide transitions and smooth edges for fonts, while maintaining a basic set of visual effects.
   - **Custom** You can customize the visual effects by selecting or clearing the visual effects options in the Performance Options dialog box. If you clear all options, Windows does not use visual effects.
5. When you have finished changing visual effects, click Apply. Click OK twice to close the open dialog boxes.

Setting Application Performance

Application performance is related to processor-scheduling caching options that you set for the Windows 7 system. Processor scheduling determines the responsiveness of applications that are running interactively (as opposed to background applications that might be running on the system as services). You control application performance by completing the following steps:

1. In Control Panel, click System And Security, and then click System.
2. In the System console, click Change Settings, or click Advanced System Settings in the left pane.
3. To display the Performance Options dialog box, click the Advanced tab in the System Properties dialog box, and then click Settings in the Performance panel.
4. The Performance Options dialog box has several tabs. Click the Advanced tab.

5. In the Processor Scheduling panel, you have the following options:
   - **Programs** To give the active application the best response time and the greatest share of available resources, select Programs. Generally, you'll want to use this option for all Windows 7 workstations.
   - **Background Services** To give background applications a better response time than the active application, select Background Services. Generally, you'll want to use this option for Windows 7 computers running as servers (meaning they have serverlike roles and are not being used as Windows 7 workstations). For example, a Windows 7 computer might be the print server for a department.
6. Click OK.

Configuring Virtual Memory

Virtual memory enables you to use disk space to extend the amount of available RAM on a system by writing RAM to disks through a process called *paging.* With paging, a set amount of RAM, such as 4,096 MB, is written to the disk as a paging file, where it can be accessed from the disk when needed in place of physical RAM.

An initial paging file is created automatically for the drive containing the operating system. By default, other drives don't have paging files, so you must create these paging files if you want them. When you create a paging file, you set an initial size and a maximum size. Paging files are written to the volume as a file named Pagefile.sys.

REAL WORLD **Windows 7 does a much better job than its predecessors of automatically managing virtual memory. Typically, Windows 7 allocates virtual memory in an amount at least as large as the total physical memory installed on the computer. This helps to ensure that paging files don't become fragmented, which can result in poor system performance. If you want to manually manage virtual memory, you can reduce fragmentation by setting an initial page file size that is at least as large as the total physical memory. For computers with 4 GB or less of RAM, you should set the maximum size to at least twice the total physical memory. For computers with more than 4 GB of RAM, you should set the maximum size to at least 1.5 times total physical memory. This can help ensure that the paging file is consistent and can be written to contiguous file blocks (if possible, given the amount of space on the volume).**

You can manually configure virtual memory by completing the following steps:

1. In Control Panel, click System And Security, and then click System.
2. In the System console, click Change Settings, or click Advanced System Settings in the left pane.
3. Click the Advanced tab in the System Properties dialog box.
4. Click Settings in the Performance section to display the Performance Options dialog box.

5. Click the Advanced tab, and then click Change to display the Virtual Memory dialog box, shown in Figure 6-18. The following information is provided:
   - **Drive [Volume Label] and Paging File Size (MB)** Shows how virtual memory is currently configured on the system. Each volume is listed with its associated paging file (if any). The paging file range shows the initial and maximum size values set for the paging file.
   - **Paging File Size For Each Drive** Provides information on the currently selected drive and enables you to set its paging file size. Space Available indicates how much space is available on the drive.
   - **Total Paging File Size For All Drives** Provides a recommended size for virtual RAM on the system and tells you the amount currently allocated. If this is the first time you're configuring virtual RAM, note that the recommended amount has already been given to the system drive (in most instances) and that this is indicated by the selection of the System Managed Size option.

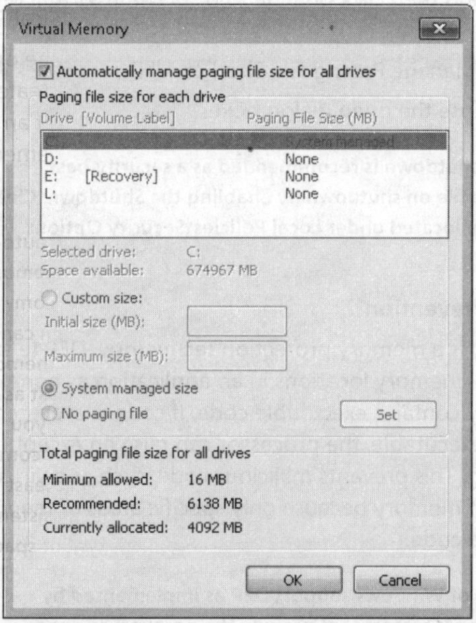

FIGURE 6-18 Virtual memory extends the amount of physical memory (RAM) on a system.

6. By default, Windows 7 manages the paging file size for all drives. If you want to manually configure virtual memory, clear the Automatically Manage Paging File Size For All Drives check box.
7. In the Drive list box, select the volume you want to work with.
8. Select Custom Size, and then enter an initial size and a maximum size.

9. Click Set to save the changes.
10. Repeat steps 7 through 9 for each volume you want to configure.
11. Click OK, and if prompted to overwrite an existing Pagefile.sys file, click Yes.
12. If you updated the settings for a paging file that is currently in use, you'll see a prompt explaining that you need to restart the system for the changes to take effect. Click OK.
13. Click OK twice to close the open dialog boxes. When you close the System utility, you'll see a prompt stating that the changes will not be applied until you restart your computer.

You can have Windows 7 automatically manage virtual memory by following these steps:

1. Click the Advanced tab in the System Properties dialog box.
2. Click Settings in the Performance section to display the Performance Options dialog box.
3. Click the Advanced tab, and then click Change to display the Virtual Memory dialog box.
4. Select the Automatically Manage Paging File Size For All Drives check box.
5. Click OK three times to close the open dialog boxes.

TIP **Clearing the page file on shutdown is recommended as a security best practice. You can clear the page file on shutdown by enabling the Shutdown: Clear Virtual Memory Pagefile option, located under Local Policies\Security Options.**

Configuring Data Execution Prevention

Data Execution Prevention (DEP) is a memory protection technology. DEP tells the computer's processor to mark all memory locations in an application as nonexecutable unless the location explicitly contains executable code. If code is executed from a memory page marked as nonexecutable, the processor can raise an exception and prevent the code from executing. This prevents malicious code, such as a virus, from inserting itself into most areas of memory because only specific areas of memory are marked as having executable code.

NOTE **Thirty-two-bit versions of Windows support DEP as implemented by Advanced Micro Devices (AMD) processors that provide the no-execute page-protection (NX) processor feature. Such processors support the related instructions and must be running in Physical Address Extension (PAE) mode to support large memory configurations. Sixty-four-bit versions of Windows also support the NX processor feature but do not need to use PAE to support large memory configurations.**

To be compatible with DEP, applications must be able to explicitly mark memory with the Execute permission. Applications that cannot do this will not be compatible with the NX processor feature. If you are experiencing memory-related problems running applications, you should determine which applications are having problems and configure them as exceptions rather than completely disabling execution protection. In this way, you still get the benefits of memory protection and can selectively disable memory protection for programs that aren't running properly with the NX processor feature.

Execution protection is applied to both user-mode and kernel-mode programs. A user-mode execution protection exception results in a STATUS_ACCESS_VIOLATION exception. In most processes, this exception will be an unhandled exception and will result in the termination of the process. This is the behavior you want because most programs violating these rules, such as a virus or worm, will be malicious in nature.

Execution protection for kernel-mode device drivers, unlike protection for applications, cannot be selectively disabled or enabled. Furthermore, on compliant 32-bit systems, execution protection is applied by default to the memory stack. On compliant 64-bit systems, execution protection is applied by default to the memory stack, the paged pool, and the session pool. A kernel-mode execution protection access violation for a device driver results in an ATTEMPTED_EXECUTE_OF_NOEXECUTE_MEMORY exception.

You can determine whether a computer supports DEP by using the System utility. If a computer supports DEP, you can also configure it by completing the following steps:

1. In Control Panel, click System And Security, and then click System.
2. In the System console, click Change Settings, or click Advanced System Settings in the left pane.
3. Click the Advanced tab in the System Properties dialog box, and then in the Performance panel, click Settings to display the Performance Options dialog box.
4. Click the Data Execution Prevention tab. The text at the bottom of this tab specifies whether the computer supports execution protection.
5. If a computer supports execution protection and is configured appropriately, you can configure DEP by using the following options:
   - **Turn On DEP For Essential Windows Programs And Services Only** Enables DEP only for operating system services, programs, and components. This is the default setting and is recommended for computers that support execution protection and are configured appropriately.
   - **Turn On DEP For All Programs Except Those I Select** Configures DEP and allows for exceptions. Select this option, and then click Add to specify programs that should run without execution protection. In this way, execution protection will work for all programs except those you have listed.
6. Click OK.

Configuring System and User Environment Variables

System and user environment variables are configured by means of the Environment Variables dialog box, shown in Figure 6-19. To access this dialog box, click the Advanced tab in the System Properties dialog box, and then click the Environment Variables button.

NOTE **When you create or modify system environment variables, the changes take effect when you restart the computer. When you create or modify user environment variables, the changes take effect the next time the user logs on to the system.**

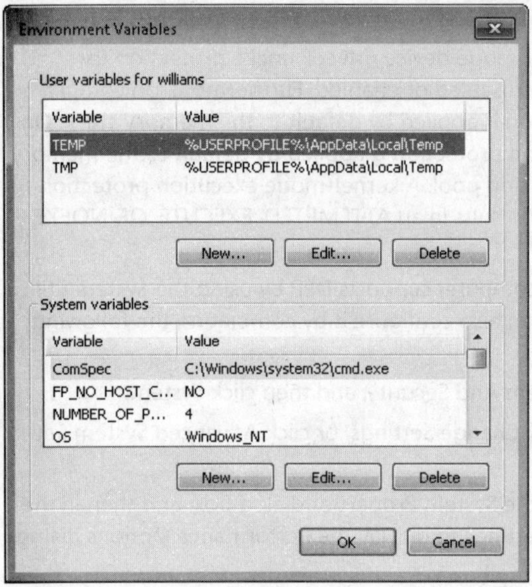

FIGURE 6-19 The Environment Variables dialog box lets you configure system and user environment variables.

CREATING AN ENVIRONMENT VARIABLE

You can create an environment variable by completing the following steps:

1. Click New under User Variables or under System Variables, whichever is appropriate. This opens the New User Variable dialog box or the New System Variable dialog box, respectively.
2. In the Variable Name field, type the variable name. In the Variable Value field, type the variable value. Click OK.

REAL WORLD **The command path for executables is managed through the PATH variable. You can edit this variable to update the command path as discussed in the section "Managing the Command Path" in Chapter 9.**

You can access Group Policy and use a preference item to create an environment variable on computers throughout a domain by completing the following steps:

1. Open a Group Policy object (GPO) for editing in the Group Policy Management Editor. To configure preferences for computers, expand Computer Configuration\Preferences\Windows Settings, and then select Environment. To configure preferences for users, expand User Configuration\Preferences\Windows Settings, and then select Environment.
2. Right-click the Environment node, point to New, and then select Environment Variable. This opens the New Environment Properties dialog box.
3. From the Action list, select Create. Next, select User Variable to create a user variable or System Variable to create a system variable.
4. In the Name field, type the variable name. In the Value field, type the variable value.
5. Use the options on the Common tab to control how the preference is applied. In most cases, you'll want to create the new variable only once. If so, select Apply Once And Do Not Reapply.
6. Click OK. The next time policy is refreshed, the preference item will be applied as appropriate for the Group Policy object in which you defined the preference item.

EDITING AN ENVIRONMENT VARIABLE

You can edit an environment variable by completing the following steps:

1. Select the variable in the User Variables or System Variables list box.
2. Click Edit under User Variables or under System Variables, whichever is appropriate. The Edit User Variable dialog box or the Edit System Variable dialog box opens.
3. Type a new value in the Variable Value field, and then click OK.

You can access Group Policy and use a preference item to update an environment variable on computers throughout a domain by completing the following steps:

1. Open a Group Policy object (GPO) for editing in the Group Policy Management Editor. To edit preferences for computers, expand Computer Configuration\Preferences\Windows Settings, and then select Environment. To edit preferences for users, expand User Configuration\Preferences\Windows Settings, and then select Environment.
2. Right-click the Environment node, point to New, and then select Environment Variable. This opens the New Environment Properties dialog box.
3. From the Action list, select Update to update the variable, or select Replace to delete and then re-create the variable. Next, select User Variable to create a user variable or System Variable to create a system variable.

4. In the Name field, type the name of the variable to update. In the Value field, type the variable value.
5. Use the options on the Common tab to control how the preference is applied. In most cases, you'll want to create the new variable only once. If so, select Apply Once And Do Not Reapply.
6. Click OK. The next time policy is refreshed, the preference item will be applied as appropriate for the GPO in which you defined the preference item.

DELETING AN ENVIRONMENT VARIABLE

You can delete an environment variable by selecting it and clicking Delete. To delete an environment variable on computers throughout a domain using Group Policy, complete the following steps:

1. Open a Group Policy object (GPO) for editing in the Group Policy Management Editor. To configure preferences for computers, expand Computer Configuration\Preferences\Windows Settings, and then select Environment. To configure preferences for users, expand User Configuration\Preferences\Windows Settings, and then select Environment.
2. Do one of the following:
   - If a preference item already exists for the variable, double-click the variable name to open the related Properties dialog box. Select Delete in the Action list. On the Common tab, set the appropriate options, such as Apply Once And Do Not Reapply, and then click OK.
   - If a preference item doesn't already exist for the variable, you need to create one using the techniques discussed previously. Be sure to select Delete in the Action list and select the appropriate options on the Common tab.

Configuring System Startup and Recovery

System startup and recovery properties are configured by means of the Startup And Recovery dialog box, shown in Figure 6-20. To open this dialog box, click the Advanced tab in the System Properties dialog box and then click the Settings button in the Startup And Recovery panel.

SETTING STARTUP OPTIONS

The System Startup area of the Startup And Recovery dialog box controls system startup. In a computer with multiple bootable operating systems, to set the default operating system, select one of the operating systems listed under Default Operating System. The startup options change the configuration settings used by the Windows Boot Manager.

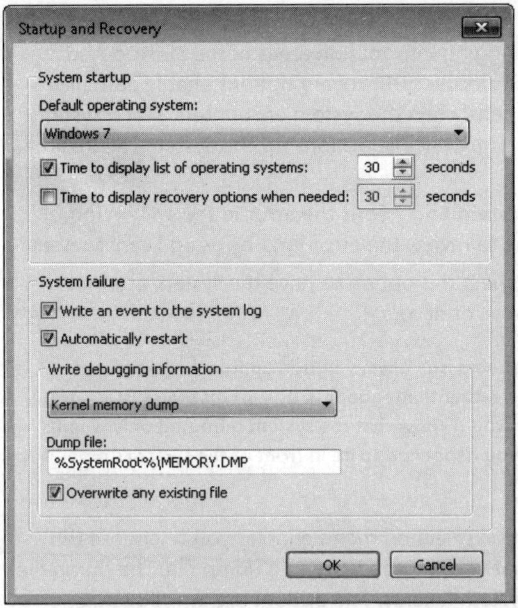

FIGURE 6-20 The Startup And Recovery dialog box lets you configure system startup and recovery procedures.

At startup of a computer with multiple bootable operating systems, Windows 7 displays the startup configuration menu for 30 seconds by default. You can change this by taking either of the following actions:

- Boot immediately to the default operating system by clearing the Time To Display List Of Operating Systems check box.
- Display the available options for a specific amount of time by ensuring that the Time To Display List Of Operating Systems check box is selected, and then setting a time delay in seconds.

Generally, on most systems you'll want to use a value of 3 to 5 seconds. This period is long enough for a user to make a selection, yet short enough to expedite the system startup process.

When the system is in a recovery mode and booting, a list of recovery options might be displayed. As you can with the standard startup options, you can configure recovery startup options in one of two ways. You can set the computer to boot immediately using the default recovery option by clearing the Time To Display Recovery Options When Needed check box, or you can display the available options for a specific amount of time by selecting Time To Display Recovery Options When Needed and then setting a time delay in seconds.

SETTING RECOVERY OPTIONS

The System Failure and Write Debugging Information areas of the Startup And Recovery dialog box control system recovery. Recovery options enable administrators to control precisely what happens when the system encounters a fatal system error (also known as a Stop error). The available options for the System Failure area are as follows:

- **Write An Event To The System Log** Logs the error in the system log, which allows administrators to review the error later by using Event Viewer.
- **Automatically Restart** Select this option to have the system attempt to reboot when a fatal system error occurs.

NOTE **Configuring automatic reboots isn't always a good approach. Sometimes you might want the system to halt rather than reboot to ensure that the system gets proper attention. Otherwise, you would know that the system rebooted only when you viewed the system logs or if you happened to be in front of the system's monitor when it rebooted.**

The Write Debugging Information selection menu enables you to choose the type of debugging information that you want to write to a dump file. The dump file can in turn be used to diagnose system failures. The options are as follows:

- **None** Use this option if you don't want to write debugging information.
- **Small Memory Dump** Use this option to dump the physical memory segment in which the error occurred. This dump is 256 kilobytes (KB) in size.
- **Kernel Memory Dump** Use this option to dump the physical memory area being used by the Windows kernel. The size of the dump file depends on the size of the Windows kernel.

If you elect to write a dump file, you must also specify a location for it. The default dump locations are %SystemRoot%\Minidump for small memory dumps and %SystemRoot%\Memory.dmp for all other memory dumps. You'll usually want to select Overwrite Any Existing File as well. This option ensures that any existing dump files are overwritten if a new Stop error occurs.

BEST PRACTICES **The dump file can be created only if the system is properly configured. The system drive must have a sufficiently large memory-paging file (as set for virtual memory on the Advanced tab), and the drive where the dump file is written must have sufficient free space as well. With a kernel-only dump, you must have 35 to 50 percent of the amount of RAM available for the dump file. For example, my system has 4,096 MB of RAM, so 2,048 MB of free space must be available to correctly create a kernel-only dump of debugging information.**

The System Protection Tab

The System Protection tab in the System Properties dialog box, shown in Figure 6-21, provides options for managing the configuration of System Restore. In Windows 7, System Restore includes Previous Versions as a subcomponent. The sections that follow discuss techniques for working with and configuring System Restore. Using restore points to recover a computer is discussed in Chapter 17.

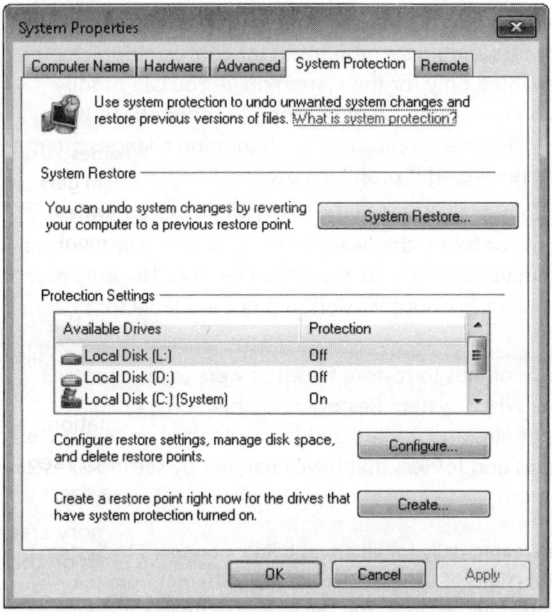

FIGURE 6-21 System Restore manages restore points on a per-drive basis.

Working with System Restore and Previous Versions

With System Restore enabled, a computer creates periodic snapshots of the system configuration, previous versions of files, or both. These snapshots are called *restore points*. System settings tracked include Windows settings and lists of programs that have been installed. If the computer has problems starting or isn't working properly because of a system configuration change, you can use a restore point to restore the system configuration to the point at which the snapshot was made. For example, suppose your system is working fine and then you install a new service pack release for Microsoft Office. Afterward, the computer generates errors and Office applications won't run. You try to uninstall the update, but that doesn't work, so you decide to run System Restore. Using System Restore, you can restore the system by using a snapshot taken prior to the update.

NOTE **System Restore can provide several different types of restore points. One type, System Checkpoint, is scheduled by the operating system and occurs at regular intervals. Another type of snapshot, Installation Restore Point, is created automatically based on events that are triggered by the operating system when you install applications. Other snapshots, known as Manual Restore Points, are created by users. You should recommend that users create Manual Restore Points prior to performing an operation that might cause problems on the system.**

System Restore manages restore points on a per-drive basis. Each drive with critical applications and system files should be monitored for configuration changes. By default, System Restore is enabled only for the system drive. You can modify the System Restore configuration by turning on monitoring of other drives. If a drive isn't configured for System Restore monitoring, configuration changes are not tracked, and the disk cannot be recovered if problems occur.

In Windows 7, previous versions of files and folders are created automatically as part of a restore point. Any file or folder that was modified since the last restore point was created is saved and made available as a previous version. The only exceptions are for system files and folders. Previous versions are not available for system folders, such as C:\Windows.

You can use previous versions of files to restore files that were inadvertently modified, deleted, or damaged. When System Restore is enabled on a drive, Windows 7 makes copies daily of files and folders that have changed on that drive. You can also create copies of files and folders that have changed by setting a restore point on the System Protection tab.

NOTE **Protection points are created daily for all drives being monitored by System Restore. However, only those versions of files that are actually different from the current version are stored as previous versions. You can enable or disable previous versions on a per-drive basis by enabling or disabling System Restore on that drive. Previous versions are saved as part of a volume's automatically or manually created protection points.**

Configuring System Restore

You control how System Restore works by using the System Restore tab of the System Properties dialog box. The system process responsible for monitoring configuration and application changes is the System Restore Service. This service is configured for automatic startup and runs under the LocalSystem account. System Restore won't work properly if this service isn't running or configured appropriately.

System Restore saves system checkpoint information for all monitored drives and requires at least 300 MB of disk space on the system volume to save restore points. System Restore reserves additional space for restore points as necessary, up to 100 percent of the total disk capacity, but this additional space is always available for user and application storage. System Restore frees up additional space for you as necessary. If System Restore runs out of available space, the operating system overwrites previously created restore points.

You can configure the amount of disk space used by System Restore. By default, System Restore reserves at least 1 percent of the total disk capacity for saving restore points. For example, on a hard disk with a total capacity of 930 GB, System Restore would reserve 9.3 GB of disk space by default.

Complete the following steps to configure System Restore for each drive:

1. In Control Panel, click System And Security, and then click System.
2. In the System console, click System Protection in the left pane.
3. To configure System Restore for a volume, select the volume in the Protection Settings list, and then click Configure. This displays the System Protection For dialog box, shown in Figure 6-22.

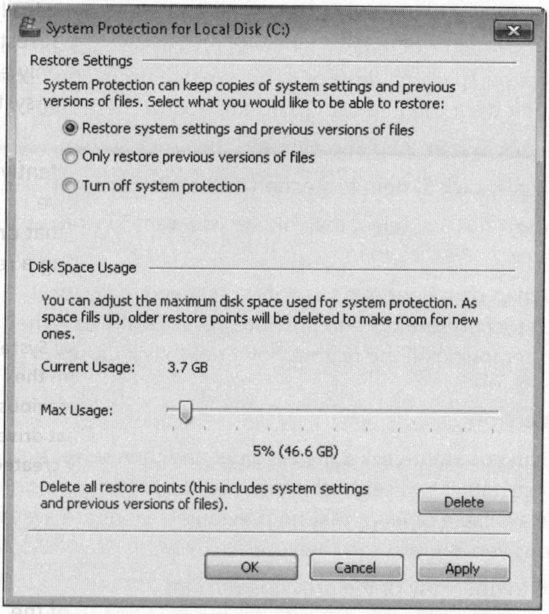

FIGURE 6-22 Configure System Restore on a per-drive basis.

4. Choose one of the following options:
   - **Restore System Settings And Previous Versions Of Files** Choose this option to keep copies of system settings and previous versions of files. This option is recommended for the system volume to ensure that you can restore the computer and recover previous versions of important data files.
   - **Only Restore Previous Versions Of Files** Choose this option to keep previous versions of files but not keep copies of system settings. This

option is recommended for nonsystem volumes so that you can recover previous versions of important data files.

- **Turn Off System Protection** Choose this option to turn off System Restore. This option is not recommended because you will not be able to restore the computer or recover previous versions of files.

5. If you've enabled system protection, you can use the Disk Space Usage slider to adjust the maximum disk space that System Restore can use. If the maximum size is reached, System Restore deletes older restore points to make room for new ones.
6. Click OK. (If you've turned off system protection, Windows removes all saved system settings and previous versions of files, and you must confirm that you want to do this by clicking Yes. When Windows finishes removing all the restore point data, click Close.)

If you are using System Restore to protect a computer and are absolutely certain the system is in a stable state, you can remove all saved system settings and previous versions of files to recover space on disks or to ensure that users don't apply a restore point that you don't want them to use. To do this, follow these steps:

1. In Control Panel, click System And Security, and then click System.
2. In the System console, click System Protection in the left pane.
3. In the Protection Settings list, select the volume you want to work with, and then click Configure.
4. Click Delete, and then click Continue to confirm that you really want to delete all saved system settings and previous versions of files. When Windows finishes removing all the restore point data, click Close.

Restoring a Previous Version

In Windows Explorer, when you right-click a file or folder and then select Properties, you see a Previous Versions tab. If you select this tab, you see previous versions of the file or folder that are available or learn that no previous versions are available. After you select a previous version, you can then use:

- The Open button to open any of the previous versions.
- The Copy button to create a copy of a previous version.
- The Restore button to revert the file or folder to a selected previous version.

There are several possible reasons you might not see a previous version of a file on your computer:

- System Restore might not be enabled on the volume. If System Restore isn't enabled on a volume, Windows 7 doesn't create previous versions, and therefore files don't have any previous versions.
- The file might be an offline file. Offline files are copies of network files. Client computers do not create previous versions of offline files. Previous versions may be available on the server where the file is stored, however.

- The file might be a system file. Previous Versions does not create copies of system files. Changes made to system files are tracked with restore points, and you must recover the computer to the restore point to go back to a previous state.
- The folder in which the file was stored has been deleted. In this case, you must open the properties for the folder that contained the folder that was deleted. Use this folder's Previous Versions tab to restore the folder, and then access the folder to recover the previous version of the file you are looking for.
- No restore point has been created since the file was created and saved.

The Remote Tab

The Remote tab in the System Properties dialog box controls Remote Assistance invitations and Remote Desktop connections. These options are discussed in the section "Managing Remote Access to Workstations" in Chapter 5.

Configuring Power Management Settings

Power management settings control the behavior of a computer in different power use situations, such as when it is plugged in or running on a battery. Although all computers should be configured with power management settings to save energy, power management settings on laptops help to balance performance against energy usage. In some cases, you'll want to reduce laptop responsiveness and overall performance to increase the battery life, enabling the laptop user to run the laptop on battery for longer periods of time. In other cases, you might want to ensure moderate performance and a moderate battery life, or you might want to ensure maximum performance regardless of how this impacts battery life.

The core aspects of power management are managed using power plans. Like power schemes in Windows XP and earlier versions of Windows, power plans are collections of power management settings that control power usage and consumption. A computer can have multiple power plans, but only one can be active at any given time. In addition to power plans, most computers have preset behaviors for when the power button is pressed and for when the sleep button is pressed, and laptops have a default action for when you close the laptop's lid. Typically, closing a laptop's lid puts it into sleep mode, pressing and holding the power button shuts down a computer, and pressing the sleep button puts a computer into sleep mode. Through systemwide settings for power options, you can customize the power button and password-protection-on-wakeup behavior to meet the needs of individual users or groups of users.

Managing Power Options from the Command Line

Windows 7 includes the Power Configuration (Powercfg.exe) utility for managing power options from the command line. You can view a list of parameters for this utility by typing **powercfg /?** at a command prompt. The parameters you'll work with most often include:

- **–a** Lists the available sleep states on the computer and the reasons why a particular sleep state is not supported.
- **–d [guid]** Deletes the power plan specified by the globally unique identifier (GUID).
- **–devicequery all_devices_verbose** Lists detailed power support information for all devices on the computer. Be sure to redirect the output to a file because this list is very long and detailed.
- **–energy** Checks the system for common configuration, device, and battery problems and then generates an HTML report in the current working directory.
- **–h** Toggles the hibernate feature on or off.
- **–l** Lists the power plans configured on a computer by name and GUID.
- **–q [guid]** Lists the contents of the power plan specified by the GUID. If you don't provide a GUID, the contents of the active power plan are listed.
- **–requests** Displays all power requests made by device drivers. If there are pending requests for the display, these requests would prevent the computer from automatically powering off the displays. If there are pending requests for any device including the display, these requests would prevent the computer from automatically entering a low-power sleep state.
- **–s [guid]** Makes the power plan specified by the GUID the active power plan.
- **–x [setting] [value]** Sets the specified value for the specified setting in the active power plan.

NOTE **By default, Windows 7 computers use hybrid sleep instead of hibernate. Hibernate should not be configured without first determining compatibility.**

The following is a sample listing returned by typing **powercfg –l** at a command prompt:

```
Existing Power Schemes (* Active)
-----------------------------------
Power Scheme GUID: 381b4222-f694-41f0-9685-ff5bb260df2e (Balanced)
Power Scheme GUID: 8c5e7fda-e8bf-4a96-9a85-a6e23a8c635c (High performance)
Power Scheme GUID: a1841308-3541-4fab-bc81-f71556f20b4a (Power saver)
Power Scheme GUID: c1d97820-3148-42a9-a587-75d618a9bb2b (Graphics Dept) *
```

The active plan is marked with an asterisk. From this listing, you can determine that this computer has four power plans and the active power plan is the Graphics Dept plan.

If you want to configure power plans or modify power settings using Powercfg, you need to do so by using an elevated command prompt. When a parameter requires a GUID, the easiest way to obtain this value is to type **powercfg –l** at an elevated command prompt, and then copy the value for the appropriate power plan. For example, if you want to make the Balanced plan the default plan for the computer in the previous example, you would type the following at an elevated command prompt:

```
powercfg -s 381b4222-f694-41f0-9685-ff5bb260df2e
```

You determine the power modes a computer supports by typing **powercfg –a** at a command prompt. Powercfg will list exactly what modes are and aren't supported, such as:

```
The following sleep states are available on this system: Standby (S1 S3)
Hibernate Hybrid Sleep
The following sleep states are not available on this system: Standby (S2)
The system firmware does not support this standby state.
```

If a computer has problems entering sleep or hibernate mode, you can use powercfg –a to possibly determine what is causing the problem. If the firmware doesn't support a particular mode, you may in some (limited) cases be able to update the firmware to gain support for a particular mode. If a device that doesn't support a particular mode is causing a problem, you may be able to remove the device and replace it with a compliant device.

Any time you want to evaluate a computer's power configuration and device compatibility, you can generate a Power Efficiency Diagnostics report by entering **powercfg –energy** at a command prompt. When you run powercfg –energy, the report is generated as an HTML document called Energy-Report.html. In the report you'll see the results of power management compliance for devices. Any device that doesn't support power management appropriately will be listed along with the error details. For example, if a USB device doesn't properly enter the Suspend state, you'll see the detailed information about the errors encountered and the device configuration. If a power management capability has been disabled due to a compatibility issue, you'll see this. For example, if the PCI Express Active-State Power Management feature isn't supported on the hardware and the feature has been disabled because of this, you'll see this listed in the report. Warnings and additional information about devices and compatibility are provided as well, including details on supported sleep states and processor power management capabilities.

REAL WORLD **For laptops, important information is provided on battery charging and battery life. If a battery is nearing or at the end of its useful life, you'll be able to tell this because the battery life is limited and the battery details will show the battery isn't holding a charge like it should. You'll then know you need to replace the laptop's battery.**

To dig even deeper into power management issues, you can get comprehensive power support details for every device on the computer by entering the following command:

```
powercfg -devicequery all_devices_verbose > power.txt
```

where Power.txt is the name of the file in the current working directory in which the power information will be saved.

When you've configured Windows PowerShell for remoting, you can easily execute Powercfg on multiple remote computers. To do this, enter the name of each remote computer to check on a separate line in a file called Computers.txt, and then save this file. Then open an elevated administrator PowerShell prompt and enter the following commands:

```
$comp = get-content c:\computers.txt
$s = new-pssession -computername $comp
invoke-command -session $s { powercfg.exe -energy }
```

Here, C:\Computers.txt is the path to the Computers.txt file. Update this path as appropriate for where you saved the file. On each computer, an Energy-Report.html file will be created in the default directory for the user account used to access the computer. If you would rather not have to retrieve the HTML document from each computer, you can write the report to a share and base the report name on the computer name as shown in the following example:

```
$comp = get-content c:\computers.txt
$s = new-pssession -computername $comp
invoke-command -session $s { powercfg.exe -energy -output
"\\fileserver46\data\$env:computername.html"}
```

Here, you write the report to the \\fileserver46\data share and name the file using the value of the ComputerName environment variable. Note that when you work with PowerShell and are referencing commands with executables, you must specify the .exe file extension with the program name.

Working with Power Plans

On laptops and Tablet PCs, the notification area of the taskbar includes a Power icon. Moving the mouse pointer over this icon shows the battery state and the power plan you are using. You can right-click the Power icon to display a shortcut menu with options for quickly accessing the Power Options utility. Out of the box, Windows 7 has three preferred power plans:

- **Balanced** A power usage plan that balances energy consumption and system performance. The processor speeds up when more resources are used and slows down when less are needed. This is the default power plan. Use this plan for users who work with a wide variety of applications, including those that are moderately graphics intensive, such as Microsoft Office PowerPoint, and those that are not graphics intensive, such as Microsoft Office Word and Microsoft Office Outlook.

- **High Performance** A high-power usage plan that optimizes the computer for performance at a direct cost to battery life. This plan ensures that you always have enough power for using graphics-intensive programs or playing multimedia games. Use this plan when performance is essential and users work primarily with graphics-intensive applications or applications that perform complex arithmetic calculations.
- **Power Saver** A low-power usage plan designed to reduce power consumption. This plan slows down the processor to maximize the battery life. Use this plan for users who work primarily with non–graphics intensive applications, such as Microsoft Word and Microsoft Outlook.

Power plan settings are divided into two general categories: basic and advanced. Basic power settings control when a computer turns off its display and when it turns itself off. By default, with the Balanced plan, Windows 7 turns off the display after 10 minutes of inactivity and puts the computer in sleep mode after 30 minutes of inactivity. With the Power Save plan, Windows 7 turns off the display after 5 minutes of inactivity and puts the computer in sleep mode after 15 minutes of inactivity. With the High Performance plan, Windows 7 turns off the display after 15 minutes of inactivity but never automatically puts the computer in sleep mode.

Advanced power settings determine precisely whether and when power management components on a computer are shut down and how those components are configured for performance. The advanced power settings available depend on the computer's configuration and include:

- **Battery\Reserve Battery Level** Determines the percentage of battery remaining that initiates reserve power mode. Typically, the default value is 7 percent, meaning the computer will enter reserve power mode when there is 7 percent of battery power remaining. Although you can set any percentage, a reserve level of 5 to 18 percent is often best.
- **Desktop Background Settings\Slide Show** Determines whether the slide show feature for the desktop background is available or paused. The default setting is Available. If you set this option to Paused, background slide shows on the desktop will be disabled.
- **Display\Turn Off Display After** Determines whether and when a computer's display is turned off to conserve power. Use a setting of Never to disable this feature. Use a specific value in minutes to determine how long the computer must be inactive before the display is turned off.
- **Hard Disk\Turn Off Hard Disk After** Determines whether and when a computer's hard disk is turned off to conserve power. Use a setting of Never to disable turning off the hard disk. Use a specific value in minutes to determine how long the computer must be inactive before the hard disk is turned off. Windows 7 provides a combo box for setting numeric values. Clicking and holding the up or down arrow enables you to rapidly scroll through

values. If you scroll down from 1, the next value is Never. You can also type a value. If you enter a value of 0, this is interpreted as Never.

- **Multimedia Settings\When Playing Video** Determines the power optimization mode used when playing video. If you set this option to Optimize Video Quality, the computer will use the best playback quality possible for video. If you set this option to Balanced, the computer will use a balanced approach, adjusting playback quality to some degree to save power. If you set this option to Optimize Power Savings, the computer will actively adjust the playback quality to save power.
- **Multimedia Settings\When Sharing Media** Determines what the computer does when a device or another computer plays media from the computer. If you set this option to Allow The Computer To Enter Away Mode, the computer will not enter sleep mode when sharing media with other devices or computers. If you set this option to Allow The Computer To Sleep, the computer can enter sleep mode after an appropriate period of inactivity regardless of whether media is being shared with other computers or devices. If you set this option to Prevent Idling To Sleep, the computer will enter sleep mode when sharing media with other devices or computers only if a user puts the computer in sleep mode.
- **PCI Express\Link State Power Management** Determines the power saving mode to use with Peripheral Component Interconnect (PCI) Express devices connected to the computer. You can set this option to Off, Moderate Power Savings, or Maximum Power Savings.
- **Power Buttons And Lid\Power Button Action** Specifies the action to take when someone pushes and holds the computer's power button. You can set this option to Do Nothing, Sleep, Hibernate, or Shutdown.
- **Power Buttons And Lid\Sleep Button Action** Sets the default action for the sleep button. Use this setting to override the computer's default action. You can set this option to Do Nothing, Sleep, or Hibernate. You cannot, however, use an option that is not supported by the computer.
- **Processor Power Management\Maximum Processor State** Sets a maximum or peak performance state for the computer's processor. To save power and reduce energy consumption, lower the permitted maximum performance state. But you lower the performance state at a direct cost to responsiveness and computational speed. Although reducing the maximum processing power to 50 percent or below can cause a significant reduction in performance and responsiveness, it can also provide a significant power savings.
- **Processor Power Management\Minimum Processor State** Sets a minimum performance state for the computer's processor. To save power and reduce energy consumption, lower the permitted minimum performance state—but you lower the performance state at a direct cost to

responsiveness and computational speed. For example, a value of 5 percent would lengthen the time required to respond to requests and process data while offering substantial power savings. A value of 50 percent helps to balance responsiveness and processing performance while offering a moderate power savings. A value of 100 percent would maximize responsiveness and processing performance while offering no power savings.

- **Processor Power Management\System Cooling Policy** Determines whether the operating system increases the fan speed before slowing the processor. If you set this option to Passive, this feature is limited, and the processor may run hotter than normal. If you set this option to Active, this feature is enabled to help cool the processor.
- ***PlanName*\Require A Password On Wakeup** Determines whether a password is required when a computer wakes from sleep. You can set this option to Yes or No. With domain computers, this option is set to Yes and can be controlled only through Group Policy.
- **Sleep\Allow Hybrid Sleep** Specifies whether the computer uses Windows 7 sleep mode rather than the sleep mode used in earlier versions of Windows. You can set this value to On or Off. Hybrid sleep mode puts the computer in a low-power consumption state until the user resumes using the computer. When running on battery, laptops and Tablet PCs continue to use battery power in the sleep state but at a very low rate. If the battery runs low on power while the computer is in the sleep state, the current working environment is saved to the hard disk, and then the computer is shut down completely. This final state is similar to the hibernate state used with Windows XP.
- **Sleep\Allow Wake Timers** Determines whether timed events should be allowed to wake the computer from a sleep state. If you set this option to Disable, timed events won't wake the computer. If you set this option to Enable, timed events can wake the computer.
- **Sleep\Hibernate After** Determines whether and when a computer hibernates to conserve power. When a computer goes into hibernation, a snapshot of the user workspace and the current operating environment is taken by writing the current memory to disk. When a user turns the computer back on, reading the memory from disk restores the user workspace and operating environment. In Windows 7, this setting isn't normally used because the standard configuration is to sleep after a period of inactivity. Use a setting of Never to disable this feature. Use a specific value in minutes to determine how long the computer must be inactive before the computer hibernates.
- **Sleep\Sleep After** Determines whether and when a computer enters a sleep state to conserve power. Use a setting of Never to disable this feature. Use a specific value in minutes to determine how long the computer must be inactive before the computer enters a sleep state.

- **USB Settings\USB Selective Suspend Setting** Determines whether the USB selective suspend feature is available. If you set this option to Disabled, selective suspend will not be used with USB devices. If you set this option to Enabled, selective suspend can be used with USB devices.
- **Wireless Adapter Settings\Power Saving Mode** Specifies the power saving mode to use with any wireless adapters connected to the computer. You can set this option to Maximum Performance, Low Power Saving, Medium Power Saving, or Maximum Power Saving.

As you can see, the advanced power settings control every facet of power management. The differences in the advanced settings are what really set the power plans apart from each other. For example, while the High Performance plan ensures performance by allowing the computer's processor to always run at 100 percent power consumption, the Power Saver and the Balanced plans reduce energy consumption by configuring the processor to use a minimum power consumption rate of 5 percent and a maximum rate of 100 percent.

When configuring power plans, it is important to allow components to turn off after periods of inactivity. Turning off components separately enables a computer to progressively go into sleep mode. When a computer is fully in sleep mode, all power-manageable components are switched off so that the computer uses less power. When the computer is brought out of sleep mode, the components, such as the monitor and hard disks, are turned back on, restoring the user workspace. You should configure sleep mode so that when a laptop is running on batteries, it goes into power conservation mode when the user is away from the laptop for a relatively short period of time, such as 20 or 30 minutes.

Because a computer can have multiple power plans, each plan can be optimized for the way a laptop is used at a particular time. You can configure multiple power plans for different situations. At home or in the office, laptops might need different power management configurations than they do when users are giving presentations. In one case, you might want to configure the laptop to quickly conserve energy when running on batteries. In another case, you might want to ensure that the laptop never turns off its hard disk or wireless adapters.

Selecting and Optimizing Power Plans

Although computers can have multiple power plans, only one plan can be active at any given time. To select or optimize a power plan, follow these steps:

1. In Control Panel, click System And Security, and then click Power Options.
2. As shown in Figure 6-23, you can specify the power plan to use by selecting it in the Preferred Plans list.

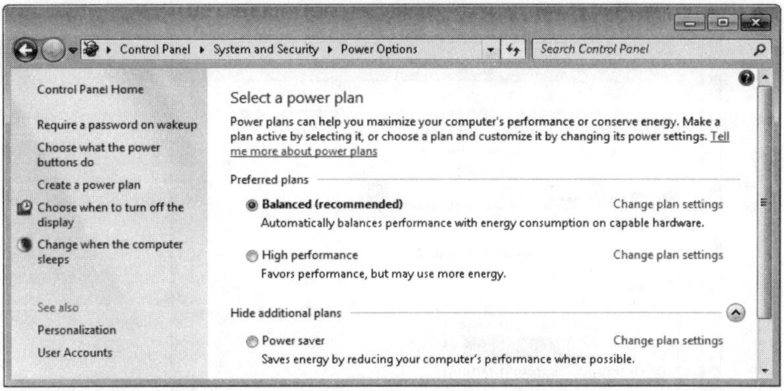

FIGURE 6-23 Choose a power plan.

3. Click Change Plan Settings for the plan you want to work with. This displays the Edit Plan Settings page, shown in Figure 6-24.

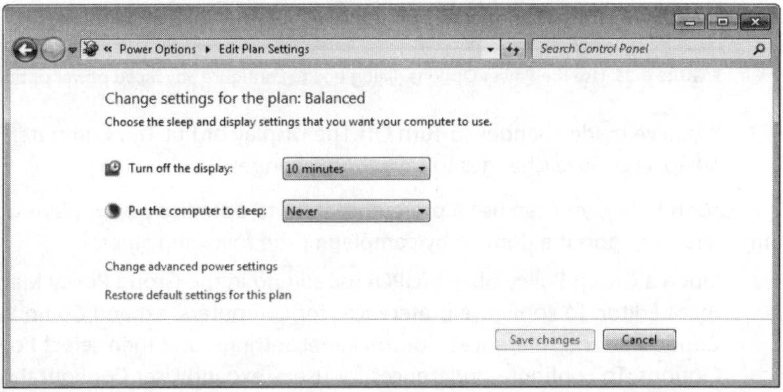

FIGURE 6-24 Configure power plan settings.

4. Use the Turn Off The Display list to specify whether or when the computer's display automatically turns off. Choose Never to disable this feature.
5. Use the Put The Computer To Sleep list to specify whether or when the computer automatically enters sleep mode. Choose Never to disable this feature.
6. If you want to configure advanced options, click Change Advanced Power Settings. Use the settings in the Power Options dialog box, shown in Figure 6-25, to configure the advanced settings. Click OK to save any changes you've made.

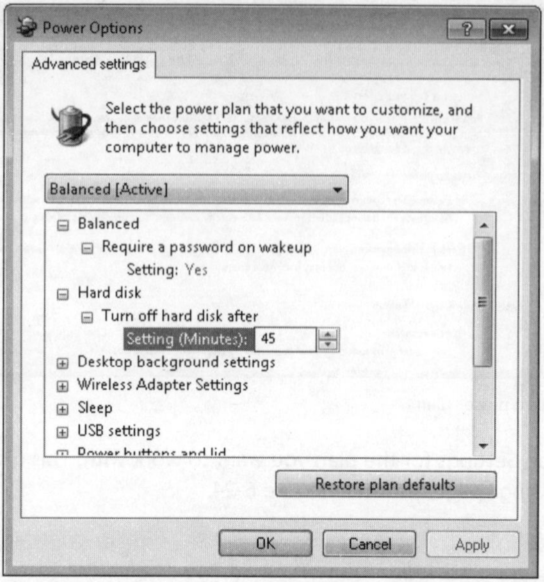

FIGURE 6-25 Use the Power Options dialog box to configure advanced power options.

7. If you've made changes to Turn Off The Display or Put The Computer To Sleep, click Save Changes to save these changes.

In Group Policy, you can use a preference item to optimize power plans on computers throughout a domain by completing the following steps:

1. Open a Group Policy object (GPO) for editing in the Group Policy Management Editor. To configure preferences for computers, expand Computer Configuration\Preferences\Control Panel Settings, and then select Power Options. To configure preferences for users, expand User Configuration\Preferences\Control Panel Settings, and then select Power Options.
2. Right-click the Power Options node, point to New, and then click Power Plan (Windows Vista And Later). This opens the New Power Plan Properties dialog box.
3. From the Action list, select Update to update the power plan's settings or select Replace to delete the power plan and then re-create it exactly as you specify.
4. From the selection list, choose the power plan you want to work with, such as Balanced.
5. To set the plan as the active plan, select the Set As The Active Power Plan check box.
6. Use the options provided to configure the settings for the power plan.

7. Click OK. The next time policy is refreshed, the preference item will be applied as appropriate for the Group Policy object in which you defined the preference item.

Creating Power Plans

In addition to the preferred power plans included with Windows 7, you can create power plans as needed. To create a power plan, follow these steps:

1. In Control Panel, click System And Security, and then click Power Options.
2. In the left pane, click Create A Power Plan. This displays the Create A Power Plan page, shown in Figure 6-26.

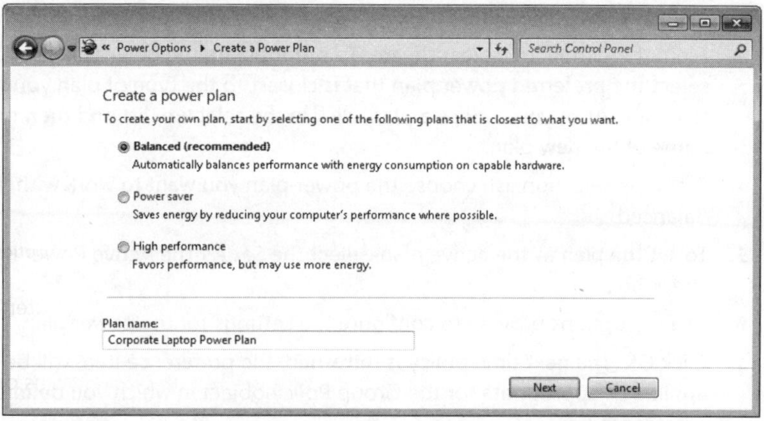

FIGURE 6-26 Create a power plan.

3. To prepopulate the power plan settings, select the preferred power plan that is closest to the type of plan you want to create.
4. In the Plan Name field, type a descriptive name for the plan, and then click Next. This displays the Edit Plan Settings page.
5. Use the Turn Off The Display list to specify whether or when the computer's display automatically turns off. Choose Never to disable this feature.
6. Use the Put The Computer To Sleep list to specify whether or when the computer automatically enters sleep mode. Choose Never to disable this feature.
7. Click Create to create the plan. The Power Options page is displayed with updates to include the plan you created as a new preferred plan that replaces the plan you selected previously. You'll find the original preferred plan under Show Additional Plans. Click the Expand button on the right to display the original plan.
8. The plan you created is selected by default. Click Change Plan Settings for this plan to display the Edit Plan Settings page, and then click Change Advanced Power Settings to display the Power Options dialog box.

9. After you configure the advanced power options as appropriate, click OK to save any changes you've made.

You can access Group Policy and use a preference item to create power plans on computers throughout a domain by completing the following steps:

1. Open a Group Policy object (GPO) for editing in the Group Policy Management Editor. To configure preferences for computers, expand Computer Configuration\Preferences\Control Panel Settings, and then select Power Options. To configure preferences for users, expand User Configuration\Preferences\Control Panel Settings, and then select Power Options.
2. Right-click the Power Options node, point to New, and then select Power Plan (Windows Vista And Later). This opens the New Power Plan Properties dialog box.
3. From the Action list, select Create. To prepopulate the power plan settings, select the preferred power plan that is closest to the type of plan you want to create. After you choose a plan, click in the selection list and then type the name of the new plan.
4. From the selection list, choose the power plan you want to work with, such as Balanced.
5. To set the plan as the active plan, select the Set As The Active Power Plan check box.
6. Use the options provide to configure the settings for the power plan.
7. Click OK. The next time policy is refreshed, the preference item will be applied as appropriate for the Group Policy object in which you defined the preference item.

Configuring Systemwide Power Button and Password Protection on Wakeup Settings

Systemwide settings for power options enable you to customize the way that the power button and password protection on wake works for all users who log on to the computer. You can configure the power button so that when it is pressed, the system shuts down, hibernates, or enters sleep mode. You can configure the computer so that when it wakes from sleep, a password is required to unlock the screen.

To set systemwide power settings, follow these steps:

1. In Control Panel, click System And Security, and then click Power Options.
2. In the left pane, click Choose What The Power Buttons Do.
3. Use the When I Press The Power Button list to specify whether the computer should do nothing, shut down, sleep, or hibernate when the power button is pressed. (See Figure 6-27.) You cannot, however, use an option that is not supported by the computer.

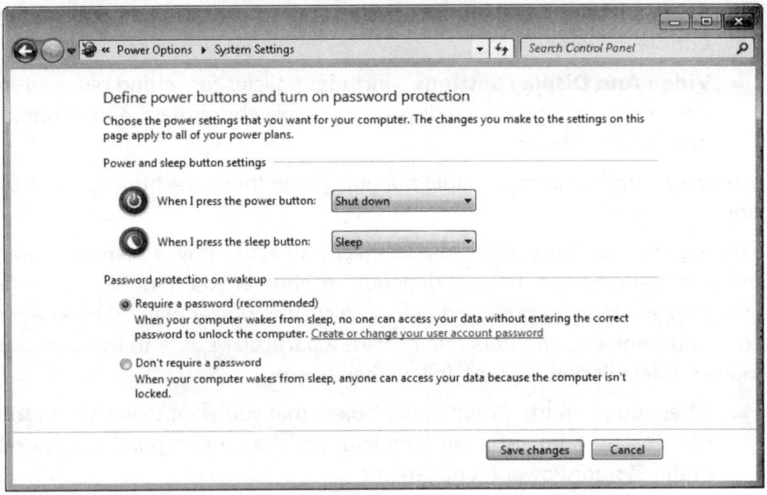

FIGURE 6-27 Set the power button, sleep button, and password-protection-on-wakeup behavior.

4. Use the When I Press The Sleep Button list to specify whether the computer should sleep, hibernate, or do nothing when the sleep button is pressed. Again, you cannot use an option that is not supported by the computer.
5. If the Password Protection On Wakeup options are not available, you need to click Change Settings That Are Currently Unavailable.
6. Use the Require A Password option to specify that the computer requires a password on wakeup. It is a good idea to prompt for a password to help ensure the security of the system.
7. Click Save Changes when you have finished making changes.

Managing Power Options in Policy Settings

In Group Policy, you'll find policy settings for managing power options in the Administrative Templates for Computer Configuration under System\Power Management. Five subnodes are provided:

- **Button Settings** Includes policies for setting plugged-in and on-battery actions for the power button, the sleep button, and the laptop lid. This also controls the way the power button works on the Tasks screen, which is displayed by pressing Ctrl+Alt+Delete.
- **Hard Disk Settings** Includes policies for setting plugged-in and on-battery actions for turning off the hard disks.
- **Notification Settings** Includes policies for controlling notifications and actions for adverse battery conditions.

- **Sleep Settings** Includes policies for setting permitted device and application sleep states.
- **Video And Display Settings** Includes policies for setting plugged-in and on-battery actions for the display, the display brightness, and desktop background slide shows.

To apply a policy setting, enable the policy, and then select the appropriate action.

Through Group Policy, you can also specify an active power plan. How you work with Power Management policies depends on whether you want to use a default power plan, an updated preferred plan, or a custom power plan that you've created. If you want all computers that process a particular policy to use one of the Windows 7 default power plans, follow these steps:

1. After you open the Group Policy object that you want to work with for editing, expand Administrative Templates policies for Computer Configuration under System\Power Management.
2. Double-click Select An Active Power Plan.
3. Select Enabled, and then use the Active Power Plan list to select the plan to use. The options are High Performance, Power Saver, and Automatic. If you choose Automatic, Windows 7 uses the Balanced power plan in most cases.
4. Click OK.

If you want all computers that process a particular policy to use an updated preferred plan or a custom power plan that you've created, follow these steps:

1. After you open the Group Policy object that you want to edit, expand Computer Configuration\Administrative Templates\System\Power Management.
2. Double-click Select A Custom Active Power Plan.
3. Select Enabled. In the Custom Active Power Plan (GUID) text box, type the GUID of the power plan to use.
4. Click OK.

TIP **To determine the GUID of a power plan, get a list of the power plans configured on a computer by typing powercfg –l at an elevated command prompt.**

Using Alarms and Configuring Alarm Actions

Alarms determine whether a laptop sounds an alarm or displays a warning message when its battery reaches a certain level. You can configure three levels of alarms and notifications for laptops:

- **Low Battery Alarm** The Low Battery Alarm is meant to alert the user when the battery power level is nearly depleted. The low-power state is activated by default when the battery has 10 percent or less power remaining. On a battery with 8 hours of useful life, 10 percent is about 48 minutes of use.

- **Critical Battery Alarm** The Critical Battery Alarm is meant to alert the user when the battery is about to fail. The critical-power state is activated by default when the battery has 3 percent or less power remaining. On a battery with 8 hours of useful life, 3 percent is about 14 minutes of use.
- **Reserve Battery Alarm** The Reserve Battery Alarm is meant to alert the user when the battery is using reserve power. The reserve-power state is activated by default when the battery has 1 percent or less power remaining. On a battery with 8 hours of useful life, 1 percent is about 5 minutes of use.

An alarm action associated with low and critical alarms enables you to dictate what specific actions the operating system should take when the alarm level is reached. Possible actions include shutting down the computer, entering sleep mode, or entering hibernate mode. Starting with Windows Vista, you could turn off low battery notifications by enabling the Turn Off Low Battery User Notification policy. In Windows 7, the reserve battery alert was added to notify users that batteries were running on reserve power. Because there are different considerations for configuring the alert levels, I'll examine each separately in the sections that follow.

Configuring Low Battery Notification and Actions

As stated previously, the low battery notification is a warning that the system is getting low on power. When entering the low-power state, the system notifies the user with either a text prompt alone or a text prompt and an audible alarm. In some cases, you might want to configure the computer to go a step further and enter standby mode in addition to or instead of giving a warning.

To configure the low battery notification and actions, follow these steps:

1. After you open the Group Policy object that you want to work with for editing, expand Administrative Templates policies for Computer Configuration under System\Power Management\Notification Settings.
2. To set the low battery notification action, double-click Low Battery Notification Action. Select Enabled, and then use the Low Battery Notification Action list to select the action, such as Sleep. Click OK.
3. To specify when the low battery alarm is triggered, double-click Low Battery Notification Level. Select Enabled, and then use the Low Battery Notification Level combo box to set the appropriate alarm level. Click OK.

TIP **The default low battery alarm level is based on the total battery life and typically is 10 percent. On most systems, this is an appropriate value. However, I've found that on some systems, especially those with poor batteries, this isn't enough, and I increase the level to between 12 and 15 percent. In contrast, on energy-efficient systems or those with two batteries, the default value is often too much. Here, I adjust the level so that the user is notified when about 20 minutes of battery power remains.**

4. By default, users are notified when a computer's battery runs low. If you want to disable user notification for a low battery condition, double-click Turn Off Low Battery User Notification, click Enabled, and then click OK.

Configuring Critical Battery Alarms

Critical battery alarms are designed to ensure that systems enter an appropriate mode prior to running out of power. When entering a critical-power state, the system notifies the user and then enters sleep mode. In sleep mode, the computer's power-manageable components shut off to conserve power. I often configure the low-power alarm so that the computer enters sleep mode. I then configure the critical-power alarm to have the computer enter hibernation mode or shut down. This takes power management to the next level and helps preserve the system before power is completely exhausted.

To configure the critical battery actions, follow these steps:

1. After you open the Group Policy object that you want to work with for editing, expand Administrative Templates policies for Computer Configuration under System\Power Management\Notification Settings.
2. To set the critical battery notification action, double-click Critical Battery Notification Action. Select Enabled, and then use the Critical Battery Notification Action list to select the action, such as Hibernate or Shut Down. Click OK.
3. To specify when the critical battery alarm is triggered, double-click Critical Battery Notification Level. Select Enabled, and then use the Critical Battery Notification Level combo box to set the appropriate alarm level. Click OK.

TIP **The default critical alarm level is based on the total battery life and typically is 3 percent. In most cases, this value is appropriate. However, if you plan for the computer to go into hibernation or shut down, you might want to reduce this value. You also want to take into account the battery life. If a computer has a long battery life, the default typically is too high, but if a computer has a short battery life, it might not be high enough. I usually set the critical power alarm so that the alarm action is triggered when there are 6 to 8 minutes of power remaining.**

Configuring Reserve Power Mode

Reserve power mode is designed to notify users that the battery is operating on reserve power. To configure reserve battery notification, follow these steps:

1. After you open the Group Policy object that you want to edit, expand Administrative Templates policies for Computer Configuration under System\Power Management\Notification Settings.
2. To specify when the reserve battery alarm is triggered, double-click Reserve Battery Notification Level. Select Enabled, and then use the Reserve Battery Notification Level combo box to set the appropriate alarm level. Click OK.

CHAPTER 7

Customizing the Desktop and the User Interface

As an administrator, you'll often be asked to help users customize their desktops and user profile data. You might even be asked to create for new users a default working environment that closely maps to a corporate standard or reflects core user preferences. One way to create a default working environment is to create a default user account, log on as that user, set up the environment as necessary, and then use the account and its associated profile as the starting point for new accounts.

Windows 7 provides a whole new level of desktop and screen customization options. Although these options are useful, they can cause problems that you might be asked to help resolve. You might also see users struggling to fix these issues on their own, so you might want to lend a hand. This chapter focuses on the configuration and troubleshooting of the following areas:

- Menus, the taskbar, and toolbars
- Desktop themes and backgrounds
- Custom desktop content

- Screen savers
- Display appearance and settings

Optimizing Windows 7 Menus

The Start menu and its related menus are designed to provide easy access to applications and utilities installed on a system. Unfortunately, the more applications and utilities you install, the more cluttered the menu system becomes. To help users escape the clutter and better use the menu system, this section focuses on techniques you can use to optimize menus.

Customizing the Start Menu Options

Windows 7 provides excellent control over the Start menu. You can choose which commands appear on the Start menu and how they are arranged. You can add options for Control Panel, Devices And Printers, Network Connections, and other key tools. You can also enable or disable personalized menus on the All Programs menu.

To change the Start menu options, follow these steps:

1. Right-click Start on the taskbar, and then click Properties. The Taskbar And Start Menu Properties dialog box is displayed with the Start Menu tab selected by default.
2. On the Start Menu tab, use the Power Button Action list to select the action to use when the power button is pressed. Options include Switch User, Log Off, Lock, Restart, Sleep, and Shut Down. In a 24x7 environment, or when multiple users log on to the same computer, switching users, logging off, or locking the system may be viable alternatives to shutting down the computer. If you change the default action, you can shut down the computer by clicking Start and then clicking Shutdown.
3. Click Customize. This displays the Customize Start Menu dialog box, shown in Figure 7-1.
4. Use the options in the dialog box to control the general appearance of the Start menu.
5. Click OK, and then click OK again to close the Taskbar And Start Menu Properties dialog box.

In the Customize Start Menu dialog box, most of the options control which commands appear on the Start menu and how they are arranged. Some items have the suboptions Display As A Link, Display As A Menu, and Don't Display This Item. Display As A Link specifies that an item, such as Control Panel, will appear as a separate option that opens a window when selected. Display As A Menu specifies that an item will provide access to a submenu that allows you to choose from its related options. Don't Display This Item removes the item from the Start menu.

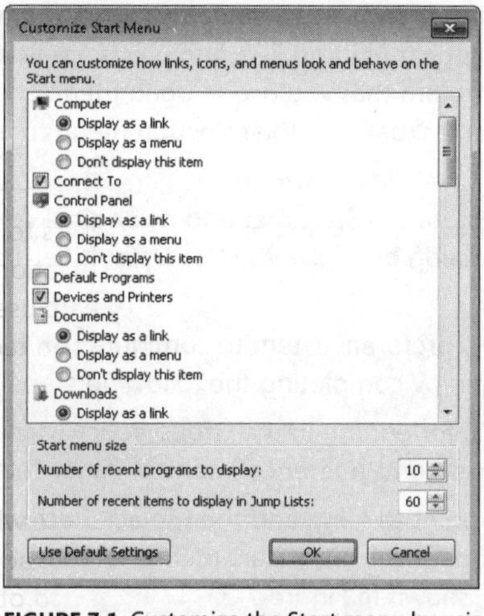

FIGURE 7-1 Customize the Start menu by using this dialog box.

Other Customize Start Menu dialog box options you'll see include the following:

- **Enable Context Menus And Dragging And Dropping** When this option is selected, users can right-click to display a shortcut menu and use drag and drop. Typically, you'll want to enable this option unless there is a specific security reason to disable it.
- **Highlight Newly Installed Programs** When this option is selected, menus for recently installed applications are highlighted, as are the menu options.
- **Open Submenus When I Pause On Them With The Mouse Pointer** Controls the behavior of menus. When this option is selected, menus open when you point to them. Otherwise, menus open only when you click them.
- **Sort All Programs Menu By Name** Controls whether menu items are organized alphabetically or by the order of installation. When this option is selected, menu items are sorted alphabetically. When this option is not selected, menu items are listed in the order of installation.
- **Use Large Icons** Controls the size of icons for menu options. To reduce the size of icons used on menus, clear this option. Otherwise, select this option to display standard-size icons on menus.
- **Number Of Recent Programs To Display** Controls the number of shortcuts to recently used programs that appear in the most frequently used list on the Start menu. Use the selection menu to assign a value from 0 to 30. The actual number of programs listed in the most frequently used list depends on the screen resolution as well as the number of items in the pinned items list, which appears above the most frequently used list on the Start menu.

- **Number of Recent Items To Display In Jump List** Controls how many shortcuts to recently used items appear in jump lists. Jump lists are lists of recent items organized by the program that you use to open them. They can appear on the Start menu and the taskbar. Use the selection menu to assign a value from 0 to 60.

If you make a mistake and want to restore the Start menu to its original configuration, open the Customize Start Menu dialog box, click the Use Default Settings button, and then click OK twice.

You can access Group Policy and use a preference item to configure the Start menu on computers throughout a domain by completing the following steps:

1. Open a Group Policy object (GPO) for editing in the Group Policy Management Editor. Expand User Configuration\Preferences\Control Panel Settings.
2. Right-click the Start Menu node, point to New, and then select Start Menu (Windows Vista And Later). This opens the New Start Menu (Windows Vista And Later) Properties dialog box, shown in Figure 7-2.

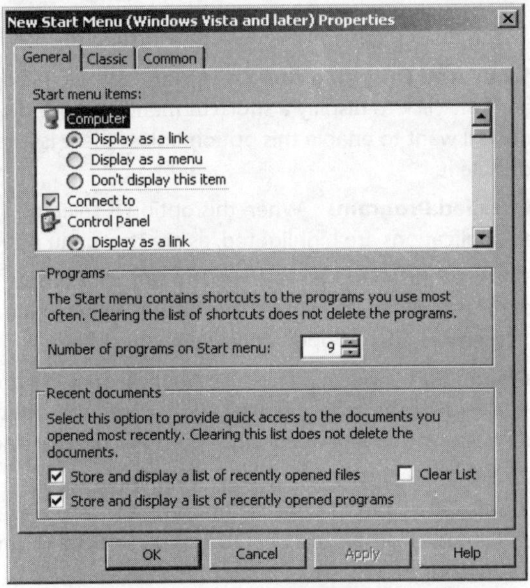

FIGURE 7-2 Create a Start menu preference.

3. Use the options provided to configure the Start menu as you'd like it to appear on users' computers. Every setting in the interface is processed by the client computer and applied, even if you don't specifically set the related value. This effectively overwrites all existing settings for this interface on the user's desktop.

4. Use the options on the Common tab to control how the preference is applied. Often, you'll want to apply your standardized Start menu options only once. If so, select Apply Once And Do Not Reapply.
5. Click OK. The next time policy is refreshed, the preference item will be applied as appropriate for the Group Policy object in which you defined the preference item.

Modifying Menus and Their Options

In the Windows 7 file system, the Start menu is represented by a pair of folders, each with the name Start Menu. Programs that are made available only to the currently logged on user are placed in the Start Menu folder that is located within the profile data for that user (%UserProfile%\AppData\Roaming\Microsoft\Windows\Start Menu). Programs that are available to any user who logs on to the computer are placed in the Start Menu folder for all users (%SystemDrive%\ProgramData\Microsoft\Windows\Start Menu).

During system startup, Windows 7 merges the contents of both Start Menu folders to create the Start menu. Below each Start Menu folder, you'll find a Programs folder. The contents of these folders and the shortcuts in them determine the structure of the Programs menu. Each folder within the Programs folders represents a menu. Shortcuts within these folders represent menu options and act as pointers to the programs you want to launch. If you want to modify menus and their options, you have several choices. You can work directly with the appropriate file system representation of the Start menu, or you can work with the menu system itself.

Rearranging Items on the Start Menu

The easiest way to change the position of menus and options within menus on the Start menu is to use the menu system. The technique you use is as follows:

1. Click Start, and then point to All Programs.
2. Point to the item that you want to change.
3. Press and hold down the left mouse button.
4. Drag the item to a new location on any menu or submenu—simply point to a submenu to open it. A horizontal line shows where the selected item will be placed.
5. Release the mouse button.

NOTE **Administrator permissions are required to move menu items. In many cases, the current user must log off and then log back on to see the menu changes.**

You can drag items to the upper-left corner of the Start menu, where they will remain displayed. This area of the Start menu is known as the *pinned items list*. When you have the mouse pointer in the proper location, you'll see the horizontal position line that highlights where the item will be placed when you release the mouse button. Other techniques for adding and removing items to the pinned items list include:

- To add items to the pinned items area, right-click the item and then select Pin To Start Menu.
- To remove items from the pinned items area, right-click the item on the menu and then select Remove From This List. There is also an Unpin From Start Menu command on this shortcut menu. This command will delete the entry from the pinned items list, but if the item has been recently used, it might then appear in the most frequently used list. Using the Remove From This List command ensures that will not happen.

Reorganizing Menu Options

The contents of the All Programs menu are normally sorted with submenus at the top and menu options below. Within each of those two categories, the menu's contents are listed alphabetically.

Menus and menu options are automatically resorted whenever new menus or menu items are added or whenever you move items. If menus and menu items aren't sorted alphabetically, someone probably cleared the Sort All Programs Menu By Name option in the Customize Start Menu dialog box for the current user. To re-alphabetize the entire All Programs menu and keep it alphabetized from now on, follow these steps:

1. Right-click Start on the taskbar, and then click Properties. The Taskbar And Start Menu Properties dialog box is displayed with the Start Menu tab selected by default.
2. Click Customize. Scroll down through the list of options in the Customize Start Menu dialog box, and then select Sort All Programs Menu By Name.
3. Click OK twice.

Adding, Modifying, and Deleting Menus

As mentioned earlier, the Start menu is represented in the file system as a folder that can be accessed through the profile data for a particular user and a folder that can be accessed through the profile data for all users. To access the Start Menu folder for the current user, right-click the Start button on the taskbar, click Open Windows Explorer, and then browse to the hidden %UserProfile%\AppData\Roaming\Microsoft\Windows\Start Menu folder. To access the Start Menu folder for all users, right-click the Start button on the taskbar, click Open Windows Explorer, and then browse to the hidden %SystemDrive%\ProgramData\Microsoft\Windows\Start Menu folder. Once you open a Start Menu folder, you can perform all the normal folder operations to update the Start menu, including the following:

- Add new menus to the All Programs menu by creating folders within the Programs folder or any subfolder of the Programs folder (except Startup).

- Modify menus by moving folders or shortcuts to new locations within the Programs folder.
- Rename folders or shortcuts to update their names on the All Programs menu. Another way to rename items is through the menu system. With the All Programs menu active, right-click the item you want to rename, and then click Rename. Type a new name for the item, and then click OK.

NOTE **If you cannot view or browse hidden folders, you need to change the folder options for Windows Explorer. To do this, choose Folder And Search Options from the Organize menu. On the View tab, select the Show Hidden Files, Folders, And Drives option, and then click OK.**

CAUTION **Delete any unwanted folders or shortcuts to remove the related menus or menu options from the All Programs menu. Another way to delete items is through the menu system. With the All Programs menu open, right-click the item you want to delete, and then click Delete. Don't rename or remove the Startup folder. This folder holds shortcuts for programs that should load automatically at startup. If you alter this folder, Windows 7 might not be able to use it. Additionally, you shouldn't rename or remove the Administrative Tools menu. The availability of the Administrative Tools menu is controlled through Taskbar And Start Menu Properties.**

Adding Menu Options to the Start Menu

Menu options are represented as shortcuts in the Windows 7 file system. This means you can create menu options simply by adding shortcuts to the Programs folder or its subfolders. After you create a shortcut, you can update its properties to include comments that are displayed when someone points to the option on the Start menu. The complete steps to create a menu option that is unique to the currently logged on user are as follows:

1. Right-click the Start button on the taskbar, click Open Windows Explorer, and then browse to the hidden %UserProfile%\AppData\Roaming\Microsoft\Windows\Start Menu\Programs folder.
2. In the left pane of Windows Explorer, select the folder to which you want to add the menu option.
3. In the Contents or View pane, right-click an open area, point to New, and then click Shortcut. This starts the Create Shortcut wizard.
4. In the field provided, type the file path to the program or file you want to associate with the shortcut. (If you don't know the file path, click Browse, and then use the Browse For Files Or Folders dialog box to locate the item you want to use.)
5. Click Next, and then type a name for the shortcut. The value you enter is the name that will appear on the Start menu.

6. Click Finish. If you want to enter comments for the shortcut, right-click the shortcut, and then click Properties. On the Shortcut tab, enter the comments in the Comment field, and then click OK.

Displaying the Administrative Tools Menu

The Administrative Tools menu is not displayed by default in Windows 7. If you want to display this menu on your computer or for a user with administrator privileges, you need to customize the Start menu.

You can add the Administrative Tools menu to either the Start menu or to the Start menu and the All Programs submenu of the Start menu by completing the following steps:

1. Right-click Start, and then click Properties. The Taskbar And Start Menu Properties dialog box is displayed with the Start Menu tab selected by default.
2. Click Customize. Scroll down the list until you can see the System Administrative Tools heading.
3. At this point, you have two options:
   - If you want to display the Administrative Tools menu as a submenu of the All Programs menu, select Display On The All Programs Menu.
   - If you want to display the Administrative Tools menu directly on the Start menu and as a submenu of the All Programs menu, select Display On The All Programs Menu And The Start Menu.
4. Click OK twice.

Working with Menus, Desktops, and Startup Applications

In the Windows operating system, menus, desktops, and startup applications are all configured with shortcuts, and it is the location of the shortcut that determines how the shortcut is used. For example, if you want to add a menu option for a user, you add a shortcut to the user's Programs or Start Menu folder. These shortcuts then appear on the user's menu. If you want to configure startup applications for all users, you add shortcuts to the AllUsersStartup folder. These applications then automatically start when a user logs in to the system locally.

Creating Shortcuts for Menus, Desktops, Startup, and More

In Windows Explorer, you can create menus, desktops, and startup applications for individual users by logging on to their computer and creating shortcuts in the appropriate locations. In Group Policy, you can create shortcuts for menus, desktops, startup applications, and more by using Shortcuts preferences, and these preference items are applied automatically to all users and computers that process the related GPO.

To configure Shortcuts preferences, follow these steps:

1. Open a Group Policy object (GPO) for editing in the Group Policy Management Editor. To configure preferences for computers, expand Computer Configuration\Preferences\Windows Settings, and then select Shortcuts. To configure preferences for users, expand User Configuration\Preferences\Windows Settings, and then select Shortcuts.
2. Right-click the Shortcuts node, point to New, and then select Shortcut. This opens the New Shortcut Properties dialog box, shown in Figure 7-3.
3. In the Action list, select Create, Update, or Replace as appropriate. Then complete the other options as discussed in this section.
4. Use the options on the Common tab to control how the preference is applied. Often, you'll want to apply a shortcut only once. If so, select Apply Once And Do Not Reapply.
5. Click OK. The next time policy is refreshed, the preference item will be applied as appropriate for the Group Policy object in which you defined the preference item.

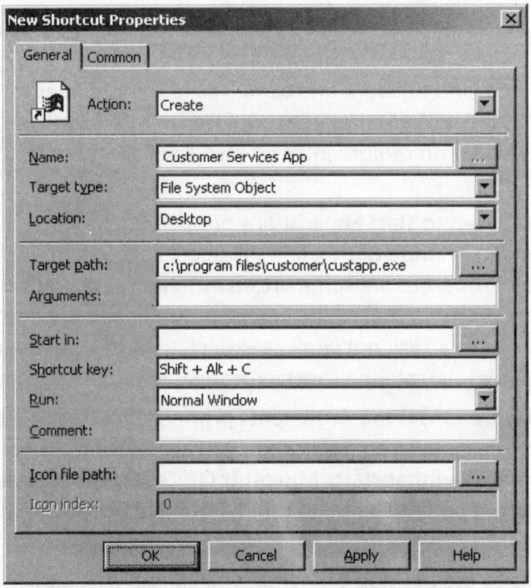

FIGURE 7-3 Create a shortcut using a preference item.

In the Location list, you'll see a list of special folders that you can use with shortcuts. Table 7-1 provides a summary of these folders.

TABLE 7-1 Special Folders for Use with Shortcuts

SPECIAL FOLDER	USAGE
AllUsersDesktop	Desktop shortcuts for all users.
AllUsersPrograms	Programs menu options for all users.
AllUsersStartMenu	Start menu options for all users.
AllUsersStartup	Startup applications for all users.
Desktop	Desktop shortcuts for a specific user.
Explorer Favorites	Favorites menu shortcuts for a specific user.
Explorer Links	Favorite links for a specific user.
Fonts	Fonts folder shortcuts for a specific user.
Programs	Programs menu options for a specific user.
Recent	Recently used document shortcuts for a specific user.
SendTo	SendTo menu shortcuts for a specific user.
StartMenu	Start menu shortcuts for a specific user.
Startup	Startup applications for a specific user.

Shortcuts can point to local and network files as well as to remote Internet resources. Shortcuts for working with local or network files are referred to as *link shortcuts*. Shortcuts for working with remote Internet resources are referred to as *URL shortcuts*.

Link shortcuts are usually used to start applications or open documents rather than access a URL in a browser. Because of this, link shortcuts have different properties than URL shortcuts. The properties are summarized in Table 7-2. If you set any property incorrectly or set a property that isn't supported by a linked application, the shortcut may not be created or may not work as expected. In this case, you need to correct the problem and try to create the shortcut again.

One of the most valuable options is the Arguments property. You can use this property to set arguments to pass in to an application you are starting. Using this property, you can create a shortcut that starts Microsoft Office Word and opens a document by setting the target path for Word and the argument for the document to open.

When you add shortcuts to the desktop or menus, you can set a hotkey sequence that activates the shortcut. The hotkey sequence must be specified with at least one modifier key and a key designator. The following modifier keys are available:

- **ALT** The Alt key
- **CTRL** The Ctrl key

- **SHIFT** The Shift key
- **EXT** The Windows key

TABLE 7-2 Link Shortcut Properties

PROPERTY	DESCRIPTION	SAMPLE VALUE
Arguments	Arguments to pass to an application started through the shortcut.	"C:\Gettingstarted.doc"
Comment	Sets a descriptive comment for the shortcut.	"Opens the Getting Started Document"
Icon File Path	Sets the location of an icon for the shortcut. If not set, a default icon is used.	"C:\Program Files\Internet Explorer\Iexplore.exe"
Icon Index	Sets the index position of the icon for the shortcut. Few applications have multiple icons indexed, so the index is almost always 0.	"0"
Location	Specifies where the shortcut should be created.	"Desktop"
Name	Sets the name of the shortcut.	"Getting Started"
Run	Sets the window style of the application started by the shortcut. The available styles are Normal Window, Minimized, and Maximized.	"Normal Window"
Shortcut Key	Sets a hotkey sequence that activates the shortcut. This property can only be used with desktop shortcuts and Start menu options.	"ALT+SHIFT+Z"
Start In	Sets the working directory of the application started by the shortcut.	"C:\Working"
Target Path	Sets the path of the file to execute.	"%WinDir%\Notepad.exe"
Target Type	Specifies the type of shortcut you are creating. Choose File System Object for link shortcuts, URL for URL shortcuts, and Shell Object for Explorer shell shortcuts.	"File System Object"

Modifier keys can be combined in any combination, such as ALT+CTRL or SHIFT+CTRL, but the combination shouldn't duplicate key combinations used by other shortcuts. Key designators include the alphabetic characters (A–Z) and numeric characters (0–9), as well as Backspace, Clear, Delete, Escape, End, Home, Return, Space, and Tab. For example, you could create a shortcut that uses the hot-key sequence SHIFT+ALT+G.

When you create shortcuts for applications, the applications normally have a default icon that is displayed with the shortcut. For example, if you create a shortcut for Internet Explorer, the default icon is a large E. When you create shortcuts to document files, the Windows default icon is used in most cases.

If you want to use an icon other than the default icon, you can use the Icon Location property. Normally, the icon location equates to an application name, such as Iexplore.exe or Notepad.exe, and the icon index is set to 0. Windows has to be able to find the executable. If the executable can't be found in the path, the icon can't be set. Because of this, be sure to enter the full path to the executable.

The working directory sets the default directory for an application. This directory is used the first time a user opens or saves files.

URL shortcuts open Internet documents in an appropriate application. For example, Web pages are opened in the default browser, such as Internet Explorer. With URL shortcuts, you can't use the Arguments, Start In, Run, or Comment properties.

Creating Menus and Menu Options

Using preferences, you can easily add menu options to existing top-level menus, such as All Programs or the Start menu. To do this, simply create a shortcut that sets the Programs or Start Menu folder as its location.

Using preferences you also can create new menus. To create menus, you use a Folders preference to add a folder to an existing special folder, such as Start Menu or Programs. After you create a menu, you can add options to it. You do this by creating shortcuts that point to a location in the new menu.

Through preferences, you can update or replace the properties of any shortcut or menu option. You do this by creating a new shortcut with the same name as the old shortcut and setting the action as Update or Replace.

You can delete shortcuts and menu options by creating a preference with the action set to Delete. You delete menus by using a Folders preference that has a Delete action.

Adding and Removing Startup Applications

Administrator-installed or user-installed applications that run in the background can be managed through the Startup folder. Startup programs that are made available only to the currently logged on user are placed in the Startup folder that is located within the profile data for that user (%UserProfile%\AppData\Roaming\Microsoft\Windows\Start Menu\Programs), and startup programs that are available to any user that logs on to the computer are placed in the Startup folder for all users (%SystemDrive%\ProgramData\Microsoft\Windows\Start Menu\Programs).

To add or remove startup programs for all users, follow these steps:

1. Right-click the Start button on the taskbar, click Open Windows Explorer, and then browse to the hidden %SystemDrive%\ProgramData\Microsoft\Windows\Start Menu folder.
2. In the left pane, click the Programs folder under Start Menu, and then click Startup.
3. You can now add or remove startup programs for all users. To add startup programs, create a shortcut to the program that you want to run. To remove a startup program, delete its shortcut from the Startup folder.

To add or remove startup programs for a specific user, follow these steps:

1. Log on as the user whose startup applications you want to manage. Right-click the Start button on the taskbar, click Open Windows Explorer, and then browse to the hidden %UserProfile%\AppData\Roaming\Microsoft\Windows\Start Menu folder.
2. In the left pane, click the Programs folder under Start Menu, and then click Startup.
3. You can now add or remove startup programs for this user. To add startup programs, create a shortcut to the program that you want to run. To remove a startup program, delete its shortcut from the Startup folder.

NOTE **Technically, you don't need to log on as the user to manage that user's startup applications—it's just easier if you do. If you can't log on as the user, access the Users folder on the system drive and work your way down through the user profile data folders. These are listed by account name.**

Using Group Policy preferences, you specify applications that should be started after a user logs on by creating shortcuts in the AllUsersStartup and Startup folders. The AllUsersStartup folder sets startup applications for all users that log on to a system. The Startup folder sets startup applications for the current user.

When you create a shortcut for startup applications, the only options you need to set in most cases are Name, Target Type, Location, and Target Path. Occasionally you may also want to set a working directory for an application or specify startup arguments.

If you later want to remove a startup application, you delete it by creating a preference with the action set to Delete.

Customizing the Taskbar

The taskbar provides quick access to frequently needed information and active applications. You can change the taskbar's behavior and properties in many ways. This section explores key techniques you can use to do this.

Understanding the Taskbar

The taskbar is one of the least appreciated areas of the Windows desktop. Users and administrators tend to pay very little attention to its configuration, yet we use it day in and day out, relying on it for quick access to just about everything we do with the Windows operating system. If you find that users are having frequent problems accessing Windows features or running applications, you can help them by tailoring the taskbar to their needs. The Windows taskbar can contain several toolbars that can assist the user in different ways.

Sometimes, you can provide tremendous productivity increases simply by adding a frequently used item to the taskbar. For example, most people spend a lot of time finding and reading documents. They browse the Web or their corporate intranet to find the latest information. They open documents in Microsoft Word, Excel, PowerPoint, or other applications, finding documents individually or starting applications to read those documents as well. By adding an Address bar to the taskbar, users can access documents directly and launch the appropriate application automatically. They just need to type the document path and press Enter. As time passes, the history feature of the Address bar tracks more and more of the user's previously accessed documents, making it easier to find the information the user needs.

Pinning Shortcuts to the Taskbar

Windows 7 does not have a Quick Launch toolbar. Instead, Windows 7 allows you to pin commonly used programs directly to the taskbar. You can do this whenever you are working with the Start menu. Simply right-click an item you want to add to the taskbar, and then click Pin To Taskbar. Once you pin an item to the taskbar, you can change the item's position on the taskbar by clicking and dragging the program's icon. To unpin an item, right-click the item on the taskbar, and then click Unpin This Program From Taskbar.

Changing the Taskbar's Size and Position

By default, the taskbar appears at the bottom of the screen and is sized so that one row of options is visible. As long as the taskbar's position isn't locked, you can dock it at any edge of the Windows desktop and resize it as necessary. To move the taskbar, simply click it and drag it to a different edge of the desktop. As you drag the taskbar, you'll see the taskbar at the edge of the Windows desktop, and when you release the mouse button, the taskbar will appear in the new location. To resize the taskbar, move the mouse pointer over the taskbar's edge, and then drag it up or down.

Auto Hiding, Locking, and Controlling Taskbar Visibility

When you want to control the visibility of the taskbar, you have several options. You can enable the Auto Hide feature to hide the taskbar from view when it is not in use. You can lock the taskbar so that it can't be resized or repositioned. You can also make the taskbar appear in a specific location and with a specific appearance. Once the taskbar is positioned and sized the way a user wants it, you should lock it. In this way, the taskbar has a fixed location, and users don't have to hunt for it.

To configure the taskbar, follow these steps:

1. Right-click the taskbar, and then click Properties.
2. Select the Taskbar tab in the Taskbar And Start Menu Properties dialog box.
3. Select the appropriate Taskbar Appearance options. You can lock the taskbar, auto-hide the taskbar, and use small icons.
4. Use the Taskbar Location On Screen list to select the location for the taskbar on the desktop. You can select Bottom, Left, Right, or Top.
5. Use the Taskbar Buttons list to specify whether taskbar buttons are combined and labels are hidden. Choose Always Combine, Hide Labels to always combine buttons of the same type and hide their labels. Choose Combine When Taskbar Is Full to combine buttons only when the taskbar is full. Choose Never Combine to never combine buttons.
6. Select Use Aero Peek To Preview The Desktop to temporarily minimize open windows and display the desktop when you place your mouse on the far end of the taskbar.
7. Click OK.

TIP **Locking the taskbar is one of the most useful taskbar options. If you lock the taskbar once it is optimized, users will have fewer problems caused by accidentally altering taskbar options. Locking the taskbar doesn't prevent users from changing the taskbar on purpose. If users really want to change the taskbar, all they need to do is right-click the taskbar, select Properties, and then clear Lock The Taskbar.**

Controlling Programs in the Notification Area

The notification area or system tray is the area on the far right of the taskbar that shows the system clock and notification icons from applications. The two standard notification icons are for Action Center and the Network console. When you point to icons in the notification area, a tooltip provides information about the state of the application. To control an application in this area, right-click the application icon to display a menu of available options. Each application has a different menu of options, most of which provide quick access to routine tasks.

You can optimize the notification area by setting properties that control whether system icons—such as for the clock, volume, and network—are displayed and whether application icons are displayed or hidden.

Controlling Icon Display in the Notification Area

The notification area can display both application and system icons. Icons for applications appear in the notification area for several reasons. Some programs, such as Action Center, are managed by Windows itself, and their icons appear periodically when notifications are pending. Other types of programs, such as an antivirus program, are configured to load at startup and then run in the background. You can often enable or disable the display of icons through setup options for the related applications, but Windows 7 provides a common interface for controlling icon display in the notification area. You can specify whether and how icons are displayed on a per-application basis.

To control the display of icons in the notification area, follow these steps:

1. Right-click the taskbar, and then click Properties.
2. Select the Taskbar tab in the Taskbar And Start Menu Properties dialog box.
3. Under Notification Area, click Customize to display the Notification Area Icons page, as shown in Figure 7-4.

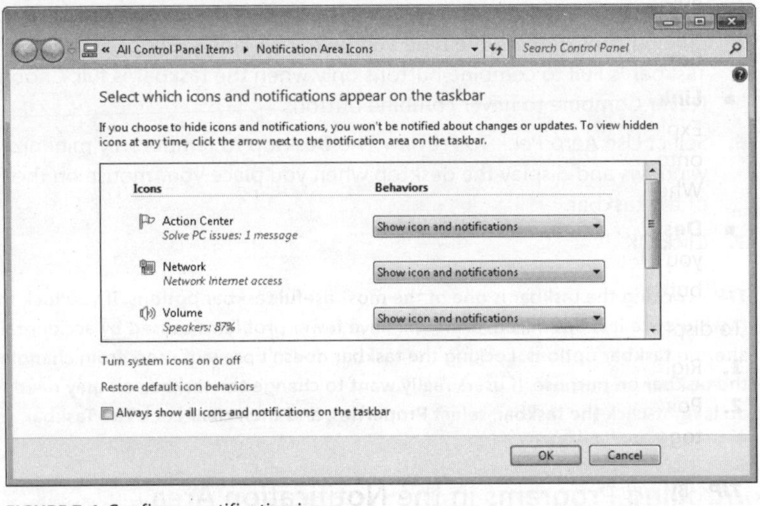

FIGURE 7-4 Configure notification icons.

4. If you want all icons to be displayed, select Always Show All Icons And Notifications On The Taskbar, and then click OK. Skip the remaining steps.
5. If you want to customize the appearance of icons, clear Always Show All Icons And Notifications On The Taskbar. You can now optimize the notification behavior. Each entry in the left column has a selection menu in the right column with the following options:
   - **Hide Icon And Notifications** Never displays the icon and notifications
   - **Only Show Notifications** Displays only notifications

- **Show Icon And Notifications** Always displays the icon and notifications

6. When you have finished updating the notification entries, click OK twice.

Optimizing Toolbars

Several toolbars are available for the taskbar. The toolbar that most users are familiar with is the Quick Launch toolbar—available in prior versions of Windows but not in Windows 7— that provided quick access to commonly used programs and the Windows desktop. The taskbar can display any of several toolbars that come with Windows 7, and users can create their own toolbars as well.

Displaying Toolbars

Toolbars available for the taskbar include:

- **Address** Provides an Address box into which you can type a URL or other address that you want to access, either on the Web, on the local network, or on the local computer. When full file paths are specified, the default application for the file is launched to display the specified file.
- **Links** Provides access to the Links folder on the Favorites menu for Internet Explorer. To add links to files, Web pages, or other resources, drag shortcuts onto the Links toolbar. To remove links, right-click the link and click Delete. When prompted, confirm the action by clicking Yes.
- **Desktop** Provides access to all the shortcuts on the local desktop so that you don't have to minimize application windows or click the Show Desktop button on the right end of the taskbar to access them.

To display or hide individual toolbars, follow these steps:

1. Right-click the taskbar to display the shortcut menu.
2. Point to Toolbars, and then select the toolbar name in the list provided. This toggles the toolbar on and off.

TIP **By default, a name label is displayed for all toolbars. You can turn off the name label by right-clicking the toolbar and then choosing Show Title to clear that command. If the taskbar is locked, you must first unlock it by clearing Lock The Taskbar on the shortcut menu.**

Creating Personal Toolbars

You can create personal toolbars for users as well. Personal toolbars are based on existing folders, and their buttons are based on a folder's contents. The toolbars you might create most often are ones that point to shared folders on the network. For example, if all users have access to CorpData, a shared folder in which corporate information is stored, and UserData, a folder in which personal information is stored, you can add toolbars to the taskbar that point to these resources. When users want to access one of these folders, they can simply click the corresponding toolbar button.

You can create personal toolbars by completing these steps:

1. Right-click the taskbar to display the shortcut menu. Point to Toolbars, and then click New Toolbar. This displays the New Toolbar—Choose A Folder dialog box, which is similar to the Open dialog box.
2. Use the options provided to navigate to and select the folder you want to use as a basis for a toolbar.
3. When you click Select Folder, the folder is displayed as a new toolbar on the taskbar. If you add shortcuts to the toolbar view, the shortcuts are added to the folder. Similarly, if you delete items from the toolbar view, the items are removed from the folder.

NOTE **When it comes to personal toolbars, there's good news and bad news. The good news is that most users find them valuable. The bad news is that if a user decides to close the toolbar, it must be re-created before it can be viewed on the taskbar again.**

Working with Desktop Themes

Desktop themes are combinations of backgrounds plus sets of sounds, icons, and other elements that help personalize the desktop and the operating environment. Administrators tend to hate themes; users tend to love them. In this section, you'll learn how to apply themes, how to tailor individual theme options, and how to delete themes.

Applying and Removing Themes

Several types of themes are available. Some themes are installed with the operating system. To apply a theme, follow these steps:

1. Right-click an open area of the desktop, and then click Personalize. This opens the Personalization console in Control Panel, shown in Figure 7-5.
2. Use the theme list to select the theme you want to use. If you want to use a theme from the Microsoft Web site, click Get More Themes Online to open the Microsoft Web site in your default browser. To use an online theme, select it, and then click Save. When prompted, select a save location. When the download is complete, click Open in the Download Complete dialog box. The theme is now available for use and applied.
3. The lower portion of the Personalization console provides appearance options for the selected theme. To change one of these items, click it.

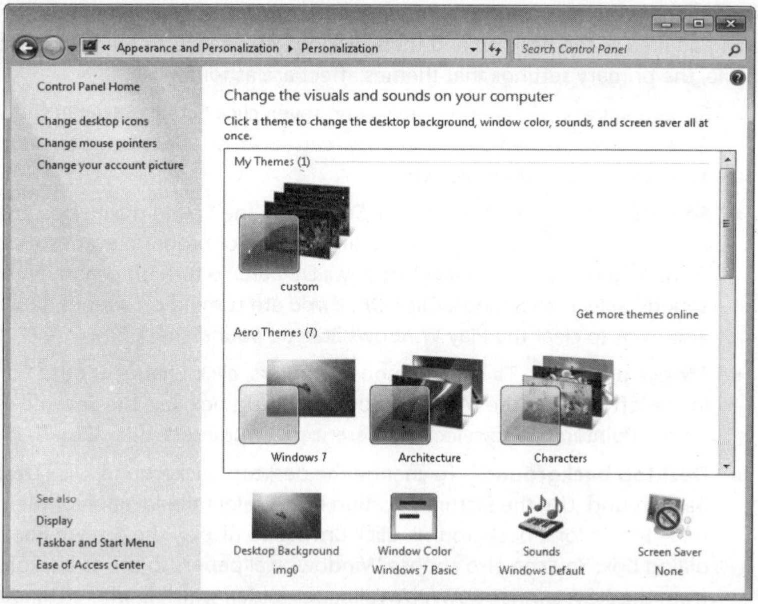

FIGURE 7-5 Use the Personalization console to access dialog boxes for configuring themes, display settings, and more.

To restore the original desktop theme, follow these steps:

1. Right-click an open area of the desktop, and then click Personalize.
2. Select Windows 7 or Windows 7 Basic as the theme.

TIP **Because the display of themes is controlled by the Themes service, you can stop this service if you need to quickly turn off themes without changing their configuration, such as when you are troubleshooting or trying to resolve an issue. To stop the Themes service, type the following command at an elevated command prompt: net stop themes. To restart the Themes service, type the following command at an elevated command prompt: net start themes.**

Tailoring and Saving Themes

When you apply a theme to the Windows desktop, many different system settings can be affected. Typically, users might like a theme but dislike a specific aspect of it, such as the sounds. To fix this, you can change the system setting the user doesn't like and then save the updated theme so that he or she can restore it in the future.

You manage themes using the Personalization console, which you open by right-clicking an area of the desktop and then clicking Personalize. In the Personalization console, the primary settings that themes affect are as follows:

- **Screen savers** To change the screen saver, click Screen Saver. In the Screen Saver Settings dialog box, select a screen saver, or select None to remove the screen saver, and then click OK.
- **Sounds** To change sounds, click Sounds. In the Sound dialog box, use the Sound Scheme list box to select a different set of program event sounds. To restore the default, select Windows Default. To turn off program event sounds, select No Sounds. Click OK. If you are turning off sounds, you might also want to clear the Play Windows Startup Sound check box.
- **Mouse pointers** To change mouse pointers, click Change Mouse Pointers in the left pane. In the Mouse Properties dialog box, use the Scheme list box on the Pointers tab to select a different set of pointers. Click OK.
- **Desktop background** To change the desktop background, click Desktop Background. Use the Picture Location list to select the location of the pictures to use for a background. Click Browse to display the Browse For Folder dialog box. You can also choose Windows wallpapers to use as backgrounds from the %SystemRoot%\Web\Wallpaper folder, which is where standard backgrounds included with Windows 7 are stored by default. Click the background you want to use, set the picture position, and then click Save Changes.
- **Color schemes** To change color schemes, click Window Color. Click the color you want to use. Select or clear Enable Transparency, and then click Save Changes.

Deleting Custom Themes

Themes that users install from other locations can take up a lot of space on the hard disk. To delete a theme and remove the theme-related files, follow these steps:

1. Right-click an open area of the desktop, and then click Personalize.
2. Under My Themes, right-click the theme to be deleted, and then click Delete Theme. Windows removes that theme's definition file and the theme-related media files.

TIP **By default, definition files for themes installed by Windows are located in the %WinDir%\Resources\Themes folder, and themes created by users are stored in their user profile. If you want to determine the total space used by themes, check the space used by these folders and their subdirectories. You shouldn't delete files from these folders manually. Instead, use the technique just described.**

Optimizing the Desktop Environment

When you open programs or folders, they appear on the desktop. You can arrange open programs and folders on the desktop by right-clicking an empty area of the taskbar and then selecting Cascade Windows, Show Windows Stacked, or Show Windows Side By Side. If you click Show The Desktop, Windows minimizes all open windows and displays the desktop. Clicking Show Open Windows restores the minimized windows to their previous states.

You can put files, folders, and shortcuts on the desktop. Any file or folder you save on the desktop appears on the desktop. Any file or folder you drag from a Windows Explorer window to the desktop stays on the desktop. To add a shortcut to a file or folder to the desktop, right-click the file or folder, point to Send To, and then click Desktop (Create Shortcut).

Beyond these basic techniques, Windows 7 provides many additional ways to optimize the desktop environment. One technique is to add a background containing a corporate logo or other symbol to the standard desktop build. This is particularly useful with loaner laptops; for example, you can create a logo with a message such as "Technology Department Loaner." Another technique is to use Windows gadgets to add custom content directly to the desktop.

Setting the Desktop Background

Windows 7 provides multiple sets of background images and groups these images into named sets according to the folders in which the image files are stored. On the computer's hard disk, background images are stored in subfolders of the %WinDir%\Web\Wallpaper folder. Each folder represents a named set. For example, images in the Landscapes folder are displayed in the Landscapes set of background images.

Background images can be created as .bmp, .gif, .jpg, .jpeg, .dib, and .png files. If you add an image in one of these formats to any of the subfolders in the %WinDir%\Web\Wallpaper folder, the image will be available as part of that set. If you want to create a new set, simply create a folder under the %WinDir%\Web\Wallpaper folder and add the appropriate images to this folder.

To set the background for the desktop, follow these steps:

1. Right-click an open area of the desktop, and then click Personalize. In the Personalization console, click Desktop Background. This displays the Desktop Background page, shown in Figure 7-6.
2. When you select Windows Desktop Backgrounds as the Picture Location, Windows 7 organizes desktop backgrounds into sets of similar images. Use the scroll bar to navigate between sets, such as Architecture or Nature.
3. Click the image you want to use as the background. If you can't find a background that you want to use, click Browse to search for a background on the file system or network.

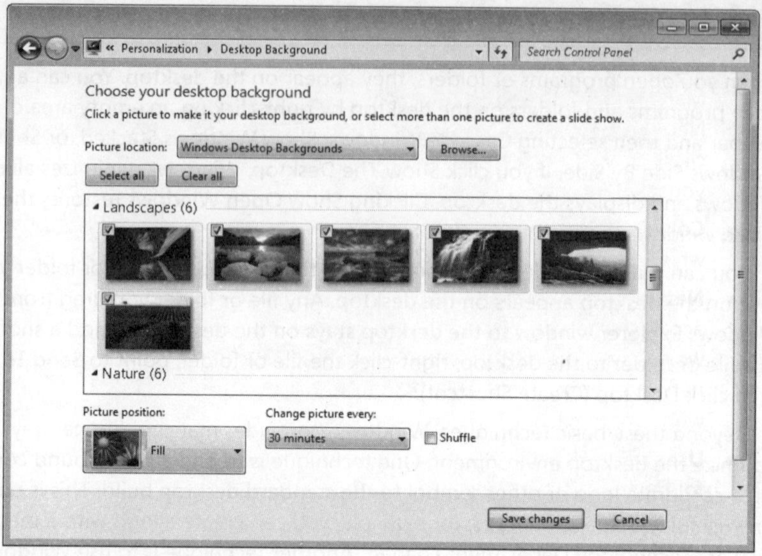

FIGURE 7-6 Select which desktop background to use.

4. Use the Picture Position options to select a display option for the background. Picture Position options include:
   - **Center** Centers the image on the desktop background. Any area that the image doesn't fill uses the current desktop color.
   - **Fill** Fills the desktop background with the image. The sides of the image may be cropped.
   - **Fit** Fits the image to the desktop background. Current proportions are maintained. This is a good option for photos and large images that you want to see without stretching or expanding.
   - **Stretch** Stretches the image to fill the desktop background. The current proportions are maintained as best as possible, but the height is stretched to fill any remaining gaps.
   - **Tile** Repeats the image so that it covers the entire screen. This is a good option for small images and icons.
5. When you are finished updating the background, click Save Changes.

Working with the Default Desktop Icons

By default, only the Recycle Bin is added to the desktop. Double-clicking the Recycle Bin icon opens a window where you can view files and folders you've marked for deletion. By selecting Empty The Recycle Bin, you permanently delete all the items in the Recycle Bin.

Other common desktop icons you can add to the desktop are as follows:

- **Computer** Double-clicking the Computer icon opens a window where you can access hard disk drives and devices with removable storage. Right-clicking the Computer icon and clicking Manage opens the Computer Management console. Right-clicking the Computer icon and clicking Map Network Drive enables you to connect to shared network folders. Right-clicking the Computer icon and clicking Disconnect Network Drive enables you to remove a connection to a shared network folder.
- **Control Panel** Double-clicking the Control Panel icon opens Control Panel, which provides access to system configuration and management tools.
- **Network** Double-clicking the Network icon opens a window where you can access the computers and devices on your network. Right-clicking the Network icon and clicking Map Network Drive enables you to connect to shared network folders. Right-clicking the Network icon and clicking Disconnect Network Drive enables you to remove a connection to a shared network folder.
- **User's Files** Double-clicking the User's Files icon opens your personal folder.

You can add or remove common desktop icons by following these steps:

1. Right-click an open area of the desktop, and then click Personalize. This displays the Personalization console.
2. In the left pane, click Change Desktop Icons. This displays the Desktop Icon Settings dialog box, shown in Figure 7-7.

FIGURE 7-7 Use the Desktop Icon Settings dialog box to select the desktop icons to display and set their appearance.

3. The Desktop Icon Settings dialog box has check boxes for each of the default icons. Clear the corresponding check box to remove an icon. Select the check box to add an icon.
4. Click OK.

You can hide all desktop icons by right-clicking an open area of the desktop, pointing to View, and selecting Show Desktop Icons. If you repeat this procedure and select Show Desktop Icons a second time, all the hidden desktop icons are restored.

If you no longer want an icon or a shortcut on the desktop, right-click it and then click Delete. When prompted, confirm the action by clicking Yes. Note that if you remove an icon representing a file or folder from the desktop, the file or folder (and its contents) are deleted.

Screen Saver Dos and Don'ts

Screen savers are designed to turn on when a computer has been idle for a specified period of time. The original job of the screen saver was to prevent image burn-in on CRT monitors by displaying a continuously changing image. With today's monitors, burn-in is no longer a problem, but screen savers are still around. The primary benefit they offer today is the ability to password-lock computers automatically when the screen saver turns on.

Configuring Screen Savers with Password Protection

Password protecting a screen saver deters unauthorized users from accessing a computer, which can protect both the personal data of the user and the intellectual property of an organization. As an administrator, you should ensure that the computers you deploy have password-protected screen savers enabled.

You can password protect a screen saver by performing the following steps:

1. Right-click an open area of the desktop, and then click Personalize.
2. Click the Screen Saver link to display the Screen Saver Settings dialog box, shown in Figure 7-8.

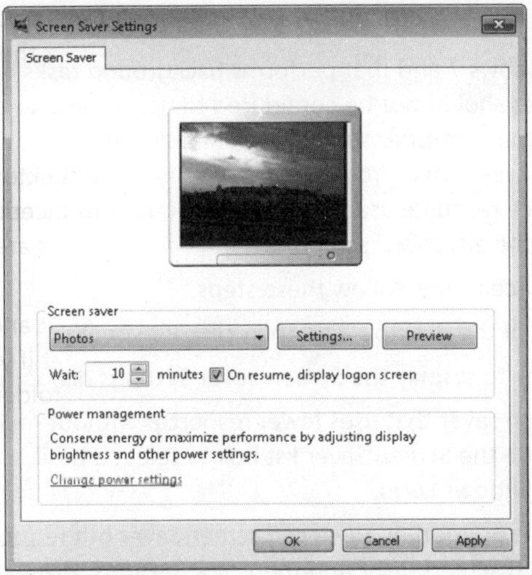

FIGURE 7-8 Set a screen saver with password protection for user and organization security.

3. Use the Screen Saver list box to select a screen saver. To disable the screen saver, select None and skip the remaining steps.

   REAL WORLD **Unfortunately, screen savers can use up a lot of a computer's resources, increasing both the energy usage of the computer (which otherwise would be idle) and its memory and processor usage. Some screen savers, particularly the three-dimensional ones such as 3D Text, can cause the processor to run at a high utilization percentage. The reason for this is that three-dimensional designs are very complex, and the computer must make a lot of computations to maintain and update the screen saver image. For tips on reducing resource usage when screen savers turn on, see the following sections, "Reducing Screen Saver Resource Usage" and "Setting Energy-Saving Settings for Monitors."**

4. Select On Resume, Display Logon Screen.
5. Use the Wait box to specify how long the computer must be idle before the screen saver is activated. A reasonable value is between 10 and 15 minutes.
6. Click OK.

NOTE **One of the best screen savers is the Photos screen saver, which displays a slide show of photos from the Pictures library by default, but you can select any other folder. By editing the settings, you can set the slide show speed and choose to shuffle the pictures rather than display them in sequence.**

Reducing Screen Saver Resource Usage

A computer that is running Windows 7 and that performs background tasks or network duties such as print services should not be configured to use a complex screen saver, such as 3D Text. Instead, the computer should be configured with a basic screen saver, such as the Blank screen saver. You can also modify the settings for advanced screen savers to reduce resource usage. Typically, you do this by reducing the redraw and refresh rates of the advanced screen saver.

To reduce screen saver resource usage, follow these steps:

1. Right-click an open area of the desktop. and then click Personalize.
2. Click the Screen Saver link to display the Screen Saver Settings dialog box.
3. If you want to use a screen saver that uses fewer resources without making configuration changes, use the Screen Saver list box to select a basic screen saver, such as Blank or Windows Logo.
4. If you want to use 3D Text or another advanced screen saver but reduce its resource usage, select that screen saver and then click Settings. Use the Settings dialog box to reduce the values for Resolution, Size, Rotational Speed, or similar fields that affect the drawing or refreshing of the screen saver.
5. Click OK to close each of the open dialog boxes.

Setting Energy-Saving Settings for Monitors

Many newer monitors have energy-saving features that cause them to shut off after a certain period of inactivity. Enabling this feature can reduce the organization's electricity bill because monitors typically use a lot of electricity to stay powered up. On some systems, this feature might have been automatically enabled by the operating system during installation. This depends, however, on the operating system properly detecting the monitor and installing any necessary drivers.

On a portable laptop computer running on batteries, saving energy is especially important. By configuring the monitor to shut off when the computer is idle, you can save the battery life and extend the available battery time for when the laptop is unplugged.

To manage a monitor's energy settings, follow these steps:

1. Right-click an open area of the desktop, and then click Personalize.
2. Click the Screen Saver link to display the Screen Saver Settings dialog box.
3. Click Change Power Settings. The Power Options console in Control Panel is displayed.
4. In the left pane, click Choose When To Turn Off Display.
5. Use the selection list provided to specify when the monitor should be turned off to save energy. By default, all the standard power plans turn off the computer's monitor after 20 minutes.

6. Click Save Changes.

NOTE If the computer is connected to a monitor that doesn't support energy-saving settings, some power options might be unavailable. If you are configuring the computer in a build area and are using a different monitor than the one the user will have, you might want to obtain the user's monitor or a similar monitor and repeat this process.

REAL WORLD Typically, you'll want to turn off the monitor after 15 to 20 minutes of idle time. On my office computer, I turn on the screen saver after 7 minutes and then turn off the monitor after 15 minutes of idle time. On my laptop, I use settings of 5 minutes and 10 minutes, respectively.

Modifying Display Appearance and Video Settings

The display appearance and video settings have a major impact on the look and feel of the Windows 7 desktop and its graphical elements. Appearance options control window, button, color, and font settings. Video settings control screen resolution, color quality, refresh frequency, hardware acceleration, and color management.

Configuring Window Color and Appearance

The Windows Aero interface is an enhanced interface that provides features such as transparent window frames, live previews, smoother window dragging, animated window closing and opening, and more. As part of the setup process, Windows 7 runs a performance test and checks the computer to see whether it meets the basic requirements for Windows Aero, which include:

- Support for Windows Display Driver Model (WDDM). WDDM 1.0 was introduced with Windows Vista. In Windows 7, display drivers that support WDDM 1.1 will offer improved performance while also reducing the per-window memory usage by up to 50 percent.
- Support for DirectX implemented in a graphics processing unit (GPU) with at least 128 MB of graphics memory. WDDM 1.1 supports DirectX 11. DirectX 11 offers enhancements and performance improvements over its predecessors.

REAL WORLD You can quickly determine how much graphics memory is available and whether a computer's display adapter supports WDDM by using Performance Information And Tools. In Control Panel, in the View By options, click either Small Icons or Large Icons to open All Control Panel Items, click Performance Information And Tools, and then click the View And Print Detailed Performance And System Information link. In the Component list, under Graphics, you'll see the display adapter type and the level of WDDM support. In the expanded list under Graphics,

you'll see additional details, including the amount of dedicated graphics memory and the DirectX version supported.

On compliant systems, Windows 7 uses the Aero design by default for its windows and dialog boxes. With Aero, three key areas of the display appearance can be optimized: color schemes, window transparency, and color intensity. To configure these display options, follow these steps:

1. Right-click an open area of the desktop, and then click Personalize.
2. Click the Window Color link to display the Window Color And Appearance page, shown in Figure 7-9.
3. Change the color of windows by clicking one of the available colors. To make your own color, click Show Color Mixer, and then use the Hue, Saturation, and Brightness sliders to create a custom color.
4. To enable transparent glass (on computers that have graphics cards with sufficient memory to support this feature), select Enable Transparency. The edges of windows will then be semitransparent, letting you see through them.

   TIP **Transparency uses more resources than most graphics features, especially on a computer with a WDDM 1.0 display driver. If users have performance issues related to memory or the processor, you might want to disable transparency. For WDDM 1.1, performance is greatly enhanced and transparency uses fewer resources.**

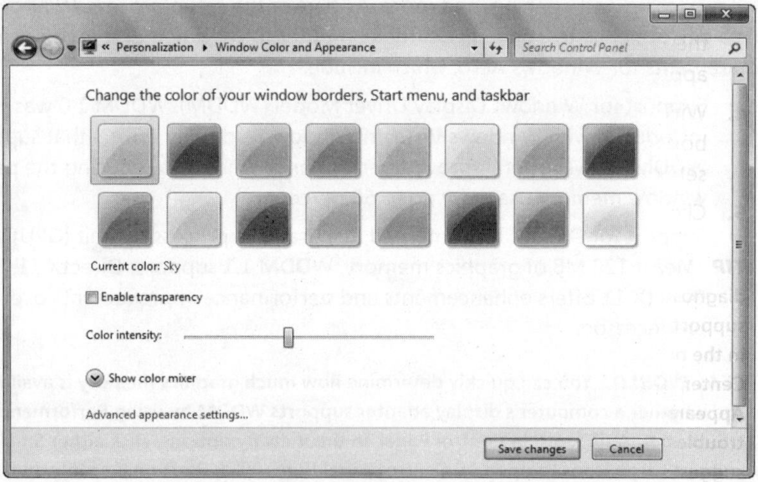

FIGURE 7-9 Configure the visual appearance of the display using the options on the Window Color And Appearance page.

5. Use the Color Intensity slider to set the strength of the color and the level of transparency. Increase the intensity to make the color stronger and to reduce the transparency. Reduce the intensity to make the color dimmer and the transparency greater.
6. Click Save Changes.

If you prefer, you can use the classic style windows and dialog boxes. When you do so, however, the appearance of most windows and dialog boxes is changed substantially. Additionally, desktop compositing is disabled, which removes features like transparency and Aero glass. To configure Windows 7 to use the classic display appearance, follow these steps:

1. Right-click an open area of the desktop, and then click Personalize.
2. Click the Windows 7 Basic theme or an Ease Of Access theme.
3. Now when you select Personalize and click the Window Color link, the classic Window Color And Appearance dialog box is displayed.

When working with any display appearance style, you can override default settings for individual graphical elements, such as the desktop or message boxes, using the Advanced Appearance dialog box. To open and work with this dialog box, follow these steps:

1. Right-click an open area of the desktop, and then click Personalize.
2. Click the Window Color link, and then click Advanced Appearance Settings.
3. Use the Item list to select the items that you want to modify, and then set the size, color, and font options you want to use. (For some items, not all these options will be available.) Changes you make are recorded when you make them, enabling you to configure multiple elements before clicking OK to apply the changes.
4. With graphical elements that contain system text, you can use the Font list box to select the typeface to use and the related Size and Color list boxes to set the size and color of the font, respectively.
5. Click OK, and then click Save Changes.

TIP **Windows 7 includes a troubleshooter for Windows Aero that can help users diagnose and resolve problems they are experiencing without needing technical support. To access the troubleshooter, the user should click the Action Center icon in the notification area of the taskbar and then click Open Action Center. In Action Center, click the Troubleshooting link to display all available troubleshooters. Under Appearance And Personalization, click Display Aero Desktop Effects. When the Aero troubleshooter starts, the user should follow the series of prompts. By default, any suggested fixes are applied automatically. If the problem cannot be resolved automatically, the user will see the message Troubleshooting Could Not Fix The Problem. The problem identified will be listed under Problems Found. Have the user click View Detailed Information to display more information on why the problem could not be resolved. If you want the user to be able to send you a report on the problem**

after he has tried to resolve it automatically, have the user start the Problem Steps Recorder prior to starting the troubleshooter. For more information about the Problem Steps Recorder, see the section "Managing Remote Access to Workstations" in Chapter 5.

Optimizing Display Readability

Regardless of whether users have 27-inch widescreens or 19-inch displays, you may find that users have difficulty reading text on the screen. Often, the readability of text on the screen decreases when you increase the display resolution, which results in the text on the screen becoming smaller. To understand why this happens, you need to understand how DPI works.

When you print documents on a printer, the number of dots per inch (DPI) determines the print quality. Generally, the higher the DPI, the better the quality of the printed document, because images and text look crisper as you use more dots per inch. For example, a high-resolution picture printed at its normal size using 1200 × 600 DPI generally looks much better than the same picture printed at 300 × 300 DPI. However, if you use scaling to print a 2 × 3–inch picture at 6 × 9 inches, you often get a poor result because the scaled image looks grainy.

For Windows computers, 96 DPI is the default for most monitors, and Windows 7 displays all user interface (UI) elements, including text, at 96 DPI by default. When you change the display resolution, you change the scaling at which UI elements are displayed. For example, if a monitor has an optimal resolution of 1920 × 1200 and you use a display resolution of 800 × 600, the UI elements will seem large and grainy because you've caused the display to scale 800 × 600 pixels into a space optimized for 1920 × 1200 pixels.

Generally, you can determine the optimal resolution by multiplying a monitor's screen width by 96 and a monitor's screen height by 96. For example, a 27-inch widescreen monitor may have a screen that is 20 inches wide and 12.5 inches high. If so, the optimal display resolution is 1920 × 1200. However, at that size, text and UI elements on the screen may seem small, and you may need to make adjustments to improve readability. One way to do this is in an application. For example, in Microsoft Word, users can use the Zoom combo box to scale text to a readable size.

Windows allows you to use scaling to increase the size of text and other items on the screen. When you use scaling in this way, Windows magnifies the size of text and UI elements to the scale you choose. Each account on a computer has a separate setting for scaling. You can specify the scaling to use for text and UI elements by following these steps:

1. In Control Panel, click Appearance And Personalization. Under the Display heading, click Make Text And Other Items Larger Or Smaller.
2. The default scaling options allow you to choose a 100-percent scale (the default), a 125-percent scale, or a 150-percent scale. To use one of these scaling options, make a selection, and then click Apply.

3. To choose a custom setting of between 100 percent and 500 percent, click Set Custom Text Size (DPI) in the left pane, and then use the Scale combo box to select or specify a scale.
4. You need to log off the user and then log on the user again for the changes to take effect.

CAUTION **If you choose a setting higher than 200 percent, UI elements and text may be scaled so large that you cannot work with the computer. You may even be unable to get back into Control Panel to restore the original scaling. If you have a scaling issue, enter dpiscaling at a command prompt or in the Search box on the Start menu. This will open the Display page directly, and you can then reset the scaling.**

REAL WORLD **If you've enabled scaling and the text in an application is blurred or unreadable, you may want to disable display scaling for that application. To do this, right-click the application shortcut, and then click Properties. On the Compatibility tab, select Disable Display Scaling On High DPI Settings, and then click OK.**

Configuring Video Settings

Video settings control screen resolution, color quality, refresh rate, hardware acceleration, and color management. This section focuses on making sure that Windows 7 has correctly identified the video card and monitor and on optimizing various video settings.

Checking the Current Video Adapter and Monitor

Every computer has a monitor driver and a video adapter driver. The monitor driver tells Windows about the capabilities of the monitor. The video adapter (or display) driver tells Windows about the capabilities of the graphics card.

Proper display is dependent on the computer using accurate information about the video adapter and the monitor. Different driver files are installed depending on which video adapter and monitor models Windows 7 detects on a system. These drivers are extremely important in determining which display resolutions, color depths, and refresh rates are available and appropriate for the system. If the adapter and monitor aren't detected and configured properly, Windows 7 won't be able to take advantage of their capabilities.

Current settings for the video adapter or monitor can be wrong for many reasons. Sometimes, Plug and Play doesn't detect the device, and a generic device driver is used. At other times, Windows 7 detects the wrong type of device, such as a different model. In this case, the device will probably work, but some features won't be available.

To check the current video adapter and monitor configured for a computer, follow these steps:

1. Right-click an open area of the desktop, and then click Screen Resolution.
2. On the Screen Resolution page, shown in Figure 7-10, the currently identified monitors are listed in the Display list. The resolution and orientation are listed in the Resolution and Orientation lists. If the correct monitor isn't displayed or you want to examine the monitor settings further, see the section "Changing the Monitor" later in this chapter.

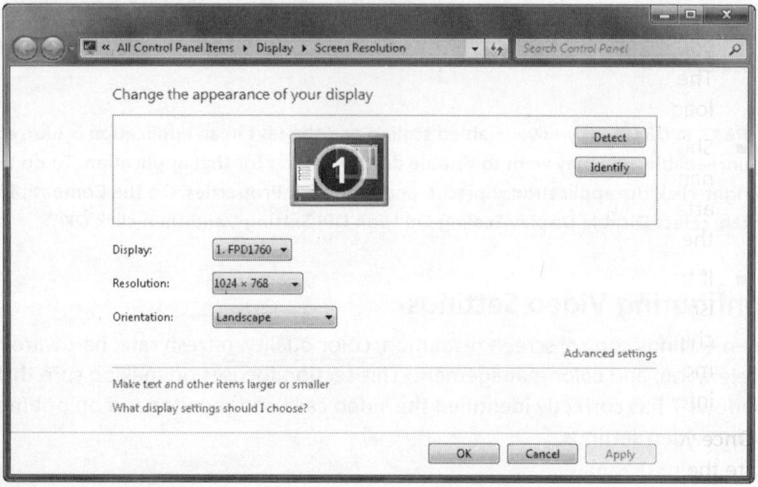

FIGURE 7-10 Check the monitor and video adapter configuration.

3. Select a monitor in the Display list, and then click the Advanced Settings link. The video adapter for the monitor is listed. If the correct video adapter isn't displayed or you want to examine the driver settings further, see the next section, "Changing the Video Driver."
4. Click OK twice.

Changing the Video Driver

If you followed the previous instructions and the video driver shown does not match the make and model installed on the computer, you might want to try to install a different driver. For example, if the computer has a generic S3 video driver configured and you are sure the computer has an NVIDIA GeForce video adapter, you should change the video driver.

To determine whether the video card make and model are correct, you need to know how the system is configured. The system documentation can tell you which video adapter is installed. Other administrators are also useful resources. Typically, someone else on the technology team will know immediately what video adapter is installed on a particular type of computer. If you can't figure out the make and model of the video adapter, you have several options. If the current settings are working, you can leave the display settings alone. You can also try the following techniques to determine the video adapter's make and model:

- Shut down the computer, and then turn it back on (but don't use the Restart option to do this because some computers may not fully initialize when you select Restart). Watch the screen when the computer is first turned on. The name of the video card might appear briefly before Windows 7 begins loading.
- Shut down the computer, and then remove the computer cover. Locate the name and model number on the video adapter itself. If the monitor is still attached to the rear of the computer, the video adapter is the card to which the monitor cable is connected.
- If the video adapter is built into the computer's motherboard (meaning there isn't a separate card), check the motherboard to see whether you can find a chip that lists the video information on it, or write down the motherboard model number and visit the manufacturer's Web site to see whether the information is available.

Once you determine the video adapter's make and model, see whether you can locate the necessary drivers on the manufacturer's Web site. Some video adapters come with installation discs. On the disc, you might find a setup program. Run this program to install the video driver. If the installation disc contains the drivers but no setup program, you need to install the drivers manually.

When you are ready to install the video adapter driver, follow these steps:

1. Right-click an open area of the desktop. and then click Screen Resolution.
2. On a system with multiple monitors or video cards, use the Display list to select the monitor with which you want to work.
3. Click Advanced Settings. On the Adapter tab, shown in Figure 7-11, note the current information in the Adapter Type and Adapter Information panels. Click Properties.

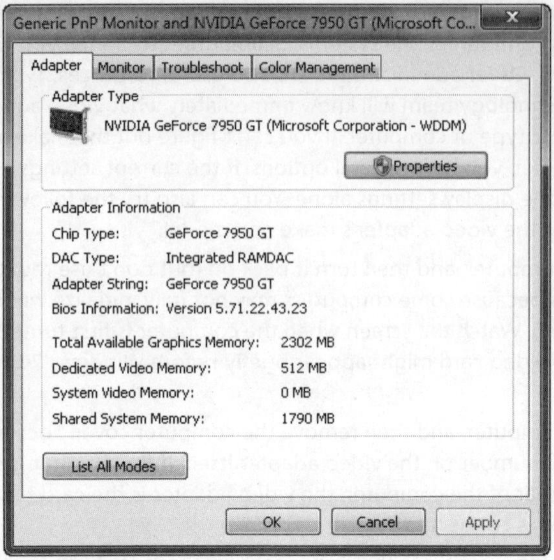

FIGURE 7-11 Note the current adapter information.

4. On the Driver tab, click Update Driver. This starts the Update Driver Software wizard.
5. Specify whether you want to search for the driver automatically or browse for the driver.
6. If you elect to search for the driver automatically, Windows 7 looks for a more recent version of the device driver and installs the driver if it is found. If a more recent version of the driver is not found, Windows 7 keeps the current driver. In either case, click Close to complete the process, and then skip the remaining steps.
7. If you choose to browse for the driver, you are given the following options:
   - **Search for the driver** If you want to search for the driver, click Browse to select a search location. Use the Browse For Folder dialog box to select the start folder for the search, and then click OK. Because all subfolders of the selected folder are searched automatically, you can select the drive root path, such as C, to search an entire drive.
   - **Choose the driver to install** If you want to choose the driver to install, click Let Me Pick From A List Of Device Drives On My Computer. The wizard then displays a list of compatible hardware. Click the device that matches your video card. To view a wider array of choices, clear the Show Compatible Hardware check box. You'll then see a list of all video card manufacturers. Scroll through the list of manufacturers to find the manufacturer of the device, and then choose the appropriate device in the right pane.

8. After selecting a device driver, continue through the installation process by clicking Next. Click Close when the driver installation is complete. If the wizard can't find an appropriate driver, you need to obtain one and then repeat this procedure. Keep in mind that in some cases you need to restart the system to activate the newly installed or updated device driver.

Changing the Monitor

The overall display quality is controlled by the combined capabilities of a computer's monitor and video adapter. Most computers have at least one monitor connection available. The type of connections supported may include the following:

- High-Definition Multimedia Interface (HDMI) is the current digital standard for connecting video devices. HDMI can be used for computer displays, but it is better suited to other high-end video devices. While HDMI can be adapted to a Digital Video Interface (DVI) connection, most computers that have an HDMI connector also have at least one DVI connector.
- Digital Video Interface is the digital standard for computer-generated text and graphics. There are several formats for DVI. DVI-I and DVI-A can be adapted to VGA. However, DVI-D cannot be adapted to VGA. Dual Link DVI supports high-resolution monitors and is required on some very large displays for optimum picture quality. Because DVI cables can support one or more of these types at the same time, you should check your cables carefully to be sure you're using the correct ones.
- Fifteen-pin Video Graphics Array (VGA) is the analog standard for connecting monitors to computers. Nine-pin VGA cables exist and are compatible with the 15-pin connector. It is still very common for monitors to have this connector, but newer connections like DVI and HDMI are recommended if available.

NOTE **A computer's monitor may have shipped with a VGA cable connected to it. If it is not the optimal connection type and the cable is designed to be removed, remove the VGA cable.**

TIP **Many computers have inputs for DisplayPort adapters. A DisplayPort adapter supports automatic adaptation to VGA, DVI, or HDMI depending on what type of display is connected to the port and what type of adapter is used between the display connector and the input connector on the back of the computer.**

If a computer has a Plug and Play monitor, Windows 7 might have detected it and installed it properly, or it might have installed a similar driver but not the one that matches the monitor's make and model. For the best quality, Windows 7 should use the driver designed for the applicable monitor. Otherwise, the display mode, color depth, refresh rate, and color-matching options might not be appropriate for the monitor.

To change the monitor setup, follow these steps:

1. Right-click an open area of the desktop, and then click Screen Resolution.
2. On a system with multiple monitors or video cards, use the Display list to select the monitor with which you want to work.
3. Click Advanced Settings. On the Monitor tab, click Properties.
4. On the Driver tab, click Update Driver. This starts the Update Driver Software wizard.
5. Continue with the driver update as described in steps 5–8 of the previous procedure.

Configuring Multiple Monitor Support

Most modern computers come with a video adapter that supports two monitors. You'll know this because the adapter will have multiple monitor connection ports. On these computers, you can connect multiple monitors and then extend a user's desktop across those monitors so that the user can see more information at one time. If you've connected multiple monitors to a computer, the Screen Resolution page will show one box for each monitor. The first monitor is labeled 1, the second is labeled 2, and so on. If you click the monitor box, you can work with the monitor in the same way you would if you had selected the monitor from the Display list.

If a monitor you've connected doesn't have its own box, check the monitor connection and then turn the monitor on. Then, when you click the Detect button, Windows should automatically detect the monitor.

If you've connected multiple monitors and are unsure which monitor is which, you can click the Identify button to display the numeric identifier of each monitor on the monitor's screen. The numeric identifier appears as a large white numeral. If you find that the screens are represented in a different position than they are configured, you can drag the monitor boxes on the Screen Resolution page so that their position matches the physical layout of the monitors.

After you configure the monitors, you may want to extend the display across their screens. To do this, click the box representing the second monitor (or select the second monitor in the Display list), and then select Extend These Displays from the Multiple Displays list. Generally, you will want screen 1 to be marked This Is Currently Your Main Display.

Changing the Screen Resolution and Color Quality

Screen resolution and color quality are key factors affecting display appearance. Screen resolution is the number of pixels that make up the display. Color quality is the number of colors that can be displayed simultaneously on the screen.

A low-end monitor has resolutions of 640 × 480, 800 × 600, and 1024 × 768. High-end monitors have additional resolutions of 1280 × 1024, 1600 × 1200, 1920 × 1200, 2048 × 1536, and sometimes even higher. The best resolution to use depends on the size of the monitor and what the user plans to do with the computer. Designers and developers who need a large screen area will appreciate a higher resolution, such as 1920 × 1200. They can then see more of what they're working with on the screen. Users who spend most of their time reading e-mail or working with Word documents might prefer a lower resolution, such as 1280 × 1024. At that resolution, screen elements are easier to see, and users will have less eyestrain. On a widescreen monitor, be sure to select a resolution that is appropriate for widescreen viewing.

Color quality depends greatly on screen resolution settings. Color quality can range from 16 colors for standard VGA monitors to 4 billion colors (32-bit) for high-end monitors. Most video cards display fewer colors when you set the screen resolution higher. This means that a computer might be able to use 16-bit, 24-bit, or 32-bit color, but the screen resolution often must be decreased to achieve the highest color quality. In most cases, the higher the color quality you can set, the better. Keep in mind that the amount of video memory required to maintain the video display is determined by multiplying the number of pixels on the screen (based on screen resolution) by the number of bits per pixel (determined by color quality). Furthermore, the maximum combination of resolution and color quality allowed is a function of the video memory on the video adapter.

You can set the screen resolution and color quality by completing the following steps:

1. Right-click an open area of the desktop, and then click Screen Resolution.
2. On a system with multiple monitors or video cards, use the Display list to select the monitor with which you want to work.
3. Click Resolution, and then use the Resolution slider to set the display size, such as 1024 × 768 pixels.
4. To set the bit depth for color, click Advanced Settings. On the Monitor tab, use the Colors list box to select a color quality, such as True Color (32-bit).
5. Click OK twice.

Changing the Display Refresh Rate

The refresh rate is the rate at which the screen is repainted. The higher the refresh rate, the less flicker there is in the display. If you've ever seen video footage of a computer system with a monitor that seemed to be scrolling or blinking, it appeared this way because the computer's refresh rate was out of sync with the video recording speed. Your eyes don't notice the flicker as much, but a low refresh rate (under 72 Hz) can sometimes make your eyes tired if you look at the display too long.

To view or set the refresh rate for a video card, follow these steps:

1. Right-click an open area of the desktop, and then click Screen Resolution.
2. On a system with multiple monitors or video cards, use the Display list to select the monitor with which you want to work.

3. Click Advanced Settings. On the Adapter tab, click List All Modes. The resolution sizes and refresh rates supported by the monitor are listed.
4. On the Monitor tab, use the Screen Refresh Rate list box to set the refresh rate.

CAUTION **In many cases, the Hide Modes That This Monitor Cannot Display check box is disabled so that it cannot be selected. If you are able to clear this check box, keep in mind that if the refresh rate exceeds the capabilities of the monitor or the video card, the screen can become distorted. Additionally, running the computer at a higher refresh rate than it supports can damage the monitor and video adapter.**

Troubleshooting Display Problems

As I stated previously, every computer has a monitor driver and a video adapter driver. The monitor driver tells Windows about the capabilities of the monitor. The video adapter (or display) driver tells Windows about the capabilities of the graphics card.

Clearly, the monitor driver and video adapter driver have important roles on a computer. When you are installing video components or updating a computer, you should be sure that the computer has drivers that have been tested in your environment and proven to be reliable. If you suspect a problem with the drivers, update the drivers if possible. If you suspect the problem is due to the configuration of the computer, start the computer in safe mode and then modify the default settings.

Before you start detailed diagnostics and troubleshooting, determine what programs the user has been running. Programs created for computers prior to Windows XP may cause compatibility issues. Close all running programs and check questionable programs to see what display mode they are using. If a program requires an alternate display mode, and switching into and out of this display mode is causing problems, you may be able to configure compatibility settings to resolve the problem. Right-click the application shortcut, and then click Properties. In the Properties dialog box, select the Compatibility tab. On the Settings panel, choose the appropriate option, such as Run In 640x480 Screen Resolution. If you are unsure which compatibility settings to use, right-click the application shortcut, click Troubleshoot Compatibility, and then follow the prompts in the Program Compatibility wizard.

Many problems with monitors have to do with the connection between the monitor and the computer. If the monitor displays blotches, color spots, diagonal lines or horizontal bars or has other similar display problems, you'll want to check the monitor connection first. After you are sure the connections are okay, turn the monitor off for at least 10 seconds, and then turn the monitor back on. If you still are experiencing problems and think the problem has to do with the monitor itself, you can try to resolve the problem through additional troubleshooting.

Monitor flicker or jitter or a shaky image can be caused by configuration issues as well as positional issues. If the monitor refresh rate is causing the problem, you can resolve it by changing the refresh rate settings as discussed previously in the section "Changing the Display Refresh Rate." If a positional issue is causing the problem, you can resolve the problem by moving the cables and devices that may be causing electromagnetic interference, including power cables for other devices, large speakers, or desk lamps. If the problem persists, make sure the monitor has a shielded cable and that it is positioned away from air conditioning units, large fluorescent lights, and so on.

If the monitor has built-in controls, check for an auto-tuning setting. Often, this will be a separate button, and when you push this button the monitor will automatically adjust itself.

If blotches of color, colors spots, or lines are the problem and resetting the connections doesn't work, you may need to perform a monitor degauss. This operation removes the build-up of stray magnetic fields around the monitor, which can distort the video image. Some monitors autodegauss by turning the monitor off and then on, some have a manual control only, and some combine both of these features. You may find a control labeled Degauss, or there may be a menu option within the monitor's software controls. While the monitor is degaussing, the screen may become distorted temporarily. This is normal behavior during the degauss process. If you manually degauss, wait 15 to 20 minutes before attempting a second degauss.

If problems persist, connect the monitor directly to the computer. Remove any extension cables connected between the monitor and the video adapter. Also remove any antiglare screens or other similar devices that cover the monitor's screen. Check the video data cable for bent, broken, or missing pins. Although some pins are missing as part of the design, other pins that are missing or bent will cause display problems. If there are bent pins and the pins are repairable, turn the monitor off, unplug the monitor from the power source, and use tweezers or pliers to straighten the pins.

CHAPTER 8

Managing Hardware Devices and Drivers

Managing a computer's hardware configuration is largely about installing and maintaining operating system components, hardware devices, and device drivers. However, managing the hardware configuration of computers running Windows 7 is very different from managing the configuration of computers running Windows XP or earlier releases of Windows. As with Windows Vista, many aspects of Windows 7 are automatically monitored and updated and don't need to be configured or maintained in the same way as they were in earlier releases of Windows. Windows 7 uses the following:

- Built-in diagnostics to monitor hardware devices, physical memory, networking, and performance
- Problem reporting to try to automatically resolve configuration and performance issues
- Problem diagnosis to offer solutions to issues that cannot be automatically resolved
- Automatic updating of operating system components
- Driver updating to obtain necessary drivers and driver updates for detected hardware devices

From the moment you install Windows 7, these features start working to help you monitor and maintain computers. As an administrator, you can use these features to help guide your configuration and maintenance efforts. Separate tools are provided for managing the areas monitored by diagnostics, including hardware diagnostics, memory diagnostics, networking diagnostics, and performance diagnostics.

For configuring and maintaining hardware devices and drivers, you can also use Device Manager, Devices And Printers, and the Add A Device wizard. You'll use these tools whenever you install, uninstall, or troubleshoot hardware devices and drivers. Other tools are available for managing specific types of hardware devices, such as keyboards and sound cards. To manage automatic updating and driver updating, you use Windows Update, which is provided as a Control Panel utility.

Working with the Automated Help System

The many enhancements to Automated Help and Support in Windows 7 fundamentally change how the operating system works and how you support it. As an administrator, you should be sure to understand how the Help architecture works and how it can be configured.

Using Automated Help And Support

Like Windows Vista, Windows 7 includes an extensive diagnostics and problem-resolution architecture. Although Windows XP and earlier releases of Windows include some Help and diagnostics features, those features are, for the most part, not self-correcting or self-diagnosing. Windows 7, on the other hand, can detect many types of hardware, memory, and performance issues and resolve them automatically or help users through the process of resolving them.

Windows 7 includes more reliable and better performing device drivers that prevent many common causes of hangs and crashes. Improved input/output (I/O) cancellation for device drivers ensures that the operating system can recover gracefully from blocking calls and that fewer blocking disk I/O operations occur.

To reduce downtime and restarts required for application installations and updates, Windows 7 can use the update process to mark in-use files for update and then automatically replace the files the next time an application is started. In some cases, Windows 7 can save the application's data, close the application, update the in-use files, and then restart the application. To improve overall system performance and responsiveness, Windows 7 uses memory more efficiently, provides ordered execution for groups of threads, and provides new process-scheduling mechanisms. By optimizing memory and process usage, Windows 7 ensures that background processes have less impact on system performance.

Windows 7 provides improved guidance on the causes of unresponsive conditions. By including additional error-reporting details in the event logs, Windows 7 makes it easier to identify and resolve issues. To automatically recover from service failures, Windows 7 uses service-recovery policies more extensively than did previous versions. When recovering a failed service, Windows 7 automatically handles both service and nonservice dependencies as well. Windows 7 starts any dependent services and system components prior to starting the failed service.

In Windows XP and earlier releases of Windows, an application crash or hang is marked as Not Responding, and it is up to the user to exit and then restart the application. Windows 7 attempts to resolve the issue of unresponsive applications by using Restart Manager. Restart Manager can shut down and restart unresponsive applications automatically. Thanks to Restart Manager, you might not have to intervene to try to resolve issues with frozen applications.

Failed installations and nonresponsive conditions of applications and drivers are also tracked through Action Center. In these cases, the built-in diagnostics mechanisms can sometimes provide a problem response. You can view a list of current problems at any time by doing one of the following:

- Click the Action Center icon in the notification area of the taskbar, and then click Open Action Center.
- In Control Panel, click System And Security, and then click Action Center.

In Action Center, shown in Figure 8-1, you can see a list of problems organized into two broad areas: Security and Maintenance.

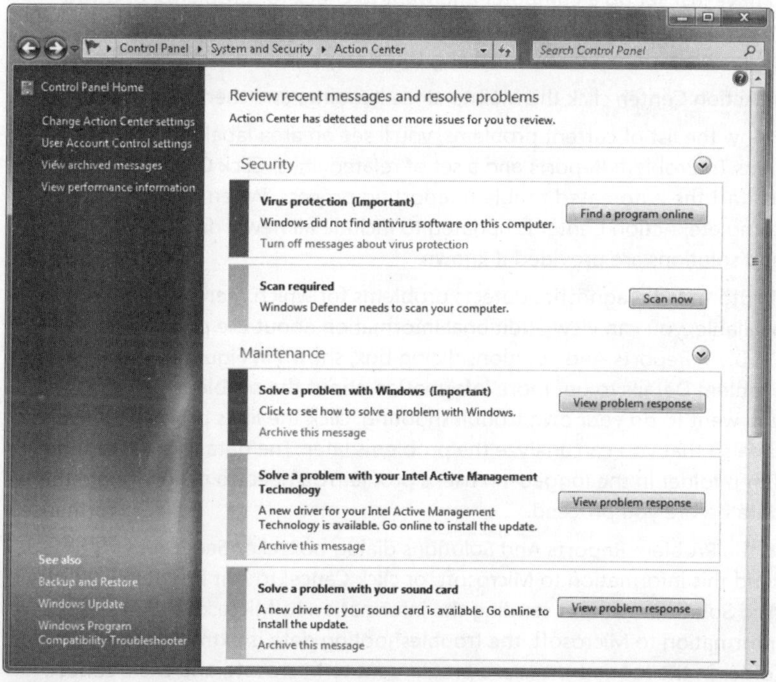

FIGURE 8-1 Check for known problems using Action Center.

Problems are color-coded:

- Red is a warning about an important problem that needs your attention. For example, if the computer doesn't have virus protection software, this is a red warning.

- Orange is a caution about a problem that you might want to look at. For example, if a computer hasn't been scanned recently by Windows Defender, this is an orange warning.

You can click the Security or Maintenance heading to expand the section and view more detailed information. Expanding the Security area displays information about the following:

- The status of the network firewall, Windows Update, virus protection, and malware protection
- The configuration of Internet security settings, User Account Control, and Network Access Protection

Expanding the Maintenance area displays information about the following:

- Links for managing the configuration of problem reports
- The status of Windows Backup and required actions for Windows Update
- The status of troubleshooting and links for changing the settings

If you have just set up a computer and want to check for problems, or if you suspect a computer has problems that haven't been diagnosed, you can initiate automatic problem detection by following these steps:

1. In Action Center, click the Maintenance heading, and then scroll down.
2. Below the list of current problems, you'll see an area labeled Check For Solutions To Problem Reports and a set of related links. Click Check For Solutions to start the automated problem reporting process. When this process is complete, Action Center is updated to include all newly discovered problems, and solutions are provided if known.
3. If automated diagnostics detects problems for which there are no solutions available, you can view additional information about the problems. In the Problem Reports And Solutions dialog box, shown in Figure 8-2, click View Problem Details to get more information about the problems detected. If you want to do your own troubleshooting, click the links provided to extract data so that you can analyze the problems later. The data is extracted to the Temp folder in the logged-on user's profile. You need to make a copy of this data before you proceed.
4. In the Problem Reports And Solutions dialog box, click Send Information to send this information to Microsoft, or click Cancel to exit Problem Reports And Solutions without sending the information to Microsoft. If you send the information to Microsoft, the troubleshooting data is extracted to the Temp folder in the logged-on user's profile, sent to Microsoft, and then deleted from the Temp directory. The amount of data extracted and sent can be a significant amount.

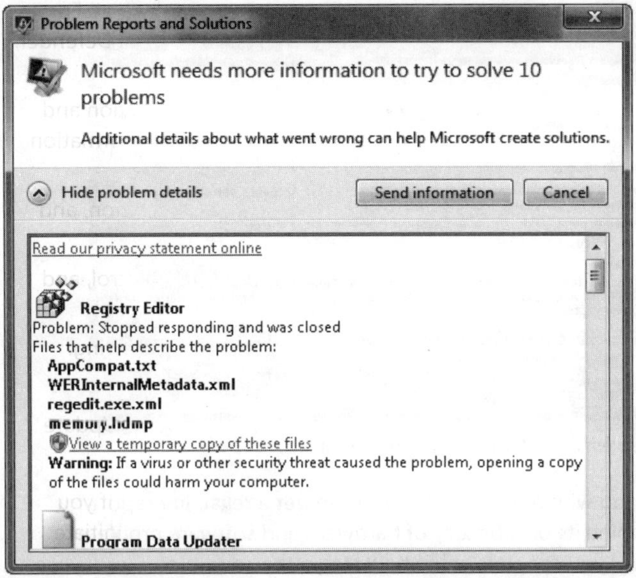

FIGURE 8-2 Review detected problems for which there are no available solutions.

In Action Center, you can resolve detected problems that have known solutions by following these steps:

1. Each problem has a solution button. With Security problems, you can typically find programs online or scan the computer using protection software. With Maintenance problems, you generally click the View Problem Response button to display a page providing more information about the problem.
2. When you view the More Information page, shown in Figure 8-3, keep the following in mind: When a driver or software issue is causing a problem, you'll find a link to download and install the latest driver or software update. When a configuration issue is causing a problem, you'll find a description of the problem and a step-by-step guide for modifying the configuration to resolve the problem.
3. When you have resolved a problem by installing a driver or software update, you can elect to archive the message for future reference by selecting the Archive This Message check box before you click OK to close the More Information page.

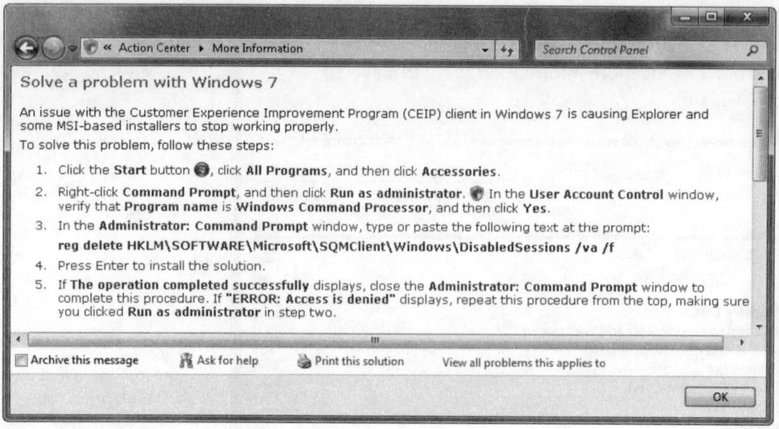

FIGURE 8-3 Resolve the problem by performing the required actions.

When you are working with Action Center, you can get a reliability report for the computer to determine its past history of hardware and software problems. By reviewing this history, you can determine how stable the computer is and what devices or programs have caused problems. To access and work with Reliability Monitor, follow these steps:

1. In Action Center, click the Maintenance heading, and then scroll down.
2. Below the list of current problems, you'll see an area labeled Check For Solutions To Problem Reports and a set of related links. Click View Reliability History.
3. As shown in Figure 8-4, you then see a graphical depiction of the computer's stability. You can view the history by days or weeks. The default view is days. To view the history by weeks, click the Weeks option for View By. The computer's stability is graphed with values ranging from 0, meaning poor reliability, to 10, meaning excellent reliability.
4. Events that could have affected stability are shown in the graph with information and warning icons, respectively. Clicking an icon displays details for the event in the Reliability Details list. As shown in the figure, events are listed by source, summary, and date. Under Action, you'll see a link. If Windows was able to resolve the problem automatically, you'll see the View Problem Response link. Clicking the link displays information on how Windows resolved the problem. In other cases you'll see the View Technical Details link. Clicking this link provides more information about the stability issue (see Figure 8-5).

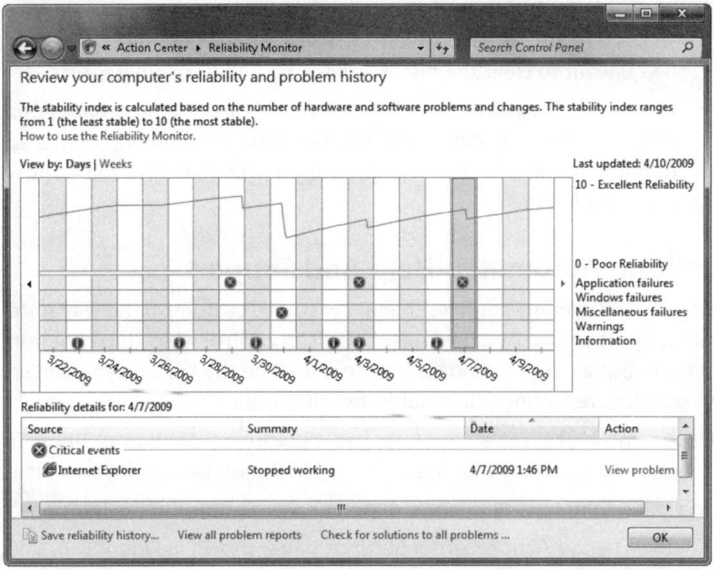

FIGURE 8-4 Review the graphical depiction of the computer's stability.

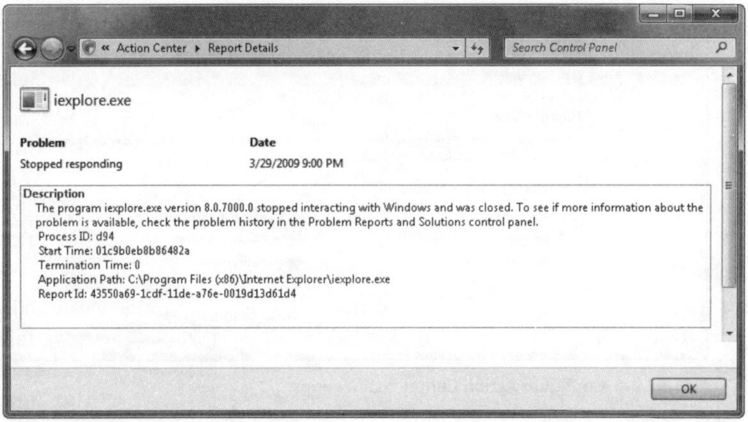

FIGURE 8-5 Review the report details to get more information.

5. At the bottom of the Reliability Monitor window are these additional options:

- **Save Reliability History** Allows you to save complete details about the computer's stability for future reference. The information is saved as a Reliability Monitor report and is formatted as XML. Click Save Reliability History, and then use the dialog box provided to select a save location and file name for the report. You can view the report in Internet Explorer by double-clicking the file.

- **View All Problem Reports** Opens the Problem History window that shows a history of all problems that have been identified and their status. If you want to clear the history, click Clear All Problem Reports.
- **Check For Solutions To All Problems** Starts the automated problem reporting process. When this process is complete, Action Center is updated to include all newly discovered problems, and solutions will be provided if known.

Customizing Automated Help And Support

Windows 7 provides many controls that allow you to customize the way Automated Help And Support works. At a basic level, you can control which types of notification messages are displayed in Action Center. To fine-tune the feature, you can control the ways problem reporting and troubleshooting work.

Each user who logs on to a computer has separate notification settings. To specify the types of notifications that are displayed in Action Center, follow these steps:

1. In Action Center, click Change Action Center Settings in the left pane.
2. On the Change Action Center Settings page, shown in Figure 8-6, select the check boxes for the types of notifications you want the user to see, and clear the check boxes for the types of notifications you don't need the user to see.

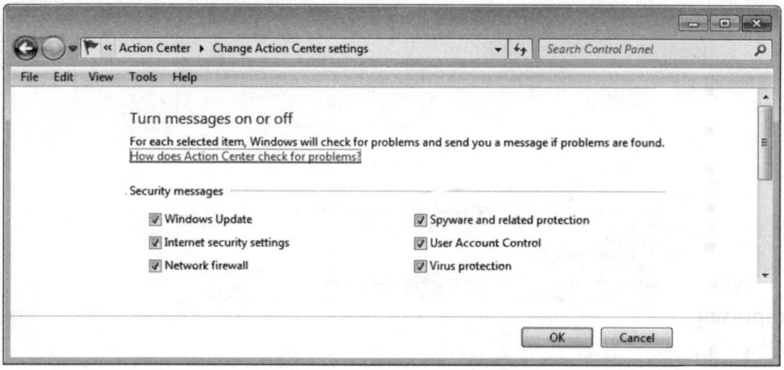

FIGURE 8-6 Configure Action Center notifications.

3. By default, usage information is sent to Microsoft as part of the Customer Experience Improvement Program. If you don't want to participate in this program, click Customer Experience Improvement Program Settings, click No, I Don't Want To Participate In The Program, and then click Save Changes.
4. Click OK.

In a standard configuration, each user who logs on to a computer has separate problem reporting settings. However, administrators also can specify that all users have the same reporting settings. To customize the way problem reporting works for the currently logged-on user or for all users, follow these steps:

1. In Action Center, click Change Action Center Settings in the left pane.
2. On the Change Action Center Settings page, under Related Settings, click Problem Reporting Settings.
3. You see the current configuration of problem reporting for the logged-on user. If you are able to modify the settings, the computer is configured so that each user can choose his or her problem report settings. If the settings are unavailable, the computer is configured so that all users have the same problem report settings.
4. If the computer has per-user problem report settings, select the problem report settings you want to use for the currently logged-on user, and then click OK to save the settings. The options are:
   - Automatically Check For Solutions
   - Automatically Check For Solutions And Send Additional Report Data, If Needed
   - Each Time A Problem Occurs, Ask Me Before Checking For Solutions
   - Never Check For Solutions
5. If the computer has per-computer problem report settings, click Change Report Settings For All Users, select the problem report settings you want to use for all users, and then click OK to save the settings. The options are:
   - Automatically Check For Solutions
   - Automatically Check For Solutions And Send Additional Data, If Needed
   - Each Time A Problem Occurs, Ask Me Before Checking For Solutions
   - Never Check For Solutions
   - Allow Each User To Choose Settings

When problem reporting is enabled, you can exclude programs from problem reporting. To do this, follow these steps:

1. In Action Center, click Change Action Center Settings in the left pane.
2. On the Change Action Center Settings page, under Related Settings, click Problem Reporting Settings. Next, click Select Programs To Exclude From Reporting.
3. On the Advanced Problem Reporting Settings page, you see a list of any programs that are currently excluded. You can now do the following:
   - Add programs to exclude them from reporting. Click Add, use the dialog box provided to navigate to and select the executable (.exe) file for the program, and then click Open.
   - Remove programs to stop excluding them from reporting. Click the program in the list provided, and then click Remove.

Each user who logs on to a computer has separate troubleshooting settings. To configure how troubleshooting works, follow these steps:

1. In Action Center, click the Maintenance heading, and then scroll down.
2. Below the list of current problems, you'll see an area labeled Troubleshooting: System Maintenance. Click Change Troubleshooting Settings.
3. On the Change Settings page, shown in Figure 8-7, you'll see the current settings for troubleshooting. By default, Windows periodically checks for routine maintenance issues and displays reminders when the System Maintenance troubleshooter can resolve problems. For example, the troubleshooter might notify the user that there are unused files and shortcuts that can be cleaned up.

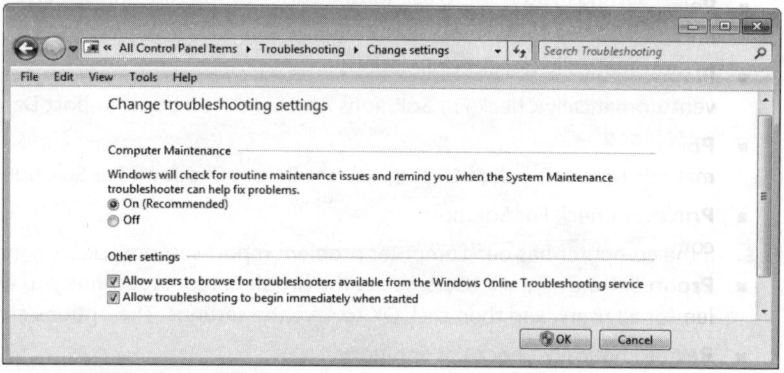

FIGURE 8-7 Specify how troubleshooting works.

4. Periodically, Microsoft may provide additional troubleshooters online. By default, users can browse for and use these troubleshooters. If you don't want the user to be able to browse for and use these troubleshooters, clear the Allow Users To Browse For Troubleshooters Available From The Windows Online Troubleshooting Service check box.
5. By default, when the user starts a troubleshooter, troubleshooting begins automatically. If you'd rather have the user confirm that he wants to start troubleshooting, clear the Allow Troubleshooting To Begin Immediately When Started check box.
6. Click OK to save your settings.

Automated troubleshooting is a feature made possible by Windows PowerShell 2.0 and related system services. As long as PowerShell is installed (it is installed by default) and the required services are available, automated troubleshooting will work. Standard troubleshooters include the following:

- **Aero troubleshooter** Diagnoses and resolves problems that prevent the computer from properly using Windows Aero.

- **Hardware And Device troubleshooter** Diagnoses and resolves problems that prevent the computer from properly using a device.
- **Homegroup Networking troubleshooter** Diagnoses and resolves problems that prevent the computer from sharing files in a homegroup.
- **Internet Connectivity troubleshooter** Diagnoses and resolves problems that prevent the computer from connecting to the Internet and accessing the Web.
- **Maintenance troubleshooter** Performs routine maintenance if the user does not.
- **Network Adapter troubleshooter** Diagnoses and resolves problems related to Ethernet, wireless, and other network adapters.
- **Performance troubleshooter** Diagnoses and resolves problems that are impacting the overall performance of the computer.
- **Play Sound troubleshooter** Diagnoses and resolves problems that prevent the computer from playing sound.
- **Power troubleshooter** Diagnoses and resolves problems that affect power management, sleep, hibernation, and resume.
- **Printer troubleshooter** Diagnoses and resolves problems that prevent the computer from using a printer.
- **Program Compatibility troubleshooter** Diagnoses and resolves problems that prevent a program from running on the computer.
- **Record Sound troubleshooter** Diagnoses and resolves problems that prevent the computer from recording sound.
- **Web Browsing Safety troubleshooter** Identifies issues with settings that could compromise the security of the computer and the safety of the user when browsing the Web.
- **Windows Media troubleshooter** Diagnoses and resolves problems that prevent the computer from playing music or DVDs. Can also be used to reset Windows Media Player to its default settings.

In Action Center, you can access any of the available troubleshooters by scrolling down and then clicking Troubleshooting. Clicking Troubleshooting opens the Troubleshooting window. As shown in Figure 8-8, troubleshooters are organized by category. These categories include the following:

- **Programs** For troubleshooting compatibility issues with applications designed for earlier versions of Windows.
- **Hardware And Sound** For troubleshooting issues with hardware devices, audio recording, and audio playback.
- **Network And Internet** For troubleshooting issues with connecting to networks and accessing shared folders on other computers.

- **Appearance And Personalization** For troubleshooting issues with the display's appearance and personalization settings. To quickly resolve display issues with Aero, click Display Aero Desktop Effects.
- **System And Security** For troubleshooting issues with Windows Update, power usage, and performance. Click Run Maintenance Tasks to clean up unused files and shortcuts and perform other routine maintenance tasks.

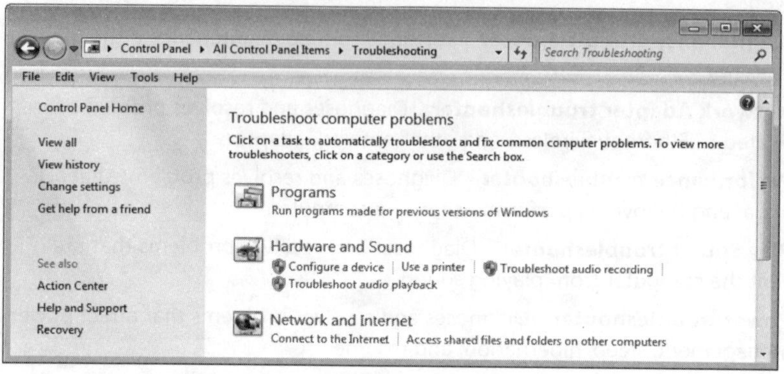

FIGURE 8-8 View and work with troubleshooters.

By default, Windows looks for updates to troubleshooters online and automatically installs them. If you prefer not to do this, clear the Get The Most Up-To-Date Troubleshooters From The Windows Online Troubleshooting Service check box.

In Group Policy, you can configure how automated troubleshooting and diagnostics work by using the Administrative Templates policies for Computer Configuration under System\Troubleshooting And Diagnostics. See Table 1-4 for information on each related policy. Table 8-1 lists related Administrative Templates policies.

TABLE 8-1 Policies for Managing Action Center and Related Features

POLICY NAME	DESCRIPTION	ADMINISTRATIVE TEMPLATES LOCATION
Troubleshooting: Allow Users To Access Online Troubleshooting Content On Microsoft Servers From The Troubleshooting Control Panel	If you enable or don't configure this policy, users who are connected to the Internet can access and search for troubleshooting content. Users can access this content by clicking Yes when prompted in Action Center to get the most up-to-date troubleshooting content.	Computer Configuration under System\Troubleshooting And Diagnostics\Scripted Diagnostics

POLICY NAME	DESCRIPTION	ADMINISTRATIVE TEMPLATES LOCATION
Troubleshooting: Allow Users To Access And Run Troubleshooting Wizards	If you enable or don't configure this policy, users can access and run the troubleshooting tools in Action Center.	Computer Configuration under System\Troubleshooting And Diagnostics
Remove The Action Center Icon	If you enable this policy, the Action Center icon is not displayed in the notification area of the taskbar, although this doesn't prevent users from accessing Action Center through Control Panel. Otherwise, the Action Center icon is displayed.	User Configuration under Start Menu And Taskbar
Turn Off Windows Customer Experience Improvement Program	If this policy is enabled, users are opted out of the program. If this policy is disabled, users are opted into the program.	Computer Configuration under System\Internet Communication Management\Internet Communication Settings
Turn Off Access To The Solutions To Performance Problems Section	If this policy is enabled, users won't be able to access solutions to performance problems. Otherwise, users can access this.	User and Computer Configuration under System\Performance Control Panel
Notify Blocked Drivers	If this policy is enabled or not configured, Windows will notify users about drivers blocked due to compatibility problems.	Computer Configuration under System\Troubleshooting And Diagnostics\Application Compatibility Diagnostics
Detect Application Failures Caused By Deprecated COM Objects	If you enable or do not configure this policy, Windows will detect programs trying to create deprecated COM objects and notify users.	Computer Configuration under System\Troubleshooting And Diagnostics\Application Compatibility Diagnostics

POLICY NAME	DESCRIPTION	ADMINISTRATIVE TEMPLATES LOCATION
Detect Application Failures Caused By Deprecated Windows DLLs	If you enable or do not configure this policy, Windows will detect programs trying to use deprecated DLLs and notify users.	Computer Configuration under System\Troubleshooting And Diagnostics\Application Compatibility Diagnostics
Turn Off Application Compatibility Engine	If this policy is enabled, Windows does not check the compatibility database prior to starting applications.	Computer Configuration under Windows Components\Application Compatibility
Turn Off Program Compatibility Assistant	If this policy is enabled, Windows does not monitor user-initiated programs for known compatibility issues at run time.	User and Computer Configuration under Windows Components\Application Compatibility
Configure Report Queue	If this policy is enabled and configured, allows an administrator to configure queuing and notification related to error reporting.	User and Computer Configuration under Windows Components\Windows Error Reporting\Advanced Error Reporting Settings
Disable Windows Error Reporting	If this policy is enabled, Windows Error Reporting will not send any information to Microsoft. Otherwise, Windows Error Reporting will send information.	User and Computer Configuration under Windows Components\Windows Error Reporting

Working with Support Services

To support automated diagnostics and problem resolution, Windows 7 provides separate components and tools for working with and managing diagnostics, problem reporting, and user assistance. These components all rely on the availability of the support services installed with the operating system. If you access the Services node under Services And Applications in the Computer Management administrative tool, you'll find a bundle of services dedicated to system support.

Table 8-2 provides an overview of key support services in Windows 7. Problem detection, troubleshooting, and resolution features are largely supported by the Diagnostic Policy Service and the Diagnostic System Host services. A third, related service, the Diagnostic Service Host service, starts only as needed.

TABLE 8-2 Support Services in Windows 7

NAME	DESCRIPTION
Application Experience	Processes application compatibility cache requests for applications
Application Information	Allows users to run applications with additional administrative privileges
Application Management	Processes installation, removal, and enumeration requests for software deployed through Group Policy
Background Intelligent Transfer Service	Transfers files in the background using idle network bandwidth
Desktop Window Manager Session Manager	Provides essential desktop services required for user switching and other desktop management features
Diagnostic Policy Service	Enables problem detection, troubleshooting, and resolution for Windows components
Diagnostic Service Host	Enables diagnostics that need to run in a LocalService context
Diagnostic System Host	Enables diagnostics that need to run in a LocalSystem context
Problem Reports and Solutions Control Panel Support	Provides support for system-level problem reports
Program Compatibility Assistant Service	Provides support for the Program Compatibility Assistant
Secondary Logon	Enables starting processes under alternate credentials
Superfetch	Helps maintain and improve performance by prefetching component and application data based on usage patterns
System Event Notification Service	Monitors system events and provides notification services

NAME	DESCRIPTION
Task Scheduler	Enables a user to configure and schedule automated tasks
Themes	Enables the computer to use themes and provides the user experience for themes management
User Profile Service	Responsible for loading and unloading user profiles during logon and logoff
Windows Error Reporting Service	Allows errors to be reported when programs stop responding and allows solutions to be retrieved
Windows Event Log	Responsible for logging events
Windows Management Instrumentation	Provides system management information
Windows Modules Installer	Supports Windows updates of recommended and optional components
Windows Remote Management	Enables Windows PowerShell remoting and the WS-Management protocol for remote management
Windows Time	Used to synchronize system time with world time
Windows Update	Enables updating of Windows components and other programs

As you can see from the number of support services, the automated Help system built into Windows 7 is fairly complex. The system is designed to automatically monitor system health, perform preventative maintenance, and report problems so that they can be resolved. Related performance and reliability data can be tracked in Performance Monitor and in Reliability Monitor.

Support services provide the foundation for the enhanced support features in Windows 7. If critical services are not running or not configured properly, you might have problems using certain support features. You can view these and other services in Computer Management by completing the following steps:

1. On the Administrative Tools menu, click Computer Management. Alternatively, in Control Panel, click System And Security, click Administrative Tools, and then double-click Computer Management.
2. Right-click the Computer Management entry in the console tree, and then click Connect To Another Computer. You can now select the system whose services you want to view.
3. Expand the Services And Applications node by clicking the plus sign (+) next to it. Select Services, as shown in Figure 8-9. You should now see a complete

list of services installed on the system. By default, this list is organized by service name. The key fields in this dialog box are used as follows:

- **Name** The name of the service. Only services installed on the system are listed here. Double-click an entry to configure its startup options.
- **Description** A short description of the service and its purpose.
- **Status** Whether the status of the service is started, paused, or stopped. (Stopped is indicated by a blank entry.)
- **Startup Type** The startup setting for the service. Automatic services are started at bootup. Users or other services start manual services. Disabled services are turned off and can't be started while they remain disabled.
- **Log On As** The account the service logs on as. The default in most cases is the LocalSystem account.

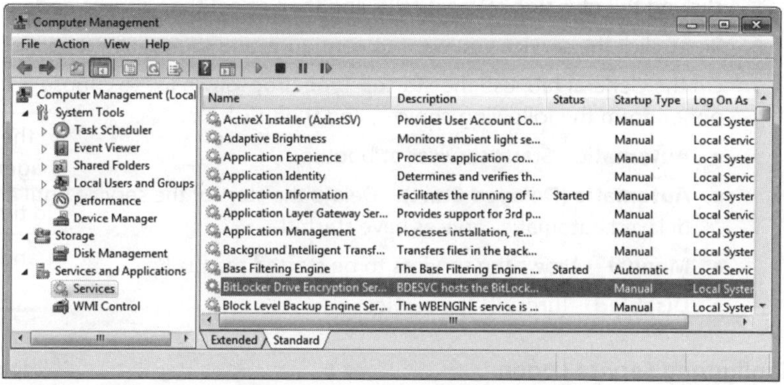

FIGURE 8-9 Use the Services view to manage services on Windows 7.

4. The Services pane has two views: Extended and Standard. To change the view, use the tabs at the bottom of the Services pane. In Extended view, quick links are provided for managing services. Click Start to start a stopped service. Click Restart to stop and then start a service. If you select a service in Extended view, you'll see a service description that details the service's purpose.

Starting, Stopping, and Pausing Services

As an administrator, you'll often have to start, stop, or pause Windows 7 services. To start, stop, or pause a service, follow these steps:

1. In Computer Management, expand the Services And Applications node by clicking the plus sign (+) next to it, and then select the Services node.
2. Right-click the service you want to manipulate, and then select Start, Stop, or Pause.

NOTE You can also choose Restart to have Windows stop and then start the service after a brief pause. Additionally, if you pause a service, you can use the Resume option to resume normal operation. When services that are set to start automatically fail, the status is blank, and you'll usually receive notification about this. Service failures can also be logged to the system's event logs. In Windows 7, you can configure actions to handle service failure automatically. For example, you can have Windows 7 attempt to restart the service for you.

Configuring Service Startup

You can set Windows 7 services to start manually or automatically. You can also turn them off permanently by disabling them. You configure service startup by following these steps:

1. In Computer Management, expand the Services And Applications node by clicking the plus sign (+) next to it, and then select the Services node.
2. Right-click the service you want to configure, and then click Properties.
3. On the General tab, use the Startup Type drop-down list to choose a startup option from the following choices, and then click OK.
   - **Automatic** Starts services at bootup.
   - **Automatic (Delayed Start)** Delays the start of the service until all non-delayed automatic services have started.
   - **Manual** Allows the services to be started manually.
   - **Disabled** Turns off the service.

Configuring Service Logon

You can configure Windows 7 services to log on as a system account or as a specific user. To do either of these, follow these steps:

1. In Computer Management, expand the Services And Applications node by clicking the plus sign (+) next to it, and then select the Services node.
2. Right-click the service you want to configure, and then click Properties.
3. Select the Log On tab. Do one of the following, and then click OK.
   - Select Local System Account if you want the service to log on using the system account (the default for most services). If the service provides a user interface that can be manipulated, select Allow Service To Interact With Desktop to allow users to control the service's interface.
   - Select This Account if you want the service to log on using a specific user account. Be sure to type an account name and password in the text boxes provided. Use the Browse button to search for a user account.

Configuring Service Recovery

Windows 7 automatically configures recovery for critical system services during installation. In most cases, you'll find that critical services are configured to restart automatically if the service fails. You cannot change these settings because they are not available.

To configure recovery options for any other service, follow these steps:

1. In Computer Management, expand the Services And Applications node by clicking the plus sign (+) next to it, and then select the Services node.
2. Right-click the service you want to configure, and then click Properties.
3. Click the Recovery tab.
4. You can now configure recovery options for the first, second, and subsequent recovery attempts. The following options are available:
   - **Take No Action** The operating system won't attempt recovery for this failure but might still attempt recovery of previous or subsequent failures.
   - **Restart The Service** Stops and then starts the service after a brief pause.
   - **Run A Program** Allows you to run a program or a script in case of failure. The script can be a batch program or a Windows script. If you select this option, set the full file path to the program you want to run, and then set any necessary command-line parameters to pass in to the program when it starts.
   - **Restart The Computer** Shuts down and then restarts the computer. Before you choose this option, double-check the computer's Startup and Recovery options. You want the system to select defaults quickly and automatically.

   TIP **When you configure recovery options for critical services, you can try to restart the service on the first and second attempts and then reboot the computer on the third attempt.**

5. Configure other options based on your previously selected recovery options, and then click OK. If you elected to run a program as a recovery option, you need to set options in the Run Program panel. If you elected to restart the service, you need to specify the restart delay. After stopping the service, Windows 7 waits for the specified delay period before trying to start the service. In most cases, a delay of 1 to 2 minutes is sufficient.

Disabling Unnecessary Services

As an administrator, your job is to ensure computer and network security, and unnecessary services are a potential source of security problems. For example, in many of the organizations that I've reviewed for security problems, I've found users' computers running Worldwide Web Publishing Service, Simple Mail Transfer

Protocol (SMTP), and File Transfer Protocol (FTP) Publishing Service when these services weren't needed. Unfortunately, these services can allow anonymous users to access computers and can also open the computer to attack if not properly configured.

If you find unnecessary services, you have a couple of options. For services installed through features, you can remove the related feature to remove the unnecessary component and its related services. You can also simply disable the services that aren't being used.

To disable a service, follow these steps:

1. In Computer Management, expand the Services And Applications node by clicking the plus sign (+) next to it, and then select the Services node.
2. Right-click the service you want to configure, and then click Properties.
3. On the General tab, select Disabled from the Startup Type drop-down list.

Disabling a service doesn't stop a running service; it prevents it from being started the next time the computer is booted, which means that the security risk still exists. To address this, click Stop on the General tab in the Properties dialog box, and then click OK.

Managing Services Using Preferences

Rather than managing services on individual computers, you can use Group Policy preference items to configure services on any computer that processes a particular Group Policy object (GPO). When you configure a service through preferences, the default value in most instances is No Change, meaning the setting is changed only if you specify a different value. As you can when you are configuring services manually, you can use Group Policy preferences to do the following:

- Start, stop, and restart services.
- Set startup to manual, automatic, automatic (delayed start), or disabled.
- Specify the logon account to use.
- Set recovery options to handle service failure.

To create a preference item to control a service, follow these steps:

1. Open a GPO for editing in the Group Policy Management Editor. Expand Computer Configuration\Preferences\Control Panel Settings.
2. Right-click the Services node, point to New, and then click Service. This opens the New Service Properties dialog box, shown in Figure 8-10.
3. In the Service Name field, type the name of the service you want to configure. The service name is not the same as the display name. If you are unsure of the service's name, click the Options button to the right of the field, and then select the service from the list of available services on your management computer. Keep in mind that some services running on your management computer might not be available on users' computers and vice versa.

4. Use the options provided to configure the service as you want it to be configured on users' computers. Settings are processed only if you select a value other than No Change.
5. Use the options on the Common tab to control how the preference is applied. Often, you'll want to apply the service configuration only once. If so, select Apply Once And Do Not Reapply.
6. Click OK. The next time policy is refreshed, the preference item will be applied as appropriate for the GPO in which you defined the preference item.

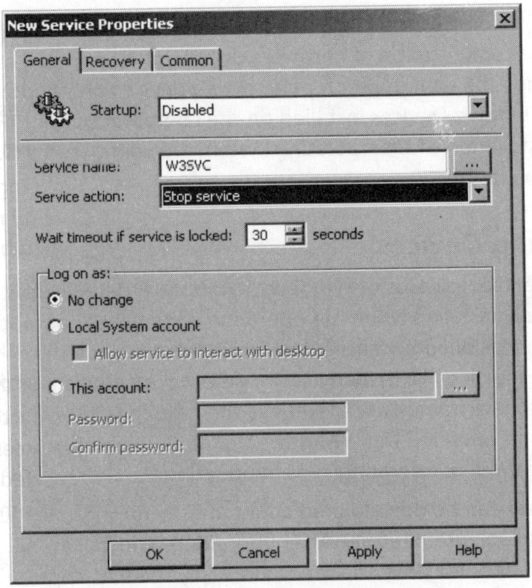

FIGURE 8-10 Customize services for a GPO.

Installing and Maintaining Devices: The Essentials

Many different types of devices can be installed in or connected to computers. The following are the key device types:

- **Cards/adapters** Circuit cards and adapters are plugged into expansion slots on the motherboard inside the computer case or, for a laptop, into expansion slots on the side of the system. Most cards and adapters have a connector into which you can plug other devices.
- **Internal drives** Many different types of drives can be installed, from CD drives, DVD drives, and Zip drives to floppy disks and hard disks. Internal drives usually have two cables. One cable attaches to the motherboard, to other drives, or to interface cards. The other cable attaches to the computer's power supply.

- **External drives and devices** External drives and devices plug into ports on the computer. The port can be standard, such as LPT1 or COM1; a port that you added with a circuit card; or a high-speed serial port, such as a universal serial bus (USB) port or an IEEE-1394 port (commonly called a FireWire port). Printers, scanners, USB flash drives, and most digital cameras are external devices.
- **Memory** Memory chips are used to expand the total amount of physical memory on the computer. Memory can be added to the motherboard or to a particular device, such as a video card. The most commonly used type of memory is random access memory (RAM).

You don't manage the configuration of hardware devices on Windows 7 in the same way that you manage the configuration of hardware devices on Windows XP and earlier releases of Windows. Devices installed on the computer but not detected during an upgrade or installation of the operating system are configured differently from new devices that you install.

Installing Preexisting Devices

Unlike Windows XP and earlier releases of Windows, Windows 7 detects devices that were not automatically installed when the operating system was upgraded or installed. If a device wasn't installed because Windows 7 didn't include the driver, the built-in hardware diagnostics will, in many cases, detect the hardware and then use the automatic update framework to retrieve the required driver the next time Windows Update runs, provided that Windows Update is enabled and you've allowed driver updating as well as operating system updating.

Although driver updates can be downloaded automatically through Windows Update, they are not installed automatically. After upgrading or installing the operating system, you should check for driver updates and apply them as appropriate before trying other techniques to install device drivers. The basic steps of checking for updates are as follows (a complete discussion of working with automatic updating is covered in Chapter 17, "Handling Maintenance and Support Tasks"):

1. Click Start, and then click Control Panel.
2. In Control Panel, click System And Security, and then click Windows Update.
3. In Windows Update, click the Check For Updates link.

Typically, device driver updates are seen as optional updates. The exceptions are for essential drivers, such as those for video, sound, and hard disk controllers. To address this, you should view all available updates on a computer, rather than only the important updates, to determine whether device driver updates are available. To install available device driver updates, follow these steps:

1. Click Start, and then click Control Panel.
2. In Control Panel, click System And Security, and then click Windows Update.
3. In Windows Update, click Check For Updates in the left pane. When Windows 7 finishes checking for updates, you might find that Windows

Update states that no important updates are available, as shown in Figure 8-11.

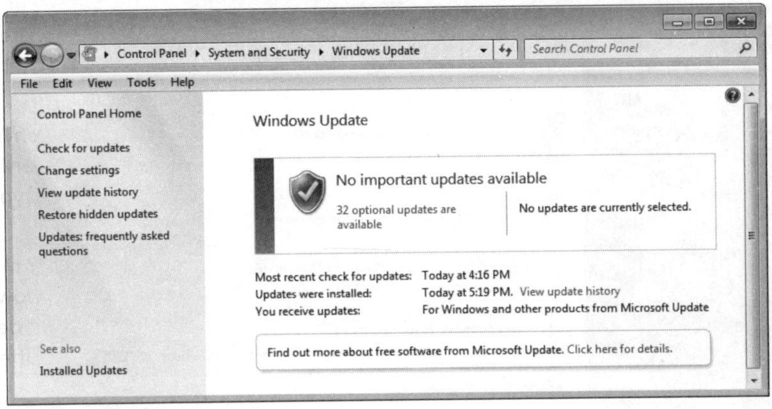

FIGURE 8-11 Check for updates.

4. Because driver updates are usually listed as optional, you should note whether any optional updates are available. If optional updates are available and you click the related link, you might find that the optional update is a driver update, as shown in Figure 8-12.

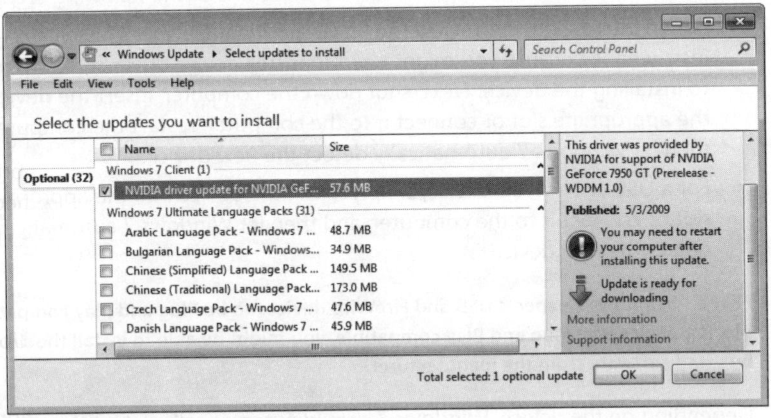

FIGURE 8-12 Select the update to install.

5. By default, optional updates are not selected for installation. To ensure that an update is installed, select the related check box, and then click OK to download and install the selected updates.

After you've installed the device driver, Windows 7 should detect the hardware within several minutes and install the device automatically. If Windows 7 detects the device but isn't able to install the device automatically, you might find a related solution in Action Center. In Figure 8-13, Windows has found updates for several device drivers that should resolve problems with the related hardware.

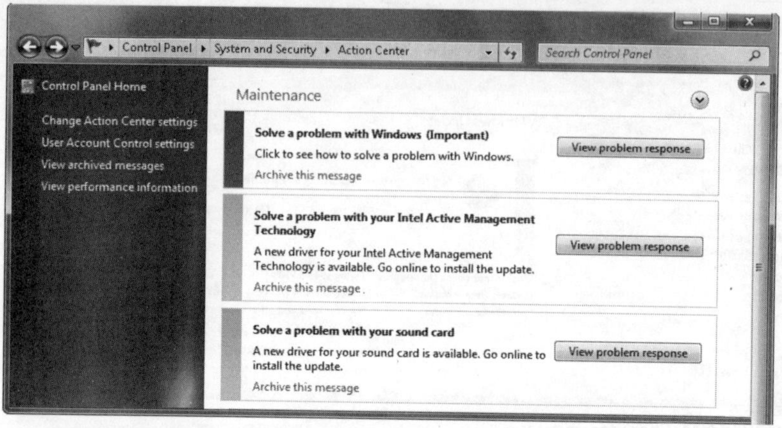

FIGURE 8-13 Check Action Center for updates that may solve a problem with a device.

Installing Internal, USB, and FireWire Devices

Most available new devices are Plug and Play compatible. This means that you should be able to install new devices easily by using one of the following techniques:

- For an internal device, review the hardware manufacturer's installation instructions because you might need to install device driver software prior to installing the device. Next, shut down the computer, insert the device into the appropriate slot or connect it to the computer, restart the computer, and then let Windows 7 automatically detect the new device.
- For a USB or FireWire device, simply insert the device into the appropriate slot or connect it to the computer, and then let Windows 7 automatically detect the new device.

NOTE **Windows 7 expects USB and FireWire devices to be Plug and Play compatible. If a device isn't Plug and Play compatible, you might be able to install the device by using software from the manufacturer.**

Depending on the device, Windows 7 should automatically detect the new device and then automatically install a built-in driver to support it, as shown in Figure 8-14. As shown in Figure 8-15, the Driver Software Installation component handles the installation task. The device should then run immediately without any problems. Well, that's the idea, but it doesn't always work that way. The success of automatic detection and installation depends on the device being Plug and Play compatible and a device driver being available.

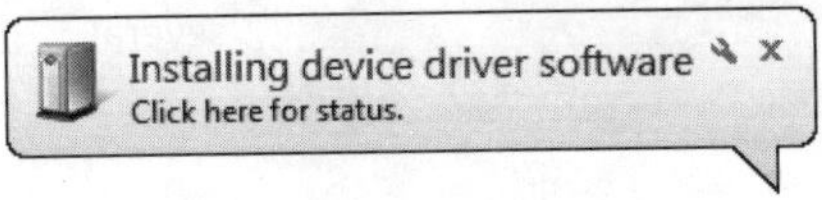

FIGURE 8-14 Windows detects the device.

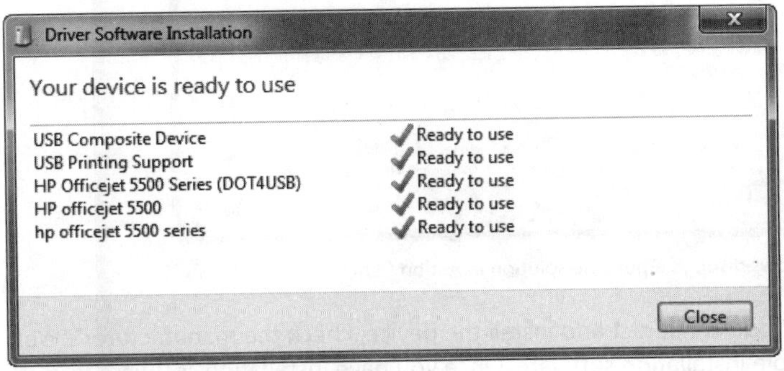

FIGURE 8-15 Windows installs the device.

Windows 7 includes many device drivers in a standard installation, and most of the time the device should be installed automatically. If driver updating is allowed through Windows Update, Windows 7 checks for drivers automatically when you connect a new device or when Windows 7 first detects the device. Because Windows Update does not automatically install device drivers, you need to check for available updates to determine if there is a driver for you to install.

> ***NOTE*** **For details on whether to use Windows Update to check for drivers automatically, see the section "The Hardware Tab" in Chapter 6. As discussed in Chapter 17, Windows Update must be enabled for this feature to work.**

Windows 7 might automatically detect the new device, but the Driver Software Installation component might run into problems installing the device. If this happens, you'll see errors similar to those shown in Figure 8-16. In this case, you should be redirected immediately to Action Center. If a possible solution is available, Windows 7 displays the solution, as shown in Figure 8-17.

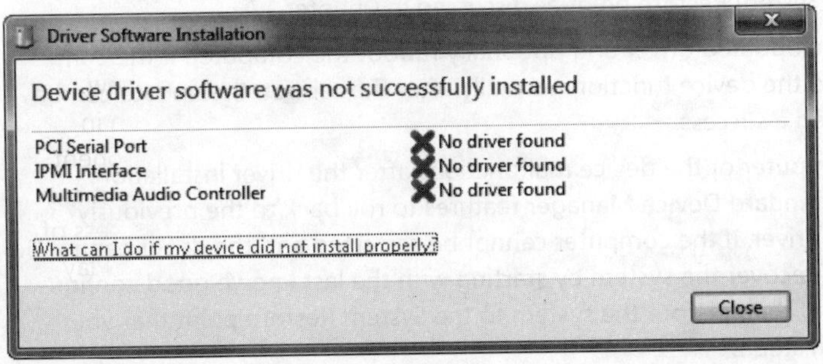

FIGURE 8-16 Windows fails to install the device.

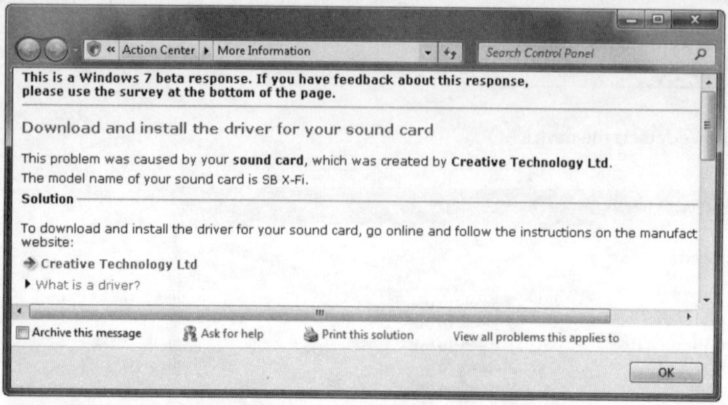

FIGURE 8-17 Windows displays a possible solution in Action Center.

If Windows 7 doesn't detect and install the device, check the manufacturer's Web site for compatible installation software. Once you have installation software for the device, run it, and then follow the prompts. The device should then be installed properly.

NOTE **If Windows cannot install a device, there might be a problem with the device itself or the driver or a conflict with existing hardware. For additional details on troubleshooting, see the section "Troubleshooting Hardware" later in this chapter.**

Once you've successfully installed a device, you need to periodically perform maintenance tasks for the device and its drivers. When new drivers for a device are released, you might want to test them in a development or support environment to see whether the drivers resolve problems that users have been experiencing. If the drivers install without problems and resolve outstanding issues, you might want to install the updated drivers on computers that use this device. The driver update procedure should be implemented as follows:

1. Check the device and driver information on each system prior to installing the new driver. Note the location, version, and file name of the existing driver.
2. Create a System Restore point as discussed in Chapter 17.
3. Install the updated driver and optionally reboot the computer. If the computer and the device function normally after the reboot, the update can be considered a success.
4. If the computer or the device malfunctions after the driver installation, use the standard Device Manager features to roll back to the previously installed driver. If the computer cannot be restarted and the driver cannot be restored, recover the system by starting with the last known good configuration, and then restore the system to the System Restore point that you created in step 2.

Installing Wireless, Network, and Bluetooth Devices

You can connect most wireless, network, and Bluetooth devices to a computer, including wireless network, storage, phone, keyboard, mouse, and media-extender devices. Often, these devices include installation software, but before you use the installation software, you should be sure it is compatible with Windows 7. If it isn't, you should check the device manufacturer's Web site for updated software.

Some devices connect directly to a computer. Others connect to a computer via a network. To connect a wireless or Bluetooth device directly to a computer, do the following:

1. Most wireless and Bluetooth devices require you to connect a receiver to the computer. Some devices might share a receiver. For example, with a wireless keyboard and mouse desktop pack, you might need to plug a shared receiver into a USB slot on the computer.
2. Position the computer and receiver so that the receiver is within range of the device you want to connect to. For example, a keyboard or mouse might need to be within 6 feet of the receiver, but the receiver for a wireless adapter might need to be within 100 feet of a wireless router.
3. Configure the device as necessary, and check that it is powered on. If you're trying to add a wireless network device, it must be configured for your wireless network before you can add it to a computer. Some wireless network devices need to be put into a discovery mode known as Wireless Protected Setup (WPS) before they can be detected.
4. The device should be detected and installed automatically. If the device isn't detected and installed, click Start, and then click Devices And Printers. In Devices And Printers, shown in Figure 8-18, be sure that the device isn't already listed as available. If the device isn't available yet, click Add A Device, and then follow the prompts.
5. If you have trouble connecting the device, try the following as part of troubleshooting:
   - Make sure the device isn't turned off, low on battery power, or in sleep mode. Some wireless devices have a button on them that you need to push to force a connection. Others, such as a Bluetooth phone, might have a setting in their software menu that you need to select to make them available. The receiver for a device might also have a button that you can press to force the receiver to scan for compatible wireless devices.
   - If wireless and Bluetooth capability is integrated into the computer, make sure the wireless or Bluetooth transmitter is turned on. Many laptops have an external switch for turning the transmitter on or off.
   - If you suspect that the device is out of range, try moving it closer to the computer. If there's a wall between the device and the computer, try putting the device and the computer in the same room.

- If a positional issue is causing the problem, you can resolve the problem by moving the cables and devices that could be causing electromagnetic interference, including power cables for other devices, large speakers, or desk lamps. If the problem persists, make sure the device is positioned away from air conditioning units, microwave ovens, and so on.

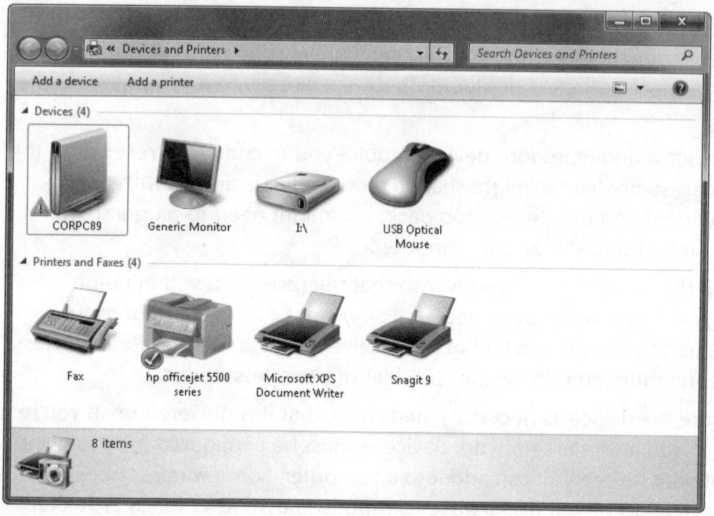

FIGURE 8-18 Check for the device in Devices And Printers.

To connect a wired or wireless device to a computer via a network, do the following:

1. Connect the device to the network and turn it on. Then configure its initial settings as appropriate for the network. For example, you might need to configure TCP/IP settings to use Dynamic Host Configuration Protocol (DHCP), or you might need to use a static IP address.
2. Wait up to 30 seconds for the device to be detected. The device should be detected and installed automatically. If the device isn't detected and installed, click Start, and then click Devices And Printers. In Devices And Printers, check whether the device is already listed as available. If the device isn't available yet, click Add A Device, and then follow the prompts.
3. If you have trouble connecting the device, try the following as part of troubleshooting:
   - Make sure that a firewall isn't blocking connectivity to the device. You might need to open a firewall port to allow access between the computer and the device.
   - Make sure the device is turned on and connected to the same network as the computer. If your network consists of multiple subnets connected together, try to connect the device to the same network subnet.

- Make sure the device is configured to broadcast its presence on the network. Most network devices automatically do this.
- Make sure the network device has an IP address and proper network settings. With DHCP, network routers assign IP addresses automatically as devices connect to the network.

NOTE **Not all detectable devices can be added to a computer. To find out if a device is able to be connected to your computer, check the information that came with the device or go to the manufacturer's Web site.**

REAL WORLD **Network discovery affects whether your computer can find other computers and devices on the network and whether other computers on the network can find your computer. By default, Windows Firewall blocks network discovery, but you can enable it by following these steps:**

1. **In Control Panel, click Network And Internet.**
2. **Click Network And Sharing Center.**
3. **In the left pane, click Change Advanced Sharing Settings.**
4. **Under Network Discovery, click Turn On Network Discovery, and then click Save Changes.**

Installing Local and Network Printers

You can connect printers to computers in several different ways. Which option you choose depends on the printer. Some printers connect directly to a computer and are referred to as *local printers.* Others connect to a computer via a network and are referred to as *network printers.* Network printers include all printers on a network, such as Bluetooth and wireless printers, as well as printers that are connected to another computer and shared on the network.

Most printers have installation software that you use to initially configure the printer. For a printer that connects directly to a computer, you usually run this software once, and the software sets up the printer and configures a connection to the printer so that it can be used. For a network printer, you usually run this software once on your management computer to prepare the printer for use and then create connections to the printer on each computer that will use the printer.

Setting Up a Local Printer

With a printer that has a USB connection, you connect the printer directly to the computer, and Windows should automatically detect and install it. If your printer connects using a serial or parallel port, you might have to install the printer manually. To install a printer manually, follow these steps:

1. Power on the printer. Click Start, and then click Devices And Printers. In Devices And Printers, check that the printer isn't already listed as available. If the printer isn't available yet, install it by following the remaining steps in this procedure.

2. In Devices And Printers, click Add A Printer. In the Add Printer wizard, click Add A Local Printer.
3. In the Use An Existing Port list, select the port to which the printer is connected, and then click Next.
4. Select the printer manufacturer and model, and then click Next.
5. If the printer isn't listed but you have the installation media, click Have Disk, and then browse to the folder where the printer driver is stored. For help, consult the printer manual.
6. If you don't have the installation media, click Windows Update, and then wait while Windows checks for available drivers.
7. Complete the additional steps in the wizard, and then click Finish. You can confirm the printer is working by printing a test page.

You can manage local printers using Group Policy preferences. I recommend this approach only for situations in which when you can carefully target computers so that only computers that actually have local printers are configured.

To create a preference item to create, update, replace, or delete local printers, follow these steps:

1. Open a Group Policy object (GPO) for editing in the Group Policy Management Editor. To configure preferences for computers, expand Computer Configuration\Preferences\Control Panel Settings, and then select Printers. To configure preferences for users, expand User Configuration\Preferences\Control Panel Settings, and then select Printers.
2. Right-click the Printers node, point to New, and then click Local Printer. This opens the New Local Printer Properties dialog box.
3. In the New Local Printer Properties dialog box, select Create, Update, Replace, or Delete in the Action list.
4. In the Connection field, enter the name of the printer. If you are creating a printer, this is the name that will be used for the new local printer. If you are updating, replacing, or deleting a printer, this name must match the targeted local printer.
5. In the Port list, select the port to which the local printer is connected.
6. In the Printer Path field, type the UNC path to a shared printer that is of the same type as the local printer you are configuring. The preference item will use this as an installation source for the printer driver.
7. Use the options on the Common tab to control how the preference is applied. Because you are enforcing a control, you will generally want to apply the setting every time Group Policy is refreshed. In this case, do not select Apply Once And Do Not Reapply.
8. Click OK. The next time policy is refreshed, the preference item will be applied as appropriate for the GPO in which you defined the preference item.

To create a preference item to manage a shared local printer, follow these steps:

1. Open a Group Policy object (GPO) for editing in the Group Policy Management Editor. Expand User Configuration\Preferences\Control Panel Settings, and then select Printers.
2. Right-click the Printers node, point to New, and then click Shared Printer. This opens the New Shared Printer Properties dialog box.
3. In the New Shared Printer Properties dialog box, select Create, Update, Replace, or Delete in the Action list. If you are creating a Delete preference, you can specify that you want to delete all shared printer connections by setting the action to Delete and selecting Delete All Shared Printer Connections.
4. In the Share Path field, type the UNC path of the shared printer.
5. Optionally, set the printer as the default printer. If you are creating, updating, or replacing a shared printer connection and want the connection to be available each time the user logs on, choose the Reconnect option.
6. Optionally, choose a local port to which you want to map the shared connection. If you are using the Delete action, the shared printer associated with that local port is deleted. Alternatively, with the Delete action you can elect to unmap all local ports.
7. Use the options on the Common tab to control how the preference is applied. Because you are enforcing a control, you will generally want to apply the setting every time Group Policy is refreshed. In this case, do not select Apply Once And Do Not Reapply.
8. Click OK. The next time policy is refreshed, the preference item will be applied as appropriate for the GPO in which you defined the preference item.

Setting Up a Wireless, Bluetooth, or Network Printer

If a printer uses a wireless or Bluetooth connection, you can prepare the computer and the printer as you would any similar device. Use the techniques discussed in the section "Installing Wireless, Network, and Bluetooth Devices" except connect to the printer in the same way you connect to a network printer.

To connect to a network printer, click Start, and then click Devices And Printers. In Devices And Printers, be sure that the printer isn't already listed as available. If the printer isn't available yet, follow these steps to connect to it:

1. In Devices And Printers, click Add A Printer. In the Add Printer wizard, click Add A Network, Wireless Or Bluetooth Printer.
2. In the list of available printers, select the printer you want to use, and then click Next.
3. If prompted, install the printer driver on your computer.
4. Complete the additional steps in the wizard, and then click Finish. You can confirm the printer is working by printing a test page.

5. If you have trouble connecting to the printer, try the following as part of troubleshooting:
   - Be sure that a firewall isn't blocking connectivity to the printer. You might need to open a firewall port to enable access between the computer and the printer.
   - Be sure the printer is turned on and connected to the same network as the computer. If your network consists of multiple subnets connected together, try to connect the printer to the same network subnet.
   - Be sure the printer is configured to broadcast its presence on the network. Most network printers automatically do this.
   - Be sure the printer has an IP address and proper network settings. With DHCP, network routers assign IP addresses automatically as printers connect to the network.

You can manage network printers using Group Policy preferences. To create, update, replace, or delete a connection to a network printer, follow these steps:

1. Open a Group Policy object (GPO) for editing in the Group Policy Management Editor. To configure preferences for computers, expand Computer Configuration\Preferences\Control Panel Settings, and then select Printers. To configure preferences for users, expand User Configuration\Preferences\Control Panel Settings, and then select Printers.
2. Right-click the Printers node, point to New, and then click TCP/IP Printer. This opens the New TCP/IP Printer Properties dialog box.
3. In the New TCP/IP Printer Properties dialog box, select Create, Update, Replace, or Delete in the Action list.
4. Do one of the following:
   - If you want to connect to the printer by IP address, enter the IP address in the IP Address field.
   - If you want to connect to the printer by its DNS name, select Use DNS Name, and then enter the fully qualified domain name of the printer.
5. In the Local Name field, enter the local name of the printer. If you are creating a printer connection, this is the name that will be displayed on users' computers. If you are updating, replacing, or deleting a printer connection, this name must match the targeted printer.
6. In the Printer Path field, type the UNC path to a shared printer that is the same type of printer as the network printer you are configuring. The preference item will use this printer as an installation source for the printer driver.
7. Optionally, set the printer as the default printer.
8. Use the options on the Port Settings tab to specify the protocol, port number, and other options used by the printer.

9. Use the options on the Common tab to control how the preference is applied. Because you are enforcing a control, you will generally want to apply the setting every time Group Policy is refreshed. In this case, do not select Apply Once And Do Not Reapply.
10. Click OK. The next time policy is refreshed, the preference item will be applied as appropriate for the GPO in which you defined the preference item.

Getting Started with Device Manager

You use Device Manager to view and configure hardware devices. You'll spend a lot of time working with this tool, so you should get to know it before working with devices.

To access Device Manager and obtain a detailed list of all the hardware devices installed on a system, complete the following steps:

1. On the Administrative Tools menu, click Computer Management. Alternatively, in Control Panel, click System And Security, click Administrative Tools, and then double-click Computer Management.

   NOTE **To work with a remote computer, right-click the Computer Management entry in the console tree, and then click Connect To Another Computer. Choose Another Computer, and then type the fully qualified name of the computer you want to work with, or click Browse to search for the computer you want to work with. Click OK.**

2. In the Computer Management console, click the plus sign (+) next to the System Tools node, and then select Device Manager. As shown in Figure 8-19, you should see a complete list of devices installed on the system. By default, this list is organized by device type.

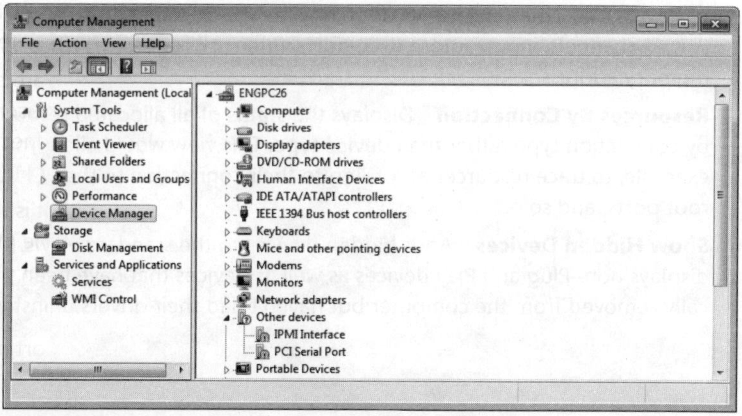

FIGURE 8-19 Use Device Manager to work with hardware devices.

3. Click the plus sign (+) next to a device type to see a list of the specific instances of that device type. Select a device to work with it.

Once you open Device Manager, you can work with any of the installed devices. If you right-click a device entry, a shortcut menu is displayed. The options available depend on the device type, but they include the following:

- **Properties** Displays the Properties dialog box for the device
- **Uninstall** Uninstalls the device and its drivers
- **Disable** Disables the device but doesn't uninstall it
- **Enable** Enables a device if it's disabled
- **Update Driver Software** Starts the Hardware Update wizard, which you can use to update the device driver
- **Scan For Hardware Changes** Tells Windows 7 to check the hardware configuration and determine whether there are any changes

TIP **The device list shows warning symbols if there are problems with a device. A yellow warning symbol with an exclamation point indicates a problem with a device. A red X indicates a device that was improperly installed or disabled by the user or an administrator for some reason.**

You can use the options on the View menu in the Computer Management console to change the default settings for which types of devices are displayed and how the devices are listed. The options are as follows:

- **Devices By Type** Displays devices by the type of device installed, such as disk drive or printer. The device name is listed below the type. This is the default view.
- **Devices By Connection** Displays devices by connection type, such as devices connected to a computer's PCI bus.
- **Resources By Type** Displays the status of allocated resources by the type of device using the resource. Resource types are direct memory access (DMA) channels, input/output (I/O) ports, interrupt requests (IRQ), and memory addresses.
- **Resources By Connection** Displays the status of all allocated resources by connection type rather than device type. This view would allow you, for example, to trace resources according to their connection to the PCI bus, root ports, and so on.
- **Show Hidden Devices** Adds hidden devices to the standard views. This displays non–Plug and Play devices as well as devices that have been physically removed from the computer but haven't had their drivers uninstalled.

Working with Device Drivers

For each hardware component installed on a computer, there is an associated device driver. The job of the device driver is to describe how the operating system uses the hardware abstraction layer (HAL) to work with a hardware component. The HAL handles the low-level communications tasks between the operating system and a hardware component. By installing a hardware component through the operating system, you are telling the operating system about the device driver it uses, and from then on the device driver loads automatically and runs as part of the operating system.

Device Driver Essentials

Windows 7 includes an extensive library of device drivers. In the base installation of the operating system, these drivers are maintained in the file repository of the driver store. Some service packs you install will include updates to the driver store. On 32-bit computers, you'll find the 32-bit driver store in the %SystemRoot%\System32\DriverStore folder. On 64-bit computers, you'll find the 64-bit driver store in the %SystemRoot%\System32\DriverStore folder and the 32-bit driver store in the %SystemRoot%\SysWOW64\DriverStore folder. The DriverStore folder also contains subfolders for localized driver information. You'll find a subfolder for each language component configured on the system. For example, for localized U.S. English driver information, you'll find a subfolder called en-US.

Every device driver in the driver store is certified to be fully compatible with Windows 7 and is digitally signed by Microsoft to assure the operating system of its authenticity. When you install a new Plug and Play–compatible device, Windows 7 checks the driver store for a compatible device driver. If one is found, the operating system automatically installs the device.

Every device driver has an associated Setup Information file. This file ends with the .inf extension and is a text file containing detailed configuration information about the device being installed. The information file identifies any source files used by the driver as well. Source files have the .sys extension. You might also find .pnf and .dll files for drivers, and some drivers have associated component manifest (.amx) files. The manifest file is written in XML, includes details about the driver's digital signature, and might also include Plug and Play information used by the device to automatically configure itself.

Every driver installed on a system has a source (.sys) file in the Drivers folder. When you install a new device driver, the driver is written to a subfolder of the Drivers folder, and configuration settings are stored in the registry. The driver's .inf file is used to control the installation and write the registry settings. If the driver doesn't already exist in the driver store, it does not already have an .inf file or other related files on the system. In this case, the driver's .inf file and other related files are written to a subfolder of DriverStore\FileRepository when you install the device.

Using Signed and Unsigned Device Drivers

Every device driver in the driver cache is digitally signed, which indicates that the driver has passed extensive testing by the Windows Hardware Quality Lab. A device driver with a digital signature from Microsoft should not cause your system to crash or become unstable. The presence of a digital signature from Microsoft also ensures that the device driver hasn't been tampered with. If a device driver doesn't have a digital signature from Microsoft, it hasn't been approved for use through testing or its files might have been modified from the original installation by another program. This means that unsigned drivers are much more likely than any other program you've installed to cause the operating system to freeze or the computer to crash.

To prevent problems with unsigned drivers Windows 7 warns you by default when you try to install an unsigned device driver. Windows can also be configured to prevent installation of certain types of devices. To manage device driver settings for computers throughout an organization, you can use Group Policy. When you do this, Group Policy specifies whether and how devices can be installed.

You can configure device installation settings on a per-computer basis using the Administrative Templates policies for Computer Configuration under System\Device Installation.

> ***TIP*** **If you're trying to install a device and find that you can't, device installation restrictions may be in place in Group Policy. You must override Group Policy to install the device.**

Tracking Driver Information

Each driver being used on a system has a driver file associated with it. You can view the location of the driver file and related details by completing the following steps:

1. Start Computer Management. In the Computer Management console, click the plus sign (+) next to the System Tools node.
2. Select Device Manager. You should now see a complete list of devices installed on the system. By default, this list is organized by device type.
3. Right-click the device you want to manage, and then click Properties. The Properties dialog box for that device opens.
4. On the Driver tab, click Driver Details to display the Driver File Details dialog box. As shown in Figure 8-20, the following information is displayed:
   - **Driver Files** Displays the full file paths to locations where the driver files exist
   - **Provider** The creator of the driver
   - **File Version** The version of the file

FIGURE 8-20 The Driver File Details dialog box displays information on the driver file paths, the provider, and the file versions.

Installing and Updating Device Drivers

To keep devices operating smoothly, it's essential that you keep the device drivers current. You install and update drivers by using the Found New Hardware, Add Hardware, and Update Driver Software wizards. By default, these wizards can search for updated device drivers in the following locations:

- The local computer
- A hardware installation CD
- The Windows Update site or your organization's Windows Update server

In Group Policy, several policies control how information about devices is obtained and how Windows searches for drivers:

- **Turn Off Access To All Windows Update Features under Computer Configuration\Administrative Templates\System\Internet Communication Management\Internet Communication Settings** If this policy setting is enabled, all Windows Update features are blocked and not available to users. Users will also be unable to access the Windows Update Web site.
- **Turn Off Windows Update Device Driver Searching under Computer Configuration\Administrative Templates\System\Internet Communication Management\Internet Communication Settings** By default, Windows Update searching is optional when installing a device. If you enable this setting, Windows Update will not be searched when a new device is installed. If you disable this setting, Windows Update will always be searched when a new device is installed if no local drivers are present.
- **Specify Driver Source Search Order under Computer Configuration\Administrative Templates\System\Device Installation** If you disable or do not configure this policy setting, you can set the source location search order for device drivers on each computer. If you enable this policy, you can

specify that Windows Update should be searched first, last, or not at all when driver software is being located during device installation.

- **Configure Device Installation Time-Out under Computer Configuration\Administrative Templates\System\Device Installation** If you disable or do not configure this policy, Windows 7 waits 5 minutes for a device installation task to complete before terminating the installation. If you enable this policy, you can specify the amount of time Windows 7 waits before terminating the installation.
- **Prevent Device Metadata Retrieval From The Internet under Computer Configuration\Administrative Templates\System\Device Installation** If you disable or do not configure this policy, Windows 7 retrieves device metadata for installed devices from the Internet and uses the information to help keep devices up to date. If you enable this policy setting, Windows 7 does not retrieve device metadata for installed devices from the Internet.

You can install and update device drivers by completing the following steps:

1. Start Computer Management. In the Computer Management console, click the plus sign (+) next to the System Tools node.
2. Select Device Manager in the Computer Management console. You should see a complete list of devices installed on the system. By default, this list is organized by device type.
3. Right-click the device you want to manage, and then click Update Driver Software. This starts the Update Driver Software wizard.

   BEST PRACTICES **Updated drivers can add functionality to a device, improve performance, and resolve device problems. However, you should rarely install the latest drivers on a user's computer without testing them in a test environment. Test first, then install.**

4. As shown in Figure 8-21, you can specify whether you want to install the drivers automatically or manually by selecting the driver from a list or specific location.

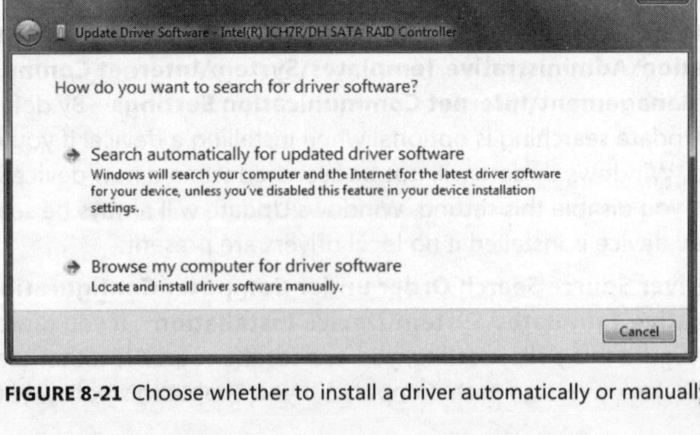

FIGURE 8-21 Choose whether to install a driver automatically or manually.

5. If you elect to install the driver automatically, Windows 7 looks for a more recent version of the device driver and installs the driver if it finds one. If a more recent version of the driver is not found, Windows 7 keeps the current driver. In either case, click Close to complete the process, and then skip the remaining steps.
6. If you chose to install the driver manually, you can do the following:
   - **Search for the driver.** Click Browse to select a search location. Use the Browse For Folder dialog box to select the start folder for the search, and then click OK. Because all subfolders of the selected folder are searched automatically, you can select the drive root path, such as C, to search an entire drive.
   - **Choose the driver to install.** Click Let Me Pick From A List Of Device Drivers On My Computer. The wizard then shows a list of compatible hardware. Click the device that matches your hardware. To view a wider array of choices, clear the Show Compatible Hardware check box. You'll see a full list of manufacturers for the type of device you are working with. As shown in Figure 8-22, scroll through the list of manufacturers to find the manufacturer of the device, and then select the appropriate device in the right pane.

FIGURE 8-22 Select the appropriate device driver for the device you're adding.

NOTE **If the manufacturer or device you want to use isn't listed, insert your device driver disk into the floppy drive or CD-ROM drive, and then click the Have Disk button. Follow the prompts.**

7. After selecting a device driver through a search or a manual selection, continue through the installation process by clicking Next. Click Close when the driver installation is complete. If the wizard can't find an appropriate driver,

you need to obtain one and then repeat this procedure. Keep in mind that in some cases you need to restart the system to activate the newly installed or updated device driver.

Enabling and Disabling Types of Devices

Using Group Policy preferences, you can manage which hardware devices can be used on computers a Group Policy object (GPO) applies to. You manage devices by enabling or disabling them according to the following:

- **Device class** A device class encompasses a broad range of similar devices, such as all DVD/CD-ROM drives.
- **Device type** A device type applies to specific devices within a device class, such as the NEC DVD-ROM RW ND-3530A ATA device.

NOTE **If you want to manage devices by type, you need to configure a management computer with the devices you plan to work with and then create the preference items on that computer. A management computer is a computer with management options installed, including the Remote Server Administrator Tools.**

To create a preference item to enable or disable devices by class or type, follow these steps:

1. Open a GPO for editing in the Group Policy Management Editor. To configure preferences for computers, expand Computer Configuration\Preferences\Control Panel Settings, and then select Devices. To configure preferences for users, expand User Configuration\Preferences\Control Panel Settings, and then select Devices.
2. Right-click the Devices node, point to New, and then click Device. This opens the New Device Properties dialog box.
3. In the New Device Properties dialog box, select one of the following options in the Action list:
   - **Use This Device (Enable)** Choose this option if you want to enable devices by class or type.
   - **Do Not Use This Device (Disable)** Choose this option if you want to disable devices by class or type.
4. Click the Options button to the right of Device Class, and then do one of the following:
   - Select a device class to manage devices by class.
   - Expand a device class node, and then select a device type to manage devices by type.
5. Use the options on the Common tab to control how the preference is applied. Because you are enforcing a control, you will generally want to apply the setting every time Group Policy is refreshed. In this case, do not select Apply Once And Do Not Reapply.

6. Click OK. The next time policy is refreshed, the preference item will be applied as appropriate for the GPO in which you defined the preference item.

Restricting Device Installation Using Group Policy

In addition to code signing and search restrictions, Group Policy settings can be used to allow or prevent installation of devices based on device class. Devices that are set up and configured in the same way are grouped into a device setup class. Each device setup class has a globally unique identifier (GUID) associated with it. To restrict devices using Group Policy, you need to know the GUID for the device setup class that you want to restrict.

The registry contains a key for each standard device setup class under HKEY_LOCAL_MACHINE\SYSTEM\CurrentControlSet\Control\Class. The registry keys are named according to the class GUID. When you select a class GUID registry key, the Class value specifies the device setup class that the GUID identifies. For example, if you select {4d36e965-e325-11ce-bfc1-08002be10318}, you'll find that the device setup class is for CD-ROM devices.

The policy settings for managing device installation are found under Computer Configuration\Administrative Templates\System\Device Installation\Device Installation Restrictions and include the following:

- Allow Administrators To Override Device Installation Restriction Policies
- Allow Installation Of Devices That Match Any Of These Device IDs
- Allow Installation Of Devices Using Drivers That Match These Device Setup Classes
- Prevent Installation Of Devices Not Described By Other Policy Settings
- Prevent Installation Of Devices That Match Any Of These Device IDs
- Prevent Installation Of Removable Devices
- Time (In Seconds) To Force Reboot When Required For Policy Changes To Take Effect

You can configure these policies by completing the following steps:

1. Open a Group Policy object (GPO) for editing in the Group Policy Management Editor.
2. Expand Computer Configuration, Administrative Templates, System, Device Installation, Device Installation Restrictions.
3. Double-click the appropriate policy to view its Properties dialog box.
4. Set the state of the policy as Not Configured if you don't want the policy to be applied, Enabled if you want the policy to be applied, or Disabled if you want to block the policy from being used (all as permitted by the Group Policy configuration).

5. If you are enabling the policy and it has a Show option, click the Show button to use the Show Contents dialog box to specify which device IDs should be matched to this policy, and then click OK. In the Registry Editor, the GUID for a device setup class is the entire key name, including the curly braces ({ and }). You can copy the key name and paste it into the Show Contents dialog box by following these steps:
   a. Open the Registry Editor by clicking Start, typing **regedit** in the Search box, and then pressing Enter.
   b. In the Registry Editor, right-click the key name, and then select Copy Key Name.
   c. In the Show Contents dialog box, click twice in the Value field so that the cursor changes to an insertion point. Right-click, and then click Paste.
   d. Delete the path that precedes the GUID value. The value you delete should be HKEY_LOCAL_MACHINE\SYSTEM\CurrentControlSet\Control\Class\.
   e. If you want to add the GUID for another device setup class, repeat steps b–d.
6. Click OK.

Rolling Back Drivers

Sometimes you'll find that a device driver you installed causes device failure or other critical problems on a system. Don't worry: you can recover the system and use the previously installed device driver. To do this, follow these steps:

1. If you are having problems starting the system, you need to boot the system in safe mode as discussed in the section "Troubleshooting Startup and Shutdown" in Chapter 17.
2. Start Computer Management. In the Computer Management console, click the plus sign (+) next to the System Tools node.
3. Select Device Manager in the Computer Management console. You should now see a complete list of devices installed on the system. By default, this list is organized by device type.
4. Right-click the device you want to manage, and then click Properties. This opens the Properties dialog box for the device.
5. Click the Driver tab, and then click Roll Back Driver. When prompted to confirm the action, click Yes.
6. Click Close to close the driver's Properties dialog box.

NOTE **If the driver file hasn't been updated, a backup driver file won't be available. In this case, the Roll Back Driver button will be unavailable.**

Removing Device Drivers for Removed Devices

Usually when you remove a device from a system, Windows 7 detects this action and automatically removes the drivers for that device. However, sometimes when you remove a device, Windows 7 doesn't detect the change, and you must remove the drivers manually. You can remove device drivers by completing the following steps:

1. Start Computer Management. In the Computer Management console, click the plus sign (+) next to the System Tools node.
2. Select Device Manager in the Computer Management console.
3. Right-click the device you want to remove, and then click Uninstall.
4. When prompted to confirm the action, click OK.

Uninstalling, Reinstalling, and Disabling Device Drivers

Uninstalling a device driver uninstalls the related device. When a device isn't working properly, sometimes you can completely uninstall the device, restart the system, and then reinstall the device driver to restore normal operations. You can uninstall and then reinstall a device by completing the following steps:

1. Start Computer Management. In the Computer Management console, click the plus sign (+) next to the System Tools node.
2. Select Device Manager in the Computer Management console. You should see a complete list of devices installed on the system. By default, this list is organized by device type.
3. Right-click the device you want to manage, and then click Uninstall.
4. When prompted to confirm the action, click OK.
5. Reboot the system. Windows 7 should detect the presence of the device and automatically reinstall the necessary device driver. If the device isn't automatically reinstalled, reinstall it manually as discussed in the section "Installing and Updating Device Drivers" earlier in the chapter.

To prevent a device from being reinstalled automatically, disable the device instead of uninstalling it. You disable a device by right-clicking it in Device Manager and then clicking Disable.

Enabling and Disabling Hardware Devices

When a device isn't working properly, you might want to uninstall or disable it. Uninstalling a device removes the driver association for the device, so it temporarily appears that the device has been removed from the system. The next time you restart the system, Windows 7 might try to reinstall the device. Typically, Windows 7 reinstalls Plug and Play devices automatically, but it does not automatically reinstall non–Plug and Play devices.

Disabling a device turns it off and prevents Windows 7 from using it. Because a disabled device doesn't use system resources, you can be sure that it isn't causing a conflict on the system.

You can uninstall or disable a device by completing the following steps:

1. Start Computer Management. In the Computer Management console, click the plus sign (+) next to the System Tools node.
2. Select Device Manager in the Computer Management console. You should see a complete list of devices installed on the system. By default, this list is organized by device type.
3. Right-click the device you want to manage, and then select one of the following options:
   - Uninstall
   - Disable
4. If prompted to confirm the action, click Yes or OK as appropriate.

Troubleshooting Hardware

Built-in hardware diagnostics in Windows 7 can detect many types of problems with hardware devices. If a problem is detected, you might see a Problem Reports And Solutions balloon telling you there is a problem. Clicking this balloon opens Action Center. The Problem Reports And Solutions console can also be accessed in Control Panel by clicking the System And Security link and then selecting Action Center.

Whenever a device is installed incorrectly or has another problem, Device Manager displays a warning icon indicating that the device has a problem. If you double-click the device, an error code is displayed on the General tab of the device's Properties dialog box. As Table 8-3 shows, this error code can be helpful when trying to solve device problems as well. Most of the correction actions assume that you've selected the General tab in the device's Properties dialog box.

TABLE 8-3 Common Device Errors and Techniques to Resolve Them

ERROR MESSAGE	CORRECTION ACTION
This device is not configured correctly. (Code 1)	Obtain a compatible driver for the device, and then click Update Driver to start the Update Driver Software wizard.
The driver for this device might be corrupted, or your system might be running low on memory or other resources. (Code 3)	Click the Update Driver button on the Driver tab to run the Update Driver Software wizard. You might see an Out of Memory message at startup because of this error.

ERROR MESSAGE	CORRECTION ACTION
This device cannot start. (Code 10)	Click the Update Driver button on the Driver tab to run the Update Driver Software wizard. Don't try to automatically find a driver. Instead, choose the manual install option, and then select the device.
This device cannot find enough free resources that it can use. (Code 12)	Resources assigned to this device conflict with another device, or the firmware is incorrectly configured. Check the firmware, and check for resource conflicts on the Resources tab in the device's Properties dialog box.
This device cannot work properly until you restart your computer. (Code 14)	Typically, the driver is installed correctly, but it will not be started until you restart the computer.
Windows cannot identify all the resources this device uses. (Code 16)	Check whether a signed driver is available for the device. If one is available and you've already installed it, you might need to manage the resources for the device. Check the Resources tab in the device's Properties dialog box.
Reinstall the drivers for this device. (Code 18)	After an upgrade, you might need to log on as an administrator to complete device installation. If this is not the case, click Update Driver on the Driver tab to reinstall the driver.
Your registry might be corrupted. (Code 19)	Remove and reinstall the device. This should clear out incorrect or conflicting registry settings.
Windows is removing this device. (Code 21)	The system will remove the device. The registry might be corrupted. If the device continues to display this message, restart the computer.
This device is disabled. (Code 22)	This device has been disabled using Device Manager. To enable it, click the Enable Device button on the General tab of the device's Properties dialog box.
This device is not present, is not working properly, or does not have all its drivers installed. (Code 24)	This might indicate a bad device or bad hardware. This error code can also occur with legacy devices; upgrade the driver to resolve.

ERROR MESSAGE	CORRECTION ACTION
The drivers for this device are not installed. (Code 28)	Obtain a compatible driver for the device, and then click Update Driver to start the Update Driver Software wizard.
This device is disabled because the firmware of the device did not give it the required resources. (Code 29)	Check the device documentation on how to assign resources. You might need to upgrade the firmware or enable the device in the system firmware.
This device is not working properly because Windows cannot load the drivers required for this device. (Code 31)	The device driver might be incompatible with Windows 7. Obtain a compatible driver for the device, and then click Update Driver to start the Update Driver Software wizard.
A driver for this device was not required and has been disabled. (Code 32)	A dependent service for this device has been set to Disabled. Check the event logs to determine which services should be enabled and started.
Windows cannot determine which resources are required for this device. (Code 33)	This might indicate a bad device or bad hardware. This error code can also occur with legacy devices; upgrade the driver and/or refer to the device documentation on how to set resource usage.
Windows cannot determine the settings for this device. (Code 34)	The legacy device must be manually configured. Verify the device jumpers or firmware settings, and then configure the device resource usage by using the Resources tab in the device's Properties dialog box.
Your computer's system firmware does not include enough information to properly configure and use this device. (Code 35)	This error occurs on multiprocessor systems. Update the firmware; check for a firmware option to use multiprocessor specification (MPS) 1.1 or MPS 1.4. Usually you want MPS 1.4.
This device is requesting a PCI interrupt but is configured for an ISA interrupt (or vice versa). (Code 36)	Legacy device interrupts are not shareable. If a device is in a PCI slot, but the slot is configured in firmware as reserved for a legacy device, this error might be displayed. Change the firmware settings.
Windows cannot initialize the device driver for this hardware. (Code 37)	Run the Update Driver Software wizard by clicking the Update Driver button on the Driver tab.

ERROR MESSAGE	CORRECTION ACTION
Windows cannot load the device driver for this hardware because a previous instance of the device driver is still in memory. (Code 38)	A device driver in memory is causing a conflict. Restart the computer.
Windows cannot load the device driver for this hardware. The driver might be corrupted or missing. (Code 39)	Check to be sure that the hardware device is properly installed and connected and that it has power. If it is properly installed and connected, look for an updated driver or reinstall the current driver.
Windows cannot access this hardware because its service key information in the registry is missing or recorded incorrectly. (Code 40)	The registry entry for the device driver is invalid. Reinstall the driver.
Windows successfully loaded the device driver for this hardware but cannot find the hardware device. (Code 41)	If the device was removed, uninstall the driver, reinstall the device, and then click Scan For Hardware Changes to reinstall the driver. If the device was not removed or doesn't support Plug and Play, obtain a new or updated driver for the device. To install non–Plug and Play devices, use the Add Hardware wizard. In Device Manager, click Action, and then click Add Legacy Hardware.
Windows cannot load the device driver for this hardware because there is a duplicate device already running in the system. (Code 42)	A duplicate device was detected. This error occurs when a bus driver incorrectly creates two identically named devices, or when a device with a serial number is discovered in a new location before it is removed from the old location. Restart the computer to resolve this problem.
Windows has stopped this device because it has reported problems. (Code 43)	The device was stopped by the operating system. You might need to uninstall and then reinstall the device. The device might have problems with the no-execute processor feature. In this case, check for a new driver.

ERROR MESSAGE	CORRECTION ACTION
An application or service has shut down this hardware device. (Code 44)	The device was stopped by an application or service. Restart the computer. The device might have problems with the no-execute processor feature. In this case, check for a new driver.
Currently, this hardware device is not connected to the computer. (Code 45)	When you start Device Manager with the environment variable DEVMGR_SHOW_NONPRESENT_DEVICES set to 1, any previously attached devices that are not present are displayed in the device list and assigned this error code. To clear the message, attach the device to the computer or start Device Manager without setting this environment variable.
Windows cannot gain access to this hardware device because the operating system is in the process of shutting down. (Code 46)	The device is not available because the computer is shutting down. When the computer restarts, the device should be available.
Windows cannot use this hardware device because it has been prepared for safe removal, but it has not been removed from the computer. (Code 47)	If you used the Safe Removal application to prepare the device for removal, or pressed a physical eject button, you'll see this error when the device is ready for removal. To use the device again, unplug it, and then plug it in again, or restart the computer.
The software for this device has been blocked from starting because it is known to have problems with Windows. Contact the hardware vendor for a new driver. (Code 48)	The driver for this device is incompatible with Windows and has been prevented from loading. Obtain and install a new or updated driver from the hardware vendor.
Windows cannot start new hardware devices because the system hive is too large (exceeds the Registry Size Limit). (Code 49)	The system hive has exceeded its maximum size and new devices cannot work until the size is reduced. Devices that are no longer attached to the computer but are still listed in the system hive might cause this error. Try uninstalling any hardware devices that you are no longer using.

CHAPTER 9

Installing and Maintaining Programs

Administrators and support staff often install and configure applications that are used on desktop computers. You need to install and configure applications before deploying new computers, install new applications on computers when the programs are requested, and update applications when new versions become available. Also, as users install additional applications, you might be called on to help troubleshoot installation problems or to help uninstall programs. Most program installation problems are fairly easy to solve if you know what to look for. Other problems are fairly difficult to resolve and require more work than you might expect. In this chapter, you'll learn how User Account Control (UAC) affects how you install and run applications and about techniques for installing, uninstalling, and maintaining programs.

Managing Application Virtualization and Run Levels

User Account Control (UAC) changes the way that applications are installed and run, where applications write data, and what permissions applications have. In this section, I'll look at how UAC affects application installation, from application security tokens to file and registry virtualization to run levels. This information is essential when you are installing and maintaining applications on Windows 7.

Application Access Tokens and Location Virtualization

All applications used with Windows 7 are divided into two general categories:

- **UAC-compliant** Any application written specifically for Windows Vista or Windows 7 is considered a compliant application. Applications certified as complying with the Windows 7 architecture have the UAC-compliant logo.
- **Legacy** Any application written for Windows XP or an earlier version of Windows is considered a legacy application.

The distinction between UAC-compliant applications and legacy applications is important because of the architectural changes required to support UAC. UAC-compliant applications use UAC to reduce the attack surface of the operating system. They do this by preventing unauthorized programs from installing or running without the user's consent and by restricting the default privileges granted to applications. These measures make it harder for malicious software to take over a computer.

NOTE **The Windows 7 component responsible for UAC is the Application Information service. This service facilitates the running of interactive applications with an "administrator" access token. You can see the difference between the administrator user and standard user access tokens by opening two Command Prompt windows, running one with elevation (right-click, and then click Run As Administrator), and the other as a standard user. In each window, type whoami /all and compare the results. Both access tokens have the same security identifiers (SIDs), but the elevated, administrator user access token will have more privileges than the standard user access token.**

All applications that run on Windows 7 derive their security context from the current user's access token. By default, UAC turns all users into standard users even if they are members of the Administrators group. If an administrator user consents to the use of her administrator privileges, a new access token is created for the user. It contains all the user's privileges, and this access token—rather than the user's standard access token—is used to start an application or process.

In Windows 7, most applications can run using a standard user access token. Whether applications need to run with standard or administrator privileges depends on the actions the application performs. Applications that require administrator privileges, referred to as *administrator user applications,* differ from applications that require standard user privileges, referred to as *standard user applications,* in the following ways:

- Administrator user applications require elevated privileges to run and perform core tasks. Once started in elevated mode, an application with a user's administrator access token can perform tasks that require administrator privileges and can also write to system locations of the registry and the file system.

- Standard user applications do not require elevated privileges to run or to perform core tasks. Once started in standard user mode, an application with a user's standard access token must request elevated privileges to perform administration tasks. For all other tasks, the application should not run using elevated privileges. Further, the application should write data only to nonsystem locations of the registry and the file system.

Applications not written for Windows 7 run with a user's standard access token by default. To support the UAC architecture, these applications run in a special compatibility mode and use file system and registry virtualization to provide "virtualized" views of file and registry locations. When an application attempts to write to a system location, Windows 7 gives the application a private copy of the file or registry value. Any changes are then written to the private copy, and this private copy is then stored in the user's profile data. If the application attempts to read or write to this system location again, it is given the private copy from the user's profile to work with. By default, if an error occurs when the application is working with virtualized data, the error notification and logging information show the virtualized location rather than the actual location that the application was trying to work with.

Application Integrity and Run Levels

The focus on standard user and administrator privileges also changes the general permissions required to install and run applications. In Windows XP and earlier versions of Windows, the Power Users group gave users specific administrator privileges to perform basic system tasks when installing and running applications. Applications written for Windows 7 do not require the use of the Power Users group. Windows 7 maintains it only for legacy application compatibility.

As part of UAC, Windows 7 by default detects application installations and prompts users for elevation to continue the installation. Installation packages for UAC-compliant applications use application manifests that contain run-level designations to help track required privileges. Application manifests define the application's privileges as one of the following:

- **RunAsInvoker** Run the application with the same privileges as the user. Any user can run the application. For a standard user or a user who is a member of the Administrators group, the application runs with a standard access token. The application runs with higher privileges only if the parent process from which it is started has an administrator access token. For example, if you open an elevated Command Prompt window and then launch an application from this window, the application runs with an administrator access token.
- **RunAsHighest** Run the application with the highest privileges of the user. The application can be run by both administrator users and standard users. The tasks the application can perform depend on the user's privileges. For a standard user, the application runs with a standard access token. For a user who is a member of a group with additional privileges, such as the Backup

Operators, Server Operators, or Account Operators group, the application runs with a partial administrator access token that contains only the privileges the user has been granted. For a user who is a member of the Administrators group, the application runs with a full administrator access token.

- **RunAsAdmin** Run the application with administrator privileges. Only administrators can run the application. For a standard user or a user who is a member of a group with additional privileges, the application runs only if the user can be prompted for credentials required to run in elevated mode or if the application is started from an elevated process, such as an elevated Command Prompt window. For a user who is a member of the Administrators group, the application runs with an administrator access token.

To protect application processes, Windows 7 labels them with integrity levels ranging from high to low. Applications that modify system data, such as Disk Management, are considered high integrity. Applications performing tasks that could compromise the operating system, such as Windows Internet Explorer 8 in Windows 7, are considered low integrity. Applications with lower integrity levels cannot modify data in applications with higher integrity levels.

Windows 7 identifies the publisher of any application that attempts to run with an administrator's full access token. Then, depending on that publisher, Windows 7 marks the application as belonging to one of the following three categories:

- Windows Vista / Windows 7
- Publisher verified (signed)
- Publisher not verified (unsigned)

To help you quickly identify the potential security risk of installing or running the application, a color-coded elevation prompt displays a particular message depending on the category to which the application belongs:

- If the application is from a blocked publisher or is blocked by Group Policy, the elevation prompt has a red background and displays the message "The application is blocked from running."
- If the application is administrative (such as Computer Management), the elevation prompt has a blue-green background and displays the message "Windows needs your permission to continue."
- If the application has been signed by Authenticode and is trusted by the local computer, the elevation prompt has a gray background and displays the message "A program needs your permission to continue."
- If the application is unsigned (or is signed but not yet trusted), the elevation prompt has a yellow background and red shield icon and displays the message "An unidentified program wants access to your computer."

Prompting on the secure desktop can be used to further secure the elevation process. The secure desktop safeguards the elevation process by preventing spoofing of the elevation prompt. The secure desktop is enabled by default in Group

Policy, as discussed in the section "Optimizing User Account Control and Admin Approval Mode" in Chapter 5.

Setting Run Levels

By default, only applications running with a user's administrator access token run in elevated mode. Sometimes, you'll want an application running with a user's standard access token to be in elevated mode. For example, you might want to start the Command Prompt window in elevated mode so that you can perform administration tasks.

In addition to application manifests (discussed in the previous section), Windows 7 provides two different ways to set the run level for applications:

- Run an application once as an administrator.
- Always run an application as an administrator.

To run an application once as an administrator, right-click the application's shortcut or menu item, and then click Run As Administrator. If you are using a standard account and prompting is enabled, you are prompted for consent before the application is started. If you are using a standard user account and prompting is disabled, the application will fail to run. If you are using an administrator account and prompting for consent is enabled, you are prompted for consent before the application is started.

Windows 7 also enables you to mark an application so that it always runs with administrator privileges. This approach is useful for resolving compatibility issues with legacy applications that require administrator privileges. It is also useful for UAC-compliant applications that normally run in standard mode but that you use to perform administration tasks. As examples, consider the following:

- A standard application written for Windows 7 is routinely run in elevated mode and used for administration tasks. To eliminate the need to right-click the application shortcut and choose Run As Administrator before running the application, you can mark it to always run as an administrator.
- An application written for Windows XP or an earlier version of Windows requires administrator privileges. Because this program is configured to use standard mode by default under Windows 7, the program isn't running properly and is generating numerous errors. To resolve the compatibility problem, you could create an application compatibility shim using the Windows Application Compatibility Toolkit (ACT) version 5.5 or later. As a temporary solution, you can mark the application to always run as an administrator.

NOTE **You cannot mark system applications or processes to always run with administrator privileges. Only nonsystem applications and processes can be marked to always run at this level.**

REAL WORLD **The Windows Application Compatibility Toolkit (ACT) is a solution for administrators that requires no reprogramming of an application. ACT can help you resolve common compatibility problems. For example, some programs run only on a specific operating system or when the user is an administrator. Using ACT, you can create a shim that responds to the application inquiry about the operating system or user level with a True statement, which allows the application to run. ACT also can help you create more in-depth solutions for applications that try to write to protected areas of the operating system or use elevated privileges when they don't need to. ACT can be downloaded from the Microsoft Download Center (*http://download.microsoft.com*).**

You can mark an application to always run as an administrator by following these steps:

1. On the Start menu, locate the program that you want to always run as an administrator.
2. Right-click the application's shortcut, and then click Properties.
3. In the Properties dialog box, click the Compatibility tab, shown in Figure 9-1.

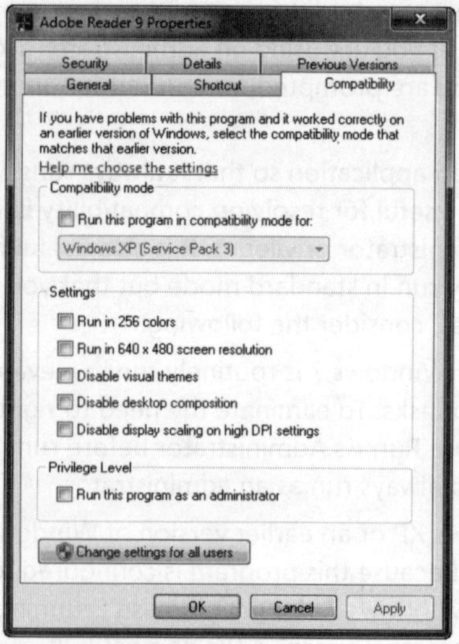

FIGURE 9-1 Access the Compatibility tab.

4. Do one of the following:
   - To apply the setting to the currently logged-on user, select the Run This Program As An Administrator check box, and then click OK.
   - To apply the setting to all users on the computer and regardless of which shortcut is used to start the application, click Change Setting For All Users to display the Properties dialog box for the application's .exe file, select the Run This Program As An Administrator check box, and then click OK twice.

NOTE **If the Run This Program As An Administrator option is unavailable, it means that the application is blocked from always running at an elevated level, the application does not require administrator credentials to run, or you are not logged on as an administrator.**

The application will now always run using an administrator access token. Keep in mind that if you are using a standard account and prompting is disabled, the application will fail to run.

Optimizing Virtualization and Installation Prompting for Elevation

With regard to applications, two areas of User Account Control can be customized:

- Automatic installation detection and prompting
- Virtualization of write failures

In Group Policy, you can configure these features by using the Administrative Templates policies for Computer Configuration under Windows Settings\Security Settings\Local Policies\Security Options. The security settings are as follows:

- **User Account Control: Detect Application Installations And Prompt For Elevation** Determines whether Windows 7 automatically detects application installation and prompts for elevation or consent. (This setting is enabled by default in Windows 7.) If you disable this setting, users are not prompted, in which case, the users will not be able to elevate permissions by supplying administrator credentials.
- **User Account Control: Virtualize File And Registry Write Failures To Per-User Locations** Determines whether file and registry virtualization is on or off. Because this setting is enabled by default, error notifications and error logging related to virtualized files and registry values are written to the virtualized location rather than the actual location to which the application was trying to write. If you disable this setting, the application will silently fail when trying to write to protected folders or protected areas of the registry.

In a domain environment, you can use Active Directory–based Group Policy to apply the security configuration you want to a particular set of computers. You can also configure these settings on a per-computer basis by using local security policy. To do this, follow these steps:

1. Click Start, point to All Programs, Administrative Tools, and then click Local Security Policy. This starts the Local Security Policy console.
2. In the console tree, under Security Settings, expand Local Policies, and then select Security Options.
3. Double-click the setting you want to work with, make any necessary changes, and then click OK.

Installing Programs: The Essentials

Program installation is fairly straightforward. Not so straightforward are troubleshooting the many things that can go wrong and fixing problems. To solve problems that might occur, you first need to understand the installation process. In many cases, the typical installation process starts when Autorun is triggered. Autorun in turn invokes a setup program. Once the setup program starts, the installation process can begin. Part of the installation process involves checking the user's credentials to ensure that he or she has the appropriate privileges to install the program and prompting for consent if the user doesn't. As part of installing a program, you might also need to make the program available to all or only some users on a computer.

Occasionally, Windows might not be successful in detecting the required installation permissions. This can occur if the installation manifest for the program has an embedded RequestedExecutionLevel setting that has a value set as RequireAdministrator. Because the RequestedExecutionLevel setting overrides what the installer detects in Windows, the installation process fails any time you run the installer with standard user permissions. To solve this problem, back out of the failed installation by exiting, canceling the installation, or taking another appropriate action. Next, locate the executable file for the installer. Right-click this file, and then click Run As Administrator to restart the installation process with administrator privileges.

Additionally, it is important to understand that in Windows 7 and Windows Server 2008 Release 2, Application Control policies replace Software Restriction policies. Software Restriction policies control the applications that users can install and run on Windows 2000, Windows XP, and Windows Vista. Application Control policies control the applications that users can install and run on Windows 7 and Windows Server 2008 Release 2. Keep the following in mind:

- When you are editing a Group Policy object (GPO), you can create and manage Software Restriction policies by using settings for computers under Computer Configuration\Policies\Windows Settings\Security Settings\Software Restriction Policies and settings for users under User Configuration\Policies\Windows Settings\Security Settings\Software Restriction Policies. Enforcement settings control how restrictions are applied. Designated file types determine what is and what is not considered an executable program.
- When you are editing a GPO, you can create and manage Application Control policies by using settings for computers under Computer Configuration\Policies\Windows Settings\Security Settings\Application Control Policies. You can now create separate rules for executable files, Windows installer files, and script files. Rules can be applied by publisher, file path, or file hash. A publisher rule gives you the most flexibility, enabling you to specify which products and versions to allow. For example, you could allow Microsoft Word 2003 or later.

Working with Autorun

When you insert an application CD or DVD into a CD or DVD drive, Windows 7 checks for a file named Autorun.inf. If present, Autorun.inf specifies the action that the operating system should take and might also define other installation parameters. Autorun.inf is a text-based file that can be opened in any standard text editor. If you were to examine the contents of one, you'd see something similar to the following code:

```
[autorun]
OPEN=SETUP.EXE AUTORUN=1
ICON=SETUP.EXE,4
SHELL=OPEN
DisplayName=Microsoft Digital Image Suite 9
ShortName=PIS
PISETUP=PIP\pisetup.exe
```

This Autorun.inf file opens a file named Setup.exe when the CD or DVD is inserted into the CD or DVD drive. Because Setup.exe is an actual program, this program is invoked. The Autorun.inf file also specifies an icon to use, the status of the shell, the program display name, the program's short name, and an additional parameter, which in this case is the location of another setup program to run.

The file that Autorun.inf specifies to open won't always be a program. Consider the following example:

```
[autorun]
OPEN=Autorun\ShelExec default.htm
```

This Autorun.inf file executes via the shell and opens a file named Default.htm in the computer's Web browser. It's important to note that even in this case, the document opened in the Web browser contains links that point to a setup program.

> ***TIP*** **With an application CD or DVD in a drive, you can restart the Autorun process at any time. Simply open and then close the drive bay.**

Application Setup and Compatibility

Most applications have a setup program that uses InstallShield, Wise Install, or Microsoft Windows Installer. When you start the setup program, the installer helps track the installation process and should also make it possible to easily uninstall the program when you need to. If you are installing an older application, the setup program might use an older version of one of these installers, and this might mean the uninstall process won't completely uninstall the program.

Even if you are absolutely certain that a program has a current installer, you should consider the possibility that you will need to recover the system if something goes wrong with the installation. To help ensure that you can recover your system, check that System Restore is enabled for the drive on which you are installing the program so that System Restore can create an automatic checkpoint before installing the program.

While the installers for most current programs automatically trigger the creation of a restore point before making any changes to a computer, the installers for older programs might not. You can manually create a restore point as discussed in Chapter 17, "Handling Maintenance and Support Tasks." Then, if you run into problems, you can try to uninstall the program or use System Restore to recover the system to the state it was in prior to the program's installation.

Before installing any application, you should check to see whether it is compatible with Windows 7. To determine compatibility, you can do the following:

- Check the software packaging, which should specify whether the program is compatible. Look for the Windows 7 logo.
- Check the software developer's Web site for a list of compatible operating systems.

NOTE **As part of the compatibility check, look for updates or patches for the program. If any are available, install them after installing the program.**

Windows 7 attempts to recognize potential compatibility problems before you install applications. If it detects one, you might see a Program Compatibility Assistant dialog box after you start a program's installer. Often, this dialog box contains information about the known compatibility issues with the program, and in many cases it displays a possible solution. For example, you might be advised to install the latest service pack for the program before running the program on the computer. In some cases, the Program Compatibility Assistant might display the message "This program is blocked due to compatibility issues." Here, the program is blocked because it causes a known stability issue with Windows, and you can't create an immediate fix to work around the problem. Your only options are to click the Check For Solutions Online button or click Cancel. If you check for solutions online, the typical solution requires you to purchase an updated version of the program. If you cancel, you stop the installation process without checking for possible solutions.

If the installation continues but fails for any reason before it is fully complete (or to properly notify the operating system regarding completion), you'll also see a Program Compatibility Assistant dialog box. In this case, if the program installed correctly, click This Program Installed Correctly. If the program didn't install correctly, click Reinstall Using Recommended Settings to allow the Program Compatibility Assistant to apply one or more compatibility fixes, and then try again to run the installer.

When you start programs, Windows 7 uses the Program Compatibility Assistant to automatically make changes for known compatibility issues as well. If the Program Compatibility Assistant detects a known compatibility issue when you run an application, it notifies you about the problem and provides possible solutions for resolving the problem automatically. You can then allow the Program Compatibility

Assistant to reconfigure the application for you, or you can manually configure compatibility as discussed in the section "Configuring Program Compatibility" later in this chapter.

For legacy applications, you can also use the Compatibility Administrator (Compatadmin.exe), provided in the Windows Application Compatibility Toolkit, to create an application manifest that sets the application's run level. The Compatibility Administrator can also help identify other types of compatibility issues with legacy applications. The Windows Application Compatibility Toolkit (ACT) can be downloaded from the Microsoft Download Center (*http://download.microsoft.com*).

Making Programs Available to All or Selected Users

Usually when you install a program, the program is available to all users on a computer. This occurs because the program's shortcuts are placed in the Start Menu\Programs folder (%SystemDrive%\ProgramData\Microsoft\Windows\Start Menu\Programs) for all users so that any user who logs on to the system has access to the program. Some programs prompt you during installation to choose whether you want to install the program for all users or only for the currently logged-on user. Other programs simply install themselves only for the current user.

If setup installs a program so that it is available only to the currently logged-on user and you want other users to have access to the program, you need to take one of the following actions:

- Log on to the computer with each user account that should have access to the program, and then rerun setup to make the program available to these users. You also need to run setup again when a new user account is added to the computer and that user needs access to the program.
- For programs that don't require per-user settings to be added to the registry before running, you can in some cases make the program available to all users on a computer by adding the appropriate shortcuts to the Start Menu\Programs folder for all users. Copy or move the program shortcuts from the currently logged-on user's profile to the Start Menu\Programs folder for all users.

If you want to make a program available to all users on a computer, you can copy or move a program's shortcuts by completing the following steps:

1. Right-click the Start button, and then click Open Windows Explorer. In Windows Explorer, navigate to the currently logged on user's Programs folder. This is a hidden folder under %UserProfile%\AppData\Roaming\Microsoft\Windows\Start Menu.
2. In the Programs folder, right-click the folder for the program group or the shortcut you want to work with, and then click Copy or Cut on the shortcut menu.

3. Next, navigate to the all-users Start Menu\Programs folder. This hidden folder is under %SystemDrive%\ProgramData\Microsoft\Windows\Start Menu.

4. In the Programs folder, right-click an open space, and then click Paste. The program group or shortcut should now be available to all users of the computer.

NOTE **In the %SystemDrive%\Users folder, you'll find a folder called All Users. If you are aware of this folder, you might wonder why you didn't copy the program's shortcut for all users to a subfolder of this folder. Well, the reason is that %SystemDrive%\Users\All Users is a symbolic link to %SystemDrive%\ProgramData. A symbolic link is a pointer to where a folder actually exists. When you are working with the command prompt (Cmd.exe), you can view symbolic links and reparse points (junctions) in the current directory by entering dir /al.**

If you want to make a program available only to the currently logged-on user rather than all users on a computer, you can move a program's shortcuts by completing the following steps:

1. Right-click the Start button, and then click Open Windows Explorer. In Windows Explorer, navigate to the all-users Start Menu folder. This hidden folder is under %SystemDrive%\ProgramData\Microsoft\Windows\Start Menu.
2. In the Programs folder, right-click the folder for a program group or the program shortcut that you want to work with, and then click Cut.
3. In Windows Explorer, navigate to the currently logged-on user's Programs folder. This is a hidden folder under %UserProfile%\AppData\Roaming\Microsoft\Windows\Start Menu.
4. In the Programs folder, right-click an open space, and then click Paste. The program group or shortcut should now be available only to the currently logged-on user.

NOTE **Moving a program group or shortcut hides the fact that the program is available on the computer—it doesn't prevent other users from running the program by using the Run dialog box or Windows Explorer.**

Deploying Applications Through Group Policy

You can make applications available to users over the network through Group Policy. When you use Group Policy to deploy applications, you have two distribution options:

- The first option is to assign the application to users or computers. When an application is assigned to a computer, it is installed the next time the computer is started and is available to all users of that computer the next time users log on. When an application is assigned to a user, it is installed the next time the user logs on to the network. An assigned application can also be configured to be installed on first use. In this configuration, the application is made available through shortcuts on the user's desktop or Start menu. With install-on-first-use configured, the application is installed when the user clicks a shortcut to launch the application.

- The second option is to publish the application and make it available for installation. When you publish an application, the application can be made available through extension activation. With extension activation configured, the program is installed when a user opens any file with an extension associated with the application. For example, if a user double-clicks a file with a .doc or .docx extension, Microsoft Word could be installed automatically.

You deploy applications for computers using a Microsoft Windows Installer Package (.msi file) and policies under Computer Configuration\Policies\Software Settings\Software Installation You deploy applications for users using a Windows Installer Package (.msi file) and policies under User Configuration\Policies\Software Settings\Software Installation. The basic steps required to deploy applications through Group Policy are as follows:

1. For clients to access the Windows Installer Package, it must be located on a network share. As necessary, copy the Windows Installer Package (.msi file) to a network share that is accessible by the appropriate users.
2. In the Group Policy Management Editor, open the Group Policy object (GPO) from which you want to deploy the application. After it is deployed, the application is available to all clients to which the GPO applies. This means the application is available to computers and users in the related domain, site, or organizational unit (OU).
3. Expand Computer Configuration\Policies\Software Settings or User Configuration\Policies\Software Settings, right-click Software Installation, point to New, and then click Package.
4. Use the Open dialog box to locate the Windows Installer Package (.msi file) for the application, and then click Open. You are then given the choice to select the deployment method: Published, Assigned, or Advanced.
5. To publish or assign the program, select Published or Assigned, and then click OK. If you are configuring computer policy, the program is available the next time a computer affected by the GPO is started. If you are configuring user policy, the program is available to users in the domain, site, or OU the next time users log on. Currently logged-on users need to log off and then log on.
6. To configure additional deployment options for the program, select Advanced. You can then set additional deployment options as necessary.

Configuring Program Compatibility

If you want to install 16-bit or MS-DOS-based programs, you might need to make special considerations. Additionally, to get older programs to run, you might sometimes need to adjust compatibility options. Techniques for handling these situations are discussed in the following sections.

Special Installation Considerations for 16-Bit and MS-DOS-Based Programs

Many 16-bit and MS-DOS-based programs that don't require direct access to hardware can be installed and run on Windows 7 without any problems. However, most 16-bit and MS-DOS-based programs do not support long file names. To help ensure compatibility with these programs, Windows 7 maps long and short file names as necessary. This ensures that long file names are protected when they are modified by a 16-bit or an MS-DOS-based program. Additionally, it is important to note that some 16-bit and MS-DOS-based programs require 16-bit drivers, which are not supported on Windows 7. As a result, these programs won't run.

Most existing 16-bit and MS-DOS-based programs were originally written for Windows 3.0 or Windows 3.1. Windows 7 runs these older programs using a virtual machine that mimics the 386-enhanced mode used by Windows 3.0 and Windows 3.1. Unlike on other recent releases of Windows, on Windows 7 each 16-bit and MS-DOS-based application runs as a thread within a single virtual machine. This means that if you run multiple 16-bit and MS-DOS-based applications, they all share a common memory space. Unfortunately, if one of these applications hangs or crashes, it usually means the others will as well.

You can help prevent one 16-bit or MS-DOS-based application from causing others to hang or crash by running it in a separate memory space. To do this, follow these steps.

1. Right-click the program's shortcut icon, and then click Properties. If the program doesn't have a shortcut, create one, and then open the shortcut's Properties dialog box.
2. On the Shortcut tab, click the Advanced button. This displays the Advanced Properties dialog box.
3. Select the Run In Separate Memory Space check box.
4. Click OK twice to close all open dialog boxes and save the changes.

NOTE **Running a program in a separate memory space uses additional memory. However, you'll usually find that the program is more responsive. Another added benefit is that you are able to run multiple instances of the program—as long as all the instances are running in separate memory spaces.**

TIP The Windows 7 command prompt (Cmd.exe) is a 32-bit command prompt. If you want to invoke a 16-bit MS-DOS command prompt, you can use Command.com. Type **command** in the Run dialog box.

Forcing Program Compatibility

Some programs won't install or run on Windows 7 even if they work on previous versions of the Windows operating system. If you try to install a program that has known compatibility problems, Windows 7 should display a warning prompt telling you about the compatibility issue. In most cases, you should not continue installing or running a program with known compatibility problems, especially if the program is a system utility such as an antivirus program or a disk partitioning program, because running an incompatible system utility can cause serious problems. Running other types of incompatible programs can also cause problems, especially if they write to system locations on disk.

That said, if a program will not install or run on Windows 7, you might be able to run the program by adjusting its compatibility settings. Windows 7 provides two mechanisms for managing compatibility settings. You can use the Program Compatibility wizard, or you can edit the program's compatibility settings directly by using the program's Properties dialog box. Both techniques work the same way. However, the Program Compatibility wizard is the only way you can change compatibility settings for programs that are on shared network drives, CD or DVD drives, or other types of removable media drives. As a result, you can sometimes use the Program Compatibility wizard to install and run programs that would not otherwise install and run.

Using the Program Compatibility Wizard

You can only configure compatibility settings for programs you've installed. You can't configure compatibility settings for programs included with the operating system. To try to automatically detect compatibility issues using the Program Compatibility wizard, follow these steps.

1. Locate the program shortcut by navigating the menus under Start, All Programs. Right-click the program shortcut, and then click Troubleshoot Compatibility. This starts the Program Compatibility wizard, shown in Figure 9-2.

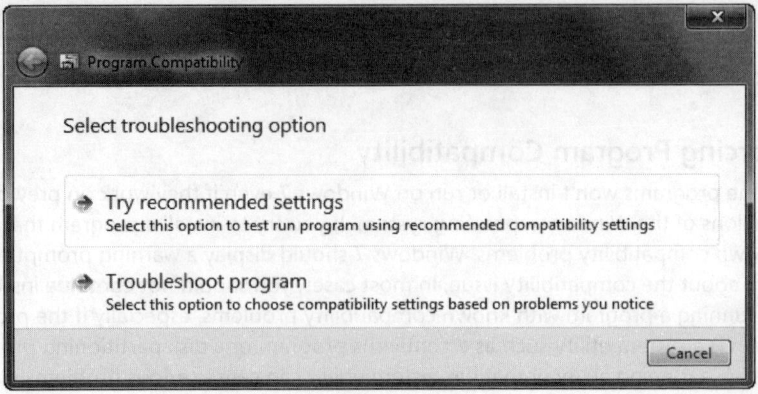

FIGURE 9-2 Troubleshoot program compatibility issues.

2. The wizard automatically tries to detect compatibility issues. To try to run the program you are troubleshooting with the recommended fixes, click Try Recommended Settings. Next, review the settings that will be applied, and then click Start The Program.
3. After running the program, click Next, and then do one of the following:
   - Click Yes, Save These Settings For This Program if the compatibility settings resolved the problem and you want to keep the settings.
   - Click No, Try Again Using Different Settings if the compatibility settings didn't resolve the problem and you want to repeat this process from the beginning.
   - Click No, Report The Problem To Microsoft And Check Online For A Solution if the compatibility settings didn't resolve the problem and you'd like to check for an online solution.
   - Click Cancel if you want to discard the compatibility settings and exit the wizard.

To perform advanced troubleshooting and use the Program Compatibility wizard to specify the compatibility settings to use, follow these steps:

1. Locate the program shortcut by navigating the menus under Start, All Programs. Right-click the program shortcut, and then click Troubleshoot Compatibility. This starts the Program Compatibility wizard.
2. Click Troubleshoot Program. On the What Problems Do You Notice? page, you can specify information about problems you've seen. The selections you make determine the wizard pages you see when you click Next. They include the following:
   - **The Program Worked On Earlier Versions Of Windows But Won't Install Or Run Now** If you select this option, you are prompted on one of the subsequent wizard pages to specify which version. Because your

choice sets the compatibility mode, choose the operating system for which the program was designed. When running the program, Windows 7 simulates the environment for the specified operating system.

- **The Program Opens But Doesn't Display Correctly** If you are trying to run a game, an educational program, or any other program that requires specific display settings, such as a program designed for Windows 98, you can select this option and then choose the type of display problem you are seeing. Your selections restrict the video display: when you use 256 colors, 640 × 480 screen resolution, or both, Windows restricts the video display. This can help with programs that have problems running at higher screen resolutions and greater color depths. Your selections can also disable themes, desktop compositing (which prevents special visual effects on the desktop), and display scaling of high dots-per-inch (DPI) settings.
- **The Program Requires Additional Permissions** If you choose this option, the program will be configured to run with administrator privileges.
- **I Don't See My Problem Listed** If you choose this option, the wizard displays optional pages for operating system and display issue selection. The wizard also sets the program to run as an administrator. Ultimately, choosing this option has the same effect as if you had selected all three of the previous options.

3. Review the compatibility settings that will be applied. If you don't want to apply these settings, click Cancel and repeat this procedure to select different options. If you want to apply these settings, click Start The Program, and the wizard runs the program with the compatibility settings you specified.
4. After running the program, click Next to continue. When you continue, you are prompted to confirm whether the changes fixed the problem. Do one of the following:
   - If the compatibility settings resolved the problem and you want to keep the settings, click Yes, Save These Settings For This Program.
   - If the compatibility settings didn't resolve the problem and you want to repeat this process from the beginning, click No, Try Again Using Different Settings.
   - If the compatibility settings didn't resolve the problem and you'd like to check for an online solution, click No, Report The Problem To Microsoft And Check Online For A Solution.
   - If you want to discard the compatibility settings and exit the wizard, click Cancel.

NOTE **If you've configured alternate display settings for an application, the application will run in the alternate display mode whenever you start it. To restore the original display settings, simply exit the program.**

Setting Compatibility Options Directly

If a program you have already installed won't run correctly, you might want to edit the compatibility settings directly rather than through the wizard. To do this, follow these steps.

1. Right-click the program's shortcut icon, and then click Properties.
2. In the Properties dialog box, click the Compatibility tab. Any option you select is applied to the currently logged-on user for the application shortcut. To apply the setting to all users on the computer and regardless of which shortcut is used to start the application, click Change Setting For All Users to display the Properties dialog box for the application's .exe file, and then select the compatibility settings that you want to use for all users who log on to the computer.

   NOTE **Programs that are part of the Windows 7 operating system cannot be run in Compatibility mode. The options on the Compatibility tab are not available for built-in programs.**

3. Select the Run This Program In Compatibility Mode For check box, and then use the selection menu to choose the operating system for which the program was designed.
4. If necessary, use the options in the Settings panel to restrict the video display settings for the program. Select 256 colors, 640 × 480 screen resolution, or both, as required.
5. If necessary, you can also disable visual themes, desktop compositing, and display scaling of high DPI settings.
6. Click OK. Double-click the shortcut to run the program and test the compatibility settings. If you still have problems running the program, you might need to modify the compatibility settings again.

Managing Installed and Running Programs

Windows 7 provides several management tools for working with programs. These tools include:

- **Task Manager** Provides options for viewing and managing running programs as well as options for viewing resource usage and performance
- **Programs** Provides tasks for viewing installed programs, adding and removing programs, viewing installed updates, and more
- **Default Programs** Helps you track and configure global default programs for the computer, personal default programs for individual users, AutoPlay settings for multimedia, and file associations for programs

- **Windows Features** Helps you view and manage the Windows components installed on a computer
- **Assoc** Helps you view and manage file type associations
- **Ftype** Helps you view and manage file type definitions

These tools and related configuration options are discussed in the sections that follow.

Managing Currently Running Programs

In Windows 7, you can view and work with a computer's currently running programs and processes by using Task Manager. You can open Task Manager by pressing Ctrl+Alt+Delete and then selecting Start Task Manager. As Figure 9-3 shows, Task Manager has two tabs for working with running programs:

- **Applications** Lists applications that are currently running in the foreground by name and status (such as Running or Not Responding). To exit a program, which might be necessary when it is not responding, click the program in the Task list, and then click End Task.
- **Processes** Lists all background and foreground applications running on the computer by image name, user name, and resource usage. To stop a process, click the process, and then click End Process.

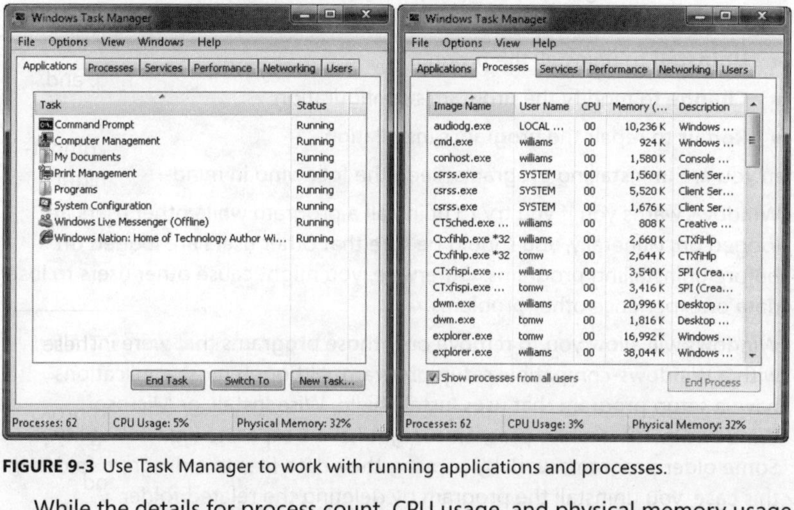

FIGURE 9-3 Use Task Manager to work with running applications and processes.

While the details for process count, CPU usage, and physical memory usage are for the computer as a whole, the processes are only listed for the currently logged-on user and the operating system by default. To see running processes for all users, you must click Show Processes From All Users.

TIP On the Processes tab, you can manage processes in additional ways by right-clicking a process and selecting from an extended list of options. The options include Open File Location, which opens the folder containing the executable file for the process in Windows Explorer; End Process Tree, which stops the process and all dependent processes; Create Dump File, which creates a memory dump file for the selected process; and Properties, which opens the Properties dialog box for the executable file.

Managing, Repairing, and Uninstalling Programs

Windows 7 considers any program you've installed on a computer or made available for a network installation to be an installed program. In Windows XP and earlier versions, you use the Add Or Remove Programs utility to install and manage applications. In Windows 7, you use the setup program that comes with the application to install applications, and you use the Installed Programs page in Control Panel to manage applications.

You can use the Installed Programs page to view, add, remove, or repair installed programs by following these steps:

1. Click Start, and then click Control Panel. In Control Panel, click Programs.
2. Click Programs And Features. You should see a list of installed programs.
3. In the Name list, right-click the program you want to work with, and then click one of the following commands:
   - **Uninstall** to uninstall the program
   - **Change** to modify the program's configuration
   - **Repair** to repair the program's installation

When you are uninstalling programs, keep the following in mind:

- Windows warns you if you try to uninstall a program while other users are logged on. Generally, you should be sure that other users are logged off before uninstalling programs. Otherwise, you might cause other users to lose data or experience other problems.
- Windows will allow you to remove only those programs that were installed with a Windows-compatible setup program. Although most applications have a setup program that uses InstallShield, Wise Install, or Microsoft Windows Installer, older programs might have a separate uninstall utility. Some older programs work by copying their data files to a program folder. In this case, you uninstall the program by deleting the related folder.
- Many uninstall programs leave behind data either inadvertently or by design. As a result, you often find folders for these applications within the Program Files folder. You could delete these folders, but they might contain important data files or custom user settings that could be used again if you reinstall the program.

- Sometimes, the uninstall process fails. Often, you can resolve any problem simply by rerunning the uninstaller for the program. Occasionally, you might need to clean up after the uninstall process. This might require removing program files and deleting remnants of the program in the Windows registry. A program called the Windows Installer Cleanup utility can help you clean up the registry. For more information on the utility and to download the software, see the article on the Microsoft support Website at *http://support.microsoft.com/kb/290301*).

Designating Default Programs

Default programs determine which programs are used with which types of files and how Windows handles files on CDs, DVDs, and portable devices. You configure default programs based on the types of files those programs support, either globally for all users of a computer or only for the current user. Individual user defaults override global defaults. For example, you could select Windows Media Player as the global default for all types of files it supports, and then all users of the computer would use Windows Media Player to play the sound, audio, and video files it supports. If a specific user wanted to use Apple iTunes instead as the default player for sound and audio files, you could configure iTunes to be that user's default player for the types of media files it supports.

You can configure global default programs for all the users of a computer by following these steps:

1. Click Start, and then click Control Panel. In Control Panel, click Programs.
2. Click Default Programs, and then click Set Program Access And Computer Defaults. You'll see the dialog box shown in Figure 9-4.

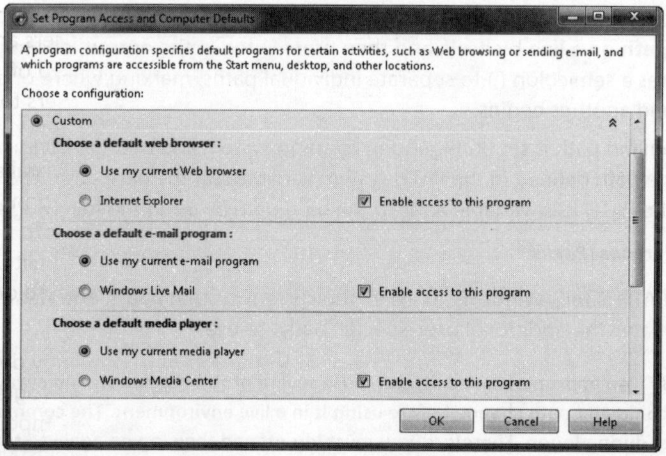

FIGURE 9-4 Choose a global default configuration.

3. Choose a configuration from one of the following options:
   - **Microsoft Windows** Sets the currently installed Windows programs as the default programs for browsing the Web, sending e-mail, playing media files, and so on.
   - **Non-Microsoft** Sets the currently installed programs as the default programs for browsing the Web, sending e-mail, playing media files, and so on.
   - **Custom** Enables you to choose programs as the defaults for browsing the Web, sending e-mail, playing media files, and so on.
4. Click OK to save the settings.

To override global defaults, you can set default programs for individual users. You can configure default programs for the current user by following these steps:

1. Click Start, and then click Control Panel. In Control Panel, click Programs.
2. Click Default Programs, and then click Set Your Default Programs.
3. Select a program you want to work with in the Programs list.
4. If you want the program to be the default for all the file types and protocols it supports, click Set This Program As Default.
5. If you want the program to be the default for specific file types and protocols, click Choose Defaults For This Program. Select the file extensions for which the program should be the default, and then click Save.

Managing the Command Path

Windows uses the command path to locate executables. You can view the current command path for executables by using the PATH command. In a command shell, type **path** on a line by itself, and then press Enter. In a Windows PowerShell console, type **$env:path** on a line by itself, and then press Enter. In the output, observe that Windows uses a semicolon (;) to separate individual paths, marking where one file path ends and another begins.

The command path is set during logon by using system and user environment variables. The path defined in the PATH system variable sets the base path. The path defined in the PATH user variable adds to the base path by using the following syntax:

```
%PATH%;AdditionalPaths
```

Here, %PATH% tells Windows to insert the current system paths, and *AdditionalPaths* designates the additional user-specific paths to use.

CAUTION **An improperly set path can cause severe problems. You should always test any command path change before using it in a live environment. The command path is set during logon. Therefore, you must log off and then log on again to see the effects of the revised path.**

Don't forget about the search order that Windows uses. Paths are searched in order, with the last path in the PATH user variable being the last one searched. This can sometimes slow the execution of your programs and scripts. To help Windows find your programs and scripts faster, you should consider placing a required path earlier in the search order.

Be careful when setting the command path. It is easy to overwrite all path information accidentally. For example, if you don't specify %PATH% when setting the user path, you will delete all other path information. One way to ensure that you can easily re-create the command path is to keep a copy of the command path in a file.

- When you are working with the command prompt, you can write the current command path to a file by entering **path > orig_path.txt**. Keep in mind that if you are using a standard command prompt rather than an administrator command prompt, you won't be able to write to secure system locations. In this case, you can write to a subdirectory to which you have access or to your personal profile. To write the command path to the command-shell window, type **path**.
- When you are working with the PowerShell console, you can write the current command path to a file by entering **$env:path > orig_path.txt**. If you are using a standard console rather than an administrator console, you won't be able to write to secure system locations. In this case, you can write to a subdirectory to which you have access or to your personal profile. To write the command path to the PowerShell window, type **$env:path**.

At the command prompt or in the PowerShell window, you can modify the command path by using the Setx.exe utility. You also can edit the command path by completing the following steps:

1. In Control Panel, click System And Security, and then click System.
2. In the System console, click Change Settings, or click Advanced System Settings in the left pane.
3. On the Advanced tab in the System Properties dialog box, click the Environment Variables button.
4. Select the PATH variable in the System Variables list. Under System Variables, click Edit.
5. By default, the path value is selected. Without pressing any other key, press the Right Arrow key. This should remove the selection highlight and place the insertion point at the end of the variable value.
6. Type a semicolon, and then enter a path to insert. Repeat as necessary, and then click OK three times.

In Group Policy, you can use a preference item to modify the command path. Follow these steps:

1. Open a Group Policy object (GPO) for editing in the Group Policy Management Editor. To configure preferences for computers, expand Computer

Configuration\Preferences\Windows Settings, and then select Environment. To configure preferences for users, expand User Configuration\Preferences\ Windows Settings, and then select Environment.

2. Right-click the Environment node, point to New, and then click Environment Variable. This opens the New Environment Properties dialog box.
3. In the Action list, select Update to update the path variable, or select Replace to delete and then re-create the path variable. Next, select User Variable to work with user variables.
4. In the Name field, type **Path**. In the Value field, type the variable value. Typically, you'll enter **%PATH%;** followed by the paths you want to add, using a semicolon to separate each path. If the affected computers have existing PATH user variable definitions, you must provide the related paths to ensure that these paths are retained.
5. Use the options on the Common tab to control how the preference is applied. In most cases, you'll want to create the PATH variable only once (rather than have Group Policy re-create the variable each time policy is refreshed). If so, select Apply Once And Do Not Reapply.
6. Click OK. The next time policy is refreshed, the preference item will be applied as appropriate for the GPO in which you defined the preference item.

CAUTION **Incorrectly setting the path can cause serious problems. Before deploying an updated path to multiple computers, you should test the configuration. One way to do this is to create a GPO in Active Directory that applies only to an isolated test computer. Next, create a preference item for this GPO, and then wait for a policy to refresh or apply policy using GPUpdate. If you are logged on to the computer, you need to log off and then log back on before you can confirm the results.**

Managing File Extensions and File Associations

File extensions and file associations also are important for determining how programs run. The types of files that Windows considers to be executables are determined by the file extensions for executables. File extensions allow users to execute a command by using just the command name. File associations are what allow users to double-click a file and open the file automatically in a related application. Two types of file extensions are used:

- **File extensions for executables** Executable files are defined with the %PATHEXT% environment variable and can be set using the Environment Variables dialog box or with Group Policy preference items in much the same way as the PATH variable. You can view the current settings by typing **set pathext** at the command line or by typing **$env:pathext** at a PowerShell prompt. The default setting is PATHEXT=.COM;.EXE;.BAT;.CMD;.VBS;.VBE;.JS;.JSE;.WSF;.WSH;.MSC. With this setting, the command line knows which files are executable and which files are not, so you don't have to specify the file extension at the command line.

- **File extensions for applications** File extensions for applications are referred to as file associations. File associations are what enable you to pass arguments to executables and to open documents, worksheets, or other application files by double-clicking their file icons. Each known extension on a system has a file association that you can view at a command prompt by typing **assoc** followed by the extension, such as **assoc .doc** or **assoc .docx**. Each file association in turn specifies the file type for the file extension. This can be viewed at a command prompt by typing **ftype** followed by the file association, such as **ftype Word.Document.8** or **ftype Word.Document.12**.

NOTE **Assoc and Ftype are internal commands for the command shell (Cmd.exe). To use the Assoc command in PowerShell, enter cmd /c assoc followed by the extension, such as cmd /c assoc .doc. To use the Ftype command in PowerShell, enter cmd /c ftype followed by the file association, such as cmd /c ftype Word.Document.8.**

With executables, the order of file extensions in the %PATHEXT% variable sets the search order used by the command line on a per-directory basis. Thus, if a particular directory in the command path has multiple executables that match the command name provided, a .com file would be executed before an .exe file and so on.

Every known file extension on a system has a corresponding file association and file type—even extensions for executables. In some cases, the file type is the extension text without the period followed by the keyword file, such as cmdfile, exefile, or batfile, and the file association specifies that the first parameter passed is the command name and that other parameters should be passed on to the application. For example, if you type **assoc .exe** to see the file associations for .exe executables, you then type **ftype exefile**. You'll see the file association is set to the following:

```
exefile="%1" %*
```

Thus, when you run an .exe file, Windows knows the first value is the command that you want to run and anything else provided is a parameter to pass along.

File associations and types are maintained in the Windows registry and can be set using the Assoc and Ftype commands, respectively. To create the file association at the command line, type **assoc** followed by the extension setting, such as **assoc .pl=perlfile**. To create the file type at the command line, set the file-type mapping, including how to use parameters supplied with the command name, such as **ftype perlfile=C:\Perl\Bin\Perl.exe "%1" %***.

You also can associate a file type or protocol with a specific program by completing the following steps:

1. Click Start, and then click Control Panel. In Control Panel, click Programs.
2. Click Default Programs, and then click Associate A File Type Or Protocol With A Program.

3. On the Set Associations page, current file associations are listed by file extension and the current default for that extension. To change the file association for an extension, click the file extension, and then click Change Program.
4. Do one of the following:
   - The Recommended Programs list shows programs that are registered in the operating system as supporting files with the selected extension. Click a recommended program to set it as the default for the selected extension, and then click OK.
   - The Other Programs list shows programs that might also support the selected extension. Click a program to set it as the default for the selected extension, and then click OK. Alternatively, click Browse to locate another program to use as the default.

In Group Policy, you can use a preference item to create new file types and file associations. To create a preference item for a new file type, follow these steps:

1. Open a Group Policy object (GPO) for editing in the Group Policy Management Editor. Expand Computer Configuration\Preferences\Control Panel Settings, and then select Folder Options.
2. Right-click the Folder Options node, point to New, and then click File Type. This opens the New File Type Properties dialog box.
3. In the Action list, select Create, Update, Replace, or Delete.
4. In the File Name Extension field, type the extension of the file type without the period, such as **pl**.
5. In the Associated Class list, select a registered class to associate with the file type.
6. Use the options on the Common tab to control how the preference is applied. In most cases, you'll want to create the new variable only once. If so, select Apply Once And Do Not Reapply.
7. Click OK. The next time policy is refreshed, the preference item will be applied as appropriate for the GPO in which you defined the preference item.

To create a preference item for a new file association, follow these steps:

1. Open a Group Policy object (GPO) for editing in the Group Policy Management Editor. Expand User Configuration\Preferences\Control Panel Settings, and then select Folder Options.
2. Right-click the Folder Options node, point to New, and then click Open With. This opens the New Open With Properties dialog box.
3. In the Action list, select Create, Update, Replace, or Delete.
4. In the File Name Extension field, type the extension of the file type without the period, such as **pl**.

5. Click the Browse (...) button to the right of the Associated Program field, and then use the Open dialog box to select the program to associate with the file type.
6. Optionally, select Set As Default to make the associated program the default for files with the previously specified file extension.
7. Use the options on the Common tab to control how the preference is applied. In most cases, you'll want to create the new variable only once. If so, select Apply Once And Do Not Reapply.
8. Click OK. The next time policy is refreshed, the preference item will be applied as appropriate for the GPO in which you defined the preference item.

Configuring AutoPlay Options

In Windows 7, AutoPlay options determine how Windows handles files on CDs, DVDs, and portable devices. You can configure separate AutoPlay options for each type of CD, DVD, and media your computer can handle by following these steps:

1. Click Start, and then click Control Panel. In Control Panel, click Programs.
2. Click Default Programs, and then click Change AutoPlay Settings. This displays the AutoPlay page in Control Panel.
3. As shown in Figure 9-5, use the media selection list to set the default AutoPlay option for each media type.

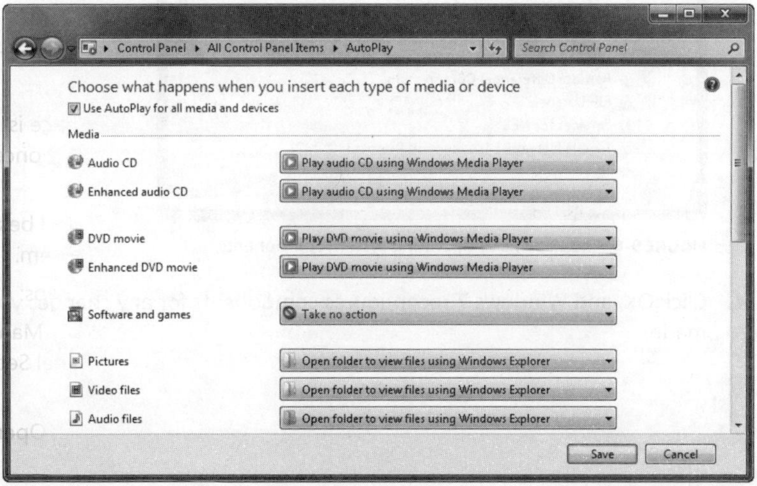

FIGURE 9-5 Set AutoPlay options for CDs, DVDs, and portable devices.

4. Click Save to save your settings.

Adding and Removing Windows Features

In Windows XP and earlier versions of Windows, you use the Add/Remove Windows Components option of the Add Or Remove Programs utility to add or remove operating system components. In Windows Vista and Windows 7, operating system components are considered Windows features that can be turned on or off rather than added or removed.

You can turn on or off Windows features by following these steps:

1. Click Start, and then click Control Panel. In Control Panel, click Programs.
2. Under Programs And Features, click Turn Windows Features On Or Off. This displays the Windows Features dialog box.
3. As shown in Figure 9-6, select the check boxes for features to turn them on, or clear the check boxes for features to turn them off.

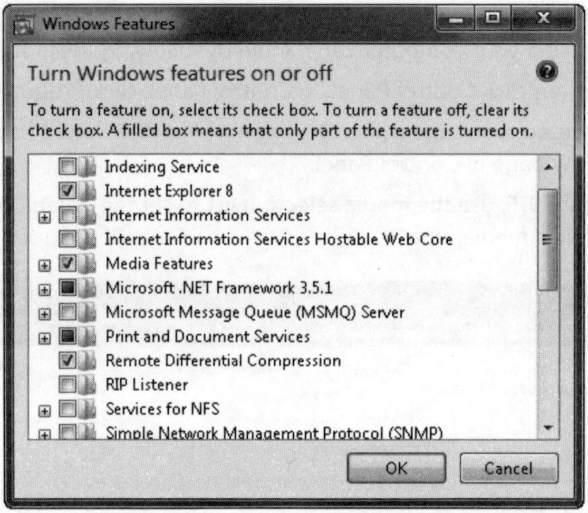

FIGURE 9-6 Add or remove operating system components.

4. Click OK, and Windows 7 reconfigures components for any changes you made.

CHAPTER 10

Managing Firmware, Boot Configuration, and Startup

As surprising as it may seem, when a computer fails to boot or experiences a Stop error that crashes the operating system, the most basic element involved in starting a computer and booting to an operating system—the firmware—is often overlooked as a possible cause. This happens because most people dig in and begin troubleshooting Windows without looking at the firmware. The trouble with this approach is that many computer problems originate in firmware, either because the firmware itself is flawed or because the firmware has been improperly configured. To distinguish between problems in firmware and problems in the operating system, you need to understand how the startup process works and what occurs during each of its phases. You also need to understand firmware itself. Primed with a solid understanding of these subjects, you'll be better prepared to diagnose and resolve related problems.

Navigating and Understanding Firmware Options

The startup process involves firmware, firmware interfaces, and an operating system. During startup, firmware is the first code that runs. Firmware performs basic initialization of the computer and provides the services that allow a computer to start loading an operating system.

Platform firmware is implemented in motherboard-chipsets. There are many types of motherboard-chipsets, and although older motherboard-chipsets might not be updatable, most newer ones have updatable firmware. Chipset firmware is separate and different from the computer's underlying firmware interface.

Firmware Interface Types and Boot Data

Every computer has firmware, yet it is the interface between the platform firmware and the operating system that handles the startup process. The way a firmware interface works and the tasks it performs depend on the type of firmware interface. Currently, the prevalent firmware interfaces are:

- Basic input/output system (BIOS)
- Extensible Firmware Interface (EFI)
- Unified Extensible Firmware Interface (UEFI)

A computer's BIOS, EFI, or UEFI provides the hardware-level interface between hardware components and software. Like chipsets themselves, BIOS, EFI, and UEFI can be updated. Because firmware development was a fast-changing area between 2005 and 2009, white papers and other technical information written prior to or during this time are likely to be outdated and inaccurate with respect to current implementations. It is important to keep the following in mind:

- Most technical documentation refers to a computer's firmware interface simply as *firmware*. For example, the documentation specifies to make "such and such a change in firmware" or to "check firmware." Technically, you make the change in the firmware *interface*, and the firmware interface makes the change in firmware.
- UEFI is both a type of firmware interface and an industry standard. UEFI as a firmware interface is modular and does not necessarily serve the same purpose or provide the same functionality as BIOS or EFI. UEFI as a standard is designed to provide extensible and testable interfaces.

It is also important to understand that BIOS, EFI, and UEFI work in distinctly different ways. BIOS is based on x86, 16-bit real-mode architecture and was originally designed to get a computer started after the computer was powered on. This is why BIOS performs firmware-to-operating-system interfacing and platform initialization.

Regardless of the firmware interface type, Windows 7 uses a pre–operating system boot environment. The boot environment is an extensible abstraction layer that allows the operating system to work with multiple types of firmware interfaces without requiring the operating system to be specifically written to work with these firmware interfaces. Within the boot environment, startup is controlled by using the parameters in the boot configuration data (BCD) store.

All computers running Windows Vista, Windows 7, and Windows Server 2008 have a BCD store. The BCD store is contained in a file called the BCD registry. The location of this registry depends on the computer's firmware:

- On BIOS-based operating systems, the BCD registry file is stored in the \Boot\Bcd directory of the active partition.
- On EFI-based operating systems, the BCD registry file is stored on the EFI system partition.

Entries in the BCD store identify the boot manager to use during startup and the specific boot applications available. The default boot manager is the Windows Boot Manager. Windows Boot Manager controls the boot experience and enables you to choose which boot application is run. Boot applications load a specific operating system or operating system version. For example, the boot application for Windows 7 is the Windows Boot Loader. This allows you to boot BIOS-based and EFI-based computers in much the same way.

Typically, you can press F8 or F12 during startup of the operating system to access the Advanced Boot Options menu and then use this menu to select one of several advanced startup modes, including Safe Mode, Enable Boot Logging, and Disable Driver Signature Enforcement. These advanced modes temporarily modify the way the operating system starts to help you diagnose and resolve problems. However, they don't make permanent changes to the boot configuration or to the BCD store.

Boot Services, Run-Time Services, and Beyond

BIOS manages the preboot data flow between the operating system and attached devices, such as the video adapter, keyboard, mouse, and hard disk. When BIOS initializes a computer, it first determines whether all attached devices are available and functioning, and then it begins to load the operating system.

Over the years, these basic features of BIOS were expanded to encompass the following:

- **Boot services** Refers to the collection of interfaces and protocols that are present in the boot environment. The services at a minimum provide an operating system loader with access to platform capabilities required to complete the operating system boot. These services are also available to drivers and applications that need access to platform capabilities. Boot services are terminated after the operating system takes control of the computer.
- **Run-time services** Refers to the interfaces that provide access to underlying platform-specific hardware, such as timers, that might be useful during operating system run time. These services are available during the boot process but also persist after the operating system loader terminates boot services.
- **Advanced Configuration and Power Interface (ACPI)** Refers to a table-based interface to the system board that enables the operating system to implement operating system–directed power management and system configuration.

- **Services for System Management BIOS (SMBIOS)** Refers to a table-based interface that is required by the Wired for Management Baseline (WMB) specification and used to relate platform-specific management information to the operating system or to an operating system–based management agent.

Generally, computers with BIOS use hard disks that have master boot record (MBR) partitions. To break free of the 16-bit roots of BIOS, Intel developed EFI as a new firmware implementation for its 64-bit Itanium-based processors. EFI is based on x64, 64-bit real-mode architecture. As with BIOS, EFI performs firmware-to-operating-system interfacing, platform initialization, and other functions. With the introduction of EFI, Intel also provided a new particular table architecture for hard disks, called the GUID partition table (GPT). Generally, computers with EFI use hard disks that have GPT partitions.

Unified EFI

As Intel began developing EFI, Intel developers and others around the world began to recognize the need to break the tie between firmware and processor architecture. This led to the development of UEFI. The UEFI 2.0 specification was finalized in January 2006, revised in January 2007 as UEFI 2.1, and revised again in September 2008 as UEFI 2.2. The UEFI specifications define a model for the interface between operating systems and platform firmware. The interface consists of data tables that contain platform-related information as well as boot and run-time service calls that are available to the operating system and its loader. The interface is independent of the processor architecture. Because UEFI abstracts the processor architecture, UEFI works with computers that have 32-bit, 64-bit, or an alternative architecture. As with EFI, computers with UEFI generally use hard disks that have GPT partitions. However, UEFI doesn't replace all the functionality in either BIOS or EFI and can, in fact, be wrapped around BIOS or EFI.

REAL WORLD **The UEFI 2.2 specification is over 2,000 pages long. To save you a tremendous amount of reading, I've summarized its core capabilities here.**

In UEFI, the system abstraction layer (SAL) is the firmware that abstracts platform implementation differences and provides the basic interface to all higher-level software. UEFI defines boot services and run-time services.

UEFI boot services include:

- Event, timer, and task priority services that create, wait for, signal, check, and close events; set timers; and raise or restore the priority of tasks.
- Memory allocation services that allocate or free memory pages, get memory maps, and allocate or free pooled memory.
- Driver model boot services that handle protocol interfaces for devices, open and close protocol streams, and connect or disconnect from controllers.
- Image services that load, start, and unload images.

- Miscellaneous services that set watchdog timers, copy and set memory, install configuration tables, and perform cyclic redundancy checking (CRC) calculations.

UEFI run-time services include:

- Variable services that get, set, and query variables.
- Time services that get and set time and get and set wakeup time.
- Virtual memory services that set virtual address mapping and convert memory pointers.
- Miscellaneous services that reset the computer, return counters, and pass information to the firmware.

UEFI defines architecture-independent models for EFI loaded images, device paths, device drivers, driver signing, and secure boot. It also defines the following:

- Console support, which allows simple text and graphics output.
- Human Interface Infrastructure support, which describes the basic mechanisms for managing user input and provides definitions for related protocols, functions, and type definitions that can help abstract user input.
- Media support, which allows I/O access to file systems, files, and media devices.
- PCI, SCSI, and iSCSI bus support, which allows I/O access across a PCI, SCSI, or iSCSI bus as well as SCSI or iSCSI boot.
- USB support, which allows I/O access over USB host controllers, USB buses, and USB devices.
- Compression support, which provides algorithms for compressing and decompressing data.
- ACPI table support, which allows installation or removal of an ACPI table.
- EFI byte code virtual machine support, which allows loading and executing EFI device drivers.
- Network protocol support, which defines the Simple Network Protocol (SNP), Preboot Execution Environment (PXE), and Boot Integrity Services (BIS) protocols. SNP provides a packet-level interface to network adapters. PXE is used for network access and network booting. BIS is used to check the digital signature of a data block against a digital certificate for the purpose of checking integrity and authorization. PXE uses BIS to check downloaded network boot images before executing them.
- Managed network protocol support, which defines the Managed Network Service Binding Protocol (MNSBP) and the Managed Network Protocol (MNP). These services allow multiple event-driven drivers and applications to access and use network interfaces simultaneously. MNSBP is used to locate communication devices that are supported by an MNP drive and manage instances of protocol drivers. MNP is used by drivers and applications to perform raw asynchronous network-packet I/O.

- Network addressing protocol support, which defines the following protocols: Address Resolution Protocol Service Binding Protocol (ARPSBP), ARP, DHCPv4, DHCPv4 service binding, DHCPv6, and DHCPv6 service binding,
- Miscellaneous network protocol support, which defines the following protocols: virtual LAN configuration, EAP/EAP management, TCPv4, TCPv4 service binding, TCPv6, TCPv6 service binding, IPv4, IPv4 service binding and configuration, IPv6, IPv6 service binding and configuration, IPSec configuration, FTPv4, FTPv4 service binding, UDPv4, UDPv4 service binding, UDPv6, UDPv6 service binding, Multicast TFTPv4, and Multicast TFTPv6.

To be clear, UEFI is not designed to replace either BIOS or EFI. While UEFI uses a different interface for boot services and run-time services, some platform firmware must perform the functions that BIOS and EFI need for system configuration and setup because UEFI does not do this. For this reason, UEFI is often implemented on top of traditional BIOS and EFI, in which case, UEFI takes the place of the initialization entry points into BIOS or EFI.

Navigating Startup and Power States

When a computer is first started, the firmware interface activates all the hardware required by the computer to boot, including:

- Motherboard-chipsets
- Processors and processor caches
- System memory
- Graphics and audio controllers
- Internal drives
- Internal expansion cards

After the firmware interface completes this process, it transfers control of the computer to the operating system. The firmware interface implementation determines what happens next.

- With BIOS-based computers running Windows XP and earlier versions of Windows, Ntldr and Boot.ini are used to boot into the operating system. Ntldr handles the task of loading the operating system, and Boot.ini contains the parameters that enable startup, including the identity of the boot partitions. Through Boot.ini parameters, you can add options that control the way the operating system starts, the way computer components are used, and the way operating system features are used.
- With BIOS-based computers running Windows Vista and later versions of Windows, Windows Boot Manager and Windows Boot Loader are used to boot into the operating system. Windows Boot Manager initializes the operating system by starting the Windows Boot Loader, which in turn starts the operating system by using information in the BCD store. Through the BCD

parameters, you can add options that control the way the operating system starts, the way computer components are used, and the way operating system features are used.

- With Itanium-based computers, Ia64ldr.efi, Diskpart.efi, and Nvrboot.efi are used to boot into the operating system. Ia64ldr.efi handles the task of loading the operating system, while Diskpart.efi identifies the boot partitions. Through Nvrboot.efi, you set the parameters that enable startup.
- With other EFI-based computers, Bootmgfw.efi manages the boot process and passes control to the Windows Boot Loader. Through Bcdedit.exe, you set the parameters that enable startup.
- With UEFI, UEFI boot services provide an abstraction layer. Currently, this abstraction layer is wrapped around BIOS or EFI. A computer with BIOS in its underlying architecture uses a BIOS-based approach to booting into the operating system. A computer with EFI in its underlying architecture uses an EFI-based approach to booting into the operating system.

Working with Firmware Interfaces

When you power on most computers, you can access the firmware interface by pressing the button shown for Setup in the initial display. For example, you might press F2 or Delete during the first few seconds of startup to enter the firmware interface. Firmware interfaces have control options that allow you to adjust the functionality of hardware. You can use these controls to do the following:

- Adjust LCD brightness (on laptop computers)
- Adjust the hard disk noise level
- Adjust the number of cores the processor is using and their speed
- Change the boot sequence
- Change the CMOS date and time
- Restore the firmware interface to the default configuration
- Turn on or off modular add-on devices

Firmware interfaces have the ability to report basic configuration details, including information about the following:

- AC adapter capacity (on laptop computers)
- Battery charge and health (on laptop computers)
- LCD type and native resolution (on laptop computers)
- Firmware version
- Memory
- Processors
- Storage devices
- Video chipsets

Most firmware interfaces allow you to create supervisor, user, and/or general passwords that are not accessible from the operating system. If a supervisor password is set, you need to provide the password before you can modify the firmware configuration. If a user password is set, you need to enter the password during startup before the computer will load the operating system. If you forget these passwords, you might not be able to operate the computer or change firmware settings until you clear the forgotten passwords, which generally also clears any customization you have made to the firmware interface.

A firmware interface update can often resolve problems or add features to the computer's firmware interface. If you are not experiencing problems on a computer and are not aware of any additional features in the firmware interface that are needed, you might not need to update a computer to the latest version of the firmware interface. An additional cautionary note is that if a firmware interface update is not performed properly, it can harm the computer and prevent it from starting.

Examining Firmware Interfaces

The information and configuration options available in the firmware interface depend on the computer you are working with, the type of firmware interface, and the version of the firmware interface. Most desktop computers have more configuration options than laptop computers do.

A popular firmware interface at the time of this writing is the Phoenix TrustedCore. As configured on my laptop computer, this interface provides several menu pages offering information and controls. The Information page provides basic information about the computer's configuration, including:

- CPU type, such as Intel Core2 Duo CPU T5250 at 1.50 GHz
- CPU speed, such as 1,500 MHz
- Hard disk type and model, such as IDE1, Hitachi HTS541616J9SA00
- Hard disk serial number, such as SB2553SJC9HT1D
- ATAPI model name, such as Toshiba DVDW/HD TS-L802A
- System BIOS version, such as v0.3505
- VGA BIOS version, such as nVidia 0.84.41.00.18
- Serial number
- Asset tag number
- Manufacturer name
- Universally unique identifier (UUID)

The Main page provides additional configuration information and allows you to manage key settings. On this page, you can view the following:

- System time
- System date

- System memory size
- Extended memory size
- Video memory size

You can view or set the following:

- Quiet Boot status as Enabled or Disabled. When this setting is disabled, the computer displays the diagnostic screen during boot.
- Power On Display status as Auto or Both. This setting determines how the display device is selected.
- Network Boot status as Enabled or Disabled. When this setting is enabled, the computer boots from the network.
- F12 Boot menu status as Enabled or Disabled. When this setting is enabled, the computer shows the F12 Boot menu during startup.
- D2D Recovery status as Enabled or Disabled. When enabled, this setting allows users to use disk-to-disk recovery.

The Security page allows you to view and set supervisor, user, and hard-disk passwords. The status information tells you the current state for each password, such as:

- Supervisor Password Is: Clear
- User Password Is: Clear
- Hard Disk Password Status: Clear

The following additional configuration options allow you to manage passwords:

- **Set Supervisor Password** Controls access to the firmware interface
- **Set User Password** Controls access to the computer
- **Set Hard Disk Password** Controls access to the computer's hard disk

To set a password, select the option, and then press Enter. When prompted, type the new password, and then type the new password again to confirm it. Press Enter to continue.

The Boot Priority Order allows you to view and manage the priority order for boot devices. A sample boot priority order listing follows from an Acer notebook computer:

1. IDE HDD
2. IDE CD
3. PCI DEV
4. USB HDD
5. USB CDROM
6. USB FDC
7. USB KEY

When you power on the computer, the computer tries to boot using the device listed first. If that fails, the computer tries the second boot device, and so on. You can use the Up and Down Arrow keys to select a device and then use the plus sign (+) or the hyphen (–) to move the device up or down in the list. Pressing the F or R key specifies the device as fixed or removable. Pressing the X key excludes or includes the device from the boot list. Pressing Shift+1 enables or disables the device.

The Exit page allows you to exit the firmware interface and resume startup of the computer. As with most firmware interfaces, you have several options:

- **Exit Saving Changes** Exits the firmware interface and saves your changes
- **Exit Discarding Changes** Exits the firmware interface and discards your changes
- **Discard Changes** Discards your changes without exiting the firmware interface
- **Save Changes** Saves your changes without exiting the firmware interface

Regardless of which menu page you are working with, you have a set of options that are standard in most firmware interfaces.

- Press F1 to get help.
- Press the Up or Down Arrow key to select an item.
- Press the Left or Right Arrow key to select a menu page.
- Press F5 or F6 to change values.
- Press F9 to apply setup defaults (you must confirm when prompted).
- Press Esc to exit (and then select an option to save or discard changes).
- Press Enter to apply or execute a command.
- Press F10 to save changes and exit the firmware interface. (When prompted to confirm, Yes is selected. Press Enter to save changes and exit. Press the Spacebar to select No, and then press Enter to remain in the firmware interface.)

As you can see, the configuration options here aren't very extensive. In contrast, desktop computers can have a dizzying array of options and suboptions. When you are working with a desktop computer, you'll likely find options that serve similar purposes. However, because there are few standards and conventions among firmware interface manufacturers, the options might have different labels and values.

Power States and Power Management

To better understand the hardware aspects related to boot issues, let's dig in and take a look at Advanced Configuration and Power Interface (ACPI). A computer's motherboard-chipset, firmware, and operating system must support ACPI for the related advanced power state features to work. ACPI-aware components track the power state of the computer. An ACPI-aware operating system can generate a request that the system be switched into a different ACPI mode, and the firmware interface responds by enabling the requested ACPI mode.

As shown in Table 10-1, there are six different power states, ranging from S0 (the system is completely powered on and fully operational) to S5 (the system is completely powered off). The states S1, S2, S3, and S4 are referred to as *sleep states,* in which the system appears off because of low power consumption but retains enough of the hardware context to return to the working state without a system reboot.

Motherboard-chipsets support specific power states. For example, one motherboard might support the S0, S1, S4, and S5 states but not the S2 and S3 states. In Windows operating systems, the sleep power transition refers to switching off the system to a sleep or a hibernate mode, and the wake power transition refers to switching on the system from a sleep or a hibernate mode. The sleep and hibernate modes allow users to switch off and on systems much faster than the regular shutdown and startup processes.

Thus, a computer is waking up when the computer is transitioning from the Off state (S5) or any sleep state (S1–S4) to the On state (S0). The computer is going to sleep when the computer is transitioning from the On state (S0) to the Off state (S5) or one of the sleep states (S1–S4). A computer cannot enter one sleep state directly from another; it must enter the On state before entering a different sleep state.

TABLE 10-1 Power States for ACPI in Firmware and Hardware

STATE	TYPE	DESCRIPTION
S0	On state	The system is completely operational, fully powered, and completely retains the context (such as the volatile registers, memory caches, and RAM).
S1	Sleep state	The system consumes less power than the S0 state. All hardware and processor contexts are maintained.
S2	Sleep state	The system consumes less power than the S1 state. The processor loses power, and processor context and contents of the cache are lost.
S3	Sleep state	The system consumes less power than the S2 state. Processor and hardware contexts, cache contents, and chipset context are lost. The system memory is retained.
S4	Hibernate state	The system consumes the least power compared to all other sleep states. The system is almost at the Off state. The context data is written to the hard disk, and no context is retained. The system can restart from the context data stored on the disk.
S5	Off state	The system is in a shutdown state and retains no context. The system requires a full reboot to start.

When you are working with firmware, you can go to the Power screen or a similar screen to manage ACPI and related settings. Power settings you might see include the following:

- **After Power Failure or AC Recovery** Determines the mode of operation if a power loss occurs, for which you'll see settings such as Stay Off, Last State, Power On. Stay Off means the system will remain off after power is restored. Last State restores the system to the state it was in before power failed. Power On means the system will turn on after power is restored.
- **Wake On LAN From S5 or Auto Power On** Determines the action taken when the system power is off and a PCI Power Management wake event occurs. You'll see settings like Stay Off or Power On.
- **ACPI Suspend State or Suspend Mode** Sets the suspend mode. Typically, you're able to set S1 state or S3 state as the suspend mode.

NOTE **Above, I provide two standard labels for each setting because your computer hardware might not have these exact labels. The firmware variant you are working with determines the actual labels that are associated with boot, power, and other settings.**

Because Intel and AMD also have other technologies to help reduce startup and resume times, you might also see power settings such as these for Intel:

- Enhanced Intel SpeedStep Technology (EIST), which can be either disabled or enabled
- Intel Quick Resume Technology Driver (QRTD), which can be either disabled or enabled

Enhanced Intel SpeedStep Technology (EIST or SpeedStep) allows the system to dynamically adjust processor voltage and core frequency, which can result in decreased average power consumption and decreased average heat production. When EIST or a similar technology is enabled and in use, you see two different processor speeds on the System page in Control Panel. The first speed listed is the specified speed of the processor. The second speed is the current operating speed, which should be less than the first speed. If EIST is off, both processor speeds will be equal. Advanced Settings for Processor Power Management under Power Options can also affect how this technology works. Generally speaking, you should not use this technology with Windows 7 (although you might want to use this technology with Windows Vista).

Intel Quick Resume Technology Driver (QRTD) allows an Intel Viiv technology-based computer to behave like a consumer electronic device, with instant on/off after an initial boot. Intel QRTD manages this behavior through the Quick Resume mode function of the Intel Viiv chipset. Pressing the power button on the computer or a remote control puts the computer in the Quick Sleep mode, and you can switch the computer to the Quick Resume mode by moving the mouse, pressing an on/

off key on the keyboard (if available), or pressing the sleep button on the remote control. Quick Sleep mode is different from standard sleep mode. In Quick Sleep mode, the computer's video card stops sending data to the display, the sound is muted, and the monitor LED indicates a lowered power state on the monitor, but the power continues to be supplied to vital components on the system, such as the processor, fans, and so on. This technology was originally designed for Windows XP Media Center Edition, and generally should not be used with Windows 7. (In many cases it does not work with Windows Vista. You might need to disable this feature in firmware to allow Windows Vista to properly sleep and resume.)

After you look at the computer's power settings in firmware, you should also review the computer's boot settings in firmware. Typically, you can configure the following boot settings:

- **Boot Drive Order** Determines the boot order for boot devices.
- **Boot To Hard Disk Drive** Determines whether the computer can boot to fixed disks. Can be set to Disabled or Enabled.
- **Boot To Removable Devices** Determines whether the computer can boot to removable media. Can be set to Disabled or Enabled.
- **Boot To Network** Determines whether the computer can perform a network boot. Can be set to Disabled or Enabled.
- **USB Boot** Determines whether the computer can boot to USB flash devices. Can be set to Disabled or Enabled.

As for power settings, your computer might not have the exact labels shown here, but the labels should be similar. You need to optimize these settings for the way you plan to use the computer. When you use BitLocker Drive Encryption, you should enable Boot To Removable Devices, USB Boot, or both to ensure that the computer can detect the USB flash drive with the encryption key during the boot process.

Diagnosing and Resolving Startup Problems

To diagnose and resolve startup problems, you need to understand the sequence of events that occur after you press the power button on a computer. When you press the power button, the following happens:

1. The firmware interface performs system configuration, also known as power-on self test (POST).
2. The firmware interface performs setup of the computer, also known as initialization of the computer.
3. The firmware interface passes control to the operating system loader, also known as the boot manager.

4. The boot manager starts the boot loader. The boot loader uses the firmware interface boot services to complete operating system boot and load the operating system. Loading the operating system involves:
   a. Loading (but not running) the operating system kernel, Ntoskrnl.exe.
   b. Loading (but not running) the hardware abstraction layer (HAL), Hal.dll.
   c. Loading the HKEY_LOCAL_MACHINE\SYSTEM registry hive into memory (from %SystemRoot%\System32\Config\System).
   d. Scanning the HKEY_LOCAL_MACHINE\SYSTEM\Services key for device drivers and then loading (but not initializing) the drivers that are configured for the boot class into memory. Drivers are also services (which means both device drivers and system services are prepared).
   e. Enabling memory paging.
5. The boot loader passes control to the operating system kernel.
6. The kernel and the HAL initialize the Windows executive, which in turn processes the configuration information stored in the HKEY_LOCAL_MACHINE\SYSTEM\CurrentControlSet hive and then starts device drivers and system services.
7. The kernel starts the Session Manager (Smss.exe), which in turn:
   a. Initializes the system environment by creating system environment variables.
   b. Starts the Win32 subsystem (Csrss.exe). Here, Windows switches the display output from text mode to graphics mode.
   c. Starts the Windows Logon Manager (Winlogon.exe), which in turn starts the Services Control Manager (Services.exe) and the Local Security Authority (Lsass.exe) and waits for a user to log on.
   d. Creates additional paging files that are required.
   e. As necessary, performs delayed renaming of in-use files that were updated in the previous session.
8. The Windows Logon Manager waits for a user to log on. The logon user interface and the default credential provider collect the user name and password and pass this information to the Local Security Authority for authentication.
9. The Windows Logon Manager runs Userinit.exe and the Windows Explorer shell. Userinit.exe initializes the user environment by creating user environment variables, running startup programs, and performing other essential tasks.

This sequence of events is for a cold start of a computer from power on through logon. The sequence of events varies if the computer is resuming from sleep, standby, or hibernation. The sequence of events also varies if you are starting an operating system other than Windows or a Windows operating system other than Windows Vista, Windows 7, or Windows Server 2008.

Sometimes you can identify the source of a startup problem by pinpointing where the startup process breaks. Table 10-2 lists the various startup phases and provides a possible cause of problems in each phase. The phase numbers are meant only to aid in the subsequent discussion.

TABLE 10-2 Troubleshooting Startup

PHASE	PHASE TITLE	POSSIBLE CAUSE OF PROBLEM
1	System configuration, power-on self test	Hardware failure or missing device
2	Setup, initial startup	Firmware configuration, the disk subsystem, or the file system
3	Operating system loader, boot manager	BCD data, improper operating system selection for loading, or invalid boot loader
4	Kernel, HAL, Windows executive	Driver or service configuration or service dependencies
5	Session Manager	Graphics display mode, system environment, or component configuration

Troubleshooting Startup Phase 1

When you power on a computer from a cold state, system configuration (power-on self test) occurs first. During this phase, the firmware performs initial checks of hardware, verifies that required devices are present, and reads the system configuration settings from nonvolatile memory on the motherboard. Although nonvolatile memory could be EEPROM, flash, or battery-backed RAM, it is more typically flash memory that remains even after you shut down and unplug the computer.

After the motherboard firmware performs its tests and reads its settings, add-on devices that have their own firmware, such as video cards and host controller cards, perform their tests and load their settings. If startup fails in this phase, the computer likely has a hardware failure. A required device, such as a keyboard, mouse, or hard disk, could also be missing. In most cases, the firmware interface displays an error message that indicates the problem. If video isn't working, the firmware interface might indicate the problem by emitting a series of beeps.

You can resolve a problem with a keyboard, mouse, or display by checking the device's connection to the computer. If another device is causing a problem, you might be able to resolve the problem by changing the device configuration in the firmware interface, or you might need to replace the device.

Troubleshooting Startup Phase 2

Once system configuration is complete, the computer enters the setup, or initial startup, phase. Firmware interface settings determine the devices the computer uses to start the operating system. The boot order and the boot enabled or disabled state of each device affects startup. As discussed previously, the computer tries to boot using the device listed first. If that fails, the computer tries the second boot device, and so on. If none of the configured devices are bootable, you'll see an error similar to the following:

```
Non-system disk or disk error
Replace and press any key when ready to continue
```

Here, you'll want to check the boot order and be sure it is set correctly. If you are trying to boot from CD or DVD media, check that the media is present and that CD/DVD booting is enabled. If you are trying to boot from a hard disk, make sure booting from a hard disk is enabled and listed prior to any USB or other removable media you've inserted. If you've recently installed a hard disk, power off and unplug the computer, and then verify that all cables are connected correctly and that any jumpers are configured correctly.

Because configuring boot options in firmware isn't necessarily intuitive, I'll provide examples from a cross-section of computers by various vendors. On an HP notebook computer, the boot settings are found on the Boot Options and Boot Order submenus on the System Configuration page. The Boot Options submenu has these options:

- **F10 And F12 Delay (sec)** Sets the amount of time for the user to press F10 or F12 at startup.
- **CD-ROM Boot** Enables or disables CD-ROM boot during startup.
- **Floppy Boot** Enables or disables the floppy boot during startup.
- **Internal Network Adapter Boot** Enables or disables networking booting during startup.

Use the Up and Down Arrow keys to select an option, and then press Enter to view and set the option.

On the Boot Order submenu, the boot order is listed as the following:

1. USB Floppy
2. ATAPI CD/DVD ROM Drive
3. Notebook Hard Drive
4. USB Diskette On Key
5. USB Hard Drive
6. Network Adapter (only if Internal Network Adapter Boot is enabled)

Here, you use the Up and Down Arrow keys to select a device, and then press F5 or F6 to move the device up or down in the list. It is important to note that this computer (like many newer computers) distinguishes between USB flash keys (referred to as *USB diskettes on keys*) and USB drives (referred to as *USB hard drives*). Computer users won't really see a difference between the two.

On a Dell computer, you manage boot settings on the Boot Sequence submenu under System. The boot order is listed as:

1. Onboard or USB CD-ROM Drive
2. Onboard SATA Hard Drive
3. Onboard or USB Floppy Drive (not present)
4. Onboard IDE Hard Drive (not present)
5. Add-in Hard Drive (not present)
6. USB Device (not present)
7. Add-in Hard Drive (not present)

Note that here, internal devices are listed as "Onboard." You use the Up and Down Arrow keys to select a device, and then press the U or D key to move the device up or down in the list. Press the Spacebar to exclude or include the device from the boot list. Press Delete to permanently delete the device if it is not present and you no longer want it in the list.

Under Drives, you have submenus for the following:

- **Diskette Drive** Determines how the firmware interface configures floppy drives.
- **Drive 0: SATA-0** Determines whether the firmware interface enables or disables the specified ATA or SATA device.
- **Drive 1: SATA-1** Determines whether the firmware interface enables or disables the specified ATA or SATA device.
- **SATA Operation** Controls the configuration of the hardware RAID.

Under Onboard Devices, the options on the USB Controller submenu control whether the computer can boot from USB storage devices.

TIP **More desktop computers are being shipping with hardware RAID controller cards. The Dell computer used for these examples has a hardware RAID controller card, and the options for configuring it are found on the SATA Operation submenu of the System page. Typically, RAID controller cards for desktop computers support RAID 0 and RAID 1. RAID 0 offers no data protection and simply stretches a logical disk volume across multiple physical disks. RAID 1 offers data protection by mirroring the disks. When disks are mirrored, two physical disks appear as one disk, and each disk has identical copies of any data.**

Troubleshooting Startup Phase 3

After setup, the firmware interface passes control to the boot manager. The boot manager in turn starts the boot loader.

On computers using BIOS, the computer reads information from the master boot record (MBR). Normally, the MBR is the first sector of data on the disk. The MBR contains boot instructions and a partition table that identifies disk partitions. The active partition, also known as the boot partition, has boot code in its first sector of data as well. The data provides information about the file system on the partition and enables the firmware to locate and start the Bootmgr stub program in the root directory of the boot partition. Bootmgr switches the process into 32-bit or 64-bit protected mode from real mode and loads the 32-bit or 64-bit Windows Boot Manager as appropriate (found within the stub file itself). Windows Boot Manager locates and starts the Windows Boot Loader (Winload).

Problems can occur if the active boot partition does not exist or if any boot sector data is missing or corrupt. Errors you might see include:

```
Error loading operating system
```

and

```
Invalid partition table
```

In many cases, you can restore proper operations by using the Startup Repair tool.

In contrast, computers using EFI have a built-in boot manager. When you install Windows, Windows adds an entry to the EFI boot manager with the title Windows Boot Manager, which points to the boot manager's executable file on the EFI system partition (\Efi\Microsoft\Boot\Bootmgfw.efi). The boot manager then passes control to the Windows Boot Loader.

Problems can occur if you install a different operating system or change the EFI boot manager settings. In many cases, you'll be able to restore proper operations by using the Startup Repair tool or by changing EFI boot manager settings.

Troubleshooting Startup Phase 4

The boot loader uses the firmware interface boot services to complete operating system boot. The boot loader loads the operating system kernel (Ntoskrnl.exe) and then loads the hardware abstraction layer (HAL), Hal.dll. Next, the boot loader loads the HKEY_LOCAL_MACHINE\SYSTEM registry hive into memory (from %SystemRoot%\System32\Config\System), and then it scans the HKEY_LOCAL_MACHINE\SYSTEM\Services key for device drivers. The boot loader scans this registry hive to find drivers that are configured for the boot class and loads them into memory.

Once the boot loader passes control to the operating system kernel, the kernel and the HAL initialize the Windows executive, which in turn processes the configuration information stored in the HKEY_LOCAL_MACHINE\SYSTEM\CurrentControlSet hive and then starts device drivers and system services. Drivers and services are started according to their start-type value. This value is set on the Start subkey under HKEY_LOCAL_MACHINE\SYSTEM\CurrentControlSet\Services*Name*, where *Name* is the name of the device or service. Valid values are 0 (identifies a boot driver), 1 (identifies a system driver), 2 (identifies an auto-load driver or service), 3 (identifies a load-on-demand driver or service), 4 (identifies a disabled and not-started driver or service), and 5 (identifies a delayed-start service). Drivers are started in the order boot, system, auto load, load on demand, delayed start.

Most problems in this phase have to do with invalid driver and service configurations. Some drivers and services are dependent on other components and services. If dependent components or services are not available or configured properly, this also could cause startup problems.

During startup, subkeys of HKEY_LOCAL_MACHINE\SYSTEM are used to configure devices and services. The Select subkey has several values used in this regard:

- The Current value is a pointer to the ControlSet subkey containing the current configuration definitions for all devices and services.
- The Default value is a pointer to the ControlSet subkey containing the configuration definition the computer uses at the next startup, provided that no error occurs and that you don't use an alternate configuration.
- The Failed value is a pointer to the ControlSet subkey containing a configuration definition that failed to load Windows.
- The LastKnownGood value is a pointer to the ControlSet subkey containing the configuration definition that was used for the last successful logon.

During normal startup, the computer uses the Default control set. Generally, if no error has occurred during startup or you haven't selected the last known good configuration, the Default, Current, and LastKnownGood values all point to the same ControlSet subkey, such as ControlSet001. If startup fails and you access the last known good configuration by using the Advanced Boot options, the Failed entry is updated to point to the configuration definition that failed to load. If startup succeeds and you haven't accessed the last known good configuration, the LastKnownGood value is updated to point to the current configuration definition.

Troubleshooting Startup Phase 5

During the final phase of startup, the kernel starts the Session Manager (Smss.exe). The Session Manager initializes the system environment by creating system environment variables and starting the Win32 subsystem (Csrss.exe). This is the point at which Windows switches from the text presentation mode used initially to a graphics presentation mode. Generally, if the display adapter is broken or not properly seated, the computer won't display in either text or graphics mode, but if the display adapter is configured improperly, you'll often notice this when the computer switches to graphics mode. If the display adapter is configured improperly, you'll have banding problems such as discussed in the section "Troubleshooting Display Problems" in Chapter 7.

The display is only one of several components that might first present problems during this late phase of startup. If startup fails during this phase, you can identify problem components by using boot logging. If the computer has a Stop error in this phase, use the information provided by the Stop message to help you identify the problem component.

The Session Manager starts the Windows Logon Manager (Winlogon.exe), which in turn starts the Services Control Manager (Services.exe) and the Local Security Authority (Lsass.exe) and waits for a user to log on. When a user logs on, the Windows Logon Manager runs Userinit.exe and the Windows Explorer shell. Userinit.exe initializes the user environment by creating user environment variables, running startup programs, and performing other essential tasks. The Windows Explorer shell provides the desktop, taskbar, and menu system.

If you encounter startup problems during or after logon, the problem is likely due to a misconfigured service or startup application. As part of troubleshooting, you can temporarily disable services and startup applications as discussed in the section "Managing System Boot Configuration" later in this chapter.

Managing Startup and Boot Configuration

During startup of the operating system, you can press F8 or F12 to access the Advanced Boot Options menu and then use this menu to select one of several advanced startup modes. These advanced modes don't make permanent changes to the boot configuration or to the BCD store. Tools you can use to modify the boot configuration and manage the BCD store include the Startup And Recovery dialog box, the System Configuration utility, and the BCD Editor. The sections that follow discuss how these tools are used.

Setting Startup and Recovery Options

The Startup And Recovery dialog box controls the basic options for the operating system during startup. You can use these options to set the default operating system, how long to display the list of available operating systems, and how long to display recovery options when needed. Whether or not you boot a computer to different operating systems, you'll want to optimize these settings to reduce the wait time during startup, and in this way speed up the startup process.

You can open the Startup And Recovery dialog box by completing the following steps:

1. In Control Panel, click System And Security, and then click System to display the System window.
2. In the left pane of the System window, click Advanced System Settings to display the System Properties dialog box.

3. On the Advanced tab of the System Properties dialog box, under Startup And Recovery, click Settings. This displays the Startup And Recovery dialog box, shown in Figure 10-1.

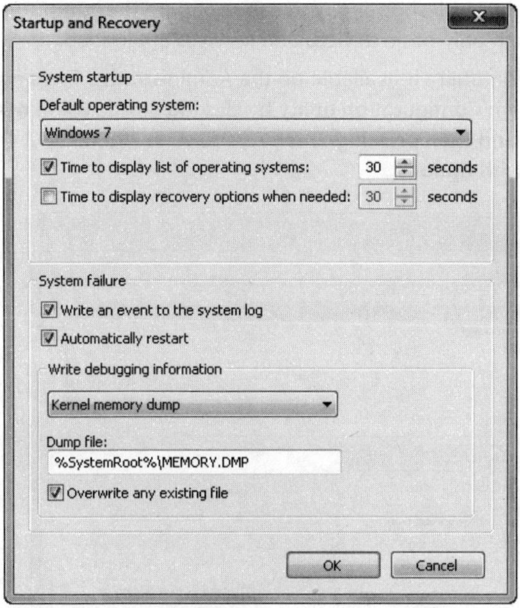

FIGURE 10-1 Configure system startup options.

4. On a computer with multiple operating systems, use the Default Operating System list to specify the operating system that you want to start by default.
5. Set the timeout interval for the operating system list by selecting the Time To Display List Of Operating Systems check box and specifying the interval in seconds. To speed up the startup process, you could use a value of 5 seconds.
6. Set the timeout interval for the recovery options list by selecting the Time To Display Recovery Options When Needed check box and specifying the interval in seconds. Again, to speed up the startup process, use a value of 5 seconds.
7. Under System Failure, select Write An Event To The System Log if you want to record events related to system failure. If you want the computer to automatically restart after a failure, select Automatically Restart.
8. Click OK to save your settings.

Managing System Boot Configuration

The System Configuration utility (Msconfig.exe) allows you to fine-tune the way a computer starts. Typically, you use this utility during troubleshooting and diagnostics. For example, as part of troubleshooting, you can configure the computer to use a diagnostic startup in which only basic devices and services are loaded.

The System Configuration utility is available on the Administrative Tools menu. You can also start the System Configuration utility by clicking Start, typing **msconfig.exe** in the Search box, and then pressing Enter. As shown in Figure 10-2, this utility has a series of tabs with options.

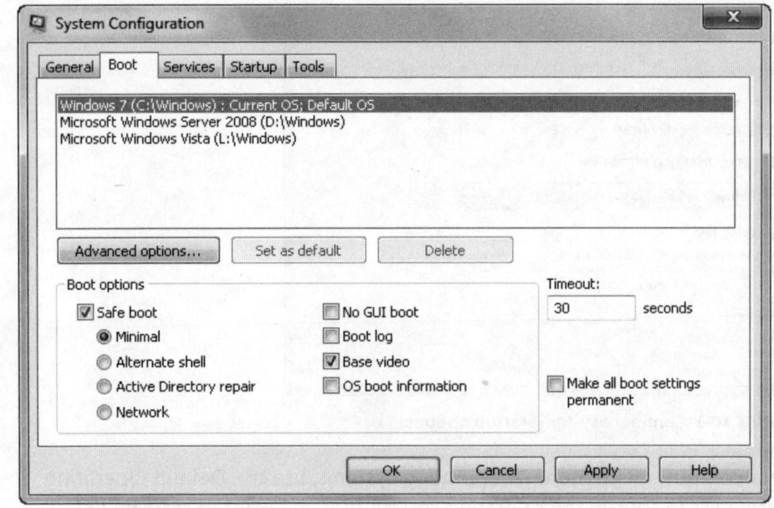

FIGURE 10-2 Use the System Configuration utility for troubleshooting.

The General tab options allow you to configure the way startup works and are the starting point for troubleshooting and diagnostics. Using these options, you can choose to perform a normal startup, diagnostic startup, or selective startup. After you restart the computer and resolve any problems, open the System Configuration utility again, select Normal Startup on the General tab, and then click OK.

The Boot tab options allow you to control the way that individual startup-related processes work. You can configure the computer to start in one of various Safe Boot modes and set additional options, such as No GUI Boot. If after troubleshooting you find that you want to keep these settings, select the Make All Boot Settings Permanent check box to save the settings to the boot configuration startup entry.

Clicking the Advanced Options button on the Boot tab displays the BOOT Advanced Options dialog box, shown in Figure 10-3. In addition to locking PCI and enabling debugging, you can use the advanced options to do the following:

- Specify the number of processors the operating system should use, regardless of whether the processors are discrete socketed CPUs or cores on a single CPU. You should use this option when you suspect a problem with additional processors that are available and you want to identify the problem as being related to multiprocessor configurations or parallelism. Consider the following scenario: A computer shipped with a single CPU that has four processor cores. A custom application used in-house for inventory management performs very poorly while running on this computer but very well on computers with single processors. You configure the computer to boot with only one processor and find the application's performance actually improves. You re-enable all the processors and let the software development team know that the application behaves as if it has not been properly optimized for parallelism.

- Specify the maximum amount of memory the operating system should use. Use this option when you suspect a problem with additional memory you've installed in a computer. Consider the following scenario: A computer shipped with 2 GB of RAM, and you installed 2 additional GB of RAM. Later, you find that you cannot start the computer. You could eliminate the new RAM as the potential cause by limiting the computer to 2,048 MB of memory.

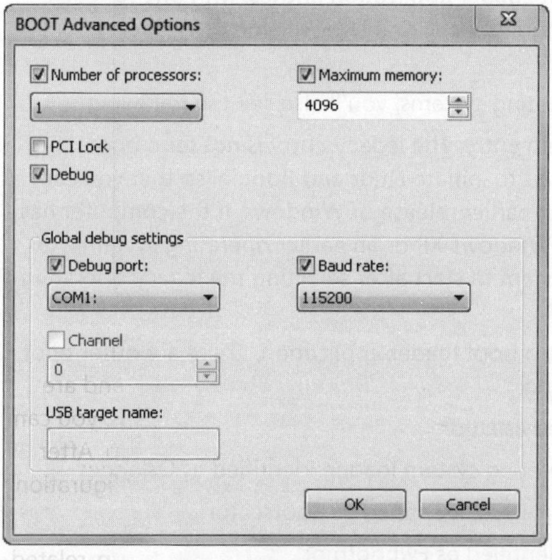

FIGURE 10-3 Use advanced boot options to help troubleshoot specific types of problems.

If you suspect that services installed on a computer are causing startup problems, you can quickly determine this by choosing a diagnostic or selective startup on the General tab. After you've identified that services are indeed causing startup problems, you can temporarily disable services by using the Services tab options and then rebooting to see if the problem goes away. If the problem no longer appears, you might have pinpointed it. You can then permanently disable the service or check with the service vendor to see if an updated executable is available. You disable a service by clearing the related check box on the Services tab.

Similarly, if you suspect applications that run at startup are causing problems, you can quickly determine this by using the options on the Startup tab. You disable a startup application by clearing the related check box on the Startup tab. If the problem no longer appears, you might have pinpointed the cause of it. You can then permanently disable the startup application or check with the software vendor to see if an updated version is available.

Keep in mind that if you use the System Configuration utility for troubleshooting and diagnostics, you should later remove your selective startup options. After you restart the computer and resolve any problems, open the System Configuration utility again, restore the original settings, and then click OK.

Using the BCD Editor

The BCD store contains multiple entries. On a BIOS-based computer, you'll see the following entries:

- One Windows Boot Manager entry. There is only one boot manager, so there is only one boot manager entry.
- One or more Windows Boot Loader application entries, with one for each instance of Windows 7, Windows Vista, or a later version of Windows installed on the computer.

On a computer with other operating systems, you'll also see the following:

- One legacy operating system entry. The legacy entry is not for a boot application. This entry is used to initiate Ntldr and Boot.ini so that you can boot into Windows XP or an earlier release of Windows. If the computer has more than one instance of Windows XP or an earlier operating system, you can select the operating system to start after selecting the legacy operating system entry.

Windows Boot Manager is itself a boot loader application. There are other boot loader applications as well, including:

- Legacy OS Loader, identified as Ntldr
- Windows Vista or later operating system loader, identified as Osloader
- Windows Boot Sector Application, identified as Bootsector
- Firmware Boot Manager, identified as Fwbootmgr
- Windows Resume Loader, identified as Resume

You can view and manage the BCD store by using the BCD Editor (Bcdedit.exe). The BCD Editor is a command-line utility. You can use the BCD Editor to view the entries in the BCD store by following these steps:

1. Click Start, point to All Programs, and then click Accessories.
2. Right-click Command Prompt, and then click Run As Administrator.
3. Type **bcdedit** at the command prompt.

Table 10-3 summarizes commands you can use when you are working with the BCD store. These commands allow you to do the following:

- Create, import, export, and identify the entire BCD store.
- Create, delete, and copy individual entries in the BCD store.
- Set or delete entry option values in the BCD store.
- Control the boot sequence and the boot manager.
- Configure and control Emergency Management Services (EMS).
- Configure and control boot debugging as well as hypervisor debugging.

TABLE 10-3 Commands for the BCD Editor

COMMAND	DESCRIPTION
/bootdebug	Enables or disables boot debugging for a boot application.
/bootems	Enables or disables Emergency Management Services for a boot application.
/bootsequence	Sets the one-time boot sequence for the boot manager.
/copy	Makes copies of entries in the store.
/create	Creates new entries in the store.
/createstore	Creates a new (empty) boot configuration data store.
/dbgsettings	Sets the global debugger parameters.
/debug	Enables or disables kernel debugging for an operating system entry.
/default	Sets the default entry that the boot manager will use.
/delete	Deletes entries from the store.
/deletevalue	Deletes entry options from the store.
/displayorder	Sets the order in which the boot manager displays the multiboot menu.
/ems	Enables or disables Emergency Management Services for an operating system entry.
/emssettings	Sets the global Emergency Management Services parameters.
/enum	Lists entries in the store.
/export	Exports the contents of the system store to a file. This file can be used later to restore the state of the system store.
/hypervisor-settings	Sets the hypervisor parameters.

COMMAND	DESCRIPTION
/import	Restores the state of the system store by using a backup file created with the /export command.
/mirror	Creates a mirror of entries in the store.
/set	Sets entry option values in the store.
/sysstore	Sets the system store device. This only affects EFI systems.
/timeout	Sets the boot manager timeout value.
/toolsdisplayorder	Sets the order in which the boot manager displays the tools menu.
/v	Sets output to verbose mode.

Managing the BCD Store

The BCD Editor is an advanced command-line tool for viewing and manipulating the configuration of the pre–operating system boot environment. Although I discuss tasks related to modifying the BCD data store in the sections that follow, you should attempt to modify the BCD store only if you are an experienced IT pro. As a safeguard, you should make a full backup of the computer prior to making any changes to the BCD store. Why? If you make a mistake, your computer might end up in a nonbootable state, and you would then need to initiate recovery.

Viewing BCD Entries

Computers can have system and nonsystem BCD stores. The system BCD store contains the operating system boot entries and related boot settings. Whenever you work with the BCD Editor, you work with the system BCD store.

On a computer with only one operating system, the BCD entries for your computer will look similar to those in Listing 10-1. As the listing shows, the BCD store for this computer has two entries: one for the Windows Boot Manager, and one for the Windows Boot Loader. Here, the Windows Boot Manager calls the boot loader and the boot loader uses Winload.exe to boot Windows 7.

LISTING 10-1 Entries in the BCD Store on a Single-Boot Computer

```
Windows Boot Manager
--------------------
identifier              {bootmgr}
device                  partition=L:
description             Windows Boot Manager
locale                  en-US
inherit                 {globalsettings}
```

```
default                    {current}
resumeobject               {1cafd2de-e035-11dd-bbf6-bdebeb67615f}
displayorder               {current}
                           {975a8204-9658-11dd-993e-9aea7965e9da}
                           {360a7720-e6ef-11dc-89b8-84b5c301f2c8}
toolsdisplayorder          {memdiag}
timeout                    30

Windows Boot Loader
-------------------
identifier                 {current}
device                     partition=C:
path                       \Windows\system32\winload.exe
description                Windows 7
locale                     en-US
inherit                    {bootloadersettings}
recoverysequence           {1cafd2e0-e035-11dd-bbf6-bdebeb67615f}
recoveryenabled            Yes
osdevice                   partition=C:
systemroot                 \Windows
resumeobject               {1cafd2de-e035-11dd-bbf6-bdebeb67615f}
nx                         OptIn
```

BCD entries for Windows Boot Manager and Windows Boot Loader have similar properties. These properties include those summarized in Table 10-4.

TABLE 10-4 BCD Entry Properties

PROPERTY	DESCRIPTION
Description	Shows descriptive information to help identify the type of entry.
Device	Shows the physical device path. For a partition on a physical disk, you'll see an entry such as partition=C:.
FileDevice	Shows the path to a file device, such as partition=C:.
FilePath	Shows the file path to a necessary file, such as \hiberfil.sys.
Identifier	Shows a descriptor for the entry. This can be a boot loader application type, such as Bootmgr or Ntldr, a reference to the current operating system entry, or the globally unique identifier (GUID) of a specific object.
Inherit	Shows the list of entries to be inherited.
Locale	Shows the computer's locale setting, such as en-US. The locale setting determines the language shown in the user interface (UI). The \Boot folder contains locale subfolders for each locale supported, and each of these subfolders have language-specific UI details for the Windows Boot Manager and the Windows Memory Diagnostic utility (Memdiag.exe).

PROPERTY	DESCRIPTION
OSDevice	Shows the path to the operating system device, such as partition=C:.
Path	Shows the actual file path to the boot loader application, such as \Windows\System32\winload.exe.

When you are working with the BCD store and the BCD Editor, you'll see references to well-known identifiers, summarized in Table 10-5, as well as GUIDs. When a GUID is used, it has the following format, where each *N* represents a hexadecimal value:

```
{NNNNNNNN-NNNN-NNNN-NNNN-NNNNNNNNNNNN}
```

such as:

```
{975a8204-9658-11dd-993e-9aea7965e9da}
```

The dashes that separate the parts of the GUID must be entered in the positions shown. Both well-known identifiers and GUIDs are enclosed in curly braces.

TABLE 10-5 Well-Known Identifiers

IDENTIFIER	DESCRIPTION
{badmemory}	Contains the global RAM defect list that can be inherited by any boot application entry.
{bootloadersettings}	Contains the collection of global settings that should be inherited by all Windows Boot Loader application entries.
{bootmgr}	Indicates the Windows Boot Manager entry.
{current}	Represents a virtual identifier that corresponds to the operating system boot entry for the operating system that is currently running.
{dbgsettings}	Contains the global debugger settings that can be inherited by any boot application entry.
{default}	Represents a virtual identifier that corresponds to the boot manager default application entry.
{emssettings}	Contains the global Emergency Management Services settings that can be inherited by any boot application entry.
{fwbootmgr}	Indicates the firmware boot manager entry. This entry is used on EFI systems.

IDENTIFIER	DESCRIPTION
{globalsettings}	Contains the collection of global settings that should be inherited by all boot application entries.
{hypervisorsettings}	Contains the hypervisor settings that can be inherited by any operating system loader entry.
{legacy}	Indicates the Windows Legacy OS Loader (Ntldr) that can be used to start Windows operating systems earlier than Windows Vista.
{memdiag}	Indicates the memory diagnostic application entry.
{ntldr}	Indicates the Windows Legacy OS Loader (Ntldr) that can be used to start Windows operating systems earlier than Windows Vista.
{ramdiskoptions}	Contains the additional options required by the boot manager for RAM disk devices.
{resumeloadersettings}	Contains the collection of global settings that should be inherited by all Windows resume-from-hibernation application entries.

When a computer has additional instances of Windows Vista, Windows 7, or later versions of Windows installed, the BCD store has additional entries for each additional operating system. For example, the BCD store might have one entry for the Windows Boot Manager and one Windows Boot Loader entry for each operating system.

When a computer has a legacy operating system installed, the BCD store has three entries: one for the Windows Boot Manager, one for the Windows Legacy OS Loader, and one for the Windows Boot Loader. Generally, the entry for the Windows Legacy OS Loader will look similar to Listing 10-2.

LISTING 10-2 Sample Legacy OS Loader Entry

```
Windows Legacy OS Loader
------------------------
identifier:             {ntldr}
device:                 partition=C:
path:                   \ntldr
description:            Earlier version of Windows
```

Although the Windows Boot Manager, Windows Legacy OS Loader, and Windows Boot Loader are the primary types of entries that control startup, the BCD store also includes information about boot settings and boot utilities. The Windows Boot Loader entry can have parameters that track the status of boot settings, such as whether No Execute (NX) policy is set to Opt In or Opt Out. The Windows Boot

Loader entry also can provide information about available boot utilities, such as the Windows Memory Diagnostic utility.

To view the actual value of the GUIDs needed to manipulate entries in the BCD store, type **bcdedit /v** at an elevated command prompt.

Creating and Identifying the BCD Store

Using the BCD Editor, you can create a nonsystem BCD store by using the following command:

```
bcdedit /createstore StorePath
```

where *StorePath* is the folder path to the location where you want to create the nonsystem store, such as:

```
bcdedit /createstore c:\non-sys\bcd
```

On an EFI system, you can temporarily set the system store device by using the /sysstore command. Use the following syntax:

```
bcdedit /sysstore StoreDevice
```

where *StoreDevice* is the actual system store device identifier, such as:

```
bcdedit /sysstore c:
```

The device must be a system partition. Note that this setting does not persist across reboots and is used only in cases where the system store device is ambiguous.

Importing and Exporting the BCD Store

The BCD Editor provides separate commands for importing and exporting the BCD store. You can use the /export command to export a copy of the system BCD store's contents to a specified folder. Use the following command syntax:

```
bcdedit /export StorePath
```

where *StorePath* is the actual folder path to which you want to export a copy of the system store, such as:

```
bcdedit /export c:\backup\bcd
```

To restore an exported copy of the system store, you can use the /import command. Use the following command syntax:

```
bcdedit /import ImportPath
```

where *ImportPath* is the actual folder path from which you want to import a copy of the system store, such as:

```
bcdedit /import c:\backup\bcd
```

On an EFI system, you can add /clean to the /import command to specify that all existing firmware boot entries should be deleted. Here is an example:

```
bcdedit /import c:\backup\bcd /clean
```

Creating, Copying, and Deleting BCD Entries

The BCD Editor provides separate commands for creating, copying, and deleting entries in the BCD store. You can use the /create command to create identifier, application, and inherit entries in the BCD store.

As shown previously in Table 10-5, the BCD Editor recognizes many well-known identifiers, including {dbgsettings}, which is used to create a debugger settings entry; {ntldr}, used to create a Windows Legacy OS entry; and {ramdiskoptions}, used to create a RAM disk additional options entry. To create identifier entries, you use the following syntax:

```
bcdedit /create Identifier /d "Description"
```

where *Identifier* is a well-known identifier for the entry you want to create, such as:

```
bcdedit /create {ntldr} /d "Earlier Windows OS Loader"
```

You can create entries for specific boot loader applications as well, including:

- **Bootsector** Identifies a real-mode boot sector application; used to set the boot sector for a real-mode application.
- **Osloader** Identifies an operating system loader application; used to load Windows Vista or later.
- **Resume** Identifies a Windows Resume Loader application; used to resume the operating system from hibernation.
- **Startup** Identifies a real-mode application; used to identify a real-mode application.

Use the following command syntax:

```
bcdedit /create /application AppType /d "Description"
```

where *AppType* is one of the previously listed application types, such as:

```
bcdedit /create /application osloader /d "Windows Vista"
```

You can delete entries in the system store by using the /delete command and the following syntax:

```
bcdedit /delete Identifier
```

If you are trying to delete a well-known identifier, you must use the /f command to force deletion, such as:

```
bcdedit /delete {ntldr} /f
```

By default, the /cleanup option is implied, which means that the BCD Editor cleans up any other references to the entry being deleted. This ensures that the data store doesn't have invalid references to the identifier you removed. Because entries are removed from the display order as well, this could result in a different default operating system being set. If you want to delete the entry and clean up all other references except the display order entry, you can use the /nocleanup command.

Setting BCD Entry Values

After you create an entry, you need to set additional entry option values as necessary. The basic syntax for setting values is:

```
bcdedit /set Identifier Option Value
```

where *Identifier* is the identifier of the entry to be modified, *Option* is the option you want to set, and *Value* is the option value, such as:

```
bcdedit /set {current} device partition=d:
```

To delete options and their values, use the /deletevalue command with the following syntax:

```
bcdedit /deletevalue Identifier Option
```

where *Identifier* is the identifier of the entry to be modified, and *Option* is the option you want to delete, such as:

```
bcdedit /deletevalue {current} badmemorylist
```

When you are working with options, Boolean values can be entered in several different ways. For True, you can use 1, On, Yes, or True. For False, you can use 0, Off, No, or False. To view the BCD entries for all boot utilities and the values for settings, type **bcdedit /enum all /v** at an elevated command prompt. This command enumerates all BCD entries regardless of their current state and lists them in verbose mode. Each additional entry has a specific purpose and lists values that you can set, including the following:

- **Resume From Hibernate** The Resume From Hibernate entry shows the current configuration for the resume feature. The pre–operating system boot utility that controls resume is Winresume.exe, which in this example is stored in the C:\Windows\System32 folder. The hibernation data, as specified in the Filepath parameter, is stored in the Hiberfil.sys file in the root folder on the OSDevice (C: in this example). Because the resume feature works differently if the computer has Physical Address Extension (PAE) and debugging enabled, these options are tracked by the Pae and Debugoptionenabled parameters.
- **Windows Memory Tester** The Windows Memory Tester entry shows the current configuration for the Windows Memory Diagnostic utility. The pre–operating system boot utility that controls memory diagnostics is

Memtest.exe, which in this example is stored in the C:\Boot folder. Because the Windows Memory Diagnostic utility is designed to detect bad memory by default, the Badmemoryaccess parameter is set to Yes by default. You can turn this feature off by entering **bcdedit /set {memdiag} badmemoryaccess NO**. With memory diagnostics, you can configure the number of passes by using Passcount and the test mix as Basic or Extended by using Testmix. Here is an example: **bcdedit /set {memdiag} passcount 2 textmix basic**.

- **Windows Legacy OS Loader** The Windows Legacy OS Loader entry shows the current configuration for the loading of earlier versions of Windows. The Device parameter sets the default partition to use, such as C:, and the Path parameter sets the default path to the loader utility, such as Ntldr.
- **EMS Settings** The EMS Settings entry shows the configuration used when booting with Emergency Management Services. Individual Windows Boot Loader entries control whether EMS is enabled. If EMS is provided by the BIOS and you want to use the BIOS settings, you can enter **bcdedit /emssettings bios**. With EMS, you can set an EMS port and an EMS baud rate as well. Here is an example: **bcdedit /emssettings EMSPORT:2 EMSBAUDRATE:115200**. You can enable or disable EMS for a boot application by using /bootems, following the identity of the boot application with the state you want, such as On or Off.
- **Debugger Settings** The Debugger Settings entry shows the configuration used when booting with the debugger turned on. Individual Windows Boot Loader entries control whether the debugger is enabled. You can view the hypervisor debugging settings by entering **bcdedit /debugsettings**. When debug booting is turned on, DebugType sets the type of debugger as SERIAL, 1394, or USB. With SERIAL debugging, DebugPort specifies the serial port being used as the debugger port, and BaudRate specifies the baud rate to be used for debugging. With 1394 debugging, you can use Channel to set the debugging channel. With USB debugging, you can use TargetName to set the USB target name to be used for debugging. With any debug type, you can use the /Noumex flag to specify that user-mode exceptions should be ignored. Here are examples of setting the debugging mode: **bcdedit /dbgsettings SERIAL DEBUGPORT:1 BAUDRATE:115200**, **bcdedit /dbgsettings 1394 CHANNEL:23**, **bcdedit /dbgsettings USB TARGETNAME:DEBUGGING**.
- **Hypervisor Settings** The Hypervisor Settings entry shows the configuration used when working with the hypervisor with the debugger turned on. Individual Windows Boot Loader entries control whether the debugger is enabled. You can view the hypervisor debugging settings by entering **bcdedit /hypervisorsettings**. When hypervisor debug booting is turned on, HypervisorDebugType sets the type of debugger, HypervisorDebugPort specifies the serial port being used as the debugger port, and

HypervisorBaudRate specifies the baud rate to be used for debugging. These parameters work the same as with Debugger Settings. Here is an example: **bcdedit /hypervisorsettings SERIAL DEBUGPORT:1 BAUDRATE:115200**. You can also use FireWire for hypervisor debugging. When you do, you must separate the word "channel" from the value with a colon as shown in this example: **bcdedit /hypervisorsettings 1394 CHANNEL:23**.

Table 10-6 summarizes key options that apply to entries for boot applications (Bootapp). Because Windows Boot Manager, Windows Memory Diagnostic, Windows OS Loader, and Windows Resume Loader are boot applications, these options apply to them as well.

TABLE 10-6 Key Options for Boot Application Entries

OPTION	VALUE DESCRIPTION
BadMemoryAccess	When true, allows an application to use the memory on the bad memory list. When false, applications are prevented from using memory on the bad memory list.
BadMemoryList	An integer list that defines the list of Page Frame Numbers of faulty memory in the system.
BaudRate	Sets an integer value that defines the baud rate for the serial debugger.
BootDebug	Sets a Boolean value that enables or disables the boot debugger.
BootEMS	Sets a Boolean value that enables or disables Emergency Management Services.
Channel	Sets an integer value that defines the channel for the 1394 debugger.
ConfigAccessPolicy	Sets the access policy to use as either DEFAULT or DISALLOWMMCONFIG.
DebugAddress	Sets an integer value that defines the address of a serial port for the debugger.
DebugPort	Sets an integer value that defines the serial port number for the serial debugger.
DebugStart	Can be set to ACTIVE, AUTOENABLE, or DISABLE.
DebugType	Can be set to SERIAL, 1394, or USB.

OPTION	VALUE DESCRIPTION
EMSBaudRate	Defines the baud rate for Emergency Management Services.
EMSPort	Defines the serial port number for Emergency Management Services.
FirstMegaBytePolicy	Sets the first megabyte policy to use as USENONE, USEALL, or USEPRIVATE.
GraphicsModeDisabled	Sets a Boolean value that enables or disables graphics mode.
GraphicsResolution	Defines the graphics resolution, such as 1024 × 768 or 800 × 600.
Locale	Sets the locale of the boot application.
Noumex	When Noumex is set to TRUE, user-mode exceptions are ignored. When Noumex is set to FALSE, user-mode exceptions are not ignored.
NoVESA	Sets a Boolean value that enables or disables the use of Video Electronics Standards Association (VESA) display modes.
RecoveryEnabled	Sets a Boolean value that enables or disables the use of a recovery sequence.
RecoverySequence	Defines the recovery sequence to use.
RelocatePhysical	Sets the physical address to which an automatically selected nonuniform memory access (NUMA) node's physical memory should be relocated.
TargetName	Defines the target name for the USB debugger as a string.
TestSigning	Sets a Boolean value that enables or disables use of prerelease test-code signing certificates.
TruncateMemory	Sets a physical memory address at or above which all memory is disregarded.

Table 10-7 summarizes key options that apply to entries for Windows OS Loader (Osloader) applications.

TABLE 10-7 Key Options for Windows OS Loader Applications

OPTION	VALUE DESCRIPTION
AdvancedOptions	Sets a Boolean value that enables or disables advanced options.
BootLog	Sets a Boolean value that enables or disables the boot initialization log.
BootStatusPolicy	Sets the boot status policy. Can be DisplayAllFailures, IgnoreAllFailures, IgnoreShutdownFailures, or IgnoreBootFailures.
ClusterMode-Addressing	Sets the maximum number of processors to include in a single Advanced Programmable Interrupt Controller (APIC) cluster.
ConfigFlags	Sets processor-specific configuration flags.
DbgTransport	Sets the file name for a private debugger transport.
Debug	Sets a Boolean value that enables or disables kernel debugging.
DetectHal	Sets a Boolean value that enables or disables HAL and kernel detection.
DriverLoad-FailurePolicy	Sets the driver load failure policy. Can be Fatal or UseErrorControl.
Ems	Sets a Boolean value that enables or disables kernel Emergency Management Services.
Hal	Sets the file name for a private HAL.
HalBreakPoint	Sets a Boolean value that enables or disables the special HAL breakpoint.
Hypervisor-LaunchType	Configures the hypervisor launch type. Can be Off or Auto.
HypervisorPath	Sets the path to a private hypervisor binary.
IncreaseUserVA	Sets an integer value (in megabytes) that increases the amount of virtual address space that the user-mode processes can use.
Kernel	Sets the file name for a private kernel.
LastKnownGood	Sets a Boolean value that enables or disables booting to the last known good configuration.
MaxProc	Sets a Boolean value that enables or disables the display of the maximum number of processors in the system.

OPTION	VALUE DESCRIPTION
Msi	Sets the message signaled interrupt (MSI) to use. Can be Default or ForceDisable.
NoCrashAuto-Reboot	Sets a Boolean value that enables or disables automatic restart on crash.
NoLowMem	Sets a Boolean value that enables or disables the use of low memory.
NumProc	Sets the number of processors to use on startup.
Nx	Controls no-execute protection. Can be OptIn, OptOut, AlwaysOn, or AlwaysOff.
OneCPU	Sets a Boolean value that forces or does not force only the boot CPU to be used.
OptionsEdit	Sets a Boolean value that enables or disables the options editor.
OSDevice	Defines the device that contains the system root.
Pae	Controls PAE. Can be Default, ForceEnable, or ForceDisable.
PerfMem	Sets the size (in megabytes) of the buffer to allocate for performance data logging.
QuietBoot	Sets a Boolean value that enables or disables the boot screen display.
RemoveMemory	Sets an integer value (in megabytes) that removes memory from the total available memory that the operating system can use.
RestrictAPIC-Cluster	Sets the largest APIC cluster number to be used by the system.
ResumeObject	Sets the identifier for the resume object that is associated with this operating system object.
SafeBoot	Sets the computer to use a Safe Boot mode. Can be Minimal, Network, or DsRepair.
SafeBoot-AlternateShell	Sets a Boolean value that enables or disables the use of the alternate shell when booted into safe mode.
Sos	Sets a Boolean value that enables or disables the display of additional boot information.
SystemRoot	Defines the path to the system root.

OPTION	VALUE DESCRIPTION
UseFirmwarePCI-Settings	Sets a Boolean value that enables or disables use of BIOS-configured Peripheral Component Interconnect (PCI) resources.
UsePhysical-Destination	Sets a Boolean value that forces or does not force the use of the physical APIC.
Vga	Sets a Boolean value that forces or does not force the use of the VGA display driver.
WinPE	Sets a Boolean value that enables or disables booting to Windows PE.

Changing Data Execution Prevention and Physical Address Extension Options

Data Execution Prevention (DEP) is a memory-protection technology. When DEP is enabled, the computer's processor marks all memory locations in an application as nonexecutable unless the location explicitly contains executable code. If code is executed from a memory page marked as nonexecutable, the processor can raise an exception and prevent the code from executing. This behavior prevents malicious application code, such as virus code, from inserting itself into most areas of memory.

For computers with processors that support the non-execute (NX) page-protection feature, you can configure the operating system to opt in to NX protection by setting the nx parameter to OptIn, or opt out of NX protection by setting the nx parameter to OptOut. Here is an example:

```
bcdedit /set {current} nx optout
```

When you configure NX protection to OptIn, DEP is turned on only for essential Windows programs and services. This is the default. When you configure NX protection to OptOut, all programs and services—not just standard Windows programs and services—use DEP. Programs that shouldn't use DEP must be specifically opted out, as discussed in the section "Configuring Data Execution Prevention" in Chapter 6. You can also configure NX protection to be always on or always off by using AlwaysOn or AlwaysOff, such as:

```
bcdedit /set {current} nx alwayson
```

Processors that support and opt in to NX protection must be running in PAE mode. You can configure PAE by setting the Pae parameter to Default, ForceEnable, or ForceDisable. When you set the pae state to Default, the operating system uses the default configuration for PAE. When you set the PAE state to ForceEnable, the operating system uses PAE. When you set the PAE state to ForceDisable, the operating system will not use PAE. Here is an example:

```
bcdedit /set {current} pae default
```

Changing the Operating System Display Order

You can change the display order of boot managers associated with a particular installation of Windows Vista, Windows 7, or a later version by using the /displayorder command. The syntax is:

```
bcdedit /displayorder id1 id2 … idn
```

where *id1* is the operating system identifier of the first operating system in the display order, *id2* is the identifier of the second, and so on. You could change the display order of the operating systems identified in these BCD entries:

```
Windows Boot Loader
--------------------
identifier              {14504de-e96b-11cd-a51b-89ace9305d5e}

Windows Boot Loader
--------------------
identifier              {8b78e48f-02d0-11dd-af92-a72494804a8a}
```

by using the following command:

```
bcdedit /displayorder {14504de-e96b-11cd-a51b-89ace9305d5e}
{8b78e48f-02d0-11dd-af92-a72494804a8a}
```

You can set a particular operating system as the first entry by using /addfirst with /displayorder, such as:

```
bcdedit /displayorder {8b78e48f-02d0-11dd-af92-a72494804a8a} /addfirst
```

You can set a particular operating system as the last entry by using /addlast with /displayorder, such as:

```
bcdedit /displayorder {8b78e48f-02d0-11dd-af92-a72494804a8a} /addlast
```

Changing the Default Operating System Entry

You can change the default operating system entry by using the /default command. The syntax for this command is:

```
bcdedit /default id
```

where *id* is the operating system ID in the boot loader entry. You could set the operating system identified in this BCD entry as the default:

```
Windows Boot Loader
--------------------
identifier              {975a8204-9658-11dd-993e-9aea7965e9da}
```

by using the following command:

```
bcdedit /default {975a8204-9658-11dd-993e-9aea7965e9da}
```

If you want to use a pre–Windows 7 operating system as the default, use the identifier for the Windows Legacy OS Loader. The related BCD entry looks like this:

```
Windows Legacy OS Loader
------------------------
identifier              {466f5a88-0af2-4f76-9038-095b170dc21c}
device                  partition=C:
path                    \ntldr
description             Earlier Microsoft Windows Operating System
```

Following this, you could set Ntldr as the default by entering:

```
bcdedit /default {466f5a88-0af2-4f76-9038-095b170dc21c}
```

Changing the Default Timeout

You can change the timeout value associated with the default operating system by using the /timeout command. Set the /timeout command to the wait time you want to use (in seconds) as follows:

```
bcdedit /timeout 30
```

To boot automatically to the default operating system, set the timeout to 0 seconds.

Changing the Boot Sequence Temporarily

Occasionally, you might want to boot to a particular operating system one time and then revert to the default boot order. To do this, you can use the /bootsequence command. Follow the command with the identifier of the operating system to which you want to boot after restarting the computer, such as:

```
bcdedit /bootsequence {975a8204-9658-11dd-993e-9aea7965e9da}
```

When you restart the computer, the computer will set the specified operating system as the default for that restart only. Then, when you restart the computer again, the computer will use the original default boot order.

CHAPTER 11

Using TPM and BitLocker Drive Encryption

Many of the security features built into the Windows 7 operating system are designed to protect a computer from attacks by individuals accessing the computer over a network or from the Internet. But what about when individuals have direct physical access to a computer or your data? In these instances, Windows security safeguards don't apply. If someone can boot a computer—even if it is to another operating system he's installed—he could gain access to any data stored on the computer, perhaps even your organization's most sensitive data. In addition, with the increased use of USB flash drives, users often take their data with them, and if they lose the USB flash drive, the data normally has no protection, meaning that anyone who finds the flash drive could read and access the data.

To protect computers and data in these instances, Windows 7 includes BitLocker Drive Encryption, BitLocker To Go, and the Trusted Platform Module (TPM) Services architecture. Together these features help protect computers and data stored on USB flash drives. BitLocker Drive Encryption is a full-volume encryption technology. BitLocker To Go is a virtual-volume encryption technology for USB flash drives. TPM is a feature you can use with BitLocker Drive Encryption to enhance security.

Creating Trusted Platforms

A computer running Windows 7 must be equipped with a compatible TPM and compatible firmware to take advantage of TPM Services. Windows 7 supports TPM version 1.2 or later and requires Trusted Computing Group (TCG)–compliant firmware. Firmware that is TCG-compliant supports the Static Root of Trust Measurement as defined by the TCG. For some configurations of TPM and BitLocker Drive Encryption, you also need to be sure that the firmware supports reading USB flash drives at startup.

TPM: The Essentials

Windows 7 includes the Encrypting File System (EFS) for encrypting files and folders. By using EFS, users can protect sensitive data so that it can be accessed only with their public key certificate. Encryption certificates are stored as part of the data in a user's profile. As long as users have access to their profiles and the encryption keys they contain, they can access their encrypted files.

Although EFS offers excellent data protection, it doesn't safeguard a computer from attack by someone who has direct physical access. In a situation in which a user loses a computer, a computer is stolen, or an attacker is logging on to a computer, EFS might not protect the data because the attacker might be able to gain access to the computer before it boots. He could then access the computer from another operating system and change the computer's configuration. He might then be able to hack into a logon account on the original operating system and log on as the user or configure the computer so that he can log on as a local administrator. Either way, the attacker could eventually gain full access to a computer and its data.

To seal a computer from physical attack and wrap it in an additional layer of protection, Windows 7 includes the Trusted Platform Module (TPM) Services architecture. TPM Services protect a computer by using a dedicated hardware component called a TPM. A TPM is a microchip that is usually installed on the motherboard of a computer, where it communicates with the rest of the system by using a hardware bus. Computers running Windows 7 can use a TPM to provide enhanced protection for data, to ensure early validation of the boot file's integrity, and to guarantee that a disk has not been tampered with while the operating system was offline.

A TPM has the ability to create cryptographic keys and encrypt them so that they can be decrypted only by the TPM. This process, referred to as *wrapping* or *binding*, protects the key from disclosure. A TPM has a master "wrapping" key called the Storage Root Key (SRK). The SRK is stored within the TPM to ensure that the private portion of the key is secure.

Computers that have a TPM can create a key that has been not only wrapped but sealed. The process of sealing the key ensures that the key is tied to specific platform measurements and can be unwrapped only when those platform measurements have the same values they had when the key was created. This is what gives TPM-equipped computers increased resistance to attack.

Because TPM stores private portions of key pairs separately from memory controlled by the operating system, keys can be sealed to the TPM to provide absolute assurances about the state of a system and its trustworthiness. TPM keys are unsealed only when the integrity of the system is intact. Further, because the TPM uses its own internal firmware and logical circuits for processing instructions, it does not rely on the operating system and is not subject to external software vulnerabilities.

The TPM can also be used to seal and unseal data that is generated outside the TPM, and this is where the true power of the TPM lies. In Windows 7, the feature that accesses the TPM and uses it to seal a computer is called BitLocker Drive Encryption. Although BitLocker Drive Encryption can be used in both TPM and non-TPM configurations, the most secure method is to use TPM.

When you use BitLocker Drive Encryption and a TPM to seal the boot manager and boot files of a computer, the boot manager and boot files can be unsealed only if they are unchanged since they were last sealed. This means that you can use the TPM to validate a computer's boot files in the pre–operating system environment. When you seal a hard disk using TPM, the hard disk can be unsealed only if the data on the disk is unchanged since it was last sealed. This guarantees that a disk has not been tampered with while the operating system was offline.

When you use BitLocker Drive Encryption but do not use a TPM to seal the boot manager and boot files of a computer, TPM cannot be used to validate a computer's boot files in the pre–operating system environment. This means that in this instance there is no way to guarantee the integrity of the boot manager and boot files of a computer.

Enabling and Using TPM

The TPM Services architecture in Windows 7 provides the basic features required to configure and deploy TPM-equipped computers. This architecture can be extended with a feature called BitLocker Drive Encryption, which is discussed in the section "BitLocker Drive Encryption: The Essentials" later in this chapter.

Before you can use TPM, you must turn on TPM in firmware and initialize the TPM for first use in software. As part of the initialization process, you set the owner password on the TPM. After TPM is enabled, you can manage the TPM configuration.

In some cases, computers that have TPM might ship with TPM turned on. In most cases, however, you'll find TPM is not turned on by default. With my computers, I needed to do the following:

1. Start the computer, and then press F2 during startup to access the firmware. In the firmware, I accessed the Advanced screen and then the Peripheral Configuration screen.
2. On the Peripheral Configuration screen, Trusted Platform Module was listed as an option. After scrolling down to highlight this option, I pressed Enter to

display an options menu. From the menu, I chose Enable and then pressed Enter.

3. To save the changes to the setting and exit the firmware, I pressed F10. When prompted to confirm that I wanted to exit, I pressed Y, and the computer then rebooted.

Windows 7 provides several tools for working with a TPM, including these:

- **Trusted Platform Module Management** A console for configuring and managing a TPM. You can access this tool by clicking Start, typing **tpm.msc** in the Search box, and then pressing Enter.
- **Initialize The TPM Security Hardware** A wizard for creating the required TPM owner password. You can access this tool by clicking Start, typing **tpminit** in the Search box, and then pressing Enter.

REAL WORLD **Access to the Trusted Platform Module Management console can be restricted in Group Policy. If you are unable to open the console, check to see if a Group Policy object (GPO) being processed includes Management Console restrictions under Windows Components\Microsoft Management Console.**

When you are working with Trusted Platform Module Management, you can determine the exact state of the TPM. If you try to start Trusted Platform Module Management without turning on TPM, you'll see an error stating this. You'll also see an error if you try to run the Initialize The TPM Security Hardware wizard without turning on TPM.

Only when you've turned on TPM in firmware will you be able to access and work with the TPM tools. When you are working with the Trusted Platform Module Management console, shown in Figure 11-1, you should note the TPM status and the TPM manufacturer information. The TPM status indicates the exact state of the TPM (see Table 11-1). The TPM manufacturer information shows whether the TPM supports specification version 1.2. Support for TPM version 1.2 or later is required.

TABLE 11-1 TPM Status Indicators and Their Meanings

STATUS INDICATOR	MEANING
The TPM is on and ownership has not been taken	The TPM is turned on in firmware but hasn't been initialized yet.
The TPM is on and ownership has been taken	The TPM is turned on in firmware and has been initialized.
The TPM is off and ownership has not been taken	The TPM is turned off in software but hasn't been initialized yet.
The TPM is off and ownership has been taken	The TPM has been initialized but is turned off in software.

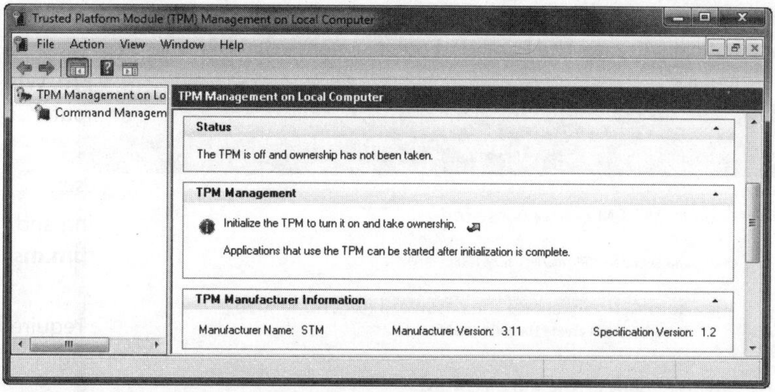

FIGURE 11-1 Use the Trusted Platform Module Management console to initialize and manage TPM.

Initializing a TPM for First Use

Initializing a TPM configures it for use on a computer. The initialization process involves turning on the TPM and then setting ownership of the TPM. By setting ownership of the TPM, you assign a password that helps ensure that only the authorized TPM owner can access and manage the TPM. The TPM password is required to turn off the TPM if you no longer want to use it and to clear the TPM before the computer is recycled. In an Active Directory domain, you can configure Group Policy to save TPM passwords.

To initialize the TPM and create the owner password, complete the following steps:

1. Start the Trusted Platform Module Management console. On the Action menu, click Initialize TPM to start the Initialize The TPM Security Hardware wizard.

   NOTE **If the Initialize The TPM Security Hardware wizard detects firmware that does not meet Windows requirements for a TPM or no TPM is found, you will not be able to continue and should check that the TPM has been turned on in firmware.**

   REAL WORLD **If a TPM was previously initialized and then cleared, you are prompted to restart the computer and follow onscreen instructions during startup to reset TPM in firmware. The wizard should start again when you next log on. However, on my systems, this did not occur. Instead, when I clicked Restart, I needed to enter firmware by pressing F2 during startup. I then needed to disable TPM, save the changes, and exit firmware. This triggered an automatic reset. After this, I needed to enter firmware by pressing F2, which let me enable TPM, save changes, and then exit firmware. This triggered another automatic reset. When the operating system loaded, I logged on and then needed to restart the Initialize The TPM Security Hardware wizard.**

2. On the Create The TPM Owner Password page, shown in Figure 11-2, click Automatically Create The Password (Recommended).

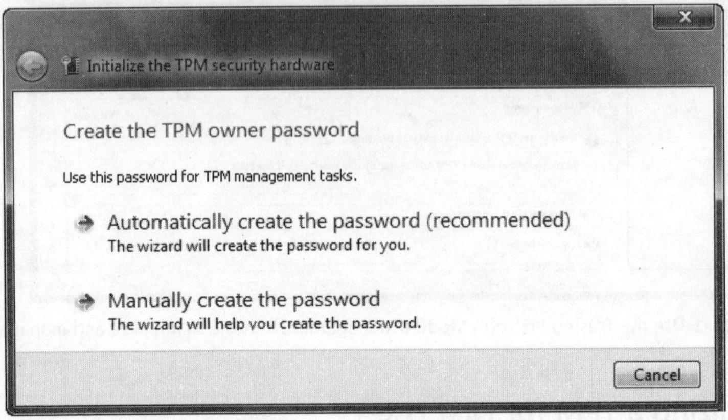

FIGURE 11-2 Initialize the TPM.

3. On the Save Your TPM Owner Password page, note the 48-character TPM owner password. Click Save The Password.
4. In the Save As dialog box, select a location to save the password backup file, and then click Save. By default, the password backup file is saved as *ComputerName*.tpm. Ideally, you should save the TPM ownership password to removable media, such as a USB flash drive.
5. On the Save Your TPM Owner Password page, click Print The Password if you want a hard copy of the password. Be sure to save the printout containing the password in a secure location, such as a safe or a locked file cabinet.
6. Click Initialize. The initialization process might take several minutes to complete. When initialization is complete, click Close. In the TPM Management console, the status should be listed as "The TPM is on and ownership has been taken."

Turning an Initialized TPM On or Off

Computers that have TPM might ship with TPM turned on. If you decide not to use TPM, you should turn off and clear the TPM. If you want to reconfigure or recycle a computer, you should also turn off and clear the TPM.

To turn off TPM, complete the following steps:

1. Start the Trusted Platform Module Management console. On the Action menu, click Turn TPM Off. This starts the Manage The TPM Security Hardware wizard.

2. On the Turn Off The TPM Security Hardware page, shown in Figure 11-3, use one of the following methods for entering the current password and turning off the TPM:
   - If you have the removable media onto which you saved your TPM owner password, insert it, and then click I Have The Owner Password File. On the Select Backup File With The TPM Owner Password page, click Browse, and then use the Open dialog box to locate the .tpm file saved on your removable media. Click Open, and then click Turn TPM Off.
   - If you do not have the removable media onto which you saved your password, click I Want To Enter The Owner Password. On the Type Your TPM Owner Password page, enter the TPM password (including dashes), and then click Turn TPM Off.
   - If you do not know your TPM owner password, click I Do Not Have The TPM Owner Password, and then follow the instructions provided to turn off the TPM without entering the password. Because you are logged on locally to the computer, you will be able to turn off the TPM.
3. In the TPM Management console, the status should be listed as "The TPM is off and ownership has been taken." Do not discard the TPM owner password file or printout. You need this information if you want to turn the TPM back on.

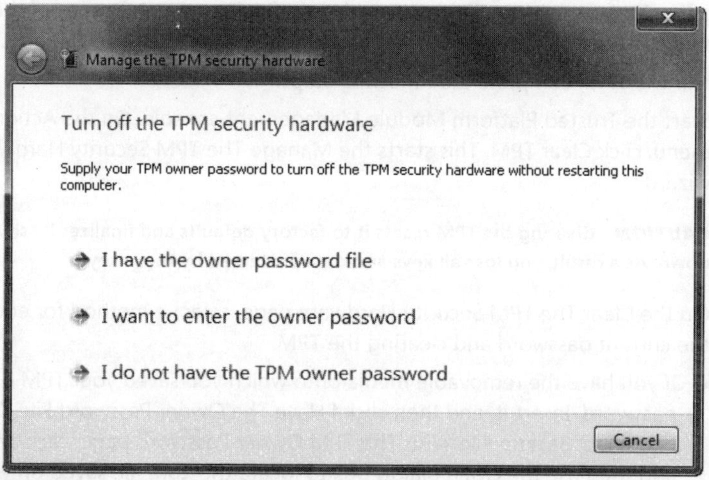

FIGURE 11-3 Click an option for turning off the TPM.

After you follow the previous procedure to turn off the TPM in software, you can turn on the TPM in software by following these steps:

1. Start the Trusted Platform Module Management console. On the Action menu, click Turn TPM On. This starts the Manage The TPM Security Hardware wizard.

2. On the Turn On The TPM Security Hardware page, use one of the following methods for entering the current TPM password and turning on the TPM:
   - If you have the removable media onto which you saved your TPM owner password, insert it, and then click I Have The Owner Password File. On the Select Backup File With The TPM Owner Password page, click Browse, and then use the Open dialog box to locate the .tpm file saved on your removable media. Click Open, and then click Turn TPM On.
   - If you do not have the removable media onto which you saved your password, click I Want To Enter The Owner Password. On the Type Your TPM Owner Password page, enter the TPM password (including dashes), and then click Turn TPM On.
   - If you do not know your TPM owner password, click I Do Not Have The TPM Owner Password, and then follow the instructions provided to turn on the TPM without entering the password. Because you are logged on locally to the computer, you will be able to turn on the TPM.
3. In the TPM Management console, the status should be listed as "The TPM is on and ownership has been taken." Do not discard the TPM owner password file or printout. You need this information if you want to manage the TPM.

Clearing the TPM

Clearing the TPM cancels the TPM ownership and finalizes the shutdown of the TPM. You should clear the TPM only when a TPM-equipped computer is to be recycled.

To clear the TPM, complete the following steps:

1. Start the Trusted Platform Module Management console. On the Action menu, click Clear TPM. This starts the Manage The TPM Security Hardware wizard.

   CAUTION **Clearing the TPM resets it to factory defaults and finalizes its shutdown. As a result, you lose all keys and data protected by those keys.**

2. On the Clear The TPM Security Hardware page, select a method for entering the current password and clearing the TPM:
   - If you have the removable media onto which you saved your TPM owner password, insert it, and then click I Have The Owner Password File. On the Select Backup File With The TPM Owner Password page, click Browse, and then use the Open dialog box to locate the .tpm file saved on your removable media. Click Open, and then click Clear TPM.
   - If you do not have the removable media onto which you saved your password, click I Want To Enter The Owner Password. On the Type Your TPM Owner Password page, enter your password (including dashes), and then click Clear TPM.

- If you do not know your TPM owner password, click I Do Not Have The TPM Owner Password, and then follow the instructions provided to clear the TPM without entering the password. Because you are logged on locally to the computer, you will be able to clear the TPM.

Changing the TPM Owner Password

You can change the TPM password at any time. To change the TPM owner password, complete the following steps:

1. Start the Trusted Platform Module Management console. On the Action menu, click Change Owner Password. This starts the Manage The TPM Security Hardware wizard.
2. On the Change TPM Owner Password page, select a method for entering the current password:
   - If you have the removable media onto which you saved your TPM owner password, insert it, and then click I Have The Owner Password File. On the Select Backup File With The TPM Owner Password page, click Browse, and then use the Open dialog box to locate the .tpm file saved on your removable media. Click Open, and then click Create New Password.
   - If you do not have the removable media onto which you saved your password, click I Want To Enter The Owner Password. On the Type Your TPM Owner Password page, enter your password (including dashes), and then click Create New Password.
3. On the Create The TPM Owner Password page, select Automatically Create The Password (Recommended), and then click Next.
4. On the Save Your TPM Owner Password page, note the 48-character TPM owner password. Click Save The Password. In the Save As dialog box, select a location to save the password backup file, and then click Save. If you are saving the password backup file to the same location and with the same name as the password file you are replacing, click Yes when prompted.
5. On the Save Your TPM Owner Password page, click Print The Password if you want a hard copy of the password. Be sure to save the printout containing the password in a secure location, such as a safe or a locked file cabinet.
6. To complete the process, click Change Password.

BitLocker Drive Encryption: The Essentials

Although BitLocker Drive Encryption and BitLocker To Go are often referred to simply as BitLocker, they are separate but similar features included in the Ultimate and Enterprise editions of Windows 7. BitLocker Drive Encryption is designed to protect the data on lost, stolen, or inappropriately decommissioned computers and is a full-volume encryption technology. BitLocker To Go is designed to protect the data on USB flash drives and is a virtual-volume encryption technology. This means that standard BitLocker encrypts an entire volume by wrapping it in protected encryption. BitLocker To Go, on the other hand, creates a virtual volume on a USB flash drive. This virtual volume is encrypted by using an encryption key stored on the USB flash drive.

Understanding BitLocker Drive Encryption

On a computer without BitLocker Drive Encryption, a user with direct physical access to the computer has a variety of ways he could gain full control and then access the computer's data, whether that data is encrypted with EFS or not. For example, a user could use a boot disk to boot the computer and reset the administrator password. A user could also install and then boot to a different operating system and then use this operating system to unlock the other installation.

BitLocker Drive Encryption prevents all access to a computer's drives except by authorized personnel by wrapping entire drives in tamper-proof encryption. If an unauthorized user tries to access a BitLocker-encrypted drive, the encryption prevents the user from viewing or manipulating the data in any way. This dramatically reduces the risk of an unauthorized person gaining access to confidential data through offline attacks.

> ***CAUTION*** **BitLocker Drive Encryption reduces disk throughput. It is meant to be used when a computer is not in a physically secure location and requires additional protection.**

BitLocker Drive Encryption can use a TPM to validate the integrity of a computer's boot manager and boot files at startup and to guarantee that a computer's hard disk has not been tampered with while the operating system was offline. BitLocker Drive Encryption also stores measurements of core operating system files in the TPM.

Every time the computer is started, Windows validates the boot files, the operating system files, and any encrypted volumes to ensure that they have not been modified while the operating system was offline. If the files have been modified, Windows alerts the user and refuses to release the key required to access Windows. The computer then goes into Recovery mode, prompting the user to provide a recovery key before it allows access to the boot volume. The Recovery mode is also used if a BitLocker-encrypted disk drive is transferred to another system.

BitLocker Drive Encryption can be used in both TPM and non-TPM computers. If a computer has a TPM, BitLocker Drive Encryption uses the TPM to provide enhanced protection for your data and to ensure early boot file integrity. These features together help prevent unauthorized viewing and accessing of data by encrypting the entire Windows volume and by safeguarding the boot files from tampering. If a computer doesn't have a TPM or its TPM isn't compatible with Windows, BitLocker Drive Encryption can be used to encrypt entire volumes, and in this way protect the volumes from tampering. This configuration, however, doesn't allow the added security of early boot file integrity validation.

On computers with a compatible TPM that is initialized, BitLocker Drive Encryption can use one of the following TPM modes:

- **TPM-Only** In this mode, only TPM is used for validation. When the computer boots, TPM is used to validate the boot files, the operating system files, and any encrypted volumes. Because the user doesn't need to provide an additional startup key, this mode is transparent to the user, and the user logon experience is unchanged. However, if the TPM is missing or the integrity of files or volumes has changed, BitLocker enters Recovery mode and requires a recovery key or password to regain access to the boot volume.
- **TPM and PIN** In this mode, both TPM and a user-entered numeric key are used for validation. When the computer boots, TPM is used to validate the boot files, the operating system files, and any encrypted volumes. The user must enter a PIN when prompted to continue startup. If the user doesn't have the PIN or is unable to provide the correct PIN, BitLocker enters Recovery mode instead of booting to the operating system. As before, BitLocker also enters Recovery mode if the TPM is missing or the integrity of boot files or encrypted volumes has changed.
- **TPM and Startup Key** In this mode, both TPM and a startup key are used for validation. When the computer boots, TPM is used to validate the boot files, the operating system files, and any encrypted volumes. The user must have a USB flash drive with a startup key to log on to the computer. If the user doesn't have the startup key or is unable to provide the correct startup key, BitLocker enters Recovery mode. As before, BitLocker also enters Recovery mode if the TPM is missing or the integrity of boot files or encrypted volumes has changed.
- **TPM and Smart Card Certificate** In this mode, both TPM and a smart card certificate are used for validation. When the computer boots, TPM is used to validate the boot files, the operating system files, and any encrypted volumes. The user must have a smart card with a valid certificate to log on to the computer. If the user doesn't have a smart card with a valid certificate and is unable to provide one, BitLocker enters Recovery mode. As before, BitLocker also enters Recovery mode if the TPM is missing or the integrity of boot files or encrypted volumes has changed.

On computers without a TPM or on computers that have incompatible TPMs, BitLocker Drive Encryption uses Startup Key Only or Smart Card Certificate Only mode. Startup Key Only mode requires a USB flash drive containing a startup key. The user inserts the USB flash drive in the computer before turning it on. The key stored on the flash drive unlocks the computer.

REAL WORLD **Although it is likely that an update or service pack for Windows 7 will enable you to use BitLocker to encrypt the USB flash drive containing your startup key, the original release of Windows 7 does not allow you to do this. For this reason, don't enable BitLocker on the USB flash drive containing your startup key.**

Smart Card Certificate Only mode requires a smart card with a valid certificate. The user validates the smart card certificate after turning on the computer. The certificate unlocks the computer.

Several important changes have been made to BitLocker Drive Encryption since the technology was first implemented on Windows Vista. For Windows 7, you can now do the following:

- Encrypt FAT volumes as well as NTFS volumes. Previously, you could only encrypt NTFS volumes. When you encrypt FAT volumes, you have the option of specifying whether encrypted volumes can be unlocked and viewed on computers running Windows Vista, Windows XP, or Windows Server 2008. This option is configured through Group Policy and is enabled when you turn on BitLocker. In the Administrative Templates policies for Computer Configuration under Windows Components\BitLocker Drive Encryption, there are separate policies for earlier versions of Windows that allow FAT-formatted fixed drives and FAT-formatted removable drives to be unlocked and viewed.
- Allow a data-recovery agent to be used with BitLocker Drive Encryption. This option is configured through Group Policy. The data-recovery agent allows an encrypted volume to be unlocked and recovered by using a recovery agent's personal certificate or a 48-digit recovery password. You can optionally save the recovery information in Active Directory. In the Administrative Templates policies for Computer Configuration, there are separate policies for operating system volumes, other fixed drives, and removable drives.
- Deny write access to removable data drives not protected with BitLocker. This option is configured through Group Policy. If you enable this option, users have read-only access to unencrypted removable data drives and read/write access to encrypted removable data drives.

In a domain, domain administrators are the default data-recovery agents. A homegroup or workgroup has no default data-recovery agent, but you can designate one. Any user you want to designate as a data-recovery agent needs a personal encryption certificate. You can generate a certificate by using the Cipher utility and then use the certificate to assign the data-recovery agent in Local Security Policy under Public Key Policies\BitLocker Drive Encryption.

Deploying BitLocker Drive Encryption

Deploying BitLocker Drive Encryption in an enterprise changes the way administrators and users work with computers. A computer with BitLocker Drive Encryption requires user intervention to boot to the operating system—a user must enter a PIN, insert a USB flash drive containing a startup key, or use a smart card with a valid certificate. Because of this requirement, after you deploy BitLocker Drive Encryption, you can no longer be assured that you can perform remote administration that requires a computer to be restarted without having physical access to the computer—someone might need to be available to type the required PIN, insert the USB flash drive with the startup key, or use a smart card with a valid certificate.

Before you use BitLocker Drive Encryption, you should perform a thorough evaluation of your organization's computers. You need to develop plans and procedures for the following:

- Evaluating the various BitLocker authentication methods and applying them as appropriate
- Determining whether computers support TPM, and thus whether you must use TPM or non-TPM BitLocker configurations
- Storing, using, and periodically changing encryption keys, recovery passwords, and other validation mechanisms used with BitLocker

You need to develop new procedures for items such as these:

- Performing daily operations with BitLocker-encrypted drives
- Providing administrative support for BitLocker-encrypted drives
- Recovering computers with BitLocker-encrypted drives

These procedures need to take into account the way BitLocker encryption works and the requirements to have PINs, startup keys, smart cards, and recovery keys available whenever you work with BitLocker-encrypted computers. After you evaluate your organization's computers and develop basic plans and procedures, you need to develop a configuration plan for implementing BitLocker Drive Encryption.

Several implementations of BitLocker Drive Encryption are available: BitLocker Drive Encryption originally released with Windows Vista, the updated version released with Windows Server 2008, and the version released with Windows 7. Although computers running Windows 7 and Windows Server 2008 Release 2 and later versions of Windows can work with any of the available versions, earlier versions of Windows can't necessarily work with the latest version of BitLocker. For example, you might need to configure Group Policy to allow access from earlier versions of Windows.

To turn on BitLocker Drive Encryption on the drive containing the Windows operating system, the drive must have at least two partitions:

- The first partition is for BitLocker Drive Encryption. This partition, designated as the active partition, holds the files required to start the operating system and is not encrypted.
- The second is the primary partition for the operating system and your data. This partition is encrypted when you turn on BitLocker.

With implementations of BitLocker prior to Windows 7, you need to create the partitions in a certain way to ensure compatibility. This is no longer the case in Windows 7. When you install Windows 7, an additional partition is created automatically during setup. By default, this additional partition is used by the Windows Recovery Environment (Windows RE). However, if you enable BitLocker on the system volume, Windows usually moves Windows RE to the system volume and then uses the additional partition for BitLocker.

Using BitLocker on a hard disk is easy. On a computer with a compatible TPM, you must initialize the TPM as discussed earlier in the section "Initializing a TPM for First Use," and then you need to enable BitLocker. On a computer without a compatible TPM, you only need to enable BitLocker on your hard disk.

You can use local Group Policy and Active Directory–based Group Policy to help manage and maintain TPM and BitLocker configurations. Group Policy settings for TPM Services are found in Administrative Templates policies for Computer Configuration under System\Trusted Platform Module Services. Group Policy settings for BitLocker are found in Administrative Templates policies for Computer Configuration under Windows Components\BitLocker Drive Encryption. There are separate subfolders for fixed data drives, operating system drives, and removable data drives.

Policies you might want to configure include the following:

- Trusted Platform Module Services policies
  - Turn On TPM Backup To Active Directory Domain Services
  - Configure The List Of Blocked TPM Commands
  - Ignore The Default List Of Blocked TPM Commands
  - Ignore The Local List Of Blocked TPM Commands
- BitLocker Drive Encryption policies
  - Choose Default Folder For Recovery Password
  - Choose Drive Encryption Method And Cipher Strength
  - Prevent Memory Overwrite On Restart
  - Provide The Unique Identifiers For Your Organization
  - Validate Smart Card Certificate Usage Rule Compliance
- Fixed Drive policies
  - Configure Use Of Smart Cards On Fixed Data Drives
  - Deny Write Access To Fixed Drives Not Protected By BitLocker
  - Allow Access To BitLocker-Protected Fixed Data Drives From Earlier Versions Of Windows
  - Configure Use Of Passwords For Fixed Data Drives
  - Configure Use Of Smart Cards On Fixed Data Drives
  - Choose How BitLocker-Protected Fixed Drives Can Be Recovered
- Operating System Drive policies
  - Require Additional Authentication At Startup
  - Allow Enhanced PINs For Startup
  - Configure Minimum PIN Length For Startup
  - Choose How BitLocker-Protected Operating System Drives Can Be Recovered
  - Configure TPM Platform Validation Profile

- Removable Data Drive policies
  - Allow Access To BitLocker-Protected Removable Data Drives From Earlier Versions Of Windows
  - Choose How BitLocker-Protected Removable Drives Can Be Recovered
  - Configure Use Of Passwords For Removable Data Drives
  - Configure Use Of Smart Cards On Removable Data Drives
  - Control Use Of BitLocker On Removable Drives
  - Deny Write Access To Removable Drives Not Protected By BitLocker

Active Directory includes TPM and BitLocker recovery extensions for Computer objects. For TPM, the extensions define a single property of the Computer object, called ms-TPM-OwnerInformation. When the TPM is initialized or when the owner password is changed, the hash of the TPM ownership password can be stored as a value of the ms-TPM-OwnerInformation attribute on the related Computer object. For BitLocker, these extensions define Recovery objects as child objects of Computer objects and are used to store recovery passwords and associate them with specific BitLocker-encrypted volumes.

To ensure that TPM and BitLocker recovery information is always available, you should configure Group Policy to save recovery information in Active Directory.

- With Turn On TPM Backup To Active Directory Domain Services, enable the policy and then use the setting Require TPM Backup To AD DS.
- With Choose How BitLocker-Protected Fixed Drives Can Be Recovered, enable the policy and accept the default options to allow data recovery agents and save the recovery information in Active Directory.
- With Choose How BitLocker-Protected Operating System Drives Can Be Recovered, enable the policy and accept the default options to allow data recovery agents and save the recovery information in Active Directory.

REAL WORLD **For Federal Information Processing Standard (FIPS) compliance, you cannot create or save BitLocker recovery passwords. Instead, you need to configure Windows to create recovery keys. The FIPS setting is located in the Security Policy Editor at Local Policies\Security Options\System Cryptography: Use FIPS Compliant Algorithms For Encryption, Hashing, And Signing.**

To configure BitLocker to use recovery keys, enable the security option System Cryptography: Use FIPS Compliant Algorithms For Encryption, Hashing, And Signing in local Group Policy or Active Directory–based Group Policy as appropriate. With this setting enabled, users can only generate recovery keys.

Managing BitLocker Drive Encryption

With Windows 7, you can configure and enable BitLocker Drive Encryption on both system volumes and data volumes. When you encrypt system volumes, you must unlock the computer at startup by using a TPM, a startup key, a startup PIN, or any required or optional combination of the three. To enforce the strictest and highest security possible, use all three authentication methods.

In the current implementation of BitLocker, you do not have to encrypt a computer's system volume prior to encrypting a computer's data volumes. When you use encrypted data volumes, the operating system mounts BitLocker data volumes as it would any other volume, but it requires either a password or a smart card with a valid certificate to unlock the drive.

The encryption key for a protected data volume is created and stored independently from the system volume and all other protected data volumes. To allow the operating system to mount encrypted volumes, the key chain protecting the data volume is stored in an encrypted state on the operating system volume. If the operating system enters Recovery mode, the data volumes are not unlocked until the operating system is out of Recovery mode.

Setting up BitLocker Drive Encryption requires these steps:

1. Partitioning a computer's hard disks appropriately and installing the operating system (if you are configuring a new computer). Windows Setup partitions the drives for you automatically. However, the volume where BitLocker data is stored must always be the active, system volume.
2. Initializing and configuring a computer's TPM (if applicable).
3. Turning on the BitLocker Drive Encryption feature (as necessary).
4. Checking firmware to ensure that the computer is set to start first from the disk containing the active, system partition and the boot partition, not from USB or CD/DVD drives (applicable only when you encrypt system volumes).
5. Turning on and configuring BitLocker Drive Encryption.

After you've turned on and configured BitLocker encryption, you can use several techniques to maintain the environment and perform recovery.

Preparing for BitLocker Drive Encryption

As discussed previously, BitLocker Drive Encryption can be used in a TPM or a non-TPM configuration. Both configurations require some preliminary work before you can turn on and configure BitLocker Drive Encryption.

With Windows 7 Ultimate and Enterprise editions, BitLocker should be installed by default. If it is not, you can install the BitLocker Drive Encryption feature by using the Add Features Wizard. You need to restart the computer to complete the installation process.

You can determine the readiness status of a computer by accessing the BitLocker Drive Encryption console. Click Start, and then click Control Panel. In Control Panel, click System And Security, and then click BitLocker Drive Encryption. If the system isn't properly configured, you'll see an error message. Note the following:

- If you see an error message related to TPM on a computer with a compatible TPM, refer to the section "Enabling and Using TPM" to learn more about TPM states and enabling TPM in firmware.
- If you see an error message related to TPM on a computer with an incompatible TPM or no TPM, you need to change the computer's Group Policy settings so that you can turn on BitLocker Drive Encryption without a TPM.

You can configure policy settings for BitLocker encryption in local Group Policy or in Active Directory–based Group Policy. In local policy, you apply the settings to the computer's local Group Policy object. For domain policy, you apply the settings to a Group Policy object processed by the computer. While you are working with domain policy, you can also specify requirements for computers with a TPM.

To configure the way BitLocker can be used with or without a TPM, follow these steps:

1. Open the appropriate Group Policy object for editing in the Group Policy Management Editor.
2. In the Administrative Templates policies for Computer Configuration under Windows Components\BitLocker Drive Encryption\Operating System Drives, double-click the setting Require Additional Authentication At Startup.
3. In the Require Additional Authentication At Startup dialog box, shown in Figure 11-4, define the policy setting by selecting Enabled.

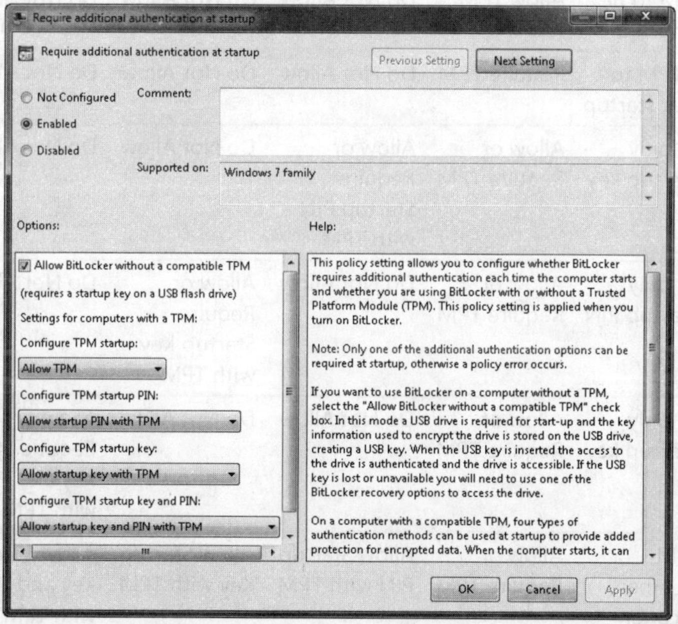

FIGURE 11-4 Choose an option for turning off the TPM.

4. Do one of the following:
   - If you want to allow BitLocker to be used without a compatible TPM, select the Allow BitLocker Without A Compatible TPM check box. This changes the policy setting so that you can use BitLocker encryption with a startup key on a computer without a TPM.
   - If you want to require BitLocker to be used with a TPM, clear the Allow BitLocker Without A Compatible TPM check box. This changes the policy setting so that you can use BitLocker encryption on a computer with a TPM by using a startup PIN, a startup key, or both.
5. On a computer with a compatible TPM, four types of authentication methods can be used at startup to provide added protection for encrypted data. These authentication methods can be allowed or required. Use Table 11-2 to help you configure how TPM is used with the available authentication methods.

TABLE 11-2 Common Options for Using TPM with BitLocker

	SETTING FOR			
WHEN THE COMPUTER STARTS	**CONFIGURE TPM STARTUP**	**CONFIGURE TPM STARTUP PIN**	**CONFIGURE TPM STARTUP KEY**	**CONFIGURE TPM STARTUP KEY AND PIN**
Allow TPM to be used at startup	Allow TPM	Do Not Allow	Do Not Allow	Do Not Allow
Require TPM to be used at startup	Require TPM	Do Not Allow	Do Not Allow	Do Not Allow
Use TPM only with a startup key	Allow or Require TPM	Allow or Require Startup PIN with TPM	Do Not Allow	Do Not Allow
Use TPM only with a startup PIN	Allow or Require TPM	Do Not Allow	Allow or Require Startup Key with TPM	Do Not Allow
Use TPM only with a startup key and PIN	Allow or Require TPM	Do Not Allow	Do Not Allow	Allow or Require Startup Key and PIN with TPM
Allow TPM with any other authentication method	Allow or Require TPM	Allow Startup PIN with TPM	Allow Startup Key with TPM	Allow Startup Key and PIN with TPM

6. Click OK to save your settings. This policy is enforced the next time Group Policy is applied.
7. Close the Group Policy Management Editor. To apply Group Policy immediately to the computer you are logged on to, click Start, type **gpupdate.exe /force** in the Search box, and then press Enter.

Computers that have a startup key or a startup PIN also have a recovery password or certificate. The recovery password or certificate is required in the event of the following:

- Changes are made to the system startup information
- The encrypted drive must be moved to another computer
- The user is unable to provide the appropriate startup key or PIN

The recovery password or certificate should be managed and stored separately from the startup key or startup PIN. Although users are given the startup key or startup PIN, administrators should be the only ones with the recovery password or certificate. As an administrator, you need the recovery password or certificate to unlock the encrypted data on the volume if BitLocker enters a locked state. Generally, unless you use a common data-recovery agent, the recovery password or certificate is unique to this particular BitLocker encryption. This means you cannot use it to recover encrypted data from any other BitLocker-encrypted volume—even from other BitLocker-encrypted volumes on the same computer. To increase security, you should store startup keys and recovery data apart from the computer.

When BitLocker is installed, the BitLocker Drive Encryption console is available in Control Panel. Your configuration options for BitLocker depend on whether the computer has a TPM and on how you've configured Group Policy.

Enabling BitLocker on Nonsystem Volumes

Encrypting a nonsystem volume protects the data stored on the volume. Any volume formatted with FAT, FAT32, or NTFS can be encrypted with BitLocker. The length of time it takes to encrypt a drive depends on the size of the drive, the processing power of the computer, and the level of activity on the computer.

Before you enable BitLocker, you should configure the appropriate Fixed Data Drive policies and settings in Group Policy and then wait for Group Policy to be refreshed. If you don't do this and you enable BitLocker, you might need to turn BitLocker off and then turn BitLocker back on because certain state and management flags are set when you turn on BitLocker.

If you dual boot a computer or move drives between computers, the Allow Access To BitLocker-Protected Fixed Data Drives From Earlier Versions Of Windows setting in Group Policy can ensure that you have access to the volume on other operating systems and computers. Unlocked drives are read-only. To ensure that you can recover an encrypted volume, you should allow data-recovery agents and store recovery information in Active Directory.

To enable BitLocker encryption on a nonsystem volume, follow these steps:

1. Click Start, and then click Computer. Right-click the data volume, and then click Turn On BitLocker. BitLocker then initializes the drive.

   NOTE **If BitLocker is already enabled, the Manage BitLocker option is displayed instead of Turn On BitLocker.**

2. On the Choose How You Want To Unlock This Drive page, shown in Figure 11-5, choose one or more for the following options, and then click Next:
   - **Use A Password To Unlock The Drive** Select this option if you want the user to be prompted for a password to unlock the drive. Passwords allow a drive to be unlocked in any location and to be shared with other people.
   - **Use My Smart Card To Unlock The Drive** Select this option if you want the user to use a smart card and enter the smart card PIN to unlock the drive. Because this feature requires a smart card reader, it is normally used to unlock a drive in the workplace and not for drives that might be used outside the workplace.
   - **Automatically Unlock This Drive On This Computer** Select this option if you want the drive to be unlocked automatically once the computer starts and the operating system loads. This option is available only when you've encrypted the system volume.

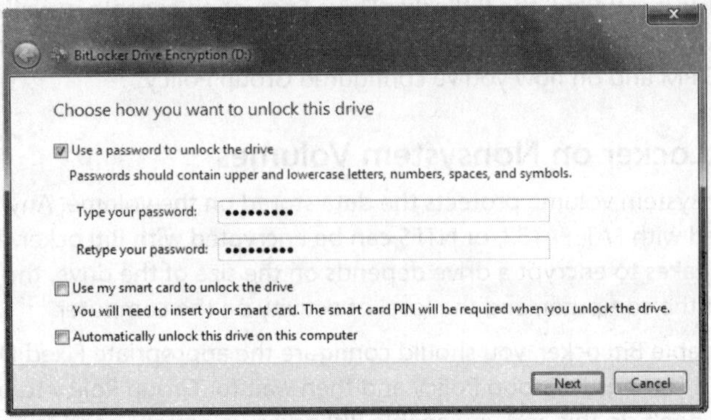

FIGURE 11-5 Choose an option for unlocking a drive.

3. On the How Do You Want To Store Your Recovery Key page, click Save The Recovery Key To A USB Flash Drive.
4. In the Save A Recovery Key To A USB Drive dialog box, choose the location of your USB flash drive, and then click Save. Do not remove the USB drive with the recovery key.
5. You can now optionally save the recovery key to a folder, print the recovery key, or both. For each option, click the option, and then follow the wizard's

steps to set the location for saving or printing the recovery key. When you have finished, click Next.

6. On the Are You Ready To Encrypt This Drive page, click Start Encrypting. How long the encryption process takes depends on the size of the drive and other factors.

Enabling BitLocker on USB Flash Drives

Encrypting USB flash drives protects the data stored on the volume. Any USB flash drive formatted with FAT, FAT32, or NTFS can be encrypted with BitLocker. The length of time it takes to encrypt a drive depends on the size of the drive, the processing power of the computer, and the level of activity on the computer.

Before you enable BitLocker, you should configure the appropriate Removable Data Drive policies and settings in Group Policy and then wait for Group Policy to be refreshed. If you don't do this and you enable BitLocker, you might need to turn BitLocker off and then turn BitLocker back on because certain state and management flags are set when you turn on BitLocker.

To be sure that you can recover an encrypted volume, you should allow data-recovery agents and store recovery information in Active Directory. If you use a flash drive with earlier versions of Windows, the Allow Access To BitLocker-Protected Removable Data Drives From Earlier Versions Of Windows policy can ensure that you have access to the USB flash drive on other operating systems and computers. Unlocked drives are read-only.

To enable BitLocker encryption on a USB flash drive, follow these steps:

1. Insert the USB flash drive, click Start, and then click Computer.
2. Right-click the USB flash drive, and then click Turn On BitLocker. BitLocker initializes the drive.
3. On the Choose How You Want To Unlock This Drive page, choose one or more for the following options, and then click Next:
   - **Use A Password To Unlock This Drive** Select this option if you want the user to be prompted for a password to unlock the drive. Passwords allow a drive to be unlocked in any location and to be shared with other people.
   - **Use My Smart Card To Unlock The Drive** Select this option if you want the user to use a smart card and enter the smart card PIN to unlock the drive. Because this feature requires a smart card reader, it is normally used to unlock a drive in the workplace and not for drives that might be used outside the workplace.
4. On the How Do You Want To Store Your Recovery Key page, click Save The Recovery Key To A File.
5. In the Save BitLocker Recovery Key As dialog box, choose a save location, and then click Save.

6. You can now print the recovery key if you want to. When you have finished, click Next.
7. On the Are You Ready To Encrypt This Drive page, click Start Encrypting. Do not remove the USB flash drive until the encryption process is complete. How long the encryption process takes depends on the size of the drive and other factors.

The encryption process does the following:

1. Adds an Autorun.inf file, the BitLocker To Go reader, and a Read Me.txt file to the USB flash drive.
2. Creates a virtual volume with the full contents of the drive in the remaining drive space.
3. Encrypts the virtual volume to protect it. USB flash drive encryption takes approximately 6 to 10 minutes per gigabyte to complete. The encryption process can be paused and resumed provided that you don't remove the drive.

As a result, when AutoPlay is enabled and you insert the encrypted drive into a USB slot on a computer running Windows 7, Windows 7 runs the BitLocker To Go reader, which in turn displays the dialog box shown in Figure 11-6. When you are prompted, enter the password, smart card PIN, or both to unlock the drive. Optionally, select Automatically Unlock On This Computer From Now On to save the password in an encrypted file on the computer's system volume. Finally, click Unlock to unlock the volume so that you can use it.

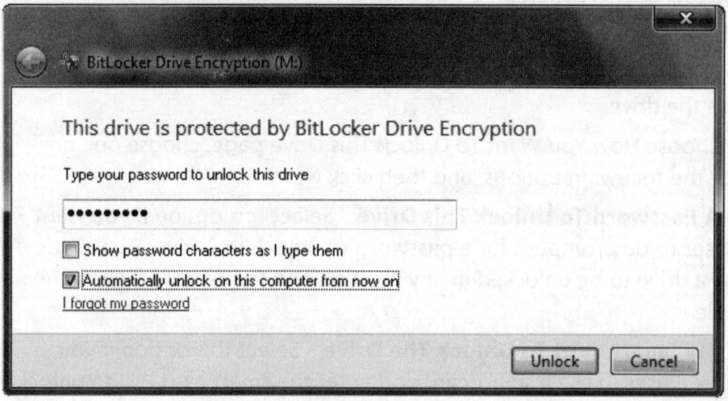

FIGURE 11-6 Unlock the encrypted drive.

Enabling BitLocker on System Volumes

Before you can encrypt a system volume, you must remove all bootable media from a computer's CD/DVD drives as well as all USB flash drives. You can then enable BitLocker encryption on the system volume by completing the following steps:

1. Click Start, and then click Computer. Right-click the system volume, and then click Turn On BitLocker. Windows checks the computer and the drive to ensure that BitLocker can be enabled. Click Next.

   NOTE **If BitLocker is already enabled, the Manage BitLocker option is displayed instead of Turn On BitLocker.**

2. On the Preparing Your Drive For BitLocker page, click Details to review how Windows will prepare your drive. Generally, Windows uses an existing drive or unallocated space on the system drive for the required BitLocker partition. If Windows RE is in this partition, Windows moves Windows RE to the system volume and then uses this additional partition for BitLocker.
3. Click Next to prepare the drive for BitLocker. When this process is complete, click Next again.
4. As Figure 11-7 shows, you can now configure BitLocker startup preferences. Continue as discussed in the separate procedures that follow.

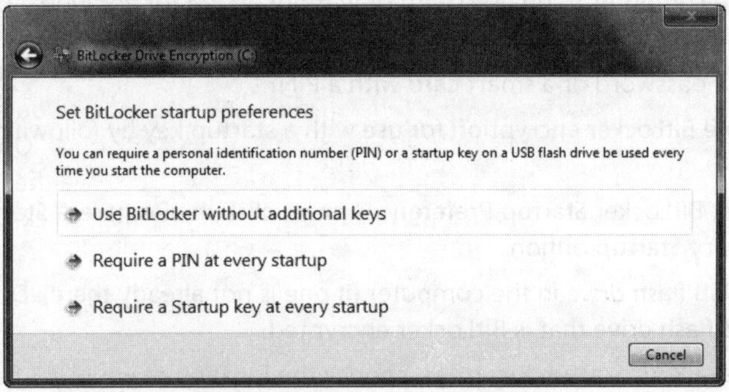

FIGURE 11-7 Configure BitLocker startup preferences.

You can use BitLocker to provide basic integrity checks of the volume without requiring any additional keys. In this configuration, BitLocker protects the system volume by encrypting it. This configuration does the following:

- Grants access to the volume to users who can log on to the operating system.
- Prevents those who have physical access to the computer from booting to an alternate operating system to gain access to the data on the volume.
- Allows the computer to be used with or without a TPM for additional boot security
- Does not require a password or a smart card with a PIN.

To use BitLocker without any additional keys, follow these steps:

1. On the Set BitLocker Startup Preferences page, click Use BitLocker Without Additional Keys.
2. On the How Do You Want To Store Your Recovery Key page, click Save The Recovery Key On A USB Flash Drive.

3. In the Save A Recovery Key To A USB Drive dialog box, choose the location of your USB flash drive, and then click Save. Do not use a USB flash drive that is BitLocker encrypted.
4. You can now optionally save the recovery key to a folder, print the recovery key, or both. Click an option, and then follow the wizard steps to set the location for saving or printing the recovery key. When you have finished, click Next.
5. On the Encrypt The Drive page, click Start Encrypting. How long the encryption process takes depends on the size of the drive and other factors.

To enhance security, you can use BitLocker with a PIN or startup key. This configuration does the following:

- Grants access to the volume only to users who can provide a valid key.
- Prevents those who have physical access to the computer from booting to an alternate operating system to gain access to the data on the volume.
- Allows the computer to be used with or without a TPM for additional boot security
- Requires a password or a smart card with a PIN.

You can enable BitLocker encryption for use with a startup key by following these steps:

1. On the Set BitLocker Startup Preferences page, click the Require A Startup Key At Every Startup option.
2. Insert a USB flash drive in the computer (if one is not already there). Do not use a USB flash drive that is BitLocker encrypted.
3. On the Save Your Startup Key page, choose the location of your USB flash drive, and then click Save.
4. Next, you need to save the recovery key. Because you should not store the recovery key and the startup key on the same media, remove the USB flash drive and insert a second USB flash drive.

   NOTE **The startup key is different from the recovery key. If you create a startup key, this key is required to start the computer. The recovery key is required to unlock the computer if BitLocker enters Recovery mode, which might happen if BitLocker suspects the computer has been tampered with while the computer was offline.**

5. On the How Do You Want To Store Your Recovery Key page, click Save The Recovery Key To A USB Flash Drive.
6. In the Save A Recovery Key To A USB Drive dialog box, choose the location of your USB flash drive, and then click Save. Do not remove the USB drive with the recovery key.
7. You can now optionally save the recovery key to a folder, print the recovery key, or both. Click an option, and then follow the wizard's steps to set the

location for saving or printing the recovery key. When you have finished, click Next.

8. On the Encrypt The Volume page, confirm that Run BitLocker System Check is selected, and then click Continue.
9. Confirm that you want to restart the computer by clicking Restart Now. The computer restarts, and BitLocker ensures that the computer is BitLocker compatible and ready for encryption. If the computer is not ready for encryption, you will see an error and need to resolve the error status before you can complete this procedure. If the computer is ready for encryption, the Encryption In Progress status bar is displayed. You can monitor the status of the disk volume encryption by pointing to the BitLocker Drive Encryption icon in the notification area. By double-clicking this icon, you can open the Encrypting dialog box and monitor the encryption process more closely. You also have the option to pause the encryption process. Volume encryption takes approximately 1 minute per gigabyte to complete.

   By completing this procedure, you have encrypted the operating system volume and created a recovery key unique to that volume. The next time you turn on your computer, the USB flash drive with the startup key must be plugged into a USB port on the computer. If you do not have the USB flash drive containing your startup key, you will need to use Recovery mode and supply the recovery key to gain access to the data.

You can enable BitLocker encryption for use with a startup PIN by following these steps:

1. On the Set BitLocker Startup Preferences page, select the Require A PIN At Every Startup option.
2. On the Type Your Startup PIN page, enter and confirm the PIN. The PIN can be any number you choose and must be 4 to 20 digits in length. The PIN is stored on the computer.
3. Insert a USB flash drive on which you want to save the recovery key, and then click Set PIN. Do not use a USB flash drive that is BitLocker encrypted.

   Continue with steps 5 to 9 in the previous procedure.

When the encryption process is complete, you have encrypted the entire volume and created a recovery key unique to this volume. If you created a PIN or a startup key, you are required to use the PIN or startup key to start the computer. Otherwise, you will see no change to the computer unless the TPM changes or cannot be accessed, or if someone tries to modify the disk while the operating system is offline. In this case, the computer enters Recovery mode, and you need to enter the recovery key to unlock the computer.

Managing and Troubleshooting BitLocker

You can determine whether a system volume, data volume, or inserted USB flash drive uses BitLocker by clicking Start, Control Panel, and then System And Security. Double-click BitLocker Drive Encryption, and you'll see the status of BitLocker on each volume, as shown in Figure 11-8.

The BitLocker Drive Encryption service must be started for BitLocker to work properly. Normally, this service is configured for manual startup and runs under the LocalSystem account.

To use smart cards with BitLocker, the Smart Card service must be started. Normally, this service is configured for manual startup and runs under the LocalService account.

After you create a startup key or PIN and a recovery key for a computer, you can create duplicates of the startup key, startup PIN, or recovery key as necessary for backup or replacement purposes. To do this, click Start, and then click Computer. Right-click the volume, and then click Manage BitLocker. If BitLocker is turned off, the Turn On BitLocker option is displayed instead.

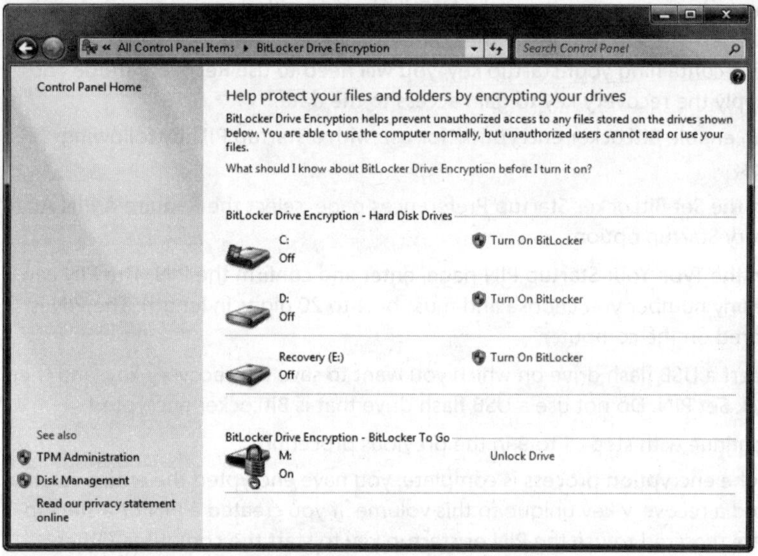

FIGURE 11-8 Review the current status of BitLocker for each volume.

The management options provided depend on the type of volume you are working with and the encryption settings you choose. The available options include the following:

- **Add A Password To Unlock The Drive** Allows you to add an encryption password. Click this option, and then type and confirm the new password. Click Next, and then click OK.

- **Change Password To Unlock The Drive** Allows you to change the encryption password. Click this option, and then type and confirm the new password. Click Next, and then click OK.
- **Remove Password From This Drive** Click this option to remove the encryption password requirement for unlocking the drive.
- **Add A Smart Card To Unlock The Drive** Allows you to add a smart card for unlocking the drive. Click this option, and then follow the prompts.
- **Remove Smart Card From This Drive** Click this option to remove the smart card requirement for unlocking the drive.
- **Change Smart Card For This Drive** Allows you to change the smart card used to unlock the drive. Click this option, and then follow the prompts.
- **Save Or Print Recovery Key Again** Allows you to save or print the recovery key. Click this option, and then follow the prompts.
- **Automatically Unlock This Drive On This Computer** Click this option to turn on automatic unlocking of the drive.
- **Turn Off Automatic Unlocking For This Drive On This Computer** Click this option to turn off automatic unlocking of the drive.

Recovering Data Protected by BitLocker Drive Encryption

If you've configured BitLocker Drive Encryption and the computer enters Recovery mode, you need to unlock the computer. To unlock the computer using a recovery key stored on a USB flash drive, follow these steps:

1. Turn on the computer. If the computer is locked, the computer opens the BitLocker Drive Encryption Recovery console.
2. When you are prompted, insert the USB flash drive that contains the recovery key, and then press Enter.
3. The computer will unlock and reboot automatically. You do not need to enter the recovery key manually.

If you saved the recovery key file in a folder on another computer or on removable media, you can use another computer to open and validate the recovery key file. To locate the correct file, find Password ID on the recovery console displayed on the locked computer and write down this number. The file containing the recovery key uses this Password ID as the file name. Open the file and locate the recovery key.

To unlock the computer by typing the recovery key, follow these steps:

1. Turn on the computer. If the computer is locked, the computer opens the BitLocker Drive Encryption Recovery console.
2. Type the recovery key, and then press Enter. The computer will unlock and reboot automatically.

A computer can become locked if a user tries to enter the recovery key but is unsuccessful. In the recovery console, you can press Esc twice to exit the recovery prompt and turn off the computer. A computer might also become locked if an error related to TPM occurs or boot data is modified. In this case, the computer halts very early in the boot process, before the operating system starts. At this point, the locked computer might not be able to accept standard keyboard numbers. If that is the case, you must use the function keys to enter the recovery password. Here, the function keys F1–F9 represent the digits 1 through 9, and the F10 function key represents 0.

Disabling or Turning Off BitLocker Drive Encryption

When you need to make changes to TPM or make other changes to the system, you might first need to temporarily turn off BitLocker encryption on the system volume. You cannot temporarily turn off BitLocker encryption on data volumes; you can only decrypt data volumes.

To temporarily turn off BitLocker encryption on the system volume, follow these steps:

1. Click Start, Control Panel, System And Security, and then double-click BitLocker Drive Encryption.
2. For the system volume, click Turn Off BitLocker Drive Encryption.
3. In the What Level Of Decryption Do You Want dialog box, click Disable BitLocker Drive Encryption.

   By completing this procedure, you have temporarily disabled BitLocker on the operating system volume.

To turn off BitLocker Drive Encryption and decrypt a data volume, follow these steps:

1. Click Start, Control Panel, System And Security, and then double-click BitLocker Drive Encryption.
2. For the appropriate volume, click Turn Off BitLocker Drive Encryption.
3. In the What Level Of Decryption Do You Want dialog box, click Decrypt The Volume.

To turn off BitLocker Drive Encryption and decrypt a USB flash drive, follow these steps:

1. Click Start, Control Panel, System And Security, and then double-click BitLocker Drive Encryption.
2. For the appropriate volume, click Turn Off BitLocker Drive Encryption.
3. In the What Level Of Decryption Do You Want dialog box, click Decrypt The Volume.

CHAPTER 12

Managing Disk Drives and File Systems

Most computers have several types of drives, including internal disk drives and removable media drives. An internal hard disk drive is typically the primary storage device. In most cases, the first hard disk drive installed is designated Disk 0. If additional hard disk drives are installed, they are designated Disk 1, Disk 2, and so on. This chapter discusses tools and techniques for managing disk drives and file systems. You'll learn how to partition and format disks and how to convert disks from one disk type to another. You'll also learn about Windows 7 features that affect how drivers are used, including Windows ReadyBoost, Windows ReadyDrive, and Windows SuperFetch.

Disk Management Essentials

Windows 7 enables you to designate a physical drive as a basic disk or a dynamic disk.

- **Basic disks** The disk type used most often in the past, a basic disk can on Windows 7 be divided into one or more partitions. A partition is a logical section of a disk that operates as if it were a physically separate disk. To use a partition, you must format it to use a particular file system (FAT, FAT32, or NTFS) and assign it a drive designator. The formatted partition is then referred to as a basic volume, and you can access it as a local disk on the computer. Windows 7 supports both primary and extended partitions on basic disks. A primary partition is used to start the operating system. You access a primary partition directly by its drive designator. You cannot subdivide a primary partition. An extended partition, on the other hand, is accessed indirectly. After you create an extended partition, you must divide it into one or more logical drives. You can then access the logical drives independently of each other.
- **Dynamic disks** Introduced in Windows 2000, dynamic disks enable you to perform most common disk maintenance tasks without having to restart the computer. Like a basic disk, a dynamic disk can be divided. However, dynamic disks are divided into volumes rather than partitions. A volume is very similar to a partition. The most commonly used type of volume is a simple volume. A simple volume is a volume on a single disk, which can be used to start the operating system and for general data storage. Other types of volumes can be used as well, including those that enable you to extend a single volume across several disks (a spanned volume). As with a partition or a logical drive, you must format a volume on a dynamic disk and assign it a drive designator before you can use it. The formatted volume is referred to as a dynamic volume, and you can access it as a local disk on the computer. When a dynamic volume combines space from multiple physical drives, it still appears as a single local disk and is accessed by a single drive designator.

NOTE **With FAT, the number of bits used with the file allocation table determines the variant you are working with and the maximum volume size. FAT16, also known simply as FAT, defines its file allocation tables using 16 bits. Volumes that are 4 gigabytes (GB) or less in size are formatted with FAT16. There's also a 32-bit version of FAT, known as FAT32. FAT32 defines its file allocation tables using 32 bits, and you can create FAT32 volumes that are 32 GB or less using the Windows format tools. Although Windows can mount larger FAT32 volumes created with third-party tools, you should use NTFS for volumes larger than 32 GB.**

You can change storage types from basic to dynamic and from dynamic to basic. When you convert a basic disk to a dynamic disk, partitions are changed to volumes of the appropriate type automatically and data is not lost. Converting a dynamic disk to a basic disk isn't so easy. You need to delete the volumes on the dynamic disk before you can change the disk type to a basic disk. Deleting the volumes destroys the information they contain, and the only way to get it back is to restore the data from a backup.

In addition to a disk type, all disks have a partition style, which is either master boot record (MBR) or GUID partition table (GPT). Although both 32-bit and 64-bit editions of Windows 7 support MBR and GPT partitions, the GPT partition style is not recognized by Windows XP and earlier releases of Windows.

The MBR contains a partition table that describes where the partitions are located on the disk. In this partition style, the first sector on a hard disk contains the master boot record and a binary code file called the *master boot code* that's used to boot the system. This sector is not partitioned and is hidden from view to protect the system.

With the MBR partitioning style, disks support volumes of up to 4 terabytes (TB) and use one of two types of partitions—primary or extended. Each MBR drive can have up to four primary partitions or three primary partitions and one extended partition. Primary partitions are drive sections that you can access directly for file storage. You make a primary partition accessible to users by creating a file system on it. Unlike primary partitions, extended partitions cannot be accessed directly. Instead, you can configure extended partitions with one or more logical drives that are used to store files. Being able to divide extended partitions into logical drives allows you to divide a physical drive into more than four sections.

GPT was originally developed for high-performance Itanium-based computers. GPT is recommended for disks larger than 2 TB on x86 and x64 systems or for any disks used on Itanium-based computers. The key difference between the GPT partition style and the MBR partition style is how partition data is stored. With GPT, critical partition data is stored in the individual partitions, and redundant primary and backup partition tables are used for improved structural integrity.

Although underlying differences exist between the GPT and MBR partitioning styles, most disk-related tasks are performed in the same way. This means that once you set up and configure your drives it usually won't matter whether the disk is using MBR or GPT. That said, keep the following in mind:

- Basic MBR disks can have up to four primary partitions—or three primary partitions and one extended partition, with one or more logical drives in the extended partition—and dynamic MBR disks can have an unlimited number of volumes.
- GPT disks support partitions of up to 18 exabytes (EB) in size and up to 128 partitions. Computers using GPT disks have two required partitions and one or more optional OEM or data partitions. The required partitions are the EFI system partition (ESP) and the Microsoft Reserved (MSR) partition. Although the optional partitions that you see depend on the system configuration, the optional partition type you see most often is the primary partition. Primary partitions are used to store user data on GPT disks.

- On an x86-based or x64-based computer with BIOS, you can use MBR for booting or for data disks and GPT only for data disks. On an Itanium-based computer or x64-based computer with EFI, you can have both GPT and MBR disks, but you must have at least one GPT disk that contains the ESP and either a primary partition or a simple volume that contains the operating system for booting.

Windows 7 provides several tools for working with a computer's disks. The first and most often overlooked is the Computer console. Other tools include Disk Management, FSUtil, and DiskPart. Partitions and volumes on MBR and GPT disks can be formatted using FAT, FAT32, and NTFS. When you create partitions or volumes in Disk Management, you have the opportunity to format the disk and assign it a drive letter or a mount point as part of the volume creation process. Although Disk Management lets you format the partitions and volumes on MBR disks using FAT, FAT32, and NTFS, only NTFS can be used to format partitions and volumes on GPT disks. If you want to format GPT disks by using FAT or FAT32, you must use either the Format or DiskPart command at the command prompt.

You can change partition table styles from MBR to GPT or from GPT to MBR. Changing partition table styles is useful when you want to move disks between x86-based computers and Itanium-based computers or you receive new disks that are formatted for the wrong partition table style. You can convert partition table styles only on empty disks, however. This means that the disks must be either new or newly formatted. You could, of course, empty a disk by removing its partitions or volumes.

Using the Computer Console

To access the Computer console, click Start, and then click Computer. You can use the Computer console to quickly determine the available storage devices on a computer. As Figure 12-1 shows, the Computer console provides the following details:

- **Hard Disk Drives** Lists the local disks available on the computer. Right-click a disk to display available management options, including Explore, which opens the disk in Windows Explorer with a complete Folders view. Explore is much more convenient than Open, which opens the disk in Windows Explorer but doesn't display a complete Folders view.
- **Devices With Removable Storage** Lists the removable storage devices on the computer, including CD, DVD, USB flash drives, and floppy disk drives. Right-click a device to display available management options, including Eject, which is convenient for ejecting current media so that new media can be inserted.

  TIP **Universal serial bus (USB) flash drives and FireWire/USB-attached external hard drives are being used more and more in place of floppy disks and other types of removable media. If a computer has a USB or FireWire port, you can easily connect or disconnect a drive. Before you disconnect a USB or FireWire**

drive, you should ensure that it is in a safe state. The Eject option provides one way to do this. Right-click the disk designator in Windows Explorer or any related view, such as the Devices With Removable Storage list, and then click Eject. As long as the drive is not in use, you should be able to safely disconnect the drive.

- **Network Location** Lists any mapped network drives. A network drive provides access to a shared folder or a disk on another computer. You can connect network drives by right-clicking Computer on the Start menu and then clicking Map Network Drive to start the Map Network Drive Wizard. To disconnect a network drive, right-click Computer on the Start menu, and then click Disconnect Network Drive to open the Disconnect Network Drive dialog box.

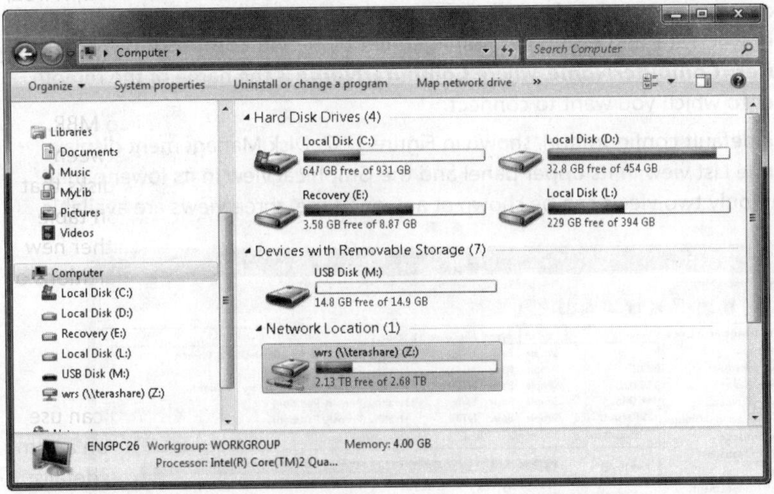

FIGURE 12-1 The Computer console provides easy access to a computer's storage devices.

Using Disk Management

When you want to configure drives, the tool of choice is Disk Management. Disk Management provides the tools you need to manage disks, partitions, volumes, logical drives, and their related file systems. Disk Management is a Microsoft Management Console (MMC) snap-in that can be accessed through a preconfigured console included with Windows or added to any custom console you've created. Using Disk Management, you can perform the following tasks:

- Determine the capacity, free space, status, and other properties of disks
- Create partitions and logical drives on basic disks
- Create volumes on dynamic disks
- Extend volumes to increase their size

- Format volumes and specify the file system to use as FAT, FAT32, or NTFS
- Assign drive letters and paths to volumes
- Convert basic disks to dynamic disks and vice versa

Disk Management is included in the Computer Management console. You can start Computer Management at an elevated command prompt by typing **compmgmt.msc**. Alternatively, right-click Computer on the Start menu, click Manage to start Computer Management, and then select Disk Management in the left pane of the Computer Management window.

When you start Computer Management, you are automatically connected to the local computer. To examine drives on another computer, right-click the Computer Management entry in the console tree, and then click Connect To Another Computer on the shortcut menu. You can now choose the system whose drives you want to examine. From the command line, you can connect to another computer when starting Computer Management by typing **compmgmt.msc /computer=*ComputerName***, where ***ComputerName*** is the name of the remote computer to which you want to connect.

In the default configuration, shown in Figure 12-2, Disk Management displays the Volume List view in its upper panel and the Graphical view in its lower panel. Although only two views can be shown at any one time, three views are available.

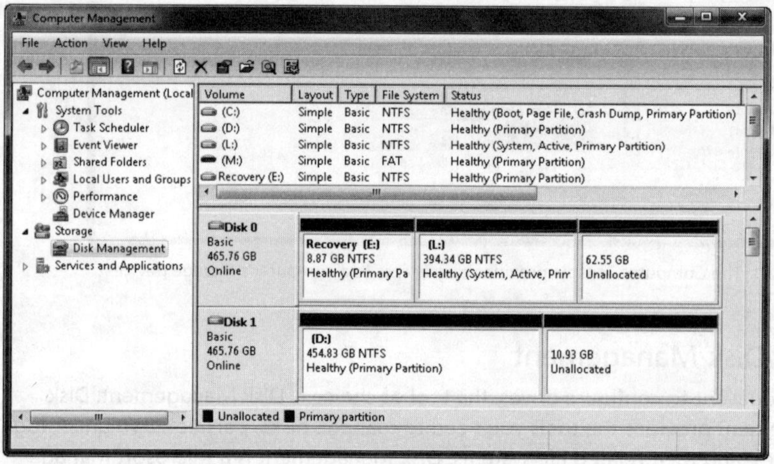

FIGURE 12-2 Use Disk Management to manage disk configurations.

- **Volume List view** Provides a detailed summary of the drives on the computer. Clicking a column label, such as Layout or Status, allows you to sort the disk information based on that column.
- **Graphical view** Provides a graphical overview of the physical and logical drives available. Summary information for the physical disk devices includes the disk number and device type, such as basic, removable, or CD-ROM;

the disk capacity; and the status of the disk device, such as online or offline. Additional details are also provided for each logical disk on the physical disk, including the drive letter and text label for the associated partition or volume; the file system type, such as FAT, FAT32, or NTFS; the size of the drive section in megabytes (MB); and the local disk status, such as healthy or unhealthy.

- **Disk List view** Provides summary information about physical drives. This information includes the disk number and device type, such as basic, removable, or CD-ROM; the disk capacity; the size of unallocated space on the disk (if any); the status of the disk device, such as online or offline; and the device interface type, such as integrated device electronics (IDE), small computer system interface (SCSI), universal serial bus (USB), or FireWire (1394).

You can change the view for the top or bottom pane by using options on the View menu. To change the top view, click View, choose Top, and then select the view you want to use. To change the bottom view, click View, choose Bottom, and then select the view you want to use.

As you can see, the available views provide overviews of available disks. To get more detailed information on a local disk, right-click it in the Volume List view, and then click Properties. You'll see a dialog box much like the one shown in Figure 12-3. This is the same dialog box that you can access from Windows Explorer (by right-clicking the top-level icon for the drive, and then clicking Properties). Use the Customize tab to select a view template to determine what folders look like in Windows Explorer's Contents pane.

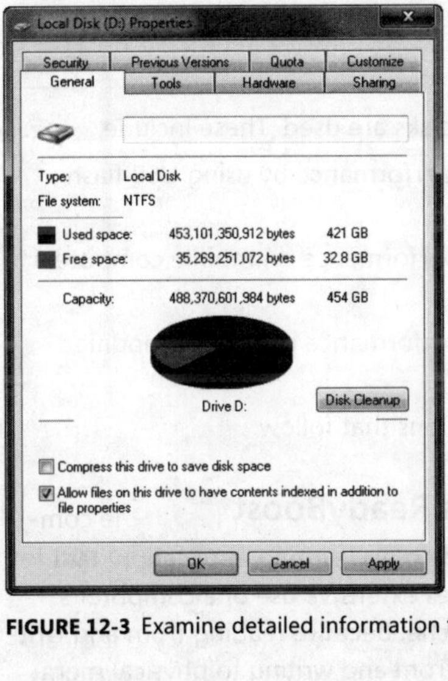

FIGURE 12-3 Examine detailed information for a drive in the Properties dialog box.

Using FSUtil and DiskPart

Windows 7 provides several command-line tools for working with disks, including the following:

- **FSUtil** Meant to be used by support professionals who need to manage disks at a fairly low level. Using FSUtil, you can examine and work with metadata and other information related to disks, including update sequence number (USN) change journals, reparse points, and hard links. You can also obtain detailed sector and cluster information, such as the number of free or reserved sectors on a disk. To learn more about FSUtil, type **fsutil** at an elevated command prompt.
- **DiskPart** A text-mode command interpreter that you can use to manage disks, partitions, and volumes from the command prompt. Not only can DiskPart perform many of the same operations as Disk Management, but it can also be used with scripts to automate disk management processes. You start DiskPart by typing **diskpart** at an elevated command prompt. You will then be at the DISKPART> prompt. If you type **help** and then press Enter, you will see a list of available commands and a description of their usage.

NOTE **Unlike Disk Management, which provides a friendly interface and is fairly easy to use, FSUtil and DiskPart are complex tools meant for advanced administrators. Their use is covered in detail in *Windows Command-Line Administrator's Pocket Consultant,* Second Edition (Microsoft Press, 2008). You'll find a detailed example of using DiskPart in the section "Marking a Partition as Active" later in this chapter.**

Improving Disk Performance

Windows 7 has several features that affect how disks are used. These include:

- **Windows ReadyBoost** Boosts system performance by using USB flash devices as additional sources for caching
- **Windows ReadyDrive** Boosts system performance on mobile computers equipped with hybrid drives
- **Windows SuperFetch** Boosts system performance by using a modified memory management algorithm

Each of these features is discussed in the sections that follow.

Understanding and Using Windows ReadyBoost

A computer's disk drives aren't used just for reading and writing application data and user documents. The operating system makes extensive use of a computer's disk drives for paging files and for the system cache. Because reading from and writing to a disk is significantly slower than reading from and writing to physical memory (RAM), these operations can cause a bottleneck that degrades performance.

Windows 7 includes Windows ReadyBoost as a way to reduce the impact related to reading and writing the system cache.

With Windows ReadyBoost, USB flash devices with sufficiently fast memory are used to extend the disk-caching capabilities of the computer's main memory. Using flash devices for caching allows Windows 7 to make random reads faster by caching data on the USB flash device instead of a disk drive. Because this caching is applied to all disk content, not just the page file or system dynamic-link libraries (DLLs), the computer's overall performance is boosted because flash devices can be read up to 10 times faster than physical disk drives.

USB flash devices that can be used with Windows ReadyBoost include USB 2.0 flash drives, Secure Digital (SD) cards, and CompactFlash cards. These devices must have sufficiently fast flash memory and be at least 256 MB or larger in size. To enhance performance, I recommend purchasing USB flash devices with high-speed memory. If the flash device has both slow and fast flash memory, only the fast flash memory portion will be used for boosting performance. From 230 MB to 4,094 MB of flash memory can be reserved on a USB flash device for ReadyBoost. A recommended amount of memory to use is from one to three times the available system memory. However, keep in mind that as of the time of this writing, the most you can reserve is 4,094 MB.

Memory on USB flash devices is primarily used for random input/output (I/O) because most flash devices are slower than a disk drive for sequential I/O. Windows ReadyBoost maximizes performance by automatically passing large, sequential read requests to the computer's disk drive for servicing. To allow a USB flash device to be removed at any time, all data writes are made to the hard disk before being copied to the flash device. This means all data stored on the flash device is duplicated on the hard disk, and there is no potential for data loss when removing the flash device. Additionally, because the flash device's memory might contain sensitive information, Windows ReadyBoost encrypts the data so that it can be used only with the computer on which it was originally written.

Enabling and Configuring ReadyBoost

With Windows ReadyBoost, USB flash devices with sufficiently fast flash memory can be used as additional sources of system cache. When you insert a USB flash device into a USB 2.0 or higher port, Windows 7 analyzes the speed of the flash memory on the device. If the flash memory performs at a sufficiently high speed, the computer's physical memory can be extended to the USB flash device. In most cases, you'll want the flash memory to be at least as fast as the computer's bus speed.

> ***TIP*** **Windows can incorrectly flag a device as failing to meet the performance requirements. If a device fails the initial performance test, you can retest the device by using the ReadyBoost tab. In Windows Explorer, right-click the device, and then click Properties. In the Properties dialog box, click the ReadyBoost tab, and then click Test Again.**

The following steps show how you can enable and configure how Windows ReadyBoost works the first time you use a USB flash device with a computer:

1. Insert a USB flash device into a USB 2.0 or higher port. The AutoPlay dialog box should be displayed automatically (unless you've changed the AutoPlay defaults in Control Panel).
2. When you click Speed Up My System Using Windows ReadyBoost, the device's Properties dialog box opens to the ReadyBoost tab, shown in Figure 12-4. Do one of the following, and then click OK:
   - If you want the device to automatically reserve the maximum amount of space for ReadyBoost, select Dedicate This Device To ReadyBoost. Choosing this setting does not prevent a user from writing files to the device. It simply configures ReadyBoost to use as much space as can be reserved.
   - If you want to use less space than the maximum possible, select Use This Device, and then use the Space To Reserve For System Speed slider or combo box to set the amount of space to use with ReadyBoost. If you reserve less than the total amount of space available, the free space can be used for files and data.

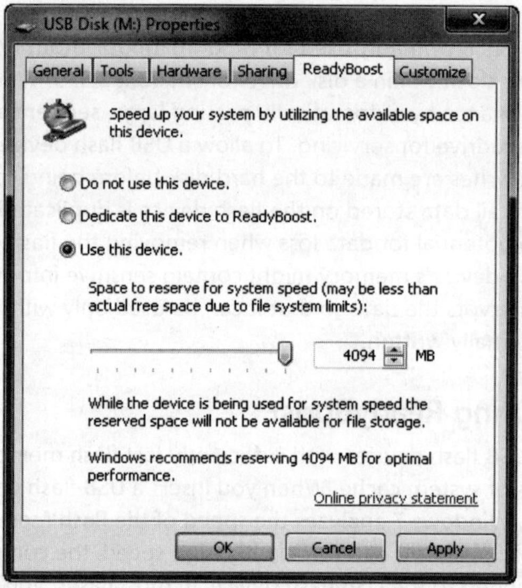

FIGURE 12-4 Configure Windows ReadyBoost settings.

Windows 7 extends the computer's physical memory to the device. The default configuration enables Windows ReadyBoost to reserve all available space on the device for boosting system speed.

REAL WORLD **To use a USB flash device with ReadyBoost, the device must have at least 2.5 megabits per second (Mbps) throughput for 4-kilobyte (KB) random reads and 1.75 Mbps throughput for 512-KB random writes. Although you can enable ReadyBoost on a device you've encrypted with BitLocker To Go, keep in mind that encryption and decryption processes can affect read/write performance. If you use BitLocker To Go and ReadyBoost, I recommend that you also automatically unlock the device when the device is inserted. Otherwise, the user has to validate the device prior to getting the performance benefits of ReadyBoost.**

To use Windows ReadyBoost with a USB flash device that you have already inserted or that you previously declined to use with Windows ReadyBoost, follow these steps:

1. Click Start, and then click Computer.
2. Right-click the USB flash device in the Devices With Removable Storage list, and then click Properties.
3. On the ReadyBoost tab, configure the options as discussed in step 2 of the previous procedure. Click OK.

For USB flash devices that do not support ReadyBoost, you cannot enable the device. You can safely remove a USB flash device that uses ReadyBoost at any time without losing data or negatively impacting the system. However, when the device is removed, system performance returns to its normal level—the performance level experienced without the device. To safely remove the device, follow these steps:

1. Open Windows Explorer or another Explorer view, such as Computer.
2. Right-click the device, and then click Eject. If you've opened files on the device or opened the device for viewing in Windows Explorer, you might need to close files and Explorer windows before you can eject the device.

Understanding and Using Windows ReadyDrive

Windows ReadyDrive improves performance on mobile computers equipped with hybrid drives. A hybrid drive is a drive that uses both flash RAM and a physical drive for storage. Because flash RAM is much faster than a physical disk, mobile computers running Windows 7 write data and changes to data to the flash memory first and periodically sync these writes and changes to the physical disk. This approach reduces the spinning of the physical drive and thus saves battery power.

The flash RAM on hybrid drives can be used to provide faster startup and resume from sleep or hibernation. In this case, the information needed for starting or resuming the operating system is written to the flash RAM prior to shutting down, entering sleep, or going into hibernation. When you start or wake the computer, this information is read from the flash RAM.

You do not need to enable ReadyDrive. ReadyDrive is enabled for use automatically on mobile computers with hybrid drives.

Understanding and Using Windows SuperFetch

Windows 7 improves performance and responsiveness by changing the way user processes and background processes are used. In Windows XP, user processes and background processes have the same memory-use prioritization: user processes and background processes are both loaded into memory as they are used. Because there is no prioritization, there is often contention for memory, and performance lags often occur as well because background processes remain resident in memory after they run. Therefore, data for user processes must be loaded into memory when it is requested. Windows 7 corrects this issue by ensuring that background processes are unloaded after they run and when data for user processes is reloading into memory.

In Windows XP, user processes and background processes have the same I/O priority, which often results in conflicts and poor read/write performance. Windows 7 corrects this by implementing high-priority I/O and low-priority I/O queues. High-priority I/O is used by user processes for read and write operations to physical drives. Low-priority I/O is used by background process read and write operations to physical drives.

> ***NOTE*** **With Windows 7, many services and routine housekeeping tasks run as background processes. For example, on Windows 7, Disk Defragmenter is scheduled to run automatically to periodically defragment disks. When Disk Defragmenter runs, it runs as a background process and uses low-priority I/O.**

The key feature that makes memory and I/O prioritization work is Windows SuperFetch. Windows SuperFetch improves system performance by using a modified memory-management algorithm. Unlike the memory-management algorithm in Windows XP and earlier versions of Windows, SuperFetch optimizes memory usage based on the way the current user is using the computer. SuperFetch does this by performing the following tasks:

- **Differentiating between user applications and background services running on the computer** SuperFetch makes the computer more responsive to user requests by prioritizing the current user's processes over background tasks. Because user processes always have priority over background tasks, background tasks do not take up all the processor time and the system remains responsive to user requests.
- **Optimizing memory for users after running background tasks** Housekeeping tasks on Windows 7 make better use of process idle time than they did on earlier versions of Windows. More system and maintenance tasks, such as Disk Defragmenter and Disk Backup, run during idle time. When the computer is idle, background processes run as they normally would. However, when background processes end, SuperFetch repopulates memory to the state it was in prior to running the background processes. This ensures that memory is optimized for user processes and that the computer is responsive to user requests.

- **Tracking the most frequently used applications and anticipating user needs** SuperFetch keeps track of which applications users run most frequently and also tracks when those applications are typically used. SuperFetch then uses the tracking information to preload the application and ready it for use when it expects that the user will need the application. This ensures faster startup for applications and faster user switching over time.
- **Taking advantage of the low-priority I/O designation** SuperFetch takes advantage of the high-priority I/O and low-priority I/O queues in Windows 7 to improve read/write times for user processes and improve a computer's overall responsiveness. When multiple processes are competing for I/O, high-priority processes always get more I/O time than low-priority processes do. As a result, user processes and applications have better performance, and there is less contention for I/O time when both user processes and background processes are running.

All versions of Windows 7 support SuperFetch. As an administrator, you should understand how SuperFetch works and the way it is configured. Some basic characteristics of SuperFetch follow.

- Runs as a service named SuperFetch. This service runs automatically at startup and logs on using the LocalSystem account.
- Uses the Svchost.exe executable, running in a network-restricted mode. This means SuperFetch can access only the local computer and doesn't have access to any networks to which the computer might be connected.
- Depends on the Filter Manager component for proper operations. Filter Manager provides file information and file-system information needed by SuperFetch, and it is installed automatically with the operating system.
- Writes prefetch data to the %SystemRoot%\Prefetch folder. The prefetch data is used to quickly start applications. Within the Prefetch folder, you'll also find several database files used to track application usage history and speed up application performance. Application faults are also tracked in a database history file.

NOTE **The Prefetch folder is self-maintaining. There's no need to delete it or empty its contents.**

When you make major changes to the operating system, install service packs or updates, or install or reconfigure applications, users may occasionally experience slow startup. The extent to which this occurs depends on how extensive the changes are and how much memory-usage information SuperFetch has to rebuild. Sometimes, such as when you install a new service pack, several restarts are required over time to normalize the startup speed.

Working with Basic and Dynamic Disks

Not that long ago, all Windows computers shipped with their hard disks configured as basic disks. Now, because people want larger or more robust disks, computer manufacturers have responded by shipping more computers with their hard disks configured as dynamic disks. Instead of having a single 500-GB drive, a new computer might have a spanned disk with 1,000 GB, where two 500-GB physical drives act as a single logical disk. In this scenario, disk spanning is used to make multiple disks appear to be a single disk. One way to implement this on Windows 7 is to use dynamic disks.

As more and more computers are shipped with dynamic disks, you might wonder whether your computers that use basic disks should be converted to dynamic disks. In some cases, the need for standardization might prompt your decision. For example, for better manageability, you might want all desktops in a particular department to have the same configuration. In other cases, IT management might direct the change because the conversion from basic disks to dynamic disks can be considered an upgrade process. (That is, you are moving computers from an older disk type to a newer disk type.) However, before you decide to move from one disk type to another, you should understand what is involved, what features are supported, and what features are not supported.

A basic disk is a physical disk that has one or more basic volumes that can be configured as primary partitions, plus an optional extended partition consisting of logical drives. A primary partition is a drive section that you can access directly for file storage. Each physical drive can have up to four primary partitions. You make a primary partition accessible to users by creating a file system on it. In place of one of the four permitted primary partitions, you can create an extended partition (meaning that the basic disk could have up to three primary partitions and one extended partition). Unlike with primary partitions, you can't access extended partitions directly. Instead, you can configure extended partitions with one or more logical drives that are used to store files. Being able to divide extended partitions into logical drives enables you to divide a physical drive into more than four sections. For example, you could create logical drives F, G, and H in a single extended partition.

A dynamic disk is a physical disk that has one or more dynamic volumes. Unlike a basic disk, a dynamic disk can have an unlimited number of volumes—any one of which can be extended or used as a system volume. Although basic disks can be used with any Windows-based operating system, dynamic disks can be used only with Windows 2000 or later releases. For example, if Disk 0 is a dynamic disk, you cannot boot that disk to Windows 98.

A key advantage of dynamic disks used to be their ability to combine physical disks using the spanning, striping, or mirroring features of Windows. However, Windows 7 allows you to span, stripe, or mirror basic disks as well. When you span or stripe drives, you create a single volume that extends from one disk to other disks, using all or part of each disk in the set. The difference between spanning and striping is how data is written. Windows 7 recognizes spanned disks in the same way it would a single partition, and write operations to the spanned disk are made to the entire partition randomly. With striping, Windows 7 writes a portion of the data to each of the underlying disks that make up the volume. In most cases, striping gives you faster read/write access to data because data is read from and written to multiple disks. With mirroring, two drives are combined to create a single fault-tolerant volume. If any one volume fails, the other volume in the set is still available, and the volume can be recovered.

CAUTION **Technically, disk striping is redundant array of independent disks (RAID) level 0 (RAID-0), and disk mirroring is RAID level 1 (RAID-1). Although disk mirroring is fault tolerant, neither disk striping nor spanning provides fault tolerance, and the failure of any disk in the set causes the volume to fail.**

Now, because you can span, stripe, and mirror drives using the basic disk type, the key features that distinguish dynamic disks from basic disks are enhanced error correction and detection and the ability to modify disks without having to restart the computer. Other features available on a disk depend on the disk formatting, such as whether you are using FAT, FAT32, or NTFS.

When you format a disk with a file system, the file system structures the disk using clusters, which are logical groupings of sectors. FAT, FAT32, and NTFS use a fixed sector size of 512 bytes but allow the cluster size to be variable. For example, the cluster size might be 4,096 bytes, so if there are 512 bytes per sector, each cluster is made up of eight sectors.

Table 12-1 provides a summary of the default cluster sizes for FAT16, FAT32, exFAT, and NTFS. You have the option of specifying the cluster size when you create a file system on a disk, or you can accept the default cluster-size setting. Either way, the cluster sizes available depend on the type of file system you are using.

REAL WORLD **Four FAT file systems are used by Windows platforms: FAT12, FAT16, FAT32, and exFAT. The difference between FAT12, FAT16, and FAT32 is the number of bits used for entries in their file allocation tables, namely 12, 16, or 32 bits. From a user's perspective, the main difference in these file systems is the theoretical maximum volume size, which is 16 MB for a FAT12 volume, 4 GB for FAT16, and 2 TB for FAT32. When the term FAT is used without an appended number, it generally refers to both FAT16 and FAT32. Extended FAT, or exFAT, is a new version of FAT for removable media. It is available with Windows Vista Service Pack 1 or later, Windows 7, and Windows Server 2008. Although exFAT retains the ease-of-use advantages of FAT32, it overcomes the 4-GB file-size limit and the 32-GB volume-size limit of FAT 32 file systems. The exFAT format also supports allocation unit sizes of up to 32,768 KB. The exFAT format is designed so that it can be used with and easily moved between any compliant operating system or device. This gives exFAT an advantage over FAT.**

TABLE 12-1 Default Cluster Sizes for FAT16, FAT32, exFAT, and NTFS

	CLUSTER SIZE			
VOLUME SIZE	**FAT16**	**FAT32**	**exFAT**	**NTFS**
7 MB to 16 MB	512 bytes	Not supported	Not supported	512 bytes
17 MB to 32 MB	512 bytes	Not supported	Not supported	512 bytes
33 MB to 64 MB	1 KB	512 bytes	4 KB	512 bytes
65 MB to 128 MB	2 KB	1 KB	4 KB	512 bytes
129 MB to 256 MB	4 KB	2 KB	4 KB	512 bytes
257 MB to 512 MB	8 KB	4 KB	32 KB	512 bytes
513 MB to 1,024 MB	16 KB	4 KB	32 KB	1 KB
1,025 MB to 2 GB	32 KB	4 KB	32 KB	2 KB
2 GB to 4 GB	64 KB	4 KB	32 KB	4 KB
4 GB to 8 GB	Not supported	4 KB	32 KB	4 KB
8 GB to 16 GB	Not supported	8 KB	32 KB	4 KB
16 GB to 32 GB	Not supported	16 KB	32 KB	4 KB
32 GB to 2 TB	Not supported	*	*	4 KB

**Using the Windows formatting tools you are limited to 32 GB. Larger volumes can be created using third-party tools.*

The important thing to know about clusters is that they are the smallest unit in which disk space is allocated. Each cluster can hold one file at most. So, if you create a 1 kilobyte (KB) file and the cluster size is 4 KB, there will be 3 KB of empty space in the cluster that isn't available to other files. That's just the way it is. If a single cluster isn't big enough to hold an entire file, the remaining file data goes into the next available cluster and then the next, until the file is completely stored. For FAT, for example, the first cluster used by the file has a pointer to the second cluster, and the second cluster has a pointer to the next, and so on until you get to the final cluster used by the file, which has an end-of-file (EOF) marker.

The disk I/O subsystem manages the physical structure of disks. Windows manages the logical disk structure at the file system level. The logical structure of a disk relates to the basic or dynamic volumes you create on a disk and the file systems with which those volumes are formatted. You can format both basic volumes and dynamic volumes using FAT or NTFS. Each file system type has a different structure, and there are advantages and disadvantages of each as well.

Although you can use both basic and dynamic disks on the same computer, the disks that make up a volume must use the same disk type. For example, if you have striped Disk 0 and Disk 1, which were created under Windows NT 4.0, you can use these drives under Windows 7. If you want to upgrade Disk 0 to the dynamic disk type, you must also upgrade Disk 1. Converting from basic to dynamic and vice versa is covered in the section "Converting a Basic Disk to a Dynamic Disk or Vice Versa" later in this chapter. Remember that although you can convert the disk type from basic to dynamic and preserve the data on the disk, you must delete any existing partitioning on a dynamic disk before you can convert from dynamic to basic. Deleting the partitioning destroys any data on the associated disks. Finally, dynamic disks cannot be created on any removable-media drives or on any disk on a portable computer. Laptops, Tablet PCs, and other types of portable computers can have only basic disks.

> ***CAUTION*** **Be careful when working with laptops. Some laptop configurations might make Disk Management think that you can convert a basic disk to a dynamic disk. This can occur on computers that do not support Advanced Power Management (APM) or Advanced Configuration and Power Interface (ACPI). Although support for dynamic disks might seem to be enabled, this is an error, and trying to convert a basic disk to a dynamic disk on one of these laptops could corrupt the entire disk.**

> ***NOTE*** **External hard drives attached via FireWire, USB, or eSATA can in some cases be converted to dynamic disks. Microsoft Knowledge Base article 299598, "How To: Convert an IEEE 1394 Disk Drive to a Dynamic Disk Drive in Windows XP," details how this can be done. However, this article doesn't provide enough cautions. The external hard drive must be used only with a single computer. If you think you will need to move the drive to another computer in the future, you shouldn't convert it to a dynamic disk. Further, before attempting to convert any external hard drive attached via FireWire or USB, you should back up the data. If possible, perform the conversion on an identical but nonessential drive in a development or testing environment and then test the drive operation.**

Using Basic and Dynamic Disks

When it comes to using basic and dynamic disks, you perform several related tasks, such as initializing new disks, setting a drive as active, or changing the drive type. Before performing these tasks, however, you should understand what the active, boot, system, and other drive designations mean.

Understanding Drive Designations

Whether working with basic or dynamic disks, you should pay particular attention to five special types of drive sections on MBR disks.

- **Active** The active partition or volume is the drive section from which an x86-based computer starts. If the computer uses multiple operating systems, the active drive section must contain the startup files for the operating system you want to start and it must be a primary partition on a basic disk or a simple volume on a dynamic disk. The active partition is not normally marked as such in Disk Management. In most cases, it is the primary partition or the first simple volume on Disk 0. However, if you change the default configuration, you will see an Active label.

CAUTION With removable media disks, you might see an Active status, which shouldn't be confused with the Active label associated with an active partition. Specifically, USB and FireWire card readers that use CompactFlash or other types of cards are displayed as having an Active status when media is inserted and the related drive is online. It is also important to note that in some cases, a removable media drive might be listed as Disk 0. In this case, you need to look for the active partition on the first physical hard disk according to its disk number. For example, if the computer has Disk 0, Disk 1, and Disk 2, and the first physical disk in sequence is Disk 1, the active partition is most likely on the first primary partition or simple volume on Disk 1.

- **System** The system partition or volume contains the hardware-specific (bootstrap) files needed to load the operating system. The system partition or volume can be mirrored but can't be part of a striped or spanned volume. The system partition is labeled as such in the Status field in Disk Management's Volume List and Graphical views.
- **Boot** The boot partition or volume contains the operating system and its support files. The boot partition or volume can be mirrored but can't be part of a striped or spanned volume. On most systems, system and boot are the same partition or volume. Although it seems that the boot and system partitions are named backward, this convention has been used since Windows NT was introduced and has not changed. Like the active partition, the boot partition is not normally marked as such in Disk Management. In most cases, it is the primary partition or the first simple volume on Disk 0. However, if the operating system is installed on a different partition or volume, you might see a Boot label.
- **Page file** A page file partition or volume contains a paging file used by the operating system. Because a computer can page memory to multiple disks, according to the way virtual memory is configured, a computer can have multiple page file partitions or volumes. However, depending on the service packs configured, the computer might only report the primary volume being used as a paging file. See the section "Configuring Virtual Memory" in Chapter 6 for details about using and configuring paging files.
- **Crash dump** The crash dump partition or volume is the one to which the computer attempts to write dump files in the event of a system crash. As discussed in Chapter 6 in the section "Configuring System Startup and Recovery," dump files can be used to diagnose the causes of system failure.

By default, dump files are written to the %SystemRoot% folder, but they can be located on any partition or volume.

Each computer has one active, one system, one boot, and one crash dump partition or volume and these partitions or volumes can be combined. The page file designation is the only drive designation that you might see on multiple partitions or volumes.

Installing and Initializing New Physical Disks

Windows 7 makes it much easier to add new physical disks to a computer. After you install the disks following the disk manufacturer's instructions, you need to log on and start Disk Management. If the new disks have already been initialized, meaning they already have disk signatures allowing them to be read and written to, they should be brought online automatically if you choose Rescan Disks from the Action menu. If you are working with new disks that have not been initialized, meaning they don't have disk signatures, Disk Management will start the Initialize And Convert Disk Wizard as soon as Disk Management starts and detects the new disks.

You can use the Initialize And Convert Disk Wizard to initialize the disks by completing the following steps:

1. Click Next to exit the Welcome page. On the Select Disks To Initialize page, the disks you added are selected for initialization automatically, but if you don't want to initialize a particular disk, you can clear the related option.
2. Click Next to display the Select Disks To Convert page. This page lists the new disks as well as any nonsystem or boot disks that can be converted to dynamic disks. The new disks aren't selected by default. If you want to convert the disks, select them, and then click Next.
3. The final page shows you the options you've selected and the actions that will be performed on each disk. If the options are correct, click Finish. The wizard then performs the designated actions. If you've elected to initialize a disk, the wizard writes a disk signature to the disk. If you've elected to convert a disk, the wizard converts the disk to a dynamic disk after writing the disk signature.

If you don't want to use the wizard, you can close it and use Disk Management instead to view and work with the disk. In the Disk List view, the disk is marked with a red icon that has an exclamation point, and the disk's status is listed as Not Initialized. Right-click the disk's icon, and then click Initialize Disk. Confirm the selection (or add to the selection if more than one disk is available for initializing), and then click OK to start the initialization of the disk. Conversion to a dynamic disk would proceed as discussed in the section "Converting a Basic Disk to a Dynamic Disk or Vice Versa."

Changing a Disk's Partition Table Style

You can change partition table styles from MBR to GPT or from GPT to MBR. Changing partition table styles is useful when you want to move disks between computers that have different processor architectures or you receive new disks that are formatted for the wrong partition table style. You can convert partition table styles only on empty disks, however. This means the disks must be either new or newly formatted. You could, of course, empty a disk by removing its partitions or volumes.

You can use both Disk Management and DiskPart to change the partition table style. To use Disk Management to change the partition style of an empty disk, start Computer Management from the Administrative Tools menu or type **compmgmt.msc** in the Search box on the Start menu and then press Enter. In Computer Management, expand the Storage node, and then select Disk Management. All available disks are displayed. Right-click the disk to convert in the Graphical view, and then click Convert To GPT Disk or Convert To MBR Disk, as appropriate.

To use DiskPart to change the partition style of an empty disk, invoke DiskPart by typing **diskpart**, and then select the disk you want to convert. For example, if you want to convert Disk 2, type **select disk 2**. After you select the disk, you can convert it from MBR to GPT by typing **convert gpt**. To convert a disk from GPT to MBR, type **convert mbr**.

Marking a Partition as Active

You don't normally need to change a partition's designation. If you are using only Windows 7 or if you are multibooting to Windows 7 and any other Windows operating system, you do not have to change the active partition, On an x86-based computer, the active partition is typically the primary partition or the first simple volume on Disk 0. If you install Windows 7 on drive C and Windows 2000 or a later version on a different partition, such as drive D, you don't need to change the active partition to boot Windows 7 or the other operating system. However, if you want to boot a non-Windows operating system, you usually have to mark its operating system partition as active and then reboot to use that operating system.

> ***NOTE*** **Only primary partitions can be marked as active. You can't mark logical drives as active. You can't mark volumes as active. When you upgrade a basic disk containing the active partition to a dynamic disk, this partition becomes a simple volume that's active automatically.**

To mark a partition as active, complete the following steps:

1. Make sure that the necessary startup files are on the primary partition that you want to make the active partition. For Windows NT, Windows 2000, and Windows XP, these files are Boot.ini, Ntdetect.com, Ntldr, and Bootsect.dos. You might also need Ntbootdd.sys.
2. Start Disk Management by typing **diskmgmt.msc** at an elevated command prompt.

3. Right-click the primary partition you want to mark as active, and then click Mark Partition As Active.

CAUTION **If you mark a partition or volume as active, Disk Management might not let you change the designation. As a result, if you restart the computer, the operating system might fail to load. The only workaround I've found is to use DiskPart to make the appropriate changes either before rebooting or before using the Startup Repair tool following a failed start.**

Listing 12-1 shows a sample DiskPart session for setting the active partition. As you can see, when you first start DiskPart, it shows the DiskPart program name and the version you are using, as well as the name of the computer. You then select the disk you want to work with and list its partitions. In this example, you select Disk 0 to work with, list its partitions, and then select Partition 1. Once you've selected a disk and a partition on that disk, you can work with that partition. Simply type the Active command at this point and press Enter to set the partition as active. When you have finished, quit DiskPart using the Exit command.

NOTE **This example uses Disk 0. On your system, Disk 0 might not be the one you want to work with. You can use the List Disk command to list the available disks and then use the information provided to determine which disk to work with.**

LISTING 12-1 Using DiskPart to Set the Active Partition

```
C:>diskpart

Microsoft DiskPart version 6.1.7200
Copyright (C) 1999-2008 Microsoft Corporation.
On computer: ENGPC85

DISKPART> select disk 0

Disk 0 is now the selected disk.

DISKPART> list partition

  Partition ###  Type              Size     Offset
  -------------  ----------------  -------  -------
  Partition 1    Primary           932 GB   1024 KB

DISKPART> select partition 1

Partition 1 is now the selected partition.

DISKPART> active

DiskPart marked the current partition as active.

DISKPART> exit
```

Converting a Basic Disk to a Dynamic Disk or Vice Versa

The easiest way to convert a basic disk to a dynamic disk or vice versa is to use Disk Management. When you upgrade to a dynamic disk, partitions are automatically changed to volumes of the appropriate type. Any primary partitions become simple volumes. Any logical drives in an extended partition become simple volumes. Any unused (free) space in an extended partition is marked as Unallocated. You can't change these volumes back to partitions. Instead, you must delete the volumes on the dynamic disk and then change the disk back to a basic disk. Deleting the volumes destroys all the information on the disk.

Before you convert a basic disk to a dynamic disk, you should be sure that you don't need to boot the computer to a previous version of Windows. You should also be sure that the disk has 1 MB of free space at the end of the disk. Although Disk Management reserves this free space when creating partitions and volumes, disk management tools on other operating systems might not; as a result, the conversion will fail. It is also important to note the following restrictions:

- You can't convert removable media to dynamic disks. You can configure removable media drives only as basic drives with primary partitions.
- You can convert disks' non-system and non-boot partitions that are part of spanned or striped volumes. These volumes become dynamic volumes of the same type. However, you must convert all drives in the set together.

To convert a basic disk to a dynamic disk, complete the following steps:

1. In Disk Management, either in the Disk List view or in the left pane of the Graphical view, right-click a basic disk that you want to convert, and then click Convert To Dynamic Disk.
2. In the Convert To Dynamic Disk dialog box, select the check boxes for the disks you want to convert, as shown in Figure 12-5. If you're upgrading a striped volume originally created on Windows NT, be sure to select all the basic disks in this set. You must convert the set together.

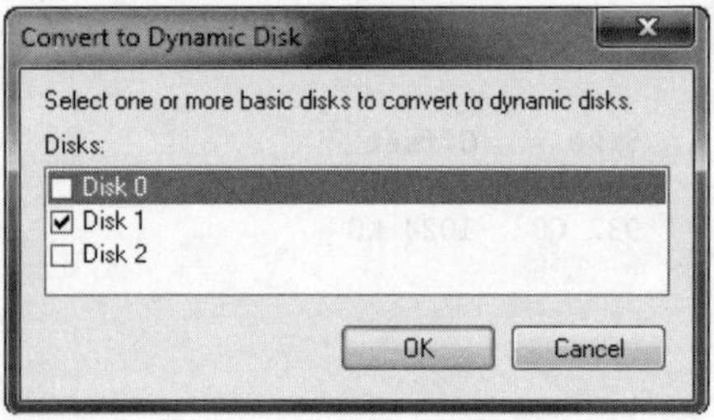

FIGURE 12-5 Select the basic disk to convert.

3. If the disk you are converting has no formatted volumes, clicking OK converts the disk, and you do not need to follow the remaining steps. If the disk you are converting has formatted volumes, clicking OK displays the Disks To Convert dialog box. Follow the remaining steps to complete the conversion.
4. The Disks To Convert dialog box shows the disks you're converting so that you can confirm the conversion. Notice the value in the Will Convert column, which should be Yes as long as the disk meets the conversion criteria, and then click Details to see the volumes on the selected drive. When you are ready to continue, click OK to close the Convert Details dialog box.
5. To begin the conversion, click Convert. Disk Management warns you that once you convert the disk, you won't be able to boot previous versions of Windows from volumes on the selected disks. Click Yes to continue.
6. Next, you are warned that file systems on the disks to be converted will be dismounted, meaning they will be taken offline and be inaccessible temporarily. Click Yes to continue. If a selected drive contains the boot partition, the system partition, or a partition in use, Disk Management will need to restart the computer, and you will see another prompt.

To convert a dynamic disk to a basic disk, complete the following steps:

1. Before you can change a dynamic disk to a basic disk, you must delete all dynamic volumes on the disk. Because this destroys all the data on the volumes, you should back up the volumes and then verify the backups before making the change.
2. When you are ready to start the conversion process, start Disk Management. In Disk Management, right-click the disk you want to convert, and then click Convert To Basic Disk. This changes the dynamic disk to a basic disk, and you can then create new partitions and logical drives on the disk.

Working with Disks, Partitions, and Volumes

Before you can store data on a physical disk, you must prepare the disk by setting a disk type, partitioning its space, assigning a drive designator, and formatting its partitions or volumes.

After partitioning a disk, you must assign each partition or volume a drive designator. The drive designator can be a letter or a path. You use drive letters to access file systems in various partitions on physical drives. Generally speaking, the drive letters A through Z are available. However, the drive letter A is usually assigned to a system's floppy drive. If the system has a second floppy drive or another removable-media drive, the letter B is usually assigned to it (or unassigned otherwise). The drive letter C is usually assigned to the first partition or volume created on Disk 0. The drive letter D is usually assigned to the first CD-ROM or DVD-ROM drive. Thus, on most systems, the drive letters E through Z are available. If you need additional volumes, you can create them using drive paths.

A drive path is set as a folder location on an existing local disk. For example, you could mount additional drives as C:\Docs1, C:\Docs2, and C:\Docs3. Drive paths can be used with basic and dynamic disks. The only restriction for drive paths is that you mount them on empty folders that are on NTFS-formatted local disks.

Formatting a partition or a volume sets the file system that will be used and creates the necessary file structures. In general, you can format a partition or a volume as FAT, FAT32, or NTFS. There are restrictions and requirements for the use of each, however.

FAT, also referred to as FAT16, is a 16-bit file system designed to be used with volume sizes of up to 4 GB. FAT uses a boot sector that stores information about the disk type, the starting and ending sectors, and the active partition. FAT gets its name from the file allocation table it uses to track the cluster locations of files and folders. There is a primary table and a duplicate table. The duplicate is used to restore the primary table if it becomes corrupted. FAT also has the capability to mark clusters (sections of disk containing data) as unused, in use, bad, or reserved. This helps to make FAT a fairly robust file system. FAT is best with volumes of 2 GB or less, and it has a maximum file size of 2 GB. FAT can also be used with floppy disks and removable disks.

FAT32 is a 32-bit version of FAT16, with some additional features and capabilities. Like FAT16, FAT32 uses a primary and a duplicate file allocation table. FAT32 can also mark clusters as unused, in use, bad, or reserved, and it too can be used with floppy disks and removable disks. FAT32 has a minimum volume size of 33 MB, a maximum volume size of 32 GB, and a maximum file size of 4 GB. This means that FAT32 can be used with considerably larger partitions and volumes than FAT16.

NOTE **The 4-GB maximum file-size limitation for FAT32 is specific to Windows 2000 and later versions of Windows. With FAT32, some earlier versions of Windows can create volumes of larger size, as can other operating systems.**

NTFS is very different from FAT16 and FAT32. Instead of using a file allocation table, NTFS uses a relational database to store information about files and folders. This database is called the master file table (MFT), and it stores a record of each file and folder on a volume, as well as additional information that helps to maintain the volume. Overall, the MFT makes NTFS much more reliable and recoverable than FAT16 or FAT32. NTFS can recover from disk errors more readily than FAT16 and FAT32 can, and NTFS generally has fewer disk problems.

NTFS has a maximum volume size of 2 TB (terabytes, or trillion bytes) or higher (depending on disk configuration) and a maximum file size that is limited only by the volume size. Although you can't use NTFS with floppy disks, you can use NTFS with removable disks. Additionally, unlike FAT16 and FAT32, which have limited security features (namely that you can mark a file only as read-only, hidden, or system), NTFS has advanced security that lets you use permissions to set specific file and folder access. NTFS supports many other advanced features, including compression, encryption, and disk quotas.

NOTE Several versions of NTFS have been implemented. NTFS 4 was first available with Windows NT. NTFS 5 was first available with Windows 2000. NTFS 5.1 was first available with Windows XP. Because most current computers have NTFS 5 or later, I focus on NTFS 5 and later in this book. Also, if you upgrade a system with a version older than the current version, you are given the opportunity to convert existing NTFS volumes to the latest version during installation. In most cases, you want to do this because it ensures support for the latest NTFS features.

Partitioning Disks and Preparing Them for Use

Disk Management is the primary tool that you use to partition disks and prepare them for use. Using Disk Management, you can partition disks, assign drive designators, and format partitions and volumes. Disk Management's command-line counterparts include DiskPart for partitioning and drive-designator assignment and Format for formatting.

Creating Partitions, Logical Drives, and Simple Volumes

Windows 7 simplifies the Disk Management user interface by using one set of dialog boxes and wizards for both partitions and volumes. The first three volumes on a basic drive are created automatically as primary partitions. If you try to create a fourth volume on a basic drive, the remaining free space on the drive is converted automatically to an extended partition with a logical drive of the size you designate. You designate the size by using the new volume feature it created in the extended partition. Any subsequent volumes are created in the extended partitions and logical drives automatically.

NOTE As discussed previously, an MBR drive can have four primary partitions. However, if you create a fourth primary partition, you are unable to further divide the drive, and this is why Windows 7 automatically creates an extended partition. The extended partition allows you to create multiple logical drives within the partition.

In Disk Management, you create partitions, logical drives, and simple volumes by completing the following steps:

1. In Disk Management's Graphical view, right-click an unallocated or free area, and then click New Simple Volume. This starts the New Simple Volume Wizard. Read the Welcome page, and then click Next.
2. The Specify Volume Size page, shown in Figure 12-6, specifies the minimum and maximum size for the volume in megabytes and lets you size the volume within these limits. Size the partition in megabytes using the Simple Volume Size field, and then click Next.

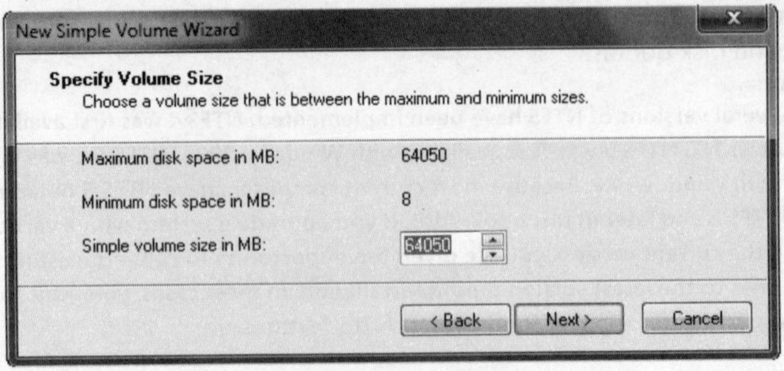

FIGURE 12-6 Set the size of the volume.

3. On the Assign Drive Letter Or Path page, shown in Figure 12-7, specify whether you want to assign a drive letter or path, and then click Next. The available options are as follows:
   - **Assign The Following Drive Letter** Select an available drive letter in the selection list provided. By default, Windows 7 selects the lowest available drive letter and excludes reserved drive letters as well as those assigned to local disks or network drives.
   - **Mount In The Following Empty NTFS Folder** Choose this option to mount the partition in an empty NTFS folder. You must then type the path to an existing folder or click Browse to search for or create a folder to use.
   - **Do Not Assign A Drive Letter Or Drive Path** Choose this option if you want to create the partition without assigning a drive letter or path. Later, if you want the partition to be available for storage, you can assign a drive letter or path at that time.

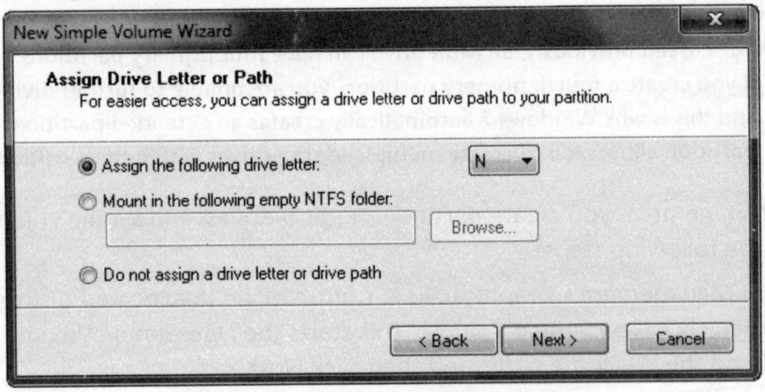

FIGURE 12-7 Assign the drive designator or choose to wait until later.

NOTE Volumes don't have to be assigned a drive letter or a path. A volume with no designators is considered to be unmounted and is for the most part unusable. An unmounted volume can be mounted by assigning a drive letter or a path at a later date. See the section "Assigning, Changing, or Removing Drive Letters and Paths" later in this chapter.

4. Use the Format Partition page, shown in Figure 12-8, to determine whether and how the volume should be formatted. If you want to format the volume, choose Format This Volume With The Following Settings, and then configure the following options:
   - **File System** Sets the file system type as FAT, FAT32, or NTFS. NTFS is selected by default in most cases. If you create a file system as FAT or FAT32, you can later convert it to NTFS by using the Convert utility. You can't, however, convert NTFS partitions to FAT or FAT32.
   - **Allocation Unit Size** Sets the cluster size for the file system. This is the basic unit in which disk space is allocated. The default allocation unit size is based on the size of the volume and, by default, is set dynamically prior to formatting. To override this feature, you can set the allocation unit size to a specific value. If you use many small files, you might want to use a smaller cluster size, such as 512 or 1,024 bytes. With these settings, small files use less disk space.
   - **Volume Label** Sets a text label for the partition. This label is the partition's volume name and by default is set to New Volume. You can change the volume label at any time by right-clicking the volume in Windows Explorer, choosing Properties, and typing a new value in the Label field provided on the General tab.
   - **Perform A Quick Format** Tells Windows 7 to format without checking the partition for errors. With large partitions, this option can save you a few minutes. However, it's usually better to check for errors, which enables Disk Management to mark bad sectors on the disk and lock them out.
   - **Enable File And Folder Compression** Turns on compression for the disk. Built-in compression is available only for NTFS. Under NTFS, compression is transparent to users and compressed files can be accessed just like regular files. If you select this option, files and directories on this drive are compressed automatically. For more information on compressing drives, files, and directories, see the section "Compressing Drives and Data" later in this chapter.

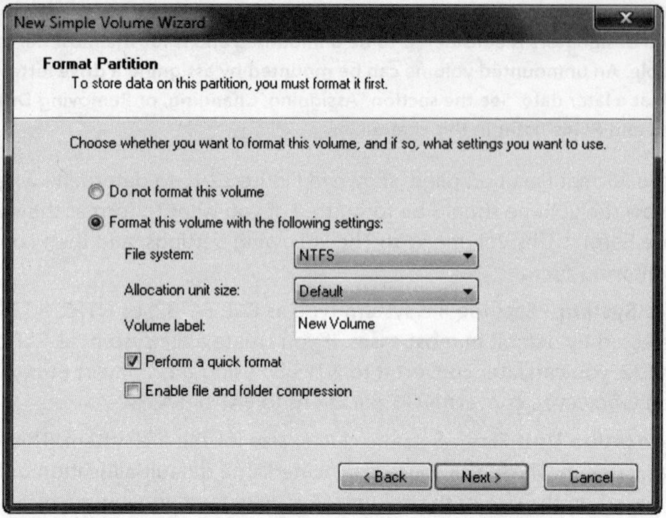

FIGURE 12-8 Set the formatting options for the partition.

5. Click Next, confirm your options, and then click Finish.

Creating Spanned and Striped Volumes

With spanning and striping, you create a single volume that extends across multiple disks. When working with spanning and striping, keep the following in mind:

- A spanned volume uses free space on multiple disks of the same type. If you have unallocated space on two or more disks of the same type, you can combine this space to create a spanned volume. A spanned volume has no fault tolerance and has average read/write performance. Files are written to the entire spanned volume randomly. If any one of the disks fails, the entire volume fails as well, and all data is lost.
- A striped volume uses free space on multiple disks and stripes the data as it is written. Striping gives you faster read/write access to data because data is read from and written to multiple disks. For example, with a three-disk striped volume, data from a file will be written to Disk 1, then to Disk 2, and then to Disk 3 in 64-KB blocks. Like a spanned volume, a striped volume has no fault tolerance, so if any one of the disks fails, the entire volume fails as well, and all data is lost.

NOTE **If you have only one disk available, you will not be able to create a spanned or striped volume. Also note that simple and spanned volumes can be extended to increase their volume size. Striped volumes, however, cannot be extended. When you create a striped volume, you should be very certain that the volume size is what you want to use. Otherwise, you might have to delete and then re-create the striped volume.**

In Disk Management, you create spanned or striped volumes on disks by completing the following steps:

1. In Disk Management's Graphical view, right-click an unallocated area, and then click New Spanned Volume or New Striped Volume, as appropriate. Read the Welcome page, and then click Next. Keep in mind that although Windows 7 supports spanning and striping on basic disks, some basic disks cannot be spanned or striped.
2. On the Select Disks page, shown in Figure 12-9, select the disks that will be part of the volume and specify the size of the volume segments on those disks. The disks must be the same disk type, either basic or dynamic. Click Next.

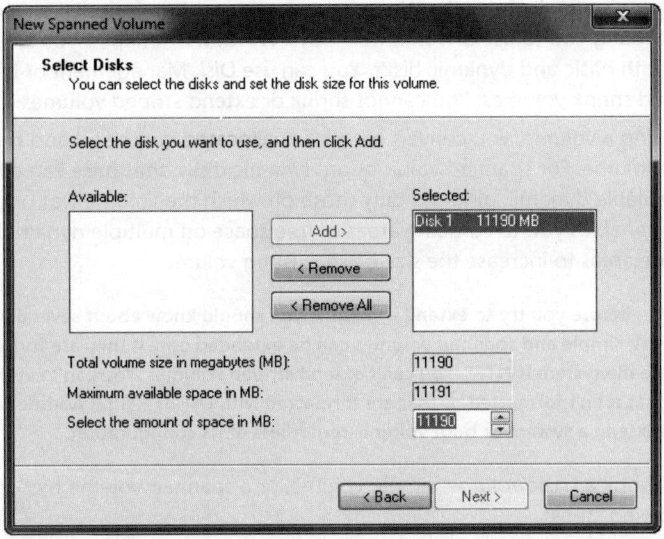

FIGURE 12-9 Specify the amount of space to use for each volume.

Available disks are shown in the Available list. Select a disk in this list, and then click Add to add the disk to the Selected list. If you make a mistake, you can remove a disk from the Selected list by selecting the disk and then clicking Remove.

Specify the space that you want to use on each disk by selecting each disk in the Selected list and then using the Select The Amount Of Space In MB field to specify the amount of space to use. Keep in mind that the Maximum field shows you the largest area of free space available on the selected disk, and the Total Volume Size field shows the total disk space currently allocated to the volume.

TIP **There's a quick way to use the same amount of space on all selected disks. To do this, highlight each disk by pressing Shift and then clicking the first disk and the last disk in the Selected list. Now, when you set the amount of space to use, you'll set the amount for all selected disks.**

3. Follow steps 3–5 in the previous section, "Creating Partitions, Logical Drives, and Simple Volumes."

Shrinking or Extending Volumes

Windows 7 doesn't user Ntldr and Boot.ini to load the operating system. Instead, Windows 7 has a preboot environment in which Windows Boot Manager is used to control startup and load the boot application you've selected. The Windows Boot Manager also finally frees the Windows operating system from its reliance on MS-DOS, enabling you to use drives in new ways. Windows 7 enables you to extend and shrink both basic and dynamic disks. You can use Disk Management or DiskPart to extend and shrink volumes. You cannot shrink or extend striped volumes.

In extending a volume, you convert areas of unallocated space and add them to the existing volume. For spanned volumes on dynamic disks, the space can come from any available dynamic disk, not only those on which the volume was originally created. This enables you to combine areas of free space on multiple dynamic disks and use those areas to increase the size of an existing volume.

CAUTION **Before you try to extend a volume, you should know about several limitations. First, simple and spanned volumes can be extended only if they are formatted and the file system is NTFS. You can't extend striped volumes. You can't extend volumes that aren't formatted or that are formatted with FAT or FAT32. Additionally, you can't extend a system or boot volume, regardless of its configuration.**

You can shrink a basic volume, simple volume, or a spanned volume by completing the following steps:

1. In Disk Management, right-click the volume that you want to shrink, and then click Shrink Volume. This option is available only if the volume meets the previously discussed criteria.
2. In the field provided in the Shrink dialog box, shown in Figure 12-10, enter the amount of space by which to shrink the disk. The Shrink dialog box provides the following information:
   - **Total Size Before Shrink In MB** Lists the total capacity of the volume in MB. This is the formatted size of the volume.
   - **Size Of Available Shrink Space In MB** Lists the maximum amount by which you can shrink the volume. This doesn't represent the total amount of free space on the volume; rather, it represents the amount of space that can be removed, not including any data reserved for the master file table, volume snapshots, page files, and temporary files.

- **Enter The Amount of Space To Shrink In MB** Lists the total amount of space that will be removed from the volume. The initial value defaults to the maximum amount of space that can be removed from the volume. For optimal drive performance, you should ensure that the volume has at least 10 percent of free space after the shrink operation.
- **Total Size After Shrink In MB** Lists what the total capacity of the volume in MB will be after you shrink the volume. This is the new formatted size of the volume.

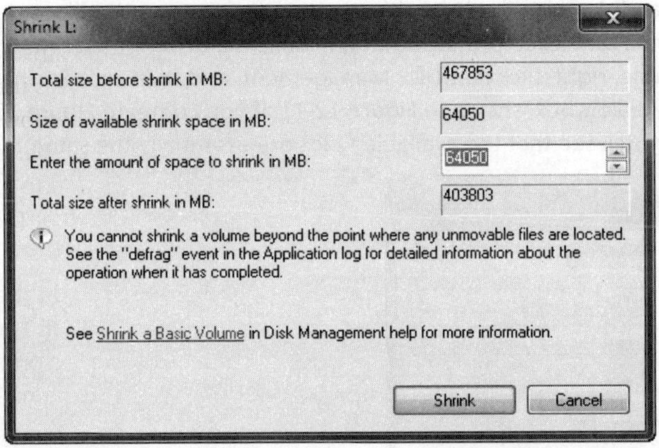

FIGURE 12-10 Specify the amount of space by which to shrink a volume.

3. Click Shrink.

You can extend a basic volume, simple volume, or a spanned volume by completing the following steps:

1. In Disk Management, right-click the volume that you want to extend, and then click Extend Volume. This option is available only if the volume meets the previously discussed criteria and free space is available on one or more of the system's disks.
2. In the Extend Volume Wizard, read the introductory message, and then click Next.
3. On the Select Disks page, shown earlier in Figure 12-9, select the disk or disks from which you want to allocate free space. Any disks currently being used by the volume will automatically be selected. By default, all remaining free space on those disks will be selected for use.
4. You can specify the additional space that you want to use on other disks by performing the following tasks:
   - In the Available list, click the disk, and then click Add to add the disk to the Selected list.

- Select each disk in the Selected list, and then use the Select The Amount Of Space In MB field to specify the amount of unallocated space to use on the selected disk.

5. Click Next, confirm your options, and then click Finish.

Formatting Partitions and Volumes

When you format a partition or a volume, you create a file system that can be used to store data and that permanently deletes any existing data in the associated section of the physical disk. This is high-level formatting that creates the file system structure rather than low-level formatting that initializes a drive for use. To format a partition or a volume, right-click it in Disk Management, and then click Format. This opens the Format dialog box, shown in Figure 12-11. If you compare Figure 12-11 with Figure 12-8, you'll see that the available fields are essentially the same.

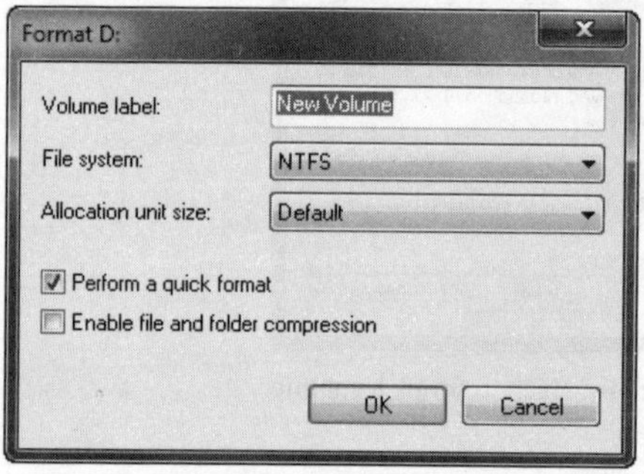

FIGURE 12-11 Use the Format dialog box to format a partition or a volume by specifying its file system type and volume label.

After selecting the appropriate options, click OK. Because formatting a partition destroys any existing data, Disk Management gives you one last chance to stop the procedure. Click OK to start formatting the partition. Disk Management then changes the status of the drive to reflect the formatting and, unless you are using the Perform A Quick Format option, the percentage of completion. When formatting is complete, the drive status will change to indicate that formatting is complete.

Assigning, Changing, or Removing Drive Letters and Paths

Each primary partition, logical drive, or volume on a computer can be assigned one driver letter and one or more drive paths, provided that the drive paths are mounted on empty NTFS folders. Once assigned, the drive letter or path remains the same each time you start the computer. Except on partitions or volumes that are designated as system or boot, you can change the drive letter or path assignment at any time. You can also remove a drive letter or path assignment, except on partitions or volumes that are designated as system or boot.

NOTE The drive letter or path assignment for the system or boot volume can be changed only by editing the registry. The procedure for making the change for Windows 2000 is described in Microsoft Knowledge Base article 223188. The procedure for making the change for Windows 7 is the same. However, it is important to be aware that if anything goes wrong during this procedure, you will probably be unable to boot the system and might have to recover the computer from backups.

To manage a partition's or a volume's drive letters or paths, go to Disk Management. In either the Volume List view or the Graphical view, right-click the partition or volume you want to configure, and then click Change Drive Letter And Paths. This opens the dialog box shown in Figure 12-12. You can now perform the following actions:

- **Add a drive path** Click Add, select Mount In The Following Empty NTFS Folder, and then type the path to an existing folder. You can also click Browse to search for or create a folder.
- **Remove a drive path** Select the drive path to remove, click Remove, and then click Yes.
- **Assign a drive letter** Click Add, select Assign The Following Drive Letter, and then choose an available letter to assign to the drive.
- **Change the drive letter** Select the current drive letter, and then click Change. Select Assign The Following Drive Letter, and then choose a different letter to assign to the drive.
- **Remove a drive letter** Select the current drive letter, click Remove, and then click Yes.

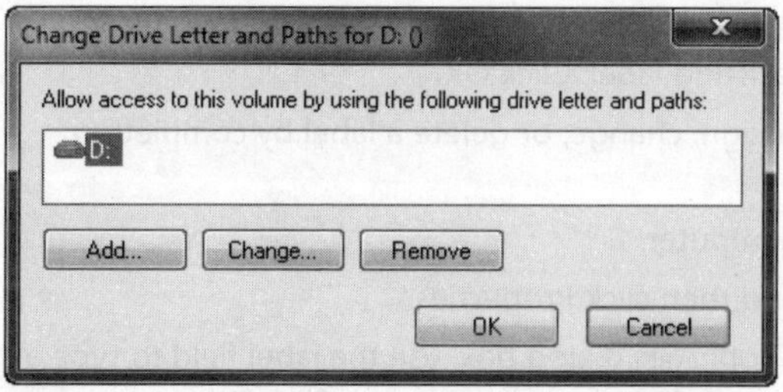

FIGURE 12-12 Use this dialog box to change or remove drive letter and path assignments.

NOTE If you try to change the letter of a drive that's in use, Windows 7 displays a warning. You need to exit programs that are using the drive and try again or allow Disk Management to force the change by clicking Yes when prompted.

REAL WORLD If the drive letter you want to use isn't available, it means it is in use or reserved for another purpose. Sometimes, you can resolve this problem by swapping drive letters. For example, if drive D is being used by the CD-ROM drive and drive E is a local disk, you might want to swap these letters so that D is used by

the local disk and E is used by the CD-ROM drive. To do this, you must remove the drive letter assigned to the CD-ROM and free drive letter D for use. Next, set the drive letter assignment for the local disk to D. This frees up E, which you can assign to the CD-ROM drive. Keep in mind that changing the letter of a drive can have unintended consequences. For example, the path to an application might be stored in the registry with the drive letter. This path would no longer be valid if you change the drive letter. Shortcuts to files or programs on the drive would be affected by the drive letter change as well and would need to be modified or re-created.

Assigning, Changing, or Deleting a Volume Label

A volume label is a text descriptor for a partition or a volume. The volume label is displayed when the drive is accessed in various Windows 7 utilities, such as Windows Explorer and Computer, and is designed to provide additional descriptive information about the contents of a drive.

> ***NOTE*** **With FAT and FAT32, the volume label can be up to 11 characters in length and can include spaces. With NTFS, the volume label can be up to 32 characters in length. FAT and FAT32 don't allow you to use some special characters, including * / \ [ ] : ; | = , . + " ? < >, that NTFS does allow.**

You can assign, change, or delete a volume label using either Disk Management or Windows Explorer. In Disk Management, you can assign, change, or delete a label by completing the following steps:

1. Right-click the partition or volume you want to work with, and then click Properties.
2. On the General tab of the Properties dialog box, use the label field to type a new label or to delete the existing label. Click OK.

In Windows Explorer, you can assign, change, or delete a label by completing these steps:

1. Click Start, and then click Computer.
2. Right-click the drive icon, and then click Properties.
3. On the General tab of the Properties dialog box, use the label field to type a new label for the volume or to delete the existing label. Click OK.

Deleting Partitions, Volumes, and Logical Drives

To change the configuration of an existing drive that's fully allocated, you might need to delete existing partitions, logical drives, or volumes. Because this deletion is irreversible, you should always back up and verify any important files and folders before deleting a partition, a logical drive, or a volume. If a computer has spanned or striped volumes, be careful when deleting volumes. Deleting any volume in a set erases the entire volume set, meaning the entire volume and all its data are lost.

CAUTION **Deleting a partition, a logical drive, or a volume is a drastic step that cannot be reversed. It removes the associated file system, and all data in the file system is lost.**

NOTE **To protect the integrity of the system, you can't delete the system or boot partition. However, Windows 7 lets you delete the active partition or volume if it is not designated as boot or system. Always check to be sure that the partition or volume you are deleting doesn't contain important data or files.**

You can delete a primary partition, a volume, or a logical drive by completing the following steps:

1. In Disk Management, right-click the partition, volume, or drive you want to delete, and then click Explore. Using Windows Explorer, move all the data to another volume or verify an existing backup to ensure that the data was properly saved.
2. In Disk Management, right-click the partition, volume, or drive again, and then click Delete Partition, Delete Volume, or Delete Logical Drive, as appropriate.
3. Click Yes to confirm that you want to delete the selected item.

Deleting an extended partition is a slightly different operation from deleting a primary partition or a logical drive. To delete an extended partition, you must first delete all the logical drives on the partition by following the steps in the preceding procedure. You can then select the extended partition area itself and delete it.

Converting a Volume to NTFS

Windows 7 provides a command-line utility for converting FAT or FAT32 volumes to NTFS. This utility, named Convert (Convert.exe), is located in the %SystemRoot%\System32 folder. When you convert a volume using this tool, the file and directory structure is preserved and no data is lost.

CAUTION **Windows 7 doesn't provide a utility for converting NTFS to FAT or FAT32. The only way to go from NTFS to FAT or FAT32 is to delete the partition by following the steps outlined in the previous section and then re-create the partition as a FAT or FAT32 volume.**

If you want to convert a drive, use the following syntax at an elevated command prompt:

```
convert volume /FS:NTFS
```

where *volume* is the drive letter followed by a colon (:), a drive path, or a volume name. For example, if you want to convert drive D to NTFS, you would use the following command:

```
convert D: /FS:NTFS
```

The complete syntax for the *Convert* command is:

```
convert volume /FS:NTFS [/V] [/X] [/CvtArea:filename] [/NoSecurity]
```

These options and switches are used as follows:

- **volume** Sets the volume to work with and must include the full drive designator (the drive letter followed by a colon). You also can specify a mount point or volume name.
- **/FS:NTFS** Converts the designated volume to NTFS. This is the only file system option.
- **/V** Sets verbose mode, which provides more detail in the output.
- **/X** Forces the volume to dismount before the conversion (if necessary).
- **/CvtArea:*filename*** Specifies a contiguous file in the root directory to be the placeholder for the NTFS system files stored on the MFT. If you omit a file name, Convert uses the default configuration and reserves 12.5 percent of the partition or volume size. This helps to prevent fragmentation of the MFT.
- **/NoSecurity** Sets the NTFS security settings on all files and folders so that the Everyone group can access them. This effectively makes the entire file system accessible to anyone who can access the system locally or remotely.

Before starting the conversion, the Convert command checks whether the drive has enough free space to perform the conversion. Generally, Convert needs a block of free space that's equal to roughly 25 percent of the total space used on the drive. For example, if the drive stores 100 MB of data, Convert needs about 25 MB of free space. If there isn't enough free space, Convert cancels the operation and tells you that you need to free up some space. On the other hand, if there is enough free space, Convert initiates the conversion. Be patient. The conversion process takes several minutes (longer for large drives). Don't access files or applications on the drive while the conversion is in progress.

NOTE **Before using the Convert command, double-check whether the partition is being used as the active boot partition or a system partition containing the operating system. With Intel x86 systems, you can convert the active boot partition to NTFS. Doing so requires that the system gain exclusive access to this partition, which can be obtained only during startup. Thus, if you try to convert the active boot partition to NTFS, Windows 7 displays a prompt asking if you want to schedule the drive to be converted the next time the system starts. If you click Yes, you can restart the system to begin the conversion process. Often several restarts of a system are required to completely convert the active boot partition. Don't panic. Let the system proceed with the conversion.**

REAL WORLD You can improve performance on the volume using the /CvtArea option so that space for the MFT is reserved. This option helps prevent fragmentation of the MFT. How? Over time, the MFT might grow larger than the space allocated to it. The operating system must then expand the MFT into other areas of the disk. Although the Windows 7 Disk Defragmenter utility can defragment the MFT, it cannot move the first section of the MFT, and it is very unlikely there will be space after the MFT because this will be filled by file data.

To help prevent fragmentation in some cases, you might want to reserve more space than the default (12.5 percent of the partition or volume size). For example, you might want to increase the size of the MFT if the volume will have many small or average-size files rather than a few large files. To specify the amount of space to reserve, you can use FSUtil to create a placeholder file equal in size to that of the MFT you want to create. You can then convert the volume to NTFS and specify the name of the placeholder file to use with the /CvtArea option.

Here, I use FSUtil to create a 1.5 GB (1,500,000,000 bytes) placeholder file named Temp.txt:

```
fsutil file createnew c:\temp.txt 1500000000
```

To use this placeholder file for the MFT when converting drive C to NTFS, you would type the following command:

```
convert c: /fs:ntfs /cvtarea:temp.txt
```

Notice that the placeholder file is created on the partition or volume that is being converted. During the conversion process, the file is overwritten with NTFS metadata and any unused space in the file is reserved for future use by the MFT.

Recovering a Failed Simple, Spanned, or Striped Volume

Basic partitions and simple volumes are fairly easy to troubleshoot and recover because only one disk is involved. Spanned or striped volumes, on the other hand, might have multiple disks, and the failure of any one disk makes the entire volume unusable. The drive status might show that the drive is Missing, Failed, Online (Errors), Offline, or Unreadable.

You might see the Missing (and sometimes Offline) status if drives have been disconnected or turned off. If the drives are part of an external storage device, check the storage device to ensure that it is connected properly and has power. Reconnecting the storage device or turning on the power should make the drives accessible. You then must start Disk Management and rescan the missing drive. Right-click the missing drive, and then click Rescan Disks. When Disk Management finishes, right-click the drive, and then click Reactivate.

You might see the Failed, Online (Errors), and Unreadable status notifications if a drive has I/O problems. As before, try rescanning the drive and then try to reactivate it. If the drive doesn't come back to the Healthy state, you might need to replace it.

TIP Sometimes you might need to reboot the computer to get a disk back online. If this still doesn't resolve the problem, check for problems with the drive, its controller, and the cables. Also make sure that the drive has power and is connected properly.

Using Disk Mirroring

With disk mirroring, you use identically sized volumes on two different drives to create a redundant data set. The drives are written with identical sets of information, and if one of the drives fails, you can still obtain the data from the other drive.

Although disk mirroring offers fault tolerance, the major drawback to disk mirroring is that it effectively cuts the amount of storage space in half. For example, to mirror a 500 GB drive, you need another 500 GB drive. That means you use 1,000 GB of space to store 500 GB of information.

Creating Mirrored Volumes

You create a mirror set by following these steps:

1. In the Disk Management Graphical view, right-click an area marked Unallocated on a disk, and then click New Mirrored Volume. This starts the New Mirrored Volume Wizard. Read the Welcome page, and then click Next.
2. Create the volume as described in the section "Creating Spanned and Striped Volumes" earlier in the chapter. The key difference is that you must create two volumes of identical size, and these volumes must be on separate drives. You won't be able to continue past the Selected Disks window until you select the two disks that you want to work with.
3. As with other RAID techniques, mirroring is transparent to users. Users see the mirrored set as a single drive that they can access and use like any other drive.

NOTE The status of a normal mirror is Healthy. During the creation of a mirror, you'll see a status of Resynching, which tells you that Disk Management is creating the mirror.

Rather than create a new mirrored volume, you can use an existing volume to create a mirrored set. To do this, the volume you want to mirror must be a basic partition or simple volume, and you must have an area of unallocated space on a second drive of equal or larger size than the existing volume.

In Disk Management, you can mirror an existing volume by following these steps:

1. Right-click the basic partition or simple volume you want to mirror, and then click Add Mirror. This displays the Add Mirror dialog box.
2. In the Disks list, select a location for the mirror, and then click Add Mirror. Windows 7 begins the mirror creation process. In Disk Management, you'll

see a status of Resynching on both volumes. The disk on which the mirrored volume is being created has a warning icon.

Breaking a Mirrored Set

You may want to or need to break a mirrored set. For example, if you no longer want to mirror your drives, you can break a mirror, which allows you to use the disk space for other purposes. If one of the mirrored drives in a set fails, disk operations can continue, but at some point you'll need to fix the mirror, and to do this you must break the mirror and then reestablish it. Although breaking a mirror doesn't delete the data in the set, you should always back up the data before you perform this procedure. This ensures that if you have problems, you can recover your data.

In Disk Management, you can break a mirrored set by following these steps:

1. Right-click one of the volumes in the mirrored set, and then click Break Mirrored Volume.
2. Confirm that you want to break the mirror by clicking Yes. If the volume is in use, you'll see another warning dialog box. Click Yes to confirm that it's okay to continue.

   Windows 7 breaks the mirror, creating two independent volumes.

Removing a Mirrored Set

In Disk Management, you can remove one of the volumes from a mirrored set. When you do this, all data on the mirror you remove is deleted, and the space it used is marked as Unallocated.

To remove a mirror, follow these steps:

1. In Disk Management, right-click one of the volumes in the mirrored set, and then click Remove Mirror. This displays the Remove Mirror dialog box.
2. In the Remove Mirror dialog box, select the disk from which to remove the mirror.
3. Confirm the action when prompted. All data on the removed mirror is deleted.

Moving a Dynamic Disk to a New System

An important advantage of dynamic disks over basic disks is that you can easily move dynamic disks from one computer to another. For example, after setting up a computer, if you decide that you don't really need an additional hard disk, you can move it to another computer where it can be better used. Before moving disks, you should complete the following steps:

1. Open Disk Management on the computer where the dynamic disks are currently installed and check their status. The status should be Healthy. If it isn't, you should fix any problems before moving the disks.

CAUTION **Drives with BitLocker Drive Encryption cannot be moved using this technique. Windows 7 Enterprise and Ultimate editions include BitLocker Driver Encryption that wraps drives in a protected seal so that any offline tampering is detected and results in the disk being unavailable until an administrator unlocks it. For more information about BitLocker Drive Encryption, see Chapter 11, "Using TPM and BitLocker Drive Encryption."**

2. Check the hard disk subsystems on the original computer and on the computer to which you want to transfer the disk. Both computers should have identical hard disk subsystems. If they don't, the Plug and Play ID on the system disk from the original computer won't match what the destination computer is expecting. As a result, the destination computer won't be able to load the right drivers, and boot might fail.
3. Check whether any dynamic disks that you want to move are part of a spanned, extended, or striped set. If they are, you should make a note of which disks are part of which set and plan on moving all disks in a set together. If you move only part of a disk set, be aware of the consequences. For spanned, extended, or striped volumes, moving only part of the set makes the related volumes unusable on the current computer and on the computer to which you are planning to move the disks.

When you are ready to move the disks, complete the following steps:

1. On the original computer, start Computer Management. Then, in the left pane, select Device Manager. In the Device list, expand Disk Drives. This shows a list of all the physical disk drives on the computer. In turn, right-click each disk that you want to move, and then click Uninstall. If you are unsure which disks to uninstall, right-click each disk, and then click Properties. In the Properties dialog box, click the Volumes tab, and then click Populate. This shows you the volumes on the selected disk.
2. Next, select the Disk Management node in Computer Management on the original computer. Right-click each disk that you want to move, and then click Remove Disk.
3. Once you perform these procedures, you can move the dynamic disks. If the disks are hot-swappable and this feature is supported on both computers, remove the disks from the original computer and then install them on the destination computer. Otherwise, turn off both computers, remove the drives from the original computer, and then install them on the destination computer. When you have finished, restart the computers.
4. On the destination computer, open Disk Management, and then click Rescan Disks on the Action menu. When Disk Management finishes scanning the disks, right-click any disk marked Foreign, and then click Import. You should now be able to access the disks and their volumes on the destination computer.

NOTE The volumes on the dynamic disks should retain the d had on the original computer. If a drive letter is already used c computer, a volume receives the next available drive letter. If a previously did not have a drive letter, it does not receive a driv moved to another computer. Additionally, if automounting is aren't automatically mounted, and you must manually mount drive letters.

Troubleshooting Common Disk Problems

Windows 7 makes extensive use of disk drives during startup and normal operations. You can often dramatically improve operating system and application performance by optimizing a computer's disk drives. You should focus on disk space usage, disk errors, and disk fragmentation. You might also want to compress data to reduce the space used by data files, freeing up space for additional files.

NOTE **Disk maintenance tools, such as Disk Cleanup, Check Disk, and Disk Defragmenter, take advantage of new resource prioritization features in Windows 7, as discussed in the section "Understanding and Using Windows SuperFetch." These changes enable these tools to run in the background to take advantage of system idle time while running. As a result, users get a consistently good performance level even when background maintenance tasks are running.**

You should closely monitor disk space usage on all system drives. As drives begin to fill up, their performance and the performance of the operating system as a whole can be reduced, particularly if the system runs low on space for storing virtual memory or temporary files. One way to reduce disk space usage is to use the Disk Cleanup tool to remove unnecessary files and compress old files. For details on using this tool, see the section "Working with Disk Cleanup" in Chapter 6. To eliminate the need to remind users to run Disk Cleanup, you can schedule Disk Cleanup to run regularly, as discussed in the section "Scheduling Maintenance Tasks" in Chapter 17.

Using Disk Management, you can determine the status of disks and the volumes they contain. Disk status is displayed in Graphical view below the physical disk number and in the Disk List view in the Status field. Volume status is displayed as part of the volume information in Graphical view and in the Status column in Volume List view.

Table 12-2 lists status messages you might see for disks. You'll find a diagnosis and suggested corrective action in the Resolution column.

STATUS	DESCRIPTION	RESOLUTION
Unrecognized	The disk is of an unknown type and can't be used on the system. A drive from a non-Windows system might display this status.	If the disk is from another operating system, don't do anything. You can't use the drive on the computer, so try a different drive.
Not Initialized	The disk doesn't have a valid signature. A drive from a non-Windows system might display this status.	If the disk is from another operating system, don't do anything. You can't use the drive on the computer, so try a different drive. To prepare the disk for use on Windows 7, right-click the disk, and then click Initialize Disk.
No Media	No media has been inserted into the CD-ROM or removable drive, or the media has been removed. Only CD-ROM and removable disk types display this status.	Insert a CD-ROM, a floppy disk, or a removable disk to bring the disk online. With FireWire/USB card readers, this status is usually but not always displayed when the card is removed.

Table 12-3 lists status messages you might see for volumes. You'll find a diagnosis and suggested corrective action in the Resolution column.

TABLE 12-3 Understanding and Resolving Volume Status Issues

STATUS	DESCRIPTION	RESOLUTION
Data Incomplete	Spanned volumes on a foreign disk are incomplete. You must have forgotten to add the other disks from the spanned volume set.	Add the disks that contain the rest of the spanned volume and then import all the disks at one time.
Data Not Redundant	Fault-tolerant volumes on a foreign disk are incomplete. You must have forgotten to add the other disks from a mirror set.	Add the remaining disk and then import all the disks at one time.

STATUS	DESCRIPTION	RESOLUTION
Failed	An error disk status. The disk is inaccessible or damaged.	Ensure that the related disk is online, and, as necessary, right-click the disk and then click Reactivate Disk. Right-click the volume, and then click Reactivate Volume. You might need to check the disk for a faulty connection.
Formatting	A temporary status that indicates the volume is being formatted.	The progress of the formatting is indicated as the percent complete, unless the Perform A Quick Format option was selected.
Healthy	The normal volume status.	The volume doesn't have any known problems. You don't need to take any corrective action.
Healthy (At Risk)	Windows had problems reading from or writing to the physical disk on which the volume is located. This status appears when Windows encounters errors.	Right-click the disk, and then click Reactivate Disk. If the disk continues to have this status or has this status periodically, the disk might be failing and you should back up all data on the disk.
Healthy (Unknown Partition)	Windows does not recognize the partition. This can occur because the partition is from a different operating system or is a manufacturer-created partition used to store system files.	No corrective action is necessary.
Initializing	A temporary status that indicates the disk is being initialized.	The drive status should change after a few seconds.
Resynching	A temporary status that indicates that a mirror set is being resynchronized.	Progress is indicated as the percent complete. The volume should return to Healthy status.

STATUS	DESCRIPTION	RESOLUTION
Stale Data	Data on foreign disks that are fault tolerant are out of sync.	Rescan the disks or restart the computer, and then check the status. A new status should be displayed, such as Failed Redundancy.
Unknown	The volume cannot be accessed. It might have a corrupted boot sector.	The volume might have a boot sector virus. Check it with an up-to-date antivirus program. If no virus is found, boot from the Windows 7 CD-ROM and use the Recovery Console's Fixmbr command to fix the master boot record.

Repairing Disk Errors and Inconsistencies

Windows 7 includes feature enhancements that reduce the amount of manual maintenance you must perform on disk drives. The following enhancements have the most impact on the way you work with disks:

- Transactional NTFS
- Self-healing NTFS

Transactional NTFS allows file operations on an NTFS volume to be performed transactionally. This means programs can use a transaction to group together sets of file and registry operations so that all of them succeed or none of them succeed. While a transaction is active, changes are not visible outside the transaction. Changes are committed and written fully to disk only when a transaction is completed successfully. If a transaction fails or is incomplete, the program rolls back the transactional work to restore the file system to the state it was in prior to the transaction.

Transactions that span multiple volumes are coordinated by the Kernel Transaction Manager (KTM). The KTM supports independent recovery of volumes if a transaction fails. The local resource manager for a volume maintains a separate transaction log and is responsible for maintaining threads for transactions separate from threads that perform the file work.

Traditionally, you have had to use the Check Disk tool to fix errors and inconsistencies in NTFS volumes on a disk. Because this process can disrupt the availability of Windows systems, Windows 7 uses self-healing NTFS to protect file systems without having to use separate maintenance tools to fix problems. Because much of the self-healing process is enabled and performed automatically, you might need to perform volume maintenance manually only when you are notified by the operating system that a problem cannot be corrected automatically. If such an error occurs, Windows 7 notifies you about the problem and provides possible solutions.

Self-healing NTFS has many advantages over Check Disk, including the following:

- Check Disk must have exclusive access to volumes, which means system and boot volumes can be checked only when the operating system starts up. On the other hand, with self-healing NTFS, the file system is always available and does not need to be corrected offline (in most cases).
- Self-healing NTFS attempts to preserve as much data as possible if corruption occurs and reduces failed file system mounting that previously could occur if a volume was known to have errors or inconsistencies. During restart, self-healing NTFS repairs the volume immediately so that it can be mounted.
- Self-healing NTFS reports changes made to the volume during repair through existing Chkdsk.exe mechanisms, directory notifications, and update sequence number (USN) journal entries. This feature also allows authorized users and administrators to monitor repair operations through Verification, Waiting For Repair Completion, and Progress Status messages.
- Self-healing NTFS can recover a volume if the boot sector is readable but does not identify an NTFS volume. In this case, you must run an offline tool that repairs the boot sector and then allow self-healing NTFS to initiate recovery.

Although self-healing NTFS is a terrific enhancement, at times you might want to (or might have to) manually check the integrity of a disk. In these cases, you can use Check Disk (Chkdsk.exe) to check for and, optionally, repair problems found on FAT, FAT32, and NTFS volumes. Although Check Disk can check for and correct many types of errors, the utility primarily looks for inconsistencies in the file system and its related metadata. One of the ways Check Disk locates errors is by comparing the volume bitmap to the disk sectors assigned to files in the file system. Beyond this, the usefulness of Check Disk is rather limited. For example, Check Disk can't repair corrupted data within files that appear to be structurally intact.

Checking for Disk Errors

You should periodically use the Check Disk tool to check the integrity of disks. Check Disk examines disks and can correct many types of common errors on FAT16, FAT32, and NTFS drives. One of the ways Check Disk locates errors is by comparing the volume bitmap with the disk sectors assigned to files in the file system. Check Disk can't repair corrupted data within files that appear to be structurally intact, however. You can run Check Disk from the command line or through a graphical interface.

Running Check Disk from the Command Line

You can run Check Disk from an elevated command prompt or within other tools. At the elevated command prompt, you can test the integrity of drive C by typing the following command:

```
chkdsk C:
```

Check Disk then performs an analysis of the disk and returns a status message regarding any problems it encounters. Unless you specify further options, Check Disk won't repair problems, however. To find and repair errors on drive C, use this command:

```
chkdsk /f C:
```

When you use this command, Check Disk performs an analysis of the disk and then repairs any errors it finds, provided that the disk isn't in use. If the disk is in use, Check Disk displays a prompt that asks whether you want to schedule the disk to be checked the next time you restart the system. Click Yes to schedule this check.

The complete syntax for Check Disk is as follows:

```
CHKDSK [volume[[path]filename]] [/F] [/V] [/R] [/X] [/I] [/C]
  [/L[:size]]
```

The options and switches for Check Disk are used as follows:

- **volume** Sets the volume to work with
- **path/filename** Specifies files to check for fragmentation (FAT16 and FAT32 only)
- **/F** Fixes errors on the disk
- **/V** Displays the full path and name of every file on the disk (FAT16 and FAT32); displays cleanup messages if any (NTFS)
- **/R** Locates bad sectors and recovers readable information (implies /F)
- **/X** Forces the volume to dismount first if necessary (implies /F)
- **/I** Performs a minimum check of index entries (NTFS only)
- **/C** Skips checking of cycles within the folder structure (NTFS only)
- **/L:*size*** Sets the log file size (NTFS only)
- **/B** Re-evaluates bad clusters on the volume (NTFS only; implies /R)

Running Check Disk Interactively

You can also run Check Disk interactively using Windows Explorer. To use Windows Explorer to check disk drives on the local computer, follow these steps:

1. Click Start, and then click Computer. Under Hard Disk Drives, right-click a drive, and then click Properties.

2. On the Tools tab, click Check Now. This displays the Check Disk dialog box, shown in Figure 12-13.

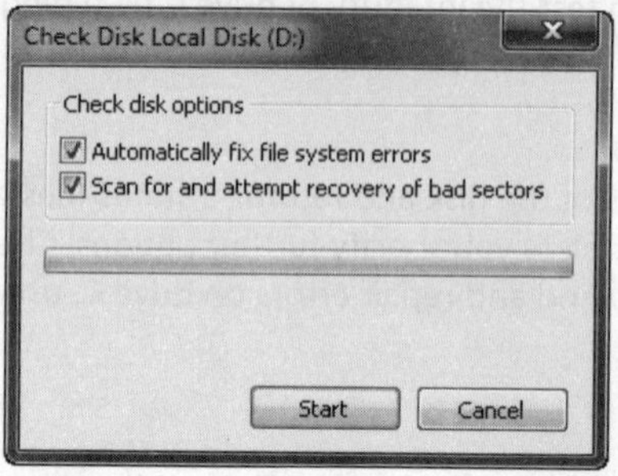

FIGURE 12-13 Check Disk is available by clicking Check Now in the Properties dialog box. Use it to check a disk for errors and repair them.

3. To check for errors without repairing them, click Start without selecting either of the check boxes in the Check Disk dialog box.
4. To check for errors and attempt to resolve them, select either or both of the following options, and then click Start.
   - **Automatically Fix File System Errors** Specifies whether Windows 7 repairs file system errors it finds
   - **Scan For And Attempt Recovery Of Bad Sectors** Specifies whether Windows 7 checks for bad sectors and attempts to recover readable information from them
5. If the disk is in use, Check Disk displays a prompt that asks whether you want to schedule the disk to be checked the next time you restart the system. Click Yes to schedule this check.
6. When Check Disk finishes analyzing and repairing the disk, click OK.

Defragmenting Disks

Any time you add files to or remove files from a drive, the data on the drive can become fragmented. When a drive is fragmented, large files can't be written to a single continuous area on the disk. As a result, the operating system must write the file to several smaller areas on the disk, which means more time is required to read the file from the disk. To reduce fragmentation, Windows 7 can manually or automatically defragment disks periodically using Disk Defragmenter. The more frequently data is updated on drives, the more often you should run this tool.

You can manually defragment a disk by following these steps:

1. In Computer Management, select the Storage node and then the Disk Management node. Right-click a drive, and then click Properties.

2. On the Tools tab, click Defragment Now. Disk Defragmenter analyzes the computer's disks to determine whether any disks need to be defragmented. If so, it recommends that you defragment now.
3. In the Disk Defragmenter dialog box, click Defragment Now. When prompted, select the disks to defragment, and then click OK.

NOTE **Depending on the size of the disk, defragmentation can take several hours. You can click Cancel Defragmentation at any time to stop defragmentation.**

When you enable automatic defragmentation, Windows 7 runs disk defragmenter automatically at 1:00 A.M. every Wednesday. As long as the computer is on at the scheduled run time, automatic defragmentation will occur. You can configure and manage automated defragmentation by following these steps:

1. In Computer Management, select the Storage node and then the Disk Management node. Right-click a drive, and then click Properties.
2. On the Tools tab, click Defragment Now. This displays the Disk Defragmenter dialog box, shown in Figure 12-14.

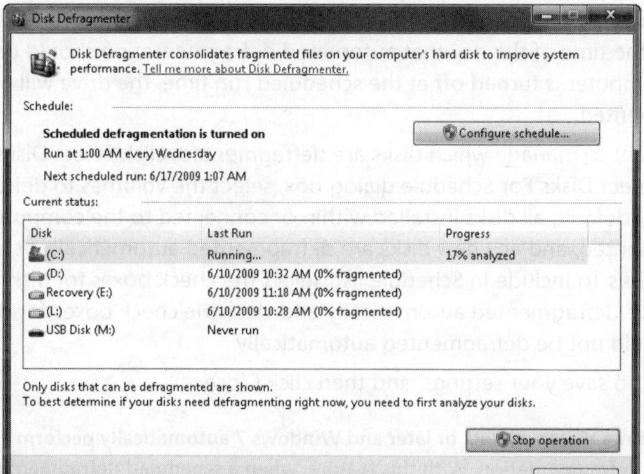

FIGURE 12-14 Use Disk Defragmenter to analyze and defragment disks.

3. If you want to modify the run schedule, click Configure Schedule. This displays the Modify Schedule dialog box, shown in Figure 12-15. To cancel automated defragmentation, clear Run On A Schedule, click OK, click Close, and then skip the remaining steps. To enable automated defragmentation, select Run On A Schedule. The default schedule or the run schedule that was last set is shown.

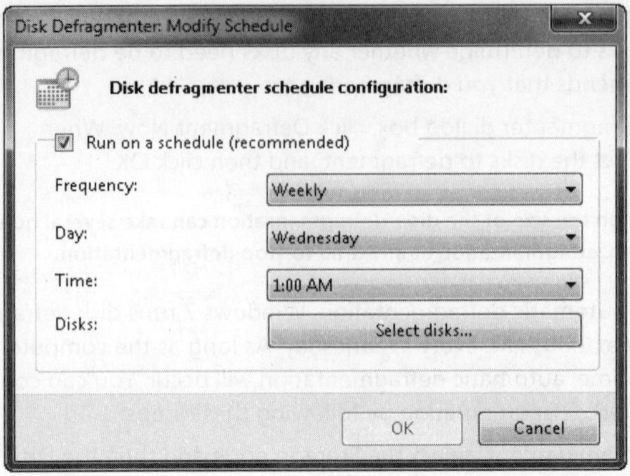

FIGURE 12-15 Specify the run schedule for automated defragmentation.

4. In the Frequency list, you can choose Daily, Weekly, or Monthly as the run schedule. If you choose a weekly or monthly run schedule, you need to select the run day of the week or month from the Day list. Finally, the Time list lets you set the time of the day that automated defragmentation should occur. If the computer is turned off at the scheduled run time, the drive will not be defragmented.
5. If you want to manage which disks are defragmented, click Select Disks. In the Select Disks For Schedule dialog box, select the volumes to defragment. By default, all disks installed within or connected to the computer are defragmented, and any new disks are defragmented automatically as well. In the Disks To Include In Schedule list, select the check boxes for disks that should be defragmented automatically and clear the check boxes for disks that should not be defragmented automatically.
6. Click OK to save your settings, and then click Close.

NOTE **Windows Vista with SP1 or later and Windows 7 automatically perform cyclic pickup defragmentation. With this feature, when a scheduled defragmentation pass is stopped and rerun, the computer automatically picks up the next unfinished volume in line to be defragmented.**

Resynchronizing and Repairing a Mirrored Set

Windows 7 automatically synchronizes mirrored volumes on drives. However, data on mirrored drives can become out of sync. For example, if one of the drives goes offline, data is written only to the drive that's online.

You can resynchronize and repair mirrored sets, but you must rebuild the set using disks with the same partition style—either MBR or GPT. You need to get both drives in the mirrored set online. Because a disk in the set has failed, the mirrored set's status should read Failed Redundancy. The corrective action you take depends on the failed volume's status:

- If the status is Missing or Offline, make sure that the drive has power and is connected properly. Then start Disk Management, right-click the failed volume, and then click Reactivate Volume. The drive status should change to Regenerating and then to Healthy. If the volume doesn't return to the Healthy status, right-click the volume, and then click Resynchronize Mirror.
- If the status is Online (Errors), right-click the failed volume, and then click Reactivate Volume. The drive status should change to Regenerating and then to Healthy. If the volume doesn't return to the Healthy status, right-click the volume, and then click Resynchronize Mirror.
- If one of the drives shows a status of Unreadable, you might need to rescan the drives on the system by choosing Rescan Disks from Disk Management's Action menu. If the drive status doesn't change, you might need to reboot the computer.
- If one of the drives still won't come back online, right-click the failed volume, and then click Remove Mirror. Next, right-click the remaining volume in the original mirror, and then click Add Mirror. You now need to mirror the volume on an unallocated area of this or a different drive. If you don't have unallocated space on this drive or another drive, you need to create space by deleting other volumes or replacing the failed drive.

Repairing a Mirrored System Volume to Enable Boot

The failure of a mirrored drive might prevent your system from booting. Typically, this happens when you're mirroring the system or boot volume, or both, and the primary mirror drive has failed.

When you mirror a system volume, the operating system should add an entry to the system's boot manager that allows you to boot to the secondary mirror. Resolving a primary mirror failure is much easier with this entry in the boot manager file than without it because all you need to do is select the entry to boot to the secondary mirror. If you mirror the boot volume and a secondary mirror entry is not created for you, you can modify the boot entries in the boot manager to create one using the BCD Editor (Bcdedit.exe).

If a system fails to boot to the primary system volume, restart the system and select the Boot Mirror – Secondary Plex option for the operating system you want to start. The system should start up normally. After you successfully boot the system to the secondary drive, you can schedule the maintenance necessary to rebuild the mirror if you want to. You'll need to follow these steps:

1. Shut down the system, replace the failed volume or add a hard disk drive, and then restart the system.
2. Break the mirror set, and then re-create the mirror on the drive you replaced, which is usually Drive 0. Right-click the remaining volume that was part of

the original mirror, and then click Add Mirror. This displays the Add Mirror dialog box.

3. In the Disks list, select a location for the mirror, and then click Add Mirror. Windows 7 begins the mirror creation process. In Disk Management, you'll see a status of Resynching on both volumes. The disk on which the mirrored volume is being created has a warning icon.
4. If you want the primary mirror to be on the drive you added or replaced, use Disk Management to break the mirror again. Make sure that the primary drive in the original mirror set has the drive letter that was previously assigned to the complete mirror. If it doesn't, assign the appropriate drive letter.
5. Right-click the original system volume, and then click Add Mirror. Now re-create the mirror.
6. Check the boot configuration and be sure that the original system volume is used during startup. You may need to modify the boot configuration to ensure this.

Working with Removable Storage Devices

Removable storage devices can be formatted with NTFS, FAT, FAT32, and exFAT. You connect external storage devices to a computer instead of installing them inside the computer. This makes external storage devices easier and faster to install than most fixed disk drives. Most external storage devices have a universal serial bus (USB) or a FireWire interface. When working with USB and FireWire, the transfer speed and overall performance of the device from a user's perspective depend primarily on the version supported.

Currently, several versions of USB and FireWire are used, including USB 1.0, USB 1.1, USB 2.0, FireWire 400, and FireWire 800. USB 2.0 is the industry standard, and it supports data transfers at a maximum rate of 480 megabits per second (Mbps), with sustained data transfer rates usually from 10 to 30 Mbps. The actual sustainable transfer rate depends on many factors, including the type of device, the data you are transferring, and the speed of a computer. Each USB controller on a computer has a fixed amount of bandwidth that all devices attached to the controller must share. The data transfer rates will be significantly slower if a computer's USB port is an earlier version than the device you are using. For example, if you connect a USB 2.0 device to a USB 1.0 port or vice versa, the device operates at the significantly reduced USB 1.0 transfer speed.

USB 1.0, 1.1, and 2.0 ports all look alike. The best way to determine which type of USB ports a computer has is to refer to the documentation that came with the computer. Newer LCD monitors have USB 2.0 ports to which you can connect devices as well. When you have USB devices connected to a monitor, the monitor acts like a

USB hub device. As occurs with any USB hub device, all devices attached to the hub share the same bandwidth and the total available bandwidth is determined by the speed of the USB input to which the hub is connected on a computer.

FireWire (IEEE 1394) is a high-performance connection standard that uses a peer-to-peer architecture in which peripherals negotiate bus conflicts to determine which device can best control a data transfer. Several versions of FireWire are currently used, including FireWire 400 and FireWire 800. FireWire 400 (IEEE 1394a) has maximum sustained transfer rates of up to 400 Mbps. FireWire 800 (IEEE 1394b) has maximum sustained transfer rates of up to 800 Mbps. As with USB devices, if you connect a FireWire 800 device to a FireWire 400 port or vice versa, the device operates at the significantly reduced FireWire 400 transfer speed.

FireWire 400 and FireWire 800 ports and cables have different shapes, making it easier to tell the difference between them—if you know what you're looking for. With that said, FireWire 400 ports and cables look exactly like early versions of FireWire that were implemented prior to the finalization of the IEEE 1394a and IEEE 1394b specifications. FireWire cables and ports that have four pins and four connectors lack bus power. FireWire 400 cables and ports have six pins and six connectors. FireWire 800 cables and ports have nine pins and nine connectors.

Before you purchase an external device for a computer, you should consider what interfaces your computer supports and the interfaces the device uses. In some cases, you might be able to get a device with a dual interface that supports USB 2.0 and FireWire 400, or a triple interface that supports USB 2.0, FireWire 400, and FireWire 800. A device with dual or triple interfaces will give you more options.

In the Computer console or Disk Management, you can work with removable disks by right-clicking a disk and then using the following commands:

- Click Open or Explore to examine the disk's contents in Windows Explorer.
- Click Format to format removable disks as discussed in the section "Formatting Partitions and Volumes" earlier in the chapter. Removable disks generally are formatted with a single partition.
- Click Properties to view or set properties. On the General tab of the Properties dialog box, you can set the volume label as discussed in the section "Assigning, Changing, or Deleting a Volume Label" earlier in the chapter.

When you work with removable disks, you can customize disk and folder views. To do this, right-click the disk or folder, and then click the Customize tab. You can then specify the default folder type to control the default details displayed. For example, you can set the default folder type as Documents or Pictures And Videos. You can also set folder pictures and folder icons.

Removable disks support network file and folder sharing. You configure sharing on removable disks in the same way that you configure standard file sharing. You can assign share permissions, configure caching options for offline file use, and limit the number of simultaneous users. You can share an entire removable disk as well as individual folders stored on the removable disk. You can also create multiple share instances.

Removable disks differ from standard NTFS sharing in that there isn't necessarily an underlying security architecture. With exFAT, FAT, or FAT32, folders and files stored do not have any security permissions or features other than the basic read-only or hidden attribute flags that you can set.

Working with Data CDs and DVDs

CD and DVD disc images are often stored as ISO files. Windows 7 has built-in capabilities to recognize ISO images and burn them to CD or DVD. Windows 7 also has built-in CD and DVD burning features that you can use to create CDs and DVDs. Before you burn data CDs and DVDs, you should familiarize yourself with the disc types and disc file system options that are available.

Disc Burning: The Essentials

By default, when you insert a blank CD or DVD, Windows 7 shows a Burn button on the Windows Explorer toolbar. Clicking this button starts the Burn A Disc Wizard, which you can use to create a data disc. Keep in mind that computer CD and DVD players are different from players for homes or cars. Typically, your computer CD/DVD player is designed to read commercially produced CD-ROMs and DVD-ROMs as well as computer-burned CDs and DVDs in specific formats, but a home or car CD or DVD player won't necessarily be able to recognize a CD or DVD you create on a computer.

Most CD/DVD burners support multiple disc types. Windows 7 natively supports burning data CDs to CD-R, CD+R, and CD-RW and burning data DVDs to DVD-R, DVD-RW, DVD+R, DVD+RW, and DVD-RAM. DVDs can be single-sided and single-layered or single-sided and dual-layered. Windows 7 also natively supports Blu-ray. If a computer has a Blu-ray player, you might also be able to burn Blu-ray discs.

Windows 7 supports two approaches to burning discs:

- Disc mastering
- Live file system

Most Windows programs create data discs using a mastered approach, and discs are written in an appropriate file system format automatically. With a mastered approach, you select a collection of files that you want to copy to a disc and then burn all the files at once. When you are burning large collections of files, this is a convenient approach, with the added bonus of compatibility with any computer or device that supports the type of data disc you are using.

When you burn files to data discs using mastering, you burn files in a session. In many CD/DVD burning programs, you have the option of leaving a session open in order to add files later, and then you close the session when you are done adding files. By closing the session, you finalize the disc and allow it to be read on other computers and devices. Otherwise, while a session is open, the disc can be read only on a compatible computer.

In contrast, a data disc with a live file system works like any other type of removable storage, such as a USB flash key or a removable disk drive. You can add files to the disc without having to burn them simply by copying and pasting files or by dragging and dropping files. If the disc is re-recordable, you can remove files by selecting them and deleting them. If you eject the disc, you can insert it into your CD/DVD drive later and continue to use it like removable storage.

Data discs with a live file system are formatted using the Universal Disc Format (UDF) rather than the standard CD File System (CDFS). Generally, only computers can read UDF-formatted data discs. Windows 7 supports burning data discs in several UDF versions, including:

- **UDF 1.5** A format compatible with Windows 2000 and later versions of Windows. It might not be compatible with Windows 98 or Apple computers.
- **UDF 2.0** A format compatible with Windows XP and later versions of Windows. It might not be compatible with Windows 98, Windows 2000, or Apple computers.
- **UDF 2.01** The default format, which includes a major update that you'll want to take advantage of in most cases. This format is compatible with Windows XP and later versions of Windows. It might not be compatible with Windows 98, Windows 2000, or Apple computers.
- **UDF 2.5** A format optimized for Windows Vista and later. It might not be compatible with earlier versions of Windows or Apple computers.

Burning ISO Images to Disc

You can burn an ISO image to a disc by completing the following steps:

1. Insert a blank disc into your CD/DVD burner. If the AutoPlay dialog box is displayed, click the Close button (the red button with the X).
2. In Windows Explorer, double-click the .iso file that you want to use to create a data CD or DVD.
3. In the Windows Disc Image Burner dialog box, shown in Figure 12-16, use the Disc Burner list to select the CD/DVD burner, and then click Burn.

FIGURE 12-16 Burn ISO images to disc.

Burning Mastered Discs

You can burn a mastered disc by completing the following steps:

1. Insert a blank disc into your CD/DVD burner. Do one of the following:
   - In the AutoPlay dialog box, select Burn Files To Disc Using Windows Explorer.
   - If the AutoPlay dialog box is not displayed, click Start, and then click Computer. In the Computer window, right-click the CD/DVD burner, and then click Open AutoPlay. In the AutoPlay dialog box, select Burn Files To Disc Using Windows Explorer.
2. In the Burn A Disc Wizard, shown in Figure 12-17, type a disc title. To create a mastered disc, select With A CD/DVD Player. When you click Next, the data disc is opened in Windows Explorer. The Files Ready To Be Written To The Disc pane displays an empty burn list. Don't close this window.
3. Using Windows Explorer, select and copy files to the burn list. Files in the burn list are copied from their original location and written as temporary files to a temporary folder. This temporary folder is created in the user's personal profile. Copies of these files are created to be sure that all the files are in one place and that you have appropriate permissions to access the files before trying to burn the disc.
4. When you are ready to continue, click Burn To Disc. In the Burn To Disc wizard, the disc title is set using the title you provided previously, and the recording speed is set to the maximum speed supported by the CD/DVD drive.

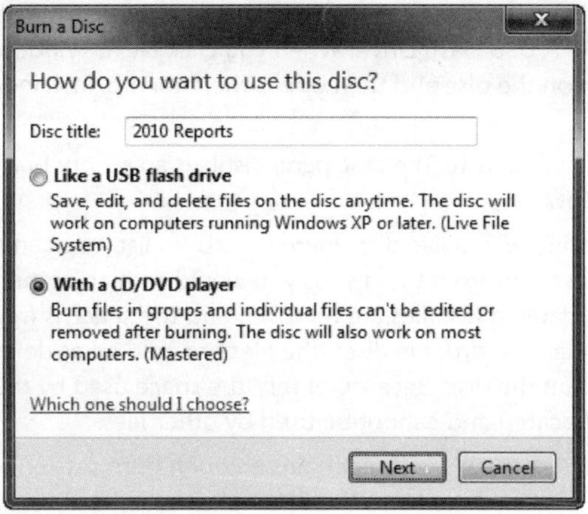

FIGURE 12-17 Prepare to burn data to a disc.

5. When you click Next, Windows 7 adds the files you selected to a disc image and then writes the files to your data disc. When finished burning the disc, Windows 7 automatically ejects the disc by default. Also by default, the temporary files are deleted, and you can then click Finish to exit the Burn To Disc wizard. If you want to burn the same files to another disc, select the Yes, Burn These Files To Another Disc check box before clicking Finish.

If an error occurs while burning, you'll see an error message. You'll have the option of trying again with a different disc, deleting the temporary files that have not burned, or saving all the temporary files and trying to burn them later. If you try again, make sure you select a slower burn speed. Although your CD/DVD drive may be able to burn at a high speed, the disc itself may not be rated for burning at the speed you selected.

Generally, if you see a burn error, only a portion of your files will have been written to the disc. If the burn session is still open, you can try to burn to the disc again. Occasionally, you may find that you have to use a new blank disc.

Burning Discs with Live File Systems

You can burn a data disc with a live file system by completing the following steps:

1. Insert a blank disc into your CD/DVD burner. Do one of the following:
   - In the AutoPlay dialog box, select Burn Files To Disc Using Windows Explorer.
   - If the AutoPlay dialog box is not displayed, click Start, and then click Computer. In the Computer window, right-click the CD/DVD burner, and then click Open AutoPlay. In the AutoPlay dialog box, select Burn Files To Disc Using Windows Explorer.

2. In the Burn a Disc Wizard, type a disc title. To create a UDF disc with a live file system, select Like A USB Flash Drive. When you click Next, Windows creates a live file system on the disc and then opens the data disc in Windows Explorer.
3. The Files Ready To Be Written To The Disc pane displays an empty burn list. Don't close this window.
4. Because you are working with a live disc, there is no burn list. You can now add files to and remove files from the disc as you would with any other disc device. With re-recordable discs, files are removed and the space is freed for other files. With standard recordable discs, the files are marked as deleted but actually still exist on the disc. Because of this, the space used by the deleted files is still allocated and cannot be used by other files.
5. While the disc is inserted, Windows 7 maintains an open burn session for the disc. If you eject the live data disc, Windows 7 closes the burn session so that you can use the disc with other computers. From then on, whenever you insert the disc, you can add or remove files using Windows Explorer. Windows will open another burn session only if you modify the disc's contents. As before, you can close the session by ejecting the disc. You can also close a burn session by right-clicking the CD/DVD drive in the Computer window and then clicking Close Session.

Changing the Default Burning Options

You can change a computer's default burning options by completing the following steps:

1. Click Start, and then click Computer. In the Computer Window, right-click the CD/DVD drive, and then click Properties.
2. On the Recording tab, use the Disc Burning list to set the default burner on a computer with multiple disc burners.
3. Use the options provided to specify where temporary files are stored.
4. If you don't want mastered discs to be ejected automatically after they are burned, clear the related check box.
5. By default, Windows closes discs with live file systems when you eject them. To confirm or modify this behavior, click Global Settings. In the Global Settings dialog box, specify whether and when sessions are closed using the options provided, and then click OK.
6. Click OK to save your settings.

Managing Disk Compression and File Encryption

When you format a drive for NTFS, Windows 7 allows you to enable disk compression or file encryption. You use compression to reduce the disk space that files require, and you use encryption to add an extra layer of protection to your data. Disk compression and file encryption are mutually exclusive. You can use one feature or the other, and neither feature is affected by BitLocker Drive Encryption, which encrypts disks at the volume level and protects a computer from external tampering prior to startup of the operating system.

Compressing Drives and Data

With compression, all files and directories stored on a drive are automatically compressed when they're created. Because this compression is transparent to users, compressed data can be accessed just like regular data. The difference is that you can store more information on a compressed drive than you can on an uncompressed drive.

> ***REAL WORLD*** **Although compression is certainly a useful feature when you want to save disk space, you can't encrypt compressed data. Compression and encryption are mutually exclusive alternatives for NTFS volumes. You can't use both techniques. For more information on encryption, see the section "Encrypting Drives and Data" later in the chapter. If you try to compress encrypted data, Windows 7 automatically decrypts the data and then compresses it. Likewise, if you try to encrypt compressed data, Windows 7 uncompresses the data and then encrypts it.**

Compressing Drives

To compress a drive and all its contents, follow these steps:

1. In Windows Explorer or Disk Management, right-click the drive that you want to compress, and then click Properties.
2. Select Compress Drive To Save Disk Space, and then click OK.

Compressing Directories and Files

If you decide not to compress a drive, Windows 7 lets you selectively compress directories and files. To compress a file or directory, follow these steps:

1. In Windows Explorer, right-click the file or directory that you want to compress, and then click Properties.
2. On the General tab of the Properties dialog box, click Advanced. In the Advanced Attributes dialog box, select the Compress Contents To Save Disk Space check box, as shown in Figure 12-18. Click OK twice.

FIGURE 12-18 Compress the selected file or directory.

For an individual file, Windows 7 marks the file as compressed and then compresses it. For a directory, Windows 7 marks the directory as compressed and then compresses all the files in it. If the directory contains subfolders, Windows 7 displays a dialog box that allows you to compress all the subfolders associated with the directory. Simply select Apply Changes To This Folder, Subfolders, And Files, and then click OK. Once you compress a directory, any new files added or copied to the directory are compressed automatically.

NOTE **If you move an uncompressed file from a different drive, the file is compressed. However, if you move an uncompressed file to a compressed folder on the same NTFS drive, the file isn't compressed. Note also that you can't encrypt compressed files.**

Expanding Compressed Drives

You can remove compression from a drive by following these steps:

1. In Windows Explorer or Disk Management, right-click the drive that contains the data you want to expand, and then click Properties.
2. Clear the Compress Drive To Save Disk Space check box, and then click OK.

TIP **Windows always checks the available disk space before expanding compressed data. You should too. If less free space is available than used space, you might not be able to complete the expansion. For example, if a compressed drive uses 150 GB of space and has 70 GB of free space available, you won't have enough free space to expand the drive.**

Expanding Compressed Directories and Files

If you decide later that you want to expand a compressed file or directory, reverse the process by following these steps:

1. Right-click the file or directory in Windows Explorer, and then click Properties.
2. On the General tab of the Properties dialog box, click Advanced. Clear the Compress Contents To Save Disk Space check box. Click OK twice.

With files, Windows 7 removes compression and expands the file. With directories, Windows 7 expands all the files within the directory. If the directory contains subfolders, you have the opportunity to remove compression from the subfolders. To do this, select Apply Changes To This Folder, Subfolders, And Files when prompted, and then click OK.

> ***TIP*** **Windows 7 also provides command-line utilities for compressing and uncompressing your data. The compression utility is called Compact (Compact.exe). The uncompression utility is called Expand (Expand.exe).**

Encrypting Drives and Data

NTFS has many advantages over other file systems that you can use with Windows 7. One of the major advantages is the capability to automatically encrypt and decrypt data using the Encrypting File System (EFS). When you encrypt data, you add an extra layer of protection to sensitive data—and this extra layer acts as a security blanket blocking all other users from reading the contents of the encrypted files. Indeed, one of the great benefits of encryption is that only the designated user can access the data. This benefit is also a disadvantage in that the user must remove encryption before authorized users can access the data.

> ***NOTE*** **As discussed previously, you can't compress encrypted files. The encryption and compression features of NTFS are mutually exclusive. You can use one feature or the other, but not both.**

Understanding Encryption and the Encrypting File System

File encryption is supported on a per-folder or per-file basis. Any file placed in a folder marked for encryption is automatically encrypted. Files in encrypted format can be read only by the person who encrypted the file. Before other users can read an encrypted file, the user must decrypt the file.

Every encrypted file has a unique encryption key. This means that an encrypted file can be copied, moved, and renamed just like any other file—and in most cases these actions don't affect the encryption of the data. (For details, see the section "Working with Encrypted Files and Folders" later in this chapter.) The user who encrypts the file always has access to the file, provided that the user's public-key certificate is available on the computer that he or she is using. For this user, the encryption and decryption process is handled automatically and is transparent.

EFS is the process that handles encryption and decryption. The default setup for EFS allows users to encrypt files without needing special permission. Files are encrypted using a public/private key that EFS automatically generates on a per-user basis.

Encryption certificates are stored as part of the data in user profiles. If a user works with multiple computers and wants to use encryption, an administrator needs to configure a roaming profile for that user. A roaming profile ensures that the user's profile data and public-key certificates are accessible from other computers. Without this, users won't be able to access their encrypted files on another computer.

> ***TIP*** **By default, the encryption algorithm used is Advanced Encryption Standard 128-bit Cyclical Bit Check (AES-128-CBC). For stricter security, Windows 7 supports the Triple DES encryption algorithm (Transport Layer Security [TLS] traffic encryption, RSA public key algorithm for TLS key exchange and authentication, and SHA-1 hashing for any TLS hashing requirements). You can use Triple DES encryption by enabling the System Cryptography: Use FIPS Compliant Algorithms For Encryption policy in Group Policy. This policy is in Computer Configuration\Windows Settings\Security Settings\Local Policies\Security Options. Regardless of the encryption algorithm you choose, administrators designated as recovery agents can decrypt files if necessary. If you enable Triple DES encryption, Internet Explorer also uses only TLS for Secure Sockets Layer (SSL), which not all Web sites support.**

Although they are separate features, both BitLocker Drive Encryption and EFS have a built-in data-recovery system to guard against data loss. This recovery system ensures that encrypted data can be recovered in the event a user's public-key certificate is lost or deleted. The most common scenario for this is when a user leaves the company and the associated user account is deleted. A manager might have been able to log on to the user's account, check files, and save important files to other folders, but if the user account has been deleted, encrypted volumes and files will be accessible only if the encryption is removed or if the files are moved to a FAT or FAT32 volume (where EFS encryption isn't supported and BitLocker encryption is not enabled).

To access encrypted files after the user account has been deleted, you need to use a recovery agent. Recovery agents have access to the file encryption key necessary to unlock data in encrypted files. To protect sensitive data, however, recovery agents don't have access to a user's private key or any private key information.

Windows 7 will encrypt volumes without designated BitLocker recovery agents, but Windows 7 won't encrypt files without designated EFS recovery agents. EFS recovery agents are designated automatically, and the necessary recovery certificates are generated automatically as well. This ensures that encrypted files can always be recovered.

Recovery agents are configured at two levels:

- **Domain** The recovery agent for a domain is configured automatically when the first Windows 7 domain controller is installed. By default, the recovery agent is the domain administrator. Through Group Policy, domain administrators can designate additional recovery agents. Domain administrators can also delegate recovery-agent privileges to designated security administrators.
- **Local computer** When a computer is part of a workgroup or in a standalone configuration, the recovery agent is the administrator of the local computer by default. Additional recovery agents can be designated. Further, if you want local recovery agents in a domain environment rather than domain-level recovery agents, you must delete the recovery policy from the Group Policy for the domain.

You can delete recovery agents if you don't want to use them. However, if you delete all recovery agents for EFS, EFS will no longer encrypt files. One or more recovery agents must be configured for EFS to function.

Encrypting Directories and Files

With NTFS volumes, Windows 7 lets you select files and folders for encryption. When you encrypt files, the file data is converted to an encrypted format that can be read only by the person who encrypted the file. Users can encrypt files only if they have the proper access permissions. When you encrypt folders, the folder is marked as encrypted, but only the files within it are actually encrypted. All files that are created in or added to a folder marked as encrypted are encrypted automatically.

To encrypt a file or directory, follow these steps:

1. Right-click the file or directory that you want to encrypt, and then click Properties.
2. On the General tab of the Properties dialog box, click Advanced, and then select the Encrypt Contents To Secure Data check box. Click OK twice.

NOTE **You can't encrypt compressed files, system files, or read-only files. If you try to encrypt compressed files, the files are automatically uncompressed and then encrypted. If you try to encrypt system files, you'll get an error.**

For an individual file, Windows 7 marks the file as encrypted and then encrypts it. For a directory, Windows 7 marks the directory as encrypted and then encrypts all the files in it. If the directory contains subfolders, Windows 7 displays a dialog box that allows you to encrypt all the subfolders associated with the directory. Simply select Apply Changes To This Folder, Subfolders, And Files, and then click OK.

NOTE On NTFS volumes, files remain encrypted even when they are moved, copied, and renamed. If you copy or move an encrypted file to a FAT, FAT32, or exFAT drive, the file is automatically decrypted before it is copied or moved. This means that you must have proper permissions to copy or move the file.

Working with Encrypted Files and Folders

Previously, I said that you can copy, move, and rename encrypted files and folders just like any other files. This is true, but I qualified this by saying "in most cases." When you work with encrypted files, you'll have few problems as long as you work with NTFS volumes on the same computer. When you work with other file systems or other computers, you might run into problems. Two of the most common scenarios are these:

- **Copying between volumes on the same computer** When you copy or move an encrypted file or folder from one NTFS volume to another NTFS volume on the same computer, the files remain encrypted. However, if you copy or move encrypted files to a FAT, FAT32, or exFAT volume, the files are decrypted before transfer and then transferred as standard files. FAT, FAT32, and exFAT don't support encryption.
- **Copying between volumes on a different computer** When you copy or move an encrypted file or folder from one NTFS volume to another NTFS volume on a different computer, the files remain encrypted as long as the destination computer allows you to encrypt files and the remote computer is trusted for delegation. Otherwise, the files are decrypted and then transferred as standard files. The same is true when you copy or move encrypted files to a FAT, FAT32, or exFAT volume on another computer. FAT, FAT32, and exFAT don't support encryption.

After you transfer a sensitive file that has been encrypted, you might want to confirm that the encryption is still applied. Right-click the file, and then click Properties. On the General tab of the Properties dialog box, click Advanced. The Encrypt Contents To Secure Data option should be selected.

Configuring Recovery Policy

In domains, EFS and BitLocker recovery policies are configured automatically for domain controllers and member computers. By default, domain administrators are the designated EFS and BitLocker recovery agents for all computers in domains. In workgroups or homegroups, the local administrator is the designated EFS recovery agent for a stand-alone workstation. BitLocker has no default recovery agent for homegroups or workgroups.

Through the Group Policy console, you can view, assign, and delete recovery agents. To do that, follow these steps:

1. Open a Group Policy object (GPO) for editing in the Group Policy Management Editor.

2. Open the Encrypted Data Recovery Agents node in Group Policy. To do this, expand Computer Configuration, Windows Settings, Security Settings, Public Key Policies, and then select either Encrypting File System or BitLocker Drive Encryption, as appropriate for the type of recovery agent you want to work with.
3. The right pane lists the recovery certificates currently assigned. Recovery certificates are listed according to who issued them, to whom they are issued, expiration date, purpose, and other properties.
4. To designate an additional recovery agent, right-click the Encrypting File System or BitLocker Drive Encryption node, and then click Add Data Recovery Agent. This starts the Add Recovery Agent Wizard, which you can use to select a previously generated certificate that has been assigned to a user and then mark it as a designated recovery certificate. Click Next.
5. On the Select Recovery Agents page, click Browse Directory. In the Find Users, Contacts, And Groups dialog box, select the user you want to work with.

   NOTE **Before you can designate additional recovery agents, you must set up a root Certificate Authority (CA) in the domain. Then you must use the Certificates snap-in to generate a personal certificate that uses the EFS Recovery Agent template. The root CA must then approve the certificate request so that the certificate can be used.**

6. To delete a recovery agent, select the recovery agent's certificate in the right pane, and then press Delete. When prompted to confirm the action, click Yes to permanently and irrevocably delete the certificate. With EFS, if the recovery policy is empty (meaning that it has no other designated recovery agents), EFS will be turned off so that files can no longer be encrypted.

Sharing Decrypted Files

By default, encrypted files can be viewed only by the file owner. If you want other users to be able to access an encrypted file, you must decrypt the file or grant the users special access to the file by completing the following procedure:

1. Right-click the file or folder in Windows Explorer, and then select Properties.
2. On the General tab of the Properties dialog box, click Advanced, and then click Details in the Advanced Attributes dialog box.

   The User Access To dialog box appears. Users who have access to the encrypted file are listed by name.
3. To allow another user to access the file, click Add.
4. If a user certificate is available for the user to whom you are granting access, select the user's name in the list provided, and then click OK. Otherwise, click Find User to locate the certificate for the user.

Decrypting Files and Directories

If you decide later that you want to decrypt a file or directory, reverse the process by following these steps:

1. Right-click the file or directory in Windows Explorer.
2. On the General tab of the related Properties dialog box, click Advanced. Clear the Encrypt Contents To Secure Data check box. Click OK twice.

With files, Windows 7 decrypts the file and restores it to its original format. With directories, Windows 7 decrypts the files within the directory. If the directory contains subfolders, you have the opportunity to remove encryption from the subfolders. To do this, select Apply Changes To This Folder, Subfolders, And Files when prompted, and then click OK.

> ***TIP*** **Windows 7 also provides a command-line utility called Cipher (Cipher.exe) for encrypting and decrypting your data. Typing *cipher* at the command prompt without additional parameters shows you the encryption status of all folders in the current directory.**

CHAPTER 13

Managing File Security and Resource Sharing

Whether you are using Windows 7 in a domain, a workgroup, or a homegroup, few aspects of the operating system are more important than file security and file sharing. File security and file sharing are so interconnected that talking about one without talking about the other is difficult. File security protects important data on your systems by restricting access, and file sharing enables you to share data so that it can be accessed by other users.

File Security and Sharing Options

For computers running Windows 7, two factors control file security and sharing options: the disk format and computer settings. The format of the local disk determines the degree of file security options available. Local disks can be formatted for the FAT file system (FAT16, FAT32) or the NTFS file system. The security options on FAT and NTFS volumes differ greatly.

- With FAT, you have very limited control over file access. Files can be marked only as read-only, hidden, or system. Although these flags can be set on files and folders, anyone with access to the FAT volume can override or change these settings, which means there are no safeguards for file access or deletion. Any user can access or delete any file without restriction.
- With NTFS, you can control access to files and folders by assigning permissions that specifically allow or deny access. Permissions can be set for

individual users and for groups of users. This gives you very granular control over file and folder access. For example, you could specify that users in the Sales Managers group have full control over a folder and its files but users in the Sales Reps group have no access to the folder whatsoever.

The settings on a computer determine the way files can be shared. Windows 7 supports two file-sharing models:

- **Standard folder sharing** Enables you to share the files in any folder on a computer. Two sets of permissions are used to determine who has access to shared folders: access permissions (discussed in the section "Controlling Access to Files and Folders with NTFS Permissions" later in this chapter) and share permissions (discussed in the section "Sharing Files and Folders over the Network"). Access permissions and share permissions together enable you to control who has access to shared folders and the level of access assigned. You do not need to move the files you are sharing.
- **Public folder sharing** Enables you to share files that are in a computer's %SystemDrive%\Users\Public folder. Access permissions on the Public folder determine which users and groups have access to publicly shared files as well as what level of access those users and groups have. When you copy or move files to the Public folder, access permissions on the files are changed to match those of the Public folder. Some additional permissions are added as well. For more information, see the section "Using and Configuring Public Folder Sharing" later in this chapter.

NOTE **With standard folder sharing, local users don't have automatic access to any data stored on a computer. Local access to files and folders is fully controlled by the security settings on the local disk. If a local disk is formatted with FAT, you can use the read-only, system, or hidden flags to help protect files and folders, but you cannot restrict access. If a local disk is formatted with NTFS, you can control access by allowing or denying access to individual users and groups of users.**

With public folder sharing, files copied or moved to the Public folder are available to anyone who logs on locally regardless of whether he or she has a standard user account or an administrator user account on the computer. Network access can be granted to the Public folder. Doing so, however, makes the Public folder and its contents open to everyone who can access the computer over the network.

Unlike in Windows XP, where only one sharing model can be used at a time, in Windows 7, computers can use both sharing models at the same time. The key advantage to standard sharing is that users can share any folder on a computer and don't have to move files or folders from their current location. Public folders, on the other hand, are open drop boxes. When users copy files and folders to public folders (and public folder sharing is enabled), the files and folders are available to other users on the computer and on the network.

In Windows 7, Windows Explorer has several new options when you select folders.

- **Include In Library** Creates a link between the folder and its contents in the user's Documents, Music, Pictures, Videos, or another library folder. This lets the user browse and work with the folder's contents as if it were part of the specified library. However, any time the user works with a file in a library folder, he is actually working with the file in its original location.
- **Share With** Shares the folder using standard folder sharing. In a homegroup, users have the option to share the folder with anyone in the homegroup as read-only or read/write. In a workgroup or domain, users have the option of sharing with specific people. In any configuration, users can also select the sharing option Nobody, which effectively removes sharing.

The default sharing configuration for computers depends on whether they are members of homegroups, workgroups, or domains. When you set up a homegroup, you specify the types of files to share as well as whether to share printers. Computers that are members of the same homegroup can then automatically share files such as pictures, music, videos, documents, and printers.

Sharing folders within a homegroup as read-only or read-write is fairly straightforward. To enable sharing in a homegroup, you complete the following steps:

1. In Windows Explorer, select the folder.
2. On the toolbar, click Share With, and then select Homegroup (Read) or Homegroup (Read/Write).

This simple approach to sharing might make homegroups seem appealing to users in your office. However, it also grants very wide access to users' data and is generally inadvisable for the workplace. This is why you should encourage users in a homegroup to share with specific people rather than with everyone. Sharing with specific people is the only technique you can use in workgroups and domains.

To enable sharing with specific people, you complete the following steps:

1. In Windows Explorer, select the folder.
2. On the toolbar, click Share With, and then select Specific People. This displays the File Sharing wizard. By default, the local Administrators group is specified as the owner of the share, and the currently logged-on user is granted read/write access.
3. In the File Sharing wizard, use the options provided to choose the people to share with. For example, if you want to include all users with local accounts on the computer, enter Users, and then click Add. This is different from sharing with everyone because the Everyone group includes anyone with access permission to the computer and not just those who are domain or local users.

4. The default sharing permission is read-only. To set a permission level for a user or group, click the user or group name, and then select Read or Read/Write.
5. Click Share to share the folder, and then click Done.

To remove sharing, you complete the following steps:

1. In Windows Explorer, select the folder.
2. On the toolbar, click Share With, and then select Nobody.

By default, when you create the first standard folder share on a computer, Windows creates the File And Printer Sharing exception in Windows Firewall. This inbound exception allows other computers on the network to send inbound Server Message Block (SMB) traffic through Windows Firewall to access the share. To accommodate this, Windows opens the following ports:

- UDP port 137, which is used for NetBIOS name resolution
- UDP port 138, which is used for NetBIOS datagram transmission and reception
- TCP port 139, which is used by the NetBIOS Session service.
- Dynamic ports for ICMPv4 and ICMPv6 (which is used for echo requests if applicable)

That in a nutshell is how standard folder sharing works. Later in the chapter, I'll go into more detail about sharing with specific people. However, before anyone can share anything, network sharing must be enabled.

Network sharing settings are meant to provide the appropriate level of security for each of the various categories of networks to which a computer can connect. For this reason, Windows maintains a separate network profile for each type of network a computer uses. Generally, most network discovery and sharing settings are disabled by default. You can configure network discovery and sharing settings by following these steps:

1. Click Start, and then click Control Panel. In Control Panel, under Network And Internet, click Choose Homegroup And Sharing Options, and then click the Change Advanced Sharing Settings link.
2. Each available network profile has a separate management panel with configuration settings. Use the expand button to display the profile you want to work with.
3. Network discovery affects whether a computer can find other computers and devices on the network and whether other computers on the network can find this computer. Turn network discovery on or off by selecting the related option.
4. File and printer sharing controls whether a computer can share files and printers. Turn file and printer sharing on or off by selecting the related option.

5. Public folder sharing controls whether a computer can share files in the Public folders. Turn public folder sharing on or off by selecting an appropriate option.
6. Media streaming allows users to share music, videos, and pictures and to access music, videos, and pictures on other computers. Turn media streaming on by clicking the related button, and then configure the Media Streaming options as appropriate. Allowing other users to listen to music, play videos, and view pictures from another computer can adversely affect performance, so you might not want to enable this feature.
7. Windows uses encryption to securely transfer your shared data. By default, the encryption level is set to 128-bit encryption (in most configurations). However, you should be sure that the computers and devices you are sharing with support this level of encryption. Otherwise, select the lower encryption level or upgrade the encryption support on the other devices and computers.
8. In workgroups and homegroups, password-protected sharing allows only people with a user account and password on the local computer to access shared resources. Turn protected sharing on or off by selecting the related option.
9. Click Save Changes to save your settings.

In Group Policy, you can prevent computers from joining homegroups by enabling the Prevent The Computer From Joining A Homegroup policy. This policy is found in the Administrative Templates policies for Computer Configuration under Windows Components\Homegroup.

In Group Policy, you also can restrict the way sharing works. The key restrictions on how sharing can be used come from the Prevent Users From Sharing Files Within Their Profile policy. This policy, found in Administrative Templates policies for User Configuration under Windows Components\Network Sharing, controls whether sharing is allowed within folders associated with user profiles, primarily the %SystemDrive%\Users folder. Keep the following in mind when working with the Prevent Users From Sharing Files Within Their Profile setting:

- When this setting is Not Configured, the default state, users are allowed to share files within their profile with other users on their network, provided that a user with administrator privileges on the computer opts in for file sharing. To opt in for file sharing, an administrator has only to share a file within his or her profile.
- When this setting is Enabled, users cannot share files within their profile by using the File Sharing wizard, and the File Sharing wizard will not create shares within the %SystemDrive%\Users folder.
- When this setting is Disabled, as might be necessary to override an inherited Enabled setting, users are allowed to share files within their profile with other

users on their network, provided that a user with administrator privileges on the computer opts in for file sharing.

- To configure the Prevent Users From Sharing Files Within Their Profile policy in Group Policy, follow these steps:
  1. Open a Group Policy object (GPO) for editing in the appropriate Group Policy editor. Next, expand Administrative Templates policies for User Configuration under Windows Components\Network Sharing.
  2. Double-click Prevent Users From Sharing Files Within Their Profile.
  3. Select Not Configured, Enabled, or Disabled, and then click OK.

Although it is tempting to use public folder sharing, most organizations—even small businesses—should encourage the use of standard folder sharing for all company files and data. Simply put, standard folder sharing offers more security and better protection, and, rather than opening the floodgates to data, it closes them and blocks access appropriately. Increasing security is essential to protecting one of the most valuable assets of any organization—its data.

Share permissions are used only when a user attempts to access a file or folder from a different computer on the network, whereas access permissions are always used whether the user is logged on locally or using a remote system to access the file or folder over the network. When data is accessed remotely, first the share permissions are applied, and then the access permissions are applied.

In many ways, this means file access permissions and standard folder sharing permissions are like wrappers around your data. File access permissions, the first wrapper, protect your data with regard to local access. If a user logs on to a system locally, file access permissions can allow or deny access to files and folders. File sharing permissions, the second wrapper, are used when you want to allow remote access. If a user accesses data remotely, file sharing permissions allow or deny initial access, but because your data is also wrapped in a file security blanket, the user must successfully pass file access permissions before working with files and folders.

Controlling Access to Files and Folders with NTFS Permissions

NTFS permissions are always evaluated when a file is accessed. NTFS permissions are fairly complex, and to understand their management, you need to understand the following:

- **Basic permissions** What the basic permissions are and how they are used
- **Special permissions** What the special permissions are and how they are used
- **File ownership** What is meant by file ownership and how file ownership is used

- **Inheritance** What is meant by inheritance and how inheritance is used
- **Effective permissions** How to determine the effective permissions on files

Understanding and Using Basic Permissions

In Windows 7, the owner of a file or a folder has the right to allow or deny access to that resource, as do members of the Administrators group and other authorized users. By allowing a permission, you grant the permission to a user or a group. By denying a permission, you deny the permission to a user or a group. Keep in mind that entries that deny permissions take precedence over entries that allow permissions. As a result, if a user is a member of two groups, and one group is allowed a permission and the other is denied that permission, the user is denied that permission.

Using Windows Explorer, you can view the currently assigned basic permissions by right-clicking a file or a folder, clicking Properties, and then clicking the Security tab in the Properties dialog box.

As shown in Figure 13-1, the Group Or User Names list shows the users and groups with permissions set for the selected resource. If you select a user or a group, the assigned permissions are shown in the Permissions For list. If permissions are shaded (unavailable), it means they have been inherited from a parent folder. Inheritance is covered in detail in the section "Applying Permissions Through Inheritance" later in this chapter.

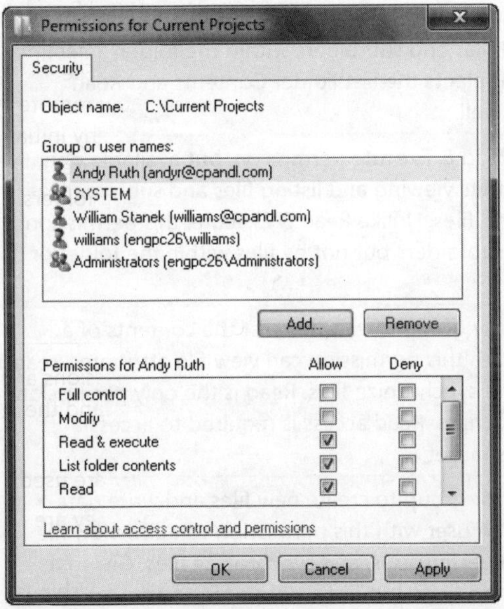

FIGURE 13-1 The Security tab shows the currently assigned basic permissions.

Working with and Setting Basic Permissions

All permissions are stored in the file system as part of the access control list (ACL) assigned to a file or a folder. As described in Table 13-1, six basic permissions are used with folders and five are also used with files. Although some permissions are inherited based on permissions of a parent folder, all permissions are defined explicitly at some level of the file system hierarchy.

TABLE 13-1 Basic File and Folder Permissions

PERMISSION	DESCRIPTION
Full Control	Grants the user or group full control over the selected file or folder and permits reading, writing, changing, and deleting files and subfolders. A user with Full Control permission for a file or folder can change permissions, delete files in the folder regardless of the permission on the files, and also take ownership of a folder or a file. Selecting this permission selects all the other permissions as well.
Modify	Allows the user or group to read, write, change, and delete files. A user with Modify permission can also create files and subfolders, but the user cannot take ownership of files. Selecting this permission selects all the permissions below it.
Read & Execute	Permits viewing and listing files and subfolders as well as executing files. If applied to a folder, this permission is inherited by all files and subfolders within the folder. Selecting this permission selects the List Folder Contents and Read permissions as well.
List Folder Contents (folders only)	Similar to the Read & Execute permission, but available only for folders. Permits viewing and listing files and subfolders as well as executing files. Unlike Read & Execute, this permission is inherited by subfolders but not by files within the folder or subfolders.
Read	Allows the user or group to view and list the contents of a folder. A user with this permission can view file attributes, read permissions, and synchronize files. Read is the only permission needed to run scripts. Read access is required to access a shortcut and its target.
Write	Allows the user or group to create new files and write data to existing files. A user with this permission can also view file attributes, read permissions, and synchronize files. Giving a user permission to write but not delete a file or a folder doesn't prevent the user from deleting the folder's or file's contents.

Equally as important as the basic permissions are the users and groups to which you assign those permissions. If a user or a group whose permissions you want to assign is already selected in the Group Or User Names list on the Security tab, you can modify the assigned permissions by clicking Edit and then using the Allow and Deny columns in the Permissions list. Select check boxes in the Allow column to add permissions, or clear check boxes to remove permissions and then click OK.

To expressly forbid a user or a group from using a permission, select the appropriate check boxes in the Deny column. Because denied permissions have precedence over other permissions, Deny is useful in two specific scenarios:

- If a user is a member of a group that has been granted a permission, but you don't want the user to have the permission and don't want to or can't remove the user from the group, you can override the inherited permission by denying that specific user the right to use the permission.
- If a permission is inherited from a parent folder and you'd rather a user or a group not have the inherited permission, you can override the allowed permission (in most cases) by expressly denying the user or group the use of the permission.

If users or groups whose permissions you want to assign aren't already available in the Group Or User Names list on the Security tab, you can easily add them. To set basic permissions for users or groups not already listed on a file or a folder's Security tab, follow these steps:

1. On the Security tab, click Edit. This displays the Permissions For dialog box.
2. In the Permissions For dialog box, click Add to display the Select Users, Computers, Service Accounts, Or Groups dialog box, shown in Figure 13-2.

FIGURE 13-2 Use the Select Users, Computers, Service Accounts, Or Groups dialog box to specify users or groups whose permissions you want to configure.

TIP **Always double-check the value of the From This Location field. In workgroups, computers will always show only local accounts and groups. In domains, this field is changeable and is set initially to the default (logon) domain of the currently logged-on user. If this isn't the location you want to use for selecting**

user and group accounts to work with, click Locations to see a list of locations you can search, including the current domain, trusted domains, and other resources that you can access.

3. Type the name of a user or a group account. Be sure to reference the user account name rather than the user's full name. When entering multiple names, separate them with semicolons.
4. Click Check Names. If a single match is found for each entry, the dialog box is automatically updated, and the entry is underlined. Otherwise, you'll see an additional dialog box. If no matches are found, you've either entered the name incorrectly or you're working with an incorrect location. Modify the name in the Name Not Found dialog box and try again, or click Locations to select a new location. When multiple matches are found, in the Multiple Names Found dialog box, select the name or names you want to use, and then click OK. The users and groups are added to the Group Or User Names list.
5. You can now configure permissions for each user and group you added by selecting an account name and then allowing or denying access permissions as appropriate.

Special Identities and Best Practices for Assigning Permissions

When you work with basic permissions, it is important to understand not only how the permissions are used but how special identities can be used to help you assign permissions. The special identities you'll see the most are Creator Owner and Users, but others are also used occasionally, as described in Table 13-2. Special identities are members of some groups automatically. To configure permissions for a special identity, enter the special identity's name as you would the name of any other user or group.

TABLE 13-2 Special Identities Used When Setting Permissions

SPECIAL IDENTITY	DESCRIPTION
Anonymous Logon	Includes any network logons for which credentials are not provided. This special identity is used to allow anonymous access to resources, such as those available on a Web server.
Authenticated Users	Includes users and computers who log on with a user name and password; does not include users who log on using the Guest account, even if the account is assigned a password.
Creator Owner	The special identity for the account that created a file or a folder. Windows 7 uses this group to identify the account that has ultimate authority over the file or folder.

SPECIAL IDENTITY	DESCRIPTION
Dialup	Includes any user who accesses the computer through a dial-up connection. This identity is used to distinguish dial-up users from other types of users.
Everyone	Includes all interactive, dial-up, and authenticated users. Although this group includes guests, it does not include anonymous users.
Interactive	Includes any user logged on locally or through a remote desktop connection.
Network	Includes any user who logs on over the network. This identity is used to allow remote users to access a resource and does not include interactive logons that use remote desktop connections.
Users	Includes authenticated users and domain users only. In Windows 7, the built-in Users group is preferred over everyone.

A solid understanding of these special identities can help you more effectively configure permissions on NTFS volumes. Additionally, whenever you work with permissions, you should keep the following guidelines in mind:

- **Follow the file system hierarchy** Inheritance plays a big part in how permissions are set. By default, permissions you set on a folder apply to all files and subfolders within that folder. With this in mind, start at the root folder of a local disk or at a user's profile folder (both of which act as top-level folders) when you start configuring permissions.
- **Have a plan** Don't set permissions without a clear plan. If permissions on folders get out of sync, and you are looking for a way to start over so that you have some continuity, you might want to configure the permissions as they should be in a parent folder and then reset the permissions on all subfolders and files in that folder using the technique discussed in the "Restoring Inherited Permissions" section of this chapter.
- **Grant access only as necessary** An important aspect of the file access controls built into NTFS is that permissions must be explicitly assigned. If you don't grant a permission to a user and that user isn't a member of a group that has a permission, the user doesn't have that permission—it's that simple. When assigning permissions, it is especially important to keep this rule in mind because it's tempting just to give users full control rather than the specific permissions they really need. Granting only the specific permissions users need to do their job is known as the *principle of least privilege*.
- **Use groups to manage permissions more efficiently** Whenever possible, you should make users members of appropriate groups and then assign permissions to those groups rather than to individual users. In this

way, you can grant permissions to new users by making them members of the appropriate groups. Then, when a user leaves or goes to another group, you can change the group membership as appropriate. For example, when Sarah joins the sales team, you can add her to the SalesUS and SalesCan groups so that she can access those groups' shared data. If she later leaves the sales team and joins the marketing team, you can remove her from the SalesUS and SalesCan groups and add her to the MarketingUS and MarketingCan groups. This is much more efficient than editing the properties for every folder Sarah needs access to and assigning permissions.

Assigning Special Permissions

Windows 7 uses special permissions to carefully control the permissions of users and groups. Behind the scenes, whenever you work with basic permissions, Windows 7 manages a set of related special permissions that specify exactly the permitted actions. The special permissions that are applied for each of the basic permissions are as follows:

- Read
  - List Folder/Read Data
  - Read Attributes
  - Read Extended Attributes
  - Read Permissions
- Read & Execute or List Folder Contents
  - All special permissions for Read
  - Traverse Folder/Execute File
- Write
  - Create Files/Write Data
  - Create Folders/Append Data
  - Write Attributes
  - Write Extended Attributes
- Modify
  - All special permissions for Read
  - All special permissions for Write
  - Delete
- Full Control
  - All special permissions listed previously
  - Delete Subfolders And Files
  - Change Permissions
  - Take Ownership

Table 13-3 describes how Windows 7 uses each special permission.

TABLE 13-3 Special Permissions for Files and Folders

SPECIAL PERMISSION	DESCRIPTION
Traverse Folder/ Execute File	Traverse Folder allows direct access to a folder in order to reach subfolders, even if you don't have explicit access to read the data the folder contains. Execute File allows you to run an executable file.
List Folder/ Read Data	List Folder lets you view file and folder names. Read Data allows you to view the contents of a file.
Read Attributes	Allows you to read the basic attributes of a file or a folder. These attributes include Read-Only, Hidden, System, and Archive.
Read Extended Attributes	Allows you to view the extended attributes (named data streams) associated with a file.
Create Files/ Write Data	Create Files allows you to put new files in a folder. Write Data allows you to overwrite existing data in a file (but not add new data to an existing file, which is covered by Append Data).
Create Folders/ Append Data	Create Folders allows you to create subfolders within folders. Append Data allows you to add data to the end of an existing file (but not to overwrite existing data, which is covered by Write Data).
Write Attributes	Allows you to change the basic attributes of a file or a folder. These attributes include Read-Only, Hidden, System, and Archive.
Write Extended Attributes	Allows you to change the extended attributes (named data streams) associated with a file.
Delete Subfolders And Files	Allows you to delete the contents of a folder. If you have this permission, you can delete the subfolders and files in a folder even if you don't specifically have Delete permission on the subfolder or the file.
Delete	Allows you to delete a file or a folder. If a folder isn't empty and you don't have Delete permission for one or more of its files or subfolders, you won't be able to delete it unless you have the Delete Subfolders And Files permission.
Read Permissions	Allows you to read all basic and special permissions assigned to a file or a folder.

SPECIAL PERMISSION	DESCRIPTION
Change Permissions	Allows you to change basic and special permissions assigned to a file or a folder.
Take Ownership	Allows you to take ownership of a file or a folder. By default, administrators can always take ownership of a file or a folder and can also grant this permission to others.
Synchronize	Allows you to synchronize an offline file or folder.

In Windows Explorer, you can view special permissions for a file or folder by right-clicking the file or folder you want to work with and then clicking Properties. In the Properties dialog box, select the Security tab and then click Advanced to display the Advanced Security Settings dialog box, shown in Figure 13-3. In this dialog box, the permissions are presented much as they are on the Security tab. The key differences are that you see individual allow or deny permission sets, whether and from where permissions are inherited, and the resources to which the permissions apply.

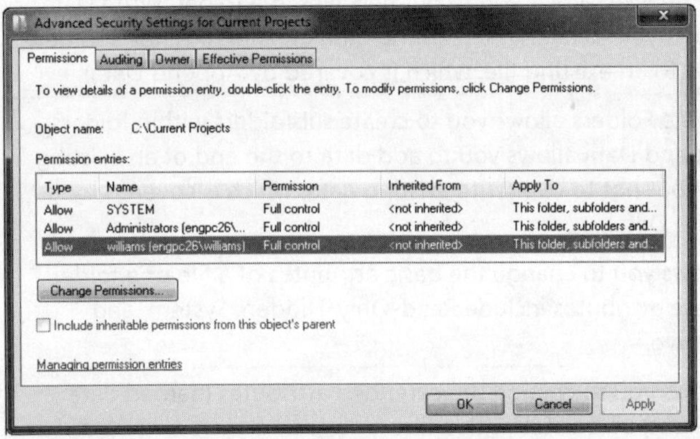

FIGURE 13-3 Use the Advanced Security Settings dialog box to configure special permissions.

Once you open the Advanced Security Settings dialog box, you need to click Change Permissions. You then see an editable version of the Permissions tab and can set special permissions by using the Add, Edit, and Remove buttons. To add a user or a group and then set special permissions for that user or group, follow these steps:

1. Click Add to display the Select User, Computer, Service Account, Or Group dialog box.
2. Type the name of a user or a group account that is a member of the selected or default domain. Be sure to reference the user account name rather than the user's full name. Only one name can be entered at a time.

3. Click OK. The Permission Entry For dialog box, shown in Figure 13-4, is displayed.

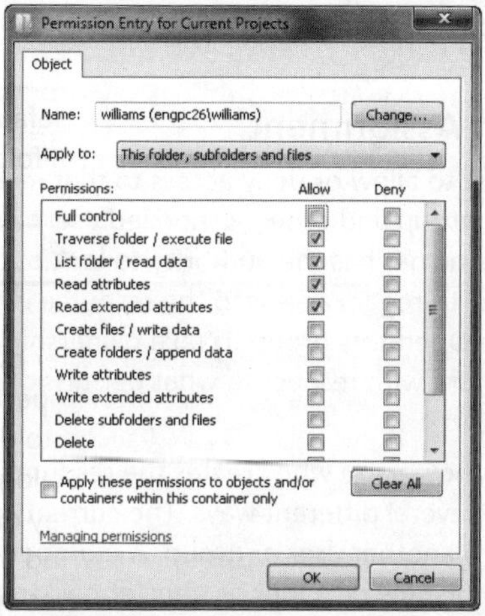

FIGURE 13-4 Configure the special permissions that should be allowed or denied.

4. Allow or deny the special permissions you want to apply. If any permissions are shaded (unavailable), they are inherited from a parent folder. You can override the inherited permission if necessary by selecting the opposite permission, such as Deny rather than Allow.

5. If the options in the Apply To list are available, choose the appropriate option to ensure that the permissions are properly inherited. The options include the following:

   - **This Folder Only** The permissions apply only to the currently selected folder.
   - **This Folder, Subfolders And Files** The permissions apply to this folder, any subfolders of this folder, and any files in any of these folders.
   - **This Folder And Subfolders** The permissions apply to this folder and any subfolders of this folder. They do not apply to any files in any of these folders.
   - **This Folder And Files** The permissions apply to this folder and any files in this folder. They do not apply to any subfolders of this folder.
   - **Subfolders And Files Only** The permissions apply to any subfolders of this folder and any files in any of these folders. They do not apply to this folder itself.
   - **Subfolders Only** The permissions apply to any subfolders of this folder but not to the folder itself or any files in any of these folders.

- **Files Only** The permissions apply to any files in this folder and any files in subfolders of this folder. They do not apply to this folder itself or to subfolders.

6. When you have finished configuring permissions, click OK.

File Ownership and Permission Assignment

The owner of a file or a folder has the right to allow or deny access to that resource. Although members of the Administrators group and other authorized users also have the right to allow or deny access, the owner has the authority to lock out non-administrator users, and then the only way to regain access to the resource is for an administrator or a member of the Restore Operators group to take ownership of it. This makes the file or folder owner important with respect to what permissions are allowed or denied for a given resource.

The default owner of a file or folder is the person who creates the resource. Ownership can be taken or transferred in several different ways. The current owner of a file or folder can transfer ownership to another user or group. A member of the Administrators group can take ownership of a file or folder or transfer ownership to another user or group—even if administrators are locked out of the resource according to the permissions. Any user with the Take Ownership permission on the file or folder can take ownership, as can any member of the Backup Operators group (or anyone else with the Restore Files And Directories user right, for that matter).

Taking Ownership of Files and Folders

If you are an administrator, an authorized user, or a backup operator, you can take ownership of a file or folder by completing the following steps:

1. In Windows Explorer, open the file or folder's Properties dialog box by right-clicking the file or folder and then clicking Properties.
2. On the Security tab, click Advanced to display the Advanced Security Settings dialog box.
3. On the Owner tab, click Edit. This opens the Advanced Security Settings dialog box for editing, as shown in Figure 13-5.
4. In the Change Owner To list, select the new owner. If you're taking ownership of a folder, you can take ownership of all subfolders and files within the folder by selecting the Replace Owner On Subcontainers And Objects option.
5. Click OK twice when you have finished.

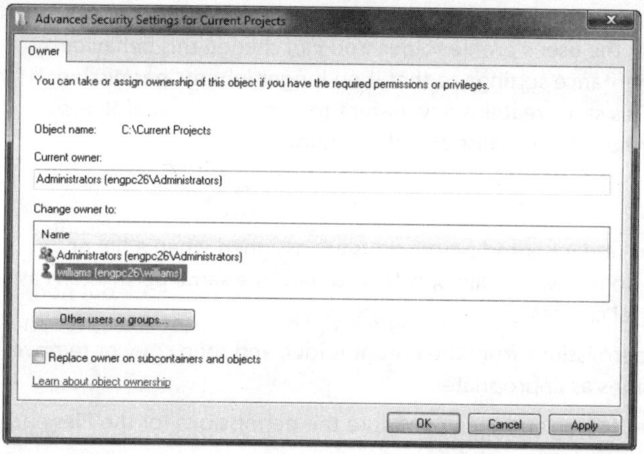

FIGURE 13-5 Use the Owner tab to take ownership of a file or a folder.

Assigning Ownership

If you are an administrator or the current owner of a file, you can assign ownership of a file or a folder to another user or group by completing these steps:

1. In Windows Explorer, open the file or folder's Properties dialog box by right-clicking the file or folder and then clicking Properties.
2. On the Security tab, click Advanced to display the Advanced Security Settings dialog box.
3. On the Owner tab, click Edit. This opens the Advanced Security Settings dialog box for editing.
4. Click Other Users Or Groups to display the Select User, Computer, Service Account, Or Group dialog box.
5. Type the name of a user or a group, and then click Check Names. If multiple names match the value you entered, you'll see a list of names and can choose the one you want to use. Otherwise, the name will be filled in for you, and you can click OK to close the Select User, Computer, Service Account, Or Group dialog box.
6. In the Change Owner To list, select the new owner. If you're assigning ownership of a folder, you can assign ownership of all subfolders and files within the folder by selecting the Replace Owner On Subcontainers And Objects option.
7. Click OK twice when you have finished.

Applying Permissions Through Inheritance

In the file and folder hierarchy used by Windows 7, the root folder of a local disk and the %UserProfile% folder are the parent folders of all the files and folders they contain by default. Any time you add a resource, it inherits the permissions of the local disk's root folder or the user's profile folder. You can change this behavior by modifying a folder's inheritance settings so that it no longer inherits permissions from its parent folder. This step creates a new parent folder, and any subfolders or files you add will then inherit the permissions of this folder.

Inheritance Essentials

Inheritance is automatic, and inherited permissions are assigned when a file or folder is created. If you do not want a file or folder to have the same permissions as a parent, you have several choices:

- Stop inheriting permissions from the parent folder, and then copy or remove existing permissions as appropriate.
- Access the parent folder, and then configure the permissions for the files and folders it contains.
- Try to override an inherited permission by selecting the opposite permission. In most cases, Deny overrides Allow.

Inherited permissions are shaded (unavailable) on the Security tab of a file or folder's Properties dialog box. Also, when you assign new permissions to a folder, the permissions propagate to the subfolders and files contained in that folder and either supplement or replace existing permissions. This propagation lets you grant additional users and groups access to a folder's resources or to further restrict access to a folder's resources independently of a parent folder.

To better understand inheritance, consider the following examples:

- On drive C, you create a folder named Data and then create a subfolder named CurrentProjects. By default, Data inherits the permissions of the C:\ folder, and these permissions are in turn inherited by the CurrentProjects folder. Any files you add to the C:\, C:\Data, and C:\Data\CurrentProjects folders have the same permissions—those set for or inherited from the C:\ folder.
- On drive C, you create a folder named Docs and then create a subfolder named Working. You stop inheritance on the Working folder by removing the inherited permissions of the parent, C:\. Any files you add to the C:\Docs\Working folder inherit the permissions of the C:\Docs folder and no other.
- On drive C, you create a folder named Backup and then create a subfolder named Sales. You add permissions to the Sales folder that grant access to members of the Sales group. Any files added to the C:\Backup\Sales folder inherit the permissions of the C:\ folder and also have additional access permissions for members of the Sales group.

REAL WORLD **Many new administrators wonder what the advantage of inheritance is and why it is used. Although inheritance occasionally seems like more trouble than it's worth, inheritance enables you to very efficiently manage permissions.**

Without inheritance, you'd have to configure permissions on every file and folder you create. If you wanted to change permissions later, you'd have to go through all your files and folders again. With inheritance, all new files and folders automatically inherit a set of permissions. If you need to change permissions, you can make the changes in a top-level or parent folder, and the changes can be automatically applied to all subfolders and files in that folder. In this way, a single permission set can be applied to many files and folders without editing the security of individual files and folders.

Viewing Inherited Permissions

To view the inherited permissions on a file or folder, right-click the file or folder in Windows Explorer, and then click Properties. On the Security tab of the Properties dialog box, click Advanced to display the Advanced Security Settings dialog box, shown earlier in Figure 13-3. The Permission column lists the current permissions assigned to the resource. If the permission is inherited, the Inherited From column shows the parent folder. If the permission is inherited by other resources, the Apply To column shows the types of resources that inherit the permission.

Stopping Inheritance

If you want a file or folder to stop inheriting permissions from a parent folder, follow these steps:

1. In Windows Explorer, right-click the file or folder, and then click Properties. On the Security tab, click Advanced.
2. On the Permissions tab, click Change Permissions. This opens the Advanced Security Settings dialog box for editing.
3. Clear the Include Inheritable Permissions From This Object's Parent check box.
4. As shown in Figure 13-6, you can now add the permissions that were previously applied or remove inherited permissions and apply only the permissions that you explicitly set on the folder or file. Click Add, and then assign additional permissions as necessary, or click Remove.

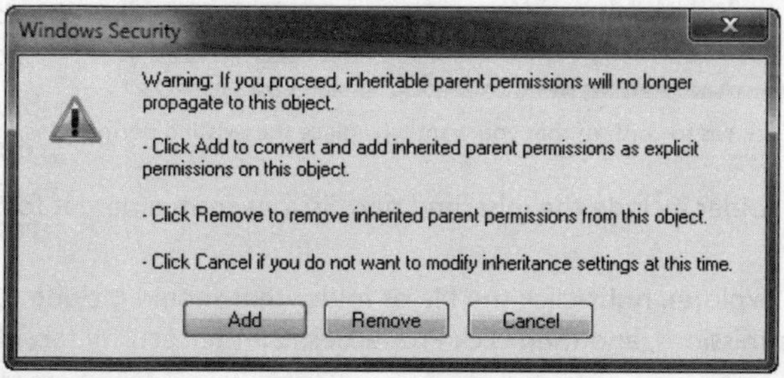

FIGURE 13-6 Copy or remove the inherited permissions.

TIP **If you remove the inherited permissions and no other permissions are assigned, everyone but the owner of the resource is denied access. This effectively locks out everyone except the owner of a folder or file. However, administrators still have the right to take ownership of the resource regardless of the permissions. Thus, if an administrator is locked out of a file or a folder and truly needs access, she can take ownership and then have unrestricted access.**

Restoring Inherited Permissions

Over time, the permissions on files and subfolders can become so dramatically different from those of a parent folder that it is nearly impossible to effectively manage access. To make managing file and folder access easier, you might want to take the drastic step of restoring the inherited permissions to all resources contained in a parent folder. In this way, subfolders and files get all inheritable permissions from the parent folder, and all explicitly defined permissions on the individual subfolders and files are removed.

To restore the inherited permissions of a parent folder, follow these steps:

1. In Windows Explorer, right-click the folder, and then click Properties. On the Security tab, click Advanced.
2. On the Permissions tab, click Change Permissions. This opens the Advanced Security Settings dialog box for editing.
3. Select Replace All Child Object Permissions With Inheritable Permissions From This Object, and then click OK.
4. As shown in Figure 13-7, you see a prompt explaining that this action will replace all explicitly defined permissions and enable propagation of inheritable permissions. Click Yes.

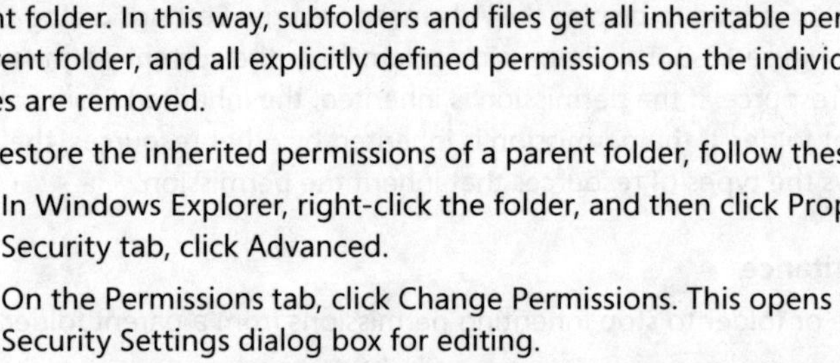

FIGURE 13-7 Click Yes to confirm that you want to replace the existing permissions.

To have a file or folder include the inherited permissions from a parent folder, follow these steps:

1. In Windows Explorer, right-click the file or folder that should include inherited permissions, and then click Properties. On the Security tab, click Advanced.

2. On the Permissions tab, click Change Permissions. This opens the Advanced Security Settings dialog box for editing.
3. Select Include Inheritable Permissions From This Object's Parent, and then click OK.

Determining the Effective Permissions and Troubleshooting

NTFS permissions are complex and can be difficult to manage. Sometimes a change—even a very minor one—can have unintended consequences. Users might suddenly find that they are denied access to files they could previously access or that they have access to files to which access should never have been granted. In either scenario, something has gone wrong with permissions. You have a problem, and you need to fix it.

You should start troubleshooting these or other problems with permissions by determining the effective permissions for the files or folders in question. As the name implies, the effective permissions tell you exactly which permissions are in effect with regard to a particular user or group. The effective permissions are important because they enable you to quickly determine the cumulative set of permissions that apply.

For a user, the effective permissions are based on all the permissions the user has been granted or denied, no matter whether the permissions are applied explicitly or obtained from groups of which the user is a member. For example, if JimB is a member of the Users, Sales, Marketing, SpecTeam, and Managers groups, the effective permissions on a file or a folder is the cumulative set of permissions that JimB has been explicitly assigned and the permissions assigned to the Users, Sales, Marketing, SpecTeam, and Managers groups. If JimB is a member of a group that is specifically denied a permission, JimB will be denied that permission as well, even if another group is allowed that permission. This occurs because deny entries have precedence over allow entries.

To determine the effective permissions for a user or a group with regard to a file or folder, complete the following steps:

1. In Windows Explorer, right-click the file or folder you want to work with, and then click Properties. In the Properties dialog box, click the Security tab, and then click Advanced to display the Advanced Security Settings dialog box.
2. Click the Effective Permissions tab, click Select, type the name of the user or group, and then click OK.
3. The effective permissions for the specified user or group are displayed using the complete set of special permissions. If a user has full control over the selected resource, he or she will have all the permissions, as shown in Figure 13-8. Otherwise, a subset of the permissions is selected, and you have to carefully consider whether the user or group has the appropriate permissions. Use Table 13-3 earlier in the chapter to help you interpret the permissions.

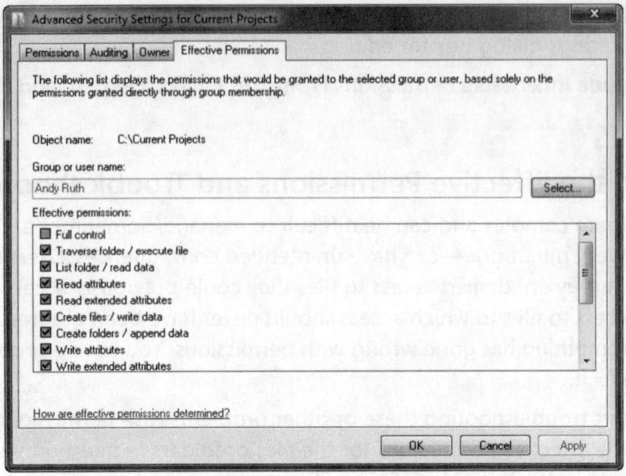

FIGURE 13-8 Any checked permissions have been granted to the specified user or group.

NOTE **You must have appropriate permissions to view the effective permissions of any user or group. It is also important to remember that you cannot determine the effective permissions for implicit groups or special identities, such as Authenticated Users or Everyone. Furthermore, the effective permissions do not take into account those permissions granted to a user because he or she is the Creator Owner.**

Sharing Files and Folders over the Network

Windows 7 supports two file-sharing models: public folder sharing and standard folder sharing. Either model or both can be used in workgroups and domains, but standard folder sharing is preferred because it is more secure than public folder sharing. Standard folder sharing enables you to use a standard set of permissions to allow or deny initial access to files and folders over a network. Standard folder sharing settings are enabled or disabled on a per-computer basis. You can turn file sharing on or off by following these steps:

1. Click Start, and then click Control Panel. In Control Panel, under the Network And Internet heading, click the Choose Homegroup And Sharing Options link, and then click Change Advanced Sharing Settings.
2. Each available network profile has a separate management panel with configuration settings. Use the expand button to display the profile you want to work with.
3. To enable file and printer sharing, select Turn On File And Printer Sharing. To disable file and printer sharing, select Turn Off File And Printer Sharing. Click Apply.

Controlling Access to Network Shares

When a user accesses a file or folder over a network and standard folder sharing is enabled, two levels of permissions are used that together determine the actions a user can perform with regard to a particular shared file or folder. The first level of permissions includes those set on the share itself. They define the maximum level of access. A user or a group can never have more permissions than those granted by the share. The second level of permissions are those set on the files and folders. These permissions serve to further restrict the permitted actions.

Three share permissions are available:

- **Owner** Users with this permission have Full Control, Read, and Change permissions, as well as the additional capabilities to change file and folder permissions and take ownership of files and folders. If you have Owner permissions on a shared resource, you have full access to the shared resource.
- **Read/Write** Users with this permission have Read and Change permissions and the additional capabilities to create files and subfolders, modify files, change attributes on files and subfolders, and delete files and subfolders. If you have Read/Write permissions on a shared resource, you can read, change, and delete data but cannot take ownership.
- **Read** Users with this permission have only Read permission. They can view file and subfolder names, access the subfolders of the share, read file data and attributes, and run program files. If you have Read permission on a shared resource, the most you can do is perform read operations.

Permissions assigned to groups work like this: If a user is a member of a group that is granted share permissions, the user also has those permissions. If a user is a member of multiple groups, the permissions are cumulative. For example, if one group has Read access and another has Read/Write access, the user will have Read/Write access. If one group has Read access and another has Owner access, the user will have Owner access.

You can override this behavior by specifically denying an access permission. Denying permission takes precedence and overrides permissions that have been granted. If you don't want a user or a group to have a permission, configure the share permissions so that the user or group is denied that permission. For example, if a user is a member of a group that has been granted Owner permissions for a share, but the user should have only Read/Write permissions, configure the share to deny Owner permissions to that user.

Creating a Shared Resource

Folders can be shared both in workgroups and domains. To share the first resource on a computer, you must be a local administrator. Sharing the first resource sets up the computer for sharing other resources and allows other users to share resources they own or to which they have appropriate access permissions.

You can create shares by using several different tools, including the following:

- **Windows Explorer** Use Windows Explorer when you want to share folders on the computer to which you are logged on.
- **Computer Management** Use Computer Management when you want to share folders on any computer to which you can connect.
- **Net Share** Use Net Share from the command line when you want to use a script to share folders. Type **net share /?** at the command prompt for the syntax of the command.

Creating a shared resource is a multipart process. First, you share the folder so that it can be accessed, and then you set the share permissions. Afterward, you should check and modify the file-system permissions as necessary. This section examines sharing a resource and setting its permissions by using Windows Explorer and Computer Management. For details on working with file system permissions, see the section "Controlling Access to Files and Folders with NTFS Permissions" earlier in this chapter.

Sharing a Resource and Setting Share Permissions in Windows Explorer

Windows Explorer supports basic sharing and advanced sharing. With basic sharing, you can share any folder except the root folder of a drive. With advanced sharing, you can share the root folder of a drive and any other folder. The root folders of drives are shared automatically as administrative shares.

To share a folder by using basic sharing, follow these steps:

1. In Windows Explorer, right-click the folder you want to share, click Share With, and then select Specific People. This opens the File Sharing wizard, shown in Figure 13-9.

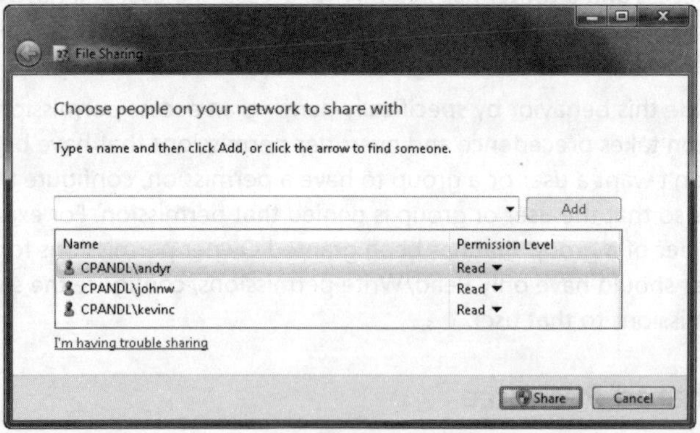

FIGURE 13-9 Use the File Sharing wizard to configure sharing of the selected file or folder.

2. Type a name, and then Click Add, or click the arrow to find someone. In workgroups, computers will always show only local accounts and groups. In

domains, you'll see local users and groups and also be able to find users in domains.

3. When you click Add, the selected users and groups are added to the Name list. You can then configure permissions for each user and group by clicking an account name to display the Permission Level options and then choosing the appropriate permission level. The options for permission levels are Read and Read/Write.
4. Finally, click Share to create the share. After Windows 7 creates the share and makes it available for use, note the share name. This is the name by which the shared resource can be accessed. If you want to e-mail a link to the shared resource to someone, click the E-mail link. If you want to copy a link to the shared resource to the Clipboard, click the Copy link. Click Done when you have finished.

NOTE **Normally, when you create a share, users access the share by using an abbreviated UNC path to the share. For example, if you share the C:\Data\Reports\ Current folder as Reports on CorPC85, users can access the folder using the UNC path \\CorPC85\Reports. However, when you share a folder within a user's profile, users access the share by using a path that is relative to the Users folder on the computer. This occurs because Windows configures sharing in relation to where the folder is located in the Users folder. For example, if MollyH shares her Documents folder on CustPC27, the UNC path to the share is \\CustPC27\Users\MollyH\ Documents.**

To share a folder using advanced sharing, follow these steps:

1. In Windows Explorer, right-click the folder you want to share, and then click Properties. This opens the folder's Properties dialog box.
2. On the Sharing tab, click Advanced Sharing. In the Advanced Sharing dialog box, select Share This Folder.
3. Windows sets the share name to the folder name by default. Either accept the default share name or enter a different name.
4. Click Permissions. Use the Permissions For dialog box to configure access permissions for the share. Click OK.
5. Click Caching. Use the Offline Settings dialog box to specify whether and how data is cached for offline use. Click OK.
6. Click OK, and then click Close.

Changing or Stopping Sharing

If you right-click a folder that is shared, point to Share With, and then click Nobody, you remove sharing settings and stop sharing the folder. To change sharing permissions, right-click the shared folder, point to Share With, and then click Specific People. You can then grant access to additional users and groups as discussed previously. To remove access for a user or group, select the user or group in the Name list, and then click Remove. When you have finished making changes, click Share to reconfigure sharing options, and then click Done.

When you are using advanced sharing, you can configure sharing by right-clicking the folder and then clicking Properties. On the Sharing tab, click Advanced Sharing. You'll then be able to enable or disable alternate shares and specify connection limits for users. You'll also be able to configure permissions and caching.

Sharing a Folder and Setting Share Permissions in Computer Management

Using Computer Management, you can share a folder on any computer to which you have administrator access. By connecting remotely to the computer rather than logging on locally, you usually save time because you don't need to access the computer or leave your desk. Follow these steps to use Computer Management to share a folder:

1. To start Computer Management, click Start, right-click Computer, and then click Manage. By default, Computer Management connects to the local computer, and the root node of the console tree displays the Computer Management (Local) label.

   TIP **If you want to use the Create A Shared Folder Wizard to share a folder on a local computer, start the wizard directly and skip steps 1–4. Simply type shrpubw at an elevated command prompt, and then click Next when the wizard starts.**

2. Right-click Computer Management in the console tree, and then click Connect To Another Computer. In the Select Computer dialog box, the Another Computer option is selected by default. Type the fully qualified domain name of the computer you want to work with, such as **engpc08.microsoft.com**, where engpc08 is the computer name and microsoft.com is the domain name. If you don't know the computer name and network discovery is enabled, click Browse to search for the computer.
3. Expand System Tools\Shared Folders, and then select Shares to display the shared folders on the system you are working with, as shown in Figure 13-10.

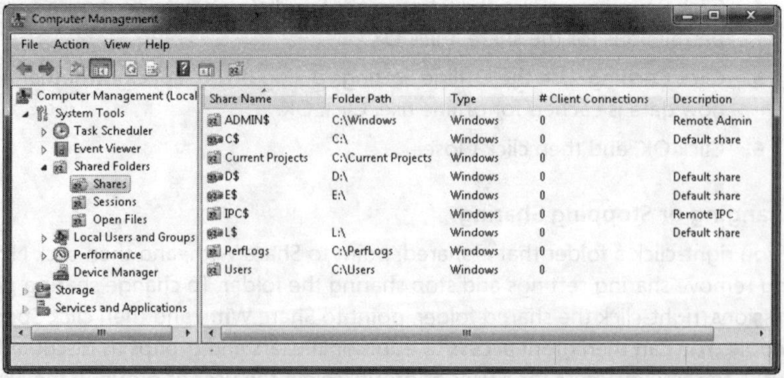

FIGURE 13-10 All available shared folders on the computer are listed on the Shares node.

4. To start the Create A Shared Folder Wizard, right-click Shares, and then click New Share. Click Next to display the Folder Path page.
5. In the Folder Path field, type the full path to the folder that you want to share, such as C:\Data. If you don't know the full path, click Browse, and then use the Browse For Folder dialog box to find the folder you want to share. The Browse For Folder dialog box also lets you create a new folder that you can then share. Click Next to display the Name, Description, And Settings page.
6. In the Share Name field, type a name for the share. Share names must be unique for each system. They can be up to 80 characters in length and can contain spaces. If you want to provide support for Windows 98, Windows Me, or Windows NT, you should limit the share name to 12 or fewer characters.
7. Type a description of the share's contents in the Share Description field.

   TIP **By default, only files and programs that users specify are available for offline use. Click Change if you want to modify the default offline files settings. You can make all files and programs available for offline use by selecting All Files And Programs That Users Open From The Shared Folder Are Automatically Available Offline, or you can make no files and programs available for offline use by selecting No Files Or Programs From The Shared Folder Are Available Offline. Click OK after making your selection.**

8. When you are ready to continue, click Next to display the Shared Folder Permissions page. The available options are as follows:
   - **All Users Have Read-Only Access** Default option. Gives users the right to view files and read data but restricts them from creating, modifying, or deleting files and folders.
   - **Administrators Have Full Access; Other Users Have Read-Only Access** Gives administrators full access to the share and gives other users read-only access. Administrators can create, modify, and delete files and folders. On NTFS, this option also gives administrators the right to change permissions and to take ownership of files and folders. Other users can only view files and read data. They can't create, modify, or delete files and folders.
   - **Administrators Have Full Access; Other Users Have No Access** Gives only administrators full access to the share.
   - **Customize Permissions** Enables you to configure access for specific users and groups, which is usually the best technique to use. To use this option, select Customize Permissions, click Custom, and then set permissions as appropriate for the share.
9. After you set up permissions on the share, click Next, and then click Finish to share the folder. Click Finish again to exit the wizard.

If you later want to stop sharing the folder, you can do this in Computer Management by right-clicking the shared folder and then clicking Stop Sharing. When prompted to confirm the action, click Yes.

Creating and Managing Shared Folders in Group Policy

You can share folders using Group Policy preferences. I recommend this approach only when you can carefully target computers so that only computers that should actually share data are configured with shared folders.

To create a preference item to create, update, replace, or delete shared folders, follow these steps:

1. Open a Group Policy object (GPO) for editing in the Group Policy Management Editor. Expand Computer Configuration\Preferences\Windows Settings, and then select Network Shares.
2. Right-click the Network Shares node, point to New, and then click Network Share. This opens the New Network Share Properties dialog box.
3. In the New Network Share Properties dialog box, select Create, Update, Replace, or Delete in the Action list.
4. In the Share Name field, type a name for the share. Share names must be unique for each system. They can be up to 80 characters in length and can contain spaces.
5. In the Folder Path field, type the full path to the folder that you want to share, such as C:\Data. If you don't know the full path, click Browse, and then use the Browse For Folder dialog box to find a folder like the one you want to share on other computers.

   REAL WORLD **If you want to use an environment variable in the folder path, press F3 to display a list of system-defined variables. Click the variable you'd like to use, such as LogOnUser. By default, variables are resolved by Group Policy before they are applied to a user's computer. To use the variable as a placeholder that is resolved on the user's computer instead, clear the Resolve Variable check box before you click Select. This inserts a placeholder for the variable to be resolved on the user's computer.**

   In Group Policy preferences, you can easily distinguish between variables resolved by Group Policy and variables resolved on a user's computer. Variables resolved by Group Policy have the syntax %*VariableName*%, such as %ProgramFiles%. Variables resolved on a user's computer have the syntax %<*VariableName*>%, such as %<ProgramFiles>%.

6. In the Comment field, type a description of the share's contents.
7. When you are updating or deleting shares, you can modify or delete all shares of a particular type rather than an individual share. You can do any or all of the following:

- Update or delete all regular shares (meaning shares that are not hidden, administrative, or special shares) by selecting Update All Regular Shares or Delete All Regular Shares.
- Update or delete all hidden shares except the administrative shares and special shares (which includes drive-letter shares, ADMIN$, FAX$, IPC$, and Print$) by selecting Update All Hidden Non-Administrative Shares or Delete All Hidden Non-Administrative Shares.
- Update or delete all administrative shares (which includes only the drive-letter shares) by selecting Update All Administrative Drive-Letter Shares or Delete All Administrative Drive-Letter Shares.

NOTE **If you want to modify special shares, such as ADMIN$, FAX$, IPC$, and Print$, or other system shares, such as SYSVOL and NETLOGON, you can create a preference item for the share and set the Share Name field to the name of the special share.**

8. Specify the number of users who can connect to the share. Select Maximum Allowed to allow the maximum number of users allowed by the operating system. Select Allow This Number Of Users to specify a limit.
9. Specify whether access controls should be used to determine whether users can see folders in the share. Select Enable if you want only users with Read permission to be able to see the folders within the share. Select Disable if you want all users to be able to see the folders within the share.
10. Use the options on the Common tab to control how the preference is applied. Because you are enforcing a control, you will usually want to apply the setting every time Group Policy is refreshed. In this case, do not select Apply Once And Do Not Reapply.
11. Click OK. The next time Group Policy is refreshed, the preference item will be applied as appropriate for the GPO in which you define the preference item.

Using and Accessing Shared Resources

Once you share a file or folder, users can connect to it as a network resource or map it to a drive letter on their machines. When a network drive is mapped, users can access it as they do a local drive on their computer.

You can map a network drive to a shared file or folder by completing the following steps:

1. Click Start, and then click Computer. In the Computer window, click the Map Network Drive button on the toolbar. This displays the Map Network Drive dialog box, shown in Figure 13-11.

   TIP **You can map or disconnect a network drive in any Windows Explorer window via the options on the Tools menu. The Tools menu is available only when classic menus are displayed in Windows Explorer. If the classic menus are**

not shown, press F10 to display them, or click Organize, click Layout, and then click Menu Bar.

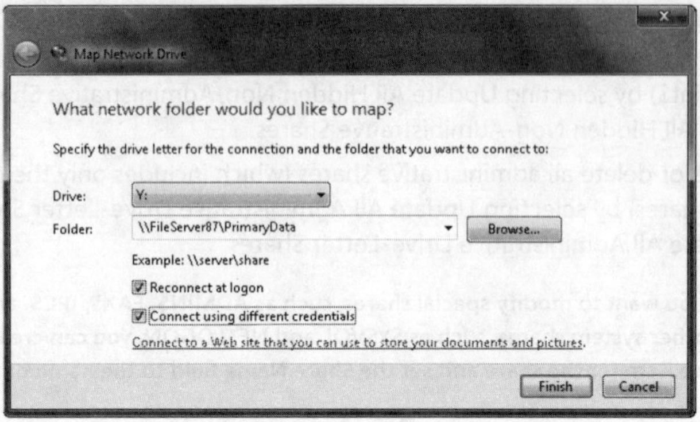

FIGURE 13-11 Map the share you want to use to a network drive.

2. Use the Drive list to select a free drive letter to use, and then click the Browse button to the right of the Folder list. In the Browse For Folder dialog box, expand the network folders until you can select the name of the workgroup or the domain with which you want to work.
3. When you expand the name of a computer in a workgroup or a domain, you'll see a list of shared folders. Select the shared folder you want to work with, and then click OK.
4. Select Reconnect At Logon if you want Windows 7 to connect to the shared folder automatically at the start of each session.
5. Click Finish. If the currently logged-on user doesn't have appropriate access permissions for the share, select Connect Using Different Credentials, and then click Finish. After you click Finish, you can enter the user name and password of the account with which you want to connect to the shared folder. Enter the user name in Domain\Username format, such as Cpandl\Williams.

If you later decide that you don't want to map the network drive, click Start, and then click Computer. Under Network Location, right-click the network drive icon, and then click Disconnect.

You can access Group Policy and use a preference item to configure the network drives on computers throughout the domain by completing the following steps:

1. Open a Group Policy object (GPO) for editing in the Group Policy Management Editor. Expand User Configuration\Preferences\Windows Settings, and then select Drive Maps.
2. Right-click the Drive Maps node, point to New, and then click Mapped Drive. This opens the New Drive Properties dialog box.

3. In the New Drive Properties dialog box, select Create, Update, Replace, or Delete in the Action list.
4. In the Location field, enter the UNC path to the network share, such as \\CorpServer45\corpdatashare, or click the Browse button to locate a share.

   REAL WORLD **If you want to use an environment variable in the share path, press F3 to display a list of system-defined variables. Click the variable you'd like to use, such as LogOnUser. By default, variables are resolved by Group Policy before they are applied to a user's computer. To use the variable as a placeholder that is resolved on the user's computer instead, clear the Resolve Variable check box before you click Select. This inserts a placeholder for the variable to be resolved on the user's computer.**

   In Group Policy preferences, you can easily distinguish between variables resolved by Group Policy and variables resolved on a user's computer. Variables resolved by Group Policy have the syntax %*VariableName*%, such as %ProgramFiles%. Variables resolved on a user's computer have the syntax %<*VariableName*>%, such as %<ProgramFiles>%.

5. Select Reconnect if you want Windows 7 to connect to the shared folder automatically at the start of each session.
6. Enter the label for the network drive in the Label As field.
7. Under Drive Letter, specify how the drive letter should be assigned. To use the first available drive letter starting after a drive letter that you specify, select Use First Available, Starting At, and then specify the starting drive letter. To always use a specific drive letter, choose Use, and then choose the drive letter. Unless you know for sure that a drive letter is available, you'll usually want to use the first available drive letter.
8. Optionally, specify the credentials to use when connecting to the network share.
   - If you want to map a network drive using credentials other than those of the user, type the credentials to be used. The password is encrypted and stored as part of the GPO in the Sysvol on domain controllers.
   - If you want to force a user to enter the required credentials, enter %<LogonUser>% in the User Name field and do not enter anything in the Password and Confirm Password fields.

NOTE **Entering the credentials for a network drive is a poor security practice that should be used only in a limited number of situations. If you use this technique, be sure to periodically change the password on the related user account and then update the passwords in your preference items that use this account.**

9. Additional options are provided for hiding or showing either the drive you are configuring or all drives. When you show or hide all drives, both network drives and physical drives are affected.

10. Use the options on the Common tab to control how the preference is applied. Because you are enforcing a control, you will usually want to apply the setting every time Group Policy is refreshed. In this case, do not select Apply Once And Do Not Reapply.
11. Click OK. The next time policy is refreshed, the preference item will be applied as appropriate for the GPO in which you defined the preference item.

Using and Accessing Shared Folders for Administration

In Windows 7, several special shares are created automatically and are intended for use by administrators or the operating system. Most of the special shares have a dollar sign ($) added to the end of their names, which hides the shares from users. As an administrator, you might occasionally need to create your own hidden shares or work with the standard special shares.

Creating a hidden share is fairly easy. All you need to do is add a dollar sign ($) to the end of the share name. For example, if you want to share the C:\Reports folder but don't want it to be displayed in the normal file share lists, name it Reports$ rather than Reports. Hiding a share doesn't control access to the share, however. Access to shares is controlled by using permissions, regardless of whether a share is visible or hidden.

Which special shares are available on a system depends on the system's configuration. This means that some computers might have more special shares than others. The most commonly found special and administrative shares are listed in Table 13-4.

The best tools to use when you want to work with special or otherwise hidden shares are the Net Share command and Computer Management. To see a list of all shares on the local computer, including special shares for administrators, simply type **net share** at a command prompt. To see a list of all shares available on any computer on the network, complete the following steps:

1. To start Computer Management, click Start, right-click Computer, and then click Manage. By default, Computer Management connects to the local computer, and the root node of the console tree has the Computer Management (Local) label.
2. Right-click Computer Management in the console tree, and then click Connect To Another Computer. In the Select Computer dialog box, the Another Computer option is selected by default. Type the host name or the fully qualified domain name of the computer you want to work with, such as **engpc08** or **engpc08.microsoft.com**, where engpc08 is the computer name and microsoft.com is the domain name. If you don't know the computer name and network discovery is enabled, click Browse to search for the computer you want to work with.
3. Expand System Tools and Shared Folders, and then select Shares to display a list of the shares on the system you are working with.

TABLE 13-4 Special and Administrative Shares

SHARE NAME	DESCRIPTION
C$, D$, E$, and other local disk shares	A special share to the root of a drive. All local disks, including CD/DVD-ROM drives and their shares, are known as C$, D$, E$, and so on. These shares allow members of the Administrators and Backup Operators groups to connect to the root folder of a local disk and perform administrative tasks. For example, if you map to C$, you are connecting to C:\ and have full access to this local disk.
ADMIN$	An administrative share for accessing the %SystemRoot% folder in which the operating system files reside. This share is meant to be used for remote administration. For administrators working remotely with systems, ADMIN$ provides a convenient shortcut for directly accessing the operating system folder.
IPC$	An administrative share used to support named pipes that programs use for interprocess (or process-to-process) communications. Because named pipes can be redirected over the network to connect to local and remote systems, they also enable remote administration.
PRINT$	Supports printer sharing by providing access to printer drivers. Whenever you share a printer, the system puts the printer drivers in this share so that other computers can access them as needed.

Sometimes when you are managing folders or files, you might not want users to be connected to a shared folder. For example, if you need to move files to a new location, before you move the files, you might want to ensure that no one is using them. One way to see who is working with shared folders and their related files is to examine user sessions and open files.

Every user who connects to a shared folder creates a user session. To determine who is currently connected, click Sessions under Shared Folders in the console tree. The current users are listed in the right pane. To disconnect a user and end his or her session, right-click the session entry in the right pane, click Close Session, and then click OK to confirm the action. To disconnect all user sessions, right-click Sessions in the console tree, click Disconnect All Sessions, and then click OK to confirm the action.

Every shared file that is being accessed is listed as an open file. To determine which files are open, click Open Files under Shared Folders in the console tree. The currently open files are listed in the right pane. To close an open file, right-click the related entry in the right pane, click Close Open File, and then click OK to confirm the action. To close all open files, right-click Open Files in the console tree, click Disconnect All Open Files, and then click OK to confirm the action.

Troubleshooting File Sharing

You can diagnose and resolve most issues with file sharing by doing the following:

- **Check the connectivity between the computer sharing resources and the computer from which the user is trying to access the shared resources** Both computers must be connected to the network and configured with the appropriate TCP/IP settings. Both computers must have firewall configurations that permit inbound and outbound connectivity. The computer sharing resources must have a File And Printer Sharing exception in Windows Firewall. Windows Firewall supports multiple active profiles, and the active and applicable profile must be configured correctly. If you are using third-party firewall software, inbound connections must be allowed on UDP port 137, UDP port 138, TCP port 139, and all ports for ICMPv4 and (if applicable for echo requests) ICMPv6.
- **Check the connection credentials** When both computers are members of a domain, the user should connect to the share by using domain credentials. If the user has logged on to his or her computer as a local user rather than a domain user, you want to ensure that the user connects to the share with alternative credentials and that those alternative credentials are for an appropriate user account in the appropriate domain.
- **Check the Advanced Sharing settings in Network And Sharing Center** To successfully share files on a desktop computer running Windows 7, File And Printer sharing must be enabled for the active (current) network profile and the Prevent Users From Sharing Files Within Their Profiles policy must not be enabled. Computers can be connected to multiple networks simultaneously, and the network type for each active network must be correctly configured in Network And Sharing Center.
- **Check the network type for the active network** In Network And Sharing Center, the network type on both computers must be set appropriately. If the network type is set to Public, many sharing and connection settings are locked down and restricted.
- **Check share permissions, the underlying NTFS permissions, and the access flags on files** The share permissions must be configured to grant the user access. The underlying NTFS permissions must be configured to grant the user access. Access flags on files must be cleared to remove read-only, hidden, or system flags as appropriate.

For deeper troubleshooting, you need to look at the DNS configuration of both computers as well as the domain membership of both computers. Ideally, both computers should be on the same network or on networks connected by fast Ethernet connections. Ideally, both computers should be members of the same domain or be in trusted domains.

The Server service is required to share files. On the computer sharing files, check to be sure that the Server service is running and is configured correctly. Normally, the Server service should be configured for Automatic startup and should run under the LocalSystem account. The Server service depends on a Server SMB driver being available, and you can check this dependency on the Dependencies tab in the Server Properties dialog box.

In Group Policy for the computer sharing files, ensure that the user has the Access This Computer From The Network user right. This user right is set using policies for Computer Configuration under Windows Settings\Security Settings\Local Policies\User Rights Assignment. By default, all authenticated users have this user right.

Using and Configuring Public Folder Sharing

Public folder sharing is designed to enable users to share files and folders from a single location. It enables users to quickly determine everything they've publicly shared with others and organize publicly shared files by type. In this section, I'll examine how public folder sharing works and how public folder sharing can be configured.

Using Public Folder Sharing

You can access public folders in Windows Explorer by clicking Start and then clicking Computer. In Windows Explorer, click the leftmost option button in the address list, and then click Public. With public folder sharing, you copy or move files that you want to share to a computer's %SystemDrive%\Users\Public folder.

The Public folder has several subfolders that can be used to help organize public files, including:

- **Public Desktop** Used for shared desktop items.
- **Public Documents, Public Music, Public Pictures, Public Recorded TV, Public Videos** Used for shared document and media files.
- **Public Downloads** Used for shared downloads.

Any content placed in these subfolders is available to all users who log on to the computer (and to all network users if network access has been granted to the Public folder).

By default, everyone with a user account and password on a computer can access that computer's Public folder. When you copy or move files to the Public folder, access permissions are changed to match those of the Public folder, and some additional permissions are added as well.

The default permissions for the Public folder allow local computer users to read, write, change, and delete any public files. In the Public Music, Public Pictures, and Public Videos folders, %ComputerName%\Users are granted Read & Execute and Read permissions.

The default Public folder sharing configuration can be changed in two key ways:

- Allow users with network access to view and open public files but restrict them from changing, creating, or deleting public files. When you configure this option, the implicit group Everyone is granted Read & Execute and Read permissions to public files and Read & Execute, List Folder Contents, and Read permissions on public folders.
- Allow users with network access to view and manage public files. This allows network users to open, change, create, and delete public files. When you configure this option, the implicit group Everyone is granted Full Control permissions to public files and public folders.

Configuring Public Folder Sharing

Public folder sharing settings are set on a per-computer basis. The same public folder setting is used for the Public folder and all its subfolders. You can configure public folder sharing by following these steps:

1. Click Start, and then click Control Panel. In Control Panel, click Choose Homegroup And Sharing Options under Network And Internet. Next, click the Change Advanced Sharing Settings link.
2. Expand the network profile you want to work with. Under Public Folder Sharing, select the public folder sharing option you want to use. The options available are:
   - **Turn On Sharing So Anyone With Network Access Can Read And Write Files In The Public Folders** Select this option to grant co-owner access to the public folders and all public data to anyone who can access the computer over the network. Windows Firewall settings might prevent external access.
   - **Turn Off Public Folder Sharing** Select this option to turn off network access to the public folders and allow only locally (console) logged-on users access to public data.
3. To allow only people with a user account and password on the local computer to access shared files, shared printers, and the Public folder, expand the Password Protected Sharing panel, and then select the Turn On Password Protected Sharing option.
4. Click Save Changes to save the changes.

Auditing File and Folder Access

Although access permissions help protect data, they don't indicate who was trying to access files and folders inappropriately or who's been deleting important files either accidentally or intentionally. To track who accessed files and folders and what they did, you must configure auditing for file and folder access. You can track file and folder access by enabling auditing, specifying which files and folders to audit, and then monitoring the security logs.

Enabling Auditing for Files and Folders

You configure auditing policies by using Group Policy or local security policy. Use Group Policy when you want to set auditing policies throughout the enterprise. Use local security policy when you want to set auditing policies on a specific computer, keeping in mind that local policy can be overridden by Group Policy.

To enable auditing of files and folders, do one of the following:

- To configure local policy for a specific computer, start the Local Security Policy tool by clicking Start, pointing to All Programs, Administrative Tools, and then clicking Local Security Policy. Next, expand Local Policies, and then select Audit Policy.
- To configure enterprise policy, open a Group Policy object (GPO) for editing in the Group Policy Management Editor. Next, expand Administrative Templates policies for Computer Configuration under Local Policies, and then select Audit Policy.

Next, double-click Audit Object Access. This displays the Audit Object Access Properties dialog box. Under Audit These Attempts, select the Success check box to log successful access attempts, the Failure check box to log failed access attempts, or both check boxes, and then click OK. This enables auditing, but it doesn't specify which files and folders should be audited.

Configuring and Tracking Auditing

Once you've enabled Audit Object Access, you can control whether and how folder and file usage is tracked by setting the level of auditing for individual folders and files. Keep in mind that auditing is available only on NTFS volumes and that inheritance rules apply to auditing of files and folders. This allows you, for example, to audit access to every file or folder on a volume simply by specifying that you want to audit the root folder of the volume.

You specify files and folders to audit by completing the following steps:

1. In Windows Explorer, right-click the file or folder to be audited, and then click Properties.
2. In the Properties dialog box, click the Security tab, and then click Advanced.
3. In the Advanced Security Settings dialog box, click Continue on the Auditing tab. This displays an editable version of the Auditing tab, shown in Figure 13-12.

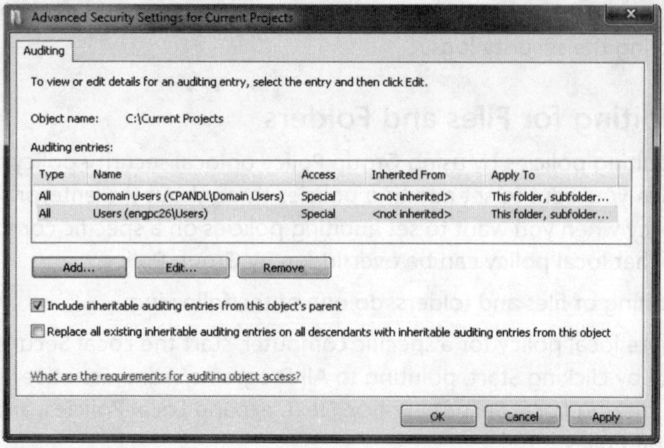

FIGURE 13-12 Review the current auditing settings and make new selections.

4. Use the Auditing Entries list to select the users, groups, or computers whose actions you want to audit. To add specific accounts, click Add, and then use the Select User, Computer, Service Account, Or Group dialog box to select an account name to add. If you want to audit actions for all users, use the special group Everyone. Otherwise, select the specific groups and users you want to audit, such as Domain Users. When you click OK, you'll see the Auditing Entry For dialog box, as shown in Figure 13-13.

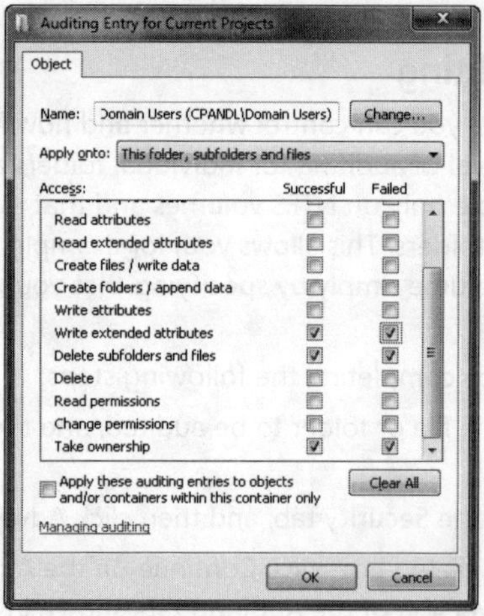

FIGURE 13-13 Specify the actions to audit for the designated user, group, or computer.

5. Use the Apply Onto list to specify how the auditing entry is to be applied.

6. The Access list allows you to specify which actions should be audited. Select the Successful or Failed check box, or both, for the events you want to audit.

The events you can audit are the same as the special permissions listed in Tables 13-1 and 13-3, except that you can't audit synchronization of offline files and folders. Click OK when you've finished. Repeat this process to audit other users, groups, or computers.

7. Before you click OK to close the Advanced Security Settings dialog box, you might want to configure inheritance. You have the same two inheritance options discussed earlier in the chapter:
   - If you want to inherit auditing settings from a parent object, be sure that the Include Inheritable Auditing Entries From This Object's Parent check box is selected.
   - If you want child objects of the current object to inherit the settings you are setting on the current folder, select the Replace All Existing Inheritable Auditing Entries... check box.

Often you'll want to track only failed actions. This way, you know if someone was trying to perform an action and failed. Keep in mind that a failed attempt doesn't always mean someone is trying to break into a file or folder. A user simply might have double-clicked a folder or file he or she doesn't have access to. In addition, some types of actions can cause multiple failed attempts to be logged even when the user performed the action only once. Regardless, you should always check multiple failed attempts because of the possibility that someone is attempting to break into a computer.

Any time files and folders that you've configured for auditing are accessed, the action is written to the system's Security log, which you can open in Event Viewer. Successful actions, such as successful file reads, cause successful events to be recorded. Failed actions, such as failed file deletions, cause failed events to be recorded.

CHAPTER 14

Maintaining Data Access and Availability

Maintaining data access and availability is a key part of user and system administration. Beyond standard file and folder management, the key tasks you'll perform frequently include configuring Windows Explorer options, managing offline file settings, working with disk quotas, and managing branch caching. Windows Explorer options control the available file and folder management features as well as the available file types. Offline file settings control the availability of files and folders when users are working offline. Quotas help limit the amount of disk space available to users. Branch caching stores downloaded documents and files locally for faster retrieval.

Configuring Windows Explorer Options

When you think about it, most of your time working with a computer is spent managing files and folders. You create files and folders to store and organize information. You move the files and folders from one location to another. You set file and folder properties, and so on. Because you spend so much time working with files and folders, a few simple techniques for effective management can go a long way toward saving you time and effort.

Customizing Windows Explorer

Windows Explorer is the tool of choice for working with files and folders. Unfortunately, its default settings are configured for the widest cross-spectrum of users and not experienced users or administrators. For example, as an administrator, you often want to see system files, such as dynamic-link library (DLL) files and files that have or haven't been compressed. By default, Windows Explorer doesn't display hidden file types or differentiate between compressed and uncompressed files.

To override the initial settings, complete the following steps:

1. In Control Panel, click Appearance And Personalization.
2. Under Folder Options, click Show Hidden Files And Folders. This displays the Folder Options dialog box with the View tab selected, as shown in Figure 14-1.

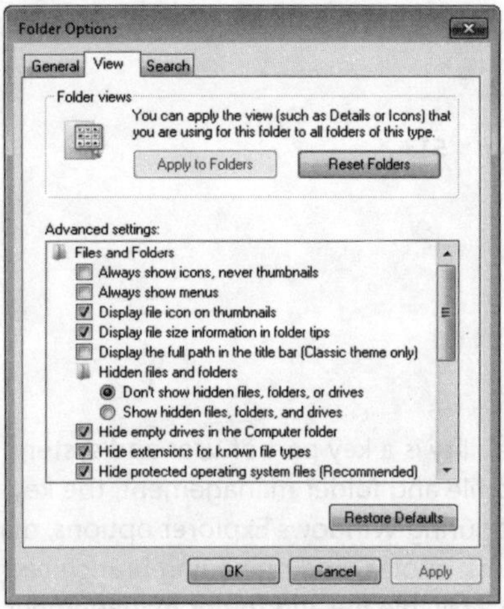

FIGURE 14-1 Set options for Windows Explorer using the Folder Options dialog box.

3. You can now customize Windows Explorer settings by using any of the following options:
   - **Always Show Icons, Never Thumbnails** By default, Windows Explorer shows large thumbnail images of the actual content for pictures and other types of files. For folders that have many pictures, this option can be annoying because Windows Explorer has to render the thumbnail representation of each image. To disable thumbnails except when you select the Thumbnails option on the View menu, select this option.
   - **Always Show Menus** By default, Windows Explorer hides the menu bar, and you must choose to display it by clicking Organize, pointing to Layout, and then clicking Menu Bar. To always display the menu bar, select this option.
   - **Display File Icon On Thumbnails** By default, Windows Explorer adds file icons to the thumbnails it displays. To display thumbnails without file icons, clear this option.

- **Display File Size Information In Folder Tips** By default, when you move the mouse pointer over a folder name or folder icon, Windows Explorer displays a tooltip showing the folder's creation date and time, the size of the folder, and a partial list of files. To display less information (only the creation date and time), clear this option.
- **Display The Full Path In The Title Bar** By default, when you press Alt+Tab to access the flip view, Windows displays the folder name when you move the mouse pointer over a Windows Explorer window. To display the actual file path instead, select this option.
- **Hidden Files And Folders** By default, Windows Explorer does not display hidden files, folders, or drives. To display hidden files, folders, and drives, select Show Hidden Files, Folders, And Drives.
- **Hide Empty Drives In The Computer Folder** By default, Windows Explorer does not display information about empty drives in the Computer window. To display information about empty drives, clear this option.
- **Hide Extensions For Known File Types** By default, Windows Explorer does not display file extensions for known file types. To display file extensions for all file types, clear this option.
- **Hide Protected Operating System Files** By default, Windows Explorer does not display operating system files. To display operating system files, clear this option.
- **Launch Folder Windows In A Separate Process** By default, Windows runs all instances of Windows Explorer in the same process. This saves memory and generally speeds up the process of opening new windows, but it also means that all instances of Windows Explorer are dependent on each other. If one instance crashes, they all crash, and if one instance is in a pending or wait state, all instances could become locked. To modify this behavior and have Windows start a new process for each instance of Windows Explorer, select this option.
- **Show Drive Letters** By default, Windows Explorer displays drive letters as part of the information on the Locations bar. Clear this option if you don't want to see drive letters.
- **Show Encrypted Or Compressed NTFS Files In Color** By default, Windows Explorer lists encrypted files and compressed files using different colors than normal files. Encrypted files are displayed with green text and compressed files are displayed using blue text. Clear this option if you don't want to use different colors.
- **Show Pop-Up Description For Folder And Desktop Items** By default, Windows Explorer shows tooltips with additional information about a file or folder when you move the mouse over the file or folder. Clear this option if you don't want to see tooltips.

- **Show Preview Handlers In Preview Pane** By default, when the Preview pane is visible, Windows Explorer displays previews of selected files and folders. Clear this option if you don't want to see previews.
- **Use Check Boxes To Select Items** By default, Windows Explorer allows you to select files, folders, and other items by using only the standard selection techniques, such as click, Shift+click, and Ctrl+click. Select this option if you want Windows Explorer to display check boxes to select multiple files.
- **Use Sharing Wizard** By default, Windows Explorer uses the File Sharing wizard for configuring file sharing, as discussed in Chapter 13, "Managing File Security and Resource Sharing." If you prefer to use only the advanced file sharing options, clear this option. When you try to share files, you need to click Advanced Sharing on the Sharing tab so that you can configure permissions, caching, and connections settings separately.
- **When Typing Into List View** By default, when you are working with the list view and press a letter key, Windows Explorer selects the first file or folder with that letter at the start of its name. If you would rather have Windows Explorer enter the text you type into the Search box, select the Automatically Type Into The Search Box option.

Configuring Advanced Windows Explorer Options

Both users and administrators spend a lot of time working with Windows Explorer or one of the related views, such as Computer. As an administrator, you'll often want to do more with Windows Explorer. You might want to perform one of the following tasks:

- Deploy computers that have certain Windows Explorer features blocked out. For example, you might want to block users' access to the Hardware tab, preventing them from viewing or changing hardware on a computer.
- Hide or restrict access to local disks. For example, you might want to prevent users from accessing the floppy disk drives on the computers that you deploy.

These and other advanced configuration options for computers are discussed in this section.

Setting Group Policy for Windows Explorer and Folder Views

As with many other Windows 7 features, you can use Group Policy to control the options available in Windows Explorer. Because many of these options extend to folder views and settings, they are useful to examine. Table 14-1 provides an overview of policies that you might want to implement and how these policies are used when they are enabled. These Administrative Templates policies for User Configuration are located in Windows Components\Windows Explorer.

TABLE 14-1 Policies for Windows Explorer

POLICY NAME	POLICY DESCRIPTION
Allow Only Per User Or Approved Shell Extensions	Shell extensions extend the feature set available in Windows Explorer. This setting permits a computer to run only shell extensions that have been approved by an administrator or that don't affect other users on that computer. Approved shell extensions must have a registry entry in HKEY_LOCAL_MACHINE\SOFTWARE\Microsoft\Windows\CurrentVersion\Shell Extensions\Approved.
Display Confirmation Dialog When Deleting Files	Displays a confirmation dialog box whenever you delete files or move files to the Recycle Bin.
Display The Menu Bar In Windows Explorer	Overrides the default configuration and displays the classic menu bar in Windows Explorer.
Hides These Specified Drives In My Computer	In Windows Explorer views, hides icons representing selected hard drives. Users can still gain access to drives through other methods.
Hides The Manage Item On The Windows Explorer Context Menu	Removes the Manage item from the shortcut menu in Windows Explorer views and the Start menu. This shortcut menu option is used to open Computer Management.
Maximum Number Of Recent Documents	Specifies the maximum number of document shortcuts that Recent Items displays. The default is 15. For this list to be available, you must select Recent Items in the Customize Start Menu dialog box.
Prevent Access To Drives From My Computer	Prevents users from accessing files on selected drives in Windows Explorer views. Users also can't use the Run or Map Network Drive commands to access files on these drives.
Remove "Map Network Drive" And "Disconnect Network Drive"	Prevents users from mapping or disconnecting network drives by using Windows Explorer. This doesn't prevent use of other techniques, such as the command prompt.
Remove CD Burning Features	Removes CD creation and modification features from Windows Explorer. Users are not prevented from using other CD burning programs.

POLICY NAME	POLICY DESCRIPTION
Remove DFS Tab	Removes the DFS tab from Windows Explorer and Windows Explorer–based windows, preventing users from using the tab to view or change distributed file system (DFS) settings. Note that the DFS tab is available only when DFS is configured in the workgroup or domain.
Remove File Menu From Windows Explorer	Removes the File menu from Windows Explorer views but doesn't prevent users from using other means to perform tasks that are available on this menu.
Remove Hardware Tab	Removes the Hardware tab from all dialog boxes, preventing users from using the tab to view, change, or troubleshoot hardware devices.
Remove Security Tab	Removes the Security tab from the Properties dialog boxes for files, folders, shortcuts, and drives. This prevents users from changing or viewing the related file and folder permissions.
Remove Windows Explorer's Default Context Menu	Prevents users from right-clicking and displaying shortcut menus on the desktop and in Windows Explorer.
Removes The Folder Options Menu Item From The Tools Menu	Prevents users from accessing the Folder Options dialog box. As a result, users can't change folder views, file types, or offline file settings. Users can still access folder options in Control Panel.
Turn Off Caching Of Thumbnail Pictures	Disables caching of thumbnail views.
Turn Off Library Features That Rely On Indexed File Data	Disables all Arrangement views except By Folder and all Search filter suggestions other than Date Modified and Size. Also disables the view of file content snippets in Content mode and the ability to stack on the Context menu.
Turn Off The Display Of Thumbnails And Only Display Icons	Disables creation and display of thumbnails when users access local computer folders. This can reduce wait times and make accessing a folder the first time faster for users, although users might need to view media files to distinguish between them.
Turn Off The Display Of Thumbnails And Only Display Icons On Network Folders	Disables creation and display of thumbnails when users access network folders. This can reduce wait times and make accessing a folder the first time faster for users, although users might need to view media files to distinguish between them.

As detailed in Table 14-1, many Windows Explorer policies control the availability of options such as menu items and tabs in dialog boxes. To configure these options for all users of a computer, follow these steps:

1. Open a Group Policy object (GPO) for editing in the Group Policy Management Editor. The related Administrative Templates policies for User Configuration are located in Windows Components\Windows Explorer.
2. Double-click the policy you want to configure. This displays a Properties dialog box. Select one of the following options:
   - **Not Configured** Specifies that no changes will be made to the registry for this policy
   - **Enabled** Enables the policy and updates the registry
   - **Disabled** Disables the policy and updates the registry
3. Click OK.

NOTE **You'll find detailed coverage of some of these policies in later sections of this chapter. In particular, be sure to read the next section, "Managing Drive Access in Windows Explorer," which covers hiding or preventing access to drives in Windows Explorer.**

As you work with policy settings related to Windows Explorer, keep in mind that the following settings do not apply to Windows Vista or Windows 7:

- **Maximum Allowed Recycle Bin Size** On Windows 7, each computer has a Recycle Bin for each configured drive, and each user who logs on locally has a separate private copy of these Recycle Bins. You can modify the Recycle Bin settings for the current user by right-clicking Recycle Bin, and then clicking Properties. On the General tab, select the Recycle Bin location that you want to work with, set the maximum allowed size, and then click OK.
- **No "Computers Near Me" In Network Locations / No "Entire Network" In Network Locations** On Windows 7, the capability to determine network topology is a built-in feature of Network And Sharing Center. The People Near Me feature, used with Windows Collaboration, identifies people using computers on the same network segment, and you can sign in automatically when Windows starts or sign in manually when you want to use Windows Collaboration.
- **Remove Search Button From Windows Explorer** Because search features are more tightly integrated in Windows 7, they are controlled in different ways. You'll find some related settings under User Configuration\Administrative Templates\Windows Components\Instant Search. Options for controlling indexing of files and folders are under Computer Configuration\Administrative Templates\Windows Components\Search.

Managing Drive Access in Windows Explorer

You might want to block access to files on certain drives or even hide certain drives on a system. You manage this through Group Policy. The policies you use are Hide These Specified Drives In My Computer and Prevent Access To Drives From My Computer.

Hiding drives prevents users from accessing them in Windows Explorer views, but it doesn't prevent them from using other techniques to access the drives. In contrast, blocking access to drives prevents users from accessing any files on the drives and ensures that these files cannot be accessed using Windows Explorer or the Run or Map Network Drive commands. It doesn't, however, hide drive icons or the folder structure in Windows Explorer.

To hide selected drives or to prevent access to files on selected drives, follow these steps:

1. Open a Group Policy object (GPO) for editing in the Group Policy Management Editor. The related Administrative Templates policies for User Configuration are located in Windows Components\Windows Explorer.
2. To hide drives, double-click Hide These Specified Drives In My Computer, and then select Enabled. Next, specify which drives you are hiding, and then click OK. Key options are the following:
   - Select Restrict All Drives to restrict access to all internal hard drives and floppy drives.
   - Select Restrict A And B Drives Only to restrict access to floppy drives.
   - Select Restrict A, B And C Drives Only to restrict access to floppy drives and drive C.
   - Select Do Not Restrict Drives to remove additional restrictions that would otherwise apply.
3. To block access to files on specific drives, double-click Prevent Access To Drives From My Computer, and then select Enabled. Next, select the drives you want to restrict access to, and then click OK.

NOTE **The List Folder Contents permission controls whether a user can see files in a folder. If you want to ensure that users cannot view the names of folders on drives, you should also hide the drives.**

Managing Offline Files

Configuring offline files is a multistep process that begins with appropriate settings in Group Policy, continues with configuring specific offline folders, and ends with setting user options for working offline. Although users who work offline primarily use laptops that they take home or to other locations, all users can benefit from offline file configurations. Configuring Group Policy for offline files is discussed in Chapter 3, "Configuring User and Computer Policies." This section provides more details about offline files and provides specific steps for configuring them.

Understanding Offline Files

Offline files enable users to store network files on their computer so that the files are available when the users are not connected to the network or there is a network outage. Once offline files are configured, Windows 7 automatically uses them whenever network files are not available. This enables users to continue working on network files without interruption. When the connection to the network is reestablished, Windows 7 synchronizes the files on the user's computer with the files in the network folder.

The way changes are applied depends on how they were made. If multiple users make changes to a particular offline file, they can use conflict resolution features to save their version of the file over the existing version, keep the existing version, or save both versions on the network. If a user deletes an offline file, the file is also deleted on the network, except if someone has modified the file on the network so that it has a more recent date and time stamp. In this exceptional case, the file is deleted from the user's computer but not from the network. If users change an offline file that someone else deletes from the network, they can choose to save their version to the network or delete it from their computer.

Windows 7 provides two key enhancements to the way offline files are used:

- **Change-only syncing** Windows 7 provides faster synchronization by syncing only the changed blocks of files. Only the changed blocks are written back to the server during synchronization.
- **Unavailable file and folder ghosting** When part of the contents of a folder is made available offline, Windows 7 creates ghosted entries of other files and folders to preserve the online context. When you are not connected to a remote location, you'll see ghost entries for online items as well as normal entries for offline items.

Both users and administrators have control over when offline files are synchronized. Automatic synchronization can be triggered by user logon and logoff and by computers entering the sleep or hibernate modes. The exact settings for automatic synchronization depend on Group Policy and user settings. For details on configuring offline files through Group Policy, see the section "Configuring Offline File Policies" in Chapter 3.

Manual synchronization is controlled through Sync Center. You can access Sync Center by clicking Start, pointing to All Programs, Accessories, and then clicking Sync Center.

Making Files or Folders Available Offline

Shared network folders can be made available for use offline. By default, all subfolders and files within the shared folders are also available offline. If necessary, you can change the availability of individual files and subfolders. To do this, you need to change the availability of each individual file or subfolder. Keep in mind that new files added to a shared folder that is designated for offline use are not automatically distributed to users working offline. The offline folder must be synchronized to obtain the updates.

You can configure offline files by using Windows Explorer or the Computer Management console. Because Computer Management enables you to work with and manage offline files on any of your network computers, it's usually the best tool to use. Making files or folders available offline is a three-step process. First you share folders, then you make those folders available for offline use, and finally, you have the users specify the files and folders they want to use offline.

Step 1: Share Folders

In the Computer Management console, you make a folder available for sharing by completing the following steps:

1. Right-click Computer Management in the console tree, and then click Connect To Another Computer. Use the Select Computer dialog box to choose the computer you want to work with.
2. In the console tree, expand System Tools and Shared Folders, and then select Shares. The current shares on the system are displayed in the details pane.
3. Right-click Shares, and then click New Share. This starts the Create A Shared Folder Wizard, which can be used to share folders as discussed in Chapter 13 in the section "Sharing a Folder and Setting Share Permissions in Computer Management."

Step 2: Make Folders Available for Offline Use

In the Computer Management console, you make a shared folder available for offline use by completing these steps:

1. Right-click Computer Management in the console tree, and then click Connect To Another Computer. Use the Select Computer dialog box to choose the computer you want to work with.
2. In the console tree, expand System Tools and Shared Folders, and then select Shares.
3. Double-click the share you want to configure for offline use. On the General tab, click Offline Settings.

4. In the Offline Settings dialog box, shown in Figure 14-2, select one of the following options:
   - **Only The Files And Programs That Users Specify Are Available Offline** Use this setting when you want users to specify any files that they want to work with offline. This is the default option and is the best choice when multiple users want to modify the same files within a folder. Once configured for manual caching, files are automatically downloaded and made available for offline use. If an older version of a document was cached previously, the older version is deleted. When using a file online, the server version always reflects that the file is in use.
   - **All Files And Programs That Users Open From The Shared Folder Are Automatically Available Offline** Use this setting for folders containing user data and programs. Opened files and program executables are automatically downloaded and made available for offline use. If an older version of a document was cached previously, the older version is deleted from the local cache. When using a file online, the server version always reflects that the file is in use. Prompts are displayed if version conflicts occur.

     With this option, you can also select Optimize For Performance to enable expanded caching of programs. Expanded caching enables programs shared over the network to be cached so that they can be run locally, which improves performance.
5. Click OK twice.

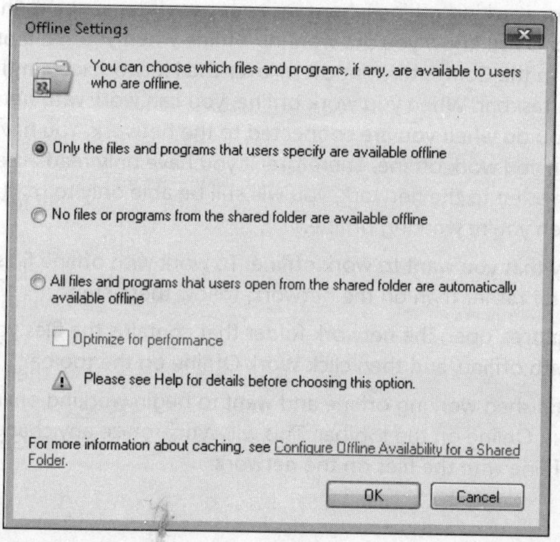

FIGURE 14-2 Configure caching options for offline files in the Offline Settings dialog box.

Step 3: Specify the Offline Files and Folders to Use

Once you've created the shares and configured offline use of those shares as appropriate, you can specify the files and folders to use offline by following these steps:

1. Map a network drive to a shared file or folder as discussed in Chapter 13 in the section "Using and Accessing Shared Resources."
2. Click Start, and then click Computer. This opens the Computer window.
3. Create the offline file cache by doing one of the following:
   - To copy the contents of a shared folder to the user's computer and make it available for offline use, under Network Location, right-click the shared location, and then click Always Available Offline.
   - To copy only a selected folder (and its contents) or a selected file to the user's computer and make it available offline, use the Computer console to locate the network file or folder, and then right-click the file or folder and click Always Available Offline.

Designating files and folders for offline use creates a local cache of the contents of the files and folders on the user's computer. It also establishes a sync partnership between the local computer and the sharing computer or extends an existing sync partnership to incorporate the additional shared files and folders. Sync partnerships can be managed using Sync Center, as discussed in "Managing Offline File Synchronization" on the next page.

Working Offline

You are considered to be working offline whenever your computer is not connected to the local area network. You know you are working offline when you see a red X over Network Drives in the Computer window or over the Network icon in the notification area of the taskbar. When you work offline, you can work with network files in the same way you do when you are connected to the network. You have the same permissions when you work offline. Therefore, if you have only read access to a file when you're connected to the network, you will still be able only to read and not modify the file when you're working offline.

You can also specify that you want to work offline. To work with offline files stored on your computer rather than on the network, follow these steps:

1. In Windows Explorer, open the network folder that contains the files you want to work with offline, and then click Work Offline on the toolbar.
2. When you are finished working offline and want to begin working online again, click Work Online on the toolbar. This will synchronize any changes you've made offline with the files on the network.

Managing Offline File Synchronization

Sync Center, shown in Figure 14-3, simplifies the management of cached offline files and folders. In Sync Center, a sync partnership is established for every shared folder that has locally cached contents. Each sync partnership has a set of properties that enables you to control whether and how syncing occurs.

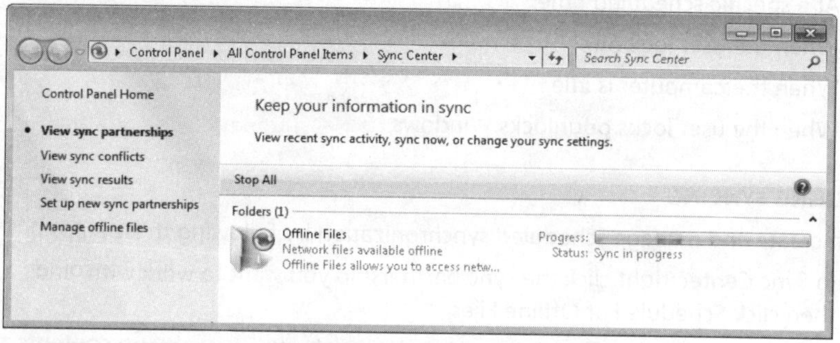

FIGURE 14-3 Use Sync Center to view and manage synchronization.

Viewing Current Sync Partnerships

You can view current sync partnerships in Sync Center by following these steps:

1. Access Sync Center by clicking Start, pointing to All Programs, Accessories, and then clicking Sync Center.
2. In Sync Center, sync partnerships are listed according to name, status, progress, conflict count, error count, and category.

After you display Sync Center, you can easily check for synchronization problems, start or stop syncing, and configure syncing.

Syncing Offline Files Manually

You can manually synchronize offline files by using either of the following techniques:

- **Sync all offline files and folders** When multiple sync partnerships have been established, you can sync all offline files and folders by opening Sync Center and then clicking Sync All. Sync All is available only when no individual sync partnerships are selected.
- **Sync a specific network share** When you want to sync the offline files and folders for a particular shared network folder, open Sync Center, click the sync partnership that you want to work with, and then click Sync.

Syncing Offline Files Automatically

Group Policy settings control how offline file synchronization works. Generally, offline files are automatically synchronized when a user reconnects to the network after being disconnected from the network or electing to work offline. You can also configure synchronization so that it occurs at one of the following times:

- At a specific scheduled time
- When the user logs on
- When the computer is idle
- When the user locks or unlocks Windows

SCHEDULING SYNCING

You can create and manage scheduled synchronization by following these steps:

1. In Sync Center, right click the sync partnership you want to work with, and then click Schedule For Offline Files.
2. If you've previously scheduled synchronization for this resource, you can:
   - **Create a new schedule** Click Create A New Sync Schedule, and then follow steps 3–7.
   - **View or edit an existing schedule** Click View Or Edit An Existing Sync Schedule, click the schedule to change, click Next, and then follow steps 3–7.
   - **Delete an existing schedule** Click Delete An Existing Sync Schedule, click the schedule to delete, and then click Delete. Click OK, and then skip the remaining steps.
3. Review the items you are configuring and clear the check boxes for any items you don't want to configure. Click Next, and then click At A Scheduled Time.
4. The Start On and At options are configured so that scheduled syncing will start immediately. (See Figure 14-4.) If you want to start scheduled syncing on a different date and time, use the options provided to change the start date and time.
5. The Repeat Every option sets the sync interval. The default interval is once every day. You can set the repeat interval to a value in minutes, hours, days, weeks, or months. Because only changes are synced, you might want to sync more frequently than you would with Windows XP. For example, with important files, you might want to sync every 3 to 4 hours.
6. Click Next.
7. Type a descriptive name for the scheduled synchronization, and then click Save Schedule.

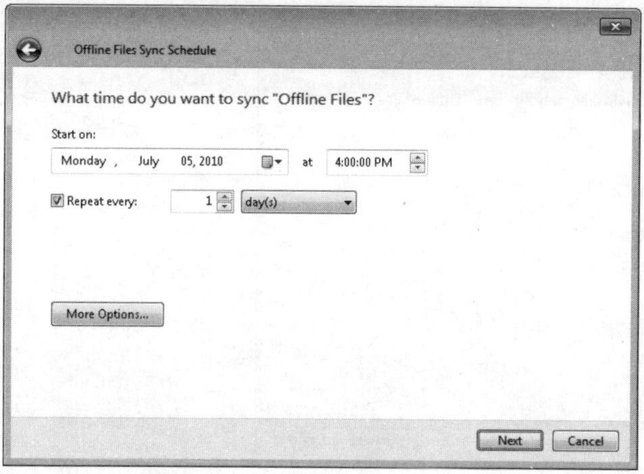

FIGURE 14-4 Create a sync schedule.

SYNCING ON AN EVENT OR ACTION

You can create and manage synchronization based on events or actions by following these steps:

1. In Sync Center, click the sync partnership you want to work with, and then click Schedule.
2. If you've previously scheduled synchronization for this resource, you can:
   - **Create a new schedule** Click Create A New Sync Schedule, and then follow steps 3 through 6.
   - **View or edit an existing schedule** Click View Or Edit An Existing Sync Schedule, click the schedule to change, click Next, and then follow steps 3 through 6.
   - **Delete an existing schedule** Click Delete An Existing Sync Schedule, click the schedule to delete, and then click Delete. Click OK, and then skip the remaining steps.
3. Review the items you are configuring, clear the check boxes for any items you don't want to configure, and then click Next. Click When An Event Occurs.
4. As shown in Figure 14-5, use the check boxes provided to specify the events and actions that start automatic syncing.
5. Click Next.
6. Type a descriptive name for the scheduled sync, and then click Save Schedule.

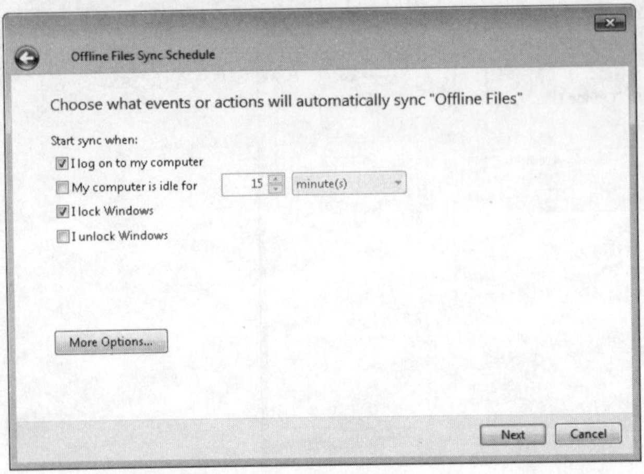

FIGURE 14-5 Sync based on events and actions.

Determining Synchronization Details, Errors, and Warnings

Synchronization results provide details, errors, and warnings. To view current sync results, open Sync Center, and then click View Sync Results. You can review sync details to determine when syncing was started, stopped, or completed. You can review errors and warnings to determine whether there are problems with the synchronization configuration.

Resolving Synchronization Conflicts

Synchronization conflicts occur if a user makes changes to a file offline that is updated online by another user. You can view and resolve synchronization conflicts by following these steps:

1. In Sync Center, click View Sync Conflicts.
2. The main pane specifies whether there are any conflicts. (See Figure 14-6.)

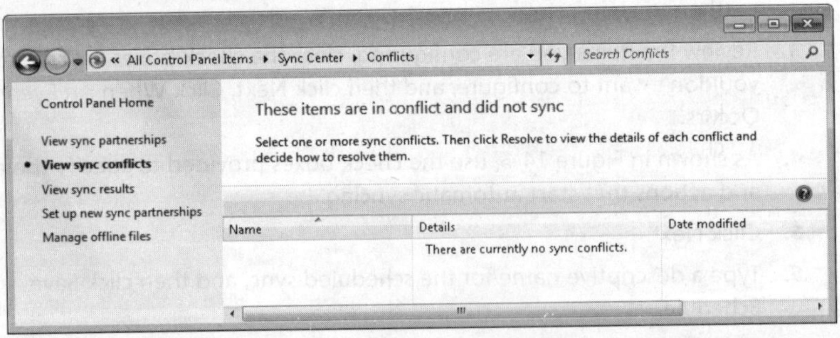

FIGURE 14-6 Conflicts are listed according to document name, file type, time, partnership, and conflict type.

3. To display the Resolve Conflict dialog box, shown in Figure 14-7, double-click a conflict you want to resolve.

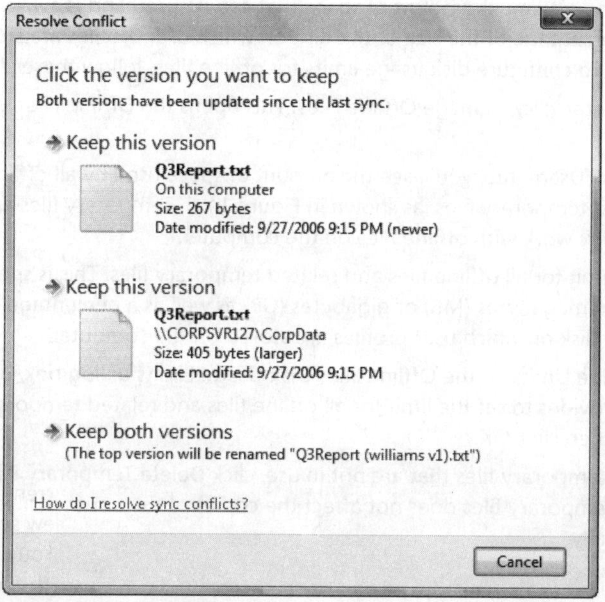

FIGURE 14-7 Use the Resolve Conflict dialog box to resolve synchronization conflicts.

4. You can now do the following:
   - Click the version you want to keep. If you want to keep the local version and overwrite the network version, click the version listed as On This Computer. If you want to keep the network version and overwrite the local version, click the version listed as being on the shared network location.
   - Click Keep Both Versions to write the local version to the shared network location with a new file name. Generally, the new file name will be the same as the old file name but with a numeric suffix indicating the version increment. If you are at all unsure about which version of a file to keep, keep both versions, and then compare the two versions carefully for changes that should be merged or discarded.

Configuring Disk Usage Limits for Offline Files

In Sync Center, you can control how much space is used and available for offline files. By default, the maximum amount of space that can be used and is available for offline files is a percentage of the size of the disk on which user profiles are stored on the computer. To configure disk usage limits for offline files, follow these steps:

1. In Sync Center, click Manage Offline Files. This opens the Offline Files dialog box.
2. On the Disk Usage tab, you'll see the amount of space used by all offline files and related temporary files, as shown in Figure 14-8. Temporary files are created as users work with offline files on the computer.
3. Note the limit for all offline files and related temporary files. This is specified as a limit in megabytes (MB) or gigabytes (GB) as well as a percentage of the size of the disk on which user profiles are stored on the computer.
4. Click Change Limits. In the Offline Files Disk Usage Limits dialog box, use the options provides to set the limit for all offline files and related temporary files, and then click OK.
5. To delete temporary files that are not in use, click Delete Temporary Files. Deleting temporary files does not affect the copies of the network files stored locally.
6. Click OK.

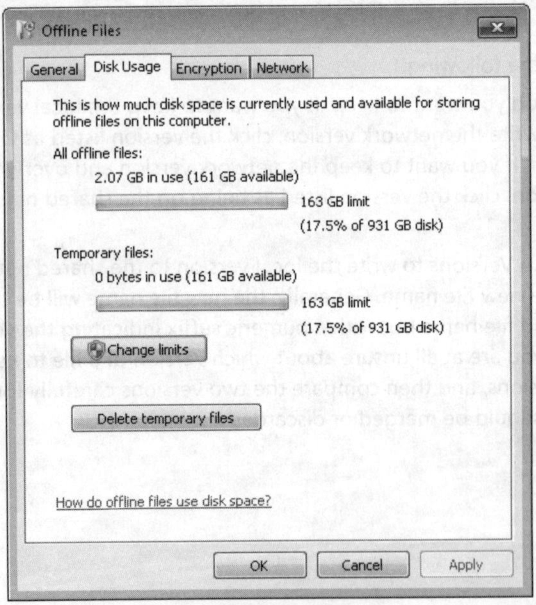

FIGURE 14-8 Configure disk limits for offline files.

Managing Encryption for Offline Files

To enhance security, you can specify whether offline files are encrypted. If you encrypt offline files, only the files stored on your computer are encrypted and not the files on the network. Users do not need to decrypt the encrypted files before working with them. Decryption is performed automatically by the operating system. To encrypt offline files, follow these steps:

1. In Sync Center, click Manage Offline Files. This opens the Offline Files dialog box.
2. On the Encryption tab, click Encrypt to encrypt all offline files, and then click OK.

If you want to disable encryption later, repeat this procedure but click Unencrypt.

Making Offline Files Unavailable

As an administrator, you can specify files that should not be available for offline use. Typically, you'll do this when a shared folder contains specific files that users shouldn't manipulate. To make a file unavailable for offline use, you should set a specific exclusion policy, as described in Chapter 3 in the section "Administratively Controlling Offline Files and Folders."

In the Computer Management console, you make a shared folder unavailable for offline use by completing these steps:

1. Right-click Computer Management in the console tree, and then click Connect To Another Computer. Use the Select Computer dialog box to choose the computer you want to work with.
2. In the console tree, expand System Tools and Shared Folders, and then select Shares.
3. Double-click the share you want to configure for offline use. On the General tab, click Offline Settings.
4. In the Offline Settings dialog box, select No Files Or Programs From The Shared Folder Are Available Offline.
5. Click OK.

To completely disable the use of offline files, complete these steps:

1. In Sync Center, click Manage Offline Files. This opens the Offline Files dialog box.
2. On the General tab, click Disable Offline Files, and then click OK.

If you want to enable offline files later, repeat this procedure but click Enable Offline Files.

Configuring Disk Quotas

The following sections discuss how to use and manage disk quotas. Disk quotas enable you to manage disk space usage and are configured on a per-volume basis. Only NTFS file system volumes can have quotas, so you can't create them for FAT16 or FAT32 volumes. The first step in configuring quotas is to enable disk quota policies as described in Chapter 3 in the section "Configuring Disk Quota Policies." Once you configure the necessary policies, you can set up quotas for specific volumes on a system.

Using Disk Quotas

Administrators use disk quotas to manage disk space usage for critical volumes, such as those that provide corporate or user data shares. When you enable disk quotas, you set a disk quota limit and a disk quota warning level. The disk quota limit sets the maximum space that can be used (which prevents users from writing additional information to a volume), logs events when a user exceeds the limit, or both. You use the disk quota warning to warn users and to log warning events when users approach their disk quota limits.

> ***REAL WORLD*** **Although most administrators configure quotas that are enforced, you can set disk quotas that are not enforced. You might wonder why you would do this. Sometimes, you might want to track disk space usage on a per-user basis and know when users have exceeded some predefined limit. Instead of denying the users additional disk space, however, you can track the overage by recording an event in the application log.**

Disk quotas apply only to standard users, not to administrators. Administrators can't be denied disk space even if they exceed enforced disk quota limits. Disk quota limits and warnings can be set in kilobytes (KB), megabytes (MB), gigabytes (GB), terabytes (TB), petabytes (PB), and exabytes (EB). In a typical environment, you'll use megabytes or gigabytes. For example, on a corporate data share that is used by members of a department, you might limit disk space usage to between 20 and 100 GB. For a user data share, you might set the level much lower, such as 5 to 20 GB, restricting the user from creating large amounts of personal data. Often, you'll set the disk quota warning as a percentage of the disk quota limit. For example, you could set the warning at 90 to 95 percent of the disk quota limit.

Because disk quotas are tracked on a per-volume, per-user basis, disk space used by one user does not affect the disk quotas for other users. Thus, if one user exceeds his limit, any restrictions applied to this user don't apply to other users. For example, if a user exceeds a 5-GB disk quota limit and the volume is configured to prevent writing over this limit, the user can no longer write data to the volume. He can, however, remove files and folders from the volume to free up disk space, move files and folders to a compressed area on the volume, or elect to compress files. Moving files to a different location on the volume doesn't affect the quota restriction. The amount of file space is the same unless the user moves uncompressed files and folders to a folder with compression. In any case, the restriction on a single user does not affect other users' ability to write to the volume (as long as the volume has free space).

You can enable disk quotas on local volumes and on remote volumes. To manage disk quotas on local volumes, you work with the local disk itself. To manage disk quotas on remote volumes, you must share the root directory for the volume and then set the disk quota on the volume. Keep in mind that when you enable disk quotas on a local volume, operating system and application program files are not included in the volume usage for the user who installed those files. Generally, system files are owned by the TrustedInstaller account, and program files are owned by the System account.

Only members of the Domain Administrators group or the local system Administrators group can configure disk quotas. Through local Group Policy, you can enable disk quotas for an individual computer. Through site, domain, or organizational unit policies, you can enable disk quotas for groups of users and computers. Keeping track of disk quotas does cause some overhead on computers, which is a function of the number of disk quotas being enforced, the total size of volumes and their data, and the number of users to which the disk quotas apply.

Although disk quotas appear to be tracked on a per-user basis, behind the scenes, Windows 7 manages disk quotas according to security identifiers (SIDs). Because disk quotas are tracked by SIDs, you can safely modify user names without affecting the disk quota configuration. Tracking by SIDs causes some additional overhead when you view disk quota statistics for users because Windows 7 must correlate SIDs to user account names so that the account names can be displayed in dialog boxes. This requires contacting the local user manager service or the domain controller as necessary. Once names are looked up, they are cached to a local file so that they are available immediately the next time they are needed. The query cache is updated infrequently, so if you notice a discrepancy between what is displayed and what is configured, you need to refresh the information. Usually, this means selecting Refresh or pressing function key F5 in the current window.

Enabling Disk Quotas on NTFS Volumes

Disk quotas are set on a per-volume basis, and only NTFS volumes can have disk quotas. The best way to configure disk quotas is through Group Policy, as discussed in Chapter 3. Once the appropriate policies are configured, you can create disk quota entries to manage per-user and per-group quotas.

If you'd rather configure quotas on each computer, you can enable disk quotas on an NTFS volume by following these steps:

1. Start Computer Management. You are connected to the local computer by default. If you want to configure disk quotas on a remote computer, right-click Computer Management in the console tree, and then click Connect To

Another Computer. In the Select Computer dialog box, select the computer you want to work with.

2. In the console tree, expand Storage, and then select Disk Management. The volumes configured on the selected computer are displayed in the details pane.
3. Using the Volume List or Graphical view, right-click the volume you want to work with, and then click Properties.
4. Click the Quota tab, shown in Figure 14-9. Select the Enable Quota Management check box.

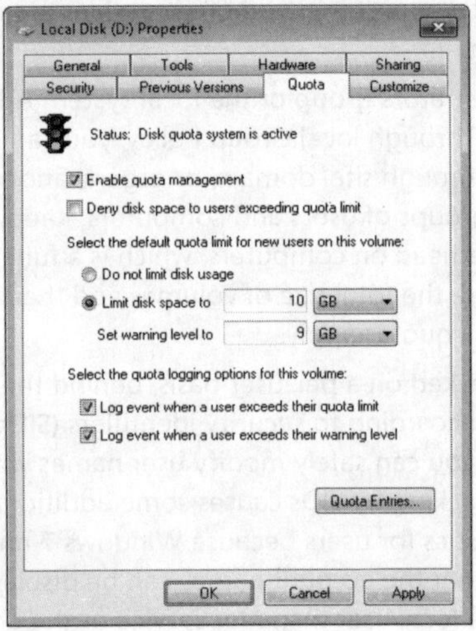

FIGURE 14-9 Once you enable quota management, you can configure a quota limit and quota warning for all users.

5. To set a default disk quota limit that is applied to each user, select Limit Disk Space To, and then use the fields provided to set a limit. Next, use the Set Warning Level To field to set the default warning limit. The disk quota warning limit should usually be 90 to 95 percent of the disk quota limit.

TIP **Although the default quota limit and warning apply to all users, you can use the Quota Entries dialog box to override the default and configure different levels for individual users. If you create many unique quota entries and don't want to re-create them on a volume with similar characteristics and usage, you can export the quota entries and import them on a different volume.**

6. To enforce the disk quota limit and prevent users from going over the limit, select the Deny Disk Space To Users Exceeding Quota Limit check box. Keep in mind that this creates a physical limitation for users but not for administrators.

7. To configure logging when users exceed a warning limit or the quota limit, use the Log Event check boxes.
8. If the quota system isn't currently enabled, you'll see a prompt asking you to enable the quota system. Click OK to allow Windows 7 to rescan the volume and update disk usage statistics. Actions can be taken against users who exceed the current limit or warning levels. These include preventing users from writing to the volume, notifying users the next time they access the volume, and logging applicable events in the application log.

Viewing Disk Quota Entries

Disk space usage is tracked on a per-user basis. When disk quotas are enabled, each user storing data on a volume has an entry in the disk quota file. This entry is updated periodically to show the current disk space used, the applicable quota limit, the applicable warning level, and the percentage of allowable space being used. As an administrator, you can modify disk quota entries to set different limits and warning levels for particular users. You can also create disk quota entries for users who have not yet saved data on a volume. By creating entries, you ensure that when a user does make use of a volume, she has an appropriate limit and warning level.

To view the current disk quota entries for a volume, follow these steps:

1. Start Computer Management. You are connected to the local computer by default. If you want to view disk quotas on a remote computer, right-click Computer Management in the console tree, and then click Connect To Another Computer. In the Select Computer dialog box, select the computer you want to work with.
2. In the console tree, expand Storage, and then select Disk Management. The volumes configured on the selected computer are displayed in the details pane.
3. Using the Volume List or Graphical view, right-click the volume you want to work with, and then click Properties.
4. On the Quota tab, click Quota Entries. This displays the Quota Entries dialog box, shown in Figure 14-10. As you can see in the figure, each quota entry is listed according to its status. The status is meant to quickly depict whether a user has gone over the limit. A status of OK means the user is working within the quota boundaries. Any other status usually means the user has reached the warning level or the quota limit.

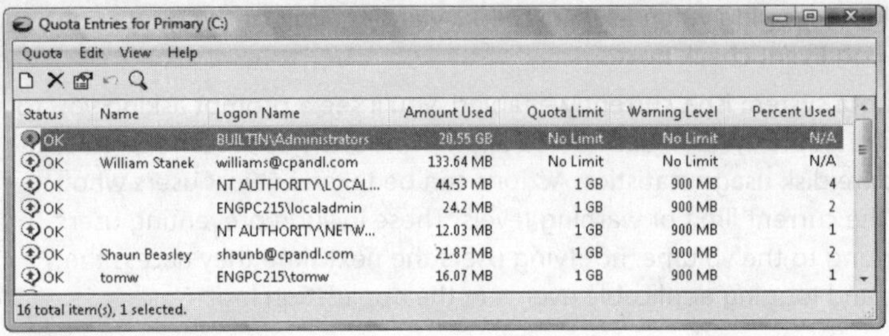

FIGURE 14-10 Disk quota entries show current disk space usage on a particular volume as well as applicable quota limits and warning levels.

Creating Disk Quota Entries

You can create disk quota entries for users who have not yet saved data on a volume as well as for users who have already saved data on a volume. This enables you to set custom limits and warning levels for any user as necessary. Usually, you'll use this feature when one user frequently stores more information than others do. For example, a graphic designer might have much larger storage needs than a customer-support person does. The good news about custom quota entries is that you can export them to other volumes, which enables you to quickly apply the same set of rules to multiple volumes.

To create a quota entry on a volume, follow these steps:

1. In Computer Management, expand Storage, and then select Disk Management. Using the Volume List or Graphical view, right-click the volume you want to work with, and then click Properties.
2. On the Quota tab, click Quota Entries. Current quota entries for all users are listed. To refresh the listing, press function key F5 or click Refresh on the View menu.
3. If the user doesn't have an existing entry on the volume, create one by clicking New Quota Entry on the Quota menu. This opens the Select Users dialog box.
4. In the Select Users dialog box, type the name of a user in the Enter The Object Names To Select field, and then click Check Names. If multiple matches are found, select the account you want, and then click OK. If no matches are found, update the name you entered and try again. Repeat this step as necessary, and then click OK.
5. Once you've selected a name, the Add New Quota Entry dialog box is displayed. You have several options. You can remove all quota restrictions for this user by selecting Do Not Limit Disk Usage. In addition, you can set a specific limit and warning level by selecting Limit Disk Space To and then entering the appropriate values in the fields provided.

6. Click OK. Close the Quota Entries dialog box, and then click OK in the Properties dialog box.

Updating and Customizing Disk Quota Entries

You can modify and customize disk quota entries for individual users at any time by following these steps:

1. In Computer Management, expand Storage, and then select Disk Management. Using the Volume List or Graphical view, right-click the volume you want to work with, and then click Properties.
2. On the Quota tab, click Quota Entries. Current quota entries for all users are listed. To refresh the list, press function key F5 or click Refresh on the View menu.
3. Double-click the quota entry for the user. This displays the Quota Settings For dialog box, which is similar to the dialog box shown in Figure 14-9.
4. To remove all quota restrictions for this user, select Do Not Limit Disk Usage.
5. To modify the current limit and warning level, select Limit Disk Space To, and then enter the appropriate values in the fields provided.
6. Click OK.

Deleting Disk Quota Entries

When you've created disk quota entries on a volume and a user no longer needs to use the volume, you can delete the associated disk quota entry. When you delete a disk quota entry, all files owned by the user are collected and displayed in a dialog box so that you can permanently delete the files, take ownership of the files, or move the files to a folder on a different volume.

To delete a disk quota entry for a user and manage the remaining files on the volume, follow these steps:

1. In Computer Management, expand Storage, and then select Disk Management. Using the Volume List or Graphical view, right-click the volume you want to work with, and then click Properties.
2. On the Quota tab, click Quota Entries. Current quota entries for all users are listed. To refresh the listing, press function key F5 or click Refresh on the View menu.
3. Select the disk quota entry that you want to delete, and then press Delete or select Delete Quota Entry from the Quota menu. You can select multiple entries by using the Shift or Ctrl key.
4. When prompted to confirm the action, click Yes. This displays the Disk Quota dialog box with a list of files owned by the selected user or users.
5. Use the List Files Owned By list to display files for the user whose quota entry you are deleting. You must then specify how to handle the files for the user.

You can handle each file separately by selecting a file and then choosing an appropriate option. Select multiple files by using the Shift or Ctrl key. The following options are available:

- **Show Folders Only** Changes the view to show only folders in which the user has files. In this way, you can delete, move, or take ownership of all the user's files in a particular folder.
- **Show Files Only** Shows all files that the user owns according to the folder in which they were created.
- **Permanently Delete Files** Select the files to delete, and then click Delete. When prompted to confirm the action, click Yes.
- **Take Ownership Of Files** Select the files that you want to take ownership of, and then click Take Ownership.
- **Move Files To** Select the files that you want to move, and then, in the field provided, enter the path to a folder on a different volume. If you don't know the path that you want to use, click Browse to display the Browse For Folder dialog box. Once you find the folder, click Move.

6. Click Close when you have finished managing the files. Provided that you've appropriately handled all user files, the disk quota entries are deleted.

Exporting and Importing Disk Quota Settings

Rather than re-create custom disk quota entries on individual volumes, you can export the settings from a source volume and import them to another volume. Both volumes must be formatted using NTFS. To export and then import disk quota entries, perform the following steps:

1. Start Computer Management. You are connected to the local computer by default. If you want to work with disk quotas on a remote computer, right-click Computer Management in the console tree, and then click Connect To Another Computer. In the Select Computer dialog box, select the computer you want to work with.
2. In the console tree, expand Storage, and then select Disk Management. The volumes configured on the selected computer are displayed in the details pane.
3. Using the Volume List or Graphical view, right-click the source volume, and then click Properties.
4. On the Quota tab, click Quota Entries. This displays the Quota Entries dialog box.
5. On the Quota menu, click Export. This displays the Export Quota Settings dialog box. Choose the location in which to save the file containing the quota settings. Specify a name for the file in the File Name field, and then click Save.

TIP **If you save the settings file to a mapped drive on the target volume, you'll have an easier time importing the settings. Quota files are usually fairly small, so you don't need to worry about disk space usage.**

6. From the Quota menu, choose Close to close the Quota Entries dialog box. Click OK to close the Properties dialog box.
7. Right-click Computer Management in the console tree. On the shortcut menu, click Connect To Another Computer. In the Select Computer dialog box, select the computer containing the target volume on which you want to use the exported settings.
8. Expand Storage, and then select Disk Management. Using the Volume List or Graphical view, right-click the target volume, and then click Properties.
9. Click the Quota tab, ensure that Enable Quota Management is selected, and then click Quota Entries. This displays the Quota Entries dialog box for the target volume.
10. On the Quota menu, click Import. In the Import Quota Settings dialog box, select the quota settings file that you saved previously. Click Open.
11. If the volume had previous quota entries, you can replace or keep existing entries. When prompted about a conflict, click Yes to replace an existing entry, or click No to keep the existing entry. The option to replace or keep existing entries can be applied to all entries on the volume by selecting Do This For All Quota Entries prior to clicking Yes or No.

Disabling Disk Quotas

You can disable quotas for individual users or all users on a volume. When you disable quotas for a particular user, that user is no longer subject to the quota restrictions, but disk quotas are still tracked for other users. When you disable quotas on a volume, quota tracking and management are completely removed. To disable quotas for a particular user, follow the technique outlined in the section "Updating and Customizing Disk Quota Entries." To disable quota tracking and management on a volume, follow these steps:

1. Start Computer Management. You are connected to the local computer by default. If you want to disable disk quotas on a remote computer, right-click Computer Management in the console tree, and then click Connect To Another Computer. In the Select Computer dialog box, select the computer you want to work with.
2. In the console tree, expand Storage, and then select Disk Management. The volumes configured on the selected computer are displayed in the details pane.
3. Using the Volume List or Graphical view, right-click the volume, and then click Properties.
4. On the Quota tab, clear the Enable Quota Management check box. Click OK. When prompted to confirm, click OK.

Using Branch Caching

Windows BranchCache is a file-caching feature that works in conjunction with Background Intelligent Transfer Service (BITS). In a domain environment, administrators at a remote office can enable branch caching to allow computers running Windows 7 or a later version to retrieve documents and other types of files from a local cache rather than retrieving files from servers over the network.

Branch caching works with files transferred using Hypertext Transfer Protocol (HTTP) and server message block (SMB). This means files transferred from both intranet Web servers and internal file servers are cached. Caching can dramatically improve response times and dramatically reduce transfer times for documents, Web pages, and multimedia content.

Branch caching can be enabled at each remote office in the company. Generally speaking, local area network (LAN) boundaries determine how the feature works after it is implemented. If a LAN is connected to the central office over a network on which the round trip network latency is more than 80 milliseconds, clients on that LAN will use the local cache when it is available. Note also that multiple LANs connected together over a fast network can also use a single local cache.

When you enable branch caching, the first time a file is accessed from an intranet Web site or file server over the network, Windows 7 transfers the file from the originating server and caches the file locally within the remote office. When the same user or a different user at the remote office accesses the file later, Windows looks for the file in the local cache. If it finds the file, Windows queries the originating server to see if the file has changed since it was cached. If the file has not changed, Windows retrieves the file from the local cache, eliminating the need to transfer the file over the wide area network. If the file has changed, Windows retrieves the file from the originating server and updates the copy of the file in the cache.

You can configure branch caching in one of two modes:

- **Distributed cache** In this mode, the user's desktop computer running Windows 7 or a later version hosts distributed file caches. A server running at the remote office is not needed because each local computer caches and sends out files.
- **Host cache** In this mode, a server running Windows Server 2008 Release 2 (or a later version) and located in the remote office hosts the local file cache. The server caches files and sends them to clients located in the remote office.

Obviously, there are advantages and disadvantages to both caching modes. With the distributed cache mode, you do not need to install a server before you can enable branch caching, but user's desktops have to maintain the cache and distribute files, which requires processing power and could adversely affect performance. With the host cache mode, you must install a server before you can enable branch caching, but once the server is up and running, all the processing and overhead for maintaining the cache is handled by the server, and this is a significant advantage over the distributed cache mode.

Keep the following in mind:

- Branch caching doesn't prevent users from saving files locally—it works with read requests, such as when a user requests a file from a file server.
- Branch caching works seamlessly with encryption and secure transfer technologies, such as SMB Signing and IPSec.
- By default, network files are cached in the remote office only when the round trip network latency is more than 80 milliseconds.
- Branch caching doesn't need to be enabled in the central office; only enable branch caching in remote offices.

You enable and configure branch caching by completing the following steps:

1. Open a Group Policy object (GPO) for editing in the appropriate Group Policy editor. The related Administrative Templates policies for Computer Configuration are located in Network\BranchCache.
2. Double-click Turn On BranchCache. In the Properties dialog box, select Enabled, and then click OK.
3. Do one of the following:
   - To enable distributed branch caching, double-click Set BranchCache Distributed Cache Mode. In the Properties dialog box, select Enabled, and then click OK.
   - To enable hosted branch caching, double-click Set BranchCache Hosted Cache Mode. In the Properties dialog box, select Enabled, type the host name of the caching server in the field provided, and then click OK.
4. If you want to specify the network latency required to trigger caching, double-click Configure BranchCache For Network Files. In the Properties dialog box, select Enabled. In the field provided, enter the round trip network latency above which network files must be cached. This value is specified in milliseconds. If you enter 0, files will always be cached.
5. If you enabled hosted branch caching, double-click Set Percentage Of Disk Space Usage For Client Computer Cache. In the Properties dialog box, select Enabled. In the field provided, enter the percentage of total disk space that client computers should dedicate to BranchCache, and then click OK. By default, the maximum cache size is 5 percent of the total disk space.

Two related policies can help you optimize branch caching for your environment:

- **Do Not Allow The BITS Client To Use Windows BranchCache** This policy is in the Administrative Templates policies for Computer Configuration under Network\Background Intelligent Transfer Service (BITS). It controls whether the BITS client uses branch caching for background transfers. Although you'll usually want the BITS client to be able to write to and retrieve files from the cache, this would include operating system files and other types of data transferred using BITS, which might create large caches and extra work for distributed caches.

- **Hash Publication For BranchCache** This policy is in the Administrative Templates policies for Computer Configuration under Network\Lanman Server. It controls whether and how BranchCache creates digital hashes for cached files. By default, digital hashes are created, and they allow clients to quickly determine whether a file in the cache is the same as the file on a server.

CHAPTER 15

Configuring and Troubleshooting TCP/IP Networking

This chapter focuses on managing network and wireless connections, which are used to communicate on a network. For networking to work properly, you must install networking components and configure network communications by using Dynamic Host Configuration Protocol (DHCP), Domain Name System (DNS), and Windows Internet Naming Service (WINS). DHCP is used for dynamic configuration of networking and Internet Protocol (IP) address settings. Both DNS and WINS provide name resolution services. DNS is the preferred service, and WINS is maintained for backward compatibility with earlier releases of the Windows operating system.

Navigating Windows 7 Networking Features

The networking features in Windows 7 are different from those in Windows XP and earlier releases of Windows. Windows 7 has a new suite of networking tools, including:

- **Network Explorer** Provides a central console for browsing computers and devices on the network

- **Network And Sharing Center** Provides a central console for viewing and managing a computer's networking and sharing configurations
- **Network Map** Provides a map of the network that depicts how computers and devices are connected
- **Network Diagnostics** Provides automated diagnostics to help resolve networking problems

Before discussing how these networking tools are used, I'll first look at the Windows 7 features on which these tools rely: network discovery, which controls the ability to see other computers and devices, and network awareness, which reports changes in network connectivity and configuration.

Understanding Network Discovery and Network Categories

The network discovery settings of the computer you are working with determine the computers and devices you can browse or view in Windows 7 networking tools. Discovery settings work in conjunction with a computer's Windows Firewall settings to block or allow the following:

- Discovery of network computers and devices
- Discovery of your computer by others

Network discovery settings are meant to provide the appropriate level of security for each type of network to which a computer can connect. Four categories of networks are defined:

- **Domain network** Intended as a designation for a network in which computers are connected to a corporate domain they belong to.
- **Work network** Intended as a designation for a network in which computers are being used in a workgroup.
- **Home network** Intended as a designation for a network in which computers are configured as members of a homegroup and are not connected directly to the public Internet.
- **Public network** Intended as a designation for a network in a public place, such as a coffee shop or airport, rather than an internal network.

NOTE **By default, discovery and file sharing are not enabled, but they can be enabled on domain, work, and home networks. By using the Network window or Advanced Sharing Settings in Network And Sharing Center, you can enable discovery and file sharing. This step reduces restrictions and permits computers on the network to discover other computers and devices on that network and share files. However, by default, discovery and file sharing are blocked on a public network. This enhances security by preventing computers on the public network from discovering other computers and devices on that network. When discovery and file sharing are disabled, files and printers that you have shared from the computer cannot be accessed from the network. Additionally, some programs might not be able to access the network.**

Because a computer saves settings separately for each category of network, you can specify different settings for blocking and allowing network traffic for each category. The first time you connect your computer to a network, you'll see a dialog box that allows you to specify whether you are at home, at work, or in a public location. Your selection sets the network category. If you change your network connection or connect to a new network, Windows 7 tries to determine the network category automatically. If Windows 7 is unable to determine the network category, it uses the public network category. If you join a computer to a domain, the network to which the computer is connected changes to a work network.

Based on the network category, Windows 7 configures settings that either turn discovery on or off. The On (enabled) state means that the computer can discover other computers and devices on the network and that other computers on the network can discover the computer. The Off (disabled) state means that the computer cannot discover other computers and devices on the network and that other computers on the network cannot discover the computer.

Working with Network Explorer

Network Explorer displays a list of discovered computers and devices on the network. You can access Network Explorer by clicking Start and then clicking Network. If you haven't added the Network option to the Start menu, you can access Network Explorer from Control Panel. In Control Panel, click Network And Internet. Under the Network And Sharing Center heading, click View Network Computers And Devices.

The network discovery settings for the computer determine which computers and devices are listed in Network Explorer. If discovery is enabled, you'll see other computers on the network, as shown in Figure 15-1. If discovery is blocked, you'll see a note about this in Network Explorer's notification area, as shown in Figure 15-2. Clicking the warning message and then selecting Turn On Network Discovery enables network discovery and opens the appropriate Windows Firewall ports so that network discovery is allowed. If no other changes have been made with regard to network discovery, the computer will be in the discovery-only state. You need to configure sharing of printers, files, and media manually, as discussed in Chapter 13, "Managing File Security and Resource Sharing."

Provided you have appropriate permissions, you can browse any computer or device listed in Network Explorer. Double-click the icon for the computer to access its shared resources. Double-click the icon for a device to access its management interface or browse its resources.

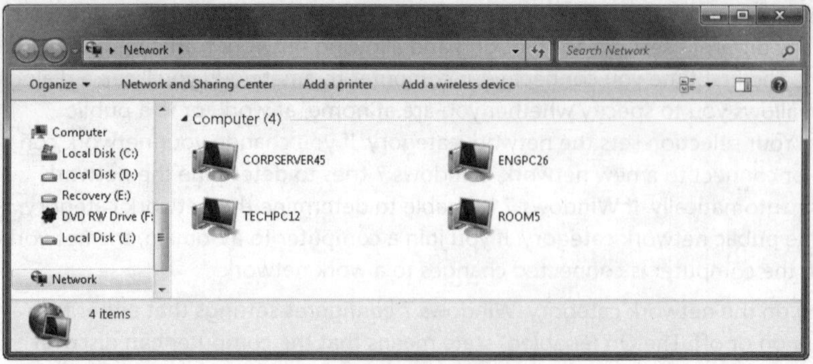

FIGURE 15-1 Use Network Explorer to allow network discovery and to browse resources as permitted by the current configuration.

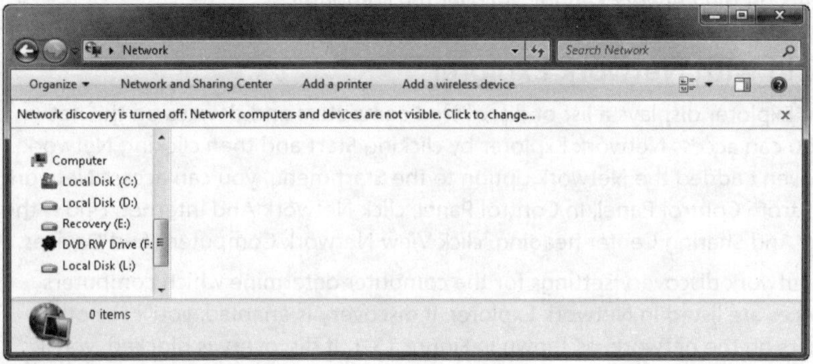

FIGURE 15-2 If network discovery is blocked, you need to enable it to view other computers and devices.

Network Explorer's toolbar provides several options:

- **Network And Sharing Center** When you want to view network status or manage network settings, click Network And Sharing Center. See the next section, "Working with Network And Sharing Center," for more information.
- **Add A Printer** Starts the Add Printer wizard. Use the wizard to add a local, network, wireless, or Bluetooth printer.
- **Add A Wireless Device** Starts the Add A Device wizard. Use the wizard to add wireless devices that were detected but not configured.

Working with Network And Sharing Center

Network And Sharing Center, shown in Figure 15-3, provides the current network status as well as an overview of the current network configuration. In Control Panel, you can access Network And Sharing Center by clicking Network And Internet and then clicking Network And Sharing Center.

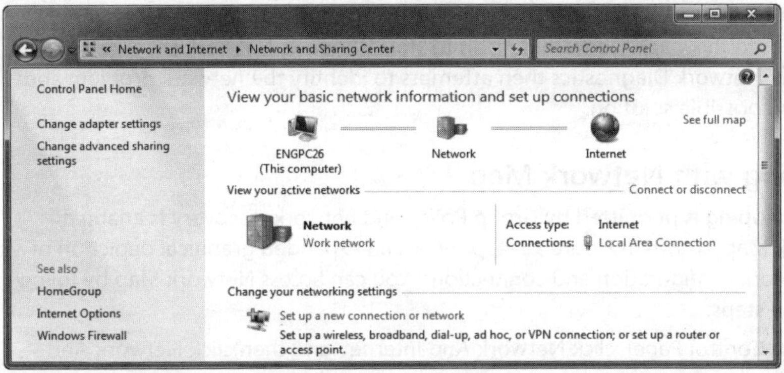

FIGURE 15-3 Use Network And Sharing Center to view the network status and details.

Network And Sharing Center has four main areas:

- **Summary network map** Provides a graphical depiction of the network configuration and connections. A normal status is indicated by a line connecting the various network segments. Any problems with the network configuration or connections are depicted with warning icons. A yellow warning icon indicates a possible configuration issue. A red X indicates a lack of a connection for a particular network segment. In Figure 15-3, the computer has a connection to the network and a connection to the Internet. Clicking See Full Map opens Network Map, which displays an expanded network view, as discussed in the next section, "Working with Network Map."
- **Active networks** Lists the currently active networks by name and provides an overview of the networks. Network names are listed in bold to the right of the network icon. If you double-click the network icon, you can specify the network name and change the network icon. The link listed below the network name shows the category of the current network, such as Work Network, Home Network, or Public Network. If you click this link, you can set the network location type.
- **Access type** Specifies whether and how the computer is connected to its current network. If the computer doesn't have Internet access, the access type is No Internet Access. The Connections field shows the names of the connections being used to connect to the active networks. If you click a connection, you can display the Status dialog box for the connection.
- **Network settings** Provides options for configuring the computer's networking settings. To configure sharing, click Change Advanced Sharing Settings in the left pane. Within the Advanced Sharing Settings window, to turn network discovery on or off, click Turn On Network Discovery or Turn Off Network Discovery, and then click Save Changes.

From Network And Sharing Center, you can attempt to diagnose a warning status. To do this, click the warning icon to start Windows Network Diagnostics. Windows Network Diagnostics then attempts to identify the network problem and provide a possible solution.

Working with Network Map

When mapping is permitted by Group Policy and network discovery is enabled, Network Map, shown in Figure 15-4, provides an expanded graphical depiction of the network configuration and connections. You can access Network Map by following these steps:

1. In Control Panel, click Network And Internet, and then click Network And Sharing Center.
2. In Network And Sharing Center, click See Full Map.

> ***NOTE*** **In a standard Windows 7 configuration, computers running Windows 7 can create a summary network map like the one available in Network And Sharing Center. More detailed network mapping, however, is permitted only when network discovery is enabled and network mapping is allowed by Group Policy.**

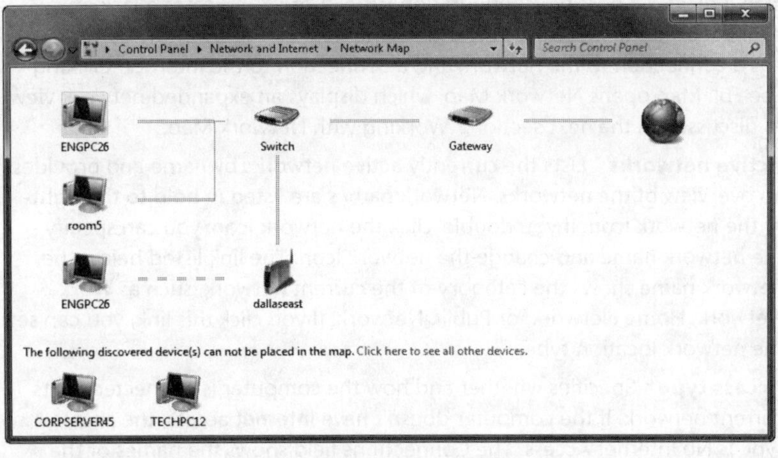

FIGURE 15-4 Use Network Map to get an expanded view of the network.

Computers and devices that are discovered and can be placed on the map are shown with lines that depict how they are connected. Computers and devices that are discovered but cannot be placed on the map are listed at the bottom of the page.

On the network map, any problems with the network configuration or connections are depicted with warning icons. A yellow warning icon indicates a possible configuration issue. A red X indicates the lack of a connection for a particular network segment. Clicking a warning icon starts Windows Network Diagnostics, which tries to identify the network problem and provide a possible solution.

> ***REAL WORLD*** **Network Map can be useful in some situations. However, because it allows discovery of an organization's internal network, which can put the network at risk, network mapping is disabled in Group Policy by default. Group Policy settings for controlling network mapping are found in the Administrative Templates policies for Computer Configuration under Network\Link-Layer Topology Discovery. For a computer to discover other computers for mapping, Turn On Mapper I/O (LLTDIO) Driver must be enabled in a Group Policy object being applied to the computer. For a computer to be discovered by other computers, Turn On Responder (RSPNDR) Driver must be enabled in a Group Policy object being applied to the computer.**
>
> **When you enable either or both of these settings, you can specify how this feature should work. In most cases, you'll want to configure the settings to allow operation while the computer is in the domain and prohibit operation while connected to a private network. Only allow operation on a public network when a specific need requires it, and then allow it only for the individual computer or computers that require mapping.**

Installing Networking Components

If you want to install networking on a computer, you must install TCP/IP networking and a network adapter. Windows 7 uses TCP/IP as the default wide area network (WAN) protocol. Networking components are normally installed during Windows 7 installation. You can also install TCP/IP networking through local area connection properties.

Working with TCP/IP and the Dual IP Stack

The TCP and IP protocols enable computers to communicate across various networks and the Internet by using network adapters, whether network interface cards, USB-attachable network adapters, PC Card network adapters, or built-in adapters on the motherboard. Windows 7 has a dual IP-layer architecture in which both Internet Protocol version 4 (IPv4) and Internet Protocol version 6 (IPv6) are implemented and share common Transport and Frame layers.

IPv4 and IPv6 are used in very different ways. IPv4 has 32-bit addresses and is the primary version of IP used on most networks, including the Internet. IPv6 has 128-bit addresses and is the next generation of IP.

IPv4's 32-bit addresses commonly are expressed as four separate decimal values, such as 127.0.0.1 or 192.168.1.20. The four decimal values are referred to as *octets* because each represents 8 bits of the 32-bit number. With standard unicast IPv4 addresses, a variable part of the IP address represents the network ID and another variable part represents the host ID. There is no correlation between a host's

IPv4 address and the internal machine (MAC) address used by the host's network adapter.

IPv6's 128-bit addresses are divided into eight 16-bit blocks delimited by colons. Each 16-bit block is expressed in hexadecimal form. With standard unicast IPv6 addresses, the first 64 bits represent the network ID and the last 64 bits represent the network interface. Here is an example of an IPv6 address:

```
FEC0:0:0:02BC:FF:BECB:FE4F:961D
```

Because many IPv6 address blocks are set to 0, a contiguous set of 0 blocks can be expressed as "::", a notation referred to as the *double-colon notation*. Using double-colon notation, the two 0 blocks in the previous address are compressed as follows:

```
FEC0::02BC:FF:BECB:FE4F:961D
```

If three or more 0 blocks are included, they would be compressed in the same way. For example, FFE8:0:0:0:0:0:0:1 becomes FFE8::1.

When networking hardware is detected during installation of the operating system, both IPv4 and IPv6 are enabled by default and there is no need to install a separate component to enable support for IPv6. The modified IP architecture in Windows 7 is referred to as the *Next Generation TCP/IP stack*. Table 15-1 summarizes the key TCP/IP enhancements implemented in the Next Generation TCP/IP stack. Table 15-2 summarizes the key TCP/IP enhancements that are specific to IPv6.

TABLE 15-1 Key TCP/IP Enhancements in the Next Generation TCP/IP Stack

FEATURES SUPPORTED	DESCRIPTION
Automatic Black Hole Router Detection	Prevents TCP connections from terminating due to intermediate routers silently discarding large TCP segments, retransmissions, or error messages.
Automatic Dead Gateway Retry	Ensures that an unreachable gateway is checked periodically to determine whether it has become available.
Compound TCP	Optimizes TCP transfers for the sending host by increasing the amount of data sent in a connection while ensuring other TCP connections are not impacted.
Extended Selective Acknowledgments	Extends the way Selective Acknowledgments (SACKs) are used, enabling a receiver to indicate up to four noncontiguous blocks of received data and to acknowledge duplicate packets. This helps the receiver determine when it has retransmitted a segment unnecessarily and adjust its behavior to prevent future retransmissions.

FEATURES SUPPORTED	DESCRIPTION
Modified Fast Recovery Algorithm	Provides faster throughput by altering the way that a sender can increase the sending rate if multiple segments in a window of data are lost and the sender receives an acknowledgment stating that only part of the data has been successfully received.
Neighbor Unreachability Detection for IPv4	Determines when neighboring nodes and routers are no longer reachable and reports the condition.
Network Diagnostics Framework	Provides an extensible framework that helps users recover from and troubleshoot problems with network connections.
Receive Window Auto Tuning	Optimizes TCP transfers for the host receiving data by automatically managing the size of the memory buffer (the receive windows) to use for storing incoming data based on the current network conditions.
Routing Compartments	Prevents unwanted forwarding of traffic between interfaces by associating an interface or a set of interfaces with a logon session that has its own routing tables.
SACK-Based Loss Recovery	Makes it possible to use SACK information to perform loss recovery when duplicate acknowledgments have been received and to more quickly recover when multiple segments are not received at the destination.
Spurious Retransmission Timeout Detection	Provides correction for sudden, temporary increases in retransmission timeouts and prevents unnecessary retransmission of segments.
TCP Extended Statistics	Helps determine whether a performance bottleneck for a connection is the sending application, the receiving application, or the network.
Windows Filtering Platform	Provides application programming interfaces (APIs) for extending the TCP/IP filtering architecture so that it can support additional features.

TABLE 15-2 Key TCP/IP Enhancements for IPv6

FEATURE SUPPORTED	DESCRIPTION
DHCPv6-Capable DHCP Client	Extends the DHCP client to support IPv6, and allows stateful address autoconfiguration with a DHCPv6 server.
IP Security	Allows use of Internet Key Exchange (IKE) and data encryption for IPv6.
IPv6 over Point-to-Point Protocol (PPPv6)	Allows native IPv6 traffic to be sent over PPP-based connections, which in turn allows remote access clients to connect with an IPv6-based Internet service provider (ISP) through dial-up or PPP over Ethernet (PPPoE)–based connections.
Link-Local Multicast Name Resolution (LLMNR)	Allows IPv6 hosts on a single subnet without a DNS server to resolve each other's names.
Multicast Listener Discovery version 2 (MLDv2)	Provides support for source-specific multicast traffic and is equivalent to Internet Group Management Protocol version 3 (IGMPv3) for IPv4.
Random Interface IDs	Prevents scanning of IPv6 addresses based on the known company IDs of network adapter manufacturers. By default, Windows 7 generates random interface IDs for nontemporary, autoconfigured IPv6 addresses, including public and link-local addresses.
Symmetric Network Address Translators	Maps the internal (private) address and port number to different external (public) addresses and ports, depending on the external destination address.

Installing Network Adapters

Network adapters are hardware devices that are used to communicate on networks. You can install and configure network adapters by completing the following steps:

1. Follow the manufacturer's instructions. For example, you might need to use the software provided by the manufacturer to modify the Interrupt setting or the Port setting of the adapter.
2. If installing an internal network interface card, shut down the computer, unplug it, and install the adapter card in the appropriate slot on the computer. When you've finished, plug in and start the computer.
3. Windows 7 should detect the new adapter during startup. If you have a separate driver disc for the adapter, you should insert it now. Otherwise, you might be prompted to insert a driver disc.

4. If Windows 7 doesn't detect the adapter automatically, follow the installation instructions in the section "Working with Device Drivers" in Chapter 8.
5. If networking services aren't installed on the system, install them as described in the next section.

Installing Networking Services (TCP/IP)

If you're installing TCP/IP after installing Windows 7, log on to the computer using an account with administrator privileges, and then follow these steps:

1. In Control Panel, click Network And Internet, and then click Network And Sharing Center.
2. In Network And Sharing Center, under View Your Active Networks, click the link for the network connection.

   TIP **If the network connection you want to work with isn't active, click Connect To A Network. In Network Connections, right-click the connection you want to work with, and then click Properties.**

3. In the Status dialog box, click Properties. This displays a Properties dialog box for the connection with the Networking tab selected, as shown in Figure 15-5.

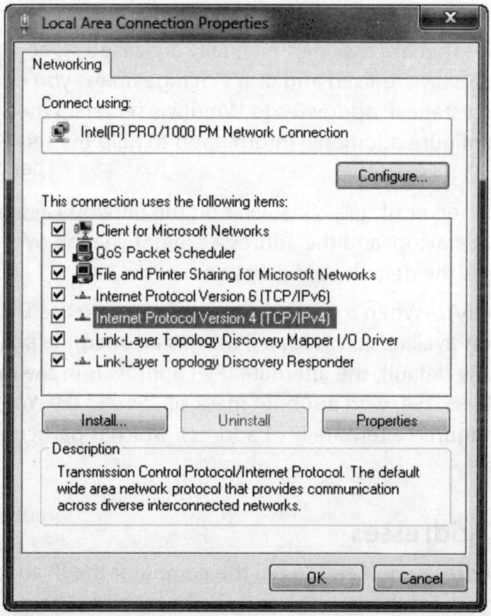

FIGURE 15-5 Use the Local Area Connection Properties dialog box to install and configure TCP/IP.

4. If Internet Protocol Version 6 (TCP/IPv6), Internet Protocol Version 4 (TCP/IPv4), or both aren't shown in the list of installed components, you need to install them. Click Install, click Protocol, and then click Add. In the Select Network Protocol dialog box, select the protocol to install, and then click OK. To install both TCP/IPv6 and TCP/IPv4, repeat this step.
5. In the Local Area Connection Properties dialog box, make sure that the following are selected, as appropriate: Internet Protocol Version 6 (TCP/IPv6), Internet Protocol Version 4 (TCP/IPv4), or both. Click OK.
6. As necessary, follow the instructions in the next section for configuring local area connections for the computer.

Configuring Local Area Connections

A local area connection is created automatically if a computer has a network adapter and is connected to a network. If a computer has multiple network adapters and is connected to a network, a local area connection is created for each adapter. If no network connection is available, you should connect the computer to the network or create a different type of connection, as explained in the section "Managing Local Area Connections" later in this chapter.

Computers use IP addresses to communicate over TCP/IP. Windows 7 provides the following ways to configure IP addressing:

- **Manually** IP addresses that are assigned manually are called *static IP addresses*. Static IP addresses are fixed and don't change unless you change them. You usually assign static IP addresses to Windows servers. When you do this, you need to configure additional information to help the server navigate the network.
- **Dynamically** A DHCP server (if one is installed on the network) assigns dynamic IP addresses at startup, and the addresses might change over time. Dynamic IP addressing is the default configuration.
- **Alternatively (IPv4 only)** When a computer is configured to use DHCPv4 and no DHCPv4 server is available, Windows 7 assigns an alternate private IP address automatically. By default, the alternate IPv4 address is in the range 169.254.0.1 to 169.254.255.254, with a subnet mask of 255.255.0.0. You can also specify a user-configured alternate IPv4 address, which is particularly useful for laptop users.

Configuring Static IP Addresses

When you assign a static IP address, you need to tell the computer the IP address you want to use, the subnet mask for this IP address, and, if necessary, the default gateway to use for internetwork communications. An IP address is a numeric identifier for a computer. IP addressing schemes vary according to how your network is configured, but they're normally assigned based on a particular network segment.

IPv6 addresses and IPv4 addresses are very different, as discussed in the section "Working with TCP/IP and the Dual IP Stack." In IPv6, the first 64 bits represent the network ID, and the remaining 64 bits represent the network interface. In IPv4, a variable number of the initial bits represent the network ID, and the rest of the bits represent the host ID. For example, if you're working with IPv4 and a computer on the network segment 10.0.10.0 with a subnet mask of 255.255.255.0, the first three octets identify the network. The network's unique ID is 10.0.10.0. The address range you have available for computer hosts is 10.0.10.1 to 10.0.10.254. In this range, the address 10.0.10.255 is reserved for network broadcasts.

If you're on a private network that is indirectly connected to the Internet, you should use private IPv4 addresses. Private network IPv4 addresses are summarized in Table 15-3.

TABLE 15-3 Private IPv4 Network Addressing

PRIVATE NETWORK ID	SUBNET MASK	USABLE IP ADDRESS RANGE	BROADCAST ADDRESS
10.0.0.0	255.0.0.0	10.0.0.0–10.255.255.254	10.255.255.255
172.16.0.0	255.240.0.0	172.16.0.0–172.31.255.254	172.31.255.255
192.168.0.0	255.255.0.0	192.168.0.0–192.168.255.254	192.168.255.255

All other IPv4 network addresses are public and must be leased or purchased. If the network is connected directly to the Internet and you've obtained a range of IPv4 addresses from your Internet service provider, you can use the IPv4 addresses you've been assigned.

Using the Ping Command to Check an Address

Before you assign a static IP address, you should make sure that the address isn't already in use or reserved for use with DHCP. You can use the Ping command to see whether an address is in use. Open a command prompt and type **ping**, followed by the IP address you want to check.

To test the IPv4 address 10.0.10.12, you would use the following command:

```
ping 10.0.10.12
```

To test the IPv6 address FEC0::02BC:FF:BECB:FE4F:961D, you would use the following command:

```
ping FEC0::02BC:FF:BECB:FE4F:961D
```

If you receive a successful reply from the ping test, the IP address is in use and you should try another one. If the request times out for all four ping attempts, the IP address isn't active on the network at this time and probably isn't in use. However, a firewall could be blocking your ping request. Your company's network administrator should also be able to confirm whether an IP address is in use.

Configuring a Static IPv4 or IPv6 Address

One local area network (LAN) connection is available for each network adapter installed. These connections are created automatically. To configure static IP addresses for a particular connection, complete the following steps:

1. In Control Panel, click Network And Internet, and then click Network And Sharing Center.
2. In Network And Sharing Center, under View Your Active Networks, click the link for the network connection.
3. In the Local Area Connection Status dialog box, click Properties. This displays the Local Area Connection Properties dialog box.
4. Double-click Internet Protocol Version 6 (TCP/IPv6) or Internet Protocol Version 4 (TCP/IPv4), depending on the type of IP address you are configuring.
5. For an IPv6 address, do the following:
   - Click Use The Following IPv6 Address, and then type the IPv6 address in the IPv6 Address text box. The IPv6 address you assign to the computer must not be used anywhere else on the network.
   - Press Tab. The Subnet Prefix Length field ensures that the computer communicates over the network properly. Windows 7 should insert a default value for the subnet prefix in the Subnet Prefix Length text box. If the network doesn't use variable-length subnetting, the default value should suffice. If the network does use variable-length subnets, you need to change this value as appropriate for your network.
6. For an IPv4 address, do the following:
   - Click Use The Following IP Address, and then type the IPv4 address in the IP Address text box. The IPv4 address you assign to the computer must not be used anywhere else on the network.
   - Press Tab. The Subnet Mask field ensures that the computer communicates over the network properly. Windows 7 should insert a default value for the subnet mask into the Subnet Mask text box. If the network doesn't use variable-length subnetting, the default value should suffice, but if it does use variable-length subnets, you need to change this value as appropriate for your network.
7. If the computer needs to access other TCP/IP networks, the Internet, or other subnets, you must specify a default gateway. Type the IP address for the network's default router in the Default Gateway text box.
8. DNS is needed for domain name resolution. Type a preferred address and an alternate DNS server address in the text boxes provided.
9. When you've finished, click OK twice, and then click Close. Repeat this process for other network adapters and IP protocols you want to configure.
10. With IPv4 addressing, configure WINS as necessary following the technique outlined in the section "Configuring WINS Resolution" later in this chapter.

Configuring Dynamic IP Addresses and Alternate IP Addressing

Although static IP addresses can be used with workstations, most workstations use dynamic or alternate IP addressing or both. You configure dynamic and alternate addressing by completing the following steps:

1. In Control Panel, click Network And Internet, and then click Network And Sharing Center.
2. In Network And Sharing Center, under View Your Active Networks, click the link for the network connection.
3. In the Local Area Connection Status dialog box, click Properties. This displays the Local Area Connection Properties dialog box, shown in Figure 15-5.

   NOTE **In the Local Area Connection Status dialog box, one LAN connection is shown for each network adapter installed. These connections are created automatically. If you don't see a LAN connection for an installed adapter, check the driver for the adapter. It might be installed incorrectly.**

4. Double-click Internet Protocol Version 6 (TCP/IPv6) or Internet Protocol Version 4 (TCP/IPv4) depending on the type of IP address you are configuring.
5. Select Obtain An IPv6 Address Automatically or Obtain An IP Address Automatically, as appropriate for the type of IP address you are configuring. If you want to, select Obtain DNS Server Address Automatically, or select Use The Following DNS Server Addresses, and then type a preferred and alternate DNS server address in the text boxes provided.
6. When you use dynamic IPv4 addressing with desktop computers, you should configure an automatic alternate address. To use this configuration, on the Alternate Configuration tab, be sure that Automatic Private IP Address is selected. Click OK twice, click Close, and then skip the remaining steps.
7. When you use dynamic IPv4 addressing with mobile computers, you usually want to configure the alternate address manually. To use this configuration, on the Alternate Configuration tab, select User Configured. Then, in the IP Address text box, type the IP address you want to use. The IP address that you assign to the computer should be a private IP address, as shown earlier in Table 15-3, and it must not be in use anywhere else when the settings are applied.
8. With dynamic IPv4 addressing, complete the alternate configuration by entering a subnet mask, default gateway, and DNS and WINS settings. When you've finished, click OK twice, and then click Close.

NOTE **You'll find more detailed information on configuring laptops in the section "Configuring Networking for Laptops" in Chapter 16.**

Configuring Multiple Gateways

To provide fault tolerance in case of a router outage, you can configure Windows 7 computers so that they use multiple default gateways. When multiple gateways are assigned, Windows 7 uses the gateway metric to determine which gateway is used and at what time. The gateway metric indicates the routing cost of using a gateway. The gateway with the lowest routing cost, or metric, is used first. If the computer can't communicate with this gateway, Windows 7 tries to use the gateway with the next lowest metric.

The best way to configure multiple gateways depends on the configuration of your network. If computers use DHCP, you probably want to configure the additional gateways through settings on the DHCP server. If computers use static IP addresses, or you want to set gateways specifically, assign them by completing the following steps:

1. In Control Panel, click Network And Internet, and then click Network And Sharing Center.
2. In Network And Sharing Center, under View Your Active Networks, click the link for the network connection.
3. In the Local Area Connection Status dialog box, click Properties. This displays the Local Area Connection Properties dialog box. (See Figure 15-5.)
4. Double-click Internet Protocol Version 6 (TCP/IPv6) or Internet Protocol Version 4 (TCP/IPv4) depending on the type of IP address you are configuring.
5. Click Advanced to open the Advanced TCP/IP Settings dialog box, shown in Figure 15-6.

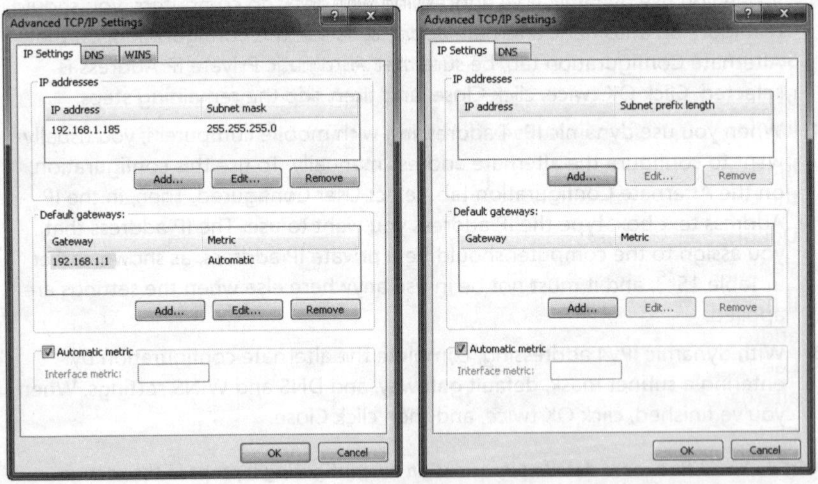

FIGURE 15-6 Use the Advanced TCP/IP Settings dialog box to configure multiple IP addresses and gateways (for IPv4 on the left, and IPv6 on the right).

6. The Default Gateways area shows the current gateways that have been manually configured (if any). You can enter additional default gateways as necessary. Click Add, and then type the gateway address in the Gateway text box.
7. By default, Windows 7 automatically assigns a metric to the gateway. You can also assign the metric manually. To do this, clear the Automatic Metric check box, and then enter a metric in the text box provided.
8. Click Add, and then repeat steps 6 and 7 for each gateway you want to add.
9. Click OK three times, and then click Close.

Configuring DNS Resolution

DNS is a host name resolution service that you can use to determine the IP address of a computer from its host name. This enables users to work with host names, such as http://www.msn.com or http://www.microsoft.com, rather than an IP address, such as 192.168.5.102 or 192.168.12.68. DNS is the primary name service for Windows 7 and the Internet.

As with gateways, the best way to configure DNS depends on the configuration of your network. If computers use DHCP, you'll probably want to configure DNS through settings on the DHCP server. If computers use static IP addresses, or you want to specifically configure DNS for an individual user or system, you should configure DNS manually.

Basic DNS Settings

You can configure basic DNS settings by completing the following steps:

1. In Control Panel, click Network And Internet, and then click Network And Sharing Center.
2. In Network And Sharing Center, under View Your Active Networks, click the link for the network connection.
3. In the Local Area Connection Status dialog box, click Properties. This displays the Local Area Connection Properties dialog box. (See Figure 15-5.)
4. Double-click Internet Protocol Version 6 (TCP/IPv6) or Internet Protocol Version 4 (TCP/IPv4) depending on the type of IP address you are configuring.
5. If the computer is using DHCP and you want DHCP to specify the DNS server address, select Obtain DNS Server Address Automatically. Otherwise, select Use The Following DNS Server Addresses, and then type a primary and an alternate DNS server address in the text boxes provided.
6. Click OK twice, and then click Close.

Advanced DNS Settings

You configure advanced DNS settings by using the DNS tab of the Advanced TCP/IP Settings dialog box, shown in Figure 15-7. You use the fields on the DNS tab as follows:

- **DNS Server Addresses, In Order Of Use** Use this area to specify the IP address of each DNS server that is used for domain name resolution. Click Add if you want to add a server IP address to the list. Click Remove to remove a selected server address from the list. Click Edit to edit the selected entry. You can specify multiple servers for DNS resolution. Their priority is determined by the order. If the first server isn't available to respond to a host name resolution request, the next DNS server in the list is accessed, and so on. To change the position of a server in the list, select it, and then use the up or down arrow button.
- **Append Primary And Connection Specific DNS Suffixes** Normally, this option is selected by default. Use this option to resolve unqualified computer names in the primary domain. For example, if the computer name Gandolf is used and the parent domain is microsoft.com, the computer name would resolve to gandolf.microsoft.com. If the fully qualified computer name doesn't exist in the parent domain, the query fails. The parent domain used is the one set in the System Properties dialog box on the Computer Name tab. (To check the settings, click System And Security in Control Panel, and then click System.)
- **Append Parent Suffixes Of The Primary DNS Suffix** This option is selected by default. Use this option to resolve unqualified computer names by using the parent/child domain hierarchy. If a query fails in the immediate parent domain, the suffix for the parent of the parent domain is used to try to resolve the query. This process continues until the top of the DNS domain hierarchy is reached. For example, if the computer name Gandolf is used in the dev.microsoft.com domain, DNS would attempt to resolve the computer name to gandolf.dev.microsoft.com. If this didn't work, DNS would attempt to resolve the computer name to gandolf.microsoft.com.
- **Append These DNS Suffixes (In Order)** Select this option to specify DNS suffixes to use for name resolution rather than resolving names through the parent domain. Click Add if you want to add a domain suffix to the list. Click Remove to remove a selected domain suffix from the list. Click Edit to edit the selected entry. You can specify multiple domain suffixes, which are used in order. If the first suffix doesn't resolve properly, DNS attempts to use the next suffix in the list. If this fails, the next suffix is used, and so on. To change the order of the domain suffixes, select the suffix, and then use the up or down arrow button to change its position.
- **DNS Suffix For This Connection** This option sets a specific DNS suffix for the connection that overrides DNS names already configured for this connection. However, you'll usually set the DNS domain name by clicking System

And Security in Control Panel, clicking System, and then clicking Change Settings. In the System Properties dialog box, click Change on the Computer Name tab, and then click More. You can now enter the primary DNS suffix for the computer in the text box provided. Click OK three times to save your changes.

- **Register This Connection's Addresses In DNS** Use this option if you want all IP addresses for this connection to be registered in DNS under the computer's fully qualified domain name. This option is selected by default.

  Dynamic DNS updates are used in conjunction with DHCP to enable a client to update its A (Host Address) record if its IP address changes and to enable the DHCP server to update the PTR (Pointer) record for the client on the DNS server. DHCP servers can also be configured to update both the A and PTR records on the client's behalf. Dynamic DNS updates are supported only by BIND 5.1 or higher DNS servers, as well as by Windows 2000 Server, Windows Server 2003, and later server versions of Windows. Windows NT Server 4 does not support this feature.
- **Use This Connection's DNS Suffix In DNS Registration** Select this option if you want all IP addresses for this connection to be registered in DNS under the parent domain.

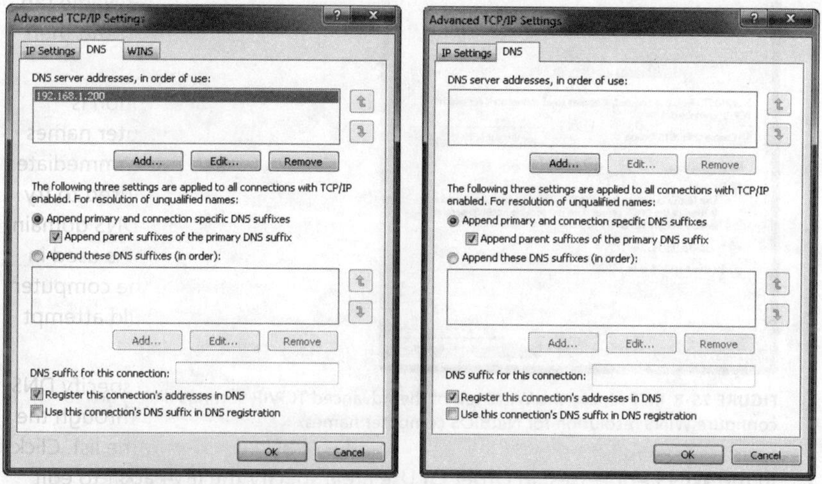

FIGURE 15-7 Use the DNS tab of the Advanced TCP/IP Settings dialog box to configure advanced DNS settings (for IPv4 on the left, and IPv6 on the right).

Configuring WINS Resolution

You use WINS to resolve NetBIOS computer names to IPv4 addresses. You can use WINS to help computers on a network determine the address of other computers on the network. If a WINS server is installed on the network, you can use the server to resolve computer names. Although WINS is supported on all versions of Windows, Windows 7 primarily uses WINS for backward compatibility.

You can also configure Windows 7 computers to use the local file LMHOSTS to resolve NetBIOS computer names. However, LMHOSTS is consulted only if normal name resolution methods fail. In a properly configured network, these files are rarely used. Thus, the preferred method of NetBIOS computer-name resolution is WINS in conjunction with a WINS server.

As with gateways and DNS, the best way to configure WINS depends on the configuration of your network. If computers use DHCP, you'll probably want to configure WINS through settings on the DHCP server. If computers use static IPv4 addresses, or you want to configure WINS specifically for an individual user or system, you should configure WINS manually.

You can manually configure WINS by completing the following steps:

1. Open the Advanced TCP/IP Settings dialog box, and then click the WINS tab. You'll see the WINS Addresses, In Order Of Use area, shown in Figure 15-8.

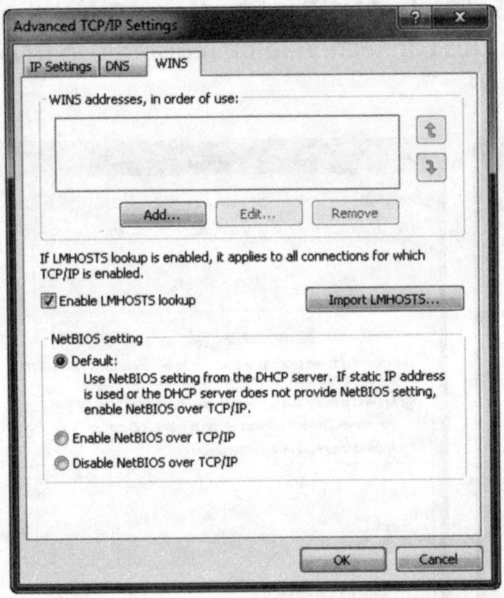

FIGURE 15-8 In IPv4, use the WINS tab of the Advanced TCP/IP Settings dialog box to configure WINS resolution for NetBIOS computer names.

2. In the WINS Addresses, In Order Of Use area, specify the IPv4 address of each WINS server that is used for NetBIOS name resolution. Click Add if you want to add a server IPv4 address to the list. Click Remove to remove a selected server from the list. Click Edit to edit the selected entry.
3. You can specify multiple servers, which are used in order, for WINS resolution. If the first server isn't available to respond to a NetBIOS name resolution request, the next WINS server in the list is accessed, and so on. To change the position of a server in the list, select it, and then use the up or down arrow button.

4. To enable LMHOSTS lookups, select the Enable LMHOSTS Lookup check box. If you want the computer to use an existing LMHOSTS file defined somewhere on the network, retrieve this file by clicking Import LMHOSTS. You generally will use LMHOSTS only when other name resolution methods fail.
5. WINS name resolution requires NetBIOS Over TCP/IP services. Select one of the following options to configure WINS name resolution using NetBIOS:
   - If you use DHCP and dynamic addressing, you can get the NetBIOS setting from the DHCP server. Select Default: Use NetBIOS Setting From The DHCP Server.
   - If you use a static IP address or the DHCP server does not provide NetBIOS settings, select Enable NetBIOS Over TCP/IP.
   - If WINS and NetBIOS are not used on the network, select Disable NetBIOS Over TCP/IP. This eliminates the NetBIOS broadcasts that would otherwise be sent by the computer.
6. Click OK three times, and then click Close. As necessary, repeat this process for other network adapters.

TIP **LMHOSTS files are maintained locally on a computer-by-computer basis, which can eventually make them unreliable. Rather than relying on LMHOSTS, be sure that your DNS and WINS servers are configured properly and are accessible to the network for centralized administration of name resolution services.**

Managing Local Area Connections

Local area connections enable computers to access resources on the network and the Internet. One local area connection is created automatically for each network adapter installed on a computer. This section examines techniques you can use to manage these connections.

Enabling and Disabling Local Area Connections

Local area connections are created and enabled automatically. If you want to disable a connection so that it cannot be used, complete the following steps:

1. In Control Panel, click Network And Internet, and then click Network And Sharing Center.
2. In Network And Sharing Center, in the left pane, click Change Adapter Settings.
3. In Network Connections, right-click the connection, and then click Disable.
4. Later, if you want to enable the connection, right-click the connection, and then click Enable.

If you want to disconnect from a network or start another connection, complete the following steps:

1. In Control Panel, click Network And Internet, and then click Network And Sharing Center.
2. In Network And Sharing Center, in the left pane, click Change Adapter Settings.
3. In Network Connections, right-click the connection, and then click Disconnect. Typically, only remote access connections have a Disconnect option.
4. Later, if you want to activate the connection, right-click the connection in Network Connections, and then click Connect.

Checking the Status, Speed, and Activity for Local Area Connections

To check the status of a local area connection, follow these steps:

1. In Control Panel, click Network And Internet, and then click Network And Sharing Center.
2. In Network And Sharing Center, under View Your Active Networks, click the link for the network connection.
3. This displays the Local Area Connection Status dialog box. If the connection is disabled or the media is unplugged, you won't be able to access this dialog box. Enable the connection or connect the network cable to resolve the problem, and then try to display the Status dialog box again.

The General tab of the Local Area Connection Status dialog box, shown in Figure 15-9, provides useful information about the following:

- **IPv4 Connectivity** The current IPv4 connection state and type. You typically see the status identified as Local when you are connected to an internal network, Internet when a computer can access the Internet, or No Network Access when not connected to a network.
- **IPv6 Connectivity** The current IPv6 connection state and type. You typically see the status identified as Local when you are connected to an internal network, Internet when a computer can access the Internet, or No Network Access when not connected to a network.
- **Media State** The state of the media. Because the Status dialog box is available only when the connection is enabled, you usually see this as Enabled.
- **Duration** The amount of time the connection has been established. If the duration is fairly short, the user either recently connected to the network or the connection was recently reset.
- **Speed** The speed of the connection. This should read 10.0 Mbps for 10-megabits-per-second (Mbps) connections, 100.0 Mbps for 100-Mbps

connections, and 1.0 Gbps for 1-gigabit-per-second (Gbps) connections. An incorrect setting can affect the computer's performance.

- **Bytes** The number of bytes sent and the number received by the connection. As the computer sends or receives packets, you'll see the computer icons indicate the flow of traffic.

FIGURE 15-9 The General tab of the Local Area Connection Status dialog box provides access to summary information regarding connections, properties, and support.

Viewing Network Configuration Information

In Windows 7, you can view the current configuration for network adapters in several ways. To view configuration settings using the Status dialog box, follow these steps:

1. In Control Panel, click Network And Internet, and then click Network And Sharing Center.
2. In Network And Sharing Center, in the left pane, click Change Adapter Settings.
3. In Network Connections, double-click the connection. This displays the Local Area Connection Status dialog box. If the connection is disabled or the media is unplugged, you won't be able to access this dialog box. Enable the connection or connect the network cable to resolve the problem, and then try to display the Status dialog box again.

4. Click Details to view detailed information about the IP address configuration, including the following:
   - **Physical Address** The machine or media access control (MAC) address of the network adapter. This address is unique for each network adapter.
   - **IPv4 Address** The IPv4 address assigned for IPv4 networking.
   - **IPv4 Subnet Mask** The subnet mask used for IPv4 networking.
   - **IPv4 Default Gateways** The IPv4 address of the default gateways used for IPv4 networking.
   - **IPv4 DNS Servers** IP addresses for DNS servers used with IPv4 networking.
   - **IPv4 WINS Servers** IP addresses for WINS servers used with IPv4 networking.
   - **IPv4 DHCP Server** The IP address of the DHCPv4 server from which the current lease was obtained (DHCPv4 only).
   - **Lease Obtained** A date and time stamp for when the DHCPv4 lease was obtained (DHCPv4 only).
   - **Lease Expires** A date and time stamp for when the DHCPv4 lease expires (DHCPv4 only).

You can also use the Ipconfig command to view advanced configuration settings. To do so, follow these steps:

1. Click Start, and then type **cmd** in the Search field.
2. Press Enter.
3. At the command line, type **ipconfig /all** to see detailed configuration information for all network adapters configured on the computer.

NOTE **The command prompt is started in standard user mode. This is not an elevated command prompt.**

Renaming Local Area Connections

Windows 7 initially assigns default names for local area connections. In Network Connections, you can rename a connection by right-clicking the connection, clicking Rename, and then typing a new connection name. If a computer has multiple local area connections, proper naming can help you and others better understand the uses of a particular connection.

Troubleshooting and Testing Network Settings

Windows 7 includes many tools for troubleshooting and testing TCP/IP connectivity. The following sections look at automated diagnostics, basic tests that you should perform whenever you install or modify a computer's network settings, and techniques for resolving difficult networking problems involving DHCP and DNS. The final section shows you how to perform detailed network diagnostics testing.

Diagnosing and Resolving Local Area Connection Problems

Occasionally network cables can become unplugged or the network adapter might experience a problem that temporarily prevents it from working. After you plug the cable back in or solve the adapter problem, the connection should automatically reconnect. You can diagnose local area connection problems by right-clicking the Network notification icon on the taskbar and clicking Troubleshoot Problems.

Windows Network Diagnostics then tries to identify the problem. As shown in Figure 15-10, a list of possible solutions is provided if identifiable configuration problems are detected. Some solutions provide automated fixes that can be executed by clicking the solution. Other solutions require manual fixes, such as resetting a network router or a broadband modem. If your actions don't fix the problem, refer to other appropriate parts of this troubleshooting section.

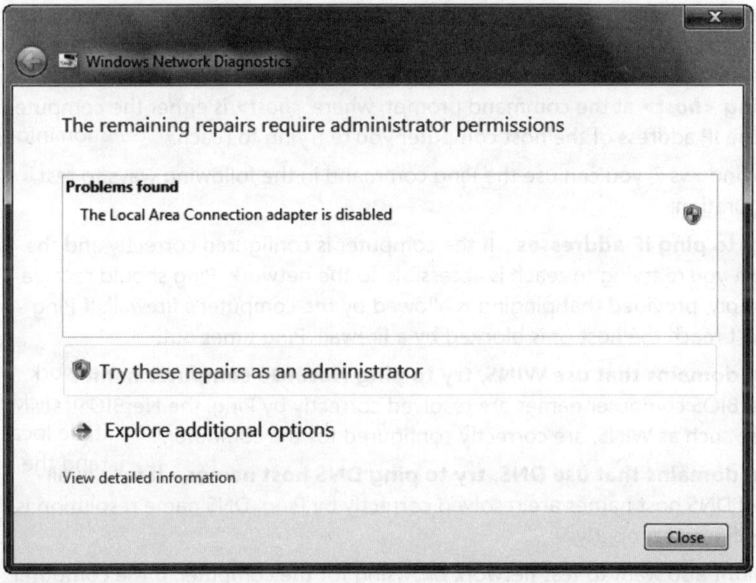

FIGURE 15-10 Resolve the problem by making a selection or performing a required action.

Diagnosing and Resolving Internet Connection Problems

Because services, protocols, and configuration settings have so many interdependencies, troubleshooting network problems can be difficult. Fortunately, Windows 7 includes a powerful network diagnostics tool for pinpointing problems that relate to the following:

- General network connectivity problems
- Internet service settings for e-mail, newsgroups, and proxies
- Settings for modems, network clients, and network adapters
- DNS, DHCP, and WINS configuration
- Default gateways and IP addresses

In Network And Sharing Center, you can diagnose Internet connection problems by clicking the red X on the network map. Windows Network Diagnostics then tries to identify the problem. If identifiable configuration problems exist, a list of possible solutions is provided. Some solutions provide automated fixes that can be executed by clicking the solution. Other solutions require manual fixes, such as resetting a network router or a broadband modem. If your actions don't fix the problem, refer to other appropriate parts of this troubleshooting section.

Performing Basic Network Tests

Whenever you install a new computer or make configuration changes to a computer's network settings, you should test the configuration. The most basic TCP/IP test is to use the Ping command to test the computer's connection to the network. To use it, type **ping <*host*>** at the command prompt, where <*host*> is either the computer name or the IP address of the host computer you're trying to reach.

With Windows 7, you can use the Ping command in the following ways to test the configuration:

- **Try to ping IP addresses** If the computer is configured correctly and the host you're trying to reach is accessible to the network, Ping should receive a reply, provided that pinging is allowed by the computer's firewall. If Ping can't reach the host or is blocked by a firewall, Ping times out.
- **On domains that use WINS, try to ping NetBIOS computer names** If NetBIOS computer names are resolved correctly by Ping, the NetBIOS facilities, such as WINS, are correctly configured for the computer.
- **On domains that use DNS, try to ping DNS host names** If fully qualified DNS host names are resolved correctly by Ping, DNS name resolution is configured properly.

You might also want to test network browsing for the computer. If the computer is a member of a Windows 7 domain and computer browsing is enabled throughout the domain, log on to the computer and then use Windows Explorer or Network Explorer to browse other computers in the domain. Afterward, log on to a different computer in the domain and try to browse the computer you just configured. These tests tell you whether DNS resolution is being handled properly in the local environment. If you can't browse, check the configuration of the DNS services and protocols.

> ***REAL WORLD*** **Access to network resources in Network Explorer is dependent on the Computer Browser service and the network discovery settings. The Computer Browser service is responsible for maintaining a list of computers on a network. If the service is stopped or isn't working properly, a computer won't see available resources in Network Explorer. You can check the status of the Computer Browser service in Computer Management. Expand Services And Applications, and then select Services in the left pane. The status of the Computer Browser service should be Started. If the status is blank, the service isn't running and should be started.**

In some cases, the Computer Browser service might be running normally, but there might not be an updated list of resources in Network Explorer. This can happen because the service performs periodic updates of the resource list rather than checking continuously for updates. If a resource you want to use isn't listed, you can wait for it to become available (which should take less than 15 minutes in most cases), or you can connect to the resource directly by using the Universal Naming Convention (UNC) name or IP address of the resource, as discussed in the section "Using and Accessing Shared Resources" in Chapter 13.

In some cases, discovering and sharing might be set to block discovery. You need to allow discovery to resolve this by following these steps:

1. In Control Panel, click Network And Internet, and then click Network And Sharing Center.
2. In Network And Sharing Center, in the left pane, click Change Advanced Sharing Settings.
3. If network discovery is turned off, click Turn On Network Discovery.

Resolving IP Addressing Problems

The current IP address settings of a computer can be obtained as described in the "Viewing Network Configuration Information" section of this chapter. If a computer is having problems accessing network resources or communicating with other computers, an IP addressing problem might exist. Take a close look at the IP address currently assigned, as well as other IP address settings, and use the following pointers to help in your troubleshooting:

- If the IPv4 address currently assigned to the computer is in the range 169.254.0.1 to 169.254.255.254, the computer is using Automatic Private IP Addressing (APIPA). An automatic private IP address is assigned to a computer when it is configured to use DHCP and its DHCP client cannot reach a DHCP server. When using APIPA, Windows 7 will periodically check for a DHCP server to become available. If a computer doesn't eventually obtain a dynamic IP address, this usually means the network connection has a problem. Check the network cable and, if necessary, trace the cable back to the switch or hub it connects to.

- If the IPv4 address and the subnet mask of the computer are currently set as 0.0.0.0, the network is either disconnected or someone attempted to use a static IP address that duplicated another IP address already in use on the network. In this case, you should access Network Connections and determine the state of the connection. If the connection is disabled or disconnected, this status should be shown. Right-click the connection, and then click Enable or Repair. If the connection is already enabled, you need to modify the IP address settings for the connection.
- If the IP address is dynamically assigned, check to be sure that another computer on the network isn't using the same IP address. You can do this by disconnecting the network cable for the computer that you are working with and pinging the IP address in question. If you receive a response from the Ping command, you know that another computer is using the IP address. This computer probably has an improper static IP address or a reservation that isn't set up properly.
- If the IP address appears to be set correctly, check the network mask, gateway, DNS, and WINS settings by comparing the network settings of the computer you are troubleshooting with those of a computer that is known to have a good network configuration. One of the biggest problem areas is the network mask. When subnetting is used, the network mask for one area of the network might be very similar to that of another area. For example, the network mask in one IPv4 area might be 255.255.255.240, and it might be 255.255.255.248 in another IPv4 area.

Releasing and Renewing DHCP Settings

DHCP servers can assign many network configuration settings automatically. These include IP addresses, default gateways, primary and secondary DNS servers, primary and secondary WINS servers, and more. When computers use dynamic addressing, they are assigned a lease on a specific IP address. This lease is good for a specific time period and must be renewed periodically. When the lease needs to be renewed, the computer contacts the DHCP server that provided the lease. If the server is available, the lease is renewed and a new lease period is granted. You can also renew leases manually on individual computers or by using the DHCP server itself.

Problems can occur during the lease assignment and renewal process that prevent network communications. If the server isn't available and cannot be reached before a lease expires, the IP address can become invalid. If this happens, the computer might use the alternate IP address configuration to set an alternate address, which in most cases has settings that are inappropriate and prevent proper communications. To resolve this problem, you need to release and then renew the DHCP lease.

Another type of problem occurs when users move around to various offices and subnets within an organization. In being moved from location to location, their computers might obtain DHCP settings from the wrong server. When the users return to their offices, the computers might seem sluggish or perform incorrectly due to the settings assigned by the DHCP server at another location. If this happens, you need to release and then renew the DHCP lease.

You can release and renew DHCP leases by completing the following tasks:

1. In Network And Sharing Center, in the left pane, click Change Adapter Settings.
2. In Network Connections, right-click the connection you want to work with, and then click Diagnose.
3. After Windows Network Diagnostics tries to identify the problem, a list of possible solutions is provided. If the computer has one or more dynamically assigned IP addresses, one of the solutions should be Automatically Get New IP Settings. Click this option.

You can also follow these steps to use the Ipconfig command to release and renew settings:

1. Start an elevated command prompt.
2. To release the current settings for all network adapters, type **ipconfig /release** at the command line. Then renew the lease by typing **ipconfig /renew**.
3. To only renew a DHCP lease for all network adapters, type **ipconfig /renew** at the command line.
4. You can check the updated settings by typing **ipconfig /all** at the command line.

REAL WORLD **If you don't release the old DHCP settings before trying to renew the DHCP settings, the computer will try to renew the settings on the network to which it was last connected. If the computer is on a new network, the computer might not be able to establish a connection to the server or device that assigned the DHCP settings previously.**

If a computer has multiple network adapters and you want to work with only one or a subset of the adapters, you can do this by specifying all or part of the connection name after the ipconfig /renew or ipconfig /release command. Use the asterisk as a wildcard character to match any characters in a connection's name. For example, if you want to renew the lease for all connections with names starting with Loc, you can type the command ipconfig /renew Loc*. If you want to release the settings for all connections containing the word Network, you can type the command ipconfig /release *Network*.

Registering and Flushing DNS

The DNS resolver cache maintains a history of DNS lookups that have been performed when a user accesses network resources using TCP/IP. This cache contains forward lookups, which provide host-name-to-IP-address resolution, and reverse lookups, which provide IP-address-to–host-name resolution. Once a DNS entry is stored in the resolver cache for a particular DNS host, the local computer no longer has to query external servers for DNS information on that host. This enables the computer to resolve DNS requests locally, which provides a quicker response.

The period of time in which entries are stored in the resolver cache depends on the Time to Live (TTL) value assigned to the record by the originating server. To view current records and see the remaining TTL value for each record, in an elevated command prompt, type **ipconfig /displaydns**. These values are given as the number of seconds that a particular record can remain in the cache before it expires. These values are continually being counted down by the local computer. When the TTL value reaches 0, the record expires and is removed from the resolver cache.

Occasionally, you'll find that the resolver cache needs to be cleared to remove old entries and enable computers to check for updated DNS entries before the normal expiration and purging process takes place. Typically, this happens because server IP addresses have changed, and the current entries in the resolver cache point to the old addresses rather than the new ones. Sometimes the resolver cache itself can become out of sync, particularly when DHCP has been misconfigured.

> ***REAL WORLD*** **Skilled administrators know that several weeks in advance of the actual change, they should start to decrease the TTL values for DNS records that are going to be changed. Typically, this means reducing the TTL from a number of days (or weeks) to a number of hours, which allows for quicker propagation of the changes to computers that have cached the related DNS records. Once the change is complete, administrators should restore the original TTL value to reduce renewal requests.**

In most cases, you can resolve problems with the DNS resolver cache by flushing the cache or reregistering DNS. When you flush the resolver cache, all DNS entries are cleared out of the cache and new entries are not created until the next time the computer performs a DNS lookup on a particular host or IP address. When you reregister DNS, Windows 7 attempts to refresh all current DHCP leases and then performs a lookup on each DNS entry in the resolver cache. By looking up each host or IP address again, the entries are renewed and reregistered in the resolver cache. You'll generally want to flush the cache completely and allow the computer to perform lookups as needed. Reregister DNS only when you suspect that there are problems with DHCP and the DNS resolver cache.

You can use the Ipconfig command to flush and reregister entries in the DNS resolver cache by following these steps:

1. Start an elevated command prompt.
2. To clear out the resolver cache, type **ipconfig /flushdns** at the command line.
3. To renew DHCP leases and reregister DNS entries, type **ipconfig /registerdns** at the command line.
4. When the tasks are complete, you can check your work by typing **ipconfig /displaydns** at the command line.

CHAPTER 16

Managing Mobile Networking and Remote Access

Users often want to connect to their organization's network from an off-site computer. To do so, they need a dial-up, broadband, virtual private network (VPN), or DirectAccess connection. Dial-up networking enables users to connect off-site computers to their organization's network by using a modem and a standard telephone line. Broadband enables users to connect off-site computers to their organization's network using high-speed digital subscriber line (DSL) routers or cable modems. VPN and DirectAccess use encryption to provide secure connectivity over an existing connection, which can be a local area, dial-up, or broadband connection. Increasingly, wireless connections are being used as well. With a wireless connection, computers establish connections by using a network adapter that has an antenna that enables it to communicate with similar wireless devices.

Configuring Networking for Laptops

Most laptops need more than one network configuration: one for the office, one for home, and maybe another for when the user is traveling. At the office, the laptop uses a dynamic IP address and network settings that are assigned by a

Dynamic Host Configuration Protocol (DHCP) server. At home, the laptop uses a static IP address and different network settings to communicate on a network and access a shared printer and a broadband Internet device. In some cases, a laptop might need to be configured to make a Wi-Fi connection using a Wi-Fi adapter card with a static IP configuration when the user is away from his or her desk and a DHCP configuration when the laptop is physically connected to the network, or vice versa. When a system uses DHCP to obtain its primary network settings, you can configure alternate network settings for those times when a DHCP server isn't available, such as when the user is traveling or at home. Systems can use alternate configurations either automatically or through user interaction. When in meeting rooms or elsewhere on the go, laptop users are also likely to need to connect to networked projectors, a task for which the Connect To A Network Projector wizard provides an easy solution.

Working with Windows Mobility Center

Windows Mobility Center provides a single location for managing mobile PC settings and includes a series of control tiles that provide quick access to the most commonly used mobile PC settings. On a laptop or a Tablet PC, you can access Windows Mobility Center by right-clicking the Power icon in the taskbar's notification area and then clicking Mobility Center. You can also click Start, Control Panel, Hardware And Sound, Windows Mobility Center.

Windows Mobility Center's control tiles enable you to adjust mobile PC settings by using options such as sliders to adjust the display's brightness, a selection list to change the power plan, and a toggle button to turn presentation settings on or off. Although the set of control tiles available depends on the type of mobile PC and the manufacturer, following are the most common control tiles:

- **Battery Status** Shows the status of the computer's battery. You can use the selection list provided to change from one power plan to another. If you've created any custom power plans, these are available as well.
- **Brightness** Enables you to manage the brightness setting for the display. If brightness is configurable on the computer, use the slider to adjust the brightness.
- **External Display** Enables you to connect to a secondary display device, which might be necessary to give a presentation. Click Connect Display to access a secondary display device connected through a cable.
- **Presentation Settings** Enables you to turn presentation mode on or off. In presentation mode, the mobile PC's display and hard disk do not enter sleep mode when the computer is inactive. Click Turn On to enter presentation mode.
- **Sync Center** Enables you to view the status of file synchronization and initiate syncing. Click Sync to start a new sync using Sync Center.

- **Volume** Enables you to manage the current volume setting. If volume is configurable on your computer, use the slider to adjust the volume.
- **Wireless Network** Enables you to view and manage the status of your wireless network connection. Click Turn Wireless On to enable your wireless connection.

Most laptop and Tablet PC manufacturers customize Windows Mobility Center by adding their own control tiles to extend these common options. For example, some HP laptops include the HP Wireless Assistant control tile, which you can use to configure wireless networking settings for the integrated wireless device.

Configuring Dynamic IP Addresses

DHCP gives you centralized control over IP addresses and TCP/IP default settings. If a network has a DHCP server, you can assign a dynamic IP address to any of the network adapter cards on a computer. Afterward, you rely on the DHCP server to supply the basic information necessary for TCP/IP networking. To enable dynamic IP addressing for both IPv4 and IPv6, separate DHCP services must be set up for both IPv4 and IPv6.

To configure dynamic IP addresses, complete these steps:

1. In Control Panel, click Network And Internet, and then click Network And Sharing Center.
2. In the left pane in Network And Sharing Center, click Change Adapter Settings.
3. Network Connections displays a list of all network connections configured for use on the computer. Right-click the connection you want to configure, and then click Properties.
4. Double-click Internet Protocol Version 4 (TCP/IPv4), or select Internet Protocol Version 4 (TCP/IPv4) and then click Properties. This displays the Internet Protocol Version 4 (TCP/IPv4) Properties dialog box, shown in Figure 16-1.
5. Select Obtain An IP Address Automatically. You can also select Obtain DNS Server Address Automatically, or select Use The Following DNS Server Addresses and then type a preferred and alternate Domain Name System (DNS) server address in the fields provided.
6. Click OK.
7. If your organization or network uses IPv6, double-click Internet Protocol Version 6 (TCP/IPv6). Select Obtain An IPv6 Address Automatically. You can also select Obtain DNS Server Address Automatically, or select Use The Following DNS Server Addresses and then type a preferred and alternate DNS server address in the fields provided. Click OK.
8. Configure alternate private IP addressing as necessary (as discussed in the next section).

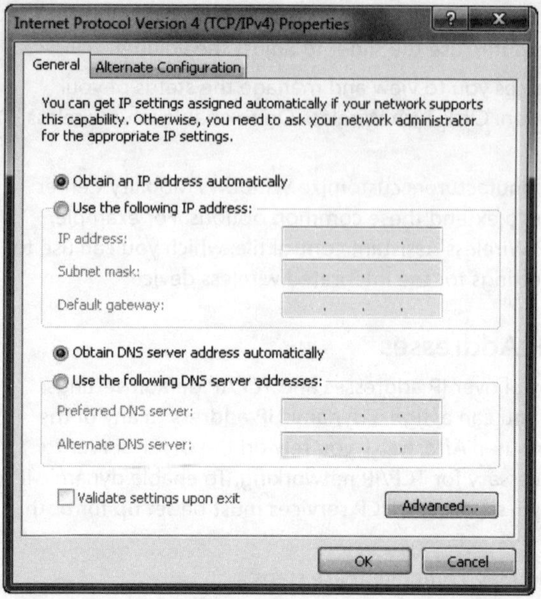

FIGURE 16-1 To use DHCP, configure the computer to obtain an IP address automatically.

Configuring Alternate Private IP Addresses

Only IPv4 connections have alternate configurations. When you use DHCP with an IPv4 connection, an automatic private IP address is assigned when the DHCP server can't be reached during startup or when the current IP address lease expires. The automatic private IP address is in the range 169.254.0.1 to 169.254.255.254, with a subnet mask of 255.255.0.0. Because the automatic private IP address configuration does not include default gateway, DNS, or Windows Internet Naming Service (WINS) server settings, a computer using the alternate IP addressing is isolated on a separate network segment in the Automatic Private IP Addressing (APIPA) range.

If you want to ensure that a computer uses specific IP address and network configuration settings when no DHCP server is available, you need to specify an alternate configuration. One of the key reasons for using an alternate configuration is to accommodate laptop users who take their computers home from work. In this way, the user's laptop can be configured to use a dynamically assigned IP address at work and an alternate IP address configuration at home. Before you get started, you might want to ask users for their home networking settings, including the IP address, gateway, and DNS server addresses required by their Internet service provider (ISP).

To configure alternate private IP addresses, complete the following steps:

1. In Control Panel, click Network And Internet, and then click Network And Sharing Center.

2. In the left pane in Network And Sharing Center, click Change Adapter Settings.
3. Network Connections displays a list of all network connections configured for use on the computer. Right-click the connection you want to configure, and then click Properties.
4. Double-click Internet Protocol Version 4 (TCP/IPv4) to open the Internet Protocol Version 4 (TCP/IPv4) Properties dialog box. You can also select Internet Protocol Version 4 (TCP/IPv4) and then click Properties.
5. If you have already configured the adapter to obtain an IP address automatically, you should be able to click the Alternate Configuration tab, shown in Figure 16-2.

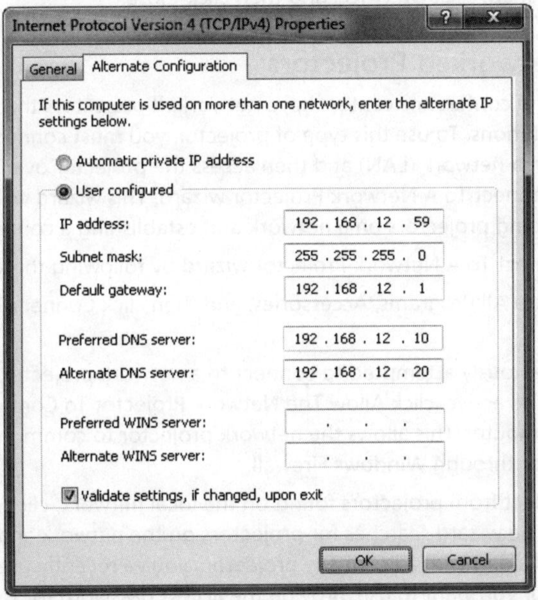

FIGURE 16-2 Use the Alternate Configuration tab to configure private IP addresses for the computer.

6. On the Alternate Configuration tab, select the User Configured option. Then, in the IP Address field, type the IP address you want to use. The IP address you assign to the computer should be a private IP address, and it must not be in use anywhere else at the time the settings are applied. Private IP addresses are normally in the range 10.0.0.1 to 10.255.255.254, 172.16.0.1 to 172.31.255.254, or 192.168.0.1 to 192.168.255.254 (excluding IP addresses reserved for network IDs and broadcasts).
7. The Subnet Mask field ensures that the computer communicates over the network properly. Windows 7 should insert a default value into this field for

the subnet mask. If the network doesn't use subnets, the default value should suffice. However, if the network does use subnets, you need to change this value as appropriate for the target network.

8. If the computer needs to access other TCP/IP networks, the Internet, or other subnets, you must specify a default gateway. Type the IP address of the network's default router in the Default Gateway field.
9. DNS servers are needed for domain name resolution. Type a preferred and an alternate DNS server address in the fields provided.
10. If WINS is used on the network for compatibility with previous versions of Windows, configure a preferred and an alternate WINS server using the fields provided.
11. When you've finished, click OK twice, and then click Close.

Connecting to Networked Projectors

Many meeting rooms and conference centers have networked projectors that are used for making presentations. To use this type of projector, you must connect your computer to the local area network (LAN) and then access the projector over the network by using the Connect To A Network Projector wizard. This wizard walks you through the steps of finding projectors on a network and establishing a connection.

You can use the Connect To A Network Projector wizard by following these steps:

1. Click Start, point to All Programs, Accessories, and then click Connect To A Network Projector.
2. If you haven't previously attempted to connect to a network projector and Windows Firewall is active, click Allow The Network Projector To Communicate With My Computer. This allows the network projector to communicate with the computer through Windows Firewall.
3. If you want to select from projectors found on the local network, click Search For A Projector. The wizard searches for projectors on the network and returns its results along with a list of any projectors you've recently used. Click the projector you want to use, provide the access password for the projector if necessary, and then click Next.
4. If you know the network address of the projector, click Enter The Projector Network Address. On the Enter The Network Address Of A Network Projector page, type the network address of the projector, such as **http://intranet.cpandl.local/projectors/confb-proj1**. Enter any required access password, and then click Connect.
5. Once you've established a connection to the projector, click Finish to exit the wizard and begin using the projector.

Understanding Mobile Networking and Remote Access

Although the underlying technologies are fundamentally different, direct-dial, broadband, VPN, and DirectAccess connections all make it possible for users to access your organization's network remotely. With a typical direct-dial network configuration, off-site users use their computer's modem and a standard telephone line to connect to a modem pool located at the office. A Windows server managing the modem pool and running Routing And Remote Access authenticates the logon ID and password and authorizes the user to connect to the internal network. The user can then access network resources just as she does when working on-site.

Figure 16-3 shows direct-dial connections using modem pools. Analog modems use dedicated telephone lines to connect users to the internal network at speeds up to 33.6 kilobits per second (Kbps) per line. Digital modems use channels of a T1 line to connect users to the internal network at speeds up to 56 Kbps per line. In a standard configuration, you might have 8, 12, or 16 modems configured in the pool, each with its own line (or channel). Typically, the modem pool has a lead number that users can call. This number connects to the first modem in the pool. When the lead number is busy, the line rolls over to the next number, which connects to the next modem in the pool, and so on, enabling users to dial a single number to gain access to all modems in the pool.

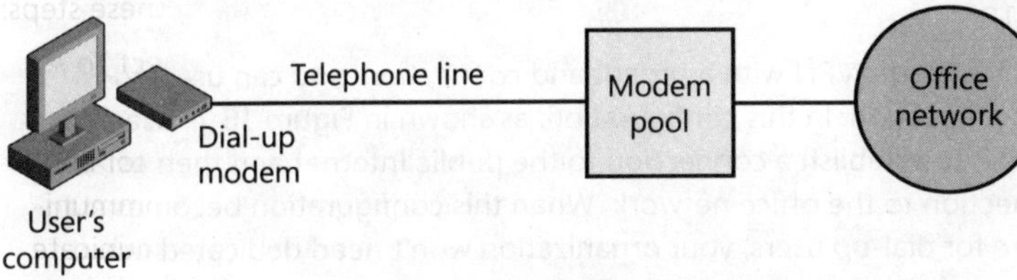

FIGURE 16-3 Use a dial-up connection to access an office network through a modem pool.

Unlike direct-dial connections, which can be made directly to the office network, broadband connections are made through an ISP's network. The user's DSL router, cable modem, or cellular modem establishes a connection to the ISP, which in turn connects the user to the public Internet. To connect to the office network, a broadband user must establish a VPN or DirectAccess connection between his computer and the office network. Figure 16-4 shows how VPN and DirectAccess work.

A VPN is an extension of a private network across the public Internet. Once a user is connected, it appears to him that he is directly connected to the office network, and he can access network resources just as he does when working on-site. These seamless connections are possible because a virtual tunnel is established between the user's computer and the office network, where the VPN technology takes care of routing information over the public Internet. One of two VPN technologies is typically used: Point-to-Point Tunneling Protocol (PPTP) or Layer 2 Tunneling Protocol (L2TP).

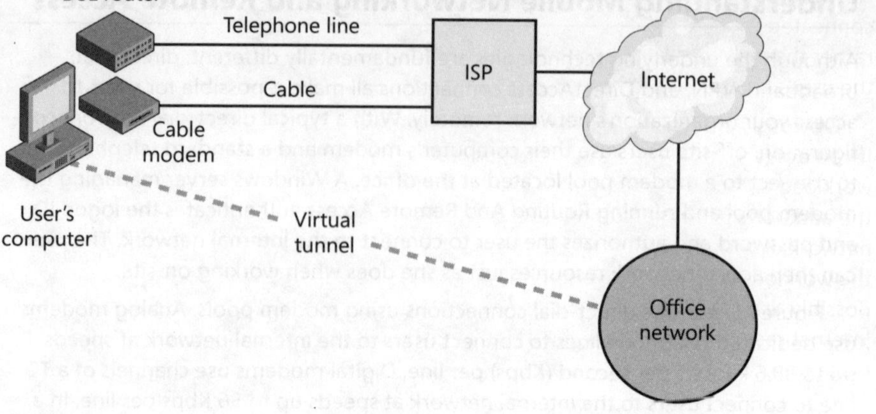

FIGURE 16-4 Use virtual tunnels to access an office network.

Both L2TP and PPTP offer encryption and protection from attacks, but only L2TP uses IP Security (IPSec) for advanced encryption, making it the more secure of the two technologies. Unfortunately, L2TP is more difficult to configure. When you use L2TP, you need to use Microsoft Certificate Services or a third-party certificate server to issue individual certificates for each system that will connect to the network using L2TP.

In addition to using a VPN with a broadband connection, you can use a VPN with a dial-up connection. In this configuration, as shown in Figure 16-4, users go through their ISP to establish a connection to the public Internet and then establish a private connection to the office network. When this configuration becomes standard procedure for dial-up users, your organization won't need dedicated private lines like those reserved for a modem pool.

DirectAccess is a new approach to virtual tunneling. Although fundamentally different from VPN, the basic idea is the same—a DirectAccess connection is an extension of a private network across the public Internet. Once a user is connected (which happens automatically after the feature is enabled), it appears to him that he is directly connected to the office network, and he can access network resources just as he does when working on-site. These seamless connections are possible because a virtual tunnel is established between the user's computer and the office network, where the DirectAccess technology takes care of routing information over the public Internet.

DirectAccess is a client-server technology that requires IPv6 and IPSec. Client computers must run the Enterprise edition of Windows 7 or later. Server computers must run Windows Server 2008 Release 2 or later. To use DirectAccess, you must set up and configure IPv6 for use by both client and server computers throughout the enterprise, including DNSv6 and DHCPv6 as appropriate.

In the Administrative Templates policies for Computer Configuration under Network\Network Connections, you can use the Route All Traffic Through The Internal

Network policy to control how DirectAccess works. By default, when a user is connected to a workplace, the user's computer accesses Internet resources directly rather than going through the workplace network. If you enable the routing policy, the user's computer accesses the Internet through the workplace network.

Obviously, both configuration approaches have advantages and disadvantages. If you don't route Internet traffic through the internal network, you reduce the workload and traffic levels on the workplace's connection to the Internet but lose the additional security and safeguards that might be in place to protect the internal network. If you route Internet traffic through the internal network, you increase the workload and traffic levels on the workplace's connection to the Internet, and possibly dramatically increase latency and response times when the user works with Internet resources, but you ensure that any additional security and safeguards in place to protect the internal network are also enforced.

Creating Connections for Remote Access

As discussed previously, you can create both dial-up and broadband connections for remote access. If you want additional security, you can also configure these connections to use VPN. Once you enable DirectAccess, DirectAccess is seamless for the user, and the user needs only to establish a connection to the Internet to access the workplace network.

Windows 7 provides a wizard for creating these connections. In most cases, you'll want to access this wizard through Network And Sharing Center. In Network And Sharing Center, click Set Up A New Connection Or Network. You can then create a dial-up, broadband, or VPN connection.

REAL WORLD **Consider whether Group Policy can help you reduce your workload. If you want to use the same connection settings on multiple computers, you can create dial-up and VPN connections using Group Policy preferences. You also can import the settings into Group Policy. Either way, the connections are then available to all computers affected by the Group Policy object. You can use this technique to deploy new connection configurations, update existing configurations when you need to make changes, and delete existing configurations and replace them with new ones.**

Creating a Dial-Up Connection

Windows 7 provides two options for making dial-up connections. You can create a dial-up connection to an ISP or a dial-up connection to a workplace. Although the connections are created using slightly different techniques, the settings for the connection options are the same, with the following exceptions:

- A dial-up connection to an ISP does *not* use the Client For Microsoft Networks component, and it redials by default if the line is dropped.

- A dial-up connection to a workplace does use the Client For Microsoft Networks component, and it does *not* redial by default if the line is dropped.

The networking component Client For Microsoft Networks enables Windows 7 systems to communicate in a Windows domain or workgroup. Because most workplaces use Windows domains or workgroups and some ISPs don't, the component is configured for workplace environments and not for ISPs.

Creating dial-up connections is a two-part process. Before you create a dial-up connection, you should check the current phone and modem options, which specify dialing rules. Once the dialing rules are configured, you can create the dial-up connection.

Working with Dialing Rules and Locations

Dialing rules are used with modems to determine how phone lines are accessed, what the caller's area code is, and what additional features should be used when dialing connections. Sets of dialing rules are saved as dialing locations in the Phone And Modem tool.

VIEWING AND SETTING THE DEFAULT DIALING LOCATION

To view and set the default dialing location, follow these steps:

1. In Control Panel, select either Large Icons or Small Icons in the View By drop-down list.
2. Click Phone And Modem. The first time you start this tool, you'll see the Location Information dialog box, shown in Figure 16-5.

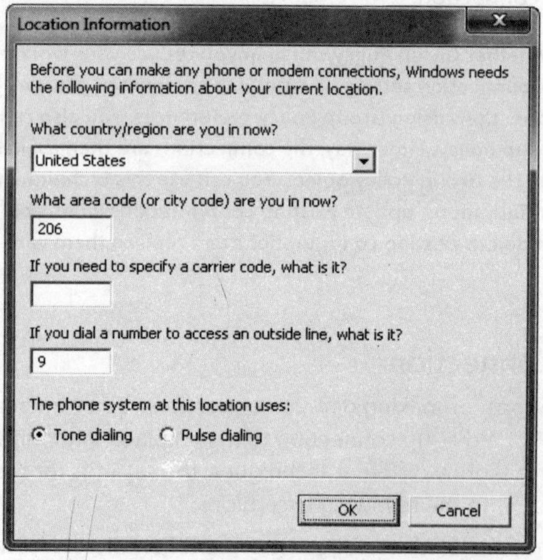

FIGURE 16-5 The first time you use Phone And Modem, you must configure the initial location.

3. Answer the following questions to configure the default location (My Location):
   - **What Country/Region Are You In Now?** Select the country or region you are in, such as United States.
   - **What Area Code (Or City Code) Are You In Now?** Type the appropriate area or city code, such as 212.
   - **If You Need To Specify A Carrier Code, What Is It?** You can specify the telephone carrier to use when dialing and establishing connections by entering its carrier code. A carrier code might be necessary if you are making long-distance or international calls.
   - **If You Dial A Number To Access An Outside Line, What Is It?** Type the number you need, if any, to access an outside line. An access number might be necessary to bypass a switch panel within a company or when dialing from a hotel.
4. In The Phone System At This Location Uses field, select Tone Dialing or Pulse Dialing. Most areas of the United States and Canada use tone dialing.
5. After you configure an initial location and click OK, you'll see the Phone And Modem dialog box, shown in Figure 16-6.

   From this point on, you no longer need to set up an initial location.

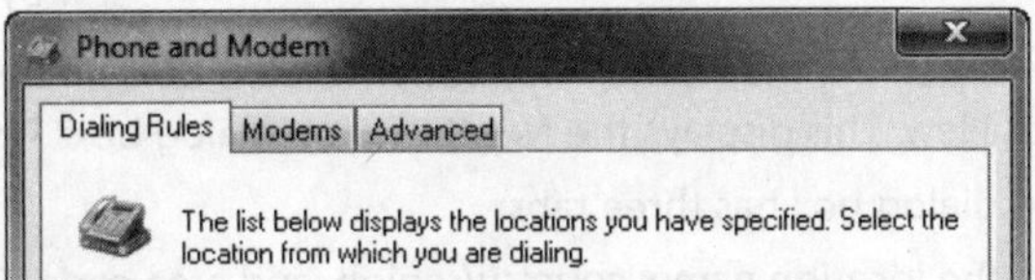

FIGURE 16-6 Check dialing rules to ensure that they are configured properly.

Locations configured for the computer are shown by name and area code in the Locations list. The location from which you are currently dialing is selected and highlighted in bold.

6. Initially, the default location is set as My Location. By selecting a different location, you can make it the current or default location. I recommend editing the default location (My Location) to rename it so that the name includes the city or office location. To view the configuration of a selected location, click Edit. To rename the location, type a new value in the Location Name field on the General tab, and then click OK.

NOTE **Of all the available dialing rules, the area code is the one you'll work with most often. During installation of the operating system, a default location might have been created with the area code specified by the person who set up the computer. In many cases, the default area code is not the one the user needs to use when dialing another location from home.**

CREATING DIALING LOCATIONS

You can create dialing locations to set unique rules for each area code from which the user makes dial-up connections. To create a dialing location, follow these steps:

1. In Control Panel, select either Large Icons or Small Icons in the View By drop-down list.
2. Click Phone And Modem. In the Phone And Modem dialog box, on the Dialing Rules tab, click New. This displays the New Location dialog box.
3. The New Location dialog box has three tabs:
   - **General** Sets the location name, country/region, and area code. On this tab, you can also set access numbers for outside lines for local or long-distance calls, disable call waiting, and specify whether tone or pulse dialing is used. Be sure to use an appropriate location name. Typically, this is the name of the city or metropolitan area from which the user is dialing.
   - **Area Code Rules** Sets rules that determine how phone numbers are dialed from the location's area code to other area codes and within the location's area code. These rules are useful when multiple area codes that are not long distance are included in the same location. They are also useful when calls within the area code might be local or long distance based on phone number prefixes.
   - **Calling Card** Sets a calling card to use when dialing from this location. Calling card information for major carriers is provided, and you can also create calling card records.
4. When you have finished creating the location, check that the default location in the Phone And Modem dialog box is correct. You might need to select a different entry. Click OK.

DELETING DIALING LOCATIONS

To delete a dialing location, follow these steps:

1. In Control Panel, select either Large Icons or Small Icons in the View By drop-down list. Click Phone And Modem.
2. In the Phone And Modem dialog box, select the location you want to permanently remove, and then click Delete. If prompted to confirm the action, click Yes.
3. Select the dialing location that you want to use as the default, and then click OK.

Creating a Dial-Up Internet Connection to an ISP

You can create dial-up connections in the following ways:

- If users are dialing up through an ISP that has point of presence (POP) locations throughout the United States and the world, you'll usually want to configure dialing rules and connections for specific locations. For example, you could create a dial-up location called Seattle and a dial-up connection called Connect To ISP In Seattle. In this configuration, you would specify the area code for Seattle as well as any special dialing rules and then configure the connection to use the ISP's access numbers for Seattle. You would also need to show users how to change their current locations for when they travel from place to place.
- If users are dialing an 800 number or long distance to access the office modem pool or a special out-of-area access number for an ISP, you'll usually want to configure separate connections rather than separate locations. Here, you would create a connection that dials long distance to establish the connection and a connection that is used when the user is in the local area. You would then need only one dialing location.

To create a dial-up Internet connection, follow these steps:

1. Before you create a dial-up connection, you should check the current phone and modem options as discussed in the section "Working with Dialing Rules and Locations" earlier in this chapter.

   NOTE **If you use dialing rules with a connection and then set area and country codes, you are enabling the connection to be used for long-distance calls, which can sometimes be very expensive. If this isn't what you want, you might want to reconsider these selections.**

2. In Network And Sharing Center, click Set Up A New Connection Or Network. This starts the Set Up A Connection Or Network wizard.
3. Select Set Up A Dial-Up Connection, and then click Next.
4. In the Dial-Up Phone Number text box, specify the phone number to dial for this connection.

5. Set account information for the connection. Enter the user name in the field provided, and then enter the password. Although you can specify that the password is remembered by selecting Remember This Password, doing so is a poor security practice because it enables anyone with access to the computer to use the connection.
6. In the Connection Name field, enter the name for the connection, such as Service Provider. Keep in mind that the name should be short (50 or fewer characters) but descriptive.
7. If you want the connection to be available to all users of the computer, select Allow Other People To Use This Connection. This option is useful when you plan to assign the connection through Group Policy and have not provided user logon information.
8. Click Connect to create the dial-up connection and establish a connection. Click Close. To test the connection settings, follow the steps outlined in the section "Establishing Connections" later in this chapter.

REAL WORLD **Most organizations use digital phone systems, which don't allow you to make an analog connection to an outside line. If this is the case at your office, you need to access an analog line before you can test the connection. Some digital phones can be equipped with digital-to-analog converters that you can use for testing dial-up connections. You might find these converters used with conference phones or fax machines, or you might find that conference phones or fax machines are already connected to analog phone lines.**

Creating a Dial-Up Connection to a Workplace

Creating a dial-up connection to a workplace is similar to creating a dial-up connection to the Internet. You create a dial-up connection to a workplace by following these steps:

1. In Network And Sharing Center, click Set Up A New Connection Or Network. This starts the Set Up A Connection Or Network wizard.
2. Select Connect To A Workplace, and then click Next. If you have a connection already, you can reconfigure that connection or create a new connection. Typically, you'll want to create a new connection, so click No, Create A New Connection.
3. On the How Do You Want To Connect page, click Dial Directly.
4. Specify the phone number to dial for this connection by using the Telephone Number text box. In the Destination Name field, type the name for the connection, such as Corporate Office or Seattle Office. Keep in mind that the name should be short (50 or fewer characters) but descriptive.

5. If you want the connection to be available to all users of the computer, select Allow Other People To Use This Connection. This option is best when you plan to assign the connection through Group Policy and have not provided user logon information.
6. If you want to use a smart card for the connection, select Use A Smart Card.
7. Click Next. Set account information for the connection. Enter the user name in the field provided, and then enter the password. Although you can specify that the password is remembered by selecting Remember This Password, this is a poor security practice because it enables anyone with access to the computer to use the connection.
8. If you are connecting to a domain, you can specify the logon domain in the Domain field.
9. Click Connect to create the connection and connect to it. In most cases, the connection will fail because you are setting up a connection for an alternate location, such as the user's home Internet connection, and these settings won't work through the organization's network. As a result, you'll have an option to click Skip to bypass connection activation. Click Close.

In Group Policy, you can create, edit, and remove dial-up connections by using network options preferences. To configure network options preferences, follow these steps:

1. Open a Group Policy object (GPO) for editing in the Group Policy Management Editor. To configure preferences for computers, expand Computer Configuration\Preferences\Control Panel Settings, and then select Network Options. To configure preferences for users, expand User Configuration\Preferences\Control Panel Settings, and then select Network Options.
2. Right-click the Network Options node, point to New, and then click Dial-Up Connection. This opens the Network Options Properties dialog box.
3. In the Action list, select Create, Update, or Replace as appropriate.
4. If you want the connection to be available to all users of the computer, select Allow Users Connection. Otherwise, select User Connection to apply the connection only to the user for whom the policy is being processed.
5. Enter a connection name and connection phone number.
6. Use the options on the Common tab to control how the preference is applied. Often, you'll want to apply a policy only once. If so, select Apply Once And Do Not Reapply.
7. Click OK. The next time Group Policy is refreshed, the preference item will be applied as appropriate for the GPO in which you defined the preference item.

Creating a Broadband Connection to the Internet

In many respects, broadband connections are much easier to configure than dial-up connections are. When you work with broadband, you don't need to set up dial-up rules or locations. You don't need to worry about calling cards, ISP access numbers, or redialing preferences, and this makes broadband much easier to work with.

Most broadband providers give users a router or a modem that users need to connect to the service provider. Each user must also have a network adapter on his or her computer, connected to a DSL router or cable modem. In this configuration, the necessary connection is established over a LAN rather than a specific broadband connection. Therefore, it is the local area connection that must be properly configured to gain access to the Internet. You won't need to create a broadband connection.

You can, however, create a specific broadband connection if needed. In some cases, you need to do this to set specific configuration options, such as secure authentication, required by an ISP, or you might want to use this technique to set the user name and password required by the broadband provider.

You create a broadband connection to the Internet by following these steps:

1. In Network And Sharing Center, click Set Up A New Connection Or Network. This starts the Set Up A Connection Or Network wizard.
2. Select Connect To The Internet, and then click Next. If you have a connection already, you can reconfigure that connection for use or create a new connection. Typically, you'll want to create a new connection, so click Set Up A New Connection Anyway. Click No, Create A New Connection, and then click Next.
3. On the How Do You Want To Connect page, click Broadband (PPPoE) to create a broadband connection to the Internet.
4. Do the following, and then click Next:
   - Set account information for the connection. Enter the user name in the field provided, and then enter the password. Although you can specify that the password is remembered by selecting Remember This Password, this is a poor security practice because it enables anyone with access to the computer to use the connection.
   - In the Connection Name field, type the name for the connection, such as Seattle Office Secure Broadband. Keep in mind that the name should be short (50 or fewer characters) but descriptive.
   - If you want the connection to be available to all users of the computer, select Allow Other People To Use This Connection. This option is best when you plan to assign the connection through Group Policy and have not provided user logon information.

5. Click Connect to create the connection and connect to it. In most cases, the connection will fail because you are setting up a connection for an alternate location, such as a remote office, and these settings won't work through the organization's network. As a result, you'll have an option to click Skip to bypass connection activation. Click Close.

   TIP **With a broadband connection, you need a DSL router or cable modem to test the connection. Be sure to configure any special settings required by the ISP, as detailed in the section "Configuring Connection Properties" later in this chapter.**

Creating a VPN Connection

VPNs are used to establish secure communications channels over an existing dial-up or broadband connection. You must know the IP address or fully qualified domain name of the remote access server to which you are connecting. If the necessary connection is available and you know the host information, you can create the connection by following these steps:

1. In Network And Sharing Center, click Set Up A New Connection Or Network. This starts the Set Up A Connection Or Network wizard.
2. To create a VPN connection, select Connect To A Workplace, and then click Next.
3. Select No, Create A New Connection, and then click Next. Note that a user will need to establish a connection to the Internet—via dial-up or broadband—before attempting to use the VPN.
4. Click Use My Internet Connection (VPN).
5. Type the IPv4 or IPv6 address or fully qualified domain name of the computer to which you are connecting, such as 157.54.0.1 or external.microsoft.com. In most cases, this address is for the remote access server configured for the office network.
6. Type a name for the connection in the Destination Name field. If the computer is configured to use a smart card for authentication, select Use A Smart Card.
7. If you want the connection to be available to all users of the computer, select Allow Other People To Use This Connection. This option is best when you plan to assign the connection through Group Policy and have not provided user logon information.
8. Click Next. A user is prompted by default for her name and password when she makes a connection. If you're creating a connection for an individual user and don't want the user to be prompted for logon information, enter the user name and password in the fields provided. Otherwise, enter only the user name and leave the password blank.

Although you can specify that the password is remembered by selecting Remember This Password, doing so is a poor security practice because it enables anyone with access to the computer to use the connection. If you don't select Remember This Password, the user is prompted for her password.

9. Specify the logon domain in the Domain field, and then click Connect. To connect to a VPN connection, you must first be connected to the dial-up or broadband connection specified earlier. In most cases, the connection will fail because you are setting up a VPN connection for an alternate location, such as the user's home Internet connection, and these settings won't work through the organization's network. Because of this, you'll have an option to click Skip to bypass connection activation. Click Close.

In Group Policy, you can create, edit, and remove VPN connections by using network options preferences. To configure network options preferences, follow these steps:

1. Open a Group Policy object (GPO) for editing in the Group Policy Management Editor. To configure preferences for computers, expand Computer Configuration\Preferences\Control Panel Settings, and then select Network Options. To configure preferences for users, expand User Configuration\Preferences\Control Panel Settings, and then select Network Options.
2. Right-click the Network Options node, point to New, and then click VPN Connection. This opens the Network Options Properties dialog box.
3. In the Action list, select Create, Update, or Replace as appropriate.
4. If you want the connection to be available to all users of the computer, select Allow Users Connection. Otherwise, select User Connection to apply the connection only to the user for whom the policy is being processed.
5. Enter a connection name and connection IP address. Alternatively, select Use DNS Name, and then enter the fully qualified domain name to use.
6. On the Security tab, select Advanced. Use the Data Encryption list to specify whether and how encryption should be used. In most cases, you'll want to require encryption. Under Logon Security, specify the security options to use.
7. Use the options on the Common tab to control how the preference is applied. Often, you'll want to apply a policy only once. If so, select Apply Once And Do Not Reapply.
8. Click OK. The next time Group Policy is refreshed, the preference item will be applied as appropriate for the GPO in which you defined the preference item.

Configuring Connection Properties

Whether you are working with dial-up, broadband, or VPN connections, you'll often need to set additional properties after creating a connection. The key properties that you will work with are examined in this section.

> ***NOTE*** **As you work with connection properties, keep in mind that VPN connections use existing connections and that the configuration of each connection is separate. With VPN, the primary connection is established first by using the settings assigned to that connection, and then the VPN connection is attempted using the VPN connection settings. With this in mind, you should configure the primary connection first and then configure the options for VPN. You should change this approach only when you are troubleshooting problems with VPN. In this case, you should start with the VPN configuration and work your way back to the settings for the primary connection.**

Configuring Automatic or Manual Connections

Windows 7 can be configured to establish dial-up, broadband, or VPN connections automatically when users access programs, such as a Web browser, that need to connect to the Internet. Automatic connections work in ways that depend on settings in the Internet Options tool. The dial-up options include the following:

- **Never Dial A Connection** Users must manually establish a connection.
- **Dial Whenever A Network Connection Is Not Present** The connection is established automatically when it's needed but only when the local area connection isn't working.
- **Always Dial My Default Connection** The default connection is always established when an Internet connection is needed (even if other connections are already established).

> ***TIP*** **The way you configure automatic connections really depends on the way your organization works. Contrary to what many administrators think, laptop users are usually less frustrated when their computers are set to never dial a connection. Users might not have access to a dial-up connection when they are out of the office, for example, and having the computer attempt to dial a connection when a user is meeting with customers or giving a presentation can be disruptive. On the other hand, if you are configuring dial-up networking for users with desktops at a remote or home office, they'll probably want to use automatic connections.**

To configure computers to connect manually, follow these steps:

1. In Control Panel, click Network And Internet. In Network And Internet, click Internet Options. In the Internet Properties dialog box, click the Connections tab, shown in Figure 16-7.
2. Select Never Dial A Connection, and then click OK.

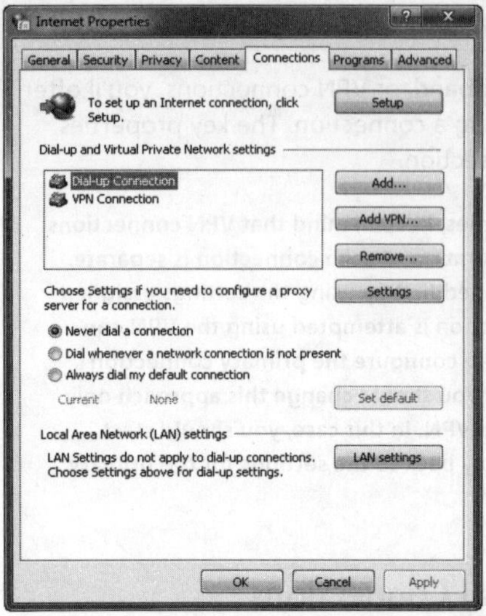

FIGURE 16-7 Configure manual or automatic connections by using the Connections tab.

You can configure automatic connections by following these steps:

1. In Control Panel, click Network And Internet. In Network And Internet, click Internet Options. In the Internet Properties dialog box, click the Connections tab.
2. Select Dial Whenever A Network Connection Is Not Present to establish a connection automatically if a local area connection isn't working. Select Always Dial My Default Connection to always attempt to establish a connection.
3. The Dial-Up And Virtual Private Network Settings list shows the dial-up, broadband, and VPN connections that are currently configured. Select the connection you want to use by default when establishing a connection, and then click Set Default.
4. Click OK.

Configuring Proxy Settings for Mobile Connections

As with connections themselves, proxy server settings can be set manually or automatically. With manual configuration, you need to configure each property step by step. With automatic configuration, the computer attempts to detect proxy server settings and then configure the appropriate options, or the computer reads a configuration script to use in configuring the proxy.

> ***NOTE*** **Proxy settings can be configured for multiple systems through Group Policy. If you elect not to configure proxy settings through Group Policy, you can configure them on a per-connection basis as discussed in this section.**

Configuration scripts can be stored in a file on the local computer or at an Internet address. Using configuration scripts can save a lot of time, especially when you consider that each connection you create is configured separately. Further, because VPN connections are established on top of an existing setting, the proxy settings for the VPN can be different from those set in the original connection.

To use automatic proxy configuration for a connection, complete the following steps:

1. In Control Panel, click Network And Internet. In Network And Internet, click Internet Options. In the Internet Properties dialog box, click the Connections tab.
2. In the Dial-Up And Virtual Private Network Settings list, select the dial-up connection that you want to configure, and then click Settings. This displays a Settings dialog box similar to the one shown in Figure 16-8.

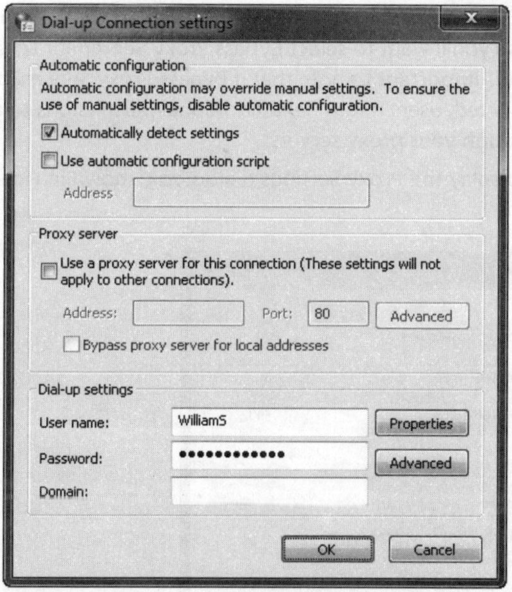

FIGURE 16-8 Proxy settings can be automatically configured through detection or scripts.

3. To attempt to automatically detect proxy settings when establishing the connection, select Automatically Detect Settings.
4. To use a configuration script, select Use Automatic Configuration Script, and then type the file path or Uniform Resource Locator (URL) for the script. With file paths, you can use environment variables, such as %UserProfile%\PROXY.VBS. With URLs, be sure to use the computer URL, such as *http://proxy.microsoft.com/proxy.vbs*.

5. To ensure that only automatic settings are used, clear the Use A Proxy Server For This Connection check box.
6. Click OK twice.

To use manual proxy configuration, complete the following steps:

1. In Control Panel, click Network And Internet. In Network And Internet, click Internet Options. In the Internet Properties dialog box, click the Connections tab.
2. In the Dial-Up And Virtual Private Network Settings list, select the dial-up connection you want to configure, and then click Settings.
3. Clear the Automatically Detect Settings and Use Automatic Configuration Script check boxes if they are selected.
4. Select Use A Proxy Server For This Connection. The Bypass Proxy Server For Local Addresses check box is not selected by default. In most cases, however, you won't want to use a proxy for requests made to servers on the same network segment, so you'll want to select Bypass Proxy Server For Local Addresses as well. It is important to note that if Bypass Proxy Server For Local Addresses is not selected, users might need additional permissions to access intranet servers through your proxy servers.
5. Click Advanced to display the Proxy Settings dialog box, shown in Figure 16-9.

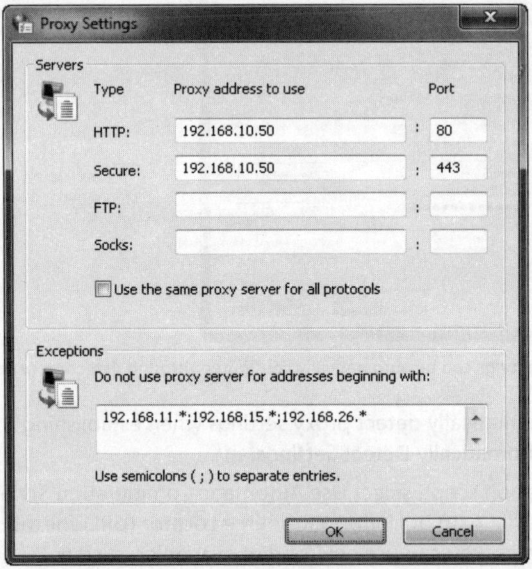

FIGURE 16-9 You can use the same proxy for all services, or you can configure multiple proxies.

6. Using the text boxes in the Servers area, set the IP address for proxies. You'll find the following two columns of text boxes:
   - **Proxy Address To Use** Sets the IP address of the related proxy server or servers. Enter the IP address for each service. If multiple proxies are configured for a particular service, type the IP address for each proxy server in the order in which you want the Web client to attempt to use them. Each address must be separated by a semicolon. If a proxy isn't configured for a service, do not fill in the related text box.
   - **Port** Sets the port number on which the proxy server responds to requests. Most proxies respond to port 80 for all requests. That said, the standard ports are port 80 for Hypertext Transfer Protocol (HTTP), port 443 for Secure Sockets Layer (SSL; listed as Secure), port 21 for File Transfer Protocol (FTP), and port 1081 for Socks. Check with your organization's Web administrator for the proper settings.
7. The Use The Same Proxy Server For All Protocols check box enables you to use the same IP address and port settings for the HTTP, SSL, FTP, and Socks services. You have the following options:
   - If your organization has one proxy server that handles all requests, select the Use The Same Proxy Server For All Protocols check box. Type the IP address that you want to use and the port number on which the server responds.
   - If you want to use a unique proxy server or servers for each type of service, clear the Use The Same Proxy Server For All Protocols check box, and then enter the necessary IP addresses and port numbers in the text boxes provided.
8. If your network has multiple segments or there are specific servers that shouldn't use proxies, enter the appropriate IP addresses or IP address ranges in the Exceptions list. Each entry must be separated by a semicolon. The asterisk (*) character can be used as a wildcard character to specify an address range of 0 through 255, such as 192.*.*.*, 192.168.*.*, or 192.168.10.*.
9. Click OK three times.

Configuring Connection Logon Information

Each connection you create has separate settings for logon information. You can set a user name, password, and domain by performing the following steps:

1. In Control Panel, click Network And Internet. In Network And Internet, click Internet Options. In the Internet Properties dialog box, click the Connections tab.
2. In the Dial-Up And Virtual Private Network Settings list, select the connection you want to configure, and then click Settings.

3. Type the user name and password for the connection in the User Name and Password text boxes.
4. If a domain name is required, enter the domain name in the Domain text box.
5. Click OK twice.

Setting a connection to use the appropriate logon information isn't the last step in ensuring a proper configuration. You should also set options that specify whether users are prompted for logon information or a phone number. If a logon domain is required to establish a connection, you should ensure that the logon domain is passed with the other logon information. By default, the domain name is not included.

To configure additional options, follow these steps:

1. In Control Panel, click Network And Internet. In Network And Internet, click Internet Options. In the Internet Properties dialog box, click the Connections tab.
2. In the Dial-Up And Virtual Private Network Settings list, select the connection you want to configure, and then click Settings.
3. In the Settings dialog box, click Properties.
4. In the Properties dialog box, click the Options tab. You can now configure the following options:
   - To display status messages while connecting, select Display Progress While Connecting.
   - To ensure that users are prompted for logon information if necessary, select Prompt For Name And Password, Certificate, Etc.
   - To ensure that the logon domain is included when requested, select Include Windows Logon Domain.
   - To prompt for a phone number when needed, select Prompt For Phone Number.
5. Click OK three times.

Configuring Redialing Options and Automatic Disconnection

For dial-up connections, you can set dialing options that enable connections to be automatically redialed when lines are busy and when the connection is dropped. To configure redialing options, follow these steps:

1. In Control Panel, click Network And Internet. In Network And Internet, click Internet Options. In the Internet Properties dialog box, click the Connections tab.
2. In the Dial-Up And Virtual Private Network Settings list, select the connection you want to configure, and then click Settings.
3. In the Settings dialog box, click Properties.

4. In the Properties dialog box, click the Options tab. Use the following settings in the Redialing Options area to configure redialing, then click OK:
   - **Redial Attempts** Sets the number of times to redial the phone number automatically. To disable redialing, enter 0 as the redial value.
   - **Time Between Redial Attempts** Sets the time to wait before redialing attempts. The available values are 1 second, 3 seconds, 5 seconds, 10 seconds, 30 seconds, 1 minute, 2 minutes, 5 minutes, and 10 minutes.
   - **Idle Time Before Hanging Up** Specifies whether Windows 7 disconnects the phone line when the connection hasn't been actively used for a specified time. The available values are Never, 1 minute, 5 minutes, 10 minutes, 20 minutes (the default), 30 minutes, 1 hour, 2 hours, 4 hours, 8 hours, and 24 hours.
   - **Redial If Line Is Dropped** Specifies whether Windows 7 attempts to redial the connection if the line is dropped. With connections to a workplace, this option is usually cleared by default. In most cases, however, you'll want to select it.
5. In the Settings dialog box, click Advanced. Select or clear Disconnect When Connection May No Longer Be Needed to specify whether Windows 7 disconnects when a user quits all Internet programs that would otherwise use the connection.
6. Click OK three times.

   TIP **If users complain about getting disconnected during dial-up sessions, the Disconnect settings can be the problem. Talk with the users about how they use the Internet and then determine whether you should change the settings to better meet their needs. Another reason for disconnection is if the Idle Time Before Hanging Up option is used.**

Setting a Connection to Use Dialing Rules

Dial-up connections can be configured with or without dialing rules. If you don't use dialing rules with a connection, the seven-digit phone number assigned to the connection is dialed at all times. When you assign dialing rules, the current dialing location determines whether the connection is attempted as a local or long-distance phone call.

To view or set the dialing rules for a connection, follow these steps:

1. In Control Panel, click Network And Internet. In Network And Internet, click Internet Options. In the Internet Properties dialog box, click the Connections tab.
2. In the Dial-Up And Virtual Private Network Settings list, select the connection you want to configure, and then click Settings.

3. In the Settings dialog box, click Properties. This displays a Properties dialog box.
4. To ensure that the connection uses the appropriate dialing rules, on the General tab, select Use Dialing Rules, and then type an area code and select a country/region code.
5. If you don't want to use dialing rules, clear the Use Dialing Rules check box.
6. Click OK three times.

Configuring Primary and Alternate Phone Numbers

With dial-up connections, you can configure two types of phone numbers: the primary number to dial whenever a connection is attempted, and alternate phone numbers to try if a primary number fails. To configure phone numbers, follow these steps:

1. In Control Panel, click Network And Internet. In Network And Internet, click Internet Options. In the Internet Properties dialog box, click the Connections tab.
2. In the Dial-Up And Virtual Private Network Settings list, select the connection you want to configure, and then click Settings.
3. In the Settings dialog box, click Properties. This displays a Properties dialog box.
4. The primary phone number is listed in the Phone Number text box. Type a new number as necessary.
5. Click Alternates. This displays the Alternate Phone Numbers dialog box. You can now manage primary and alternate phone numbers by using the following techniques:
   - To add a phone number, click Add to display the Add Alternate Phone Number dialog box. Next, enter the seven-digit alternate local number in the Phone Number text box. You can use a dash if you want to, such as 555-1234. If you want to set dialing rules, select Use Dialing Rules, and then type an area code and select a country/region code. Click OK.
   - To change the order in which numbers are dialed, select a number, and then use the up or down arrow to change its position in the Phone Numbers list. The top number in the list becomes the primary number.
   - To edit a phone number, select the number in the Phone Numbers list, and then click Edit. Then use the Edit Alternate Phone Number dialog box to change the number.
   - To remove a number, select the number in the Phone Numbers list, and then click Delete.
6. If you want to automatically use alternate numbers, select If A Number Fails, Try The Next Number. You can also have Windows 7 move a number to the

top of the list (making it the primary number) if Windows 7 is able to successfully dial it after a previous number fails. To do this, select Move Successful Numbers To Top Of The List.

7. Click OK four times.

Configuring Identity Validation

Proper identity validation is essential to maintaining the integrity of your network. When users dial in to the office, you should ensure that identities are validated securely if at all possible. This isn't the default setting for standard dial-up connections, however. With most connections, the user's logon information can be passed in clear text over the connection. If you don't allow unencrypted passwords to be used, this forces Windows 7 to attempt to pass logon information by using a secure technique, such as MS-CHAP Version 2 or Challenge Handshake Authentication Protocol (CHAP), rather than clear text. You can also configure connections to use Extensible Authentication Protocol (EAP).

With dial-up and broadband connections, you can use any of these options. With VPN, you can use only the secure techniques. When you require a secured password, you can also automatically pass the Windows logon name, password, and domain specified in the configuration. Passing the Windows logon information automatically is useful when users connect to the office and must be authenticated in the Windows domain. With both secure validation techniques, you can require data encryption and force Windows 7 to disconnect if encryption cannot be used. Data encryption is automatically used with Windows Authentication for both secured passwords and smart cards.

To configure identity validation, follow these steps:

1. In Control Panel, click Network And Internet. In Network And Internet, click Internet Options. In the Internet Properties dialog box, click the Connections tab.

2. In the Dial-Up And Virtual Private Network Settings list, select the connection you want to configure, and then click Settings.

3. In the Settings dialog box, click Properties.

4. In the Properties dialog box, click the Security tab. With VPNs, you can specify the connection protocol to use or use automatic detection. If you require secure passwords, you can also set automatic logon and require data encryption. Both options are useful when logging on to a Windows domain. The settings must be supported, however; if they aren't, users won't be able to validate their logons and connections won't be completed.

   If you use smart cards, you should also require data encryption. Data encryption is essential to ensuring the integrity and security of the data passed between the originating computer and the authenticating computer. If you select Require Encryption and the connection is not secured with encryption, the client computer will drop the connection.

5. Specify the allowed authentication protocols, and then click OK.

Configuring Networking Protocols and Components

The way in which networking protocols and components are configured depends on the type of connection. As Table 16-1 describes, dial-up connections can use either Point-to-Point Protocol (PPP) or Serial Line Internet Protocol (SLIP) as the connection protocol. Broadband connections use Point-to-Point Protocol over Ethernet (PPPoE). VPN connections use either PPTP or L2TP.

TABLE 16-1 Connection Protocol Availability by Connection Type

CONNECTION TYPE	CONNECTION PROTOCOL	DESCRIPTION
Dial-up	PPP	Used to establish connections to Windows servers over dial-up.
Dial-up	SLIP	Used to establish connections to UNIX servers over dial-up; available if you've installed third-party software.
Broadband	PPPoE	Used to establish a point-to-point broadband connection over Ethernet.
VPN	Automatic	Used to automatically detect which VPN protocol is available and establish a virtual tunnel using this protocol.
VPN	PPTP VPN	Sets the PPTP for a VPN. PPTP is an extension of PPP.
VPN	L2TP IPSec VPN	Sets the L2TP for a VPN. L2TP uses IPSec to enhance security.
DirectAccess	IPv6 over IPSec	Used to establish a secure tunnel to a workplace over an existing connection.

Three network components are used with mobile networking: Transmission Control Protocol/Internet Protocol (TCP/IP), File And Printer Sharing For Microsoft Networks, and Client For Microsoft Networks. As Table 16-2 shows, the way these components are configured by default depends on the type of connection that was created originally. You can change these settings to suit your needs. If necessary, you can also install additional networking components.

TABLE 16-2 Default Component Configuration by Connection Type

DIAL-UP COMPONENT	DESCRIPTION	BROAD-BAND	STANDARD DIAL-UP	DIAL-UP TO OFFICE	VPN
Transmission Control Protocol/ Internet Protocol (TCP/IP)	Required for network communications. By default, DHCP is used with connections unless overridden in the property settings.	Yes	Yes	Yes	Yes
File And Printer Sharing For Microsoft Networks	Enables the sharing of printers and files over the network connection; allows for mapping printers and drives.	No	No	No	Yes
Client For Microsoft Networks	Enables Windows Authentication in Windows domains; enables the computer to act as domain client.	No	No	Yes	Yes

To view or change the networking options for a connection, follow these steps:

1. In Control Panel, click Network And Internet. In Network And Internet, click Internet Options. In the Internet Properties dialog box, click the Connections tab.
2. In the Dial-Up And Virtual Private Network Settings list, select the connection you want to configure, and then click Settings.
3. In the Settings dialog box, click Properties.
4. In the Properties dialog box, click the Networking tab. You can now do the following:
   - Enable network components by selecting the related check box in the This Connection Uses The Following Items list.
   - Disable network components by clearing the related check box in the This Connection Uses The Following Items list.

> ***TIP*** **If any of the network components shown in Table 16-2 are not available and are necessary for the connection, you can install them by clicking Install on the Networking tab. Afterward, select the component type, click Add, and then select the component to use in the list provided.**

5. By default, connections use DHCP to configure network settings, including the IP address, subnet mask, default gateway, DNS servers, and WINS servers. If you want to assign a static IP address or override other default settings, select Internet Protocol Version 4 (TCP/IPv4) or Internet Protocol Version 6 (TCP/IPv6), and then click Properties. This displays a Properties dialog box that can be configured as discussed earlier in the chapter.
6. Click OK three times.

Enabling and Disabling Windows Firewall for Network Connections

With dial-up, broadband, and VPN connections, you might want to give the computer added protection against attacks by using Windows Firewall. This built-in firewall protects Windows 7 systems by restricting the types of information that can be communicated. By enforcing the appropriate restrictions, you reduce the possibility that malicious individuals can break into a system—and reducing security risks is extremely important when users are accessing the organization's network from outside your protective firewalls and proxy servers.

Windows Firewall is enabled by default for all connections and can be enabled or disabled for each type of network to which a user connects. To enable or disable Windows Firewall on a per-connection basis, follow these steps:

1. In Control Panel, click System And Security.
2. Click Windows Firewall. In the left pane of the Windows Firewall page, click Turn Windows Firewall On Or Off.
3. Windows Firewall settings for each network type to which a user can connect are listed on the Customize Settings page. Select Turn On Windows Firewall or Turn Off Windows Firewall for each network type as appropriate.
4. Click OK when you have finished.

Establishing Connections

As discussed in the section "Configuring Automatic or Manual Connections" earlier in this chapter, dial-up, broadband, and VPN connections can be established manually or automatically. The manual method lets users choose when to connect. The automatic method connects when users start a program, such as a Web browser, that requires network access.

Connecting with Dial-Up

Dial-up uses a telephone line to establish a connection between two modems. To establish a dial-up connection, follow these steps:

1. Click the Network notification icon on the taskbar. In Network Connections, click the dial-up connection you want to use, and then click Connect.

2. Confirm that the user name is correct, and then enter the password for the account if it doesn't already appear.
3. To use the user name and password whenever you attempt to establish this connection, select Save This User Name And Password For The Following Users, and then select Me Only.
4. To use the user name and password when any user attempts to establish this connection, select Save This User Name And Password For The Following Users, and then select Anyone Who Uses This Computer. Don't use this option if you plan to distribute this connection through Group Policy because you don't want to give out your connection password.
5. The Dial drop-down list shows the number that will be dialed. The primary number is selected by default. To choose an alternate number, click the drop-down list, and then select the number you want to use.
6. Click Dial. When the modem connects to the ISP or office network, you'll see a connection speed. The connection speed is negotiated on a per-call basis and depends on the maximum speed of the calling modem and the modem being called, the compression algorithms available, and the quality of the connection.

If you have problems connecting with a dial-up connection, use these tips to help you troubleshoot:

- Problem: The modem dials and reaches the other modem but cannot connect. It continues to make connection noises until you cancel the operation.

  Resolution: The phone lines are usually the source of the problem. Static or noise on the line can cause connection failures. Check the connections between the modem and the wall. Check with the phone company to see if they can test the line and resolve the problem.
- Problem: The modem dials and seems to connect, but then the service provider or office network connection is dropped unexpectedly. The connection doesn't seem to complete successfully.

  Resolution: Check your networking protocols and components as discussed in the section "Configuring Networking Protocols and Components." If these settings seem to be okay, determine whether you are passing Windows logon and domain information because this might be required. See the section "Configuring Connection Logon Information" for more details.
- Problem: The user cannot access resources in the Windows domain.

  Resolution: Client For Microsoft Networks might be required to access resources on the office network. Enable this component and ensure that the domain information is being passed as necessary.
- Problem: The user can never get through. The modem seems to be dialing the number incorrectly. You can hear it dialing too many or too few numbers.

Resolution: Check the dialing rules for the connection as well as the currently selected dialing location. Be sure that these are configured properly for the user's current location.

- Problem: A No Dial Tone message is displayed, but the modem is installed correctly and seems to be okay.

  Resolution: Check the phone cord and ensure that it is connected properly. Some modems have two line jacks, one labeled Phone/In and one labeled Line/Out. The phone cord from the wall jack should be plugged into the Line/Out jack. Some phone jacks are configured for data only, indicating a plug for a high-speed line rather than a phone or modem. Try a different jack.
- Problem: The computer freezes when the user tries to use the modem.

  Resolution: This is most likely caused by a device conflict. Follow the techniques discussed in Chapter 8, "Managing Hardware Devices and Drivers," for configuring and troubleshooting devices.
- Problem: Some services freeze or don't work.

  Resolution: Check the proxy and firewall settings. These settings can restrict the services that are available.

Connecting with Broadband

Broadband connections are established using a cable modem and a cable line or a DSL router and a telephone line. To establish a broadband connection, follow these steps:

1. Click the Network notification icon on the taskbar. In Network Connections, click the broadband connection you want to use, and then click Connect.
2. Confirm that the user name is correct, and then enter the password for the account if it doesn't already appear.
3. To use the user name and password whenever you attempt to establish this connection, select Save This User Name And Password For The Following Users, and then select Me Only.
4. To use the user name and password when any user attempts to establish this connection, select Save This User Name And Password For The Following Users, and then select Anyone Who Uses This Computer.
5. Click Connect.

If you have problems connecting with broadband, use these tips to help you troubleshoot:

- Problem: You cannot connect. The connection doesn't seem to work at all.

  Resolution: Check your network connections. Be sure that the lines connecting the DSL router or cable modem and the computer are plugged in properly.

- Problem: The connection is dropped unexpectedly. The connection doesn't seem to complete successfully.

  Resolution: Check your networking protocols and components as discussed in the section "Configuring Networking Protocols and Components." If these settings seem to be okay, determine if you are passing Windows logon and domain information because this might be required. See the section "Configuring Connection Logon Information" for more details.
- Problem: Some services freeze or don't work.

  Resolution: Check the proxy and firewall settings. These settings can restrict the services that are available.
- Problem: You cannot access resources in the Windows domain.

  Resolution: Client For Microsoft Networks might be required to access resources on the office network. Enable this component and ensure that the domain information is being passed as necessary.

Connecting with VPN

A VPN connection is made over an existing local area connection, dial-up connection, or broadband connection.

VPN connections are displayed separately from dial-up, broadband, and LAN connections. To establish a VPN connection, follow these steps:

1. Click the Network notification icon on the taskbar. In Network Connections, click the VPN connection you want to use, and then click Connect.
2. If the connection is configured to first dial another type of connection, Windows 7 tries to establish this connection before attempting the VPN connection. If prompted to establish this connection, click Yes, and then dial the connection as discussed in the section "Connecting with Dial-Up" earlier in this chapter.
3. Once the necessary connection is established, you'll see the Connect dialog box. After you confirm that the user name is correct and enter the password for the account if it doesn't already appear, click Connect.

If you have problems establishing the connection, use these tips to help you troubleshoot:

- Problem: You cannot connect. The connection doesn't seem to work at all.

  Resolution: Check your network connections. Be sure that the lines connecting the DSL router or cable modem and the computer are plugged in properly.
- Problem: You see an error message regarding the host name.

  Resolution: The host name might be incorrectly specified. Check the settings to be sure that the host name is fully expressed, such as external01.microsoft.com rather than simply external01. DNS resolutions might not be working properly either. If this is the case, enter the IP address for the host rather than the host name.

- Problem: You see an error message regarding a bad IP address.

  Resolution: Check or reenter the IP address. If the IP address is correct, TCP/IP networking might be improperly configured. Check your networking protocols and components as discussed in the section "Configuring Networking Protocols and Components." You might need to set a default gateway and a static IP address for the connection.

- Problem: A message stating that the protocol isn't supported is displayed, and the connection doesn't seem to complete successfully.

  Resolution: Set the protocol to automatic rather than to a specific setting of either PPTP or L2TP. Check the secure logon settings. They might be set to require a secure password instead of a smart card, or vice versa. If these settings seem to be okay, determine if you are passing Windows logon and domain information because this might be required. See the section "Configuring Connection Logon Information" for more details.

- Problem: You cannot map network drives or access printers.
  Resolution: File And Printer Sharing For Microsoft Networks is required to map drives and printers. Enable this component as discussed in the section "Configuring Networking Protocols and Components."

- Problem: Some services freeze or don't work.
  Resolution: Check the proxy and firewall settings. These settings can restrict the services that are available.

Wireless Networking

To make it easier for users to take their laptops with them to meetings and to other locations in the office, many organizations are implementing wireless networks. Wireless networks can be deployed and used in many different configurations. This section examines the most common configurations.

Wireless Network Devices and Technologies

When you are working with wireless networks, the most common terms you'll run across are *wireless network adapter* and *wireless access point*. Wireless adapters include PC cards for notebooks, Peripheral Component Interconnect (PCI) cards for desktops, and universal serial bus (USB) devices (which can be used with notebooks or desktops). Many of today's laptops have the wireless adapter built in. A wireless adapter uses a built-in antenna to communicate with an access point. Typically, an access point is directly connected to the organization's physical network and might also function as a network switch or hub itself, meaning it has physical ports that allow direct cable connections as well as wireless connections. Other names for access points include *wireless base stations* and *wireless gateways*.

The most widely used wireless network adapters and access points are based on the Institute of Electrical and Electronics Engineers (IEEE) 802.11 specification. Wireless devices that are based on this specification can be Wi-Fi certified to show that they have been thoroughly tested for performance and compatibility. Table 16-3 compares the features of the most-used wireless technologies based on IEEE 802.11. As the table describes, there are four standards, and each has benefits and drawbacks. It should be noted that although 802.11a wireless devices cannot interoperate with 802.11b or 802.11g devices, fewer devices use the 5-gigahertz (GHz) range, making it less likely that there will be interference with other types of wireless devices (the majority of which use the 2.4-GHz range).

TABLE 16-3 Wireless Networking Technologies

WIRELESS STANDARD	802.11A	802.11B	802.11G	802.11N
Speed	Up to 54 Mbps	Up to 11 Mbps	Up to 54 Mbps	Up to 540 Mbps
Transmission frequency	5 GHz	2.4 GHz	2.4 GHz	2.4 GHz, 5 GHz, or both
Effective indoor range	Approximately 25 to 75 feet	Approximately 100 to 150 feet	Approximately 100 to 150 feet	Approximately 200 to 300 feet
Compatibility	Incompatible with 802.11b and 802.11g devices	Can interoperate with 802.11g devices (at 11 Mbps); 802.11g wireless adapters can operate with 802.11b access points (at 11 Mbps)	Can operate with 802.11b devices (at 11 Mbps)	Can operate with 802.11b devices (at 11 Mbps) and 802.11g devices (at 54 Mbps)

Newer 802.11 transmission specifications include 802.11n. 802.11n offers speeds up to 540 megabits per second (Mbps) and can interoperate with devices using 802.11b and 802.11g. To achieve high transmission speeds, 802.11n can use multiple receivers and multiple transmitters. Each transmitter can transmit one or more streams of data. The more streams of data that a device can use across all transmitters and receivers, the higher the throughput. However, many standard 802.11n devices with multiple transmitters and receivers combine strong, weak, and reflected signals into one data stream to maximize the range.

For added security, IEEE has defined the newer 802.11i standard. Unlike the 802.11a, 802.11b, 802.11g, and 802.11n standards, the 802.11i standard isn't about transmission speeds and frequencies. 802.11i is a security standard that you can add to the existing standards. More specifically, it adds security functionality to the radio specifications of 802.11a, 802.11b, and 802.11g. This means 802.11a network adapters and access points can include the 802.11i security functionality, as can 802.11b and 802.11g wireless products.

NOTE **Keep in mind that some computers (particularly laptops) contain integrated chip sets that support multiple wireless networking technologies. Wi-Fi Protected Access Version 2 (WPA2) is the approved Wi-Fi Alliance implementation of 802.11i. WPA2 implements all mandatory elements of the 802.11i standard.**

REAL WORLD **Take a close look at compatibility issues before you deploy wireless devices that aren't based on IEEE 802.11. Increasingly, you'll see devices that achieve high speeds. Some of these devices achieve speed boosts through compression and other similar techniques while staying within the guidelines of the IEEE 802.11 specification. Others might use network technologies that are proprietary, requiring you to use that company's wireless adapters and access points to achieve the transmission improvements. For more information on wireless standards and certified devices, go to *www.wi-fi.org*.**

Wireless Security

Securing a wireless network is very different from securing a wired network. With a wired network, a cable is used to connect a computer to the network. A user must use a cable to be physically connected to the network and must have access to one of your internal switches or hubs. If an unauthorized person connects a machine to the network, it is fairly easy to determine this and trace the physical cable to the intruder's computer.

When you install wireless networking, anyone within range of one of your wireless access points has access to your network. Not only can they intercept the wireless signals that are being broadcast, they can also try to crack into the network. The bad news is that it is difficult to locate the intruder because there's no physical wire to trace. The really bad news is that if intruders can gain access to a wireless access point, they are usually inside your organization's firewall. To protect the network, you should configure its firewall if one is available and configure the wireless devices to encode all wireless transmissions.

The most basic wireless encryption scheme is Wireless Equivalency Protection (WEP). With WEP, you encrypt data using 40-bit, 128-bit, 152-bit, or higher private key encryption. With WEP, all data is encrypted using a symmetric key derived from the WEP key or password before it is transmitted, and any computer that wants to read the data must be able to decrypt it using the key. In a typical wired environment, the shared key encryption alone is sufficient to safeguard your data. In a wireless environment with high traffic volume, it is possible that someone could successfully break the shared key, and because the shared key doesn't change automatically over time, the intruder would then have access to your organization's internal network.

Because WEP provides only the most basic security, its use is strongly discouraged, except in cases where no alternative exists. The preferred alternatives to WEP are Wi-Fi Protected Access (WPA) and Wi-Fi Protected Access Version 2 (WPA2). WPA was adopted by the Wi-Fi Alliance as an interim standard prior to the ratification of 802.11i. WPA2 is based on the official 802.11i standard and is fully backward compatible with WPA.

WPA and WPA2 are able to rotate keys for added security and to change the way keys are derived. By changing the encryption keys over time and ensuring that they aren't derived in one specific way, WPA and WPA2 can improve security significantly over WEP. WPA-compatible and WPA2-compatible devices can operate in enterprise mode or in a personal, home/small office configuration, as explained in the following points:

- **Enterprise mode provides authentication using IEEE 802.1X and EAP.** In the enterprise mode, wireless devices have two sets of keys: session keys and group keys. Session keys are unique to each association between an access point and a wireless client. They are used to create a private virtual port between the access point and the client. Group keys are shared among all clients connected to the same access point. Both sets of keys are generated dynamically and are rotated to help safeguard the integrity of keys over time.
- **Personal mode provides authentication via a preshared key or password.** In a personal, home/small office configuration, WPA uses a preshared encryption key rather than a changing encryption key. Here, the user enters a master key (the group key) into the access point and then configures all the other wireless devices to use this master key. A wireless device uses the master key as a starting point to mathematically generate the session key. It then regularly changes the session key so that the same session key is never used twice. Because the key rotation is automatic, key management is handled in the background.

WPA and WPA2 are fully compatible with 802.11a, 802.11b, 802.11g, and 802.11n. Many wireless devices that shipped before WPA and WPA2 became available can be made fully compatible with WPA and WPA2 through a software upgrade. With WPA, no additional modifications are necessary. The same is not necessarily true with WPA2 because some wireless devices might require processor or other hardware upgrades to be able to perform the computationally intensive Advanced Encryption Standard (AES) encryption.

When working with WPA and WPA2, keep the following in mind:

- All products Wi-Fi certified for WPA2 are interoperable with products that are Wi-Fi certified for WPA.
- Both WPA and WPA2 have personal and enterprise modes of operation.
- Both WPA and WPA2 use 802.1X and EAP for authentication.

- WPA provides strong data encryption via Temporal Key Integrity Protocol (TKIP).
- WPA2 provides enhanced data encryption via AES, which allows WPA2 to meet the Federal Information Processing Standard (FIPS) 140-2 requirement of some government agencies.

NOTE **Both WPA and WPA2 offer a high level of security to help ensure that private data remains private and that access to wireless networks is restricted to authorized users. Only WPA2 provides strong encryption through AES, which is a requirement for some corporate and government users.**

Another advanced wireless security technology is Robust Security Network (RSN), which is supported by 802.11i-compatible devices. RSN enables wireless devices to dynamically negotiate their authentication and encryption algorithms. This means the authentication and encryption algorithms used by RSN-compatible devices can be changed. New authentication techniques and algorithms can be added to address security issues. RSN is based on EAP and AES.

Installing and Configuring a Wireless Adapter

Other than laptops with built-in wireless adapters, the two main types of wireless adapters you'll use are PC cards for notebooks and PCI cards for desktops. These adapters are the easiest to configure—and I've found them to be the most reliable. The other type of wireless adapter that you might see is a device that connects to a notebook or desktop computer with a USB cable. When using USB wireless devices, keep in mind that there are two USB specifications: USB 1.0, the original specification, and USB 2.0, the faster, newer specification. A wireless device that complies with USB 2.0 must be connected to a USB 2.0 port to function properly and at the speeds you expect.

NOTE **Wireless technology is changing so quickly that Windows 7 won't recognize most wireless devices. This can make installation more difficult because you typically cannot rely on Plug and Play. In fact, with many of the wireless adapters I've worked with, I've needed to run the installation CD prior to installing the wireless devices. This is particularly true with USB devices. Be sure to read the documentation closely.**

As part of the installation process, most installation software will help you configure the wireless device. In the process, you may need to specify the name of the wireless network to which you want to connect and the mode in which the wireless device will run. Wireless adapters can run in one of two operating modes:

- **Ad hoc** In ad hoc mode, you configure the wireless adapter to connect directly to other computers with wireless adapters.
- **Infrastructure** In infrastructure mode, you configure the wireless adapter for use on a wireless network. In this configuration, the adapter expects to connect to an access point rather than to another computer directly.

After you specify the adapter mode, you might need to specify the encryption key that will be used. If your organization uses WEP security, you will in most cases have to type the required encryption key, which is usually referred to as the *network key*. With WPA/WPA2 security, you most often use a certificate or a smart card to supply the required encryption key.

Working with Wireless Networks and Wireless Connections

Once you've completed the installation of the device, you should be able to connect over the wireless network. Much like a wired network card, which has a local area connection, a wireless network card has a wireless network connection that is in turn connected to a specific network that is designated as a public network, private network, or domain network. If a computer has both a wired and a wireless connection, it might have two active connections: one to a wired network and one to a wireless network.

Wireless network connections provide the following additional details about the network and the connection:

- The name of the wireless network in parentheses after the connection type designator.
- The current signal strength. Signal strength of one bar is poor; signal strength of five bars is excellent.
- A Disconnect link for disconnecting the wireless connection.

If you click View Status for the wireless connection, you'll see a dialog box similar to the one shown in Figure 16-10. You can use the Wireless Network Connection Status dialog box to check the status of the connection and to maintain the connection, in much the same way that you can for other types of connections. You'll also see the duration and speed of the connection.

As with local area connections, wireless network connections have configurable properties. This means that every discussion about configuring local area connection properties also applies to wireless network connections. You can do the following:

- Install and uninstall networking features for clients, services, and protocols. In the Wireless Network Connection Status dialog box, click Properties, and then click Install or Uninstall as appropriate.
- Set TCP/IPv6 and TCP/IPv4 settings for DHCP, static IP, and dynamic IP addressing. In the Wireless Network Connection Status dialog box, click Properties, and then double-click Internet Protocol Version 6 (TCP/IPv6) or Internet Protocol Version 4 (TCP/IPv4).
- Disable or diagnose wireless connections. In the Wireless Network Connection Status dialog box, click Disable or Diagnose as appropriate.

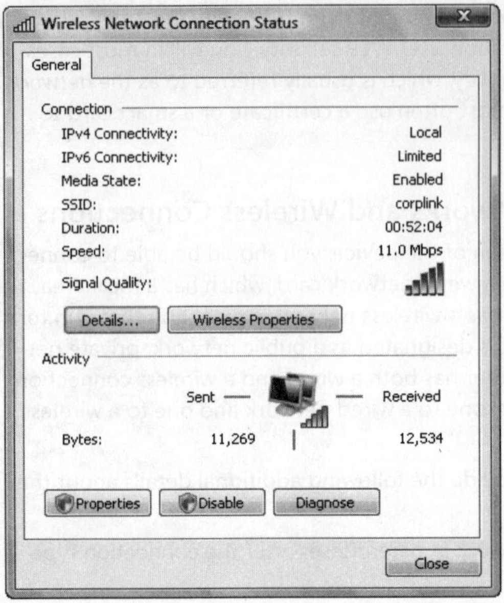

FIGURE 16-10 Determine the status and signal strength of a wireless network connection.

If you have problems establishing a wireless connection and automated diagnostics can't resolve the problem, use these tips to help you troubleshoot:

- Problem: Limited or no connectivity to the wireless network.

  Resolution: Check the signal strength. If the signal strength is low (poor), you need to move closer to the access point or redirect your antenna. For a built-in antenna, you might need to change the position of the laptop relative to the access point. The problem could also be that the network did not properly connect and configure network addressing. To check the connection state, click the connection link in Network And Sharing Center, and then review the connection status in the Status dialog box. If the media state is not set to Enabled, click Diagnose to try to resolve the problem by using automatic network diagnostics.
- Problem: Not connected or unable to connect to the wireless network.

  Resolution: If you are out of the broadcast area, your computer will not be able to connect to the wireless network. Double-click on the connection. The computer will display the Wireless Network Connection dialog box, and in the right pane you will see the message "No wireless networks were found in range." If you think this is an error, click Refresh Network List under Network Tasks. Otherwise, try moving closer to the access point or changing the position of your antenna or computer relative to the access point. The computer also might not be configured properly for establishing a wireless connection on this network.

TIP **You'll have better connection speeds—up to the maximum possible with the wireless technology you are using—when you have a stronger signal. If the signal strength is weak, the connection speed might be reduced considerably. To improve the signal strength, try moving the adapter's antenna if one is available or try changing the position of the computer relative to the access point.**

Connecting to Wireless Networks

Any wireless access point broadcasting within range should be available to a computer with a wireless adapter. By default, Windows 7 automatically determines the appropriate settings. If a connection requires a password or other credentials, you are prompted for the credentials when you try to connect to the wireless network. You can preconfigure wireless connections for users as well. This enables you to configure different authentication, encryption, and communication options as necessary.

You can preconfigure a connection for a wireless network by completing the following steps:

1. In Network And Sharing Center, click Set Up A New Connection Or Network. This starts the Set Up A Connection Or Network wizard.
2. Select Manually Connect To A Wireless Network, and then click Next.

   You now need to enter information about the wireless network to which you want to connect. Your network administrator should have this information.
3. In the Network Name box, enter the network name (also referred to as the network's secure identifier, or SSID).
4. Use the Security Type list to select the type of security being used. The encryption type is then filled in automatically for you.
5. With WEP and WPA-Personal, you must enter the required security key or password phrase in the Security Key box. For example, a WEP key typically is one of the following:
   - 5 case-sensitive characters
   - 13 case-sensitive characters
   - 10 hexadecimal, case-insensitive characters
   - 26 hexadecimal, case-insensitive characters
6. By default, the connection is started automatically whenever the user logs on. If you also want the computer to connect to the network regardless of whether the network can be reached—for example, when the computer is out of range of the wireless base—select Connect Even If The Network Is Not Broadcasting.
7. Click Next, and then click Close.

Typically, when you are within the broadcast range of a wireless network, you won't need to preconfigure a connection and can instead connect directly, letting Windows determine the correct settings. To connect to a wireless network, complete the following steps:

1. In Network And Sharing Center, click Connect To A Network. By default, all available networks are listed by name, status, and signal strength. If a network that should be available isn't listed, try clicking the Refresh button.
2. Moving the pointer over a wireless network entry displays a message box that provides the network name, signal strength, security type, radio type (the wireless standard supported), and the link's security ID.
3. You can now connect to or disconnect from a wireless network:
   - To connect to a wireless network, select the network, and then click Connect.
   - To disconnect from a wireless network, select the network, and then click Disconnect.

Managing and Troubleshooting Wireless Networking

You can manage wireless networks by using Manage Wireless Networks. To access this window, click Manage Wireless Networks in Network And Sharing Center. Manage Wireless Networks lists wireless networks in the order in which the computer should try to use the available networks. The network listed at the top of the list is tried before any others. If the computer fails to establish a connection to this network, the next network in the list is tried, and so on.

To change the preference order for a network, click it, and then use the Move Up or Move Down button to set the order in which the computer should try to use the network. As necessary, click Add to create a new wireless network that will be added to the wireless networks list, or select an existing network and click Remove to delete a listed wireless network.

Windows 7 includes many tools for troubleshooting and testing network connectivity. The section "Troubleshooting and Testing Network Settings," in Chapter 15 discusses techniques for diagnosing and resolving network issues. On wireless networks, you'll encounter similar issues. In addition to those troubleshooting techniques, you'll also want to do the following:

- Review the security configuration for the wireless network and check that the settings are correct. Reenter the security key or passphrase.
- Ensure the wireless device is positioned correctly and within range of the wireless access point. You might want to try moving the computer closer to the access point.
- Ensure there is no interference from other devices that use the same transmission range or from other devices that create magnetic fields. You might want to move or turn off devices that could be causing interference.

CHAPTER 17

Handling Maintenance and Support Tasks

Throughout this book, I've discussed support and troubleshooting techniques that you can use to administer Windows 7. In this chapter, you'll learn techniques for improving the support of computers regardless of their location and for recovering from specific types of problems. I'll start with a look at automatic updates and then look at how using the Remote Assistance feature can help you troubleshoot problems when you're not at the user's keyboard. Also, don't forget about the Problem Steps Recorder (Psr.exe). As discussed in Chapter 5, "Managing User Access and Security," you can use this tool to capture details related to the exact problem a user is having without needing access to the user's computer.

Managing Automatic Updates

The standard automatic updating feature in Windows 7 is called Windows Update. Windows Update is an enhanced version of the automatic update feature included in previous releases of Windows. Not only is Windows Update used to update the operating system, it is also used to update programs that ship with the operating system and hardware device drivers. The sections that follow discuss how Windows Update works and how it can be used to help keep a computer up to date.

Windows Update: The Essentials

Windows Update is a client component that connects periodically to a designated server and checks for updates. Once it determines that updates are available, it can be configured to download and install the updates automatically or to notify users and administrators that updates are available. The server component to which Windows Update connects is either the Windows Update Web site hosted by Microsoft (*http://windowsupdate.microsoft.com/*) or a designated Windows Update Services server hosted by your organization.

Unlike the automatic updating feature in previous versions of Windows, which only distributes and installs critical updates, Windows Update supports distribution and installation of the following:

- **Critical updates** Updates that are determined to be critical for the stability and safeguarding of a computer
- **Security updates** Updates that are designed to make the system more secure
- **Update roll-ups** Updates that include other updates
- **Service packs** Comprehensive updates to the operating system and its components, which typically include critical updates, security updates, and update roll-ups
- **Optional updates** Updates that may be useful, including updates for drivers.

A key part of the extended functionality allows Windows Update to prioritize downloads so that updates can be applied in order of criticality. This allows the most critical updates to be downloaded and installed before less critical updates. You can also control how a computer checks for new updates and how it installs them. The default polling interval used to check for new updates is 22 hours. Through Group Policy, you can change this interval. By default, every day at 3:00 A.M. local time, computers install updates they've downloaded. You can modify the installation to require notification or change the install times.

Windows 7 reduces the number of restarts required after updates by allowing a new version of an updated file to be installed even if the old file is currently being used by an application or system component. To do this, Windows 7 marks the in-use file for update and then automatically replaces the file the next time the application is started. With some applications and components, Windows 7 can save the application's data, close the application, update the file, and then restart the application. As a result, the update process has less impact on users.

REAL WORLD **Automatic updating uses the Background Intelligent Transfer Service (BITS) to transfer files. BITS is a service that performs background transfers of files and allows interrupted transfers to be restarted. BITS version 3.5, which is included with Windows 7, improves the transfer mechanism so that bandwidth is used more efficiently, which in turn means less data is transferred and the transfer is**

faster. Through Group Policy, BITS can be configured to download updates only during specific times and to limit the amount of bandwidth used. You configure these and other settings by using the Set Up A Work Schedule To Limit The Maximum Network Bandwidth Used For BITS Background Transfers policy. This policy is found in the Administrative Templates policies for Computer Configuration under Network\Background Intelligent Transfer Service (BITS) In Group Policy. Additionally, by using BITS 3.5, Windows 7 can obtain updates from trusted peers across a local area network (LAN) as well as from an update server or from Microsoft directly. Once a peer has a copy of an update, other computers on the local network can automatically detect this and download the update directly from the peer, meaning a required update may need to be transferred across the wide area network (WAN) only once rather than dozens or hundreds of times.

You can use automatic updating in several different ways. You can configure systems by using the following options:

- **Install Updates Automatically** With this option, the operating system retrieves all updates at a configurable interval (22 hours by default) and then installs the updates at a scheduled time, which by default is every day at 3:00 A.M. This configuration represents a change in behavior from Windows XP because users are not required to accept updates before they are installed. Updates are instead downloaded automatically and then installed according to a specific schedule, which can be once a day at a particular time or once a week on a particular day and time.
- **Download Updates But Let Me Choose Whether To Install Them** With this option (the default), the operating system retrieves all updates as they become available and then prompts the user when the updates are ready to be installed. The user can then accept or reject each update. Accepted updates are installed. Rejected updates are not installed, but they remain on the system so that they can be installed later.
- **Check For Updates But Let Me Choose Whether To Download And Install Them** With this option, the operating system notifies the user before retrieving any updates. If the user elects to download the updates, she still has the opportunity to accept or reject them. Accepted updates are installed. Rejected updates are not installed, but they remain on the system so that they can be installed later.
- **Never Check For Updates** When automatic updates are disabled, users are not notified about updates. Users can, however, download updates manually from the Windows Update Web site.

When Windows Update is configured for automatic download and installation, users are minimally notified of update availability or installation. Clicking a notification on the taskbar allows you to get more information about an update.

Configuring Automatic Updating

Windows 7 organizes updates into the following broad categories:

- **Important updates** Includes critical updates, security updates, update roll-ups, and service packs for the operating system and programs that ship with the operating system
- **Recommended updates** Includes updates to drivers that are provided with the operating system and recommended optional updates
- **Microsoft product updates** Includes updates for other Microsoft products that are installed on the computer as well as new optional Microsoft software
- **Point and print drivers** Includes updates to drivers that provide client-side rendering capability

NOTE **By default, Windows Update includes updates to Web compatibility lists from Microsoft. Sites listed are displayed in Compatibility view automatically. You can configure this feature by using Administrative Templates policies for Computer Configuration under Windows Components\Internet Explorer\Compatibility View.**

REAL WORLD **When you are using Home, Ultimate, or Professional editions of Windows 7, Windows Update continues to search for compatible point and print drivers if it fails to find any on the computer itself or on the Windows Update site. If the computer does not find a match, it attempts to create a mismatch connection by using any available driver that supports the hardware. However, when you are using Windows 7 Enterprise edition, you must explicitly enable the Extend Point And Print Connection To Search Windows Update policy to obtain the same behavior. This policy is found in Administrative Templates policies for Computer Configuration under Printers.**

By default, Windows 7 is configured to automatically install important updates. You can configure automatic updates on a per-computer basis by completing the following steps:

1. In Control Panel, click System And Security. Click Windows Update. This displays the Windows Update page.
2. In the left panel, click Change Settings. This displays the Change Settings page.
3. Specify whether and how updates should occur.
4. If you've enabled updates and also want to install drivers and optional updates, select the Give Me Recommended Updates The Same Way I Receive Important Updates check box.
5. If you want to allow standard users to install updates, select the Allow All Users To Install Updates On This Computer check box.

6. If you want to get updates for Microsoft products and optional Microsoft software, select the Give Me Updates For Microsoft Products And Check For New Optional Microsoft Software When I Update Windows check box.
7. Click OK.

In an Active Directory domain, you can centrally configure and manage automatic updates by using the Administrative Templates policies for both Computer Configuration and User Configuration under Windows Components\Windows Update. Table 17-1 summarizes the key policies.

TABLE 17-1 Policies for Managing Automatic Updates

POLICY	FUNCTION
Allow Automatic Updates Immediate Installation	When enabled, this setting allows automatic updates to immediately install updates that do not interrupt Windows services or require the computer to be restarted. These updates are installed immediately after they are downloaded.
Allow Non-Administrators To Receive Update Notifications	When enabled, this setting allows any user logged on to a computer to receive update notifications as appropriate for the automatic updates configuration. If disabled or not configured, only administrators receive update notifications.
Automatic Updates Detection Frequency	When enabled, this setting defines the interval to be used when checking for updates. By default, computers check approximately every 22 hours for updates. If you enable this policy and set a new interval, that interval will be used with a wildcard offset of up to 20 percent of the interval specified. This means that if you set an interval of 10 hours, the actual polling interval would depend on the computer and be between 8 and 10 hours.
Configure Automatic Updates	When you enable this setting, you can configure how automatic updates work using similar options to those described later in this chapter. You can also schedule the installation.
Delay Restart For Scheduled Installations	By default, when a restart is required after an automatic update, the computer is restarted after a 15-minute delay. To use a different delay, enable this policy, and then set the delay time.

POLICY	FUNCTION
Enable Client-Side Targeting	When enabled, this setting allows an administrator to define a target group for the current Group Policy object. Client-side targeting allows administrators to control which updates are installed on specified groups of computers. Before an update is deployed, it must be authorized for a particular target group.
Enabling Windows Update Power Management To Automatically Wake Up The System To Install Scheduled Updates	When this policy is enabled and the computer is configured for automated, scheduled installation of updates, Windows Update uses the computer's power management features to wake the computer from hibernation at the scheduled update time and then install updates. This wake-up-and-install process does not occur if the computer is on battery power.
No Auto-Restart With Logged On Users For Scheduled Automatic Updates Installations	When enabled, this setting specifies that the computer will not automatically restart after installing updates that require a restart if a user is currently logged on. Instead, the user is notified that a restart is needed. Restarting the computer enforces the updates.
Re-Prompt For Restart With Scheduled Installations	When enabled and when automatic updates are configured for scheduled installation of updates, this setting ensures the logged-on user is prompted again after a set interval if a restart was previously postponed. If this setting is disabled or not configured, the default reprompt interval of 10 minutes is used.
Remove Access To Use All Windows Update Features	When you enable this setting, all Windows Update features are removed. Users are blocked from accessing Windows Update, and automatic updating is completely disabled.
Reschedule Automatic Updates Scheduled Installations	When enabled, this setting specifies the amount of time to wait after system startup before proceeding with a scheduled installation that was previously missed.
Specify Intranet Microsoft Update Service Location	When enabled, this setting allows you to designate the fully qualified domain name of the Microsoft Update Services server hosted by your organization and of the related statistics server. Both services can be performed by one server.
Turn On Recommended Updates Via Automatic Updates	When this policy is enabled, recommended updates, including those for drivers and other optional updates, are installed along with other updates.

Checking for Updates

The main Windows Update page provides details about the last time the computer or a user checked for updates, the last time updates were installed, and the current automatic update configuration. You can determine Windows Update usage or manually check for updates by following these steps:

1. In Control Panel, click System And Security. Click Windows Update. Statistics are provided about the most recent check for updates, the last time updates were installed, and the current update configuration.
2. If you want to manually check for updates, click Check For Updates.
3. To install optional updates that may be available, click the link that shows how many optional updates are available.
4. On the Select Updates To Install page, select the updates to install, and then click OK.

Viewing Update History and Installed Updates

The Windows Update download manager tracks both successful and failed updates by using an update history log. You can access this log by following these steps:

1. In Control Panel, click System And Security. Click Windows Update.
2. In the left panel, click View Update History. This displays the View Update History page.

On the View Update History page, updates listed with a Successful status were downloaded and installed. Updates listed with an Unsuccessful status were downloaded but failed to install. To remove an update while accessing the View Update History page, click Installed Updates. Then, on the Installed Updates page, right-click the update that you do not want and click Remove.

Removing Automatic Updates to Recover from Problems

If an automatic update causes a problem on a system, don't worry. You can remove an automatic update in the same way that you uninstall any other program. Simply follow these steps:

1. In Control Panel, click System And Security. Click Windows Update.
2. Click View Update History, and then click Installed Updates.
3. To remove an update, select it in the list provided, and then click Uninstall.

Hiding Available Updates

Over time, a user might accumulate a number of updates that were intentionally not installed but still appear on the list of updates available for installation. If you or the user has reviewed the update and you don't want to install it, you can hide the update by completing the following steps:

1. In Control Panel, click System And Security. Click Windows Update.
2. Click the link telling you how many updates are available.
3. On the Select Updates To Install page, right-click the update you do not want to install, and then click Hide Update.

Restoring Declined Updates

If a user declines an update or has asked not to be notified about or install updates automatically, you can restore the updates so that they can be installed. To do this, complete the following steps:

1. In Control Panel, click System And Security. Click Windows Update.
2. Click Restore Hidden Updates.
3. On the Restore Hidden Updates page, select an update you want to install, and then click Restore.
4. Windows 7 will restore the update so that it can be selected and installed through the normal notification and installation process.

Using Remote Assistance to Resolve Problems

Remote Assistance enables support personnel to view a user's desktop and take control temporarily to resolve problems or walk the user through the execution of complex tasks. After Remote Assistance is configured locally as discussed in Chapter 5, or through Group Policy as discussed in Chapter 3, "Configuring User and Computer Policies," you can work with this feature.

Understanding Remote Assistance

Remote Assistance is a feature of Windows XP and later releases of Windows. Only users running these operating systems can initiate and respond to Remote Assistance invitations. In the enterprise, the easy way to work with Remote Assistance is as follows:

1. Be sure you are using a user account that is a member of the local Offer Remote Assistance Helpers group (or of a group that is a member of this group).
2. Be sure that Windows Firewall exceptions are created for the executable files Msra.exe and Raserver.exe, and open TCP port 135 for DCOM. Normally, these settings are configured by default through Group Policy.
3. Be sure that the other computer is configured to allow Remote Assistance, and then connect to the computer by its computer name or IP address.

With an enterprise configuration, you can provide remote assistance by following these steps:

1. Click Start, type **msra** in the Search box, and then press Enter.
2. In the Windows Remote Assistance wizard, click Help Someone Who Has Invited You.
3. Type the name or IP address of the computer you want to assist, and then click Next to connect to the computer.

Users can initiate sessions by creating an invitation request. Support personnel initiate sessions by offering help to users. Once a session is initiated, assistants can chat with users, observe their working screens, and, if permitted, control their computers.

Remote Assistance invitations can be created by using the following techniques:

- **E-mail invitation** E-mail invitations are sent as e-mail messages to a named e-mail address. An attachment provided in the message is used to initiate the Remote Assistance session. You might want to configure a standard e-mail address, such as RemoteAssist@your_company_name.com, to allow users to send invitation requests easily to the support team. If this address is configured in Microsoft Exchange Server as a distribution list that delivers the invitations to support team members or as an additional mailbox for specific team members, support staff will be able to handle requests more efficiently and users will have a standard way of requesting help.
- **File invitation** File invitations are saved as Microsoft Remote Control Incident (MsRcIncident) files. Double-clicking the file name initiates the Remote Assistance session. You can use file invitations if you are using Web-based e-mail and need to attach the invitation separately. You might also want to configure a shared folder that is automatically mapped as a network drive for users and ensure that it is accessible by support personnel. Name the share something that easily identifies it as being used for assistance requests, such as HelpDeskRequest or AssistanceInvitations.
- **Easy Connect invitation** Uses the Peer Name Resolution Protocol (PNRP) to send a Remote Assistance invitation over the Internet. Easy Connect generates an access password automatically, which allows the helper to connect directly to the computer. The helper's contact information is saved for quick reference in the future without using the password. (This technique works only when both helper and the person being assisted are using Windows 7 or later releases.)

With Windows 7, invitations must be created with a control password, which is a change made from previous releases of Windows to enhance security. The control password provides an additional layer of security in the Remote Assistance configuration, ensuring that users are authorized to provide remote assistance and that they know the invitation password. You should establish an official guideline that requires the use of invitation passwords. To streamline the invitation process, you might want to define passwords that are used with invitations. Passwords should be changed regularly, and you might want to assign different passwords to different groups within the organization.

To work properly, Remote Assistance relies on the presence of a network connection between the user's computer and the assistant's computer. Remote Assistance uses UPnP, SSDP, PNRP, and Teredo for communications. Because most firewalls do not allow these communications by default, a firewall between the two computers might prevent the assistance session, and to ensure success, an exception must be created for outbound communications from the assistant's computer to the user's computer. To configure the required Windows Firewall exception for Remote Assistance, follow these steps:

1. In Control Panel, click System And Security. Under the Windows Firewall heading, click Allow A Program Through Windows Firewall.
2. In the Allows Programs window, scroll down until you see Remote Assistance. Ensure that the Remote Assistance check box is selected.
3. Select the network types for which Remote Assistance should be allowed, and then click OK.

Remote Assistance can work through Network Address Translation (NAT) firewalls. When providing support through Remote Assistance, you'll find built-in diagnostic tools that you can run with a single click. For escalation of support issues, two different support staff can connect to a computer simultaneously. Finally, thanks to the automatic reconnect-after-restart feature, if you need to restart a computer you are assisting remotely, you won't need to reconnect to the computer manually. The Remote Assistance session is reestablished automatically after the computer reboots.

Creating Remote Assistance Invitations

To create a Remote Assistance invitation for e-mail, follow these steps:

1. In Control Panel, under the System And Security heading, click Find And Fix Problems. In the left pane of the Troubleshooting window, click Get Help From A Friend.
2. On the Remote Assistance page, click Invite Someone To Help You, and then click Use E-Mail To Send An Invitation.
3. When prompted, enter and confirm a secure password for connecting to the computer. This password is used by the person you are inviting and is only valid for the Remote Assistance session.
4. When you click Next, Windows 7 starts your default e-mail program and creates an e-mail message with the invitation. In the To field, type the e-mail address of the person you are inviting, and then click Send.

To create a Remote Assistance invitation and save it to a file, follow these steps:

1. In Control Panel, under the System And Security heading, click Find And Fix Problems. In the left pane of the Troubleshooting window, click Get Help From A Friend.
2. On the Remote Assistance page, click Invite Someone To Help You, and then click Save This Invitation As A File.
3. In the field provided, enter a path and file name for the invitation. If you specify the path to a network folder, the invitation can be accessed easily by an administrator with access to this network folder.
4. Give your helper the invitation file and the automatically generated password. This password is used by the person you are inviting and is valid only for the Remote Assistance session.

To create a Remote Assistance invitation for Easy Connect, follow these steps:

1. In Control Panel, under the System And Security heading, click Find And Fix Problems. In the left pane of the Troubleshooting window, click Get Help From A Friend.
2. On the Remote Assistance page, click Invite Someone To Help You, and then click Use Easy Connect.
3. Tell your helper the Easy Connect password. This password is generated automatically for this Remote Assistance session only.

By default, Remote Assistance invitations are valid for a maximum of 6 hours and enable support staff to remotely control a computer. You can change these settings by using the System Properties dialog box, as discussed in Chapter 5 in the section "Configuring Remote Assistance." Once you've sent the invitation by e-mail or created the invitation file, the Windows Remote Assistance dialog box is displayed, as shown in Figure 17-1. This dialog box provides the following options:

- **Cancel** Effectively cancels the Remote Assistance request by not allowing the invitation to be used to connect to the computer.
- **Request Control/Stop Sharing** Requests control of or stops sharing the computer.
- **Fit To Screen** Resizes the other person's screen to fit your window.
- **Disconnect** Ends the help session and disconnects.
- **Settings** Allows you to configure the session settings. Available settings depend on the type of computer being helped. By default, when you press the Esc key, shared control of the computer is stopped, a log of the Remote Assistance session is saved, and the bandwidth usage is configured so that full-window drag and desktop backgrounds are not enabled. For fast or slow connections, you can modify the bandwidth usage settings by using the Bandwidth Usage slider.

NOTE **By default, the Remote Assistance log is created in the %UserProfile%\Documents\Remote Assistance Logs folder on the computer of the user requesting remote assistance.**

- **Chat** Opens a chat window for sending messages between the helper and the current user of the computer.
- **Send File** Transfers a file to the other computer.

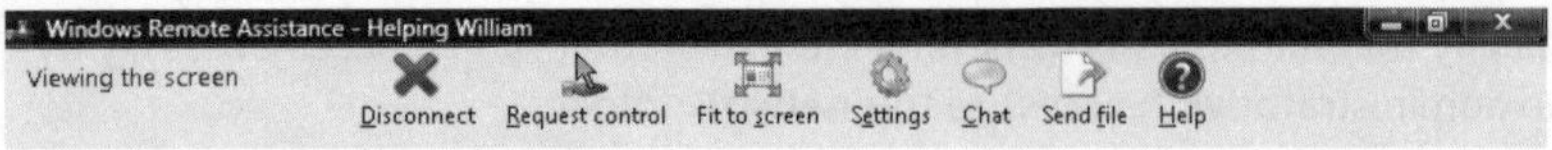

FIGURE 17-1 Manage Remote Assistance sessions.

Offering Remote Assistance or Answering a Remote Assistance Invitation

If you know that a user is having problems with her computer, you can follow these steps to offer remote assistance rather than waiting for her to send you an invitation or Easy Connect password:

1. Click Start, type **msra,** and then press Enter.
2. In the Windows Remote Assistance wizard, click Help Someone Who Has Invited You.
3. Click the Advanced Connection Option For Help Desk link.
4. Type the name or IP address of the computer you want to assist, and then click Next to connect to the computer.

If someone has already created an invitation, you can answer the invitation by double-clicking the related e-mail attachment or file. You can also answer an invitation saved to a file by following these steps:

1. Click Start, type **msra,** and then press Enter.
2. In the Windows Remote Assistance wizard, click Help Someone Who Has Invited You.
3. Click Use An Invitation File, and then use the Open dialog box to locate the invitation. Click Open.
4. When prompted, provide the necessary password for the invitation.
5. Click Finish. You are connected to the computer of the user needing assistance, provided the user hasn't canceled the invitation, the invitation hasn't expired, and Remote Assistance is allowed.

If someone is using Easy Connect and has sent you the password, you can answer the invitation by following these steps:

1. Click Start, type **msra,** and then press Enter.
2. In the Windows Remote Assistance wizard, click Help Someone Who Has Invited You.
3. Click Use Easy Connect. When prompted, provide the password for the invitation.
4. Click OK. You are connected to the computer of the user needing assistance.

Detecting and Resolving Windows 7 Errors

Any particular computer can have dozens, and in some cases hundreds, of different components, services, and applications configured on it. Keeping all these components working properly is a big job, and the built-in diagnostics features discussed previously in this book do a good job of detecting common problems and finding solutions for them. As discussed in Chapter 8, "Managing Hardware Devices and Drivers," known problems are tracked in the Problem Reports And Solutions console. Like the built-in diagnostic features, this console attempts to provide solutions to problems where possible. Not all problems can be automatically detected and resolved, and this is where the errors reported by Windows components, applications, services, and hardware devices become useful.

Using the Event Logs for Error Tracking and Diagnosis

Windows 7 stores errors generated by processes, services, applications, and hardware devices in log files. Two general types of log files are used:

- **Windows logs** Logs used by the operating system to record general system events related to applications, security, setup, and system components
- **Applications and services logs** Logs used by specific applications or services to record application-specific or service-specific events

Entries in a log file are recorded according to the warning level of the activity. Entries can include errors as well as general informational events. You'll see the following levels of entries:

- **Information** An informational event, which is generally related to a successful action
- **Audit Success** An event related to the successful execution of an action
- **Audit Failure** An event related to the failed execution of an action
- **Warning** A warning, details of which are often useful in preventing future system problems
- **Error** An error, such as the failure of a service to start

In addition to level, date, and time, the summary and detailed event entries provide the following information:

- **Source** The application, service, or component that logged the event.
- **Event ID** An identifier for the specific event.
- **Task Category** The category of the event, which is sometimes used to further describe the related action.
- **User** The user account that was logged on when the event occurred. If a system process or service triggered the event, the user name is usually that of the special identity that caused the event, such as NetworkService, LocalService, or System.
- **Computer** The name of the computer on which the event occurred.
- **Details** In the detailed entries, this provides a text description of the event, followed by any related data or error output.

Viewing and Managing the Event Logs

You can access event logs by using the Event Viewer node in Computer Management. To open Computer Management, click Start, point to All Programs, Administrative Tools, and then click Computer Management. If the Administrative Tools menu isn't accessible, you can open Computer Management by clicking Start and then clicking Control Panel. In Control Panel, click System And Security, Administrative Tools, and then Computer Management.

You can access the event logs by completing the following steps:

1. Open Computer Management. You are connected to the local computer by default. If you want to view logs on a remote computer, right-click the Computer Management entry in the console tree (left pane), and then click Connect To Another Computer. In the Select Computer dialog box, enter the name of the computer that you want to access, and then click OK.
2. Expand the Event Viewer node, and then expand the Windows Logs node, the Application And Services Logs node, or both nodes to view the available logs.
3. Select the log that you want to view, as shown in Figure 17-2.

Warnings and errors are the two key types of events you'll want to examine. Whenever these types of events occur and you are unsure of the cause, double-click the entry to view the detailed event description. Note the source of the error and attempt to resolve the problem by using the techniques discussed in this book. To learn more about the error and steps you can take to resolve it (if necessary), you can click the Event Log Online link provided in the error description or search the Microsoft Knowledge Base for the event ID or part of the error description.

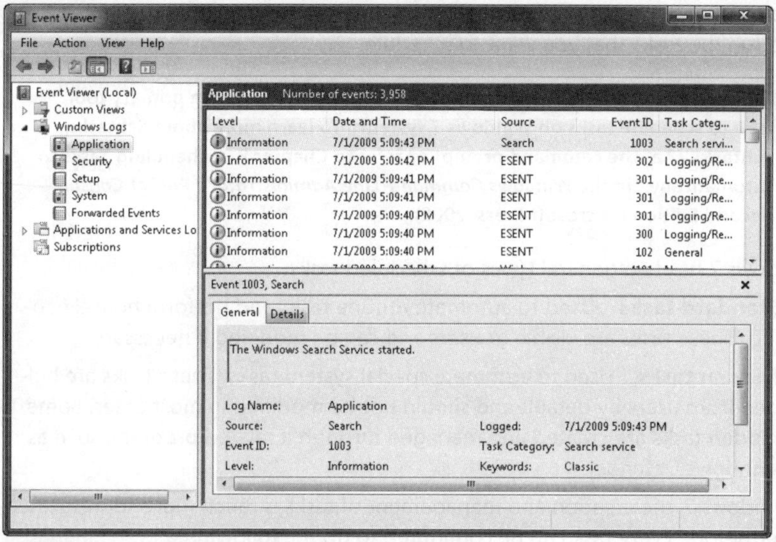

FIGURE 17-2 Event Viewer displays events for the selected log.

Scheduling Maintenance Tasks

When you manage desktop and laptop systems, you'll often want to perform routine maintenance tasks on a periodic or recurring basis. To do this, you can use the Task Scheduler service to schedule one-time or recurring tasks to run automatically. You automate tasks by running command-shell scripts, Windows Script Host (WSH) scripts, or applications that execute the necessary commands for you. Unlike earlier releases of Windows, Windows 7 includes an extensive library of preconfigured tasks. These tasks handle everything from uninstalling a Bluetooth device to defragmenting disks to performing Windows Defender scans.

Understanding Task Scheduling

Windows 7 provides several tools for scheduling tasks, including the Task Scheduler and the Schtasks command-line tool. Both can be used for scheduling tasks on local and remote systems. The Task Scheduler includes several wizards for scheduling tasks that provide point-and-click interfaces for task assignment. Schtasks is the command-line counterpart.

Both scheduling tools use the Task Scheduler service to monitor the system clock and run tasks at specified times. The Task Scheduler service logs on as the LocalSystem account by default. This account usually doesn't have adequate permissions to perform administrative tasks. To overcome this problem, each task can be set to run as a specific user, and you set the user name and password to use when you create the task. Be sure to use an account that has adequate user privileges and access rights to run the tasks that you want to schedule.

> ***NOTE*** **The focus of this section is on the Task Scheduler. This is the primary tool you'll use to schedule tasks on Windows 7 systems. To learn more about Schtasks, type schtasks /? at the command prompt or refer to Chapter 9, "Scheduling Tasks to Run Automatically," in the *Windows Command-Line Administrator's Pocket Consultant,* Second Edition (Microsoft Press, 2008).**

Windows 7 has two general types of scheduled tasks:

- **Standard tasks** Used to automate routine tasks and perform housekeeping. These tasks are visible to users and can be modified if necessary.
- **Hidden tasks** Used to automate special system tasks. These tasks are hidden from users by default and should not be modified in most cases. Some hidden tasks are created and managed through a related program, such as Windows Defender.

In Windows 7, the creation and management of tasks is much more sophisticated than ever before. Every task can be configured to do the following:

- Run only when a user is logged on, or run regardless of whether a user is logged on
- Run with standard user privileges, or run with the highest privileges required (including administrator privileges)

Because tasks created on Windows 7 are not compatible with earlier releases of Windows, you cannot copy a Windows 7 task to a computer running an earlier release of Windows and expect the task to run. However, when creating the task, you can specify that it should be created so that it is compatible with earlier releases of Windows. This allows you to use the task on computers running earlier releases of Windows.

Tasks can have many properties associated with them, including the following:

- **Triggers** Triggers specify the circumstances under which a task begins and ends. You can begin a task based on a schedule as well as on user logon, computer startup, or processor idling. You can also begin a task based on events, a user connecting or disconnecting from a Terminal Server session, or a user locking or unlocking a workstation. Tasks with event-based triggers can be the most powerful because they allow you to provide automated ways to handle errors and warnings.
- **Actions** Actions define the action a task performs when it is triggered. This allows a task to start programs, send e-mail messages, or display messages.
- **Conditions** Conditions help qualify the conditions under which a task is started or stopped once it has been triggered. You can use conditions to wake the computer to run a task and to start the computer only if a specific network connection is available. You can use conditions to start, stop, and

restart a task based on the processor idle time. For example, you might want to start a task only if the computer has been idle for at least 10 minutes, stop the task if the computer is no longer idle, and then restart the task again if the computer becomes idle once more. You can also use conditions to specify that a task should start only if the computer is on alternating current (AC) power and stop if the computer switches to battery power.

Viewing and Managing Tasks on Local and Remote Systems

The current tasks configured on a system are accessible through the Task Scheduler node in Computer Management. You can view and manage the scheduled tasks configured on a computer by completing the following steps:

1. Open Computer Management. You are connected to the local computer by default. If you want to view tasks on a remote computer, right-click the Computer Management entry in the console tree (left pane), and then click Connect To Another Computer. In the Select Computer dialog box, enter the name of the computer that you want to access, and then click OK.
2. Expand the Task Scheduler node, and then expand the Task Scheduler Library node and related subnodes as necessary to view the configured scheduled tasks.
3. Select a task to view its properties by using the tabs shown in Figure 17-3. If you want to manage the task, right-click the task and then do the following:
   - Click Delete to delete a task.
   - Click Disable to disable a task.
   - Click Properties to edit the task's properties. Make the appropriate changes in the Properties dialog box, and then click OK.
   - Click Export to export a task to a file that can be imported on another computer. After you export the task, use Computer Management to connect to the other computer, right-click the Task Scheduler Library node, and then click Import Task. You can then use the Open dialog box to locate and open the task on the other computer.
   - Click Run to run the task.
   - If the task is running, click End to stop the task.

NOTE **Although you can modify and delete user-created tasks, most tasks created by the operating system cannot be configured or deleted. If operating system tasks are not shown, you can display these tasks by clicking View and then selecting Show Hidden Tasks. Note also that when exporting tasks, the task's Configure For setting determines the operating systems with which the task can be used.**

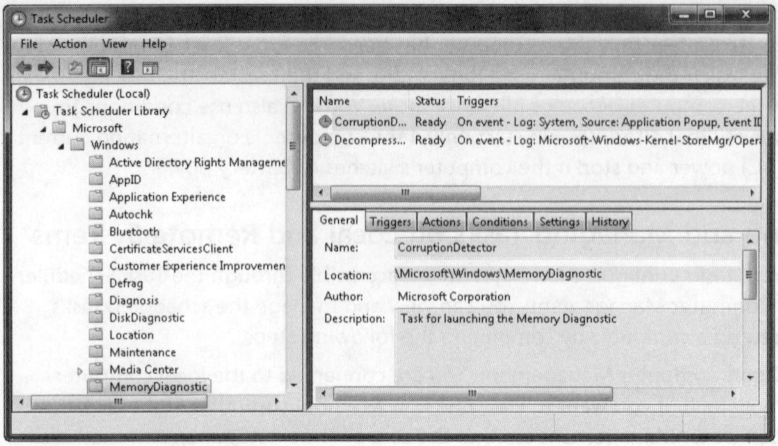

FIGURE 17-3 View and manage scheduled tasks.

You can view the scheduled tasks currently running on a computer by completing the following steps:

1. Open Computer Management. You are connected to the local computer by default. If you want to view tasks on a remote computer, right-click the Computer Management entry in the console tree (left pane), and then click Connect To Another Computer. In the Select Computer dialog box, enter the name of the computer that you want to access, and then click OK.
2. Select the Task Scheduler node to read in its attributes. Right-click the Task Scheduler node, and then select Display All Running Tasks.

Creating Scheduled Tasks

You can create a scheduled task by completing the following steps:

1. Open Computer Management. You are connected to the local computer by default. If you want to create tasks on a remote computer, right-click the Computer Management entry in the console tree (left pane), and then click Connect To Another Computer. In the Select Computer dialog box, enter the name of the computer that you want to access, and then click OK.
2. Select and then right-click the Task Scheduler node, and then click Create Task. This starts the Create Task wizard.
3. On the General tab, type the name of the task, and then set security options for running the task.
   - If the task should run under a user account other than the current user, click Change User Or Group. Use the Select User Or Group dialog box to select the user or group under which the task should run, and then provide the appropriate credentials when prompted later.

- Set other run options as necessary by using the options provided. By default, tasks run only when a user is logged on. If you want to run the task regardless of whether a user is logged on, select Run Whether User Is Logged On Or Not. You can also elect to run with highest privileges and configure the task for earlier releases of Windows.

4. On the Triggers tab, create and manage triggers by using the options provided. To create a trigger, click New, use the options provided to configure the trigger, and then click OK.
5. On the Actions tab, create and manage actions by using the options provided. To create an action, click New, use the options provided to configure the action, and then click OK.
6. On the Conditions tab, specify any limiting conditions for starting or stopping the task.
7. On the Settings tab, choose any additional optional settings for the task.
8. Click OK to create the task.

Troubleshooting Scheduled Tasks

When you configure tasks to run on a computer, you can encounter several types of problems. Some tasks won't run when they are supposed to. Others will start but won't stop. To determine the status of a task, select the task in the Task Scheduler and note the status, last run time, and last run result. If a task has a status of Queued, it is waiting to run at a scheduled time. If a task has a status of Ready, it is ready to run at its next run time. If a task should be running automatically but has a last run time of Never, you need to check the task's properties to determine why it isn't running. If the last run result is an error, you need to resolve the referenced problem so that the task can run normally.

Check a task's properties by clicking its entry in the Task Scheduler. The History tab provides detailed information on the task, from creation to its latest run time. Use the information to help you resolve problems with the task.

A task that is listed as Running might not in fact be running but instead might be a hung process. You can check for hung processes by using the Last Run Time column, which tells you when the task was started. If a task has been running for more than a day, there is usually a problem. A script might be waiting for input, the task might have problems reading or writing files, or the task might simply be a runaway task that needs to be stopped. To stop the task, right-click it in the Task Scheduler, and then click End.

Backing Up and Recovering a Computer

Windows 7 provides Backup And Restore Center as a central console for backing up and recovering a computer. You can access this console by clicking Start, clicking Control Panel, and then clicking the Back Up Your Computer link under the System And Security heading. Other tools for backing up and recovering a computer's data include Previous Versions, the Startup Repair tool, Windows Resume Loader, System Restore, and Backup. These tools are discussed in the sections that follow.

Backing Up and Recovering Files and Folders Using Previous Versions

Chapter 6, "Configuring Windows 7 Computers," introduced Previous Versions and also discussed configuring and using this feature. Although Previous Versions is not a replacement for full system backups, it can be used to create automatic backups of changed files and folders on monitored drives. If a monitored file or folder was accidentally deleted or modified, you can recover the file or folder to the previous version by using the technique discussed in Chapter 6 in the section "Restoring a Previous Version."

Recovering from a Failed Resume

When a computer running Windows 7 enters sleep mode or hibernates, a snapshot of the current state of the computer is created. For sleep mode, this snapshot is created in memory and then read from memory when a user wakes the computer. For hibernate mode, this snapshot is written to disk and then read from disk when a user wakes the computer. Both operations are handled by the Windows Resume Loader.

Problems with resuming a computer can occur for a variety of reasons, including errors in the snapshot, physical errors in memory, and physical disk errors. If there is a problem resuming after waking the computer, Windows Resume Loader will prompt you with a warning message similar to the following:

```
Windows Resume Loader
The last attempt to restart the system from its previous location failed.
Attempt to restart again?

Continue with system restart
Delete restoration data and proceed to system boot.

Enter=choose
```

To have Windows Resume Loader attempt to reload the system state again, select Continue With System Restart. To have Windows Resume Loader delete the saved state of the computer and restart the computer, select Delete Restoration

Data And Proceed To System Boot. Although the latter option, a full restart, will typically resolve the problem, it could mean losing data if work wasn't saved before the computer entered sleep or hibernate mode.

Repairing a Computer to Enable Startup

To start properly, computers running Windows 7 need access to specific system files. If a computer won't start due to a corrupted or missing system file, you can use the Startup Repair tool. Sometimes repairing a damaged or missing file won't fix all the computer's problems, and you might need to continue troubleshooting to diagnose and resolve the deeper problem.

Most other types of startup problems occur because something on the system has changed; for example, a device might have been incorrectly installed. The system configuration or registry might have been updated improperly, causing a conflict. Often you can resolve startup issues using safe mode to recover or troubleshoot system problems. When you have finished using safe mode, be sure to restart the computer using a normal startup. You will then be able to use the computer as you normally would.

In safe mode, Windows 7 loads only basic files, services, and drivers. The drivers loaded include those for the mouse, monitor, keyboard, mass storage, and base video. The monitor driver sets the basic settings and modes for the computer's monitor; the base video driver sets the basic options for the computer's graphics card. No networking services or drivers are started unless you choose the Safe Mode With Networking option. Because safe mode loads a limited set of configuration information, it can help you troubleshoot problems.

Restart a system in safe mode by completing the following steps:

1. If the computer is running but has started with errors, click Start. On the Start menu, click the Shut Down options button, and then click Restart.
2. During startup, press F8 to access the Advanced Boot Options screen. If the computer has multiple operating systems or you've installed the Recovery Console, you'll see the Windows Boot Manager screen. On the Windows Boot Manager screen, select Windows 7 as the operating system, and then press F8.
3. Use the arrow keys to select the safe mode option you want to use, and then press Enter. The safe mode option you use depends on the type of problem you're experiencing. The key options are as follows:
   - **Repair Your Computer** Loads the Startup Repair tool as discussed in the section "Repairing and Recovering a Computer" later in the chapter.
   - **Safe Mode** Loads only basic files, services, and drivers during the initialization sequence. The drivers loaded include those for the mouse, monitor, keyboard, mass storage, and base video. No networking services or drivers are started.

- **Safe Mode With Networking** Loads basic files, services, and drivers, as well as services and drivers needed to start networking.
- **Safe Mode With Command Prompt** Loads basic files, services, and drivers, and then starts a command prompt instead of the Windows 7 graphical interface. No networking services or drivers are started.

TIP **In Safe Mode With Command Prompt, you can start the Explorer shell from the command-line interface by pressing Ctrl+Shift+Esc to open Task Manager. On the File menu, click New Task (Run) to open the Create New Task window. Type explorer.exe, and then click OK.**

- **Enable Boot Logging** Allows you to create a record of all startup events in a boot log.
- **Enable Low Resolution Video** Allows you to start the system in low-resolution 640 × 480 display mode, which is useful if the system display is set to a mode that can't be used with the current monitor.
- **Last Known Good Configuration** Starts the computer in safe mode using registry information that Windows 7 saved at the last shutdown. Only the HKEY_CURRENT_CONFIG (HKCC) hive is loaded. This registry hive stores information about the hardware configuration with which you previously and successfully started the computer.
- **Disable Automatic Restart On System Failure** Prevents Windows from restarting after a crash. Otherwise, by default, Windows will restart automatically after a crash. If Windows restarts repeatedly, you might have a firmware configuration issue as discussed in Chapter 10, "Managing Firmware, Boot Configuration, and Startup."
- **Disable Driver Signature Enforcement** Starts the computer in safe mode without enforcing digital signature policy settings for drivers. If a driver with an invalid or missing digital signature is causing startup failure, this will resolve the problem temporarily so that you can start the computer and resolve the problem by getting a new driver or changing the driver signature enforcement settings.

4. If a problem doesn't reappear when you start in safe mode, you can eliminate the default settings and basic device drivers as possible causes. If a newly added device or updated driver is causing problems, you can use safe mode to remove the device, reverse the update, or install a different version of the driver software.
5. If you are still having a problem starting the system normally and suspect that problems with hardware, software, or settings are to blame, remain in safe mode and then try using System Restore to undo previous changes. See the "Backing Up and Recovering System State Using System Restore" section of this chapter.

6. If System Restore doesn't work, try modifying startup options as discussed in the section "Managing System Configuration, Startup, and Boot" in Chapter 6.

Backing Up and Recovering System State Using System Restore

The section "The System Protection Tab" in Chapter 6 introduces System Restore and also discusses configuring this feature. Restore points can be used to recover systems that are experiencing problems after a system update, software installation, hardware installation, or other change. The following sections discuss how restore points can be created manually and how systems can be recovered using restore points. Restore operations are reversible in most cases.

Understanding Restore Points

System Restore monitors the operating system for changes and creates restore points at regular daily intervals before changes are introduced. The feature works by saving a snapshot of a computer's system configuration and writing the snapshot to disk so that it can be used to recover the system to a point in time if necessary. It is important to note that System Restore does not affect personal data. You can recover a system to a restore point without affecting a user's application data, cached files, or documents. System Restore doesn't write any information to the Documents folder either.

System Restore tracks and saves configuration information separately for each drive on a computer. This means that each drive has disk space made available to System Restore, and you can turn off monitoring of individual drives as needed. If a drive is configured for System Restore monitoring, you can recover from changes if a problem occurs. If a drive isn't configured for System Restore monitoring, configuration changes are not tracked, and changes cannot be recovered if a problem occurs. On most systems, you should configure System Restore for the system drive, which stores the operating system files, and for all drives containing critical applications.

Restore points can be restored in one of three ways: by checkpoint, by date, or by event. Individual snapshots scheduled by the operating system are called *system checkpoints*. When you install Windows 7, the first snapshot—the initial system checkpoint—is created automatically. Other system checkpoints are made approximately every 24 hours. If a computer is turned off when a daily checkpoint is scheduled, System Restore creates the checkpoint the next time the computer is started.

Some snapshots are created automatically based on events that the operating system triggers when you make changes or install applications. For simplicity, I call these snapshots *installation restore points*, and there's actually a group of them, each with a different purpose. The event-based snapshots are as follows:

- **Program name installation restore points** Created prior to installing a program that uses a compatible installer. You can use installation restore points to track application installation and to restore a computer to the state it was in before the application was installed. Restoring the computer state means that all file and registry settings for the installed program are removed. It also means that programs and system files altered by the installation are restored to their previous state. Once completed, the program won't work, and you'll need to reinstall it if the user wants to use it again.

CAUTION These are called _program name installation restore points_ instead of _program uninstall restore points_ for a very good reason. The restore process doesn't uninstall all the application files. It removes file and registry settings that might affect the operation of the computer. To completely uninstall a program, you need to use the Programs tool in Control Panel.

- **Automatic update restore points** Created prior to applying an automatic update. If a computer has problems after applying an automatic update, you can use the restore point to recover the computer to its previous state. (You can also use the Programs tool to remove automatic updates.)
- **Restore operation restore points** Created prior to restoring a computer. If you find that you used the wrong restore point or that the restore point doesn't work, you can use these restore points to undo the restore operation and recover the computer to its state before you reversed the previous settings.
- **Unsigned device driver restore points** Created prior to the installation of an unsigned or uncertified driver on a computer. If a computer has problems after installing an unsigned or uncertified driver, you can use these restore points to restore the computer to its state before you installed the driver. For signed and certified drivers, the normal rollback procedure should allow you to go back to the previous driver being used.
- **Microsoft Backup tool recovery restore points** Created prior to recovering files or system data by using the Backup tool. If the recovery fails or if the computer doesn't work properly after the recovery, you can undo the changes and restore the computer to its previous state.

Users can also create snapshots manually. These snapshots are called *manual restore points*. You should recommend that users create snapshots prior to performing any operation that could cause problems on the system.

You can restore computers when they are running in normal mode or safe mode. In normal mode, a restore operation restore point is created prior to restoration of the computer. But in safe mode, the restore operation restore point is not created because changes you make in safe mode aren't tracked and you can't undo them using restore points. However, you can use safe mode to restore any previously created restore point.

Creating Manual Restore Points

You can create a manual restore point by following these steps:

1. In Control Panel, click System And Security, and then click System.
2. In the left pane, click System Protection.
3. Select the disk for which you want to create the restore point, and then click Create.
4. Enter a description for the restore point, such as Prior To Display Monitor Driver Update And Changes. Click Create.
5. When the restore point is created, click OK.

Recovering from Restore Points

To recover a computer from a restore point, follow these steps:

1. In Control Panel, under the System And Security heading, click the Back Up Your Computer link.
2. Click the Recover System Settings On Your Computer link.
3. Click Open System Restore. System Restore examines the available restore points on the computer. This process can take several minutes. When it completes, click Next.
4. System Restore recommends one or more restore points. Restore points are listed by date, time, description, and type. If you want to determine what programs the restore operation will affect, click the restore point, and then click Scan For Affected Programs.
5. If you want to see additional restore points that are available, click Show More Restore Points.
6. Click the restore point that you want to use, and then click Next.
7. Click Finish. When prompted, click Yes to confirm that you want to use the selected restore point to restore the computer's system files and settings.

During the restoration, System Restore shuts down Windows 7. After restoration is complete, Windows 7 restarts using the settings in effect at the date and time of the snapshot. After the system restarts, the System Restore dialog box is displayed again. Read the message provided, and then click Close. If Windows 7 isn't working properly, you can apply a different restore point or reverse the restore operation by repeating this procedure and selecting the restore operation that was created prior to applying the current system state.

Troubleshooting System Restore

System Restore isn't always successful in its recovery attempts. If System Restore fails to recover the computer to the point in time you are targeting, you can repeat the restore procedure to try to recover the computer. This time, select a different restore point.

Creating and Using a Backup

The Professional, Enterprise, and Ultimate editions of Windows 7 include Backup And Restore Center. You can use this tool to automate backups and to create a complete backup of a computer. You must have appropriate permissions to back up and restore files on a computer.

Configuring Backups

Windows 7 can automatically create both personal data backups and system image backups. Personal data backups are used to periodically back up pictures, music, videos, e-mail, documents, and other types of important files. System image backups are used to periodically back up the system drive, the boot drive, and other drives required for Windows to run. You can use personal data backups to restore your data. You can use system image backups to restore a computer if it stops working.

The computer must be turned on at the scheduled run time for automated backups to work. You cannot save backups to the system disk, the boot disk, or tape. You can save personal data backups to USB flash drives, CD/DVD drives, and network locations, regardless of whether they are formatted with FAT or NTFS. However, you can save system image backups only to internal drives, network locations, or USB flash drives formatted with NTFS. You also can save system image backups to CD/DVD drives.

By default, scheduled backups are created every Sunday at 7 P.M. In a workplace where computers are shut off over the weekend, you'll want to change this setting.

You can configure automated backups by following these steps:

1. In Control Panel, under the System And Security heading, click the Back Up Your Computer link.
2. If you haven't previously configured automated backups, click Set Up Backup. Otherwise, click Change Settings.
3. On the Select Where You Want To Save Your Backup page, use the options provided to specify a backup location on a local disk, a CD/DVD drive, a USB flash drive, or the network, and then click Next. With CD/DVD drives, if the backup doesn't fit on one disc, you need to be available to insert discs when prompted.
4. On the What Do You Want To Back Up page, do one of the following, and then click Next:
   - Select Let Windows Choose if you want to back up all personal data in user profile folders and libraries and also create a system image.
   - Select Let Me Choose if you want to select personal and system data to back up.
5. If you selected Let Me Choose, use the options provided to select personal data to back up. You can expand the Data Files and Computer nodes and

subnodes to select specific folders and libraries. By default, the Include A System Image check box is selected to ensure that system image backups are created (which is what you'll usually want to do). After making your selections and clearing unwanted options, click Next.

6. On the Review Your Backup Settings page, click Change Schedule. Use the options provided to set the backup schedule, and then click OK. The How Often list lets you choose Daily, Weekly, or Monthly as the run schedule. If you choose a weekly or monthly run schedule, you need to set the day of the week or month to run by using the What Day list. Finally, the What Time list lets you set the time of day when automated backup should occur. Click OK.
7. If you are creating the initial backup and saving the backup schedule, click Save Settings And Run Backup to save your settings and then have Windows create the initial backup. If you've already created the initial backup for the computer, you'll see the Save Settings And Exit option instead.

Once you've configured automated backups, you can use the settings to run a backup manually at any time. Simply open Backup And Restore, and then click Back Up Now. If you want to manually create a system image backup, follow these steps:

1. In Control Panel, under the System And Security heading, click the Back Up Your Computer link. In the left pane, click Create A System Image.
2. On the Where Do You Want To Save The Backup page, use the options provided to specify a backup location. Click Next.
3. On the Which Drives Do You Want To Include In The Backup page, the computer's system drive is selected by default. You cannot change this selection, but you can add other drives to the backup image by selecting the related check boxes. Click Next to continue.
4. Click Start Backup.

Managing and Troubleshooting Backups

You can manage and troubleshoot backups by using Backup And Restore. To access this feature in Control Panel, click the Back Up Your Computer link under the System And Security heading.

Backup And Restore provides basic information about backups, including the backup location and backup size. To get more information about how disk space is used by Windows Backup, click Manage Space. In the Manage Windows Backup Disk Space dialog box, you can do the following:

- View the space usage summary.
- Browse the backup location by clicking the Browse link.
- Manage data files by clicking View Backups and then selecting backup sets to delete.
- Change settings for system image backups to save space.

To modify the run schedule, follow these steps:

1. In Control Panel, under the System And Security heading, click the Back Up Your Computer link.
2. Under Schedule, click Change Settings, and then complete steps 3–7 of the procedure describing how to configure automated backups.

To disable automated backups, follow these steps:

1. In Control Panel, under the System And Security heading, click the Back Up Your Computer link.
2. In the left pane, click Turn Off Schedule.

If Backup encounters any problems while backing up files, you'll see a warning or error message providing information about the problem encountered, as shown in Figure 17-4.

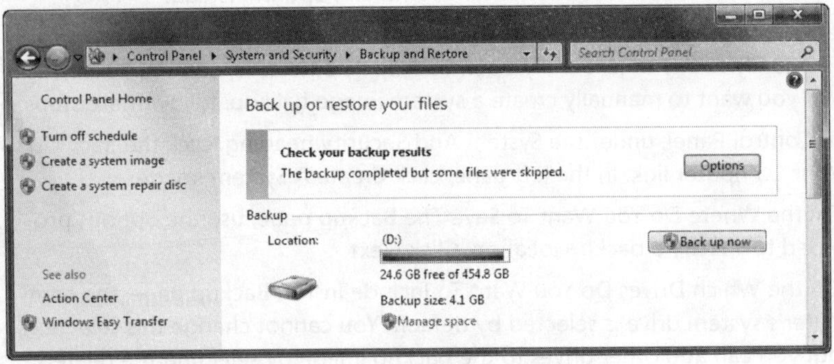

FIGURE 17-4 Use Backup And Restore Center to manage backups.

To begin troubleshooting, click Options. This opens the Windows Backup: Troubleshooting Options dialog box, shown in Figure 17-5. The options you have depend on the type of warning or error generated. With most warnings, you'll be able to view skipped files and change backup settings. With most errors, you'll be able to try to run the backup again or change the backup settings.

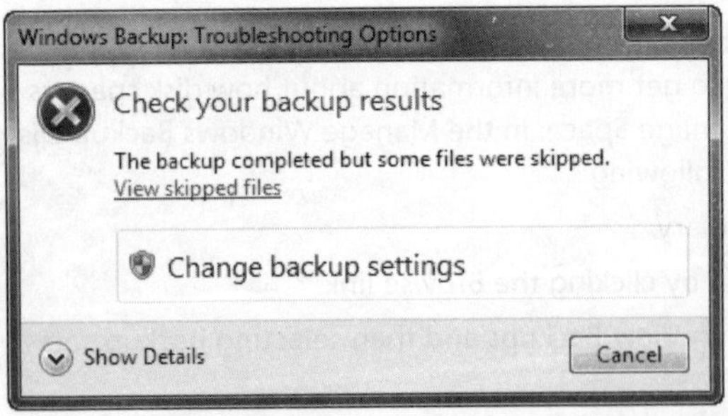

FIGURE 17-5 Begin troubleshooting to resolve backup issues.

Before you make a selection, click Show Details to get information about the backup time and backup location. If the user's computer or the server at the backup location was shut down or offline at the time of the backup, the backup would have failed and you can try to run the backup again. If the backup location doesn't have enough free space, you need to change the backup settings and pick a new backup location.

Recovering Personal Data

You can recover personal data files you've backed up by following these steps:

1. In Control Panel, under the System And Security heading, click the Back Up Your Computer link.
2. In Backup And Restore, click Restore My Files.

If the items you want to restore are stored in the current backup location, use the options in the Restore Files window to select items to restore, click Next, and then follow the prompts. The item selection options include:

- Click Browse For Files to browse your backup for files to restore. All files will be restored to their latest version.
- Click Browse For Folders to browse your backup for folders to restore. All folders and their contents will be restored to their latest version.
- Click Search to search for files and folders to restore. All selected files and folders will be restored to their latest version.
- Click Choose A Different Date to restore files from a different backup. In the Restore Files dialog box, you'll see a list of all backups by backup period. Click the backup you want to restore files from, and then browse or search for files.

If the items you want to restore are in a different location, click Select Another Backup To Restore Files From. In the Restore Files (Advanced) dialog box, you'll see a list of all backups by backup period, computer, and backup location. Click the backup you want to restore files from, and then browse or search for files.

Repairing and Recovering a Computer

When you install Windows 7, a Window Recovery Environment (Windows RE) partition is created automatically. You can use Windows RE to repair the computer by following these steps:

1. If the computer is running but has started with errors, click Start. On the Start menu, click the Shut Down options button, and then click Restart.
2. During startup, press F8 to access the Advanced Boot Options screen. If the computer has multiple operating systems, you'll see the Windows Boot Manager screen and can press F8 at that time.

3. On the Advanced Boot Options menu, use the arrow keys to select Repair Your Computer, and then press Enter.
4. The computer will load the Windows RE. In the System Recovery Options dialog box, select a language and keyboard layout, and then click Next.
5. To access recovery options, you need to log on using a local administrator account. Select the local administrator to log on as, type the password for this account, and then click OK.
6. In the System Recovery Options dialog box, note the location of the operating system, and then choose one of the following recovery options:
   - **Startup Repair** Choose this option to repair problems that prevent Windows from starting, including bad entries in the boot configuration data store, corrupted system files, and damaged boot managers. Normally, this tool is started automatically if Windows detects a fixable problem.
   - **System Restore** Choose this option to access System Restore so that you can restore Windows to an earlier point in time. If a configuration change or application installation is preventing startup and restore points are available, you can use this feature to restore Windows to a time prior to the change.
   - **System Image Recovery** Choose this option to perform a full recovery of the computer by using a system image created previously. If Startup Repair, System Restore, and other troubleshooting techniques fail to restore the computer and you have a system image for recovery, you can restore the computer from the backup image.
   - **Windows Memory Diagnostics** Choose this option if you suspect that a computer has a memory problem that is not being automatically detected.
   - **Command Prompt** Choose this option to access a command prompt and work with the commands and tools available in the recovery environment.

When you cannot recover Windows any other way, your final recovery option is to reinstall Windows 7. Before doing this, try to repair the computer by using Startup Repair and System Restore. If this fails, try to recover the computer by using a system image.

Troubleshooting Startup and Shutdown

As an administrator, you often need to troubleshoot problems with startup and shutdown. The sections that follow look at techniques for resolving common problems.

Resolving Restart or Shutdown Issues

Normally, you can shut down or restart Windows 7 by using the Shut Down options button on the Start menu. Sometimes, however, Windows 7 won't shut down or restart normally, and you must take additional actions. In those cases, follow these steps:

1. Press Ctrl+Alt+Del. The Windows screen should be displayed. Click Start Task Manager.
2. On the Applications tab, look for an application that is not responding. If all programs appear to be running normally, skip to step 5.
3. Select the application that is not responding, and then click End Task.
4. If the application fails to respond to the request, you'll see a prompt that allows you to end the application immediately or cancel the end-task request. Click End Now.
5. Try shutting down or restarting the computer. Press Ctrl+Alt+Del to display the Windows screen again, click the Shut Down options button to the right of the Shut Down button, and then click Restart or Shut Down as appropriate.

Windows 7 will also log off the current user and shut down the computer if you press the computer's power button. If any programs fail to respond, you'll have the option to force the logoff, or you can simply wait a few seconds for Windows to force the logoff.

> ***REAL WORLD*** **As a last resort, you might be forced to perform a hard shutdown by pressing and holding down the computer's power button or by unplugging the computer. If you do this, Check Disk will probably run the next time you start the computer. This allows the computer to check for errors and problems that might have been caused by the hard shutdown. If Check Disk doesn't run automatically, you might want to run it manually.**

Making Sense of Stop Errors

The "Configuring System Startup and Recovery" section in Chapter 6 details how to configure Windows 7 to write debugging information. If a major error occurs while Windows 7 is starting, installing a program, or performing another operation, you'll see a Stop error message across the entire screen. Read this information carefully and write down the following information:

- **Error name** The error name should be on the third line of the error screen and is listed in all caps, such as KERNEL_STACK_INPAGE_ERROR.
- **Troubleshooting recommendations** The error name is followed by the troubleshooting recommendations. These recommendations are based on the type of error that occurred and provide general guidelines on resolving the problem.

- **Error number** The troubleshooting recommendations are followed by technical information. On the next line after the Technical Information heading, you'll see the word Stop, an error number, and a list of error parameters. The error number following Stop is what you should write down, such as STOP: 0X00000050.
- **Driver information** Immediately following the line with the Stop error number is a line that lists the name of the driver associated with the error. This information is provided only if the error can be traced to a specific driver. Write down the driver name.

If the system is configured to write an event to the event logs if a Stop error occurs and it was possible to write the event before the system crashed completely, the error number and error parameters will be written to an event in the System log with an event source of Save Dump. The event will also specify whether a dump file was created and where it was saved if applicable.

> ***REAL WORLD*** **Windows 7 includes an Online Crash Analysis feature that allows you to send the dump file to Microsoft Product Support Services. If error reporting is enabled, you will be prompted to send this debugging information to Microsoft when you restart the system. You have the option of sending the debugging information anonymously or using your Microsoft Connect account. If you send the debugging information with your name and contact information through Microsoft Connect, a technician might contact you for further information and might also be able to suggest an action to correct the problem.**

Once you have the Stop error information, you might need to start the system in safe mode as discussed in the section "Repairing a Computer to Enable Startup" earlier in this chapter. You can then look to resolve the problem by performing the following tasks:

- **Look up the Stop error on the Microsoft Knowledge Base** Visit *support.microsoft.com* and perform a search of the Microsoft Knowledge Base using the error number as the keyword. If a known problem is related to the error code, you should find a related Knowledge Base article. As appropriate, follow the instructions given to resolve the issue.
- **Check the driver (if driver information was provided)** When you reboot the system, check the driver to be sure it is digitally signed. If the driver has been updated recently, you might consider rolling back to the previous driver version. Just because the driver is listed doesn't mean the driver is corrupt and needs replacing, however. The Stop error could have been caused by other factors.
- **Determine what has changed recently** Stop errors can be caused by both hardware and software. Closely review any programs or hardware that have been installed recently on the computer. If you added new hardware, check to be sure that the hardware is installed correctly; that the latest, signed drivers are installed; and that the hardware is properly configured.

If you added new software, check to be sure that the installation completed successfully. You might also want to check for updates or patches to the software.

- **Check system resources** Stop errors can occur if the system becomes critically low of RAM or disk space. Once you get the system started, check the drives to determine the amount of free space available and, as necessary, free additional disk space using Disk Cleanup or other tools. Also open Task Manager by pressing Ctrl+Alt+Del and clicking Start Task Manager. Look at the Performance tab to check the amount of physical and virtual RAM available. If very little memory is available, determine which programs are using memory and whether there are problem programs, such as adware or spyware, running.
- **Repair system files** Stop errors can be caused by damaged or improper versions of system files. If you suspect a system file is the cause of the problem and the system won't boot properly, you might need to repair the operating system or reinstall the operating system using the repair options discussed in the section "Repairing a Computer to Enable Startup."
- **Check hardware and firmware** Stop errors can be caused by faulty hardware. If a computer frequently crashes, you might want to examine the hardware closely. Check the hardware drivers first; a driver might be causing the Stop errors. Check the physical hardware. Look specifically at the hard disks, RAM, CPU, and graphics card. A hard disk might be going bad, RAM might be defective, the CPU might have overheated, or the graphics card might be incompatible with Windows 7. Also look at the firmware. Check the settings carefully. You might check whether an update is available from the motherboard's manufacturer.

Index

Symbols and Numbers

A

C

E

G

H

I

J

K

L

N

O

P

V

W

X

About the Author

WILLIAM R. STANEK (*www.williamstanek.com/*) has more than 20 years of hands-on experience with advanced computer programming and software development. He is a leading technology expert, an award-winning author, and a pretty-darn-good instructional trainer. Over the years, his practical advice has helped millions of programmers, developers, and network engineers all over the world. He has written more than 100 books. His recent books include *Active Directory Administrator's Pocket Consultant, Windows Group Policy Administrator's Pocket Consultant, Windows PowerShell 2.0 Administrator's Pocket Consultant*, and *Windows Server 2008 Inside Out* (all from Microsoft Press).

William has been involved in the commercial Internet community since 1991. His core business and technology experience comes from more than 11 years of military service. He has substantial experience in developing server technology, encryption, and Internet solutions. He has written many technical white papers and training courses on a wide variety of topics. He frequently serves as a subject matter expert and consultant.

William has a BS in computer science, magna cum laude, and an MS with distinction in information systems. He is proud to have served in the Persian Gulf War as a combat crewmember on an electronic warfare aircraft. He flew on numerous combat missions into Iraq and was awarded nine medals for his wartime service, including one of the United States of America's highest flying honors, the Air Force Distinguished Flying Cross. Currently, he resides in the Pacific Northwest with his wife and children.

Follow William on Twitter at WilliamStanek.

